The three Stauffenberg brothers, Berthold, Alexander and Claus, were inseparable both emotionally and intellectually. Their view of human existence was rooted in their south German aristocratic background, in classical antiquity, and in Christian culture, as well as in the nineteenth and twentieth centuries. Pindar, Dante, Hölderlin and Stefan George were their principal literary heroes; Alexander, Caesar, Frederick II, Napoleon and Gneisenau were their models in generalship and statesmanship.

This 'family biography' describes the brothers' youth and formative years, their association with the circle of the poet Stefan George, and their professional and political development. Their professions and their political and military environments led them to take fundamental positions on the military ethos and on their government's and Hitler's tyranny.

The military career of Claus, Count Stauffenberg and his fight to overthrow Hitler, culminating in the attempted assassination and coup of 20 July 1944, provide the focus for the book. It is based on the most comprehensive collection of sources yet used, including family papers, correspondence, and information from numerous contemporaries, with a unique collection of illustrative material.

Stauffenberg

Stauffenberg

A Family History, 1905–1944

PETER HOFFMANN

McGill University

CAMBRIDGE
UNIVERSITY PRESS

Published by the Press Syndicate of the University of Cambridge
The Pitt Building, Trumpington Street, Cambridge CB2 1RP
40 West 20th Street, New York, NY 10011-4211, USA
10 Stamford Road, Oakleigh, Melbourne 3166, Australia

Originally published in German as *Claus Schenk Graf von Stauffenberg und seine Brüder*
by Deutsche-Verlags-Anstalt, Stuttgart, 1992
and © 1992 Deutsche Verlags-Anstalt GmbH, Stuttgart
First published in English by Cambridge University Press 1995 as *Stauffenberg*
Revised and translated by the author

English translation © Peter Hoffmann 1995

Printed in Great Britain at the University Press, Cambridge

A catalogue record for this book is available from the British Library

Library of Congress cataloguing in publication data
Hoffmann, Peter, 1930–
[Claus Schenk Graf von Stauffenberg und seine Brüder. English]
Stauffenberg: a family history, 1905–1944 / Peter Hoffmann.
p.   cm.
Includes bibliographical references and index.
ISBN 0 521 45307 0
1. Schenk von Stauffenberg, Claus Philipp, Graf, 1907–1944.
2. Schenk von Stauffenberg, Claus Philipp, Graf, 1905–1944 – Family.
3. Anti-Nazi movement – Germany – Biography.
4. Revolutionaries – Germany – Biography.
5. Hitler, Adolf, 1889–1945 – Assassination attempt, 1944 (July 20).
I. Title.
DD247.S342H6413   1995
943.08–DC20   94-31228   CIP

ISBN 0 521 45307 0 hardback

CE

CONTENTS

ILLUSTRATIONS

Sources of illustrations

Archiv für Kunst und Geschichte, Berlin: 46
Author's archive: 24, 27, 51
Nl BS: 9, 10, 14, 16, 21, 28, 35
National Archives, Washington D.C.: 41, 42, 50, 51
Private collections: 1–7, 12 (above), 17, 20, 22, 23 (left), 30, 32, 36, 37, 43, 44, 45, 47, 48
StGA: 8, 11, 12 (below), 13, 15, 18, 19, 23 (right), 26, 29, 39, 49
Ullstein Bilderdienst, Berlin: 25, 34, 38
Maps by Atelier Höllerer, Stuttgart

ABBREVIATIONS

AA/PA	Auswärtiges Amt/Politisches Archiv, Bonn
AB	Albrecht von Blumenthal
ADAP	Akten zur deutschen auswärtigen Politik
AHA	Allgemeines Heeresamt
AK	Armee-Korps
AM	Anneliese Edle Mertz von Quirnheim
AOK	Armee-Oberkommando
AS	Alexander Schenk, Count Stauffenberg
AÜ	Alexander, Count Üxküll
BA	Bundesarchiv, Coblenz
BA-MA	Bundesarchiv-Militärarchiv, Freiburg i.Br.
BA-Z	Bundesarchiv-Zentralnachweisstelle, Kornelimünster
BDC	Berlin Document Center, Berlin
BS	Berthold Schenk, Count Stauffenberg
ClS	Claus Schenk, Count Stauffenberg
CM	Christian Müller, *Oberst. i.G. Stauffenberg*
CP	Castrum Peregrini Foundation, Amsterdam
CS	Caroline Schenk, Countess Stauffenberg
CSA	Caroline Schenk, Countess Stauffenberg, 'Aufzeichnungen'
CSGA	Gedichtalbum aus dem Besitz Caroline Gräfin Stauffenbergs (Caroline Stauffenberg's poetry album)
CSK	Caroline Schenk, Countess Stauffenberg, Kriegstagebuch (War Diary)
CvdS	Charlotte, Countess (von der) Schulenburg
CvT	Clarita von Trott zu Solz
DAL	Deutsches Literaturarchiv, Marbach a.N.
EK	Ernst Kantorowicz
EL	Edith Landmann
ELG	Eberhard-Ludwigs-Gymnasium
EM	Ernst Morwitz
EW	Erika Wolters

F.D.R. Library	Franklin D. Roosevelt Library, Hyde Park, New York
FDS	Fritz-Dietlof, Count (von der) Schulenburg
F	Frank Mehnert
FRUS	Foreign Relations of the United States
GA	*Gesamt-Ausgabe*
GenQuM	Generalquartiermeister
GenStdH	Generalstab des Heeres
GS	General Staff
HCSt	Hans Christoph Schenk, Baron von Stauffenberg
HGr	Herresgruppe (Army Group)
HPA	Herrespersonalamt
IfMLbZKdSED, ZPA	Institut für Marxismus-Leninismus beim Zentralkomitee der Sozialistischen Einheitspartei, Zentrales Parteiarchiv
IfZ	Institut für Zeitgeschichte, Munich
JA	Johann Anton
KTB	Kriegstagebuch (War Diary)
LD	Light Division
LT	Ludwig Thormaehlen
MaS	Marlene Schenk, Countess Stauffenberg
MF	Maria Fehling
MFA	Militärgeschichtliches Forschungsamt, Freiburg i.Br.
MK	Max Kommerell
MS	Maria Schenk, Countess Stauffenberg
MSt	Michael Stettler
NA	National Archives, Washington D.C.
NL	Nachlass (personal papers)
Nl AS	Nachlass Alexander Schenk, Count Stauffenberg
Nl F	Nachlass Frank Mehnert
Nl MK	Nachlass Max Kommerell
Nl MS	Nachlass Maria Schenk, Countess Stauffenberg
NS	Nina Schenk, Countess Stauffenberg
NSDAP	Nationalsozialistische Deutsche Arbeiterpartei (German National Socialist Workers' Party)
OKH	Oberkommando des Heeres
OKW	Oberkommando der Wehrmacht
OSS Archive	Office of Strategic Services Archive, Langley, Virginia
PM	Papers of Freya von Moltke
PPa	Papers of Karl Josef Partsch
PP	Papers of Theodor Pfizer
P.R.O.	Public Record Office, London

RB	Robert Boehringer
RF	Rudolf Fahrner
RGBl.	*Reichsgesetzblatt*
RO	Rudolf Obermüller
RSHA	Reichssicherheitshauptamt
Slg	Sammlung (collection)
StG	Stefan George
StGA	Stefan George Archiv, Stuttgart
TP	Theodor Pfizer
UAT	Universitätsarchiv Tübingen
VB	*Völkischer Beobachter*
WFSt	Wehrmachtführungsstab
WK	Walter Kempner

German military ranks from *Generalmajor* up are transposed to British usage; a German *Generalmajor* will be referred to as a Brigadier, etc.

PROLOGUE

The Stauffenberg brothers were all born in the first decade of the twentieth century. As children and adolescents they were strongly influenced by three distinct elements in their background. First there was the family, with its traditional forms and values, its estates in Swabia and Franconia, its connections with the royal court of Württemberg in Stuttgart, its tradition of service to the state. Second, the spirit and teaching of their school, with its emphasis on the classics; third, the world of poetry and poets. Before all else came the service of the fatherland: as Bismarck once remarked, with the brevity that was sufficient to convey his meaning to like-minded contemporaries, there was no reason why the sons of Prussian farmers should be shot in a cause that was not Prussia's, but 'I am not speaking of the nobleman, he was born for that.'[1] However, under the National Socialist dictatorship, between 1933 and 1945, the Stauffenberg brothers, faced with crimes unparalleled in the history of mankind, were forced by their profession and their external circumstances to adopt a far more questioning attitude towards the past and present of their own nation.

What road brought Claus, Count von Stauffenberg, to the sandpile in the courtyard of the Berlin War Ministry where he was shot, and his brother, Berthold, to the hook on which he was strangled in the execution hut of Plötzensee Prison? What is the meaning of these sacrifices, and of the anguish of the survivors – the surviving brother, the mother, widows and children?

A number of difficulties lie in wait for those who seek to become familiar with the Stauffenberg brothers. They were extraordinarily unlike their contemporaries – in their own families, in the nobility, within the Catholic community, in their school, in their professions. This fact emerges strongly from the primary sources. The more closely a witness was acquainted with the Stauffenbergs, the more cautious he was in describing them, in uttering judgements beyond respect, admiration, and acknowledgement of the extraordinary in them. This was particularly true for Claus and his whole, harmonious personality. The less well a witness knew the Stauffenbergs, the more his evidence reflects his own limitations. There is an almost complete lack of negative information on Claus Stauffenberg which a sceptical researcher might well attribute to piety. But closer scrutiny reveals such scepticism to be misguided. Indeed, a very great number of the Stauffenbergs' contemporaries stressed above all their extraordinariness, both intellectual and physical.

The Stauffenbergs themselves were aware of being unlike other people, partly because of their strong family and aristocratic traditions. This may put off some present-day observers or confirm their own prejudices. Taboos against differences in natural endowments and class differences, the assumption of the equality of all human beings, can make it difficult to understand a culture which rejected comprehensive levelling. But the current hankering after a fictitious equality cannot, of course, make it any the less fictitious. Individuals have different social and cultural origins, genetic inheritances, education, positions, achievements and even privileges, if not 'rights' in a legal sense.

In a larger context, however, there were negative aspects in the Stauffenbergs' lives, which Claus Stauffenberg himself addressed: 'As General Staff officers we must all share the responsibility.'[2] Claus Stauffenberg's cousin and friend, Peter Count Yorck von Wartenburg, who was condemned to death for his own part in the attempted uprising, wrote two days before his execution that he had been driven to act 'by the feeling of the guilt which lay so heavy on us all'. Both Stauffenberg and Yorck were deeply afflicted by the number and enormity of crimes committed in the name of Germany.[3] Under interrogation by the Secret State Police Yorck singled out for his condemnation the 'extermination measures' against Jews, and to the 'People's Court' which condemned him to death by hanging he confirmed his own and his cousin Stauffenberg's loathing at the persecution which the presiding judge, Roland Freisler, referred to as 'the extermination of the Jews'.[4] Axel von dem Bussche, referring to the mass shooting of Jews he had witnessed at Dubno on 5 October 1942, declared that 'essentially, what happened on 20 July would not have happened without that'.[5] The guilt that Yorck, and also his cousin Stauffenberg, accepted was that they been too slow to oppose the evil, and that they had been inactive in helpless outrage too long after they had seen it. But it would be unhistorical to demand that an individual should always have been what he ultimately became.

The admission of shared responsibility sprang from ethical principles which raised the Stauffenbergs and their friends high above the mass of people in all classes of society. After three months of investigation following the failed uprising of 20 July 1944, the head of the Secret State Police investigating commission, SS Lieutenant-Colonel Walter von Kielpinski, summarised the results: 'The complete inner alienation from the ideas of National Socialism which characterised the men of the reactionary conspiratorial circle expresses itself above all in their position on the Jewish

Question. [. . .] they cling to the liberal position of granting to the Jews in principle the same status as to every German.'[6] Claus Stauffenberg's own utterances from April 1942 onwards, and the testimony of Berthold Stauffenberg, Alexander Stauffenberg and Peter Yorck to the Secret State Police and the 'People's Court', confirm that general finding in their individual cases.

The Stauffenbergs were not governed by a 'world view', but rather by the *rejection* of thought systems. Claus Stauffenberg never inclined towards any political party. A close friend said that if Claus had ever thought in earnest about political parties he would have formed one himself.[7] But at the end of his life he insisted that a document be drawn up containing the fundamental tenets of what it meant to be German, as he saw them.[8]

The principal motives of the Stauffenberg brothers were rooted in their awareness of belonging to a noble family with a tradition of service to the state, and in the intellectual and political history of their country. These motives were family honour, adherence to the ideals Stefan George had taught them, and the military code. All three led to the recognition of the criminal nature of Hitler's war. All three can be discerned again and again from their early youth. From about April 1942 they emerged and dominated all else.

The sources present considerable difficulties. The family's custom of maintaining a certain reticence vis-à-vis the vulgar outside world, and the secrecy which surrounded the closed circle of the friends of the poet Stefan George, both tended to keep information off the record, or to encode it. From the moment when the Stauffenberg brothers were welcomed and initiated by the 'Master', there stood between them and the rest of the world an invisible wall which could be crossed only by those who were familiar with, and sympathetic towards, the ideas of Stefan George. Those who now make the effort to penetrate this invisible wall will be surprised at the strength with which the ideas of Stefan George's circle persisted down to the Stauffenbergs' last days.

Claus Stauffenberg's decision to become a soldier had a further effect of encoding biographical information. A soldier's very readiness to die for his country sets him apart from it in his daily life and his mentality.

A third level of mystification, as far as the rest of the world was concerned, was represented by involvement with the Army General Staff. General Franz Halder, Chief of the General Staff 1938–1942, wrote to an early Stauffenberg biographer that 'because the work of the General Staff is sealed off from the public', it was effectively impossible to write its history.[9]

Joachim Kramarz wrote, in the foreword of the Stauffenberg biography he published in 1965 that, after 20 July 1944 the Secret State Police had confiscated even the smallest scrap of paper in Stauffenberg's Berlin flat and at his family home in Bamberg, so that only a very few items had survived: a few letters someone had not burned, a postcard, a few military files. In 1968 Robert Boehringer, who had inherited Stefan George's papers, made available five letters and six poems by Claus Stauffenberg. Christian Müller, who in 1970 published a long dissertation on Stauffenberg, had found a few more letters and some files of written exercises from Stauffenberg's years of training.

When the present author began to look into Stauffenberg's thinking, every corner that might have held papers seemed to have been scraped bare. But it soon became clear that much more had survived than Kramarz and Müller had turned up. The author now has originals or copies of more than sixty letters by Claus Stauffenberg and a number of further private and official documents; of hundreds of letters by Berthold and Alexander Stauffenberg, and other writings by them; and of notes, communications and correspondence from friends, guest books, and unused archival sources.

The inclusion in the research of Claus's brothers, Berthold and Alexander, proved fruitful, as did the inclusion of the other friends of Stefan George. Even certain papers confiscated by the Secret State Police from Lautlingen Manor and taken to a branch office of the Reich's Central Security Department at Markkleeberg near Leipzig in November 1944 have survived. Robert Boehringer, as Stefan George's heir, claimed them, received them in 1961, and in the 1970s transferred them to the newly founded Stefan George Archiv in Stuttgart. Contrary to reasonable expectation it proved possible to learn a good deal about Stauffenberg's tour of duty in Tunisia in 1943. Some key documents for Stauffenberg's efforts to overthrow the Hitler regime in the spring of 1944 recently became accessible in archives in Potsdam. On the other hand, a body of papers confiscated by the Gestapo has so far failed to re-surface and must be presumed lost. Many documents, letters in particular, were destroyed after 20 July 1944 by their owners who feared police searches.

It is my agreeable duty to thank more persons for their assistance than I can name in this Prologue. For the most part their names appear in the lists of sources. I am grateful above all to my father, the late Wilhelm Hoffmann, for his unfailing readiness to discuss aspects of my research and to offer thoughtful advice. Further I wish to express special thanks to Karen Bingel, Valentin Boss, the late Rudolf Fahrner, Lore Frank, Manfred Kehrig, Klemens von Klemperer, Joachim Kramarz, Richard Lamb, H. O. Malone, Rüdiger von Manstein, Frank Nicosia, the late Theodor Pfizer, Katherine Sams, Olga von Saucken, Peter Sauerbruch, Albert Schick (representing also many other members of the 10th Panzer Division) and also Bradley Smith, the numerous Stauffenberg family and particularly Nina, Countess Stauffenberg, the late Alfred, Count Stauffenberg, Berthold, Count Stauffenberg, Hans Christoph, Baron Stauffenberg. Thanks also to my colleague, the late Robert Vogel, Gemma Wolters-Thiersch, Eberhard

Zeller, the archivists of the Stefan George Archiv, the Bundesarchiv, the Bundesarchiv-Abteilungen Potsdam, the Bundesarchiv-Militärarchiv, the Bundesarchiv-Zentralnachweisstelle, the Institut für Zeitgeschichte, the Krankenbuchlager Berlin, the Deutsche Dienststelle (Wehrmacht-Auskunft-Stelle) Berlin, the Rilke-Archiv, the National Archives in Washington and the McLennan Library at McGill University. My special thanks go to my son Peter F., who read the typescript and made many valuable suggestions.

I am grateful to the Faculty of Graduate Studies and Research at McGill University for their generous support, and equally to the Social Sciences and Humanities Research Council of Canada, the Stiftung Volkswagenwerk, and the Killam Foundation.

P.H.
McGill University, Montreal, 1994

I

Childhood, a World War, and a new beginning

The recorded history of the Stauffenberg family begins in Swabia, south of the Neckar river and on the upper Danube, in the thirteenth century. During this century the power of the German kings declined, and the Counts of Zollern, like other princes, assumed the trappings of royalty. Members of the family later to be known as the 'Schenken von Stauffenberg' were appointed as cup bearers or stewards (*Schenken*), so that 'Schenk' became a clan name. Surnames were appended depending on the place of residence. One of these places was Stauffenberg, referring to one of the many cone-shaped mountains in southern Germany.[1]

By the end of the fifteenth century, 'Stauffenberg' was a permanent part of the family's name; a tradition in the family also associates it with the Staufen dynasty. The Stauffenbergs rose in the world in 1698, when Emperor Leopold I made one member a hereditary Baron (*Freiherr*), and in 1791 when Emperor Leopold II made another an hereditary Imperial Count (*Reichsgraf*).

The Stauffenberg brothers were descended from the baronial family, one of whom, Franz Ludwig Baron Schenk von Stauffenberg, had been made a hereditary count (*Graf*) of the Kingdom of Bavaria by King Ludwig II in 1874. As a member of the Bavarian parliament (*Landtag*), he had campaigned for the repeal of the death penalty, 'purely as a matter of humanity'. His family had acquired Amerdingen Manor (near Nördlingen) through marriage in 1566, and had added Greifenstein near Bamberg, Jettingen near Günzburg, and Lautlingen near Ebingen on the southern slopes of the Schwäbische Alb in the seventeenth and eighteenth centuries. Over three centuries, members of the clan served as cathedral canons in Bamberg, Würzburg and Augsburg, and as administrators in the government of the prince-bishop of Bamberg; one of them was himself a prince-bishop.

The father of the Stauffenberg brothers, Alfred Schenk, Count von Stauffenberg, owner of Lautlingen, was a grandson of the first Bavarian count. He attained the rank of major in the army of the King of Württemberg and served the royal court at Stuttgart as Lord Chamberlain from 1908. After the well-loved King abdicated at the end of November 1918,

Stauffenberg managed the private estates of the royal family until his own retirement in 1928. His inclinations were practical: he installed electric cables, repaired furniture and even grew artichokes in the harsh climate of Lautlingen; and he involved his children in these pursuits.[2] In May 1904 the Count, who was a Catholic, married the Lutheran Caroline, Countess von Üxküll-Gyllenband, daughter of an Austrian Imperial Lieutenant-Colonel and his wife Valerie, née Countess von Hohenthal, who was a descendant of Field Marshal August Neidhardt, Count von Gneisenau.[3] Caroline, Countess Stauffenberg was interested in art and contemporary literature, and remained largely unconcerned with the mysteries of the kitchen. She raised her children with loving care, spoke French and English with them as well as German, and encouraged them in intellectual pursuits. The environment of the Lord Chamberlain's household at the royal court formed their bearing and outlook. One of the brothers later reflected that the style of their upbringing had been 'monumental'.[4]

The twins, Berthold and Alexander, were born in Stuttgart on 15 March 1905. Alexander was merry, friendly, of somewhat smaller stature and slower than his brother, and musically gifted. Berthold seemed to be a dreamy introvert, with a profound expression in his beautiful eyes that frightened his mother.[5] One evening in October 1907, the twins wanted to go to the village church in Lautlingen. Their mother led them to the statue of St Mary and prompted them to fold their hands in prayer before the 'heavenly mama'. Alexander did so, but Berthold, with a serious expression, extended his little hand toward his own mother and said, 'here heavenly mama'.[6]

In Stuttgart, or in Lautlingen during the summer, Queen Charlotte of Württemberg frequently visited Caroline Stauffenberg, her close friend from the years before Caroline's marriage. The children called her 'Ke' (for *Königin,* 'queen'). Once Berthold, kissing her hand, bit her as well, and thought it a tremendously good joke when it startled her considerably.[7]

On 15 November 1907 in Jettingen, Caroline Stauffenberg bore another pair of twins, Claus Philipp and Konrad Maria. She was in her eighth month of pregnancy and happened to be staying with her mother-in-law. Konrad died a day after birth.[8] When Claus was old enough to be told about his lost twin, he lamented his loss. For a time he often brought his mother flowers for his brother's grave.[9]

Berthold directed his attention and love almost exclusively to his youngest brother. Alexander, who was more sedate and philosophical, was a little isolated. Claus's health was weaker than his brothers', but both he and Alexander were uncommonly insensitive to pain. At the age of four Claus feared neither horses nor loaded hay wagons. Climbing steep rocks around Lautlingen, he declared that he wished to be a hero. He kept up with the most daring of the village lads. In February 1913, in Silvaplana, he preferred

1. Caroline Schenk, Countess Stauffenberg (née Countess Üxküll-Gyllenband), ca. 1910

the steepest ski runs. After a minor operation in July 1914, the physician and the nurses were astonished by Claus's fortitude; he declared: 'Now I have been quite brave, and now I can be a soldier and go to all the wars when I am grown up.'[10] His elders and his contemporaries were charmed by his blond hair and big eyes; his quick intelligence made learning easy for him.

Both Alexander and Claus were pious, unlike Berthold. When Claus was three he often dreamed about death and said that he did not wish to go to heaven but wanted to 'always stay here'; or that he would go to heaven rather than to purgatory since he had been good.[11]

While Berthold was ill with diphtheria in 1913, he weighed up the prospects of negotiations to end the Second Balkan War and told his mother: 'You will see that they won't reach agreement: the Turks cannot accept the Bulgarian proposals nor the Balkan States those of Turkey, and the war will continue.' His mother worried that his intellect was developing too rapidly.[12]

Claus preferred clear, simple solutions. As a nine-year-old he commented on the Reformation: if Luther had been more patient and had persuaded the popes and the monks to behave better, there would now be only one faith

2. *Lautlingen near Ebingen on the southern slope of the Schwäbische Alb: a lino cut, ca. 1910, and a modern photograph*

3. Above: Berthold and Alexander at Lautlingen, 1908. Below, from left: Alexander, Berthold and Claus near Lautlingen, 1914

and that would be so much nicer. A year later he suggested the abolition of money: then there would be neither rich nor poor; all unhappiness in the world was caused by money, as one could see in the story of the Nibelungs.[13]

When Alexander had diphtheria in January 1917, his brothers were quarantined with Aunt Olga ('Osch'), Countess Üxküll, in her official quarters in the former 'Academy' founded by Duke Carl Eugene. In July 1918 Alexander had pneumonia followed by a pleural infection. He took communion and wanted his brothers to do the same and to pray for his recovery.[14]

The familiar places of the brothers' childhood years were the family's official residence in the Old Castle in Stuttgart, their house in Lautlingen, and their relatives' houses (all of them called *Schloss*, 'castle' in German) in Jettingen, Amerdingen and Greifenstein. The mother and children sometimes went on vacations to the North Sea or to the Alps. Gardens, salons, teas, encounters with the royal family, visits to the Wilhelma Park in Cannstatt were part of the routine.

The twins had private tutors until autumn 1913, when they began to attend the Eberhard-Ludwigs-Gymnasium, Stuttgart's foremost grammar school, with a strong emphasis on the classics.[15] At the same time, Claus began attending a private grammar school; he was delighted and excitedly competed with his brothers to learn. From 1916 he, too, attended the Gymnasium. The three brothers also played the piano and the violin; in 1917 Claus took up the cello.

In the same year, Berthold and Claus were both top of their forms; Alexander was fourteenth. In the final (leaving) examinations, Berthold's marks were on average 'good', Alexander's 'satisfactory', and Claus's were in between. Although all three wrote poems, only Alexander was a true poet. Berthold's superior intellect was clear and sharp-edged, realistic but not incapable of enthusiasm and fantasy; at the same time he was taciturn, wooden, even bashful, and socially awkward.

The family were spending their holidays in Lautlingen when they learned by telephone on 31 July 1914 that the King had left his summer residence in Friedrichshafen on Lake Constance to return to Stuttgart. The Lord Chamberlain had to return too. Groups of men and boys were standing in the street in the village, talking excitedly; weeping women stood before their front doors; there were no signs of enthusiasm. On 1 August, Countess Stauffenberg decided to return to Stuttgart with the children, as she noted in her diary: 'All this enormous frenzy in the whole world and I am walking about with the children in bright sunshine – this will not do – it is unbearable. [. . .] This evening the telephone again – everything mobilised and I wanted to leave – Alfred didn't want me to go, but in the end he permitted it.' On 2 August mother, children, their Irish governess Miss Barry and some of the servants travelled to Stuttgart in crowded railway trains, amidst rumours that Danube bridges had been destroyed and spies shot.[16]

A field hospital was set up in the Old Castle. Uncle Berthold, a Major in the 1st Uhlans, joined his regiment; his brother Alfred was eager to serve at the front; Uncle Nikolaus, Count Üxküll, was a Captain in the Austrian Imperial and Royal General Staff Corps under the General Inspector of Cavalry Carl, Count Huyn. On 13 August the news came that Clemens, Count Stauffenberg, a son of Uncle Berthold, had been shot through the lung.

On 28 August there was an air raid alert in Stuttgart and a good deal of shooting, but apparently it was 'all for nothing'. Wounded soldiers walked through the streets, amidst great public interest; announcements of victories caused general excitement. Miss Barry, who spoke only English, could no longer go out with the children and in any case had to report to the police twice daily, until she returned home in January 1915 on the news of her sister's death. Countess Stauffenberg wrote in her diary of the stunned apathy of the wounded, of the horrors of battles and losses, of her worries about her brother Nikolaus, of her wish for peace; not a word of enthusiasm for the war.

The children's reaction to the war was quite different, of course. They were 'seized by such enthusiasm' that Claus one morning came to his mother sobbing: his brothers had told him that in ten years' time they would be able to join up, but he would not. It took his mother a long time to soothe him, and she ended up promising that she would be 'heroic' and would let all her boys go. Claus prayed every evening that all the soldiers would come home again, all the wounded be healed, and every fallen soldier go to heaven. In August 1914 Alexander wrote a poem in honour of the victor of Liège, Lieutenant-General Otto von Emmich, and in 1915 one about the sunken mine layer *Königin Luise* and another on 'Germany'. Berthold and Claus wrote poems with more pathos than art about 'Our Enemies' and the submarine *U9*. Berthold became so interested in the German Navy that in November 1916 he wrote an essay on its history and presented it at school.[17]

On 22 June 1915 all the voluntary hospital helpers left the Old Castle for the summer holidays. The school year was over, Berthold had received 'his annual prize' on speech day, and mother and sons travelled to Lautlingen. The brothers fetched their dog Harro from the home farm on the Tierberg, hitched up the donkey to haul large wooden boxes from the railway station – and upset the wagon within twenty feet of the station because a wheel had come off. They contracted measles from the village children, Alex developed a bad cough, Berthold fell through a bridge-railing 'into the abyss'. After the capture of Warsaw on 7 August, and of Kovno and Brest-Litovsk on 18 and 25 August 1915, Countess Stauffenberg ordered flags to be hung and got the priest to ring the church bells. But in the spring of 1916 she recorded how

4. From left: Alexander, Claus and Berthold with their mother, at the Old Castle in Stuttgart, 1915

concerned the people were about Verdun: 'They are always saying that we shall bleed to death at Verdun.'[18]

In September 1915 the boys returned to school in Stuttgart. Occasional air raids were only mild interruptions. The high point of the autumn was a concert in the Round Hall of the Old Castle. At Christmas, after an address by Chief Court Chaplain Dr Konrad Hoffmann, the King and Queen gave gifts to two hundred children, advancing from opposite ends of a long table towards its middle. The English blockade caused food shortages, however, so that Countess Stauffenberg had to abandon her practice of giving tea every evening at Stuttgart railway station to soldiers passing through. The spring of 1916 was overshadowed by Verdun. The Stauffenberg and other children gave a concert 'for the submarines' which raised 1200 marks.[19]

In March 1917 Alfred von Hofacker fell at Verdun. He was a son of Countess Stauffenberg's sister Albertine. His brother Cäsar came home on leave from Macedonia, where he was serving with the flying corps, to Lautlingen where the Stauffenberg and Hofacker families were spending Easter. In 1918 Cäsar served with the German Military Mission in Turkey, where his Uncle Nikolaus, Count Üxküll, had replaced the Austrian Military Attaché in Constantinople at the end of 1917 and during part of 1918.

5. *Above, from left: Alexander, Claus and Berthold, in the Old Castle in Stuttgart, 1913. Below, from left: Berthold, Alexander and Claus at Lautlingen, 1917*

Cäsar was taken prisoner by French troops in October 1918 and did not return from captivity in France until March 1920.[20]

In the summer of 1917 the twins were strong enough to help the farm women with the haying and the grain harvest. They went out at half-past six to mow. Claus got the draught animals out of the stable and hitched them

6. *Above, courtyard at Lautlingen, 1917: Claus (on the donkey), Alexander (with hat) and Berthold (on box). Below: garden at Lautlingen, 1917. From left: Alexander, Claus and Berthold with their parents*

up; the twins loaded and unloaded wagons. In autumn of that year the Gymnasium was turned into a camp for captured French Army officers; the classes were moved to other school buildings. There were more air raids in November and December, trains ran late, and in January 1918 the schools closed for lack of coal. The family spent the time at Jettingen, where they were snowed in.[21]

In July 1918 Alexander was taken to hospital in Stuttgart, suffering from pleurisy. Berthold and Claus were lodged in Heutingsheim, near Ludwigsburg, with the widow of a former colleague of Count Stauffenberg in the Lord Chamberlain's office. The brothers wrote home about visits to Hoheneck, Ludwigsburg and Monrepos; about boating and bathing plans, tunnels they had dug in the new hay, the weeding of pathways and flower beds, except that 'yesterday it rained and so we couldn't and didn't have to'.[22] Claus wrote home about a lazy Thursday morning when they had dead-headed some carnations and lain in the sun, and a remarkable afternoon:

> Then a 5-times-wounded young hero, Herr von Plüskow, came to tea from Ludwigsburg with his parents. His foot is very badly hurt and he has it in splints. Three men had to carry him from the carriage into the garden. But the dauntless fellow wants to go back to the front despite his 5 wounds. His father is six feet nine inches tall and therefore the tallest soldier in the German Army. The Emperor used to take him with him as his aide-de-camp when he went abroad. Then we went into the hay and built a fine fox lair, under the hay, with three exits.[23]

On 18 July Berthold and Claus went with their father to Lautlingen and joined their cousins, the two daughters and son of Uncle Nux (Nikolaus Üxküll). Berthold wrote to Alexander telling him to get well and join them soon: then they would play robbers or wolves again; they could not read much because the Üxkülls did not read and always wanted to be entertained. On 2 August Berthold told how they had moved out of their robbers' lair, a tent, into a hut with table and wicker chairs:

> Claus led the donkey, Alex [Üxküll] sat in front, I stood on top of the furniture. That's how the voyage began. Weippert passed with the tray – and laughed, Frau Schairer came down from the garden – and laughed, Frau Müller stood in front of her house – and laughed, at the bottom of the garden sat Aunt Ida – and laughed. In short – everyone we met laughed. Slowly we approached the hut. It's a wonder that we didn't upset all our household goods. As quick as lightning everything was unloaded and put in its place. We were able to have tea inside straight away. That's the story of our move.[24]

There followed news of poor weather and welcome opportunities for reading, drinking fermented strawberry juice, helping father to do the wallpapering.

Alexander arrived in Lautlingen on 23 August, still convalescent and a little overwhelmed by his energetic brothers and cousins, but smiling quietly and happily. From the end of August to the end of September all the children were tutored by a student of classical language and literature, a girl

7. *Lautlingen, 1917. From left: Alexander, Berthold, Claus*

called Thilde Wendel. Uncle Nux came home on leave at the end of August. Aunt Alexandrine, Countess Üxküll (familiarly known as Üllas or Lasli), the head of the Württemberg Red Cross, arrived from Moscow having just witnessed the murder of the German Minister Count von Mirbach-Harff on 6 July, in the midst of the revolution; she had travelled for nine months by train and sled to the prisoner-of-war camps, crossed eastern Siberia, and had observed shocking conditions in camps holding many half-frozen and half-starved Germans: she had had only a little money, furs and boots to distribute among so many.[25]

In November 1914 the Chief of the High General Staff, Lieutenant-General von Falkenhayn, had said to Chancellor von Bethmann Hollweg that Germany would not win the war. Nevertheless, the armies of Germany and the other Central Powers had mounted bloody offensives deep into enemy territory, year after year, to force a decision. The Peace of Brest-Litovsk, signed with revolutionary Russia on 3 March 1918, did not free sufficient German forces to ensure the success of the German offensive begun eighteen days later in the west; the growing strength of the Americans more than offset French and English losses. On 8 August English, Australian and French troops achieved a decisive breach in the German front; on 13 August Lieutenant-General Ludendorff, the German Quartermaster General who acted as Chief of the General Staff, informed Chancellor

Count von Hertling that it was no longer possible to force peace upon the enemy by military offensives, nor did this seem likely to be achieved by purely defensive means: it was necessary to negotiate an armistice.[26]

Germany requested an armistice on 3 October; two days later Countess Stauffenberg and her sons learned the news during the autumn vacation on their way from Lautlingen to Jettingen. Late in the evening the mother took her children to church. Claus was in tears and said, 'my Germany cannot perish; if she goes down now, she will rise again strong and great; after all, there is still a God'. Alex was in shock and despair; Berthold said nothing.[27] On 24 October page one of the *Schwäbischer Merkur*, Württemberg's leading newspaper, carried the translated text of the note sent the previous day by the American Secretary of State Lansing, which stated that the Allies claimed the right to impose what peace terms they thought fit and refused to treat with representatives of the present German government. Only the removal of the monarchy could prevent the occupation of Germany by enemy troops. On 10 November the newspapers reported the abdication of the Emperor; on the following day the armistice was signed.

King William II of Württemberg did not want any of his subjects to shed their blood in defence of a lost cause. On 2 November he forbade the installation of machine guns in his Palace. Despite demonstrations and some turmoil on 6 November, the King, wearing civilian clothes as usual, walked alone through the streets of Stuttgart as he had always done, being greeted reverently by the populace. On 8 November the pupils of the Gymnasium were sent home early. On 9 November there were more open-air gatherings; one of the King's ministers proposed convening an assembly for the purpose of forming a republic. The King said he had been intending this for several weeks and gave the order at once.[28] At eleven in the morning a mob pushed its way into the Palace. Dr Gussmann, the King's personal physician, together with the Chief of the Royal Cabinet, Baron von Neurath, the Lord Chamberlain, Count Stauffenberg, and the servants prevented the mob from penetrating to the King's apartments. But the royal standard flying from the palace roof was replaced by a red flag and 'revolutionary sentries' were posted outside, whereupon the crowd dispersed. The King did not abdicate, but would not stay under a red flag and decided to leave Stuttgart.

The Stauffenberg family was in the midst of the upheaval. The Old Palace was in the centre of the city, only a few hundred yards from the royal residence. At ten in the morning the trams stopped running, large crowds milled around outside the Old Castle, red flags appeared, and radical speeches were made; the mob disarmed unresisting soldiers in nearby barracks and in the King's Palace. In the afternoon Countess Stauffenberg went to see the Queen. The King came into the room, looking sorrowful with tears trickling down his white beard, saying he wished it was time for their departure. He had long known that he was likely to be the last of the

Kings of Württemberg, but such an end to his reign seemed undignified and unjust at the hands of a people who had enjoyed a liberal government; and even the soldiers had all deserted him, he said, evidently having expected some show of loyalty despite his orders to avoid bloodshed.

At half-past six the King and Queen, Count Stauffenberg, the General Adjutant Lieutenant-General von Gaevernitz, and a few aides and ladies-in-waiting left in two motor-cars, escorted by revolutionary guards, for Bebenhausen, a former Cistercian monastery near Tübingen, now a royal hunting lodge. Count Stauffenberg was later described by Duke Philip, son of Duke Albrecht who would have succeeded King William II on the throne, as the most faithful of the King's men and the only one who had not lost his head during those sad days. By nine o'clock in the evening everyone had safely arrived in Bebenhausen. On 10 November there was talk of counter-revolution and of the imminent arrival of White Guards from the garrisons of Ulm and Ludwigsburg, but all remained calm.

On 11 November Germany accepted the armistice which forced her to disarm and to accept whatever conditions the victors imposed. All through 15 November, Claus strove to hold back tears: he did not want any celebration on this, the saddest birthday of his life. He was also disappointed that the King had left without a struggle.[29]

It was Count Stauffenberg who negotiated the settlement of the estate and pensions of the King and Queen with the new government of Württemberg. The formal agreement was signed on 29 November, and on 30 November the King abdicated. The royal family retained certain properties, but all the royal estates, forests and other crown properties, including the palaces in Stuttgart and Ludwigsburg, passed into state ownership. The property of the nobility was generally not expropriated, but became subject to civil law.[30]

For the Stauffenberg family a tradition going back many generations came to an end on that last day of November. For centuries they had served reigning monarchs as noble vassals and had themselves lorded over farmers and servants. Now it was the people who ruled. The thought of being the servants of the people was a strange one to them.

The beginning of January 1919 saw the 'Spartakist' (communist) uprising, in the course of which there was some shooting in Stuttgart, near the *Württemberger Zeitung* building in the Hospitalstrasse. On a particularly disturbed day Countess Stauffenberg went to the Gymnasium in the Holzgartenstrasse and fetched her sons, quite unmoved by the fact that the twins' class was sitting an examination at the time. The disorders, sporadic shooting and strikes continued through February, March and April, and noble families had good reason for concern, as Countess Stauffenberg wrote: 'Eisner shot by Count Arco in Munich [. . .] Pillage and nocturnal shootings continue – 25 aristocrats imprisoned.'[31] Most members of the nobility decided that it was dangerous to remain in the city: country estates offered greater safety, since the country folk generally remained loyal; and the presence of the family would also help protect the estates against attempts at expropriation. Representatives of the various branches of the Stauffenberg family met in Stuttgart and converted the estates which were subject to primogeniture – now forbidden by law – into a family corporation.

On 8 April Countess Stauffenberg and her sons travelled to Greifenstein via Nuremberg, which was in a state of siege. There they heard about the 'soviet republic' which had been set up in Munich; of street battles, of the Bavarian government's retreat to Bamberg, and a month later of the shooting of hostages by the Spartakists, and then of the downfall of the latter. By the end of May the family was back in Lautlingen, while a new flat, at 18 Jägerstrasse in Stuttgart, was being made ready to serve as their official residence. The political situation was chaotic. If Germany did not sign the Treaty of Versailles, French troops and Spahis (troops recruited from the French colonies) would occupy the country. On 31 May the Queen arrived by motor-car and entrusted her jewels to Countess Stauffenberg, who concealed them in her clothing and smuggled them into Switzerland for the duration.[32]

In June the boys, then at Lautlingen, were joined by the children of Uncle Nux.[33] Claus, who had embarked on his own religious observances when at the Old Castle, continued them at an 'altar' in the attic, sharing them with his eight-year-old Lutheran cousin Elisabeth ('Baby'), Countess Üxküll, 'because she knew so little about the Holy Mass'. Berthold, now fourteen, read about astronomy, geology and philosophy. Alexander read about music and about Goethe's sojourn in Weimar, and wrote poetry.

From mid-June to mid-September the three brothers were tutored by Elisabeth Dipper of Stuttgart, who was about to go to the university of Tübingen. Apparently the boys' mother had asked the head of Stuttgart's most prestigious girls' high school to suggest a candidate for this post. When Miss Dipper arrived the boys hitched the donkey to the wagon, collected her at the station, and drove back with her as fast as the donkey could go along the rough road through the village. Miss Dipper knew she was being tested, and that her authority depended on how calmly she could face up to this challenge from the three energetic youngsters.

Miss Dipper and the boys used to breakfast in the small tower at the bottom of the garden. It was just the same as at home: 'ersatz coffee, the same moist brown bread except that here it is toasted, margarine, jam'. Lessons followed in the same room. At luncheon and dinner servants went round with the dishes, there were fresh plates for every course; the children were expected to eat whatever they took onto their plates. Count Stauffenberg personally mixed the salad in a large glass bowl. The meals were rather simpler than Miss Dipper was used to, 'although perhaps finer'. Conversation often switched to English or French. Coffee was taken in the library, where the parents and other elders discussed history and current events, with the boys quietly taking in everything that was said. Those interminable meals were a nuisance, wrote Miss Dipper in a letter home, because every day the eating and the subsequent process of digestion took up at least 5½ hours. The noonday meal was followed by a nap, and the day was used up!

Count Stauffenberg was expected in the week after Miss Dipper's arrival. He had acquired a reputation for being gruff, harsh and abrupt toward his wife and sons. He was certainly displeased with the new order and described the current government as a gang of blackguards. But Countess Stauffenberg's Aunt Osch declared Count Stauffenberg 'an anachronism'.

Alexander was easily hurt by his father's critical mutterings but Claus, always ready with a philosophical insight, had a method: let father growl until he got over it! The three boys had read many books which their teacher now wanted to read herself; she discussed with them the memoirs of Carl Schurz (the American statesman) and Spengler's *Decline of the West*. Alexander composed pieces for the piano. Alex was touchingly gullible, still childlike. Because Berthold mastered all school subjects so easily Miss Dipper needed all her Greek learning to be able to answer his questions. Alex considered himself stupid, although he was merely a bit slower than his brothers. Berthold was darkly taciturn with a suggestion of arrogance, but Miss Dipper ascribed this in part to his superior intelligence. He wanted to enter the diplomatic service. Claus was constantly drawing up plans for the complete rebuilding of Lautlingen Manor, intended to go into farming, and grew many plants in his own little garden. He did not yet know that he could charm people almost at will. When in September Countess Stauffenberg proposed 'holidays' every other day for the purpose of sunbathing, Claus did not want to forego Miss Dipper's tutoring for fear of falling behind in school (though in fact there was no danger of that). They compromised: there would be lessons, but no 'homework'. Each pupil was also required to memorise a poem. Claus chose Heinrich Heine's ballad on Belshazzar, the King of Babylon who had blasphemed Jehovah and robbed the Temple, declaiming with passion:

> Belsazer ward aber in selbiger Nacht
> Von seinen Knechten umgebracht.

> (But that same night Belshazzar was slain by his servants.)

From the summer of 1919 to Count Stauffenberg's retirement in 1928 the family lived in the official residence of the President of the Ducal Revenue Office, no. 18 Jägerstrasse, Stuttgart, between vineyards and the station (the modern building by Paul Bonatz). Uncle Nux and Aunt Üllas also had flats at no. 18 Jägerstrasse.[34]

Initially, Claus stayed at Lautlingen and was taught, together with the

Üxküll children, by a new governess, Elsbet Miller, who had been sent by the head of the same Stuttgart girls' high school as Elisabeth Dipper. Berthold and Alexander went back to school in Stuttgart. Alexander came to Lautlingen the first week-end after school had begun, pale and upset because another pupil had used cogent arguments to cast doubt on the divinity of Christ: if he could not believe in it, said Alexander, he could no longer go to Holy Communion. Berthold was really an agnostic, but was interested in Master Ekkehart and St Francis of Assisi; when the master who taught Catholic dogma slandered Luther so vilely that several pupils protested, Berthold remained silent during the class, but spoke to the teacher afterward and informed him that he and his Catholic fellow pupils would no longer attend if the master continued his vulgar attacks.[35]

The great poets of the time attracted the boys. Their first love was the poetry of Hofmannsthal. Some of their teachers gathered pupils informally to read from the works of Conrad Ferdinand Meyer and Martin Heidegger; Berthold, Alexander and their friends Theodor Pfizer and Hans-Ulrich von Marchtaler met to read works by Goethe, Friedrich Hebbel and Heinrich von Kleist, and Rilke's 'Cornet'. Others set up an exhibition of prints of Expressionist paintings by artists such as Nolde, Macke and Jawlensky – though formal instruction never ventured closer to their own time than the Renaissance. At home and at school the brothers and their friends acted scenes from Hölderlin's *Empedokles*, Hofmannsthal's *Der Tod des Tizian* and Shakespeare's *Julius Caesar*.[36]

In February 1918 Dr Wilhelm, Baron von Stauffenberg, died. Since August 1914 he had been corresponding with Rilke, and after his death Countess Stauffenberg correspondend with the great poet.[37] This connection may have influenced the attitudes of the Countess and her children. After the funeral, Countess Stauffenberg wrote to Rilke that the last time she had seen Dr von Stauffenberg, in September 1917, he had told her that Rilke had just written his most exquisite work. Was it available in the book shops? She was now reading the book she had found beside Dr von Stauffenberg's bed in order to transport herself into his world. Rilke replied that even more pressing than his sorrow for his lost friend was his obligation to continue in the direction in which that magnanimous and wise friend wished him to go; he, Rilke, was most pleased to find that his own nature was urging him in the same direction. The work for which Countess Stauffenberg had displayed such an alert interest existed only in unconnected fragments, which would have been intelligible only to the well-informed friend who had learned, through various conversations, what their overall plan would be. It might be published in the distant future, and if ever it was completed, Rilke would dedicate a copy to Countess Stauffenberg. Would she let him know which book had been on Dr von Stauffenberg's bedside table?

Countess Stauffenberg answered that when she was re-reading Rilke's 'Requiem auf den Tod eines Knaben' (Requiem for a boy's death), it had occurred to her that Rilke might be able to find words of consolation, both for himself and for her, for the loss of Dr von Stauffenberg. It must be a poet's greatest privilege to find that 'a God had enabled him to give expression to his suffering'. In the stack of books beside Dr von Stauffenberg's bed there was De Coster's *Ulenspiegel*. Apart from the pile lay Arnold Bennett's *The Old Wives' Tale*: she had read it, but did not believe that Dr von Stauffenberg had any particular views on it. But he did consider Mary Hamilton's *Dead Yesterday* brilliant: its superior standard of justice and objectivity must have agreed with his own thinking.

There followed a pause in the correspondence. In January 1919 Rilke sent Countess Stauffenberg a copy of Insel's (the publishers') Almanac. The selection of contributions by himself, he wrote, was largely determined by the death of his friend. Countess Stauffenberg thanked Rilke and declared herself better prepared for future blows of fate – which she must expect as a mother of three sons in the coming difficult times. When Rilke sent her Émile Verhaeren's *Les Flammes hautes*, she thanked him and enclosed a photograph of her children on a balcony of the Old Castle in Stuttgart. Rilke wrote back: the photograph had added much to Countess Stauffenberg's letter and he now understood her anxiety about her three sons, but he also saw in the affectionate group the overriding happiness which three such handsome, richly promising lads must give her.

In 1918 another living poet touched the life of the Stauffenberg family when Bernhard, Count Üxküll, died. Count Üxküll, an officer cadet in the Prussian Field Artillery First Guards Regiment, was born in 1899; his father was a half-brother of Countess Stauffenberg's father. He had become a friend of Stefan George in 1907 through Ernst Morwitz, a judge in the Berlin High Court of Appeal. A friend of Bernhard's , Adalbert Cohrs, also in the Army, and addicted to certain drugs, had failed to return from leave on time. Bernhard had stayed with him, and they had both shot themselves.[38] However, for the time being Stefan George remained a remote presence for the Stauffenbergs.

In 1920 the Stauffenberg brothers produced one issue of a hand-written periodical they called 'Hermes'. Berthold's contribution compared the World War with the Seven Years' War, identified its causes as the existence of coalitions and well-founded mutual distrust, and regretted that the outcome was not equally favourable. Alexander contributed poems and a fragment of a fairy-tale. Claus, doubtless inspired by his father's conversation, was represented by a disquisition on unemployment benefit, stating that it would destroy Germany more horribly than any enemies could have done: socialism, Spartakism and strikes would only increase, particularly since the government would soon have to halt payments to the workers.[39]

The Reich was indeed insecure, even after painful losses of territory. France was stoking the flames of separatism in the Rhineland and in Bavaria; Poland, with British support, seized German territory in Silesia and in West Prussia, despite plebiscites favouring Germany. When in January 1921 the Entente Powers gave details of their reparation demands, this produced both despondency and the will to resist in Germany.[40]

Early in 1921 Alexander wrote to Theodor Pfizer, a friend of the Stauffenberg brothers: 'One more year like the past one and we shall be standing at the graveside of our homeland; but it is more probable that we shall see hints of a new dawn, although it may be on a distant horizon.' In the spring of 1921 Alexander read about the Battle of Salamis and declared that he thought history was good material for ballads or plays. In school he was caught reading Thomas Mann's *Tonio Kröger* in class: the teacher curled his lip and recommended 'modern' literature such as he had read in his own youth, Frenssen's *Jörn Uhl* (a rather indifferent novel) for example.[41]

In the schoolyard Alexander asked Theodor if he knew that there was one greater even than Rilke: Stefan George. In 1921 the twins and Theodor read George's book of poems, *Der Stern des Bundes*.[42]

Berthold and Alexander each developed a number of close boyhood friendships, two of which continued until their deaths. No similar relationships of Claus's are recorded, perhaps because he was often ill and absent from school, and because two schoolmates who are said to have been good friends of Claus did not live to tell their story; but mostly because Claus, who still missed his twin, attached himself to his elder brothers, even in the schoolyard during break. One day in 1923 he wrote from Lautlingen to his cousin Alexander, Count Üxküll, who was in Stuttgart. He was sorry that they had not seen each other during Alex's last visit to Lautlingen; he believed that they had much to say to each other, as they had done the last time, and they should be friends and love each other.[43] It appears that little came of this, since Alex Üxküll was rather independent. Later, until about 1928, Claus's friends were almost all friends of Stefan George and of his own elder brothers.[44] Among the elder brothers' school friends were Theodor Pfizer, the son of a judge; Hans-Ulrich von Marchtaler, son of a career army officer; Rudolf Obermüller, son of a civil servant who lived at no. 12 Jägerstrasse; Georg Federer, whose father was the Consul of Austria-Hungary; Frank Mehnert, who was born in Moscow in 1909, son of a German-Russian printer who fell serving in the German Army in the World War.

In the years up to 1923 the twins and Claus belonged to the 'New Scouts', one of several 'Youth Movement' (*Jugendbewegung*) groups represented at school. They went on walking expeditions, read round the camp-fire from Stefan George's *Der Stern des Bundes*, sang old mercenary songs, and talked about the fate of the Reich and of the national community (*Volksgemein-schaft*).[45]

Berthold's exchanges with Rudolf Obermüller afford a view of the reserved and even taciturn young Stauffenberg. Berthold gave Rudolf a photograph of himself and wrote:

> Love is the meaning of the world. In nature, who alone still offers herself to us in all her purity, I can find only beauty, joy, love. And are they not in the deepest sense one and the same? To give oneself in love, and thus to seek perfection, this shall be the way! Yours, Berthold Stauffenberg. June 1921.

It was the language of Hölderlin, from his 'Hyperion': 'Over thousands of years Love gave birth to living human beings; through friendship they will be born anew.' Stefan George wrote this variation: 'Love gave birth to the world · love will give birth to it anew.' In 1922 Berthold declared Hölderlin and George his greatest heroes.

Rudolf dedicated to Berthold his valedictory address to the final-year class of 1922; he wrote intimate 'Obituaries on Living Persons', including one for Berthold. After he had gone to study theology in Tübingen, and Berthold had matriculated at Heidelberg University in May 1923, Rudolf walked to Heidelberg to see him. Berthold informed him gently that he, unlike his friend, could not accept a compromise between classical Hellas and Christianity.[46]

By this time Berthold, Claus and Alexander had been introduced to Stefan George. Max Kommerell, who was a little older and had grown up in Cannstatt across the river from Stuttgart, was the closest of George's young friends at that time, and was adept at discovering new candidates for the poet's circle. He wrote love poems addressed to Berthold; Berthold wrote love poems addressed to George and to the fourteen-year-old Frank Mehnert.[47]

In April and June 1923, both Alexander and Berthold wrote letters explaining how they conceived their duty, in view of the state of the nation. Three years later Claus, again in a letter, explained his choice of career. All three unhesitatingly dedicated their lives to the service of the nation. Lautlingen included two leaseholds, of 150 hectares each, which could have supported a frugal rural life. But Claus, who liked farming, nonetheless considered that the only reason why noblemen should hold land was in order to ensure that they could bring up their children to public service as officers in the armed forces, civil servants or professionals. The brothers' background and upbringing, as well as their extraordinary intellectual endowments, naturally inclined them towards professions appropriate to their abilities. They were conscious of their illustrious ancestors, a prince-bishop on the Stauffenberg side and Count Gneisenau on the Üxküll side. All three claimed, as of right, a place in the first rank of those who served the nation.[48]

On 11 January 1923, French and Belgian troops occupied the Ruhr on the pretext that Germany had deliberately defaulted on reparations; in fact, she had failed to deliver a smallish quantity of timber and telegraph poles. Young Germans volunteered for National Service in droves. Everywhere defence forces were formed in conjunction with the regular forces, particularly in the universities. The Versailles Treaty prohibited the training of reserves, but after the Ruhr occupation the German authorities refused to admit Entente inspectors (who included French and Belgian officers) to Reichswehr installations. During the inspection-free months from January 1923 to the beginning of 1924, great numbers of young Germans received their basic military training, among them the Stauffenbergs and their friends.[49]

During the summer semester of 1923, Alexander and Berthold jogged around Heidelberg to get fit for their military training. Alexander wrote to Theodor Pfizer, who was in basic training in Ulm with No. 13 Infantry Regiment, that he had given up his plans for the study and practice of literature. Now that at any moment there might be 'powerful explosions and fateful decisions', 'we have no right to waste time: as things now stand, everyone has to be at the ready – all this must lead to a horrible end'. Alexander's poems of May and June 1923 speak of combat, blood, sacrifice, treading a path through ruin with sword in hand. Alexander remarked that his life was going to be enriched beyond all expectations by 'the limitless tasks which are set by the ideal of the Reich (perhaps a model for it already exists, in *Der Stern des Bundes*)'.[50] Berthold had much the same ideas: there was little point in thinking about the future, soon everything would end in utter chaos – or alternatively, in the most ghastly Americanisation. It was just as well they were going to Ludwigsburg for military training, as it might soon be needed.[51]

In this same year, which was one of rampant inflation, Berthold paid 8,425 Reichsmarks and Alexander 7,225 Reichsmarks in fees for their university courses. Berthold was reading law, but wrote in June that so far he had attended only two lectures, one of which was given by Gundolf, the literary historian and famous friend of Stefan George. Most of the time, he claimed, he spent roaming through the forests and sunning himself by the river or in a boat. Alexander thought their freedom glorious, especially since Woldemar, Count Üxküll (Bernhard's brother) was in Heidelberg. Üxküll had been among George's friends since 1907 and had recently received a doctorate in history. Alexander went for walks with him, and together they read the tragedies of Aeschylus. Alexander was looking forward to a visit from his parents, and when the train carrying Aunt Osch and the Queen stopped in Heidelberg he intended to be on the platform – but he would have to pay for his platform ticket in postage stamps, as the twenty Reichsmarks which remained to him were worth less than half a penny: 'We shall scrounge enormously from Osch.'[52]

Berthold spent some time with the training battalion of No. 13 Infantry Regiment in Schwäbisch Gmünd, but his service was cut short by an inflammation of the joints. Alexander served in the 4th (Baden) Squadron, commanded by Captain Baron Geyr von Schweppenburg, of No. 18 Cavalry Regiment in Ludwigsburg. He did not think he was cut out to be a soldier, but he enjoyed all the riding.[53]

After spending the holidays at Lautlingen, Berthold matriculated at Jena University for the winter semester 1923/24, to read law and philosophy. He thought the region lovely, and the city horrid, devoid of the atmosphere it must have had in Goethe's and Schiller's time. The sorts of people one saw all around one, including the students, were abominable: there was not a single face with whose owner one would have liked to become acquainted. Moreover, daily necessities were difficult to procure because of the inflation.[54]

Alexander matriculated the same winter at Tübingen University, where Theodor Pfizer was also reading law. He lived with Aunt Osch at no. 6 Kaiserstrasse and enrolled for lectures in civil law, social policy and Greek and Roman history. Together with Karl Schefold, a school friend, he read Homer. A sense of duty had determined his decision to read law: he wrote to his mother that he had inherited the pragmatic Stauffenberg temperament, 'which will not allow that the Menelauses and Ciceros have any relevance to the resurgence of Germany'. But by December 1923 all that had changed. History had him 'in its grip', and he hoped it would never let go.[55]

The first meeting with Stefan George gave new direction and meaning to the lives of the Stauffenberg brothers. The connection came through Dr Maria Fehling, daughter of the Mayor of Lübeck and sister of a famous theatrical director, who worked for Cotta Publishers in Stuttgart; the publisher's wife was a friend of Countess Stauffenberg's, and so Dr Fehling made the acquaintance of the Stauffenberg family. She was a friend of Dr Albrecht von Blumenthal, who was a friend of Stefan George; and she suggested that 'at least two of the brothers were suitable for the Circle'. She meant Berthold and Claus.

Berthold was introduced to Stefan George by Blumenthal in Marburg on Lahn at the end of May, in the house of Professor Friedrich Wolters, an important friend of George's. Claus was presented to Stefan George at the same time or very soon thereafter. Alexander was introduced to the poet by Woldemar, Count Üxküll, later than Berthold, but also in Marburg on Lahn and also in May 1923.[56]

Stefan George gave Berthold a nickname which was used thereafter by the poet and his friends: Adjib (the wonderful), after a ruler from the *Thousand and One Nights*, who was, like Berthold, wise and mature in youth and who, in his eagerness to rule, displaced his father. People in the streets of Munich are said to have taken Berthold for a Wittelsbach prince. In a

8. Lautlingen, 1924. From left: Claus, Berthold and Alexander with their parents

poem in *Das Neue Reich* Stefan George praised Berthold's 'majesty', his 'lordly right', his 'grace' which must not be supplanted by ideas of general equality and the happiness of the greatest number. Alexander received the name 'Offa', after the son of a king of the Angles who fought fiercely against enemies who sought to rob his father of his kingdom, and then relapsed into indolence. When 'Offa' came to see Stefan George for the second time, in March 1924, the poet said to him: 'Good God, Offa, how wooden you are!' He was more attracted to Berthold's beauty and superior intellect, and to Claus's charming radiance and uninhibited wholeness. Claus was not even given a nickname, because the poet, as one of his close friends later explained, found nothing in Claus which he would have been able or willing to mould or improve upon.[57]

Before the World War, Stefan George had claimed for himself a 'domin-ion of the spirit' (*reich des geistes*). He disdained 'clan, class and name', preferring the 'sonship' from which he himself would create his 'rulers of the world'. He esteemed nobility of character above descent and kinship. But since the revolution he had found it easier to approach and win over members of the established nobility.[58] George must have confirmed the Stauffenberg brothers in their sense of association with the imperial Staufen dynasty: otherwise Claus, in the poems he gave to George, would surely not have declared himself so openly the heir of Ottonian and Staufen kings.[59]

From this time forward, the relationship with Stefan George and his circle separated the Stauffenberg brothers from the rest of the world by an invisible, yet perceptible and impenetrable, wall. Alexander considered his encounter with the poet 'the greatest event in his life'; he called George the ruler and lord of his fate, priest, king, father, judge, sage, blazing centre, 'creator of a new world of love and ardour', 'Prince in the Reich's late glory'; above all there ruled the Great Unifier, the God Eros. As late as 1959 Alexander confessed in a public lecture his 'unreserved reverence and admiration' for Stefan George's works and praised the poet's power of moulding other people. Claus said he had 'as his teacher the greatest poet of his time'. Berthold vowed submission to his 'Lord' and 'Master', declared himself 'overpowered and spell-bound', and called George Saviour: 'You are sent as Saviour to this world.' He confessed 'arduous yearning', a feeling of striding forth 'free from sin'.[60]

Alexander's poems to Stefan George and other friends are scarcely less passionate, though much more poetic than those of Berthold – or those of Claus, who praised Eros only in a poem filled with dreams of feminine charms.[61]

The youths' bond with Stefan George was unreserved, comprehensive, deep; it was like the 'Imitation of Christ', it was love and obedience.

Admission into the Circle was sealed with a kiss, as Alexander recorded:

> [. . .] my lips inquire
> Your eye was silent· and see· the circle round
> Is written only when from mouth to mouth
> The lips speak their silent answer.[62]

The manuscripts of Berthold's, Alexander's and Claus's poems, found among Stefan George's papers, were folded and soiled at the folds: the poet must have carried them about with him for a long time.

George's own views on love were stated publicly on his behalf in 1912, by Friedrich Gundolf and Karl Wolfskehl in the *Jahrbuch für die geistige Bewegung*. He cared not if the devotion of Schiller's Don Carlos to the Marquis Posa, or that of Goethe's Ferdinand to Egmont, had anything to do with a certain 'witch-hunting law statute' in the Penal Code: this 'eros' was part of German culture and education, just like the sanctioned institution of matrimony – under cover of which every abominable and unnatural form of indecency could occur. The former eros was not to be despised because of possible excesses. In any case, it was not really a question of moral prejudice. Most humans could no more understand Dante's love for Beatrice than Shakespeare's for the 'friend' of the Sonnets: 'it is the distaste of the American, who has become devoid of passion, for every form of heroic love'. George and his friends had nothing in common with 'those wholly disagreeable people who whine for the repeal of certain penal statutes', for the most repugnant attacks 'against us' had come from precisely such circles.[63]

On 16 and 17 June 1923, Claus and his parents visited relatives in Neckarhausen and then came to see Berthold and Alexander in Heidelberg. Countess Stauffenberg called to see George, then on one of his frequent stays with Ernst Kantorowicz, the young historian, who shared a flat with Woldi (Woldemar Üxküll) at no. 12 Schloss-Wolfsbrunnenweg. She wanted to see what sort of company her sons were keeping: their enthusiastic devotion to the poet made her acutely aware that they were turning away from their youthful attachment to her toward adulthood, toward the father figure and toward the service of greater causes. The famous poet attracted her, too; but no relationship developed comparable even to that she had had with Rilke.[64]

Claus, like his brothers, had views on the purpose of life, which he had expressed even before the Ruhr occupation, and before his brothers had gone to Heidelberg and into military training. In July 1922 he wrote in a school essay that it was the natural destiny of the citizen 'in his profession to further the welfare of the state', and he subscribed to Schiller's ideals of 'freedom, order, concord' as his life's aim. In September 1922, in an essay on 'Use and Dangers of Competitive Games', he declared that their purpose was concord for the well-being of the fatherland.[65]

School fellows remember Claus as a rather frail-looking youth who loved the arts and wanted to be a musician. Only one or two saw another side. When Claus understood that his musical talents would not lead him to superior accomplishments he gave up this ambition. When he asked his classmate, Alfons Bopp (who intended to become a priest) what he considered the essential value of a human being, Bopp said it was the immortal soul; but Claus said no, accomplishment was the key.[66]

Claus also thought for a while of becoming an architect. He proclaimed this goal in a school essay of 24 January 1923, but declared there was only one calling for a man who had 'recognised the fatherland and the new Reich'; and he used the word *Kampf* (combat or struggle) three times in the first two sentences of the essay: 'To become worthy of the fatherland and of combat for the fatherland and then to sacrifice oneself to the sublime combat for the nation; to lead a life in awareness of reality and combat.' This was possible in any occupation. For his part, he intended to do it as an architect, making every building he designed a temple dedicated to the German nation. In order to better understand his own nation and other nations and their cultures, however, he also intended to study history. This was his plan now, he wrote – but he might change it later. The main thing was to follow whatever path one eventually chose with clear and manly resolution. The fundamental occupation must always be combat for the fatherland; the actual occupation must be subordinated to this guiding principle. Claus's inclination to architecture was not a passing one. Through 1923 at least he seems to have kept it, as one of his poems records:

> I often feel I must draw plans
> Of high vast palaces
> With red marble, white stairways
> And fabulous long light-strewn halls.

In his last year at school he often designed stage scenery, and even during the Second World War he liked to talk about his earlier career choice, and about building plans.[67]

The occupation of the Ruhr; passive resistance; 'black' (illicit) reserve training in the Reichswehr; communist insurrections in Saxony and Thuringia; the restiveness of the 'national combat leagues' in Bavaria; the Hitler putsch in Munich: all these events sent ripples of excitement, if no more, flowing through the schools. In some high schools in Stuttgart lapels sported ribbons in black, white and red (the colours of the Empire), or swastikas. Some pupils roughed up their 'enemies'; pupils wearing black, white and red or black, red and gold (republican) taunted each other in the street; some parents received anonymous letters warning them against patronising shops owned by Jews; a pupil was punished with two hours' solitary detention because he had sung the 'International' in the form room.[68] These incidents indicate tendencies, but they do not permit blanket judgements. Most pupils' views were influenced by those of their parents and were likely to represent the 'national' or 'patriotic' outlook, but not extreme racist or communist views.

The pupils of Claus's predominantly Catholic form later declared that their first allegiance was to their Church. But the school as a whole celebrated annually the foundation of the German state on 18 January 1871, and on flag-flying days they always hoisted a black, white and red flag besides the black, red and gold flag of the Republic, implicitly refusing to accept the latter as the official national flag. In 1923 Rudolf Griesinger, who taught French to the top form, told them that he regretted the inclusion of French literature in the curriculum: it was a waste of time. Although only two of Claus's former classmates said the Republic had a negative image in the school, the prevailing mood was one of indifference. But there was complete unity in the condemnation of the Versailles Treaty that Germany had been forced to accept under threat of military occupation. One of the teachers, Albert Ströhle, published a study of the Treaty; hundreds of thousands of copies were sold in 1923, and all the pupils were expected to own one.[69] Arthur Gutmann, who taught Catholic dogma, said that the swastika was an anti-Semitic symbol. Claus objected that it had occurred in ancient Egypt and had had nothing to do with anti-Semitism. He was, of course, familiar with the use of the swastika on books published by members of Stefan George's circle – many of whom were Jewish.[70]

There were some Jewish pupils in most forms. On the list of candidates for the final school examination from the form which included the elder Stauffenberg brothers, two boys were identified as 'Israelite'. In the corresponding list for Claus's final year there were three, and one whose last name was changed upon application from Levi to Lerse. Of the three who passed the examination at the same time as Claus, Alfred Bach became a chemical engineer, left Germany in 1932 because he saw the rise of Hitler, and died in Israel in 1960; Eduard Lowinsky became a famous musicologist at the University of Chicago and died in 1985; Erich Marx could not be traced.[71]

A classmate of Claus's recalled a mildly anti-Semitic atmosphere in his schooldays and said that he had himself rather avoided Lowinsky's company.[72] Lowinsky's parents had come from the Ukraine, and when Eduard was eight or nine he had been refused admission to the Jewish youth league 'Kameraden' because he was an Eastern Jew; he joined the Zionist organisation 'Blau-Weiss'.[73] He had no memory of any pervasive anti-Semitism at school, but he remembered expressions of prejudice by some pupils and teachers. One of his classmates was surprised to find that Lowinsky, though a Jew, had considerable will-power; when Lowinsky commented on pupils wearing swastikas, one gave him an anti-Semitic pamphlet; a music teacher wanted to know how Lowinsky, as a Jew, could be enthusiastic for the Lutheran Bach.[74]

The Stauffenbergs had nothing to do with incidents at that or any other level, nor are there any reports that they had anti-Semitic leanings. A Jewish pupil, Lothar Bauer, often came to tea at the Stauffenbergs' flat. Alfred Bach was a friend of Claus's and was often invited to no. 18 Jägerstrasse; he recalled later how impressed he had been at being invited as a Jew to birthday parties when Christian school fellows were not invited.[75] Friendships with Jews, however, do not necessarily prove an absence of prejudice.

On one occasion Eduard Lowinsky, the best musician in Claus's form, came with Claus to the Jägerstrasse, most likely as a potential pianist in a Stauffenberg trio or quartet; but Countess Stauffenberg, possibly preoccupied or absent-minded, spoke to him only briefly in the hall and did not ask him in. Claus felt embarrassed and made amends by walking for half an hour with him, back to his parents' flat, chatting enthusiastically the whole time about Gothic cathedrals.

Ever since the elder brothers had gone to Heidelberg and the three of them had met Stefan George, Claus had yearned to join his brothers and see the poet again. The school and the rather small city of Stuttgart must have been hard to tolerate; violent political disturbances, the occupation of the Ruhr by enemy forces, rumours of putsches, the brothers' approaching

9. Frank Mehnert at Lautlingen, 1924

military service, all added to Claus's restlessness. In June 1923 he visited
Alexander in Heidelberg, and another relation, Rudolf, Count Bassewitz,
who was stationed in Copenhagen as a counsellor in the German legation.[76]
    At the end of that summer, after the elder brothers had done their

military service, the family were re-united at Lautlingen; Albrecht von Blumenthal and Maria Fehling, Woldi and Theodor were house guests in September. Claus fell ill with angina, and was confined to bed when Karl Schefold came to see him to urge upon him the idea of the 'New Life of the Youth Movement' groups at school. 'Claus replied: "I do not follow ideas, but people"', by which Schefold understood him to mean, 'I follow the man who means more to me than any doctrine', namely Stefan George.[77]

Claus and Frank Mehnert, who was two years younger and attended the same Gymnasium, spent a good deal of time in each other's company. In January 1924 they read Hölderlin's *Hyperion* together. Both greatly missed Berthold, to whom Frank had formed a passionate attachment in 1922.[78] But Berthold and Alexander were in Italy that year.

2

Secret Germany

The accession of the Stauffenbergs to Stefan George's circle caused tremendous excitement among the poet's friends. The brothers' name was richly suggestive: Ernst Kantorowicz was writing a biography of the Staufen Emperor Frederick II, and the poet's own claim to the intellectual leadership of Germany bathed everything in a mystic, luminous haze. Those enveloped in it perceived it as a 'vision' of great clarity.

The Master himself wrote a poem about Berthold, referring to his 'sublimity', his 'grace' and his 'lordly right'. Albrecht von Blumenthal dedicated a series of poems to *principi iuventutis* (Berthold), calling him 'a king's son', 'invisibly crowned', 'striding through the streets of his future capital [. . .] on the way to his new throne'. Max Kommerell, a young literary historian and a very close friend of Stefan George, applied to both Berthold and Alexander epithets such as 'royal' and 'royal descendants'. He named Claus 'chief of the myth', described the 'miraculous lad' as the heir to the emperor 'in the Staufen mountain', mentioned 'secret coronation' in the same context, then further compared Claus to the god of war, and entitled allusive poems 'Songs to C.', 'Kyffhäuser' and 'The Initiation of a Hero'.[1]

In those days – until about 1929 – Kommerell was in complete harmony with the poet's thoughts and doctrine: thus the former's description of the Stauffenbergs as descendants of the Staufen dynasty was not a personal view, but had emerged from the Master's conversation. Equally, Claus's own poems are pervaded by the Master's ideas and akin to his language; the poet cherished Claus's poems and carried them about in his pocket for some considerable time. In these poems Claus declared himself and his brothers 'the blond heirs of the Staufens and Ottonians'. He referred to the Master in a poem he wrote for Berthold in 1923:

> I swore lordship to myself and to you:
> Which knowledge the Master himself revealed.

Significant ideas expressed in the poems recur in a statement of Claus's beliefs written in July 1944.[2]

In February 1924 Alexander asked Stefan George for permission to join his teacher of ancient history, Wilhelm Weber, and the lecturers Fritz Taeger and Joseph Vogt, on an Italian journey. The Master urged him to go, adding obscurely that it was 'the last opportunity'.[3]

The party left Tübingen on 24 March and travelled via Milan, Verona, Padua, Venice and Ravenna, arriving in Rome on 2 April. They stopped in a small hotel called 'Minerva' on the Piazza della Minerva, where the great classical historian Theodor Mommsen had once stayed. A church, Santa Maria sopra Minerva, stood there on the ruins of the Temple of Minerva which the Emperor Domitian had built.[4] Berthold Stauffenberg and Blumenthal had set out earlier, on 7 March, and had arrived in Rome on 18 March, where they now met Alexander. Maria Fehling arrived in Rome on 4 April. On occasions Berthold, Blumenthal and Maria Fehling would join Wilhelm Weber's group to visit a museum; Blumenthal and Maria Fehling, seized with enthusiasm, fell on their knees before some of the sculptures. On 7 April Alexander, Berthold, Blumenthal and Maria Fehling travelled to Naples, Paestum and Capri. The group from Tübingen returned home toward the end of April; Alexander stayed on in Florence for two more days and was back in Tübingen by 27 April.[5]

Berthold, Blumenthal and Maria Fehling went on to Palermo and visited the Palazzo Reale, childhood home of the Emperor Frederick II, and the cathedral to see his sarcophagus. In a museum Blumenthal met the archaeologist Erich Boehringer, who was also a friend of Stefan George. Blumenthal and Berthold then went on to Girgenti (the modern Agrigento) and Syracuse. They returned via the Brenner Pass to Munich, arriving on 10 May.[6]

In that same season others of the Master's friends, such as Ernst Kantorowicz, Erika Wolters (wife of Friedrich Wolters) and the sociologist and political scientist Kurt Singer were also in Palermo. Berthold Vallentin, a Berlin lawyer and writer, was in Sicily with his wife Diana. Erika Wolters wrote to the poet: 'I looked for Frederick II and I found the Master.' The Master, she said, had captured the magic of this wonderful country in his poems, but she had to see it for herself in order to understand it fully.[7]

There was more going on here than merely the Grand Tour of the elder Stauffenbergs.[8]

Kantorowicz stayed on in Naples for the seven hundredth anniversary of Frederick II's founding of the University on 3 May 1924. The newspapers, Kantorowicz wrote to Stefan George, were comparing Mussolini to Frederick II as the prophet of the Fascists' dream of *Italia imperiale* and revelling 'nell' ombre del Suevo gloriosissimo' (in the shadow of the most magnificent Swabian).[9]

When the friends had met in Rome there had been talk of placing a wreath on the Emperor's tomb.[10] A prefatory note to Kantorowicz's biography of Frederick II states:

> When in May 1924 the Kingdom of Italy celebrated the seven-hundredth anniversary of the University of Naples, a foundation of the Hohenstaufen Frederick II, there lay a wreath at the Emperor's sarcophagus in the Cathedral at Palermo, bearing the words:
>
> TO ITS EMPERORS AND HEROES
> THE SECRET GERMANY
>
> Not that the 'Life of Frederick II' had been inspired by this occurrence.. but it might fairly be regarded as a sign that interest in the great German rulers was stirring in other than learned circles – particularly in un-imperial times.

At the conclusion of his work, Kantorowicz again referred to his own time. The myth of the emperor who lived on in secret, waiting for deliverance, had (he remarked) long since transferred itself from Frederick II to Frederick I Barbarossa, but '"He lives and lives not".. the Sibylline oracle no longer means the Emperor but the Emperor's people.'[11]

'In other than learned circles' meant in Stefan George's circle, whose members had been responsible for the wreath. Which of the poet's friends had actually placed it remains a mystery. What is certain is that the poet supervised the preparation of Kantorowicz's manuscript, edited it in collaboration with Berthold Stauffenberg, influenced its style, and represented the author vis-à-vis the publisher, so that the latter did not know who the author was until the page-proofs were corrected.[12]

The concept of a 'secret Germany' had a long history, the most recent development of which was the national movement which had begun around 1800. Hölderlin used the idea of Germany's secret creative genius in his hymnoi 'The German's Song' and 'Germania':

> The unspoken no longer
> May remain a secret
> [. . .]
> Germania, where you are priestess and,
> Weaponless, proffer around
> counsel to kings and nations.[13]

In similar vein, Friedrich Schiller wrote of a Germany of the mind, since the political Germany lay prostrate and fragmented.[14] It was Friedrich Hebbel who, in an epigram of about 1845, initiated the political mystification of Germany: nations had their kings,

> But they also have a hidden emperor
> Who perhaps himself draws water from the well,
> Whether he be artist, sage or thinker,
> Before the century ends he alone wears the crown.[15]

Heinrich Heine wrote in 1852 'of the real Germany, the great, mysterious, as it were anonymous Germany of the German people, of the sleeping sovereigns with whose sceptre and crown the long-tailed monkeys play'.[16] Paul de Lagarde, dissatisfied with the state of the nation, wrote between 1875 and 1878: 'if only there were conspirators among us, a secret open league, which thought and prepared for the great tomorrow'; 'the Germany we love and desire to see has never existed and may never exist. The ideal is something that is and is not.'[17] In 1890 Julius Langbehn drew on Hebbel for inspiration, and considered himself to be the secret emperor.[18]

Stefan George was familiar with the works of Heine, Lagarde, Langbehn and Hölderlin. In 1904, George and his friend Karl Wolfskehl declared 'that every fruitful· every liberating thought has originated in secret circles (*cénacles*)'. A modern artist or intellectual must not be disconcerted by those who hypocritically complained that such circles lost all contact with the common people, because the masses of modern times had retained none of the vital forces of a great nation. People with understanding would not object if the contemporary intellectual overlooked the very existence of the millions with whom he was sufficiently acquainted through a few specimens – just as no judicious person in antiquity objected to the treatment of 'slaves and domestic animals (*pecus et manicipium*)'.[19]

Karl Wolfskehl, in an essay representing Stefan George's views and written in 1910, first used the expression 'secret Germany' to describe the contributors to the *Blätter für die Kunst* and its 'exclusive invited readership'. He also used it to refer to those who represented the dormant forces out of which the Image of the Nation was to rise: 'For that which is now beginning, in its half-dream, to stir beneath the barren surface crust, the *secret Germany*, the only Germany alive in these times: here, and only here, has it found a voice.' With Stefan George's support, Wolfskehl expressed both fear and hope 'that a movement from the depths – if such a thing is still possible in Europe – could issue only from Germany, from the secret Germany, for which every one of our words is spoken, from which every one of our verses draws life and rhythm, and in whose unceasing service lies felicity, torment and the sanctification of our lives'.

After Wolfskehl's essay, the expression 'secret Germany' became current in George's circle, but its use remained infrequent. More often the poet's friends, in an ironic echo of Socrates, referred to their circle as 'the state'. This alluded to the passage in Plato's *Republic* in which Glaucon says to Socrates that the 'state' which they have been discussing exists nowhere on earth, only in their words. Socrates replies: 'perhaps it is established in heaven as a model for him who will see, and seeing, follow the model. Whether it exists anywhere or ever will exist, is no matter. He will serve only this state, and never any other.' Stefan George's friends were convinced that the only living Germany, the secret Germany, had been awakened by the Master's new poetry and had been given voice in his circle alone. In this regard, Stefan George considered himself the direct continuator of Hölderlin's poetic work.[20]

In October 1928 Max Kommerell published a book describing poets in the age of Goethe as 'leaders' (*Führer*). It was published by the same firm as *Blätter für die Kunst*; and it was George who decided which of his friends' works this firm should publish. Kommerell asserted that the Germans were not yet a nation (*Volk*) in either a constitutional or an intellectual sense: they were not even in process of becoming one. The secret message about the future of Germany was that the entire nation would be deified in war. The poet Hölderlin, who had been unjustly stigmatised as faint-hearted, had

> fearlessly praised war as the supreme national [*völkische*] reality . . though, to be sure, only *that* war which was waged by a fully awakened nation. Once that nation as imagined by Hölderlin does exist: a nation among whom the gods dwell and sire their heroes, a nation whose life resembles theirs [the gods'] down to the most trivial activity: such a nation must occupy the first rank. There can be only *one* such nation in any one era . . all other nations are then in the second rank, and *it* towers over them as the hero towers over men of ordinary measure. [. . .] None of the other poets and spokesmen of his [Hölderlin's] age could impart to the German that tremendous right to power, that consciousness of exclusive value and rank [. . .] The land on which God's eagle descended knows no justice save its own, and whoever denies its sanctity will be the enemy not merely of this nation, but of God Himself.[21]

In his conclusion, Kommerell conjured up the progression from the German classical era to the sublime present, 'the today of the Master's reign' in which Stefan George was leader, and thenceforward into 'an intimately earnest morrow when youth shall feel the birth of the new fatherland in zealously burning union and in the clashing of weapons previously buried all too deep'. With George's approval, Kommerell had published a vulgarised version of views which Johann Gottlieb Fichte had expressed earlier in his 'Addresses to the German Nation'. Fichte had exhorted the Germans to cast off the yoke of Napoleon's domination: he was speaking in the Academy on Unter den Linden, in Berlin, in the winter of 1807–1808, while French occupying troops marched past the building and at times drowned out his speech with the beating of their drums. In a parallel to Rousseau's *Considérations sur le gouvernement de Pologne, et sur sa réformation projetée en avril, 1772*, Fichte used philosophical reasoning to justify the 'unavoidable' functions of language and education: the only fields of activity which the French occupiers had failed to place under their own administration. Education, Fichte asserted, offered Germans a means of bringing up a generation of patriotic citizens who would take the fate of the nation to heart and into their own hands. Fichte explained, on the basis of a theory that the German language was unadulterated by Latin influences and therefore superior to the French language, that the moral fortitude of Germany was superior to that of her enemies, and that in fact Germany had great things to offer to the rest of the world. But Fichte never encouraged Germans to seek expansion and domination over other nations for domination's sake; Kommerell did.[22]

Kommerell was well disposed toward the National Socialists, and remained so until some time after Hitler became Chancellor, while at the same time considering himself 'a-political'. But the title of his book, *Der Dichter als Führer in der deutschen Klassik* (The poet as leader in the German classical period), which was approved by Stefan George, announced a claim to leadership that openly paralleled the National Socialist claim.[23]

Stefan George also held to his use of the swastika vignette on the covers and title-pages of works brought out by the publishers of *Blätter für die Kunst*. A publisher's advertisement of 1928 stated that the swastika was frequently 'mistaken' for the National Socialist 'hooked cross': 'When this ancient (Indian) sign was named *Hakenkreuz* in October 1918 and received its contemporary meaning, the Circle of the *Blätter für die Kunst* could not abandon the signum which it had introduced long ago. Those who have even a slight acquaintance with the works published under this signum will know that they have nothing to do with politics.'[24]

Two years after Max Kommerell's book was published, Friedrich Wolters, in a history of Stefan George's Movement, asserted the intellectual leadership of the Master, and implied something more. The work was entitled *Stefan George und die Blätter für die Kunst. Deutsche Geistesgeschichte seit 1890* (Stefan George and the *Blätter für die Kunst*: German intellectual history since 1890). Stefan George edited and authorised every line. In this book, he and Wolters claimed 'the living dominion [*Reich*]' which Hölderlin had heralded and the Master had founded. Step by step the Master had rejected everything that was in decay, fostered all that was intellectually healthy, and 'made himself lord over his time: the "secret empire" resulting from his labour of forty years among the Germans' had now become visible. His hidden Germany lay in the midst of the public Germany like an open yet untrodden island – nay, in the midst of a humanity shaken to its foundations, whose leaders were driven by the unleashed forces of their time 'and knew only that they had to choose between the dreariest peace and the wildest struggle'.[25]

These books by Kommerell and Wolters illustrate what Kantorowicz called the opening of the Secret Germany to the concerns of the day. According to Kantorowicz, Stefan George intended to end this diluting tendency through his poem 'Secret Germany', in which he offered a mythical image, 'the mystery of the other *Reich*', and thereby saved it from disintegration and obfuscation. The poet reminded his readers that everything which seemed worthwhile and important today was nothing but rotting leaves in the autumn winds; only that which still rested in protective slumber, 'in the deepest inner shaft' of sacred earth, was

> Miracle inexplicable today
> Destiny for days to be.[26]

The expectations of the Master's friends extended far beyond the precincts of poetic dreaming. Their letters to Stefan George are so full of evidence of these expectations that the poet's approval must be taken as implicit. In July 1918 Ernst Morwitz, facing Germany's defeat, wrote to Stefan George on the occasion of the poet's birthday, saying that the Master and his friends must not allow external events to divert them from their position. Even if those events were on the brink of catastrophe, what Plato had said remained true, namely that important artistic events never occur without important political events:

> This war will have meaning only if it lasts so long that all decay within nations is destroyed, the classes will be interchanged and the power of the individual triumphs over mechanical organisation. This is becoming ever clearer. You will be needed in Germany, beloved![27]

Wolters wrote in his book:

> We consider it great luck that today the Poet of our nation is also profoundly a statesman who seeks and shapes earthly rule, and began to construct the kernel of his dominion at the first awakening of his poetic genius.[28]

Stefan George himself had awakened those expectations. On 16 April 1911 he had told the Romanist Ernst Robert Curtius, who visited him: 'Some think my first books were merely artistic, without impulse toward the new humanity. Quite wrong! *Algabal* is a revolutionary book. Listen to this sentence of Plato's: The rules of art change only with those of the state.'[29]

In a conversation with Berthold Vallentin in January 1920, Stefan George said that in a new yearbook he intended to take a political position and to deal with the great political movements of the time. The power of governments now was not as great as in earlier years, so that 'our forces' might be sufficient for effective action.[30] In February 1928 the Master expressed to Vallentin his concern that the ideas of his Movement might never be put in practice in Germany, but rather abroad. The Romantic Movement in France and England had produced new human and spiritual attitudes, while in Germany it had remained merely literary. Everything depended on the advent of a person who could take up the ideas and transform them into effective political action. Something of that sort might be expected from Mussolini. Then Stefan George retreated again into the esoteric, described his work as 'subterranean', declared himself unconcerned with the greater public, and left it to 'his young people' to organise and to 'move the Nation'. He himself had overcome the temptation to rush prematurely into overt activity. It would be easy for him to form some organisation, but that would only defeat his intended subterranean work.[31] Stefan George was then sixty years old and was suffering from a kidney ailment; but even in earlier years he had oscillated between life and art. He wanted results in his own time, but in public he maintained his political abstinence. Not surprisingly, there was considerable debate, and at times dispute, among his friends about whether or not they should take part in politics, particularly after the great electoral successes of the National Socialists in September 1930. Kantorowicz had earlier chided Wolters for signing nationalistic and *völkisch* manifestos, saying that one could not serve in two 'states' at the same time, or allow the values which were above all parties to be dragged through the gutter. As the National Socialists gained in strength, the attitudes of the poet and most of his friends shifted in their favour. Some of George's younger friends became passionately partisan. Their elders tolerated this because the National Socialists often talked in exactly the same way as the Poet, so that the pernicious implications of what the former said were easily overlooked.[32]

In 1928 Claus Stauffenberg said, in a letter to Max Kommerell, that if external forms existed it was only so that they could be 'recognised and controlled by those who scorn them'. Essential matters were transacted elsewhere, not in the 'external world'.[33] The Stauffenbergs inwardly distanced themselves from the 'external world', living in a tension between their secular and professional activities on the one hand and their esoteric intellectual circle on the other.

Berthold spent the winter of 1923/24 in Jena and then went to Tübingen. He read property law, together with Roman, early Byzantine, French, English and oriental history. During the winter semester 1924/25 he attended the Friedrich-Wilhelms-Universität in Berlin, and so did Theodor Pfizer. The faculty included jurists such as Viktor Bruns and Rudolf Smend, and historians such as Friedrich Meinecke, Fritz Hartung and Kurt Breysig (a friend of Stefan George); the philologist and archaeologist Werner Jaeger; the literary historian Julius Petersen; the economist Werner Sombart; the philosopher Eduard Spranger.[34] During this semester at Berlin there were frequent readings of new poetry, in the presence of Stefan George, in the studio of the sculptor Alexander Zschokke at no. 13 Fasanenstrasse, or in a porter's lodge, belonging to a large villa, which Max Kommerell had rented and in which the Master lived with Johann Anton and Kommerell from October to December 1924.[35]

For the summer semester of 1925 Berthold, Alexander, Woldi and Theodor Pfizer all moved to the University of Munich. Berthold and Theodor attended Professor Ernst Beling's lectures on the philosophy of law at seven in the morning. The Master lived in Munich during part of this time, and the brothers met with him and other friends on several occasions in April and May; Berthold introduced Frank Mehnert to the Master on 7 April.[36]

During the following winter term Berthold was back in Berlin; for the summer term of 1926 and the winter term of 1927/28 he returned with Theodor to Tübingen, where both prepared for the law qualifying examinations. Berthold passed with distinction. Then he began to learn Russian, hoping to enter the diplomatic service. At the same time he helped Stefan George, Kommerell and their friend Johann Anton ('The Prince') to edit Kantorowicz's biography of the Emperor Frederick II.

In June 1927 Berthold travelled to London, visited the museums, stayed as a guest in the homes of people to whom he had introductions, and attended cricket and tennis matches. At the end of July he visited Oxford, Bratton-Fleming and Youghal in southern Ireland. He met many people, 'all of whom say the same things· are friendly· sentimental and childlike· and eventually rather tiring'. He wrote (in Russian, for the sake of practice) to Maria (Mika) Classen, who later became his wife: 'You must believe in me· you know I am proud and my blood runs hot – and my soul envisions royal deeds – and I must wait and be patient until the time comes – this makes me restless and sometimes puts me in a dark mood'.[37]

On 19 August Berthold arrived in Frankfurt am Main and went on to Königstein im Taunus to see the Master; he then spent four weeks in Lautlingen, where he also saw Frank Mehnert, Albrecht von Blumenthal and Woldi. At the end of September he went to Berlin to work on his dissertation on the legal status of the Soviet trade missions in Germany, and in October to Paris, where he took tuition in French and Russian; three times a week he went riding. He found the literary and liberal circles in which he had contacts rather unattractive. At the end of January 1928 he wrote to Mika from Paris: 'I have nothing new to say about the French, they are so stupid, so stupid.'[38] In December 1927 Johann Anton, who expected to enter the Foreign Office, came to Paris to perfect his French. With permission from the Master, Berthold and Johann travelled together through the south of France between Biarritz and Marseilles. Berthold formed favourable impressions of the French outside Paris; the provinces seemed to have retained a natural vitality. The friends travelled via Avignon to Florence, and Berthold finally stopped at Locarno for ten days in order to visit the Master at nearby Minusio.[39]

Berthold's application to join the diplomatic service was rejected.[40] After Easter 1928 he began his *practicum* (*stage*) for the bar in the Stuttgart lower civil and criminal courts. At the end of July he went with Frank to Corsica. From 1 September to 1 November 1928 he worked in the Reutlingen high bailiff's office; from 1 November to the end of the year he was in Berlin on research leave. Back in the courts in Stuttgart, he asked Uncle Nux to inquire about his prospects of admission to the diplomatic service, and to contact Professor Otto Hoetzsch, a member of the foreign-policy committee in the Reichstag. He could not see himself wasting his best years 'entirely uselessly' in a law career; the academic study of law did not interest him at all. He had a 'lofty aim' and lived 'for a high ideal', he wrote to Mika. His intellect was sharp and penetrating; he often embarrassed his intelligent and learned, but muddled, seniors by reducing complex matters to clear terms. Like others in his generation who later lost their lives in the struggle against Hitler – Helmuth James von Moltke, Dietrich Bonhoeffer, Fritz-Dietlof, Count Schulenburg – Berthold Stauffenberg and his brother Claus were aristocrats: descendants of Gneisenau and through him related to Scharnhorst,[41] sons of a royal chamberlain. Naturally they aspired to the highest levels of public service.

On 29 January Berthold received the degree of *doctor iuris* from the University of Tübingen, and on 1 March he was appointed as an assistant in the Kaiser-Wilhelm-Institut für ausländisches öffentliches Recht und Völkerrecht (Institute for Foreign Public Law and International Law), which was housed in the Royal Palace in Berlin. It was a non-governmental agency that worked with the government, particularly with the Foreign Office; most European countries had such institutes. Berthold worked on the edition of the *Fontes Juris Gentium*, published learned articles on the Permanent Court of International Justice at The Hague, and served on the German-Polish Mixed Arbitration Board. Between Christmas and New Year's Eve he visited the Master.

On 1 July 1931, on the recommendation of his Institute, Berthold became *secrétaire-rédacteur au greffe* in the office of the *Greffier* (Chancellor) of the Permanent Court of International Justice, Åke Hammarskjöld. Berthold could have married Mika on the strength of his long-term appointment at the Permanent Court after November 1931. But both his parents and Stefan George opposed the marriage, and Berthold always paid particular deference to the Master: he always used his Christmas holidays to see him rather than Mika.[42] Besides his daily duties, he edited the official commentary on the statutes of the Court, *Statut et règlement de la Cour permanente de Justice internationale. Éléments d'interprétation.* He was also occupied with third-party challenges to the Austrian-German customs union agreement signed on 19 March 1931: the Court decided by eight votes to seven that the agreement was incompatible with the Peace of St Germain of 1919 and with the Geneva Protocol of October 1922.

Berthold's restlessness remained. When Stefan George told him that he had accomplished nothing to speak of, compared with his (George's) other friends who had written books, this brought tears to Berthold's eyes. The Master took a dim view of the Hague Court, and Berthold agreed with him, saying that international justice was a sham, as the suppression of the

10. Mika Classen and Berthold Stauffenberg at Scheveningen, ca. 1930

Austrian-German customs union showed. He wished he could devote his energies to something better, thinking sometimes that there would be 'more point in giving a proper training to [his horse] Jolly'.[43]

As for Alexander, he spent the winter of 1925/26 at the University of Jena, and was subsequently in Halle. He disliked the ambience, missed the Master and his friends, doubted that the study of the classics would help him contribute to German resurgence and to the Master's vision of a new Germany, and found life as a scholar unsatisfying; nonetheless he settled into it, apparently with the Master's encouragement, accepting Blumenthal's judgement that he was totally unsuited to anything more practical. Like Berthold, Alexander suffered under the Master's 'distressing verdict that he had not yet attained merit in "the state"'. In November 1928 he submitted his doctoral dissertation on John Malalas' chronicle of the Roman Empire from Caesar to Trajan; his supervisors judged it a 'pleasingly industrious, learned and intelligent work'. It was published as a book in 1931. Alexander Stauffenberg's second thesis (a requirement for those seeking the right to teach in universities) was on Hieron II of Syracuse, and appeared in 1933. He accepted a temporary post at the University of Würzburg, having first obtained the Master's consent; in 1936 he was appointed to a chair at Würzburg.[44]

Stefan George was seeking in every possible manner to safeguard the future of the Secret Germany, his 'state'. Before the mid-1920s he regarded the jurist Ernst Morwitz of Jewish descent as his sole heir and literary executor. From 1923 onward, Max Kommerell ('Maxim', 'The Littlest One', 'Puck') and Johann Anton ('The Prince') came to be the Master's closest friends. Morwitz considered Kommerell an opportunist who used the Master's intellect and aura to promote his own career. The fact that both Kommerell and Anton were anti-Semitic, racist and arrogantly nationalistic did not endear them to Morwitz either. It was, among other things, a reflection of changes in the general social and political climate that younger and non-Jewish friends now dominated in Stefan George's circle. But from 1929 onwards Kommerell himself eschewed the poet's company. When in 1930 the Master named Robert Boehringer, Max Kommerell and Johann Anton as a board of trustees to govern a projected foundation, to be called 'The Work of Stefan George', Kommerell told George that he needed to be independent, and could no longer offer the unconditional loyalty which was expected of him. Thereafter the poet commonly referred to him as 'The Toad'. Although George continued to respect Kommerell and was always eager to read his new works, the rift led to further separations. The poet expressed surprise that Kommerell should go on seeing friends still close to the Master without seeking a reconciliation with the latter. Eventually Alexander and Claus Stauffenberg adopted the Master's reserve; Claus was most disappointed and depressed, saying that Kommerell was like one of the Emperor Frederick II's treacherous councillors, and that one was often deserted by those whom one had most trusted. Johann Anton tried in vain to bring about a reconciliation between Kommerell and George, but, torn between Stefan George and Kommerell, he took his own life in Freiburg in February 1931.[45]

Stefan George's last will and testament named Robert Boehringer and Berthold Stauffenberg as his executors. After the poet's death Berthold named Frank Mehnert as his own successor in this capacity in case he died, and stipulated that Frank must then name a successor of his own at once. After Frank had fallen on the Russian front in 1943, Berthold named his brother Claus as his successor, with the same stipulation.[46] They were the appointed heirs of the Master's Platonic 'state', committed to the realisation of the Secret Germany.[47]

3

Reichswehr

When his brothers left home for university, Claus Stauffenberg was left alone in Stuttgart with the prospect of three more years at the Gymnasium. His health was delicate: he suffered frequently from infections and head-aches.[1] In the summer of 1924, after the tumultuous events of 1923 had subsided, inflation had been overcome and the currency stabilised, and after Claus's elder brothers had returned from their Italian tour, Claus applied for permission to sit his final examinations so that he could be done with school. His request was refused because in Württemberg the final year had to be completed before candidates could be admitted to final examinations. His application to sit the examinations in the jurisdiction of the Rhine Province of Prussia was also denied. In September he did not return to school, and in October he wrote from Lautlingen to the Master that 'all these things are relatively trivial · and are becoming more so · one thing in any case has been achieved: school is over. And what more should I want than a suitable life?' At Berthold's invitation, he wrote, he was coming to Berlin in November to stay with his brother for a week or two, and to see the Master; he planned to stay with Blumenthal in Jena during the following year, presumably to continue his studies under Blumenthal's supervision. In his letter Claus also referred to a Great Deed he was going to perform, and associated it with one of the Master's books of poems:

> I have read much in the 'Jahr der Seele' [Year of the Soul] [. . .] And the more clearly life presents itself to me · the more exaltedly human existence reveals itself and the more urgently the deed shows itself · the darker becomes one's own blood · the more remote becomes the sound of one's own words and the rarer becomes the meaning of one's own life · probably until some hour, in the harshness of its tolling and the greatness of its appearance, gives the sign. Master · I have learned too much from that poem: YOU ARE THE FOUNDATION AS I NOW PRAISE YOU. Not that my dreams were false · on the contrary · I have grown · [. . .].[2]

If Claus had held to his original intention of seeking admission to a school of architecture, he would not have needed to pass the school-leaving examination. But there is no indication that he had abandoned school

11. Lautlingen, summer 1924. From left: Frank Mehnert, Berthold, Alexander, Albrecht von Blumenthal, Claus; in front, Maria Fehling

entirely: he did not want to go through the last two years at the Gymnasium, but he did want to sit the examination. It seems, therefore, that he had long since given up his plan to become an architect and intended to pursue a military career: to become an army officer, he would need the final certificate of secondary education.

The Jena plan was abandoned. But in November 1924 Claus, his brothers, Albrecht von Blumenthal and Walter Anton were frequent visitors to Stefan George in the gatekeeper's lodge where the Master was then living with Max Kommerell and Johann Anton; Johann Anton read his own poems to the group. Stefan George summoned Ludwig Thormaehlen, a sculptor and friend, to take photographs of the little assembly. These remarkable images convey the atmosphere that prevailed there, and reveal the enthusiastic devotion which Claus and Berthold felt for the poet.[3]

Claus, always delicate, then spent a period of convalescence in Lautlingen, and went for a rest cure in the Swiss Alps. Claus found it 'wonderful', as he wrote to the Master, that Berthold came to visit him there. He was so close to Berthold that he was one of the few who 'need not fear his kingly manner or be abashed by his superior presence'. Claus kept in contact with his masters at the Gymnasium and followed the curriculum. On his return from the cure it was too late to join the top form and he worked with tutors instead.[4]

12. Above, from right: Berthold, Claus and Stefan George in the gatekeeper's lodge of the Berlin-Grunewald villa, November 1924. Below, from left: Max Kommerell, Claus, Johann Anton, Albrecht von Blumenthal (seated), Alexander, Walter Anton, Berthold

Late in August 1925, Claus and Theodor Pfizer went for an early morning stroll in the hills near Lautlingen. Claus spoke of 'the painful birth of a new Germany, of national duty and service, and of his own hopes for a career'. He spoke in general terms, making no allusion either to architecture

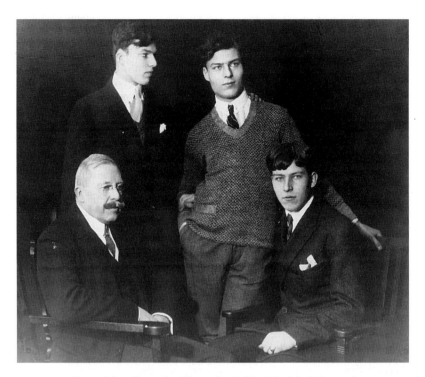

13. From right: Alexander, Claus, Berthold, with their father, ca. 1925

or to the Army. It is clear, however, that Stefan George was consulted about Claus's choice, and that he seems to have encouraged it. A poem written by Alexander Stauffenberg in August 1925 describes Claus's attraction to the soldier's life, his dreams filled with the clatter of swords and the sounds of battle. At the same time, Blumenthal wrote to the Master that Claus, whom he had seen at Lautlingen, was 'in a state of unrest which is, as so often, a reason for concern: the main cause was the soldier question'. In March 1926 Kommerell wrote to the Master that he had thought much about 'my Cl.': 'I sense his struggle from afar. May a beautiful heroic landscape emerge from his earthquakes!'[5]

On 21 October 1925 Claus Stauffenberg petitioned the Württemberg school authority for admission to final examinations in March 1926. His petition was granted two days later, and his choice of career was entered on the examination roll as 'military officer'. He passed above the class average, with marks of 'good' in French, history, geography and mathematics, 'satisfactory' in German composition, German literature, philosophy, Greek and natural history, and 'adequate' in Latin.[6]

Claus's poor health hardly seemed conducive to a military career. It must have been the main source of his own doubts, which he firmly suppressed after he had taken his decision. During his first years in the Army he suffered phases of exhaustion. In 1931, suffering from acute gastritis, he was sent to the military sanatorium in the garrison town of Kolberg (where his ancestor Gneisenau had first won military fame). With iron determination, Stauffenberg overcame his constitutional weakness.[7]

Claus Stauffenberg's father was a Major in the Royal Army of Württemberg; his father's elder brother was a Lieutenant-Colonel commanding the Bavarian Heavy Horse regiment; his mother's brother had been a Lieutenant-Colonel on the Austrian General Staff; Claus's brothers had volunteered for military training in 1923. Claus himself from an early age had talked and dreamed about becoming a soldier. As a schoolboy he had had the idea of becoming an architect, but the proposal was never more than tentative.[8] He felt a strong urge for action, he knew he could be a leader of men, and he wanted to teach and mould them. Alexander described Claus in a poem as the incarnation of the famous royal equestrian statue in Bamberg Cathedral – but also, with uncanny premonition, spoke of his

> insatiable urge
> For deeds so distant – until you find next to your heart
> Your brother sharing your destruction.[9]

Claus chose No. 17 Cavalry Regiment, which, like most regiments in the truncated post-Versailles Reichswehr, was an amalgamation of previously existing regiments. It had custody of the battle honours of several regiments of the old Army, including the Bavarian Heavy Horse whose colonel had been Uncle Berthold. This family connection improved Claus's chances of acceptance, in view of his frail health and of the fact that regiments commonly favoured relatives of their own veterans or serving members, compared to the alternative, No. 18 Cavalry Regiment in Stuttgart-Cannstatt. The regimental staff, the regimental band, and the First Squadron and the Fifth were garrisoned in Bamberg, the Second and Third Squadron in Ansbach, the Fourth and Sixth in Straubing. In 1926 the regiment belonged to the 7th (Bavarian) Division; in 1928 it became part of the 3rd Cavalry Division.[10]

Four weeks after joining his regiment, Claus Stauffenberg wrote to his father describing his motives for joining the Army – almost as though he already considered himself a personage in history. He had known all the time that it would be hard for him, since 'it is not easy for our kind to play the common man for any length of time' and on the whole to renounce the intellectual life. But he would be richly rewarded for sacrificing a few years of his youth if he could serve the Fatherland in even the smallest measure. In 1934 he wrote in a similar vein to another relative, echoing once again his essay of 1923: 'The truly aristocratic view – for us the primary consideration

14. Claus Stauffenberg at Lautlingen, 1926

15. Above: Berthold, ca. 1928. Below: Claus at Lautlingen, 1926

– demands public service of us, whatever our specific occupation.' In later years, too, he often referred to 'the aristocratic principle', and upheld it in the statement of his beliefs which he made at the beginning of July 1944.[11]

Basic training between 9 June and 7 July 1926 included joint manoeuvres with No. 18 Cavalry Regiment and mechanised troops at the Grafenwöhr training grounds east of Nuremberg, about eighteen miles from the Czech border. On 16 August the regiment began further manoeuvres as part of the 3rd Cavalry Division in the Sennelager training area in Westphalia, between Paderborn and Bielefeld. From October 1927 to August 1928 Stauffenberg attended the Infantry School at Dresden. Four officer cadets shared an apartment consisting of one bedroom and a sitting room. The day began at six with physical exercises, showers and breakfast, followed by a study hour in quarters, lectures, weapons training (on machine guns, mortars, and with the pioneer ordnance); in the afternoons there was training in infantry tactics, riding, motorcycle training, and sport.

Candidates were free to go out, but only in uniform, from six until ten in the evening (or later on Saturdays), or with permission. The weekend began on Saturday afternoon and ended at midnight on Sunday.[12]

Stauffenberg excelled in tactics. The instructor, Captain Dietl, later Lieutenant-General of Mountain Troops, would order 'situation estimate, decision, reasons'. When 'Stauff' formulated the required response with literary skill and brilliance, Dietl had nothing to add. However, Stauffenberg's marks were mixed at first. His written work often received comments such as 'marginal', 'incomplete', or 'make better use of time', 'make it more legible'. Stauffenberg's slightly untidy dress and bearing, and his irresistible laughter, could have misled some people about his uncompromising allegiance to everything that he regarded as fundamental.[13]

In his free time Stauffenberg began to learn Russian. In the evenings he often played his cello; he read the *Odyssey* and the *Iliad* in Greek, besides books on battles of annihilition or about the World War; and he 'read once again the memoirs of Napoleon and Ségur'.[14] He was on good terms with everyone, but his only close friend was a slightly older officer in his own regiment, Lieutenant Jürgen Schmidt. Schmidt was a friend of Johann Anton and a protégé of Walter Elze, the military historian and friend of Stefan George. Schmidt sent Stauffenberg, then in Dresden, some of his own poems, in which he called the younger man a warrior and hero and expressed his ardent love and devotion. It appears that Schmidt also sent Stauffenberg Friedrich Wolters's 'Four Addresses on the Fatherland', of which Stauffenberg strongly disapproved, particularly the 'philological and learned treatise on the field of honour', in which Wolters praised 'Germanic' sacrificial death in action and recommended that those who survived should be killed, or should commit suicide, so that they, too, might be admitted to Odin's company of heroes. Wolters said that the Christian Middle Ages had not attached 'ultimate ethical value' to a sacrificial death in battle, but the humanists of the Renaissance had restored it to its proper place: the religion of our time was love of the fatherland, in victory or death. Stauffenberg was evidently repelled by this nihilistic equation of life and death, which in his

16. The Infantry School, Dresden, 1928. From left: Fahnenjunker Heinz Huffmann, Stauffenberg, Rudolf Morgenstern, Henning Wilcke

view had nothing in common with the soldier's ethos. Stauffenberg thanked Schmidt, sent him some of his own 1923 poems, and asked for Schlieffen's *Cannae* and Groener's 'Testament of Count Schlieffen'. He needed them for his work, which, he assured Schmidt, was not retrospective but aimed at an application of 'images' (ideas), and at reducing phenomena to their permanent essence.[15]

At least once a month Stauffenberg attended mass at a Catholic church in Dresden, formerly the church of the King of Saxony. Occasionally he was a guest of the Duke and Duchess of Saxe-Meiningen at their castle in Thüringen. The Duke and Duchess also knew Walter Elze and Jürgen Schmidt. There is no evidence that Stauffenberg ever went to any of the frequent dancing, drinking or hunting parties of his Infantry School classmates. 'Stauff' was respected as 'different'. One of his regimental comrades called him 'a blazing sacred fire'.[16] Stauffenberg visited museums, sometimes with a fellow cadet, Manfred von Brauchitsch, a nephew of the future Commander-in-Chief of the Army; but Brauchitsch, who used to ride his motorcycle around the yard of the Infantry School while Stauffenberg was attempting to play his cello, could not understand why someone so attached to the arts had gone in for a military career. Evidently Stauffenberg had not told him why.[17] In a letter to Max Kommerell, Stauffenberg explained the difference between himself and the other officer cadets and officers. He got on perfectly well with 'subordinates, farmers and soldiers', but not with people who considered themselves to have 'the same level of education': their pride was obtuse conceit, their cameraderie pathetic egoism, their human tact consisted in familiarity, and in deriding what they could not comprehend.[18]

Stauffenberg's charm, directness and brilliance tended to dominate conversations. He liked to talk, to examine all the arguments, even to play devil's advocate against the views of his interlocutor. In 1930 his squadron commander paid tribute to his initiative, judgement, above-average tactical and technical competence, exemplary treatment of subordinates, love of horses, and interest in social, historical and religious matters, but also noted 'minor flaws': 'Conscious of his military competence and intellectual superiority, he sometimes inclines to a condescending irony, which, however, never gives offence.' His own superiority was indisputable, and perforce evoked envy as well as admiration. But Stauffenberg could be quite cutting when confronting neglect of duty or disloyalty.[19]

The other cadets knew nothing of Stauffenberg's excursions into Secret Germany. During the winter of 1927/28 he attended poetry readings with Stefan George in Berlin, with Berthold, Alexander, Blumenthal and Thormaehlen commonly in attendance. In November 1928 Stauffenberg, his brothers and several friends attended a reading of the Master's last book of poems, *Das Neue Reich* ('The New Realm'), and in February 1929 Stauffenberg was present at a reading of Kommerell's new poems, 'Dialogues at the Time of the Rebirth of Germany', which greatly moved him.

In these 'Dialogues', Goethe and Napoleon agree that their own efforts have averted the threat both of mob rule and of domination by America's 'nationless mixed race of traders', as well as the 'Hunnish hordes' of Russia, 'the end of all nobility'. When Napoleon conquered Europe, the German nation, from being 'ruler of the world', had become 'god in spirit'; but the German nation embodied the spirit 'from which the next ruler of the world will form himself'.[20] All this was, of course, approved by the Master, in whose view (shared by his friends) the Secret Germany must prepare the nation for the renewal of its visible greatness. Napoleon was to the Master's mind a hero ranking with those of Antiquity. In 1929 he told a friend, a military historian, that the Prussians ought to have made common cause with Napoleon: 'then they would have inherited everything!'[21]

Meanwhile, in 1928, Stauffenberg read military history and prepared for the final examinations at the Infantry School, made a crossing of the Elbe with his regiment and participated with No. 14 Cavalry in physically demanding manoeuvres in the Altengrabow training area. Soon he caught tonsillitis, which laid him up for four weeks, and then a sinus infection which required another four weeks' rest cure. He was grateful for the letters and poems he received from 'a very few exalted persons' like Kommerell, but was tormented by the desire for 'an hour of life in all its fulness', to embrace his beloved Kommerell and 'for a few minutes to be there only for your kisses and to hear your words', as he wrote to him:

> Can you know the life of one who has not had the fortune to give himself fully in verse, who has not experienced one hour of fulfilment, without demands, an hour of merely *being*, but only hours which drove him on and were full of questions?[22]

On 18 August 1927 Stauffenberg, still an officer cadet, was promoted from corporal to officer cadet with the rank of sergeant; on 1 August 1928 he was promoted to a grade above sergeant, and a year later he became a master sergeant.[23] In the autumn of 1928 he went to the Hanover Cavalry School. Major von Loeper, one of the instructors and later to be Stauffenberg's divisional commander, noticed that his pupil had read widely, had unusually wide-ranging interests, liked to talk, and had an extraordinary influence on his fellow cadets, often mediating in disputes. Stauffenberg's written work received better marks here than at Dresden. A study of the complicated Battle of Tannenberg (August 1914) bears the comment: 'Dates? Otherwise good and clear. Some errors in sketch.'[24]

In the examination for an officer's commission, Stauffenberg was placed sixth over all, and first in the list of cavalry officer cadets. This won him the Sword of Honour for outstanding performance, conferred on 17 August 1929, and he received the first three volumes of the history of the World War then being published by the Reich Archives. For years afterwards his parents gave him the rather expensive subsequent volumes as Christmas presents.[25] He returned to Bamberg and became a second lieutenant with effect from 1 January 1930.[26]

In January 1929 Stauffenberg wrote to Jürgen Schmidt on 'the topic that has occupied us so much', namely the Battle of Tannenberg and its analogies with the Battle of Cannae (216 BCE). In his ironically convoluted language, he announced a long-promised exposé, but claimed that his personal relationship with Schmidt, who was a protégé of the military historian Walter Elze, was getting in the way. Stauffenberg asked his friend to accept, for the time being, that his views differed from Elze's in all except purely descriptive matters: 'I struggle, and must struggle, against the tendency of those [Elze's] works [. . .] I must persist because I have a goal'.[27] Stauffenberg objected to the current widespread overvaluing of one major strategy, envelopment. Elze was all for envelopment, and accused Count Schlieffen, the Chief of the General Staff 1891–1906, of serious misunderstandings. Schlieffen had been wrong to think that the only way to win a war on two fronts was to envelop and annihilate one enemy, he had been wrong to ignore the importance of diplomacy as exemplified by Bismarck, and Germany had missed the chance of a pre-emptive strike against France at

17. Claus and Berthold with their mother at Lautlingen, 1928

the time of Russia's defeat by Japan in 1905.[28] This amounted to a suggestion that the Central Powers had lost the World War before it had even begun. Stauffenberg, who understood the importance of the creative military mind, could not accept such a suggestion. In 1934 he wrote to Frank Mehnert: 'Every one of Napoleon's battles, regardless of certain obvious errors in military art, contains more of the human element, and so does more for us, has greater significance, than the most beautiful strategy of '66 or of the "Potato War".'[29]

In October 1930 Stauffenberg wrote an essay on the battle of Issos (333 BCE), at which Alexander the Great used a 'breakthrough' method to defeat Darius III of Persia. The essay followed the prescribed structure, beginning with the two armies, their size, origin, training, combat potential, and tactics; then it considered the political and strategic background, and finally the course of the battle. Stauffenberg used the principal classical source, Flavius Arrianus. Stauffenberg, who admired in Alexander the union of statesman and military commander, the comprehensive motivation and the will to conquer, remained sceptical about any suggestion that success followed set patterns. He related Alexander's battles to the dispute in his own time between the advocates of envelopment and breakthrough. At Issos

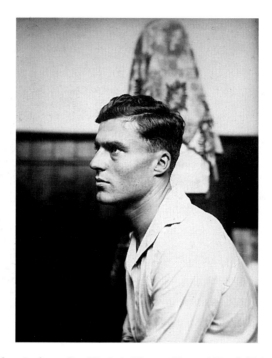

*18. Stauffenberg in the studio of Ludwig Thormaehlen and Frank Mehnert in Berlin,
ca. 1929*

there had been no alternative to breakthrough, because Darius' 600,000 men
could always have outflanked Alexander's 35,000, and also because Darius'
right flank reached the coast and his left flank the foot of the Amanos
Mountains. The point of Stauffenberg's essay was that Alexander did not
follow any set pattern, but determined where the enemy was most vulner-
able, where a decision could be forced. This meant a thrust against Darius
and his elite guard – at the very centre of the Persian army. Napoleon,
Stauffenberg explained, had followed the same principle when he led his
army directly against an opponent's capital (not a standard method in a time
of decentralised states, small armies and fortresses); similarly Schlieffen,
faced with the probability of a war on two fronts, had resolved to concentrate the majority of his forces so as to defeat the most dangerous enemy
first. Thus Alexander's choice of the breakthrough method was not based
only on the numerical relationship of the two armies, but also on their inner
conditions and interaction, and on the efficiency with which the will of the
commander could be executed.[30]

In May 1930 Stauffenberg took part in manoeuvres at Munsterlager. In
September there were exercises on the Main and Saale, during which No. 17

19. Stauffenberg (on left) ca. 1930

Cavalry of the 'Blue' forces excelled by crossing the deep river Saale without apparatus and attacking the 'Red' infantry from the rear. These manoeuvres were concluded with a gallop-past in parade formation before President von Hindenburg.[31]

On 15 November 1930, Stauffenberg became engaged to Nina, Baroness von Lerchenfeld, the daughter of a former Bavarian Royal Chamberlain and Imperial Consul General who occasionally entertained the officers of No. 17 Cavalry at his Bamberg town house. She asked Stauffenberg why he had chosen her and he replied that he judged her suitable to be the mother of his children. He told his future mother-in-law that according to Frederick the Great, an officer's wife was a necessary evil.[32] Stauffenberg's engagement was not made public, because he would have to wait until 1934 before Reichswehr rules allowed him to marry (i.e. at twenty-seven years of age or after eight years' service). But in 1933 he received a dispensation for the remaining six months, so that the wedding was held in September 1933.[33]

On 18 November 1930 Stauffenberg began a mortar course in Potsdam which familiarised him with the explosives used by sappers, and with the modern Mortar 18. When he returned to Bamberg in February 1931, he

20. *Wedding of Elisabeth, Countess Üxküll, to Paul, Baron von Handel at Berlin-Zehlendorf, 9 April 1931. Alexander and Berthold Stauffenberg are second and fourth from left in the front row; Nikolaus, Count Üxküll (Uncle Nux) is seventh from left, in uniform. In the front row, on the right, is Claus Stauffenberg with Melitta Schiller on his right*

shared a flat with Jürgen Schmidt at no. 35 Kunigundendamm, and devoted himself entirely to commanding his regiment's mortar troop.[34]

At Easter of 1931 he met with Stefan George in Berlin, together with Alexander and Frank, and in August he visited the poet's summer residence in Wasserburg on Lake Constance. In July he had sent birthday greetings to George from Bad Kolberg. In the same letter he mentioned that rumours had reached him from Berlin that the Darmstädter und National-Bank had failed on 11 July, leading to many other bank failures, while France was threatening intervention against Germany and Austria if they implemented a bilateral free-trade agreement. Stauffenberg commented that it looked as though there might be war by autumn, but thought he had learned by now that 'a few years and a few lives and personal fates' would not matter.[35]

Thirteen years after the end of the World War, Germany was still under the tutelage of the Entente. Among the armed forces, the limitations imposed by the Treaty of Versailles were keenly felt. Surrounded by the large armed forces of France, Poland and Czechoslovakia, with the promise of general disarmament unfulfilled, Germany was still allowed an Army of only 100,000 men, without tanks or aeroplanes. However, there was an almost palpable change in the military and political climate during 1931 and 1932.

Since March 1930, President von Hindenburg had been ruling the country by emergency decree through a cabinet without majority support in the Reichstag. The Chancellor, Brüning, was a World War veteran, a former machine-gun company commander; the Minister for the Armed Forces (Reichswehr) and temporary Minister of the Interior was Lieutenant-General Groener, who had succeeded Lieutenant-General Ludendorff as Quartermaster-General. On 10 October 1931 Hindenburg, who detested Hitler, at long last consented to receive him; and on that occasion Hitler also spoke with the Chief of the Reichswehr Minister's Office, Major-General von Schleicher. In the same month, at Bad Harzburg, Hitler allied his party in a National Front with the German National People's Party, the 'Stahlhelm' veterans' league, the Pan-German League and the Agrarian League, as well as other patriotic associations, and with the support of Lieutenant-Generals (ret.) von Lüttwitz and von Seeckt, attempted to dislodge the Brüning Cabinet. After bloody clashes between the SA (the National Socialist paramilitary organisation) and left-wing militants, Hitler met Schleicher again on 22 October: on this occasion Hitler acknowledged the Reichswehr's non-partisan status and reassured Schleicher and Groener about the National Socialists' campaigning methods. The Reichswehr Ministry and the Interior Ministry decided there was no threat of subversion from the Right, only from the Left, and they attempted to integrate the National Socialists into the State by declaring that there was no objection to their serving in the Reichswehr, whereas Communists would not be admitted. Relations between Hindenburg and Hitler cooled when Hitler proposed to run for president in 1932 rather than support the idea of extending Hindenburg's term by a year. In February 1932 Hindenburg declared that he would stand again in order to prevent the election of 'a representative of one-sided and extreme views' – by which he of course meant Hitler. On 26 July 1932, Groener's successor as Reichswehr Minister, Major-General von Schleicher, declared in a radio broadcast that Germany must have security: if the other powers failed to reduce their armed forces, and if the disarmament conference at Geneva continued to deny Germany 'full security and equality', then Germany would engage in 'qualitative reorganisation' of the Reichswehr. In the same address, Schleicher agreed with Hitler's views on the Reichswehr's position in the state. The speech was disseminated throughout the entire Reichswehr down to company level. On 8 August 1932 the Minister declared, in an interview published in the *New York Times*, that Germany had waited thirteen years for equal rights, and could wait no longer. On 15 October Schleicher told Baron von Neurath, the Minister for Foreign Affairs, that the Army was going to be increased to 145,000 men, involving nine heavy artillery units, twenty-two air squadrons, and a prototype tank battalion; the length of service was to be reduced to three or even two years, so that between 300,000 and 400,000 reservists would be available after five years. These measures were being discussed openly, and the Reichswehr Ministry used propaganda methods to prepare both the armed forces and the public for the proposed expansion.[36]

The great stock-market crash of 1929 and the Great Depression which followed had serious social and political consequences in Germany. By 1932 millions were unemployed and facing abject poverty. A working man with two children might receive nine Reichsmarks per week in welfare payments; out of that he would have to pay a minimal rent of four-and-a-half Reichsmarks, leaving sixteen pence per person per day to live on.[37] Election results reflected growing political radicalisation and polarisation. Many people feared a Communist revolution as that party increased its share of the popular vote from 12.6% in 1924 to 16.9% in November 1932, when over 80% of the electorate voted. The Social Democrat vote had gone from 20.5% in 1924 to 29.8% in 1928 and down again to 20.4% in November 1932. From the conservative point of view, the combined left-wing parties, with close to 50% of the popular vote, were a real menace; in fact, the Social Democrats were anathema to the Communists, since the former wanted to preserve the Weimar Republic and the latter did not. As for the National Socialists, they profited from current concerns – nationalistic resentment of the Versailles Treaty, among the well-to-do fear of social upheaval, and a general dread of Bolshevism. They had received only 6.5% of the vote in the 1924 elections and had sunk into near-oblivion with 2.6% in 1928, but in September 1930 their share jumped suddenly to 18.3%. The question was no longer whether Germany would be governed by democratic or undemocratic forces, but only whether it would be the undemocratic forces of the political Right or Left.[38]

In May 1932, Hindenburg abruptly replaced Chancellor Brüning by Major (ret.) Franz von Papen. In July 1932 Papen pleased the President by illegally dissolving the Social Democrat Prussian government. However, he could not control the mounting chaos of unemployment and virtual civil war, while Hitler took his campaign against the Papen government on to the streets. Fresh elections in November failed to provide Papen with the hoped-for broader base, and Hindenburg appointed Brigadier von Schleicher as Chancellor. Schleicher's attempts to stabilise his government failed, and Papen meanwhile put all his energy into overthrowing Schleicher. He persuaded Hindenburg to appoint Hitler as Chancellor on 30 January 1933, having Hitler form a coalition of National Socialists and members of the German National People's Party (DVNP). The DNVP held most cabinet posts, but National Socialists occupied the key posts of Speaker in the Reichstag (Göring), Chancellor (Hitler), Minister of the Interior (Dr Frick) and Prussian Interior Minister (Göring again). This gave them control over most German police. The new Reichswehr Minister, Blomberg, was a National Socialist supporter, which meant that they also had the support of the Army.[39]

Second Lieutenant Stauffenberg adopted a detached view of political matters when writing to Stefan George, although in reality he could not help being passionately involved. Like so many others, he thought that both the Treaty of Versailles and the government of the Republic were limiting the Reichswehr's ability to defend the country; but like those others, he never questioned his duty to defend the country whatever its government. Indeed, Stauffenberg's sense of fairness made him object vigorously when anyone ridiculed the flag of the Republic. But on 11 August, Constitution Day, No. 17 Cavalry Regiment preferred to celebrate the anniversary of a glorious deed by the Bavarian Lancer Brigade.[40] Stauffenberg's comrades commonly maintained, when questioned years later, that they did not often discuss politics either on or off duty; they frequently added, almost in the same breath, that many Reichswehr officers, Stauffenberg included, were fascinated by Point 22 of the National Socialist party manifesto, which called for a great national army. This applied equally to later anti-Hitler conspirators such as Lieutenant Stieff, Major Oster, Captain (General Staff) von Tresckow, Lieutenant Mertz von Quirnheim, and Stauffenberg's cousin Lieutenant (Res.) von Hofacker. Hofacker, for example, had been in a French prisoner-of-war camp from December 1918 to March 1920; he then went to university to read law, participated in the student government, and in 1922/23 helped found the first SA group at Göttingen University. Two weeks before the 1930 Reichstag elections he proclaimed that he was, 'in terms of party politics, the most decided opponent of "democracy"', and advocated the domination of the lands east of the German frontiers 'by offensive means only'. In the days leading up to the Reichstag elections of 5 March 1933 Hofacker campaigned for the National Socialists. Speaking in public, he declared that the people must empower the government 'to do away with elections once and for all, and to replace the Reichstag by a dictatorship'.[41]

Once Hitler had become Chancellor, an 'intimate relationship between the Reichswehr and the National Movement' naturally evolved, since the Minister for the Armed Forces, Fieldmarshal von Blomberg, was himself an enthusiastic supporter of Hitler's government.[42]

4

Sea change

When President von Hindenburg appointed Hitler to form a cabinet, this was not just another change of government. Many people viewed it as the long-hoped-for National Resurgence, while others saw it as a plunge into the abyss of arbitrary rule. The new rulers' resolve never to relinquish power was soon evident. The authorities immediately tightened their control over people's daily lives, and regarded outrages committed by their National Socialist supporters as necessary acts to suppress the enemies of the State.

Hitler negotiated with the Centre Party to achieve majority support for his cabinet in the Reichstag, but deliberately let the effort fail in order to obtain Hindenburg's consent to new Reichstag elections. These were set for 5 March 1933. On 20 February 1933, Hitler told a gathering of leading industrialists and businessmen that this election would be the last, and if it did not produce the desired result, this would be done by 'other means'.[1]

At the first meeting of the new cabinet, at 5 p.m. on 30 January 1933, Hitler said that he feared a general strike in protest against the new government, but that he wished to avoid using the Reichswehr to suppress strikers. Reichswehr Minister von Blomberg answered that soldiers were accustomed to considering only foreign enemies as their foes. At a luncheon given by Lieutenant-General von Hammerstein, Chief of the Army Leadership (a title imposed by the terms of Versailles for the Commander-in-Chief of the Army), in his private rooms at the War Office on 3 February, Hitler declared that rearmament against France was a priority. Internally there would be a 'purge', but this need be no concern of the Army.[2] On the following day Hindenburg, at the government's request, signed an emergency decree enabling them to prohibit political gatherings and publications of their rivals, and to prosecute virtually anyone who publicly said anything that the authorities deemed a threat to the 'vital interests of the state'. On 17 February Göring, as Prussian Minister of the Interior, ordered the Prussian police to support the 'national organisations' (SA, SS, Stahlhelm, NSDAP, DNVP), and to use their firearms against members of organisations 'hostile to the State'; he would cover for police officers who followed this directive, 'regardless of the consequences', and initiate disciplinary measures against anyone who 'displayed weakness'. Five days later, again by ministerial decree, Göring appointed 40,000 SA and SS troopers and 10,000 members of the Stahlhelm and the DNVP's German National Combat Group as deputy police officers. The SA set up their own concentration camps, hundreds of people lost their lives during the election campaign, beatings and murders were the order of the day.[3] When a Dutch anarchist set fire to the Reichstag building on 27 February, the government accused 'the Communists', pulled out an old draft decree granting emergency powers, modified it somewhat, and had it signed by the President. This 'Decree of the Reich President for the Protection of the People and the State', and 'for defence against violent Communist acts which endanger the State', came into force on 28 February: it suspended *sine die* all fundamental constitutional liberties: it permitted arrest without charge and domestic searches and seizures, and abolished freedom of property, freedom of speech and of the press, freedom of assembly and association, and freedom of communication. Certain crimes, such as treason against the government, which had hitherto been punishable by terms up to lifelong imprisonment now carried the death penalty, and the attempt to commit such crimes carried the same penalty as the accomplished act: the Penal Code, the result of legislation by the Reichstag, was changed by a mere decree so that people could be deprived of their lives.[4]

The elections on 5 March did not give Hitler's National Socialists the absolute majority they had hoped for. Despite a five-week terror campaign against the public at large, despite direct intimidation at the polling stations, the National Socialists received only 43.9% of the vote. The NSDAP-DNVP majority in the Reichstag was insufficient to pass the desired Enabling Law to give the government unlimited legislative authority. Such a law would have changed the Constitution and it therefore required a two-thirds majority. Göring manipulated the procedures by counting absent members as present; the 81 elected Communist members had been prevented from taking their seats and were not included in the count. Hitler won over the Centre Party with fraudulent promises. When the law was finally put to the vote on 23 March 1933, only the SPD voted against. This Enabling Law confirmed and extended, for a renewable four-year period, the unlimited powers the government had already acquired through emergency decrees. The Reich Government could now pass laws and conclude treaties with foreign powers without going through parliament, even if the proposed laws or treaties contravened the Constitution. In the next few weeks the government promulgated laws against criticism of the government, and set up 'Special Courts' with nearly unlimited jurisdiction to hand down sentences undefined and unlimited by any law; no appeals against the judgements of these Special Courts were allowed. On 6 July Hitler declared his revolution completed. By 14 July 1933 all political parties other than the NSDAP had either dissolved themselves or been outlawed.[5]

On 12 November 1933 Hitler had his internal and external policies approved by plebiscite. Of those eligible to vote, 96.3% did so; 95.1% of those eligible to vote voted 'yes'. In December 1933 the 'Unity of Party and State' was promulgated by law. When the SA leaders, headed by Ernst Röhm, attempted to swamp the regular Army with hundreds of thousands of SA troopers so as to gain control, Hitler had them shot, on the grounds that they were traitors posing an immediate danger to the State. Naturally the Army leaders approved of the elimination of this threat to the armed forces' role as the sole military force of the nation. After Hindenburg's death in August 1934, Hitler combined the presidency with the chancellorship.[6]

Despite his open challenge to the Versailles regime, Hitler got through the first few months of his chancellorship without provoking French intervention, a success which further consolidated his power. He delayed full-scale rearmament for the time being, until the autumn of 1933, when the western powers decided to continue denying equality to Germany. In July 1933 he concluded a concordat with the Holy See, which conferred a measure of international respectability on his regime. He said in Cabinet that the fact that the Vatican had even negotiated with his government was an 'indescribable success'. Moreover, the concordat forbade the Catholic hierarchy any involvement in political or trade union activities.

In October 1933, at the Disarmament Conference in Geneva, the French and British governments proposed to delay the granting of military equality to Germany by another four years, though it had been more or less conceded before Hitler became chancellor. France insisted that Germany must show good behaviour for an unspecified time before negotiations on armaments could be resumed. This could easily be presented as unfair discrimination. On 14 October, in a radio broadcast to the nation, Hitler deplored the treatment of Germany as a nation with inferior rights and stressed her peaceful intentions, without claiming the right to rearm; and he explained why Germany had three days earlier withdrawn from the League of Nations as well as the Disarmament Conference. The successful plebiscite on 12 November turned this diplomatic coup into a propaganda triumph.[7]

The National Socialists called their state the 'Third Reich', a term which combined and blurred the meanings of 'state' and 'empire' in an evident effort to draw legitimacy from the Holy Roman Empire and Bismarck's 'second' Empire. For Hitler this was no more than a stage on the way to greater things.[8] Certainly it was not the 'New Realm' of Stefan George's last volume of poems.

Secret Germany observed the proceedings of the new era sceptically but with interest. In the poet's circle politics had been much less taboo since the

National Socialists' electoral successes of September 1930, although there had always been an obscure suggestion of a great, possibly political, 'deed' arising from the Master's spirit.[9] The poet himself was much more interested in politics than he confessed to the public at large, or even to most of his friends. In March 1932, from his retreat at Minusio near Locarno, he observed the presidential election in Germany; he had long since declared Hindenburg, one of the candidates, a hero, and Hitler, the other serious contender, fascinated him. Even on his deathbed in the autumn of 1933, he continued to follow political developments in Germany.[10]

Among those of the Master's friends who joined the National Socialist Party were Ernst Bertram, Walter Elze, Kurt Hildebrandt, Ludwig Thormaehlen, Woldemar, Count Üxküll and Albrecht von Blumenthal; Rudolf Fahrner joined the SA on 5 February 1933. They expressed their support for the NSDAP in articles and lectures, and declared it in letters and conversations. Bertram, a literary historian, declared that the New Germany of Stefan George's vision had become reality in 1933. Thormaehlen urged his friends to join the NSDAP. The Master's friend Hildebrandt, a psychologist, said that to live and sacrifice oneself for the community was 'a celebration', and he proclaimed that he shared Plato's preference for the 'leader principle' as opposed to the 'democratic principle'. Nor did the Master object to Hildebrandt's plan to join the NSDAP, advising him only to say nothing for and nothing against the Party, and not to overlook the 'positive' element in National Socialism. Hildebrandt was also secure in the knowledge that the Master shared his own anti-Semitism.[11]

With the Master's permission, Thormaehlen's protégé Frank Mehnert sculpted a bust of Hitler which was marketed with considerable success by Hanfstaengl, the Munich art dealers. In 1936 Frank worked on a new version of the bust, and on a plaque showing Hitler's head in relief. Frank himself wanted the Secret Germany to play a leading role in events, but could not see how 'our people' could fit in with the new system. In a letter to the Master he recalled the Greek warriors of Opus, the capital of Locris, who always kept one place in their phalanx for the spirit of their founding father Ajax, one of the heroes of the Trojan War. No such place had yet been provided for 'our people'.[12]

In July 1933, when Stefan George celebrated his sixty-fifth birthday, Woldemar, Count Üxküll delivered a lecture to the students of Tübingen University which he entitled 'Stefan George's Revolutionary Ethos'. Fulminating against 'decomposition through individualism', Üxküll expounded the heroic world-view and the leader principle, long since established by the Master, and described the New Reich as the fulfilment of the Master's vision. Once again Germany would change the course of history, as she had with the great migrations, the *imperium sacrum*, the Reformation and Classicism, and the Heart of the Continent would save the World.[13] Woldi's

friends did not think much of these effusions, however. Berthold remarked
that Woldi appeared to have 'been talking a great deal · luckily he · and his
utterances · are held in extremely low regard'. Kantorowicz, who had dedicated his *Friedrich II.* to Woldi, suggested that people with more sense
needed to speak out, so as to throw some soil over 'these little heaps' and
stop them smelling.[14]

The Germanist Rudolf Fahrner was equally willing to acknowledge a
convergence between the Master's doctrines and those of the Party.
Fighting for what they had all 'sworn' to one another, he was quite drawn to
the SA brownshirts, 'who he had to believe were fulfilling the will of the
Master'.[15]

On the other hand Karl Wolfskehl, one of the Master's Jewish friends,
wrote to a Dutch friend, the poet Albert Verwey, saying that he could
overlook the National Socialists' hatred of the spirit (*Geist*), but felt his
whole being, his humanity, suffocated and poisoned by their 'indiscriminate, unrestrained hatred of the "Jew", of that chimerical yet blood-soaked
concept'. The National Socialist movement, he said, took its flavour and its
force from this wild, 'purely evil' German inhumanity. Wolfskehl castigated
the Jews around Stefan George, who lamented only their own exclusion
from the great national movement and failed to see what it was going to
mean for them.[16]

At Easter of 1933, Stefan George, together with Berthold Stauffenberg,
left Berlin for Munich. Second Lieutenant Claus Stauffenberg led the
Catholic soldiers of his regiment to mass and communion on Easter
morning, then boarded the Master's and Berthold's train in Bamberg, and
stayed with them in Munich until Monday, when his leave expired. While
the Master was in Munich, Ernst Kantorowicz showed him his draft of a
letter to the Prussian and Reich Minister for Science, Art and Public
Education, protesting against the persecution of the Jews, by reason of
which he (Kantorowicz) was requesting leave of absence from Frankfurt
University for the summer term of 1933. The Master had no objections.[17]

At the same time, Kantorowicz justified Wolfskehl's reproach. In a letter
to the Master he expressed his deep regret that as a Jew he was 'necessarily
excluded from the state, which is solely founded on race' – although, he
added, he had a growing conviction that the Master and his friends had
nothing in common with the National Socialists. While he, Kantorowicz,
had always known he would not deny his 'blood' when it was attacked, he
understood that the Master could not jeopardise 'his office' for the sake of a
few friends. Kantorowicz himself could see very few constructive features in
the new state. In the University, at least, 'attitude and mystic "feeling" –
welling up from the so-called folk consciousness – had henceforth to replace
ability · knowledge and learning'. Four weeks later Kantorowicz, sending
birthday greetings to George, wished 'that Germany might become as the

Master had dreamed'. By November Kantorowicz had concluded that this was unlikely, for the new beginning had already degenerated and turned bourgeois, so that 'the old battle lines are restored · the true movement is again in our hands'.[18]

During the summer term 1933 Kantorowicz held a seminar in his own home. He received an offer of an honorary fellowship from New College, Oxford, but decided instead to return to Frankfurt University for the winter term 1933/34. He wrote to the Master that at this time a constructive, positive theme could only lead to misunderstanding; therefore he proposed to lecture on the 'destruction of the Middle Ages', by which he meant the German 'Interregnum' of the thirteenth century. The collapse of the Staufen empire would show clearly the need for a 'Secret Germany' then – and the need for a rebirth today. Indeed, the title of his opening lecture was 'The Secret Germany'.

In his introduction, Kantorowicz said that the Secret Germany had a Trinity: Beauty, Nobility and Greatness. But the Secret Germany did not correspond at any point to contemporary Germany. The true Secret Germany was a realm both of this world and not of this world; it was near as a Last Judgement, guided by its emperors and by an intellectual nobility. Its ancestors were the gods of Hellas, the saints of the *Civitas Dei*, the medieval emperors, and Dante's *humana civilitas*. The Secret Germany no longer subscribed to the ideal of universal Christendom: the 'secret realm' of Stefan George's teachings was now confined to the German area, 'in which it was rooted and which it must shape'. Germany, like Hellas, would within a small space bring into being 'all primeval human forms and forces'. An unfathomable abyss separated the present distorted face of Germany from the greatest geniuses and heroes of the Secret Germany: Holbein, Frederick the Great, Herder, Goethe, Hölderlin, Nietzsche, Stefan George. But the best men of the nation must commit their lives to the Secret Germany so as to make it coincide in truth with the visible realm. In conclusion, Kantorowicz quoted defiantly from *Der Stern des Bundes*:

> Hinder us! indelible is the blossoming word.
> Hear us! Accept! In spite of your favour – it flowers.
> Murder us, and it flowers more richly!

Shortly after this lecture, on 11 December, Nazi boycotts forced Kantorowicz to suspend his lectures. He accepted the post at Oxford, which at least enabled him to turn his back on his hostile fatherland with his head held high.[19]

No one foresaw the dark fate of Europe's Jews more clearly than Wolfskehl. An ancestor of his, a rabbi, had come from Italy to Germany with the Emperor Otto II; his family had lived in Mainz for a thousand years. He once wrote that where he himself was, there also was the German

Geist, in defiance of the National Socialists' absurd denial of his German-ness. In 1934 he published in Berlin a collection of poems entitled 'The Voice Speaks', in which he asserted his Judaic faith and warned of the impending dangers. The reactions of the Master's friends were varied. Some believed that Wolfskehl's poems might endanger Stefan George's friends, 'blond or black, sprung from one womb, unacknowledged brethren'. Others were resolved to keep the Secret Germany free from all religions and nationalisms – including Zionism.[20]

George himself appeared impervious to the fundamental change in anti-Semitism in Germany since 30 January 1933. In September 1933 he declared that his way of life and friendships were sufficient proof of his own tolerance and indifference toward all religions.[21] In fact, anti-Semitism was so clearly a part of the mental furniture of the Master's circle that after 1945, the trustees of the poet's published works and papers sought to obscure all traces of it.[22]

In February 1933 the National Socialists began to remove political opponents and Jews from the Prussian Academy for the Arts, including such great names as Thomas Mann, René Schickele, Georg Kaiser and Franz Werfel, and replaced them with 'national' writers such as Hans Grimm and Hans Carossa. On 5 May the Prussian Minister for Sciences, Arts and Public Education, Bernhard Rust, made it known that the new Germany was anxious to bring Stefan George into the Academy. Through Morwitz, he informed George that he intended publicly to describe the poet as the forefather of the present government, and offered him both an honorary position in the Academy and a large sum of money to dispose of as he wished. If he was agreeable the President or the Chancellor would personally write the official letter.[23]

Stefan George replied on 10 May, in a letter intended for the attention of 'the appropriate government department'. He refused the honorary position 'in the so-called academy', and he refused the money, but declared his approval of the academy's 'national' orientation. He himself, he said, had administered German literature for half a century without any academy. On the positive side, he continued, he did not in the least deny his 'ancestorship of the new national movement and did not preclude his intellectual co-operation'. Furthermore: 'What I was able to do for it I have done· the young men who gather around me today share my view . . the fairytale of my being aloof has followed me throughout my entire life – it only appears to be so to unaided eyes.'

Stefan George, now almost sixty-five and in ill health, rejected a public role for himself, but supported the new government and agreed that they might say so.[24] Notwithstanding a critical remark here and there, the poet was sufficiently pleased with the new 'national movement' to state, in March 1933, that now for the first time he was hearing his views being echoed from

outside his own circle. And indeed his poems alluded to Germany's universal mission, deprecated shallow egalitarianism and affirmed the 'leader
principle'; they mentioned order, the national banner and the 'true symbol'
which it bore, and the New Reich. Ernst Morwitz lamented the fact that
young readers of Stefan George's poetry would find it hard to understand
that it had nothing in common with National Socialism; but the poet himself
made no such claim.[25] It is true that he had a low opinion of Hitler, in whom
he saw none of the greatness of a Caesar or Napoleon. Once, before Hitler
became Chancellor, the poet said that if the National Socialists came to
power, everyone in Germany would have to wear a noose around his neck,
and those who refused would be hanged immediately. He referred to the
National Socialists as hangmen, he did not want Frank to join any of their
organisations, and in April 1933 he encouraged his youngest friend, Karl
Josef Partsch, to talk Frank out of it. Robert Boehringer later characterised
the poet's position as one that neither supporters nor opponents of National
Socialism could use for their own purposes. But no one could know, said
Boehringer, whether or not the poet would have condemned the National
Socialists at some later date – thus making clear that to Boehringer's own
knowledge he had never done so. In Boehringer's view, therefore, the poet's
negative comments on the National Socialists carried little weight.[26]

At the beginning of July the poet was in his home town of Bingen to
renew his passport; he left four days before his sixty-fifth birthday. It has
been suggested that he sought to escape any official honours; but he went to
Berlin-Dahlem where his address was known to close friends, including
Morwitz, who had acted as intermediary in the exchange with the government in May 1933. Stefan George did nothing to stop his friends from
receiving and passing on any communications from the government. On the
contrary, Ludwig Thormaehlen got the impression on 12 July that the
Master was waiting for some government official to seek him out. But the
government made no effort beyond a personal telegram from Goebbels, the
Minister for Propaganda and Public Enlightenment. The poet's recent
refusal of national honours limited the government's options; there were
also those in the National Socialist Party who were suspicious of George's
apparent affinity with their ideas, and some even denounced him as
Jewish.[27]

About 25 July Stefan George travelled to Wasserburg on Lake Constance
and spent four weeks there, accompanied at various times (and sometimes
all together) by Frank Mehnert, Berthold Stauffenberg, Claus Stauffenberg
and some younger friends. On 24 August he took the ferry across the lake to
Heiden in Switzerland. According to Robert Boehringer the Master
intended mild political humour when he told him that in the middle of the
lake he had begun to breathe more easily. But in reality the poet had taken
the journey in order to exchange the sultry and oppressive lake front at

Wasserburg for the breezier uplands of Heiden. Frank deprecated any suggestion that the Master's journey constituted 'emigration'. Having spent the last months of 1931 and 1932 and the first months of 1932 and 1933 in Minusio in the Ticino, the Master began the same routine in the autumn of 1933. Up to his death on 4 December 1933 he never mentioned 'emigration'.[28]

To the Stauffenbergs, a good many National Socialist slogans sounded as though they *had* been inspired by Stefan George. When Berthold was interrogated by the Secret State Police in July 1944, he spoke for himself and for his brother Claus, saying they had approved of most of the National Socialists' domestic policies, such as the 'leader principle', the idea of 'responsible and competent leadership' linked with a 'healthy system of rank and the concept of national community', and the principle of putting the common weal above individual interests. They opposed corruption, favoured support for agriculture, approved of the racial principle and of a new German-centred legal system, and disapproved of big-city culture. But Berthold ended the list with this verdict: 'The fundamental ideas of National Socialism have in practice all been perverted into their opposites.'[29]

The Stauffenbergs were, of course, committed to their own 'Führer', Stefan George, and they were not easily dazzled by the National Socialists' appeal. Still, Alexander found the national resurgence 'distracting', and Berthold, who had never previously referred to politics in his letters to his fiancée, did so with increasing frequency after 30 January 1933.[30]

In the wake of the international crisis of October 1933, when the German government left the Geneva Disarmament Conference and the League of Nations, most Germans who worked in the Permanent Court of International Justice at The Hague left their posts. Berthold Stauffenberg felt inclined to leave, too, unless the Foreign Office wished him to stay. His work seemed to him useless in any case. He declared the entire court increasingly idiotic and the judges in a state of progressive imbecility. But in point of fact Germany had no intention of submitting to any more of the Court's decisions. Meanwhile Berthold had to think of his career; he still hoped to enter the diplomatic service.[31]

There were some among the Stauffenbergs' relatives who rejected the new government, and others who joined the National Socialist Party in the hope of influencing it for the better. Count Üxküll (Uncle Nux) joined on 1 May; his sister Alexandrine, the Red Cross officer, joined at about the same time; Franz, Baron von Stauffenberg, joined in 1937.[32] Uncle Berthold Stauffenberg, on the other hand, uttered dark threats against Hitler. When local Party leaders sought to prevail upon him to hoist a swastika flag instead of his family standard, he had a tall fir-tree cut down and set up in the pig-run, with a miniature swastika flag barely visible at its top. On 20

February 1933 he was involved in an attempted monarchist putsch in Munich, in company with the brothers Enoch and Karl-Ludwig, Baron von und zu Guttenberg.[33]

The Lerchenfelds, Nina Stauffenberg's family, evinced a more conventional toleration, or approval, of the new government. In 1938 a cousin of Nina's took his children to visit a Lerchenfeld in Bayreuth. On the occasion of Hitler's visit to Wagner's 'Haus Wahnfried', which was opposite this Lerchenfeld residence, the children lined up on the pavement in front of the garden fence so that Hitler would shake their hands for the photographers. They did not wash their hands for days afterward; one of the girls wrote Hitler's car licence number into the hem of her skirt.[34]

Claus Stauffenberg could not vote because soldiers were excluded from doing so by law, but he did not hesitate to express his views on social occasions with his regiment, or in Stefan George's circle. In April 1932 he supported Hitler's bid for the presidency. He saw Hindenburg as a 'reactionary' favoured by the narrow-minded middle classes. In 1933 Stauffenberg welcomed Hitler's appointment as Chancellor. Some contemporaries recall his reaction as 'enthusiastic'.[35]

On the evening of 30 January 1933, Stauffenberg was on his way to a social function in Bamberg when he became engulfed in an enthusiastic torchlight procession celebrating Hitler's appointment as Chancellor. Stauffenberg was in uniform and therefore immediately recognisable as an officer of the Bamberg regiment. Rather than extricating himself, he walked on at the head of the procession. When he arrived late at his destination and related the incident to his hosts and the other guests, the older ones criticised him sharply. He explained that the enthusiastic citizens would not have understood it if an officer in uniform 'in such a situation' had sidestepped the demonstration. The great soldiers of the Wars of Liberation, he said, would certainly have had a better understanding of this genuine national resurgence than did his critics.[36]

Incidents of this sort do not, however, constitute the principal evidence of Stauffenberg's views on National Socialism. A fellow officer described Stauffenberg as 'nationalist' and on the political right wing, like all officers. He was enthusiastic in his support for the new 'national' movement; he was a 'national flame', a 'sacred flame'. Stauffenberg not only supported rearmament, expansion of the Army, acquisition of heavy weapons – 'that went without saying for everyone in the Reichswehr' – he also supported non-military goals such as the unification of all national Germans within borders of the Reich. A relative of Stauffenberg's wife Nina recalls the family's surprise at his coup attempt in July 1944: many had thought of him as the only real National Socialist in the family.[37]

Stauffenberg's instructor at the Cavalry School in Hanover, Baron von Loeper, who was also his divisional commander in the Polish campaign,

21. Claus Stauffenberg at Bamberg, 1932

describes Stauffenberg as an 'uncomplicatedly cheerful, engaging person of high intelligence and native leadership qualities; his character was thoroughly decent and crystal-clear'. With his pronounced nationalism 'he had to become a victim of the Austrian Pied Piper of Braunau, just like the mass of our younger officer corps' – for in the Republic the government, the parliament, the newspapers very rarely stood up for German national interests. But, Loeper added, it was necessary to distinguish between, on the one hand, 'pure National Socialism' which attempted to combine social concerns with the national interest and to end the class struggle, and on the other hand, Hitlerism, 'which followed quite different, dictatorial, power-hungry, criminal courses'. It was a distinction which, according to Loeper, Stauffenberg did not recognise at that time.[38]

Stauffenberg was promoted to Lieutenant on 1 May 1933, a few months earlier than most of those on the same career path.[39] It was a busy time for him as commander and training officer of the mortar troop. For years he also managed the business affairs of his regimental officers' club, and he read all the military periodicals he could lay his hands on.[40]

The expansion of the armed forces, planned long before 1933, was pursued more energetically under Hitler's chancellorship. But until the end of 1933 actual expansion remained modest because Hitler needed to test the former Entente Powers' resolve to enforce the Treaty of Versailles, and because the whole issue was complicated by the ambition of Ernst Röhm, leader of the SA, to turn his organisation into the new national army, or to incorporate its greater numbers into the regular Army. Meanwhile, various measures were taken to promote the rationalisation and expansion of the Reichswehr: the replacement training structure was reorganised, along with the military districts, regions and divisional commands, and a reserve officer corps was created. Only at the end of 1933 were clear directives issued to increase the Army to 300,000 men. In the meantime the Army collaborated, at the garrison level, with its dangerous SA rivals, helping them to train, and at the same time recovering weapons and ammunition hidden when the Treaty of Versailles had come into force.[41]

In June 1933 Stauffenberg wrote to the Master with pronounced (if somewhat tortuous) scepticism. Once again, he said, it had become clear that the narrow-minded bourgeoisie could not adjust to revolution. The regime's claim to total control and its efforts at forcing everyone into line were, after all, 'not all that novel to us' (by 'us' Stauffenberg evidently meant the Army). On the other hand, it was clear that masters, not parties, made revolutions. Anyone who set his mastery on firm foundations was to be commended for his cleverness: it was an idea that ought to be borne in mind by those who tended to lose their way in definitions of 'intellectual foundations'.[42]

On 26 September 1933 Stauffenberg married the Lutheran Nina,

22. Nina and Claus Stauffenberg leaving St James's at Bamberg after their wedding on 26 September 1933

Baroness von Lerchenfeld, daughter of a Bavarian nobleman and the Baltic Baroness von Stackelberg, in St James's Catholic church in Bamberg. He wore uniform and steel helmet: 'To wed is to be on duty,' he had explained to his bride. After a reception at the 'Bamberger Hof' hotel, the couple left by train for Rome, 'to take advantage of the reasonable prices'. They had booked for an organised tour to an exhibition in Rome celebrating Mussolini's first ten years in power. They also visited churches and museums in Verona, Ostia and Florence. Berthold travelled with them as far as Bellinzona, in order to see the Master in Minusio.[43]

Stefan George had arrived there on 23 September. On 27 September Berthold found him unwell, generally weak and without appetite. Two months later Frank informed some friends that the Master's condition gave cause for concern. Robert Boehringer, Frank, the physician Walter Kempner and Clotilde Schlayer took turns at his bedside in hospital in Minusio. Karl Josef Partsch, Berthold and Alexander Stauffenberg, Albrecht von Blumenthal, Claus Stauffenberg, Walter Anton and Ludwig Thormaehlen also arrived. They were allowed a brief glimpse of the Master in his darkened room, but he was not aware of their presence. Boehringer, Frank, Berthold Stauffenberg and Walter Kempner thought it best to put off Ernst Kantorowicz and Wilhelm Stein – Jewish friends – from coming to Minusio; the older Jewish friends, Ernst Morwitz and Karl Wolfskehl, were not even informed of the Master's condition until after his death.[44]

The poet died in Minusio on 4 December 1933. Robert Boehringer, as Stefan George's heir, directed the funeral arrangements. The poet's will laid down that Berthold Stauffenberg should succeed Boehringer in the inheritance; Berthold now named Frank as his own successor. Thus Berthold and Frank henceforth had a hand in all dispositions concerning Stefan George's works and possessions. Thormaehlen, Blumenthal, Berthold, Walter Anton and others wanted to take the Master's remains back to Germany for burial. But Boehringer was able to quote the Master's pronouncement that a man ought to be buried where he had died. Eventually they all agreed that he should be buried in Minusio. Claus Stauffenberg organised the wake that was customary in the Ticino. The friends kept vigil by turns in the graveyard chapel from the evening of 4 December to the morning of 6 December.[45]

Frank and Berthold urged that President von Hindenburg should be notified. On 5 December the German Consul in Lugano asked the Minusio municipal authorities when the funeral was to take place. The friends indicated three in the afternoon of 6 December and added that additional mourners were not wanted. They then rescheduled the funeral for a quarter past eight in the morning of 6 December, without telling the authorities. But now Frank and Berthold thought it impolite to deceive the German Minister at Bern, Baron von Weizsäcker, who had been instructed by the Foreign Office to lay a wreath on behalf of the government. Boehringer, who was a friend of Weizsäcker's, informed him of the change and told him that there would be no objection to the placing of the wreath on the day after the funeral.[46]

Twenty-five friends, among them Morwitz and Wolfskehl (who had eventually been notified), attended the funeral. The large laurel wreath sent by the German government bore a black, white and red ribbon, and a red ribbon with a swastika on a white ground. Clotilde Schlayer put roses over the swastika; Frank removed them. A little later, persons unknown removed the white patch with the swastika. Frank and Karl Josef Partsch bought some white linen and black ribbon and tried to persuade the Master's cook to fashion a replacement, but she refused, so they did their own cutting and sewing and laid the result on the grave. When the largest group of friends left Locarno by train after the funeral, some of the younger ones gave each other the 'Hitler salute' with their right hands raised.[47]

5

In the Third Reich

For his friends, the Master's death threw a pall over the national resurgence. While some of them maintained a haughty distance between the poet's 'inner state' and the vulgar outer world, there was a persistent tension caused by similarities between the terminology of the esoteric sublimities of the Master's teaching and that used for the tenets of National Socialism. A good illustration of this is the genesis of Frank Mehnert's statue of a pioneer soldier, intended for erection in Magdeburg.

In 1929 Frank had abandoned his law studies to become a sculptor and Stefan George's principal companion and private secretary. In 1933, with the Master's approval, Frank entered a competition for an SA monument commissioned by the Central Prussian SA Leadership and the Prussian Minister for Science, Arts and Public Education. Since before Easter of that year, Frank had studied classical models with a view to deciding how an SA uniform might be sculpted. The monument was to be placed in front of Magdeburg Cathedral, following the removal early in 1933 of a 1929 war memorial by Ernst Barlach which its critics said symbolised defeat, and which they rejected also because it was the gift of a Social-Democratic Prussian government. The SA monument was intended to 'express the idea of national resurgence and to honour the SA troopers who had fallen in the struggle for it'. Participants in the competition were to receive one thousand marks. After the shooting of SA leaders on 30 June and 1 July 1934 Frank thought he would never see his money, but it had been posted before 30 June 1934; and in any case the monument project was not abandoned.[1]

Frank chose Claus Stauffenberg as his model. In March 1934 he came to Bamberg to work during lunch hours on the hop-floor of an abandoned brewery. But Stauffenberg refused to don an SA uniform. He wrote to Berthold: 'I have not yet quite accepted that I am to be immortalized as an S.A. man, but I console myself with the thought that this is much harder on the Nazis than it is for me.' After Frank had been working for two weeks, Stauffenberg judged the model 'fairly un-Nazi-like', adding that this was evidently intentional. Frank's entry was subsequently rejected.[2]

Through the efforts of his friends, Frank was commissioned by the City

75

23. Right: Stauffenberg as sculptor's model. Left: Frank Mehnert's pioneer statue at the Elbe bridge in Magdeburg, 1939

of Magdeburg and other sponsors to create a statue of a pioneer soldier for the east end of the bridge over the Elbe between the town and the pioneers' barracks.

Stauffenberg again served as the model. The sponsors wanted the statue to represent a common soldier. Thormaehlen, Frank's supporter and intermediary in contacts with the sponsors, believed that the statue should have an anonymous face, and that the face of a person from the Master's 'state' should not be used. Thormaehlen, Claus and Frank agreed that the statue must not have a 'plain' face that suggested low intelligence, because it would clash with the noble bearing of the statue and make it look ridiculous. But Claus and Frank insisted that the statue was to have Claus's features, and eventually Thormaehlen and the sponsors were persuaded to accept it.[3]

The statue, in shelly limestone, was unveiled on 2 December 1939. During the night of 27 to 28 March 1942 some persons unknown knocked it down and rolled the fragments into the river. The guard-post at the bridge was unoccupied at the time for reasons that remain obscure; the sentries before the pioneers' barracks had a good view over the bridge but did not notice anything, although the four-ton statue could only have been pulled

24. Detail of the pioneer statue (Magdeburg, 1982)

off its base by horses or a vehicle with a chain or steel cable. The fragments were recovered; only the right hand was missing. Frank, who in the interim had been twice wounded on the Russian front, swore revenge: 'For every statue they knock down, twelve more shall arise, each bigger and more beautiful than the last, and shall remind them every day and everywhere they go, in their cringing consciences, of their cringing inferiority.' When Frank fell near Staraja Russa on 26 February 1943, Berthold and Claus Stauffenberg sought to restore the statue, but the course of the war overtook their efforts.[4]

Stauffenberg repeatedly gave voice to his rejection of the National Socialists' more vulgar manifestations. In March 1934 he drafted a letter to the Propaganda Ministry, 'as a German and soldier', objecting vigorously to allegations printed in *Der Stürmer*, the anti-Semitic rag edited by Julius Streicher, Gauleiter of Nuremberg, to the effect that Stefan George's poetry resembled 'Jewish Dadaism', and that his real name was Heinrich Abeles (suggesting that he had been a Jew). Claus wrote to his brother Berthold begging his consent to the sending of this letter, 'since the errors and transgressions of inferior National Socialists are so easily elevated to the dignity of state law, or easily become regarded as such'. Stauffenberg's regimental commander, Colonel von Perfall, had to give his consent, too, as Claus wrote to Berthold; but Perfall knew that Claus belonged to the Master's 'state'. Stauffenberg's intervention cannot, of course, be regarded as an attack on the regime. As late as 1938, the Army High Command excluded *Der Stürmer* from the list of publications suitable for reading in the armed forces.[5] Similarly, Stauffenberg's remark that the shooting of SA leaders on 30 June and 1 July 1934 had 'finally cleared things up' can be taken only as approval of the purge, not as an attack on the regime.[6] It is a measure of his independence that he took part in horse trials organised by the SA at Heiligenhaus, whereas most of his Army comrades shunned contacts with the SA.[7]

All the cavalry regiments in the Reichswehr were gradually being converted into mechanised or armoured formations. By July 1934, No. 17 Cavalry Regiment was largely mechanised: the 4th Squadron was now an anti-tank battalion, the 3rd and 5th gave up their horses and were reorganised into a motorcycle battalion at Eisenach.[8]

From 1 October 1934 Stauffenberg served as a training officer, and from 1935 as adjutant in the Army Cavalry School in Hanover. The family lived at no. 21 Lister Kirchweg. Stauffenberg had to train four horses every day, and he rode his own horse in trials. In 1934 he beat several of the future (1936) Olympic champions in the Army. He took English lessons, read the *Daily Telegraph*, and attended lectures on geopolitics at the Hanover Institute of Technology.[9]

In 1936 Stauffenberg was senior enough to sit the Military District Examinations for admission to the War Academy. Candidates had to be familiar with all the published volumes of the Reichsarchiv's history of the World War, and they were required to read Hitler's *Mein Kampf*.[10] In February 1936 Stauffenberg had a bad fall with a horse that tended to rear. But he passed his Military District Examinations in June 1936. On the side, he collaborated in the transfer of the Cavalry School to Krampnitz, near Berlin, as part of the establishment of the German armoured forces.[11]

In the last week of June 1936, on the end-of-course excursion for trainers at the Cavalry School to the ruins of Hohentwiel Castle, which had been in the tenth century the chief residence of the Dukes of Swabia, Stauffenberg gave a talk about the Holy Roman Empire in the Staufen era. In November of the same year he wrote to a friend: 'The supreme fulfilment for the German is the Reich, indeed the universal Reich: the sacred Reich, Humanism, the classical period [of German literature].' In April 1940, in the midst of preparations for the campaign in France, Stauffenberg was working on a lecture he wanted to give to the divisional staff on the medieval concept of the Reich based on Emperor Frederick II's state papers.[12]

25. Stauffenberg with his batman, Hans Kreller, competing in horse trials at Heiligenhaus in May 1935

Stauffenberg's superior performance in the examination for a diploma in English interpretation earned him 500 marks for a fortnight's visit to England. He arrived there on 31 August 1936, visited the Tower, St Paul's Cathedral, Westminster Abbey, Westminster Hall, Buckingham Palace, the British Museum, Windsor and Eton, and on 7 September the Royal Military College at Sandhurst. He also met with the German Military Attaché, Brigadier Baron Geyr von Schweppenburg, who was a family friend. In the middle of September he took a second trip to England to take part in a fox hunt.[13]

On 6 October 1936 Stauffenberg entered the War Academy at nos. 3–4 Kruppstrasse in Berlin-Moabit, one of Berlin's industrial suburbs. His family, including his two sons Berthold and Heimeran (born in 1934 and 1936) moved into no. 20 Waltharistrasse in Berlin-Wannsee. Berthold and his wife lived nearby at no. 14 Konstanzerstrasse in Berlin-Wilmersdorf; their cousin Cäsar von Hofacker lived at no. 8 Kaiser-Wilhelm-Strasse in Berlin-Steglitz. Fritz-Dietlof, Count Schulenburg, a friend of the Stauffenbergs and Hofackers, then Deputy Chief of Police in Berlin, lived nearby at no. 15 Ithweg in Berlin-Zehlendorf. Schulenburg's father, Lieutenant-

General Friedrich, Count Schulenburg, had been Chief of the General Staff of the Army Group commanded by the Crown Prince during the World War. From 1924 to 1928 he was a Reichstag deputy for the German National People's Party, from 1933 a member of the NSDAP, and an honorary Lieutenant-General of the SS; when he died in 1939 he was given a state funeral with Hitler in attendance. Through his friend Hofacker, the younger Schulenburg knew the Stauffenbergs' uncle Nikolaus, Count von Üxküll, who lived at no. 25 Hofbauerpfad in Berlin-Zehlendorf, where Claus Stauffenberg had heated discussions with Schulenburg on military matters.[14] The Stauffenberg brothers met frequently with Uncle Nux, Cäsar von Hofacker, Schulenburg, the young diplomats Albrecht von Kessel and Adam von Trott zu Solz, the landowner and farmer Ulrich, Count von Schwerin, and the civil servant Otto Ehrensberger at the home of their cousin Peter, Count Yorck von Wartenburg, also a civil servant, at no. 50 Hortensienstrasse in Berlin-Dahlem, where they later met Helmuth James, Count von Moltke (who specialised in international law).[15]

At this time, of the thousand men who sat the qualifying examinations in a given year, the War Academy admitted one hundred, making classes of twenty to twenty-five candidates; twenty of this one hundred were eventually posted to General Staff positions on probation for about a year, and most of these twenty were ultimately appointed to the General Staff. In 1933 the War Academy course was shortened from three to two years. After the introduction of universal military service in 1935, the majority of the War Academy graduates were posted to the General Staff. By 1938 so many had graduated that the three-year course was restored. During the war, when the Army was suffering heavy casualties, the course was reduced to only a few months.[16]

Tactical exercises, in which candidates assumed various divisional staff positions, were a daily routine. Stauffenberg's tactical work was judged 'good', 'clear', 'commendably brief', but sometimes 'too optimistic' or 'superficial'.[17] The American Captain Albert Wedemeyer, one of about a dozen or so visiting War Academy students accepted each year, thought this system preferable to the far more theoretical approach that was customary at the American Staff College at Fort Leavenworth from which he had graduated. The War Academy students, he reported, practised mostly envelopment, rarely breakthrough and defence. They learned all about the campaigns of Philip of Macedonia, Alexander, Caesar, Frederick the Great and Napoleon, and about American industrial superiority as the decisive factor in the World War, but nothing about the American Civil War. Wedemeyer was impressed with the instruction in new tactics such as the deployment of airborne divisions, armoured divisions and anti-tank units, which did not even exist in the American Forces. In their second year the students were taught to lead army corps and armies, and they studied strategy, geography, demography and climate, together with the culture, politics and economics of other nations.[18]

Some seventeen pages of notes and three pages of bibliography on military economics survive among Stauffenberg's papers, which reflect his considerable interest in both politics and economics. He was impressed by statistics on American steel production, which was four times that of Germany. In conversations with Wedemeyer he showed himself familiar with John Maynard Keynes's *The Economic Consequences of the Peace* and with Keynes's view that Germany had been treated unwisely as well as unjustly in 1919. Stauffenberg, a Cavalry Captain from 1 January 1937, was also well acquainted with British and American diplomacy in the eighteenth and nineteenth centuries, and with the Founding Fathers of the United States.[19] Stauffenberg and Wedemeyer both avoided talking about German politics, but Wedemeyer detected in Stauffenberg a fundamental scepticism about the National Socialist regime, even an aversion to it.[20]

But at times, in the presence of others, Stauffenberg would talk endlessly about National Socialism, so that fellow officers on his War Academy course asked him to avoid political topics if he wanted to eat at the same table with them.[21]

Even at that time there were signs that America and Germany might soon oppose each other in war. President Roosevelt said in his 'Quarantine Speech' of 5 October 1937 that the free world must be defended against the few who would disrupt it, and that those who threatened the freedom and territory of their neighbours must be 'put in quarantine'.[22] After his return to America, Wedemeyer wrote to Stauffenberg that he would always value their friendship, but that in a war he would fight for his country in every way he could. Stauffenberg replied confirming their friendship and expressing the hope that America would use her influence to preserve the peace.[23]

Stauffenberg and his classmate and friend at the Academy, Albrecht Ritter Mertz von Quirnheim, were similarly described by another cadet as being 'cool' towards the National Socialist regime, although neither could be said to have openly opposed it. In fact, both on the whole approved of the policies of the regime until 1938; at the same time, both were careful not to reveal their innermost thoughts to potential informers. Both approved of restrictions upon the Jews in various professions and in the civil service, but at the same time both always abhorred persecutions; in April 1933 Mertz denounced the anti-Jewish 'boycott' as shameful.[24]

Mertz, incisive, unorthodox, given to satire and sarcasm, was the son of the Reich Archivist at Potsdam, Lieutenant-General Dr Hermann Ritter Mertz von Quirnheim. He had joined No. 19 (Bavarian) Infantry Regiment, received a second lieutenant's commission, was posted in 1929 to No. 8 (Prussian) Infantry Regiment, became a lieutenant in 1931 and served with

26. *Stauffenberg (above) wrote to Frank Mehnert from a General Staff journey to the East Prussian battlefields of 1914, Tannenberg and Gumbinnen. 1937*

his regiment's training battalion in Liegnitz. In 1933 he decided that the SA was the army of the future, and wanted to join it. He had himself transferred to the border garrisons in Silesia and kept in touch with the SA leaders there, particularly SA-Lieutenant-General Heines. Mertz's father arranged his transfer to No. 5 (Prussian) Infantry Regiment in Stettin; its Colonel, Max von Viebahn, restored Mertz's grasp on the fundamentals of the soldier's profession. Viebahn also gathered together the regiment's second lieutenants and explained to them the reason for Mertz's transfer. Mertz was still somewhat wild, but he began to value his training and prepared himself diligently for the Military District Examination.[25] He grew more sceptical toward the National Socialists, but he admired the clarity of Hitler's threatening 'peace speech' of 21 May 1935, in which the dictator proclaimed the new law on the armed forces and reaffirmed the German rearmament programme in response to the Franco-Russian alliance of 2 May.[26]

At the end of their first year in the War Academy, in June 1937, Stauffenberg's class went on a 'general staff ride' to the East Prussian battlefields of 1914–1915. Stauffenberg sent Frank two postcards, listing places he had visited: Königsberg, Insterburg, Rominten Heath, Masuria, Allenstein, the Tannenberg battlefields, Gumbinnen. He admired the medieval castles and cathedrals built by the Order of German Knights, but: 'The most essential and duty-binding [*verpflichtend*] monuments are the graves of German soldiers everywhere in the region.'[27]

From 1 July up to the autumn manoeuvres, the students of the War Academy served with troops using weapons of branches other than their own. Stauffenberg found that serving in an artillery regiment at Münsingen was a 'recreation' compared with the War Academy, but he noticed that the Army was suffering from growing-pains: the education and performance of the officer corps were not at all satisfactory. Between postings, from the end of July to the end of August, he was on leave in Lautlingen with his wife and children.[28] For two weeks after that he commanded a battery in No. 35 Artillery Regiment at Karlsruhe. Manoeuvres took him along the Kocher and Jagst rivers, and to the vicinity of Heidenheim, Ellwangen, Aalen and Schwäbisch Gmünd. There followed a week with No. 25 Artillery Regiment in Münsingen. After a short break there were manoeuvres in Mecklenburg. The War Academy students worked in staffs conducting operations, or refereeing them.[29]

At the end of 1937 the German Ambassador to Moscow, Friedrich Werner, Count Schulenburg, gave a lecture to the War Academy on 'German-Soviet Political Relations' in which he clearly expounded the Soviet Union's strengths and weaknesses, her expansionist tendencies, and her enormous resources of raw materials, populations and industry. He warned against taking the show-trials and executions of certain generals as a sign of weakness, and he insisted that Russia could not be measured by European standards. The Soviet Union might not be capable of aggressive war for years to come, indeed she was more likely to wait while the western powers exhausted each other; but in a defensive war the Soviet Union commanded the advantages that had served Russia so well in the past: her enormous size, her large population, the modest material requirements of

27. War Academy staff exercise, East Prussia, 1937. Facing photographer, from left: Stauffenberg, Captain Wolf von Zawadsky, Captain Georg Gartmayr, Captain Mertz von Quirnheim. Between Gartmayr and Mertz is Captain Heinrich Worgitzky

her people and their capacity for endurance.[30] Schulenburg's predictions could hardly have been more accurate. In part they must have been based on information about Hitler's intentions as revealed in the memorandum of August 1936 to Fieldmarshall von Blomberg and Lieutenant-General Göring concerning the Four-Year Plan.[31] When in 1939 Stalin concluded a non-aggression pact with Hitler which provided for the partition of Poland and for Soviet control of the Baltic states, he must have calculated that Hitler's attack on Poland would involve Germany in war with the western powers, so that the Soviet Union could expand her dominion. The Soviet attack on Finland in November 1939 supports this interpretation.

Among the twenty-three students in Stauffenberg's class, he stood out above all others, as a nobleman, as a practising Catholic, and as a humanist with intellectual interests and great eloquence, though he was cautious in giving a formal opinion. Increasingly, fellow-students and others referred to him with extraordinary respect and admiration.[32]

In 1937 Stauffenberg submitted a paper for a prize competition orgnised by the German Society for the Policy and Science of Defence, entitled 'Defence against Enemy Parachute Troops'. It was awarded first prize, and the Air Ministry had it printed for internal circulation. On 28 April 1938

Stauffenberg was invited to give a lecture on the same topic to the Lilienthal Society for Aviation Research. In July 1938 it was published in *Wissen und Wehr*.[33]

In this paper Stauffenberg considered all aspects of the matter, for which practical experience was not yet available. He considered the deployment of parachute troops in relation to other military operations behind an opponent's front line, paying attention to attainable aims, means required, and methods of deployment. He compared parachute troops to the cavalry. He noted two principal types of parachute mission: small sabotage and espionage details, and larger combat commands. The former had to be expected at all times and their detection and neutralisation required constant vigilance by anti-aircraft posts, guards at likely targets, and frequent identity checks. Defence against parachute combat troops was more difficult because the defender could not station sufficient counter-forces at every conceivable target all the time. Potential targets which were essential in case of war, or which might be attacked in conjunction with front-line operations, nevertheless had to be given careful consideration. An enemy might well sacrifice a small, highly trained force to destroy or neutralise such targets. Parachute combat troops enjoyed the advantage of surprise at first, but once landed they were slow-moving and conspicuous; they could easily be isolated from their supply lines, and prevented from retreating.

Stauffenberg's study covered the art of defence against parachute troops in realistic detail; it was the first of its kind in the German Army and received wide recognition.[34]

Another study by Stauffenberg, on cavalry, also emerged from work and conversations at the War Academy. After several revisions, and the incorporation of some suggestions from Frank Mehnert, Stauffenberg sent his work to the Chief of Cavalry Inspection in the General Army Office, Colonel von Witzleben, who passed it on to the 7th General Staff Department for War Research with a view to having it published in the *Militärwissenschaftliche Rundschau*. The paper was not accepted for publication. Some people surmised that the editors had wrongly taken Stauffenberg to be advocating a return to the obsolete cavalry arm. He had also proposed an examination of the historic foundations of the cavalry and of the reasons for its failure in the World War, suggesting that the cavalry, had it been appropriately engaged, could have won the Battle of the Marne and so the whole war. This gave the impression that Stauffenberg, a cavalry captain without front-line experience, was lecturing the generals of the World War. At the same time, the editors may have considered it unwise to publish anything which would focus attention on the panzer tactics so soon to be put into practice – for Stauffenberg, in his final draft, emphasised the cavalry-like virtues of armoured reconnaissance vehicles and postulated that tactical and operative breakthrough were almost unthinkable without a massive concentration of tanks. Strangely, he did not mention the potential use of aeroplanes and parachute troops in cavalry-like deployment.[35]

In August 1937 Stauffenberg's uncle Nikolaus, Count Üxküll, was offered a position as the Reich Prices Commissioner's liaison officer with the War Ministry. The Reich Commissioner was Josef Wagner, the former governor of Silesia in Breslau and NSDAP Regional Leader (Gauleiter) for Lower and Upper Silesia. Peter, Count Yorck, had worked in the Reich Prices Commissioner's Berlin office since 1936. Count Üxküll accepted the position, which Stauffenberg described as being 'in the centre of the navel of the Four-Year Plan' and for which he considered his uncle ideally suited, since he was an independent personality with both a military and business background.[36]

Two weeks later Stauffenberg wrote to Teske, a classmate at the War Academy whose father had just died, and explained his view of the purpose to which they had both dedicated their lives. He deplored prevailing 'conditions and tendencies', meaning that soldiers were not adequately trained, and that both recruits and officer cadets had been politicised through their previous membership of NSDAP youth organizations. Stauffenberg was motivated by 'burning anxiety and love for the cause' combined with a large measure of optimism, even though this might be vindicated 'only in future generations after renewed upheavals and changes'. In the next sentence, Stauffenberg identified 'the cause'. The only man who could claim to love 'his Fatherland, his Army' was the man who answered the challenge with his entire existence and included his private life, his family and his children as part of that responsibility. The difficulty of the immediate task could not be exaggerated, but concern with it was the basis for any hope of attaining the goal: the unity of the Army in a common cause that transcended the background and interests of individuals.[37]

On 30 December 1937, at the baptism of his brother Berthold's son at Lautlingen, Stauffenberg expressed similarly elevated views. He spoke of the convictions of his father Alfred, after whom his nephew had been named; of loyalty to the family, to the state, to the sovereign, to God, and thus to oneself. He quoted the child's grandfather: 'It does not matter what you do, only that you act decently and that you bring honour to your name.'[38]

In January 1938, Stauffenberg learned from Captain (GS) von Pezold, with whom he had served in the Bamberg regiment (and who had the information from the Vice-President of Berlin Police, Count Schulenburg), and from Schulenburg himself, the details of the intrigues by which the War Minister, Fieldmarshal von Blomberg, and the Commander-in-Chief of the Army, General von Fritsch, had been removed from their posts. Both had objected on 5 November 1937 to Hitler's announcement of an attack on Czechoslovakia and of the annexation of Austria. Stauffenberg stood up in his War Academy lecture room and demanded to be told the reasons for the Commander-in-Chief's dismissal.[39] He expressed shock and dismay to a cousin at Wilflingen and to Brigadier von Loeper, his later divisional commander; and he privately criticised the generals who failed to make a stand against the treatment to which Blomberg and Fritsch had been subjected.[40] However, Stauffenberg, like most Germans, welcomed the union of Germany and Austria in March 1938.[41]

The final staff exercise, at army-corps level, was held along the Rhine. The graduating students alternated as regimental and divisional commanders, and as personnel, quartermaster and operations officers. The main body of German land forces was presumed to be in pursuit of a defeated enemy in the east; the War Academy candidates had to conduct the defence along the Rhine. It was a familiar problem of German strategy, that of facing potential opponents on two sides: a variation of it had been put up by Lieutenant-General Beck, Chief of the General Staff, as a problem for the General Staff exercise in the spring of 1938. In the case of the War Academy staff exercise, the defence of the Rhine against the French army proved impossible while most German forces were engaged against Czechoslovakia. The German forces in the west could only attempt an orderly retreat across the Rhine into the Neckar position.[42]

During the final exercises, on 22 June, Stauffenberg not only gave his classmates a tour of medieval cathedrals and explained the architecture and history of the Holy Roman Empire, but also found time to negotiate with a Bingen town councillor regarding Stefan George's house there; to arrange for a ceremony to name a school after the poet and for the solemn gift of a portrait; and to reassure the councillor regarding Gestapo inquiries as to why the poet had not wished to be buried in Germany. On this latter point Stauffenberg commented to Frank that, since he had been an officer at the time, he was able to give testimony which no one could call into question.[43]

The War Academy farewell dinner was held in Bingen on 23 June. Stauffenberg, Mertz and Teske had produced a mildly sarirical magazine entitled 'The School of Victory', which contained character sketches and reminiscences of the graduates. It referred to Stauffenberg's interest in the operational importance of the cavalry, and suggested his loquaciousness by quoting Goethe's line 'Es bildet ein Talent sich in der Stille' – 'talent forms itself quietly'![44] Stauffenberg used the occasion, as he liked to do, to give a well-prepared speech. He delivered it in the open air, near Stahleck Castle above Bacherach on the Rhine. He referred to the River as the focus of centuries of struggle for the mastery of Europe, and described the soldier's calling as never-ending; he concluded his historical *tour d'horizon* with Napoleon's campaigns, and expressed a commitment to national independence:

I have no need to speak of the victorious progress of the timeless, homeless conqueror-emperor, which has long since been assimilated and become the model for German soldiery. Perhaps today we ought not to curse and abuse but thank him for whose greatness his own nation was too small· for having broken the empty old forms and for having given to a shrunken world the measure of his own imperial courses· and for having directed the German nation to itself and to the act of liberation![45]

Stauffenberg spoke also of his concern lest the continuous struggles in Europe should lead to a moral and religious weakening of the nations. This had been averted in 1918 because the Last Battle on the Rhine had not been fought. But what if new conflicts led the new un-European power in the East to intervene in a struggle among European nations?

On 25 June the War Academy course formally ended in Berlin. Stauffenberg finished first in his class. A fitness report on him in the General Staff List which was written at the time of his definitive posting to the General Staff in November 1939 stated: 'Good tactical ability, tirelessly industrious, great organisational talent. Above average.'[46] Since the standard of comparison was the General Staff officers themselves, these sober words were high praise. In 1943 both the Chief of the General Staff and the Army High Command Personnel Office considered Stauffenberg eligible for General Staff positions on army corps and army command staffs, with the potential to attain 'the highest military positions'. The highest military positions were those of Chief of the General Staff, Commander-in-Chief of the Army, and Supreme Commander of the Armed Forces.

On 1 August 1938 Stauffenberg was posted as quartermaster to the First Light Division in Wuppertal. Within days he had to use his training in a situation that appeared rapidly to be approaching war over Hitler's demands against Czechoslovakia.[47] Stauffenberg himself did not believe it would come to that because Hitler, who knew the horrors of war, surely could not want one, much less one which would have to be fought against the entire world.[48]

In 1934 Berthold, Count Stauffenberg, was determined not to spend the rest of his days as a researcher in the Kaiser-Wilhelm-Institut for Foreign Public and International Law, which was housed in the former Royal Palace in Berlin. The Institute's main function was to provide legal opinions in support of government policy. It prepared papers defending government policies, and published many of the papers in its own periodical, the *Zeitschrift für ausländisches öffentliches Recht und Völkerrecht*. The Institute's work was important, but it was subsidiary to that of the Foreign Office, and was thus a poor substitute for direct participation in shaping events.

In April 1935 Berthold Stauffenberg wrote to Mika, whom he later married, that after December 1933 (when the poet had died) the best part of his life lay behind him. He was working in the Institute as it were 'on the side', as if the work did not much concern him, and surely this was intolerable as a long-term prospect. He was glad that he still had 'the other obligation', the Master's legacy; but without being able 'to really produce something' he would continue to feel melancholy.[49] As his brother Claus's ambition was to join the General Staff, Berthold's was to serve in the Foreign Office.

Berthold's life did not entirely lack variety and interest. He took military training at Bamberg in September 1934, and reserve training, 'lying in the dirt' with heavy machine-guns, at Grafenwöhr at the end of November. He spent several weeks at The Hague on Institute business in October 1934, and again in October 1935.[50] Over Christmas he paid a visit to his parents at Lautlingen, visited the Master's sister at Bingen, and met with Claus, Walter Anton, Blumenthal and Frank in Berlin. He did a further three weeks' military training at Bamberg in March 1935, and reserve-officer exercises at Bamberg in September-October 1935 and in May 1936. During this tour he fell with his horse and broke a leg. He stayed at Greifenstein, his uncle's castle, until it had healed. After a family reunion in Jettingen at the end of November, which Claus also attended, Berthold met with Frank and Robert Boehringer at Minusio on the anniversary of the Master's death.[51]

Besides his hopes of entering the Foreign Service, Berthold had an opportunity to begin an academic career. He gave a trial lecture on the Permanent Court of International Justice at Munich University on 16 February 1934, and he had expectations of an appointment in international law. He would have been glad to leave Berlin, where 'everything was so different'. But he decided against becoming a university teacher, evidently after having been appointed a senior research fellow in his Institute and as co-editor of the Institute's quarterly early in 1935. He also told a friend that he feared having to talk a lot about things he had not himself researched thoroughly. Frank's presence in Berlin may also have been a factor. Berthold settled into a routine of riding at Tattersall Beerman from seven to half-past eight, and working at the Institute from eleven to six. He regarded his work as 'totally superfluous'.[52]

During this period he was obliged to write an article on the repeal of naturalisations and withdrawal of citizenship. This supplied legal opinions in support of a law of 14 July 1933 which provided for the repeal of naturalisations that had occurred between 9 November 1918 and 30 January 1933. The criteria envisaged by this law were national origin, race and culture; its particular targets were '(a) eastern Jews unless they had fought at the front in the World War on the German side or gained special merit in service to Germany; (b) persons guilty of a felony or crime, or other behaviour detrimental to the welfare of the state and the nation'. Persons resident abroad could also be deprived of German citizenship.[53]

Stauffenberg began by referring to an article in the *Revue critique de droit international* which was critical of the new German law. There was no need, Stauffenberg said, to enter upon moral arguments, since these could not be substitutes for legal ones. While the repeal of naturalisations had been unknown in German law before 14 July 1933, France had introduced a law providing for it during the World War, and other powers had followed, mainly to enable them to confiscate the property of naturalised citizens. English law was the most far-reaching. It provided for revocation of naturalisation for persons who traded with the enemy, had an evil reputation or had been convicted of crimes, or if the government considered their citizenship not 'conducive to the public good'.

The racial criterion in the German law was based on the same desire that governed the corresponding English, French or Egyptian laws, namely, to remove unwanted intruders. The racial criterion was found also in the American citizenship law which admitted 'free white persons', 'aliens of African birth' and 'persons of African descent' but excluded from naturalisation all those of Chinese, Japanese or related descent as well as (according to a Supreme Court decision of 1923) Hindus. No state had yet objected on grounds of international law to the laws of those states that provided for repeal of citizenship, so that the critique of the German law had no precedent.[54]

This example from Berthold Stauffenberg's work illustrates his situation and the – unloved – professional duties brought upon him by his decision to devote his life to the service of his nation. It illustrates also the limit of the insights that may be gained from the publications of those days. Stauffenberg was not likely to put into writing anything he did not believe to be true. Indeed, under interrogation by the Secret State Police after 20 July 1944, Berthold confirmed that he and his brother Claus had initially approved of the greater part of National Socialist domestic policies, among them 'the racial principle'; but he concluded that the fundamental ideas of National Socialism had in practice all been perverted into their opposites.[55] But as moral arguments were irrelevant to the legal considerations which it was Stauffenberg's duty to set forth, nothing about his views on the moral merits of the new law can be learned from his article. The following example of his work also makes this clear.

The German-Polish non-aggression treaty of 26 January 1934 had weakened France's 'cordon sanitaire' of states on Germany's eastern borders which were friendly to France and hostile to Germany. In May 1935 France and the Soviet Union concluded a mutual-assistance pact against an attack by a European state. This conjured up the spectre of the Franco-Russian military convention of 1894 and the road to 1914.[56] After the French Chamber of Deputies had ratified the pact on 28 February 1936, Hitler declared in the Reichstag that it effectively cancelled the Locarno Treaty

System (Rhine Pact) of 1925 which had provided for the demilitarisation of the German Rhineland. Berthold Stauffenberg was obliged at once to produce an article setting forth the legal position. It was published immediately, appearing in the second 1936 issue of the Institute's periodical.[57]

Stauffenberg explained: since the Statutes of the League of Nations left members free to determine which states were 'aggressor states' against which they wished to take military action, treaties likely to lead to such consequences made the League's arbitration procedures ineffective and therefore could not be regarded as being in conformity with its Statutes. The Rhine Pact declared itself *conforme au Pacte de la Société des Nations* as it was not directed against any state; the Franco-Soviet pact could not be consistent with the League of Nations Statutes, since it *was* directed against a state and could lead to war.

Moreover, the Franco-Soviet pact was part of that French policy which since 1919 had sought to cover all Europe with military alliances. Britain, Italy and the Soviet Union had maintained since 1922 that such mutual-assistance pacts contravened the spirit of the League of Nations Statutes because they tended to divide Europe into hostile camps. The British government had also maintained that regional pacts could help secure the peace if all their members had equal rights and military action was limited to self-defence.

The Rhine Pact, however, could not be written in such terms because France wanted it to include guarantees of demilitarisations stipulated by the Treaty of Versailles, and to recognise her right to aid her allies, Poland and Czechoslovakia. Since at the time the Rhineland was still under French military occupation, Germany had been forced by direct military pressure to accept terms both inequitable and contrary to the spirit of the League of Nations Statutes, in order to protect herself against another invasion like the occupation of the Ruhr in 1923. But in the Rhine Pact, Stauffenberg continued, Germany had accepted only the specified exceptions, Poland and Czechoslovakia. Any subsequent extension to include further alliances therefore destroyed the legal and political basis of the Locarno Treaty system.

From 1935 Stauffenberg also sat on a committee to study issues relating to the laws of war. This 'Studienausschuss KR' was formed in anticipation of war; it was an agency of the War Ministry (after January 1938, of the Armed Forces Supreme Command or OKW, which replaced the Ministry). Its work made considerable demands on Stauffenberg's time. Chaired by Admiral Gladisch, Reich Commissioner of the Superior Prize Court, the committee met in the Zeppelin Room of the Reichstag. It included members from the War Ministry, the Navy, the Air Force, the Foreign Office, the Justice Ministry, the German Defence Policy and Defence Science Society, and Stauffenberg's Institute. Stauffenberg drafted the German prize laws

(*Prisenordnung*) of 28 August 1939 which remained in force throughout the war. Henceforth the law of naval warfare was his speciality. At the beginning of the war he was appointed a commissary (*Intendanturrat*) in the international-law department in the 1st Section of Supreme Naval Command, housed at nos. 76–78 Tirpitzufer. After the defeat of France in 1940, Stauffenberg's committee was charged with re-writing, under the aspect of German supremacy, the laws of warfare on land, sea and in the air.[58]

From October 1936 Stauffenberg also sat on the Academy for German Law's committee on international law. This brought him into contact with some lawyers already in clandestine opposition to the government and working against its criminal actions in order to uphold international law. One was Helmuth James, Count von Moltke, who sat on the same two committees as Stauffenberg; another was Peter, Count Yorck von Wartenburg, who sat on the Prize Court in Hamburg with both Stauffenberg and Moltke.[59] Stauffenberg is credited by a colleague with having prevented much injustice simply by his integrity. In his quiet, firm manner again and again he held the Naval High Command to a fair conduct of naval warfare. Partly in consequence of his work, Stauffenberg became radically opposed to the government during the war. In 1943 he declared that no sacrifice would be too great to have the mass-murderers of the Jews prosecuted by German authorities, before the Allies did so after Germany's inevitable defeat.[60]

When the head of Stauffenberg's Institute, Professor Viktor Bruns, died in September 1943, Admiral Canaris, as Chief of the Armed Forces Supreme Command Foreign Countries/Counterintelligence Office, and Moltke who worked in the international-law department of Foreign Countries Group under Canaris, together with Moltke's colleague Oxé, attempted to have Berthold Stauffenberg appointed temporary head. But Telschow, the Managing Director of the Kaiser-Wilhelm Society, who was a National Socialist, prevented it.[61]

Beside his professional duties, Berthold Stauffenberg, together with Frank, Thormaehlen and Blumenthal, remained dedicated to Stefan George's works and papers, occupied with the retrieval of manuscripts from various friends (Elze, Fahrner, Wolters's daughter), with editorial work on the final volume of the complete edition of the works and with revisions of volumes to be reprinted. Robert Boehringer, the principal heir, had to leave many tasks to Berthold because he himself refused to enter Germany once the government there had begun to persecute Jews.[62]

Berthold was so deeply committed to the Master's legacy that he believed for years he could not marry his beloved Maria (Mika) Classen, because in 1932 the Master had expressed himself 'against this marriage', and had actually sent Frank to Scheveningen, where Berthold was living, to intervene.[63] When the relationship had continued for ten years, during most of which Berthold and Mika had lived apart, without prospect of any normal life together, Berthold's father fell seriously ill. Before his death on 20 January 1936, he made his sons promise to uphold the honour and greatness of the Stauffenberg clan.[64] Since he had also opposed the marriage, Mika lost all hope and tried to return to Russia. Uncle Nux dissuaded her as it were at the last minute, but Berthold now had to take a decision, and did finally marry Mika. His family gradually accepted his reasons. He discussed the matter with Frank and Blumenthal, he wrote to his brother Claus that in view of his obligations 'to the state' of Stefan George he could not regard the marriage as merely his private affair. But he insisted that important considerations superseded the objections of his friends, as well as the prescriptive year of mourning.[65] The wedding was held on 20 June 1936 in Berlin-Zehlendorf, arranged by Uncle Nux and Aunt Ida. Berthold's mother and brother Claus both attended. After a trip to Venice and Dalmatia the couple moved into no. 14 Konstanzer Strasse in Berlin-Wilmersdorf.[66]

Frank, unconditionally loyal to the Master, could not understand how Berthold could have done anything against the Master's wishes. Only two years earlier, he and Berthold had planned to share a flat. Now Frank declared that once the wedding had taken place he would not see Berthold again. Until 1939 Frank kept all cordiality out of his correspondence with Berthold. Robert Boehringer, sending Berthold his good wishes, commented that the separation was hurting Frank more than Berthold, since he had been left alone: he would probably take in someone else. But, Boehringer said, he could not get it into his head that one of the two, Berthold or Frank, would always be missing from the Minusio reunions.[67]

Alexander Stauffenberg was a lecturer in ancient history, at the universities of Würzburg and Berlin from 1931, and at Giessen during the winter 1935/36. He was appointed extraordinary professor in Würzburg University effective from the beginning of the summer semester of 1936. Before the National Socialists came to power, he was a member of the 'Wehrstahlhelm' (Veterans' Defence League), and subsequently of No. 79 SA Brigade. His Army rank in 1936 was reserve corporal; at times, as in the summer of 1938, he took part in military exercises. He worked hard and his career developed promisingly, although he was an outspoken opponent of the National Socialists from an early stage. Blumenthal, on the other hand, supported the National Socialists, but his career developed less rapidly; he spoke ill of Alexander and acted with evident jealousy. Alexander Stauffenberg openly deplored 'Albo's' commitment to National Socialism. He discerned an 'alarmingly contemporary cramped attitude' in Blumenthal and his students, 'his *völkische adlati*'. While Blumenthal was often consulted on emendations to the Master's works, Alexander was not, nor was he concerned with gathering the poet's papers. For all these reasons he had little contact with his friends in the Master's 'state'.[68]

Alexander Stauffenberg wrote his second (habilitation) dissertation on King Hieron II of Syracuse. During the 1930s he worked on various aspects of the encounter of the Germanic nations with the Roman Empire, and in the 1940s again on classical Greek history, particularly that of Trinacria (Sicily).

At the nineteenth annual meeting of the German Historical Association in Erfurt, on 5 July 1937, Alexander Stauffenberg read a paper on 'Theoderic the Great and his Roman Mission'. He disregarded and defied the Nazi heroisation of the German nations, describing Theoderic as a loyal Roman ally who, far from wishing to destroy or Germanise the Empire or even to turn part of it into an independent Germanic state, helped to preserve and renew it, and regarded the superior Roman Imperial unity as permanent. Stauffenberg concluded that the productive encounter of the Germanic nations, so early in their history, with the Roman World Empire of which the Christian religion was an integral part enabled them to fulfil their world historic mission, which was to give life and continuity to the medieval *Imperium Christianum*. The *Deutsche Allgemeine Zeitung* reported on 8 July that Stauffenberg's view of Theoderic as a Roman governor was disputed by two participants in the session as being based on the unreliable testimony of Cassiodorus; Stauffenberg had replied that there was no other testimony than Cassiodorus', and that Cassiodorus as Theoderic's chancellor could not have represented ideas that were not those of his king. The *Frankfurter Zeitung* reported that discussion of Stauffenberg's paper had, most unusually, continued through the entire three days of the annual meeting.[69]

Captain Claus Stauffenberg read his brother's paper and the news reports about it while at Lautlingen on leave on 11 July. Four days later, from the Münsingen training grounds, he wrote to Frank that 'Offa' had caused quite a flutter, as shown by the three-day discussion; and he expressed surprise at his brother's courage. But he thought Alexander's treatment of the topic focused too much on the legal points and barely touched upon 'the essentials': 'The laws of the state and its constitution are ultimately at best the expression of a general basic view; frequently they have meaning only for day-to-day politics. Thereby the work loses somewhat in force. In any case it is the best piece of his I have read in a long time.'[70]

On 11 August 1937 Alexander married Melitta Schiller in Berlin-Wilmersdorf. Her father came from a respectable Jewish family in Leipzig; the grandfather had come there from Odessa. He had converted to Lutheranism at the age of eighteen, had studied in Leipzig, served in the Prussian Army and had settled in Krotoschin as a board-of-works counsellor in the Prussian civil service. When Posen became Polish after 1918, he did not opt for German residence and citizenship because he owned a house in Krotoschin. He and his wife acquired Polish citizenship. When he retired they were unable to move to Germany, but they were allowed to draw his pension in Danzig and so settled there.

Melitta had come to Germany before the end of the World War, so that her parents' later Polish citizenship did not affect her. She studied mathematics and physics, received her degree in civil engineering from the Munich Institute of Technology in 1927, and also acquired several pilot's certificates. From 1927 she worked in aerodynamics and made test flights to check instruments for the control of dive-flying, first at the German Aviation Testing Institute at Berlin-Adlershof, then at the Askania Works at Berlin-Friedenau, and from October 1937 at the Air War Academy at Berlin-Gatow. The apparently civilian names of the first two employers were deceptive: the German government officially created its Air Force only in March 1935. Before and during the war, Melitta Schiller flew well over two thousand diving missions in 'Ju[nkers] 87' and 'Ju 88' dive-bombers, an accomplishment surpassed by only one German pilot, a man. She was given an air captain's commission in 1937, the Iron Cross class II in 1943, and the Gold Pilot's Badge with Diamonds; she was nominated for the Iron Cross I in 1944.[71]

Melitta, her parents, her brother Otto and her sisters were in danger when the Nazi authorities began to deport Jews from Germany in 1941. They were saved largely by Melitta's reputation and by the importance of her war work. They claimed they could not obtain any papers regarding their father's descent: all they had was their parents' marriage certificate, which said they were Lutherans. The parents were not deported because a neighbour and friend in Danzig held a post with sufficient influence. The sisters and their brother Otto, an agricultural expert in the Foreign Service, were all declared 'equal to Aryans' upon their application in 1944. Melitta's sister Klara, who was unmarried, was told that she must not marry a member of the SS.[72]

After the poet's death and the emigration of Wolfskehl, Morwitz and Kantorowicz, the Master's 'state' was reduced almost entirely to non-Jews. The exceptions were two younger friends, Willi Dette and Karl Josef Partsch, who found a safe haven in the Armed Forces. Partsch, to be sure, had considerable difficulties. He reached the age for military service in 1935, but despite making a formal application he was not allowed to serve because of his Jewish grandfather. The procedures permitted the intervention of an advocate: he chose Claus Stauffenberg, who wrote on his behalf, and his case was reviewed by Party bigwigs, a 'race scientist' and a high-ranking military officer. The 'race scientist' measured his skull and pronounced it 'Nordic', but Partsch was nonetheless rejected until later, during the war.[73]

The activities of the Master's 'state' are evidence of his friends' determination to perpetuate the legacy of the Secret Germany. Frank and Rudolf Fahrner were the most active and thereby contributed to shifting the internal balance. When there was a question of a word, a spelling, a comma in a revision of one of the volumes of the Complete Edition, those who had known the poet well could cite his occasional *dicta* to effect a change, or to resist one. Claus Stauffenberg participated intensively in the editorial work for the second edition of *Das Neue Reich*, as did Blumenthal.

Blumenthal was a highly qualified philologist, but not a great scholar. He based his own status in the Master's 'state' largely on the fact that he had introduced the Stauffenberg brothers. He continued in the role of mentor to Alexander and Claus for a number of years. He embraced National Socialism and sought to persuade others to do the same, citing the Master's approval. In 1937, when the ban on admissions to NSDAP membership was briefly lifted, Blumenthal was refused admission on the grounds that he was not sufficiently active on behalf of National Socialism; he lodged a complaint, and was admitted to membership two years later. He began as a lecturer in Jena in 1922, became an untenured extraordinary professor there in 1928, held a similar post in Giessen from 1938, and finally became an ordinary professor there in 1940.[74] From 1940, as far as the group of friends was concerned, he receded into the background.[75]

Rudolf Fahrner was an Austrian who had become a student of Wolters and had met Stefan George during Wolters's final illness. After six years as a lecturer he became an extraordinary professor in Heidelberg in 1934, but had to ask to be suspended for reasons of poor health in 1936. Moreover, he had a powerful enemy in Heidelberg who accused him of failure to conform to the National Socialist line of the university and of attempting instead to organise a separate Stefan-George cell for esoteric teachings.[76]

Fahrner met Frank on a visit to the Master in Munich on 28 February 1933. Through Frank he met Berthold Stauffenberg in 1935, Claus in 1936, and finally Alexander in 1941. Alexander told Fahrner of Blumenthal's destructive attacks and criticism. While Fahrner had increasingly close relations with Alexander during the war, his contacts with Claus and Berthold were few and confined to circumscribed topics and purposes.[77] In 1946 Berthold's widow asked Fahrner to write down his reminiscences of Berthold for her children, and when she repeated her request two years later, he finally replied that he would need more information about Berthold which only Mika could provide.[78]

In 1935 Frank, with Fahrner's valuable assistance, made a statue of Hindenburg, three times life-size. The Master had regarded Hindenburg as 'heroic': in his reply to the President's message of congratulation on his sixtieth birthday in 1928, he had said that he regarded Hindenburg as the only 'emblematic figure' to emerge from the World War, one who still

28. Frank Mehnert and Rudolf Fahrner with the Hindenburg statue, Magdeburg, ca. 1937

towered over the turmoil of the contemporary world. Wolters, in particular, encouraged this Hindenburg cult and conveyed it to his student, who, as an Austrian, had initially been reluctant. War Minister von Blomberg gave permission to build a 'hall of honour' for the statue within the grounds of the Magdeburg barracks and to transfer there the battle honours of the old

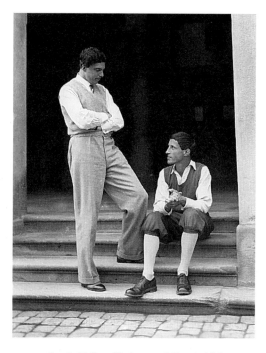

29. Berthold Stauffenberg and Frank Mehnert

Army, then in Magdeburg Cathedral. Hindenburg's son made available
articles of the Field Marshal's uniform, including his greatcoat. The 'hall of
honour' was designed by Heinrich Tessenow, Albert Speer's teacher. By the
end of August 1939, the hall and a plaster model of the statue in it stood
ready for the donors' inspection. The bronze statue was cast early in 1940,
but was then confiscated for use as war material.[79]

The soldier's life was highly regarded in the Secret Germany. Stauffenberg's career, his brothers' reserve-officer training, the statues of the
pioneer and of Hindenburg, translations from Homer and Plutarch, were all
outward manifestations of this. Fahrner, visiting Greece in 1937, sent Frank
a general-staff map of Attica to help him visualise the battlefield of Mara-
thon and the course of the battle. But the Stauffenbergs were critical of
martial attitudes that lacked the foundation of the military ethos. They
criticised Blumenthal for treating heroism and military prowess as the
essence of Sophocles' tragedies, and for making everything 'too tangible
in the Nazi manner': it was more important to set up primordial images
of man.[80]

In a book about Ernst Moritz Arndt, the influential writer and advocate
of national unity in early nineteenth-century Germany, Rudolf Fahrner

declared that Germany's renewal must be based on the agricultural life: the thoughts of other advocates of reform at that time, Stein, Scharnhorst and Gneisenau, as well as Arndt, were relevant to this. The essential elements in a state were 'heroes and peoples, leaders and followers', and Napoleon had made them visible again.[81]

Frank Mehnert and Berthold Stauffenberg read the Arndt manuscript and found themselves unable to recommend its publication to Stefan George's publisher, Bondi. But Frank was greatly impressed by Fahrner's portrait of Gneisenau in the manuscript. He urged Fahrner to develop it separately, and he drew Claus Stauffenberg into this effort.[82]

Stauffenberg read Fahrner's Gneisenau draft carefully, and read it to Karl Josef Partsch at the beginning of the summer of 1937; Stauffenberg suggested a few clarifications of terms and stylistic changes, but agreed with its substance and tenor and indeed pronounced it 'Plutarchian'. The description of the Battle of La Belle Alliance was 'at least equal to the best'. Fahrner said that Stauffenberg's participation in his Gneisenau essay had been continuous and penetrating. Partsch, too, considered the 'Gneisenau' superb.[83]

So the Gneisenau study circulated internally and became a half-secret manifesto for the 'state'. In order to get this and other efforts printed and privately disseminated, Rudolf Fahrner and Frank Mehnert founded a publishing house in Munich, Delfinverlag, whose mission was to record and pass on to younger disciples the teachings of the 'state'. 'Gneisenau' was 'published' in May 1942, in 100 copies on hand-made paper. It did not bear the author's name, for it was to be regarded as the product of the common spirit.[84] Indeed, Frank had a hand in the preface. It said that the victories against the great adversary, Napoleon, had not then or later enabled the forces of renewal in Germany to come into their own. Then, as now, a great Poet – then Goethe, now George – had appeared; then there had been an external challenge, and the nation's powers had been awakened. But those who held to the old ways, and who valued utility and material concerns more than the human spirit, had remained dull and inactive and had gained the upper hand. The renewal of the West could not arise from the French Enlightenment, but only from the forces which had originally engendered it: Antiquity, Christianity and the Germanic peoples.[85]

Gneisenau, according to Fahrner, saw the liberating force of the French Revolution: it had enabled bold men to act. Gneisenau's 'plan for the state' had been 'to place high-minded and capable men in authority' everywhere. The flower of the nation would be trained and become the army; the army would be the state, the heart of the nation. Gneisenau, said Fahrner, had told the conservatives 'who sought to smother all plans for renewal in interminable preparations for a new constitution' that he could write them ten constitutions in a single night. The success of the state depended rather on the creation of a class that would support it – and this class must be made strong enough to exert wise and firm leadership. Gneisenau had spoken of limitless forces which were slumbering, undeveloped, within the nation. According to Fahrner, the Reformers had foreseen the pernicious consequences of industrialisation and proletarianisation – the unhealthy crowding together of the unpropertied classes, the destruction of the national fabric, the boundless rule of money – and they therefore believed that handicrafts alone should provide basic material necessities such as housing, clothing, food.[86]

In memoranda written in August 1808 and 1811, Gneisenau had urged the King to proclaim a national uprising. He outlined a conspiratorial method and urged that political and military plenipotentiaries be appointed in the provinces. Stauffenberg insisted that these details of Gneisenau's 'Organisation of a Plan to Prepare the Nation for Insurrection' be eliminated from Fahrner's essay. Stauffenberg explained that whereas in Gneisenau's day there had been sufficient ethical force in society to prevent licence and chaos, and to stave off exploitation by forces with other priorities, such ethical restraints did not exist in contemporary German society. Stauffenberg believed that if Gneisenau's method were followed, there was a danger that future enemies of Germany, and supporters of anarchy both in Germany and abroad would exploit the situation.[87]

In the summer of 1808 Gneisenau also urged the King, in two memoranda, to give the country a liberal constitution with a government and administration accountable to the people's elected representatives, with equality for all classes and equal taxation of wealth. But Fahrner did not even mention these points. Whether Stauffenberg was predisposed to disregard them or was in fact kept unaware of them, Fahrner's portrait of the Stauffenberg brothers' venerable forebear was a serious distortion.[88]

Karl Josef Partsch's contribution to the works of the 'state' was to re-write the stories of Agis and Cleomenes from Plutarch's *Lives*. Frank and Claus were also involved, particularly in the description of the Battle of Sellasia. Partsch and Frank agreed that Partsch's name was to appear on the title page of the Delfinverlag edition, once difficulties arising from his partly Jewish ancestry had been resolved. They were indeed resolved, but after Frank had fallen at the front in 1943 Fahrner had the little work published under Frank's name. A copy of the private edition on hand-made paper was sent from Munich to Robert Boehringer in Geneva in October 1944.[89]

Hölderlin had planned to write an Agis tragedy, and had his Hyperion refer to Agis and Cleomenes as heroic souls greater than those of the better-known mythologies: 'Their genius was the sunset-glow of the Greek day, just as Theseus and Homer were its aurora.'[90]

The story is this. Agis, one of two kings who jointly ruled Sparta, sought to restore patriotism, hard asceticism, equality and self-sacrifice for the common good. He gave financial assistance to impoverished Spartans, and Spartan citizenship to *perioikoi*. His co-rulers preferred to line their own pockets, however, and had Agis, his mother and her mother judicially murdered. Agis' successor Cleomenes restored equality and virtue, but fell under the dominion of the Egyptians and took his own life after a failed uprising; and the Egyptians executed his mother and his children. The moral of this cruel tale is sacrifice of self for the state, for heroic Spartan ideals. It embodies a retrospective yearning for past glories, an essential element in the mentality of the Stefan George Circle.

In the five years since the Master's death, the Secret Germany had at least shown that it was still alive. Berthold Stauffenberg had advanced into the first rank among German jurists, Alexander Stauffenberg had become one of the most fearless and best-known of historians, Claus Stauffenberg had made a name for himself in military studies and had delivered a declaratory speech on 'the Rhine'. Rudolf Fahrner, Frank Mehnert and Karl Josef Partsch were engaged in artistic and literary pursuits in the spirit of the Master.

6

Crisis and war

In the summer of 1938 Hitler threatened to attack Czechoslovakia on the pretext that the 'Sudeten Germans' – the German-speaking population of Bohemia, formerly part of the Austrian Empire – were being ill-treated. There were international negotiations, the British Prime Minister, Neville Chamberlain, tried to persuade Hitler to accept a gradual absorption of the Sudetenland into the German state, and at the height of the crisis Britain mobilised her navy, France called up reservists, and Italy refused to support Germany's war policy. In the end Hitler had to accept the Sudetenland through an internationally agreed settlement.

In July 1938 Captain Count Stauffenberg served in Göppingen for ten days, then with the air group at Giessen for a week.[1] Such tours of duty were normally followed by a temporary General Staff posting, and after a year's probation by a permanent appointment on the General Staff. Because of the threat of war, the War Academy graduates' normal short tours of duty with various branches of the Armed Forces were terminated at the end of July. Stauffenberg thus received his temporary General Staff posting as a Second General-Staff officer (quartermaster) with the 1st Light Division in Wuppertal, effective from 1 August 1938. This division was one of four being newly organised as panzer divisions. Stauffenberg's duties included supply (fuel, weapons, ammunition, vehicles, food, medical requirements, transport), equipment, quarters organisation, mobilisation, evacuation, aspects of internal political and press contacts, and counter-espionage. Stauffenberg's was the most important staff position in a modern division after that of the operations officer (Ia or senior staff-officer). His logistics teacher at the War Academy used to say that future wars would be decided by the quartermasters. According to Werner Reerink, then a lieutenant and 1st special-missions staff officer (*Ordonnanzoffizier*, O 1) on the divisional staff, Stauffenberg did more to increase the division's fighting strength than anyone else.[2]

Before Stauffenberg's arrival the division had no quartermaster: he therefore had to create the section. Officers in comparable staff positions usually refused to see anyone without an appointment made through a secretary, but Stauffenberg's door always stood open, he saw anyone without formalities and with his usual cheerful expression, often smoking a black Brazil cigar; when he was standing he would bend slightly forward in a relaxed attitude. He already had the reputation of being one of the most brilliant young officers on the General Staff.[3]

When he arrived in Wuppertal, he found the town 'unimaginably proletarian· almost impossible to exist here'.[4] But he was fully occupied with his duties, which greatly interested him. As he wrote to Frank, he expected the autumn manoeuvres which began on 9 September to be 'long'. Frank understood: Stauffenberg thought war was coming.[5] Although the Munich Agreement defused the situation, Hitler did not want to give the impression that he had compromised under threat of force, and still insisted on a military occupation of the Sudeten area ceded to Germany by Czechoslovakia although the transfer of civil and military authority could have been left to commissions of experts.

The 1st Light Division moved into the 'manoeuvre' area of Kassel-Hannoversch Münden-Brakel-Warburg on 9 September along with a cavalry rifle regiment, a motorcycle infantry battalion, an armoured battalion, a reconnaissance battalion, an artillery regiment, an anti-tank battalion, a signal battalion, a pioneer battalion, and supply and medical services. They covered 255 kilometres on the first day, most motor vehicles travelling on roads, while the tanks were transported by rail. After another 207-kilometre march the division arrived in the area of Rudolstadt-Jena-Erfurt-Arnstadt. After a day's rest and another 220 kilometres they reached the area of Borna-Gera-Plauen-Chemnitz on 12 September.[6] Stauffenberg and the rest of the staff understood that 'the possibility of a wholesale war was somewhat reduced' after Prime Minister Chamberlain's meeting with Hitler at Berchtesgaden on 15 September.[7] But preparations continued. On 27 September No. 11 Panzer Regiment was added to the division, as well as No. 25 Infantry Regiment, a battalion of No. 2 Artillery Regiment, a battery of No. 38 Artillery Regiment, No. 32 Pioneer Battalion, and some frontier-guard units. On 29 September the division was poised for an attack across the Czechoslovak border. The Munich Agreement of the same day reduced the division's role to that of an occupation force guarding the border, channelling refugees and Sudeten soldiers demobilised from the Czechoslovakian Army. Stauffenberg held meetings with local authorities to secure the population's needs for coal, transport and baker's yeast. There was a shortage of horses, since most had been requisitioned by the Czechoslovakian Army; the division's diary recorded that some 'horses belonging to Jews who had fled or had been arrested' were requisitioned for municipal services in Mies. Stauffenberg declared that it was undignified for soldiers in the division to be buying up clothing material and clothing: in his view the buying power of the soldiers' German currency put the local population in the position of an underclass. If he learned of a purchase, he saw to it that the goods were returned.[8] He also sent a company from the quartermaster section to help with the potato harvest on Prince Löwenstein's farms. The divisional commander, Major-General Hoepner, and his staff were guests at Prince Löwenstein's Castle Haid on 4 October; the staff of No. 76 Artillery Regiment were quartered there for a week.[9]

On 17 October the divisional staff were back in Wuppertal; by 19 October the rest of the division had returned, and the reservists were dismissed. Seven soldiers from the division had died in road accidents, one had been shot by an officer on night duty, one had committed suicide, and a child had been killed by one of the division's vehicles.[10]

Some difficulties with fuel supplies had been experienced during the campaign. Stauffenberg and two other officers therefore devised a private wargame during subsequent quartermaster exercises: they drove a tank raid into the Urals; when it ran out of fuel in the Ukraine, they occupied Baku in a subsidiary raid and built a pipeline to the Ukraine.[11]

Since Nina Stauffenberg had complained to her husband that he was a poor correspondent, he kept a diary for her. At the end of 1943, when he took over the leadership of the anti-Hitler conspiracy, this diary was given to friends for safekeeping. In the wake of the 20 July 1944 rising the Secret State Police paid them a visit but failed to find the diary, whereupon the friends burnt it.[12] Nina Stauffenberg remembers that Stauffenberg referred in the diary to the hubris of the German actions. He did not object to the incorporation of the Sudetenland, but he was concerned about such a 'militarily irresponsible' method of provoking war, and this by no means only because German rearmament was not yet complete.[13] After the Sudeten Crisis he complained to his wife that it felt odd to have drawn the sword only to put it back in its sheath. He told his mother that one could not be altogether pleased with the German success in the crisis, since it was based on bluff.[14]

After the crisis Stauffenberg learned from the Deputy President of Berlin Police, Schulenburg, who was himself involved, that there had been plans to overthrow Hitler if he ordered an attack on Czechoslovakia – which most senior military officers believed would lead to war with France, and eventually with Britain and America. So far from declaring his approval or support, Stauffenberg actually avoided Schulenburg's society over the next few months. In his view, the political responsibility of the officer corps must be exercised by the appointed leaders and within the established structure, not by private conspiracies.[15]

As Hitler drove Germany nearer to war during the summer of 1938, the Chief of the General Staff, General Beck, had attempted to win over the Commander-in-Chief, General von Brauchitsch, and the army corps commanders for a coup d'état to prevent Hitler from waging war.[16] After a decisive meeting on 4 August 1938, when Brauchitsch failed to support him, Beck resigned. His successor, Lieutenant-General Franz Halder, tried half-heartedly to pursue Beck's plans, but they lapsed because of the Munich Agreement.

During the crisis Stauffenberg did not know of these efforts; nor was he aware of any plan for the 1st Light Division to block the road from Munich to Berlin against the SS guard regiment SS-Leibstandarte 'Adolf Hitler' during a coup d'état by Army forces in Berlin.[17]

On 9 November SA thugs smashed the windows of the many Jewish-owned shops in Wuppertal and burned the two synagogues.[18] Even though Stauffenberg apparently agreed with the general proposition to limit Jewish control of the arts and of publishing, and to expel non-German Jews, he condemned violations of law and decency. He was appalled by the pogrom of November 1938.[19]

The fates of Karl Wolfskehl, Ernst Morwitz and Ernst Kantorowicz had confronted the friends of Stefan George with the persecution of the Jews even earlier and more directly. Berthold Stauffenberg was personally affected when in 1933 the German government pressured their judge at the Permanent Court of International Justice, Professor Walther Schücking, who was of Jewish descent, to resign.[20] The 'Nuremberg Laws' of 1935 deprived all persons of Jewish origin of German citizenship and introduced severe penalties for every kind of intimate relations between Jews and non-Jews. By 1938 Jews were excluded from state schools, parks and other facilities. Alexander Stauffenberg's wife lived under threat of losing her citizenship and her job – and of being deported and murdered. Karl Josef Partsch was also in danger of being caught up in the mass murder of Jews during the war.

In the spring of 1938 Berthold Stauffenberg and Robert Boehringer disagreed on which parts of Stefan George's correspondence with Hugo von Hofmannsthal should be published. Boehringer struggled with the publisher to get the publication out in time for the Master's seventieth birthday on 12 July 1938. Berthold and Frank did not want to reveal Stefan George's embarrassingly urgent solicitation of Hofmannsthal's friendship, which Hofmannsthal had rejected, and Berthold invoked his, Robert's and Frank's common responsibility for the Master's inheritance. That Hofmannsthal was Jewish was not what concerned Frank and Berthold, but Boehringer was extremely sensitive to anything remotely suggesting anti-Semitism, maybe partly because his wife was of Jewish origin. Although his friends were not responsible for German foreign policy, it added to Boehringer's irritation. Since the Stauffenbergs and Frank had generally approved of the German regime's policy up to that time, Boehringer must have wondered if his verdict on it must also apply to them: 'I have no business with those who approve of the brown stuff.'[21]

This episode in the relations between the heirs of Stefan George may also be linked to one which concerned Karl Wolfskehl. In 1937 Wolfskehl sent some of his friends a poem called '"Life's Song." To the Germans'. Wolfskehl invoked his family's thousand-year history in Germany since his ancestor had joined the court of Otto II at Mainz, and spoke of his life among the Master's friends, ending with a derisive curse on the philistinism of the self-styled 'master humans' and their racial madness. Robert Boehringer read it to Frank at their annual meeting on the anniversary of the Master's death in Minusio in December 1937. Frank was so moved by it that he asked for a copy, which Boehringer did not feel free to give him at the time; in November 1938 Frank asked him to bring it to Minusio again. At this point, a month after the pogrom, Boehringer lent Frank his copy for a few days. After their meeting in Minusio Boehringer wrote to Frank more cordially than was his custom and ended with: 'I embrace you!' A new note of solidarity, and some cautious (because letters were subject to censorship) hints of disapproval of the German regime now crept into the Stauffenberg brothers' correspondence with Frank, Robert Boehringer and Karl Josef Partsch.[22]

Frank had lost his enthusiasm for the National Socialists, as both Boehringer and Fahrner make clear. Boehringer said simply: 'Frank relearned.' Fahrner relates how on 10 November 1938 he and Frank, in the studio at Albrecht-Achilles street in Berlin (the 'Achilleon'), took an axe to one of Frank's plaster busts of Hitler and smashed it. There was even talk of killing Hitler when he came to Magdeburg to unveil the Hindenburg statue, but the unveiling never took place. Frank remained fiercely loyal to all his Jewish friends.[23]

In December 1938 Claus Stauffenberg's family moved into a flat at no. 25 Lönsstrasse in Wuppertal-Barmen. The divisional adjutant, Captain von Blomberg, a son of the former War Minister, lived in the same building. The families became friends: Stauffenberg's children – Berthold, born in 1934, Heimeran, born in 1936 and Franz Ludwig, born in 1938 – were soon calling Mrs von Blomberg 'auntie'. She recalls Stauffenberg as a kind, generous and cultured friend who let fellow officers take precedence for Christmas furlough, and who must have found it far from easy to live among coarse soldiers.[24]

As Major (GS) Schöne, the senior staff officer in Stauffenberg's division, lived nearby, the three officers used to drive to work together in the morning; at Stauffenberg's suggestion they lunched on the same fare as the enlisted men – usually a single course. Over the fifteen-minute lunch break Stauffenberg would discourse animatedly on the latest military and political news. In the evening they drove home together.[25]

In January 1939 some twenty officers of the divisional staff, including

Schöne, Blomberg and the first special-missions officer, Lieutenant Reerink, gathered in Stauffenberg's flat to hear Rudolf Fahrner give a lecture on Gneisenau. Stauffenberg himself introduced the topic, stressing its relevance to the present.[26]

Fahrner told of Gneisenau's origins, and of how the moribund Frederick the Great refused to accept the young firebrand *à la suite*, after which Gneisenau languished for twenty years in the lower ranks of a remote garrison; and of his brilliant defence of Kolberg in 1807. Gneisenau had the roof taken off a church, filled the nave with rubble and placed two cannon on top; he made the children write paper money, procured ammunition from Sweden, engineered floods against the besieging forces, made continual sorties against them, built outworks overnight which the enemy was forced to attack as new fortresses, dictated orders while mounted on his white horse on the ramparts under fire from enemy cannon, and created pleasure groves behind the chain of outposts. Fahrner described Gneisenau's memoranda urging a national insurrection against the French, his journey to England to help strengthen the coalition against France, his draft of a campaign plan for Russia against France in 1812, his exhortations: persevere, after losing a fifth battle offer the sixth, wear the enemy down with nightly raids, raise the whole nation against the invader. Fahrner spoke of Gneisenau's 'state plan' to re-form the nation through the army and through a national insurrection. Finally he described how reforms were suppressed, how Gneisenau and other reformers were spied on by the secret police, how their correspondence was confiscated, how Fichte's 'Addresses to the German Nation' were suppressed, how Gneisenau resigned and spent the last fifteen years of his life helping Clausewitz with his work *On War*. Fahrner suggests that his lecture implied some hostility to the current regime. His hearers did not get that impression.[27]

Fahrner relates further that one wintry day in January 1939, as he walked through the forest with Stauffenberg, he asked him whether the Armed Forces could just accept the November pogrom. Stauffenberg then raised the subject of a coup d'état, mentioning that General Beck was the focus of opposition in the Armed Forces, and declaring that Major-General Hoepner was 'reliable'. Stauffenberg warned against placing confidence in other senior military men, much less in the vastly bloated Army at large: spineless people who had already twice failed to stand up to Hitler (during the Röhm and Blomberg-Fritsch crises, in 1934 and 1938 respectively) would not act any differently in future.[28] Two letters which Stauffenberg wrote in February and March 1939 largely confirm Fahrner's recollections.

From the end of 1937 into the new year, Brigadier Georg von Sodenstern, Chief of the General Staff of Army Group 2 at Frankfurt am Main, was writing an essay on 'The essence of being a soldier'.[29] He was worried by the trivialisation of the military ethos through the massive expansion of the

Army, the general pre-military training of millions of youths, and shallow
national-defence propaganda. Sodenstern submitted his essay for publication to the *Militärwissenschaftliche Rundschau*, which was edited by the 7th
Section of the Army General Staff. General Beck, then Chief of the General
Staff, wrote to Sodenstern in July 1938 that he agreed with his views, but
wished to avoid 'misinterpretations' in the current crisis. The chief of 7th
Section, Colonel Eduard Müller, wrote to Sodenstern that the Party was
trying to remove Beck and that he must be spared any additional difficulties
at the moment. Beck resigned in August 1938, and when the essay was
finally published in January 1939, there was no hostile reaction from the
Party. But the French military periodical *Cyrano* said that Sodenstern had
openly come out against the National Socialists' ideological invasion of the
Army.

In his essay, Sodenstern declared his support for the unity of National
Socialism and national defence, and for the unity of national and military
culture in the person of the 'soldier' Adolf Hitler. He sought neither
confrontation with the Party nor a special status for the Armed Forces. His
concern was for the soldier's commitment to a community of men ready to
fight and die, a readiness which set them apart from all other communities.
Men and officers must abandon all personal interests; officers must be
examples to their men in life and death. Devotion to the commander-in-
chief and death in battle must be regarded as the fulfilment of a soldier's
life. The officer needed enormous fortitude to make his commander's will
his own. A conflict between orders and his own views would make him
unable to lead convincingly: the inevitable consequence would be a rapid
decline in fighting spirit. It was therefore essential for officers and men to
have implicit trust in their leaders. Sodenstern illustrated these points by
describing a wargame played by an infantry regiment near Kiel. On the
battlefield, which covered four square kilometres, every step forward or
backward by every single man expressed the will of the general at army-
corps command post. A second lieutenant of the Blue forces was shot and
mortally wounded just outside the village of Westensee, and his command
passed to a non-commissioned officer, a blacksmith in the reserves, who
suddenly shouted 'gas!'. His men turned and ran back across the meadows,
hounded by Red machine-gun fire. A Blue corporal, his features contorted
with fury, seized a light machine-gun from a fleeing man and blasted the
Red pursuers, thus instinctively executing the general's will, and dying as
he did it. Meanwhile the commander of the reserve platoon led his men in a
counter-attack and stabilised the Blue front. While the formations for the
next day's fighting were being deployed under cover of darkness, the
general at his map-table concentrated all his energies, shook off the horror
at the terrible numbers of dead and wounded that was clutching at his
heart, and issued his orders to the thousands who must be ready to die the
next day.

Sodenstern concluded that the ethos of the soldier was the nation's most noble possession. It must not, therefore, be allowed to be an everyday topic of trivialising talk; it must be kept as a secret. War was an action not comparable to any other expression of the nation's will. War bore a stern countenance; the horror of battle made men silent.

Stauffenberg read the article and wrote to Sodenstern on 6 February, thanking him for expressing so passionately and so clearly the principles of the soldier's existential commitment, and for rejecting the vulgar propaganda about the 'nation in arms'. He could confirm in the strongest terms that he wanted to 'be led by men whose attitude commanded his respect'.

Sodenstern replied on 6 March, reiterating that the current tendency to vulgarise the military profession by turning it into a national way of life must be resisted. Far from increasing the fighting spirit, this would only prevent people from realising the sacrifices that war really involved. All men who did understand those sacrifices must hold together to 'protect the inner values of the soldier's commitment'. In masked language, Sodenstern predicted the destruction of Germany in the event of war, and called on the officer corps to close ranks against the National Socialist leadership.

Stauffenberg wrote to Sodenstern again on 13 March, phrasing carefully what he could not say in plain words. He implored Sodenstern and his fellow veterans of the World War not to stand aloof from the vast number of younger officers who looked up to them as models. He understood why older officers detested that false god, the 'masses'. But the crisis would become dangerous if those best qualified to lead lost confidence in the permanent truth of 'the aristocratic basic law, the military view of the state and of life'. The rising officer generation were already a 'mass'. But the battle would be half-won if a number – even an infinitely small number – of officers succeeded in 'awakening the incorruptible eye for what is genuine and crucial, and strengthening the immortal attitude of the officer and gentleman'. He, Stauffenberg, was 'not concerned with opposition based on class, education or profession, but only with the Reich'. Many believed that only 'the powerful effectiveness of [National Socialist] forces outside our own ranks' had rebuilt the Armed Forces, so that military men could withdraw into a narrow professionalism. But this was wrong. 'To be a soldier, especially a military leader, an officer, means to be a servant of the state, to be part of the state, and this includes overall responsibility.' The struggle had to be for the nation and the state as a whole. The officer corps was the true embodiment of the nation and the most essential pillar of the state. Therefore 'We must not only know how to fight for the Army itself: no, we must fight for our nation, for the state itself, in the knowledge that the military service and its pillar, the officer corps, represent the most essential support of the state and the true embodiment of the nation.' In the 'great battle, the national battle which decides the existence or non-existence of the nation', the responsibility would fall to the military forces in any case.

No political organisation could take responsibility away from the military forces, which therefore could not confine themselves to their own narrowly defined domain.

Turning to specific contemporary issues, Stauffenberg commented that the aloofness showed by the officer corps and its lack of support for Hitler's policy before the Munich Agreement had surely been 'politically inexpedient', but it had 'corresponded to a very true inner instinct'. It revealed a degree of disharmony between the political and the military leadership, and this was because the political leadership lacked confidence in the officer corps and had failed to allow it that measure of joint responsibility 'which is simply indispensable to the leadership of the nation in arms, which will fall to it in time of war'. Now, despite a 'different development' which was almost overpowering, Stauffenberg declared his determination 'to fight for the whole concern rather than a part'.

At about the same period Stauffenberg expressed a broadly similar, though greatly simplified, view to his bookseller in Wuppertal, begging him not to think him arrogant: he, Stauffenberg, could not be a subject of that 'petty bourgeois' Hitler, his family tradition simply forbade it.[30] But in his letters to Sodenstern Stauffenberg went much further. When he vowed to 'fight for our nation, even for the state', he suggested that the officer corps must control the fate of the nation. What he meant was that the Army should assume the leadership of the nation without Hitler and without the National Socialists.[31] When Stauffenberg castigated the failure of the 'political leadership' to involve the officer corps in larger political decisions, for example during the Sudeten Crisis of 1938, he was also echoing an essential aspect of General Beck's position.[32] Beck maintained that by geopolitical necessity the Army was Germany's right hand, and therefore the Chief of the Army General Staff must be consulted on all major internal and foreign policy decisions that might affect the Army. Beck had published a letter by Clausewitz in a special issue of *Militärwissenschaftliche Mitteilungen* in March 1937, which Stauffenberg had no doubt read. This was a letter written to Major Karl Ferdinand Heinrich von Roeder, of the Great General Staff in Berlin, on 22 December 1827: 'The art of war, vis-à-vis policy, has as its principal right and task to prevent policy from demanding things which are contrary to the nature of war, and of preventing policy based on lack of knowledge from misusing its instrument.'[33]

Stauffenberg's position was the same three or four years later, when he took his decision to attack the regime with the aim of overthrowing it. At that time he told a fellow officer who had spoken of the responsibility of the military leadership: 'We are indeed the leadership of the Army and also of the nation and we shall take control of that leadership.'[34]

On 26 September 1938 Hitler made a public speech in the Sports Palace in Berlin, in which he declared that the solution of the Sudeten Question was his 'last territorial demand in Europe'.[35] But it was not long after the annexation of the German-speaking Sudetenland, in February 1939, that he began using the Slovak nationalists to break up the Czechoslovak state. On 9 March Emil Hácha, the Czech President of Czechoslovakia, put Slovakia under martial law and dismissed the Slovak provincial government. The German press reported Czech outrages against 'Germans' and Slovaks and did its best to whip up bellicose hysteria. Germany pressed the Slovak provincial government to declare Slovakia independent, which it did on 14 March. On 15 March 1939 Hitler sent German troops to occupy Prague and the rest of Czechia. On 22 March German troops also occupied the Memel region of Lithuania. On 31 March Prime Minister Neville Chamberlain declared in the House of Commons that His Majesty's government would 'at once lend the Polish government all support in their power' if Polish independence were threatened and the Polish government considered it vital to resist with their national forces.[36] On 1 April the National Socialist Party newspaper, *Völkischer Beobachter*, carried a furious leading article by Propaganda Minister Goebbels, accusing 'cliques' in Britain and France – and even more the Americans and the Jews who pulled their strings – of 'warmongering'. But subsequent issues of the paper sought to play down the confrontation, since war with the western powers was not what Hitler wanted.[37]

Stauffenberg pronounced that Hitler had broken his word and violated the nationality principle. Frank condemned Hitler for the same reasons.[38]

On one occasion between the 'Prague' crisis and the end of May 1939, Stauffenberg met Rudolf Fahrner in Berlin, having spent an entire day riding in a tank during an exercise, and said casually but seriously: 'That lunatic will make war.' He went on to speak of the losses in the previous World War and of how dangerous it would be for a nation to sustain such losses twice in one generation.[39]

In Wuppertal in June Stauffenberg met with Partsch, who read to him from his work on Themistocles. Partsch suggested that it was time to form cells of anti-government resistance in the Army. Stauffenberg replied that this might be feasible among the workers, whose older generation had always rejected National Socialism. But the Army officers' eyes had not yet been opened: all they could see were prospects of promotion. Cells could not be formed while there was no consensus on their purpose; it would be both dangerous and hopeless.[40]

From 27 June to 13 July Stauffenberg was on leave with his family in Lautlingen. He rented a small car and went touring round Lake Constance and the Black Forest with his wife; they also visited the Romanesque monastery in Maulbronn, the ruins of the Staufen castle in Wimpfen, and Freiburg im Breisgau. From Lautlingen he wrote to Frank that Frank's and Rudolf Fahrner's translations from Homer were still in his ear and he looked forward to the next instalment. 'From 14 July I am back in Wu in order to continue preparations for an uncertain autumn to the best of my ability.'[41]

In April No. 11 Panzer Regiment and No. 65 Panzer Battalion had acquired over 250 new tanks confiscated from the Czech Skoda works, so that the First Light Division now had greater firepower than the other panzer divisions. In May the divisional staff were informed that autumn manoeuvres would be held in Silesia. On 18 August the division was put on alert, and on 19 August it departed for Neuhammer in Silesia, where it was subordinated to 15th Army Corps under Lieutenant-General Hermann Hoth.[42]

On the day before the division left Wuppertal Stauffenberg wrote to the head of the family, Uncle Berthold at Greifenstein, taking his leave, and expressing his respect for him as 'the model of a true gentleman, lord and soldier'.[43] Also on this last day in Wuppertal, Stauffenberg bought a number of works of philosophy, apologising to his bookseller for paying in banknotes, which he found as embarrassing as the idea of putting money into his doctor's palm. Saying good-bye, he added that 'in spite of it all' it was a relief to move out with his division: after all, war was his ancestral trade.[44]

On 20 August the divisional commander, Brigadier von Loeper, informed his officers of the day of the attack on Poland – 26 August.[45] On 23 August the German-Soviet non-aggression Pact was signed, leaving Poland strategically isolated. Mika wrote to Berthold that this must mean that there would be no war. On 22 August Frank's mother wrote to him that she had just heard of the Pact, and that now the peace was secured 'and Poland will soon receive her punishment'. Alexander reported for active duty as a non-commissioned officer in the reserve battery at Ansbach and hoped to be sent to the front soon. Berthold was drafted into the 1st Department of the Naval Warfare Command in Naval High Command. Alexander, Count Üxküll, Uncle Nux's son, returned from Sweden to report to his regiment, but his age-group was not being mobilised yet, so he had to fill in the time by working in the Propaganda Ministry.[46]

On the afternoon of 24 August Stauffenberg's division moved into assembly positions, with the staff quartered in a hotel in Konstadt. The attack order for 26 August was suspended during the afternoon of 25 August; No. 11 Panzer Regiment and other elements of the division were still marching toward the frontier. In the evening, three hours after the mutual assistance agreement had been signed between Britain and Poland, Hitler halted all deployments. On 26 August the division returned to its assembly positions, and reconnaissance groups that had crossed into Poland were recalled.[47] Whereas originally the infantry was to attack first and open up the Polish positions for the panzer divisions to follow, this plan was reversed in the last days before the attack.[48]

30. At the 1st Light Division's command post on the Polish border, 1 September 1939. From left: Air Force liaison officer, divisional commander Brigadier Baron von Loeper, Stauffenberg, Major Lehnert (oc divisional pioneer battalion), Lieutenant Reerink

On 1 September, the first day of the attack on Poland, the only parts of Stauffenberg's division to cross the frontier were No. 6 Artillery Battalion and the Rifle Brigade: the rest remained as a 10th Army reserve on German territory. In the afternoon the division was ordered to cross the frontier river, the Prosna. Destroyed bridges, swampy terrain and the insufficiency of pioneer troops made the crossing so difficult that only No. 6 Motorcycle Battalion, the 3rd Battalion of No. 4 Cavalry Rifle Regiment and an artillery battalion were ready to attack by 5.40 p.m. On 2 September at 5 a.m. the division attacked Wielun. Lieutenant-General von Reichenau, Commander-in-Chief 10th Army, rebuked the units for advancing too slowly and too methodically while meeting little resistance. After that the division's combat commands at times pressed forward rashly and suffered unnecessary casualties, as when Lieutenant-Colonel von Ravenstein attempted (without orders) to cross the Warthe with his group and was turned back by accurate Polish fire. By the evening of 3 September the division had successfully crossed the Warthe. On 5 September they were still being held up by fortified Polish positions east of the river.[49]

On 4 September an officer of the division had two Polish women shot out of hand without any investigation, on suspicion of having given signals to Polish artillery batteries. Stauffenberg, who had been on friendly terms with the officer, did not rest until he had been court-martialled and demoted. Later the man benefited from a general amnesty.[50]

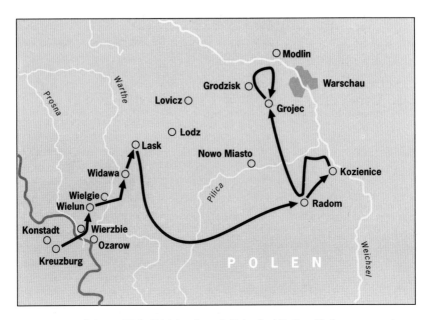

31. Progress of the 1st Light Division through Poland while Stauffenberg was serving as its quartermaster, 1 September to 2 October 1939

On 6 September the division pursued Polish forces eastwards, but at Radom they met such strong resistance that the city could not be taken until the early hours of 8 September. Stauffenberg lost his raincoat and small baggage when the car containing them was captured by Polish forces who had been overtaken by the division's rapid advance. Next the division had to destroy what Polish forces remained west of the Vistula, in the area of the German 14th Corps. On 14 September they moved into quarters near Kozienice, for a rest and for repairs to tanks and machine-guns damaged by sand.[51]

Stauffenberg wrote home on 10 September:

> It appears that we have won a great battle. We have advanced so deeply on one road that for 2 days now we have had masses of Poles on either side. There are probably several divisions. This situation is rather peculiar. At the moment the Poles are still trying to break through and will surely still cause us some casualties, but it will no longer benefit their main forces. It could turn into a Tannenberg.

On 13 and 14 September he wrote home again: the campaign had more or less been won; fighting with the outflanked and encircled Poles was nearing its end; there had been more casualties than necessary due to the inexperience of some officers, lack of information about the Polish road system, and the desperate bravery of the Polish officers. The incredibly rapid advance made it difficult for him to keep the division supplied.

Stauffenberg described the country as desolate, all sand and dust; it was astonishing that anything could be grown there.

> The inhabitants are an unbelievable rabble, very many Jews and very much mixed population. A people which surely is only comfortable under the knout. The thousands of prisoners-of-war will be good for our agriculture. In Germany they will surely be useful, industrious, willing and frugal.

Also along the division's route Stauffenberg noted, besides the prevailing 'infinite poverty, clutter and shabbiness', decayed castles and country houses with beautiful Empire and Biedermeier furniture.[52]

When they learned, on 3 September, that Britain and France had declared war, the officers of the divisional staff were dejected. Stauffenberg said that if they wanted to win it would be a question of endurance, and the war would certainly last ten years. But after the strategic defeat of Poland, he commented in a letter: 'It looks to me as if the English-French "war" was first and foremost an attempt to create a basis for negotiation. What else could it be in aid of?' In this he anticipated the view later enunciated by both Hitler and the Soviet Foreign Minister, Molotov: that the restoration of Poland could not be a realistic war aim now that Germany and Russia were in possession of all Polish territory.[53]

The division did not in fact get any rest but on 15 September moved out to join the forces encircling Warsaw. From 16 September it was strung out over twenty-five kilometres and fighting on three fronts against the defenders of Warsaw, as well as against outflanked Polish forces trying to join the Warsaw front. Several times 'the Poles, fighting with the courage of despair and having superior numbers, got us into some nasty spots'.[54]

On 17 September Stauffenberg, hearing that eastern Poland had been invaded by seven Soviet armies, mused how odd it would be to see German and Red Army soldiers fraternising in Poland. But ten days later he referred to mass executions or deportations by the Soviets in their newly acquired part of Poland:

> I do not have the impression that our friends the Bolsheviks are using kid-gloves. This war is truly a scourge of God for the entire Polish upper class. They ran from us eastward. We are not letting anyone except ethnic Germans cross the Vistula westward. The Russians will likely make short work of them, since, as is well known by now, the real danger is only in the nationalistic Polish upper class who naturally feel superior to the Russians. Many of them will go to Siberia.[55]

At about the same time, the Army High Command informed the divisional commander that within his command area 37 Jews had been shot in a cellar. Brigadier von Loeper looked into this and found that the shootings had taken place in the neighbouring sector held by SS-Leibstandarte 'Adolf Hitler'. Stauffenberg apparently did not learn of this incident.[56]

The division was withdrawn from the front on 21 September, after five days of heavy fighting between Warsaw and Modlin. They were quartered south of Grojec; the staff moved to Rykaly. The German forces took care to remove as much war booty as possible from territory which they had occupied, but had to evacuate to honour German-Soviet frontier agreements which took effect on 29 September. Stauffenberg mentioned 'unheard-of booty', war material of inestimable value to the German war economy and, most wonderfully, 'most of it English and naturally unpaid for'.[57]

The dividing line was drawn more than a hundred kilometres east of the Vistula. Stauffenberg was pleased because rivers were never good as frontiers, and besides, the available farmland would tremendously improve the German economic position. 'It is essential that we begin a systematic colonisation in Poland. But I have no fear that this will not occur.' For the enemies in the west this was 'a hard blow from behind' if they had hoped to base their war plan on the economic strangulation of Germany. They were evidently at their wits' end. French soldiers were unlikely to fight well in an attack on German territory. 'And are we to attack . . .??'[58]

Between 12 and 16 October the division returned to its home bases. Its casualties included 300 fallen soldiers. On 18 October it was renamed 6th Panzer Division. No. 11 Panzer Regiment became a permanent part of the division.[59]

Brigadier von Loeper had intended Stauffenberg to succeed Schöne as senior staff officer, but Loeper became commander of 81st Infantry Division on 25 October; his successor from 1 October was Brigadier Werner Kempf, and on 25 October Major (GS) Ulrich Bürker became senior staff officer.[60]

Stauffenberg returned from the Polish campaign flushed with the success of a well-functioning military machine. He gave an enthusiastic account to Fritz-Dietlof, Count Schulenburg, and his wife Charlotte, who thought him sadly lacking in insight into Germany's true situation.[61]

Stauffenberg was permanently posted to the General Staff in the field, effective from 1 November 1939. It is perhaps worth noting that general-staff officers were a visible elite. From the day of their permanent appointment they wore broad red stripes along the seams of their trousers. By this time Stauffenberg was living in the day-to-day expectation of joining an attack on the west with his division. Several advance orders were issued from 5 November onward and revoked at short notice, once only a few hours before the units were to be on the road.[62]

Uncle Nux and Schulenburg believed a continuation of the war would prove lethal to Germany. Uncle Nux told Theodor Pfizer that Hitler must be arrested and put on trial.[63] Peter, Count Yorck and Ulrich, Count

Schwerin knew of the crimes committed by the Germans in Poland and presumably informed Schulenburg and Üxküll. They approached Stauffenberg and suggested that he should get himself appointed adjutant to the Commander in Chief of the Army, and from that position take part in a coup d'état. Apparently Stauffenberg replied that he had not got to that point yet. The two present adjutants to the Commander in Chief were a lieutenant-colonel (GS) and a major (GS); it was unlikely that a mere captain (GS) would be appointed. But Stauffenberg told his wife that he had learned of activities tantamount to high treason and was under obligation to report them, but would not do so. He also said that it was impossible to act against Hitler while he was so successful.[64]

Both of Stauffenberg's reasons for declining indicate that he was not in principle opposed to a change of regime, but did not consider the time appropriate. All that can be gathered about Stauffenberg's character makes it impossible to assume that, while he considered the overthrow of the regime necessary, he waited for almost three years before he tried to bring it about. Another problem is the contradiction between his condemnation of the political drive to war and his enthusiastic prosecution of campaigns in the field. The answer lies in his military ethos and his confidence in the military leadership. It lies also in grievances rooted in the pre-history and history of the First World War (particularly the Treaty of Versailles); in the fact that Britain, the Dominions and France had declared war on Germany; and, marginally at least, in the effects of propaganda. Not all propaganda was untrue, however reprehensible its purpose.[65] Stauffenberg believed that the purpose of the war was 'the high aim of self-preservation' which could be attained 'only in a good long fight'.[66]

In a lengthy report dated 15 November 1939, Stauffenberg noted the lessons of the Polish campaign. His principal criticism was that the command and reporting system was adapted to static trench-warfare conditions in which distances between staffs were short and communication easy. Transport and supply, on the other hand, had been difficult because divisions could not use two or more roads, as in peace-time manoeuvres, but on the contrary often had to share one road with another division and with corps troops. Reports on supplies and requirements were commonly outdated by the time they reached higher-level quartermasters because of the rapidity of the division's combat activities. At no time during the Polish campaign did the division receive the required ammunition, rations or fuel; spare parts, weapons and mechanised equipment had not been available at all; the division was forced to cannibalise parts and components from other vehicles which were thereby rendered useless, and to steal vehicles from other formations. In the most tense combat situations and while advancing rapidly the division had had to draw supplies from army depots over great distances. No one at any level knew what stores existed or where they were.

Divisional quartermasters had drawn pistols on each other at army supply depots to secure fuel. Fuel supply rations were at best half of consumption; without the fuel supplies captured during the pursuit on the Vistula the division would have had to halt. Almost none of the division's supply lorries were cross-country vehicles. After tanks had crossed emergency bridges these were often impassable for loaded lorries. The technical troop of the quartermaster company still provided useless services such as brewers and gardeners; it ought to be re-organised as a pioneer troop. Stauffenberg called for a thorough rationalization of quartermaster procedures, standardisation of motor-vehicle production, more powerful transport vehicles, simpler and tougher tanks, improvements in artillery and machine-guns, better armament for the services in the rear.

On 24 January 1940 Stauffenberg found time, with Karl Josef Partsch, to effect the transfer of Stefan George's house in Bingen to the municipal authorities. Before handing over the keys, Stauffenberg went through the entire inventory 'down to the last broom', as Partsch wrote to Frank. The temperature was below zero in the unheated house but Stauffenberg was unperturbed, unlike the two city fathers who were stamping their freezing feet. The city fathers promised that Bingen would prove herself worthy of the great gift, and proposed adjournment to a pub, which Stauffenberg 'cleverly managed to avoid'. Instead, he and Partsch visited the graves of the Master's forbears and sister which were under a thick blanket of snow.[67]

There was so much talk among the division's officers about how much harder the coming campaign in the west would be, that the commander confronted them with a secret memorandum of 25 January 1940, entitled 'The Nature of Attack'. He said that such talk was dangerous, and contrary to the nature of attack. The purpose of a decisive attack was to achieve a breakthrough or envelopment, and to pursue the enemy to annihilation. Since the opponent in the west was equally mobile, the attack would have to be prosecuted 'continuously, with the *greatest speed* and force, *far into the depths* [of enemy territory]'.

Stauffenberg regretted that at that time the doctrines of Schlieffen, 'the untiring and incorruptible searcher after victory for an encircled Germany', had been almost forgotten.[68] He was outraged by a speech by Goebbels to the effect that the German soldier of today would fight much more bravely than the old crusading knights because he was fighting for bread and living space, not for a fiction.[69]

Stauffenberg's strong point was organisation. The Organisation Branch of the General Staff were interested in him from the moment he graduated from the War Academy, although it was considered that an appointment as quartermaster (Ib) or intelligence officer (Ic) was a necessary preliminary to a career on the General Staff. The quartermaster was as important to an armoured division as the senior staff officer (operations officer), since the

32. *At the 6th Panzer Division command post before Monthermé on the Meuse, 13 May 1940. From left: Stauffenberg, Captain (GS) Staedke, Captain von Blomberg and Brigadier Kempf*

speed and success of operations depended on the supplies of fuel and ammunition. When Stauffenberg was permanently posted to the General Staff in November 1939, Stauffenberg was judged 'a great organisational talent', 'untiringly industrious'; his tactical abilities were described as 'good'. On 5 January 1940 the divisional commander, Brigadier Kempf, said in a speech that his division had a quartermaster who, it was to be hoped, 'would never leave us'. Kempf said later that he never had to worry about supplies because 'under Stauffenberg they worked superbly'.[70]

Major (GS) Bürker was posted as senior staff officer to XVIth Army Corps from 1 February 1940. He was succeeded by Captain (GS) Helmut Staedke, formerly the quartermaster of the 4th Panzer Division. Staedke had a difficult start in the 6th Panzer Division because many of its officers had expected Stauffenberg to succeed Bürker, but Staedke had Stauffenberg's full support from his first day with the division, and they got on most amicably.[71]

The plan of campaign worked out by Army High Command and approved by Hitler was a modified Schlieffen Plan: to march through Belgium and Holland and envelop the armies of the western powers. Major-General von Manstein, Chief of the General Staff in Army Group A until 1 February 1940 and thereafter OC 38th Army Corps, considered that

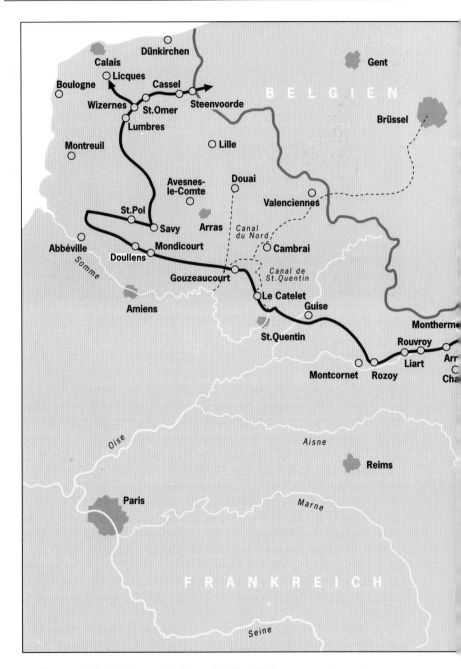

33. Progress of the 6th Panzer Division while Stauffenberg was serving as its quartermaster, 10–31 May 1940

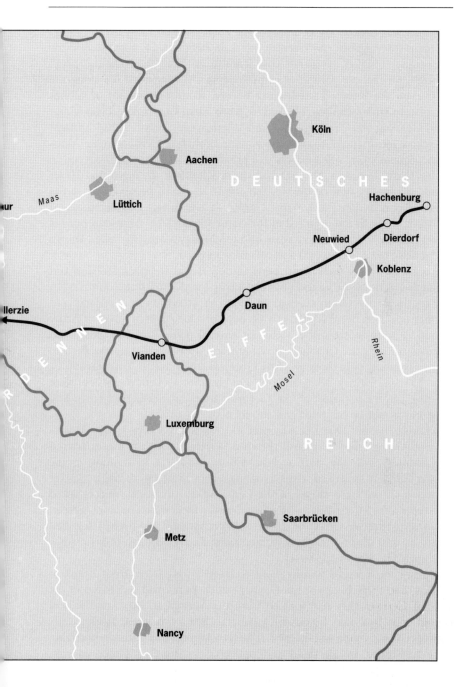

this plan was misconceived, because the enemy would most likely employ his main force against the German attack in Belgium. He suggested to his commander-in-chief, General von Rundstedt, that they should break through the chain of fortifications prolonging the Maginot Line along the Meuse, on the France-Luxembourg border. Rundstedt sought to submit this plan to Hitler, but was blocked by Army High Command. Then Major (GS) Henning von Tresckow was able to intervene. Manstein had brought Tresckow into Army Group A Operations Branch in October 1939. Manstein wrote in 1947, when he was in a prisoner-of-war camp at Bridgend in Wales: 'Now Tresckow, through his friend Schmundt, arranged that Hitler should ask for my view on the western offensive when I presented myself as Officer Commanding [38th Army Corps]. It was in fact conducted essentially according to the proposal of the Army Group [A].' Manstein put his view to Hitler on 17 February 1940; on 24 February Manstein's plan, known as 'Sichelschnitt' (sickle-cut) was officially adopted.[72]

According to the final plan, Army Group B was to attack Holland and Belgium and draw the largest possible enemy forces into those countries. In the south, Army Group C had to feign an attack on Switzerland and southern France. Between these two groups, the mechanised forces of Army Group A were to cross the Meuse at several points simultaneously and advance towards the Channel. Seven armoured divisions were assigned to Army Group A, only three to Army Group B, and none to Army Group C. The French, British, Belgian and Dutch armies, believing they were meeting the main thrust of the German attack in northern France and Belgium, would be encircled and annihilated.[73]

The 6th Panzer Division was part of 41st Army Corps under Major-General Georg-Hans Reinhardt. From 9 March to 9 May it was quartered in Limburg, with the staff at Hachenburg, and was in training in the Westerwald. It practised river crossings and breaking through bunker positions on the steep slopes of the Lahn. When divisional officers asked questions about the roads in the Ardennes, which were few and narrow, about anti-tank obstacles, or about the strength of the French fortified positions west of the Meuse, Brigadier Kempf referred them to his memorandum, 'The Nature of Attack'.[74]

During these weeks Stauffenberg received a long letter from Frank in Athens, and three books of the *Odyssey* which Frank had translated in the style of German they had learned from the Master, so that Stauffenberg should 'not lack *that* literature which, as history teaches, is especially appropriate for young war-heroes'. The translations, in a goatskin portfolio, were forwarded by Berthold and delivered by Foreign Office courier. Stauffenberg had written to Frank, telling him that he had not been in the forces which had attacked Denmark and Norway on 9 April; Frank gathered from this that Stauffenberg was impatient for action.[75]

On 8 May Stauffenberg issued advance orders for fuel supplies to cover the division's move up to the Rhine. On 9 May the divisional staff learned unofficially from No. 11 Panzer Regiment that the attack was set for 10 May, but the code-word for the division arrived only at 2 a.m. on 10 May.[76]

On 10 May the 6th Panzer Division stood ready east of Coblenz, behind the 2nd Panzer Division and two infantry divisions, as part of the 41st Army Corps which belonged to Panzer Group Kleist; this in turn, with the 4th, 12th and 16th Armies, formed Army Group A under General von Rundstedt.[77]

The division crossed the Rhine at Neuwied. Its attack troops were organized in three combat commands whose composition was modified according to need. Two of them commonly consisted of one battalion each of mounted infantry, tanks and artillery, and one company each of anti-tank and pioneer troops. The third combat command consisted initially of one battalion each of motorcycle infantry and other motorised infantry; this composition was changed after a few days to one battalion each of tanks, infantry and artillery.[78]

On the first day there were delays due to errors on the part of the 2nd Panzer Division, which was still in the area around Daun when the 6th Panzer Division was scheduled to move into it; as a result, the 6th was held up short of its goal, strung out over 120 kilometres of narrow roads in the Eifel mountains. Parts of infantry divisions got mixed up with the 6th Panzer Division combat commands, convoys of motor vehicles passed in violation of instructions, masses of vehicles stood uncamouflaged in the open, commanders failed to take action. Lieutenant-General von Kleist sharply reprimanded the divisions in an order of 0.13 a.m. on 11 May. The 6th Panzer Division reached Luxembourg, then Belgium and the French border north-east of Monthermé on the Meuse, a day later than planned, on 12 May.[79]

As expected, the bridge at Monthermé had been blown up. An attempt to cross the Meuse with air support failed; in fact German dive-bombers destroyed two of the division's armoured reconnaissance vehicles and guns and killed more than twenty of its soldiers. On 13 May, when Esebeck's combat command with its Mark IV and Mark III tanks approached within five kilometres of the river, pioneers filled inflatable floats and rafts, drove them up to the river bank in armoured personnel carriers, and under enemy fire set up a makeshift bridge for the tanks to cross moments later, while other tanks positioned on the heights east and north of Monthermé used their guns to pin down the enemy. There was an alarm that tanks were attacking the division from the rear: the senior staff officer immediately requested heavy anti-aircraft artillery to fire at the enemy tanks at point-blank range. But the 'enemy tanks' turned out to be German armoured reconnaissance cars. By late evening a small bridgehead had been secured on the south-west bank of the Meuse.[80]

In the early morning of 14 May, shortly after 3.30 a.m., enemy artillery fire destroyed the temporary bridge. Additional tanks therefore crossed on rafts, until a military bridge was completed by the afternoon. The division's heavy artillery was not yet available because the roads were jammed. The supply train under Major Erwin Topf had not arrived yet either; Stauffenberg used the divisional commander's light reconnaissance aeroplane, a Fieseler 'Stork', to look for Topf's troops, disentangled them from the infantry pushing down the road and led them up to the Meuse. Meanwhile, the division's two battalions in the bridgehead were hard pressed by the three machine-gun battalions of the (black) No. 42 Colonial Regiment in the bunkers on the heights above Monthermé.[81]

The 6th Panzer Division began its main assault on the French bunker positions on 15 May at 4.30 a.m. with artillery bombardment, advancing infantry, tanks firing their guns, and pioneers with flamethrowers. They stormed five bunkers and broke through the fortification line in the first hour of the assault. The defenders had neither sufficient forces, ammunition, anti-tank weapons nor rations. As their situation was hopeless, their regimental commander dismissed his officers and surrendered. By 11 a.m. the 6th Panzer Division's command post was several kilometres south and west of the Meuse: the division's combat commands had penetrated fifty kilometres into France. The French preparations were 'so pitiful that our operations were not effectively slowed'. A breakthrough attempt by the Germans had not been expected here: the defenders were taken completely by surprise and did not take advantage of the narrow roads and steep hills.[82]

After the first four days of the attack, Hitler concluded that the French generals had failed to understand the German strategy. Although six armoured divisions had crossed the Meuse, the French neglected the territory in front of Army Group A, continued to reinforce the Namur-Antwerp line against Army Group B, and filled the projected envelopment area with their troops. Hitler therefore assigned all additional available armoured and mechanised divisions to Army Group A.[83]

Brigadier Kempf issued an 'Order of the Day for Pursuit' on 15 May: 'The division has achieved a decisive success by breaking through the Meuse positions. I express my highest commendation to all commands involved for their outstanding performance and for their bravery. [. . .] The division will begin the pursuit of the broken enemy on the road from Monthermé through Arreux, Renwez, Chron, Sormont, Rouvroy, Liart, Le Frety, Mambressy, Rozoy, Montcornet.' On the same evening the division's combat commands reached Rozoy, having met little opposition; they occupied Montcornet after overcoming considerable resistance. The 6th Panzer

Division was at the head of the six armoured divisions that had crossed the Meuse. Shortly after midnight a radio order arrived from 41st Army Corps declaring that the day's objective was Liart. The 6th Panzer Division had passed Liart at 6 p.m.: its command post was in Raillimont. There was no more significant opposition; the attackers commonly encountered only isolated, poorly organised French units which were taken prisoner by a few energetic soldiers – who then had to leave them where they were. The division had only one goal, as Colonel von Ravenstein said in reply to a question: 'The coast!'[84]

On 16 May French bombers attacked Montcornet, Rozoy and Raillimont. But any suspicion that the enemy had laid a huge trap seemed unfounded in view of all the evidence of surprise and chaotic collapse. In the afternoon Esebeck's and Ravenstein's combat commands pushed on to the Oise. At Guise French tanks, yielding to pressure from the 8th Panzer Division north of the 6th, tried to break through southward. For the first time the 6th Panzer Division encountered French 32-ton tanks equipped with armour which their anti-tank guns could not pierce. On 17 May Lieutenant Neckenauer hit one of the French tanks with 25 shots from his anti-tank gun; only when his 26th shot hit a track did he stop the tank. But the French failed to exploit the superiority of their heavy tanks. Major-General Reinhardt promised to send 88-millimetre anti-aircraft guns which could pierce the heavy armour. But before they arrived, the heavy French tanks which were assembled west of the Oise disappeared south-westward during the night.[85]

Ravenstein's combat command again encountered some heavy French tanks at Le Catelet on 18 May. When Ravenstein's forces occupied the town after overpowering the opposition, they captured the staff of the entire French 9th Army and the commander of the French XIth Army Corps artillery, as well as many military documents. Esebeck's combat command had established a bridgehead across the St. Quentin Canal south of Cambrai by 10 p.m. On the same evening each of the two combat commands received a train of 88-millimetre anti-aircraft guns.[86]

On that day Stauffenberg wrote to his wife from a command post on the Oise to tell her that his division had come through the Eifel mountains and the Ardennes, and had crossed the Meuse, the Oise and today the Somme. The French thus far had shown no inclination to fight: they were surrendering by the thousands and streaming eastward unguarded, because guarding them would have meant halting the offensive. Stauffenberg was deeply moved by 'the incipient collapse of a great nation, not only militarily, but above all psychologically'. The British had not yet turned up; surely they must begin to give some consideration to defending their bridgehead on the Channel. He was getting little sleep, but living well: the wines were delicious. Countess Stauffenberg sent a copy of the letter to their relatives and added that the other wives were receiving letters painting much the same picture. The division had several times been the spearhead of the advance, its commander had been mentioned in dispatches, they had taken twenty thousand prisoners. It was generally remarked that the Poles had fought harder than the French, although it must be remembered that the best French troops were being encircled in the north.[87]

Major Topf described Stauffenberg in his quartermaster briefings during this campaign: tall, slim, agile, he would receive divisional and liaison officers with 'radiant courtesy', see to it that everyone was offered a glass of wine and a cigar or tobacco, make entirely unsystematic inquiries, tell anecdotes, and then suddenly and equally casually he would dictate his orders, with his left hand in his trouser pocket and a wineglass in his right, walking up and down the room.[88]

On 19 May the French counter-attacked more forcefully than they had done before, using their heaviest tanks together with infantry. An incursion by French tanks threatened to cut off Esebeck's and Ravenstein's combat commands from the rest of the division, so that the third combat command under Lieutenant-Colonel Richard Koll was sent to attack the left flank of the French southward thrust. Twenty minutes later Brigadier Kempf radioed his senior staff officer: 'Enemy attack broken, hundreds surrendering.' Many tanks and great quantities of other war material fell into German hands. Esebeck's and Ravenstein's combat commands continued to press westward and established bridgeheads on the empty Canal du Nord. The divisional command post moved to Gouzeaucourt. The advance of this day amounted to only fifteen kilometres. But despite the heavy fighting which the 6th Panzer Division had gone through, it was still fully combat-ready. Success compensated for fatigue and casualties.[89]

On 20 May Ravenstein's combat command came upon British troops for the first time, in Mondicourt, at the French 1st Army's junction with the British Expeditionary Force. 'In contrast with the French they surprised us by their tenacious fighting methods and were defeated only after an hour-long battle.' Fifty British prisoners were taken. After a refuelling stop the combat command reached Doullens, fifteen kilometres southwest of Arras, and again encountered hard-fighting British troops, while enemy bombers attacked Ravenstein's rearguard. In house-to-house combat Doullens was taken by 8 p.m. On the same evening No. 57 Panzer Reconnaissance Battalion nearly reached the coast between Abbéville and Montreuil. The 6th Panzer Division had advanced more than fifty kilometres: the strategic breakthrough had been achieved. A day of rest was declared for 21 May.[90]

Meanwhile French, British and allied forces prepared for simultaneous attacks on the southern and northern flanks of Army Group A between Arras and Valenciennes, hoping to cut off the 2nd, 6th and 8th spearhead divisions. At 1.40 p.m. on 21 May the 41st Army Corps ordered a halt of all westward movements and the formation of strong reserves. An hour later the Corps radioed: 'Alarm, alarm, alarm. Ready to move out eastward.' Two British battalions penetrated the northern flank.[91]

Stauffenberg and Staedke drove back to Corps headquarters and were ordered to send Koll's combat command toward Avesnes to secure the northern flank. The division had to turn its front northward on the St Pol-Savy line; a part of it had to retreat eastward. But no notable battle followed, for the Franco-British effort lacked force and energy. The French operating north of Panzer Group Kleist were cut off from their supply lines; the British had been preparing to leave the continent since 17 May.[92]

At noon on 22 May the 6th Panzer Division received the order to attack Calais. Esebeck's combat command reached Lumbres, forty kilometres east of Calais, by late afternoon; at 8.30 p.m. No. 57 Panzer Reconnaissance Battalion reached the heights north of Licques, and an hour later Esebeck's troops also arrived. At that moment, as the divisional war diary recorded, Major-General Reinhardt, who happened to be at the divisional command post, 'received radio orders from Group Kleist forcing him to halt the advance of the division, at the very moment when the great goal, Calais – which dominated the mind of every soldier in the division that day – was within our immediate reach'.[93]

On 23 May Halder felt certain that the 'crisis at Arras' would be over within 48 hours, and he wanted Army Group A to continue attacking so as to prevent the British and French forces from retreating through Dunkirk. On the same day Lieutenant-General Guderian, OC 19th Army Corps, demanded an immediate breakthrough to Dunkirk to complete the envelopment and annihilation.[94] But Rundstedt feared that the spearhead divisions might be cut off. Having halted Kleist's advance towards Boulogne and Calais on 22 May, he confirmed the order on 23 May, and got Hitler's approval on 24 May when Hitler visited his headquarters. Halder noted in his diary: 'The rapid left wing, which has no enemy before it, has been halted at the express wish of the Führer!' Hitler ordered Brauchitsch and Halder to reverse the campaign plan: Army Group A must hold still and become the 'anvil', while Army Group B must be the 'hammer', pounding the concentrated enemy forces. Halder also noted that Hitler did not want the final battle to take place in Flanders because National Socialist doctrine regarded the inhabitants as descendants of the Franks. In order to disguise this political consideration, Hitler claimed that the Flemish territory, with its many waterways, was unsuitable for armoured vehicle operations.[95]

On 23 May the 6th Panzer Division turned eastward: Esebeck's combat command took St Omer, and by nightfall the division's combat forces were ten kilometres east of St Omer, before Cassel. The divisional war diary records that the order on 24 May to advance on Cassel produced 'great joy', and Ravenstein's combat command immediately laid artillery on the town.

But only two hours after giving the order to attack, Corps Command countermanded it 'by order of the Führer and Supreme Commander'; only the bridgeheads on the Calais-St Omer Canal were to be held.[96]

On the same afternoon Foreign Minister von Ribbentrop, accompanied by the commander of SS Division 'Totenkopf', visited the 6th Panzer Division's command post at Wizernes and stayed for two hours. Stauffenberg wrote to his wife that he had had coffee with Ribbentrop, who made 'a tolerable impression', although 'he is certainly no great lion'. Ribbentrop also visited SS Regiment 'Deutschland', which belonged to SS Division 'Totenkopf' and was subordinated to the 6th Panzer Division to cover its northern flank; Ribbentrop's son Rudolf was serving in this SS regiment.[97]

There was no rest for the division. On 25 May it had to prepare for defence; on the 26th it was ordered back to Lumbres; as soon as it arrived it had to turn round again, because Hitler had now ordered that Dunkirk should be attacked from all sides. Having spent two days moving about – as the war diary grumpily recorded – No. 57 Panzer Reconnaissance Battalion and combat commands Esebeck and Ravenstein advanced towards Cassel from positions east of St Omer on 27 May. Corps Command named Steenvoorde, eight kilometres east of Cassel, as the next target. But British forces defended Cassel from innumerable artillery and machine-gun positions around and inside the town: 'brave' (that is, bloody) assaults made no progress, so that the division was ordered to disengage during the night, leaving a few companies to mine and guard the approaches, and to attack further eastward on the next day.[98]

On 28 May progress was again slow. But Lieutenant-General von Kleist praised 'especially the 6th Panzer Division' for having taken 36 positions on the French-Belgian border which British and French troops had defended tenaciously. On 29 May the division advanced further into Belgium. On 30 May combat commands Koll and Esebeck had to confront a British mechanised brigade of three regiments which tried to break out of Cassel and crashed into Koll's positions, fought hard for their retreat and were annihilated by Koll's combat command. The enemy lost 700 dead and 3500 prisoners here; only a few of the Cassel garrison reached Dunkirk. Brigadier Kempf reported to 41st Corps Command: 'The enemy defended himself to the last, even when his situation was hopeless. The casualties of the English brigade are uncommonly high. About fifty shot-up enemy tanks cover the battlefield.' But the 6th Panzer Division had suffered too. In the afternoon it was withdrawn from the front and moved back to St Omer. The combat troops rested on 31 May; all the others had to work on repairs.[99]

On 27 May Stauffenberg wrote his second letter from this campaign: it gave the 'sad news' of his posting to the Second (Organisation) Branch of the Army General Staff. He had to take over Group II (peacetime organisation and command structure). He found it very difficult to leave his division 'in the midst of the war and the most glorious operations', only to disappear into 'a bureaucracy'. But, of course, this posting was high recognition for Stauffenberg's abilities and performance. His division had had a part in the most decisive and successful operations in the west, and he had been 'fortunate' in his work: 'despite unimaginable speeds [of advance] the division was always excellently supplied'. Plentiful local stores provided ample rations, cargo planes brought in fuel at need, the sick and wounded were well looked after, large repair shops were set up at Namur and Charleville, and two thousand specialist technicians and mechanics were flown in. But the support services frequently had to fight off attacks, as the division's flanks were usually unprotected during the rapid advance. Quartermaster troops fought a large battle at Rouvroy and L'Echelle on 16 May and another at Honnecourt on 19 May, and on 21 May they captured a British armoured reconnaissance vehicle and its crew. They also had to weather frequent air attacks.[100]

Stauffenberg's post-action report stated that supplying a division had more to do with the military spirit of the troops than with transport, but rationalisations were still called for. The combat supply train of three to five hundred large transport vehicles was too large and unwieldy: it was 'unworkable for both organisational and military reasons' and should be eliminated. Instead, the commander of the supply train should be given five small lorry convoys. But methods for the requisitioning of supplies had improved a great deal since the Polish campaign. In the entire western campaign the division lost 446 dead, 1191 wounded, 20 missing and 438 off sick.[101]

In his letter of 27 May Stauffenberg also expressed sympathy for 'the great English tragedy'. He considered that 'the annihilation of the armies in Flanders' was a certainty, but did not think the British were defeated yet. The 'most far-reaching decisions, which will alter the face of the old world' were in preparation: after the victory in Flanders it would be the policy-makers' turn. The British faced a big decision: 'If they do not give in, there will be more hard fighting, for we shall have to make ready for the battle of annihilation against England.'

On 31 May Stauffenberg was awarded the Iron Cross First Class.[102] In the evening of the same day his division bade him farewell. The war diary recorded: 'The division's second General-Staff officer, Captain (GS) Count von Stauffenberg, who has belonged to the division since its formation and whose tireless work has bound him closely to it, is being posted to the Second Branch of the General Staff of the Army. His successor is Captain Colsman, formerly Special Missions Officer 2.'[103]

7

On the General Staff

While in France, Stauffenberg remarked that there was nothing so beautiful as a victorious campaign fought together with a friend. Two weeks after his transfer he still regretted having been pulled out of the 'most effective mobile operations which had ever been conceived'.[1] Stauffenberg was flushed with success from the campaign, and his enthusiastic energy clashed with the cool atmosphere in the General Staff. His predecessor, Captain (GS) Bernd von Pezold, a close friend from the Bamberg years, introduced him to his new duties. Pezold thought Germany could not win this war; Stauffenberg thought she could, and the friendship was slightly strained.[2] But Stauffenberg's energy was irrepressible. He wrote to his wife that after the war 'the entire existing organisation' would have to be examined, and his field of activity would have pivotal importance. His experience in organising, leading and supplying a modern armoured division would be most useful, which was why he had been sat on his new chair, he continued. He hoped to achieve a number of the changes which he had demanded in vain during his service in the field.[3]

In the same letter Stauffenberg referred, none too cautiously, to circumstances which tended to frustrate rational work. The General Staff was large, it had to co-ordinate its work with many military and government agencies at the same level, and it was dependent upon 'an absolute Führer who has very much his own ideas', so that the most diverse 'political, personal and tactical' considerations applied. Stauffenberg acknowledged that he would have to get used to having many of his efforts nullified by a sudden 'Führer's decision', or distorted by a poor compromise. The chaotic command structure of the Armed Forces was evident to Stauffenberg from the start.[4]

Stauffenberg described his branch chief, Colonel (GS) Walther Buhle, as 'an energetic, not particularly refined Swabian'; Buhle's deputy, Major (GS) Hellmuth Reinhardt, also came from Württemberg. Stauffenberg and Reinhardt had known each other for years; Reinhardt had been an older pupil at the Eberhard-Ludwigs-Gymnasium when Stauffenberg was there.

34. Stauffenberg with his sons, Franz Ludwig and Heimeran, in Wuppertal, 1940

Stauffenberg's colleague as head of Group I (war organisation) was Captain (GS) Walter Schmidt, also a Swabian. Stauffenberg jokingly pronounced the venture 'racially pure'. From the War Academy he knew Major (GS) Eberhard Finckh, who had had the bad luck to be assigned to the Quartermaster General, Brigadier Eugen Müller. Müller had asked for Stauffenberg; the latter considered Müller abominable and thought himself lucky to have escaped his clutches. Group III (engineering) was headed by Lieutenant-Colonel (GS) Hans Christ. In July 1940 Captain (GS) Albrecht Ritter Mertz von Quirnheim became head of Group IV (post-action documentation). He had served as senior staff officer in the 290th Infantry Division during the French campaign and had been awarded the Iron Cross First Class for bravery. In December he succeeded Captain (GS) Schmidt as head of Group I.[5]

When Stauffenberg joined the General Staff it was still quartered at Bad Godesberg, where it remained for three more days. It then moved to Chimay, where it stayed through June, and on 2 July to Fontainebleau.[6]

Stauffenberg had the opportunity to visit Paris frequently, mostly on business, sometimes to attend the opera. On 28 October the General Staff moved to new headquarters near Zossen south of Berlin.[7]

On 16 June France requested an armistice. Three days later Stauffenberg wrote to his wife: 'They are completely beaten, their army annihilated, a blow from which this nation will not easily recover.' In a letter written two days later he referred to the Treaty of Versailles and to the upheavals since then. It was a triumph, but one had to reflect

> how little is permanent and that the most abrupt change, even reversal, is more probable than permanence even for only a few years. If we teach our children that only constant struggle and constant striving for renewal can save us from decline – all the more so in the light of these great achievements – and that permanence, preservation and death are identical, then we shall have accomplished the greatest part of our national duty of education.

Stauffenberg's pessimism was well-founded: the war against Britain was continuing, and America was already lending her assistance.[8]

In conversation with Reinhardt at about this time, Stauffenberg attributed the campaign plan to Manstein and condemned Hitler's intervention at Dunkirk: it was, he often said, a fateful error which had allowed the defeated British army to escape. Stauffenberg spoke with contempt of Hitler's failure to pursue the enemy across the Channel.[9]

Stauffenberg was a professional and it never occurred to him to think of Hitler as one. But he recognised Hitler's 'flair for military matters'. Hitler's decision to strike at Norway had been correct, and he had realised, unlike most of his generals, that the Maginot Line could be breached. Stauffenberg told his wife: 'He made a mistake at the encirclement of Dunkirk – he will not repeat it.' Visiting his bookseller in the months after his return from France, he said that since he had been at General Staff headquarters he had changed his earlier negative view of Hitler. Being close to Hitler stimulated creative thinking; Hitler could see the overall pattern of things and he was struggling for Germany's future: it was necessary to help him win the war. Whatever he might have said about Hitler in the past: 'This man's father was not a petty bourgeois. This man's father is war.'[10]

Stauffenberg naturally did not reveal his private thoughts to everyone. Moreover, he enjoyed defending points of view opposed to those of his interlocutors. He recognised in Hitler the demon of war, but also the dilettante who failed to pursue the defeated enemy. In any case, he did not at that time hold the view that Hitler must be removed.

Hitler's orders for the mass murder of Polish intellectuals, Jews, the mentally ill, and later of the political commissars of the Red Army, were fairly well known at the highest levels of the Army High Command.[11] Stauffenberg probably received some information about the atrocities in

1939 and 1940. The available evidence shows him concerned primarily with military operations. It is not known whether Stauffenberg knew of Hitler's order of 31 March 1941 to exterminate the Communist intelligentsia and the Jews in the Soviet Union, but it seems likely in view of his duties on the General Staff. Comrades say that he became increasingly outraged at the multifarious brutality of Nazism.[12] Stauffenberg's older cousin, Cäsar von Hofacker, who worked for the military government in France, frequently complained that French goodwill was being squandered in every possible way: for example, by shooting 100 hostages for every attack on a German officer, by deporting Jews, and by plundering the country.[13] Although there are no indications that Stauffenberg learned of *systematic mass killings* of Jews and others before the spring of 1942, it is clear that in the first months of the Russian campaign his attention was drawn to the crimes committed by SS and police units behind the front lines. In the summer of 1941 Stauffenberg asked Second Lieutenant (Res.) Walther Bussmann, who worked in the Quartermaster-General's War Administration Branch 'to collect everything that implicated the SS'. Bussmann informed Stauffenberg of reports that SS and police mobile killing units (*Einsatzgruppen*) were conducting mass shootings behind the front, and Stauffenberg saw the reported figures for the victims, which ran into millions. According to Bussmann, Stauffenberg and the head of General Staff Operations Branch, Colonel (GS) Adolf Heusinger, led the demand for a revocation of the order that all captured Red Army commissars were to be shot out of hand.[14] About that time, knowledge of the secret policy of genocide had begun to spread, though mostly in the form of unverified rumour. In November 1941 Fritz-Dietlof, Count Schulenburg, informed his wife that there was a camp called Auschwitz where they were burning Jews in ovens.[15] Helmuth James, Count Moltke, who was serving in the legal branch of the OKW's Foreign Countries Group, did not find out about Auschwitz until 20 March 1942, and then it was because his brother-in-law, Hans Deichmann, worked for I.G. Farben and often had business at industrial plants in the town of Auschwitz. Deichmann told Moltke that in a camp near Auschwitz Jews were being killed by the thousands in gas-chambers.[16] Moltke searched for more information and came across the fact that on 20 January 1942 a conference had been held at a Wannsee villa to co-ordinate the 'final solution of the Jewish Question'.[17] But he still refused to believe in mass extermination until 9 October 1942, when he received a second report, which he considered authentic, about an 'SS blast-furnace' in which 6000 corpses were burned daily.[18] Although he tried to find out more and had fairly good access to information thanks to his position in the Foreign Countries Group, his knowledge was still vague. On 25 March 1943 he wrote – through his friend Dr Harry Johansson of the Nordic Ecumenical Institute in Sigtuna – to his English friend Lionel Curtis, telling him of his belief that at least nine tenths of the population do not know that we have killed hundreds of thousands of Jews [. . .] We have been informed that in Upper-Silesia a big KZ [concentration camp] is being built which is expected to be able to accommodate 40 to 50,000 men, of whom 3 to 4000 are to be killed each month. But all this information comes to me, even to me, who is seeking facts of this nature, in a rather vague and indistinct and inexact form.[19]

What could an individual do? Before 1942 only one man had given a radical answer to this question: Georg Elser, who very nearly succeeded in blowing up Hitler with a bomb in Munich in November 1939. Since then, of course, security precautions had been greatly intensified. But other determined opponents of Hitler, such as Colonel Hans Oster and Dietrich Bonhoeffer in the military counter-intelligence service, or Helmuth James, Count von Moltke and Fritz-Dietlof, Count Schulenburg, did not decide that they must try themselves to kill Hitler. In 1939, when the impending western offensive seemed certain to become a complete catastrophe, Erich Kordt and Hasso von Etzdorf, both in the Foreign Office, agreed to act as assassins, but withdrew from the brink because they felt abandoned by other conspirators, and because of the formidable obstacles posed by security precautions.[20]

Stauffenberg's reputation as a brilliant General Staff officer continued to grow. Everyone wanted to know him; even older officers, generals reporting from the front, and the Chief of the General Staff himself sought his advice. His habit of interrupting an evening's work to recite a poem by Stefan George contributed to his aura of distinctiveness and intellectuality; but there were also people who were put off by his devotion to the poet, and people who sensed that he was, in some way, leading a double life.[21]

Stauffenberg's first assignment was to help in the re-organisation of the Army from 165 into 120 divisions; the armoured divisions were to be increased from 7 to 20 and the mechanised infantry divisions from 8 to 10. His responsibilities in matters concerning the 'command structure' included co-ordination between the army group, army and army corps staffs in the field and the Home Army, supply matters, the organisation of volunteer formations, and liaison between the Army and the police, border guards, SS and SA, Ministry of the Interior, SS high command, and Supreme Command of the Wehrmacht. It was his task to suggest how authority and functions should be divided among all these organisations.[22]

Stauffenberg soon had to reverse his work on the Army's 'peace-time organisation'. From the end of June, at the latest, war in the east was being discussed among the General Staff. At the beginning of August Stauffenberg spent eight days' summer leave at Lautlingen; when he returned, he and Captain (GS) Bolko von der Heyde, who sat opposite him at their double desk, worked mainly on increasing the field army to 180 divisions,[23] and on quartermaster business for the projected war against the Soviet

35. At Lautlingen, 1940. From left: Alfred Stauffenberg, 'Duli', Alexander Stauffenberg, Berthold Stauffenberg, Nina Stauffenberg, Heimeran Stauffenberg, Claus Stauffenberg, Olga Üxküll

Union, 'Operation Barbarossa'. They were also engaged in plans for an occupation of 'armistice France' (the unoccupied portion of France which was ruled from Vichy by Marshal Pétain) in case of an enemy landing in North Africa.[24]

In September Berthold Stauffenberg wrote to his wife that no one now believed in an invasion of England: the war would take another direction. In October he said explicitly that this would be 'against the east'.[25] Frank was called up and, without enthusiasm, joined No. 309 Replacement Training Battalion in Lübben near Berlin on 3 December. Claus Stauffenberg paid him a visit there on 26 December – the Feast of St Stephen, as they noted with reference to their shared attachment to the poet. Stauffenberg had given Mertz precedence for the Christmas holidays and was unable to join his family until New Year's Eve.[26]

From mid-February 1941 German forces, commanded by Major-General Rommel, were fighting British and Dominion troops in Libya; a campaign against the British in Greece began on 6 April; and an airborne assault on British positions in Crete was launched on 20 May.[27]

In May and June when Greece was being occupied by Italian and German forces, Stauffenberg made an official trip to Thessaloniki, Athens and Crete, while Mertz went to Libya on a similar mission for the Organisation Branch.

Passing through Thessaloniki on his way back to Berlin, Stauffenberg

36. Berthold Stauffenberg in naval uniform, ca. 1940

had lunch with his cousin Alfred, Count Stauffenberg, who was to land on Crete with the paratroop assault regiment two weeks later.[28]

In Athens Stauffenberg met with Rudolf Fahrner and together they made an excursion to Coronis on the north coast of Attica.

The British forces in Greece had requisitioned and used local stores. After they had evacuated Greece, replacement shipments of 47,000 tons of grain en route from Australia, as well as 350,000 tons of grain purchased by the Greek government, were kept out of the German and Italian-occupied territories by a British blockade. A major grain-producing region of Greece had been occupied by Bulgaria. The Italian Army was the principal occupation force, but instead of fulfilling their obligations to the population they bought up supplies and even took foodstuffs out of the country; the German authorities exported some quantities of oil and raisins from Greece, but from September 1941 they procured grain for Greece from other Balkan states. Food was already in very short supply in Greece in the first days of the Italian and German occupation. Several efforts to aid Greece were made, mostly after August 1941, by the German military authorities there, and by the Bishop of Messambria, Angelo Roncalli. Fahrner wanted Stauffenberg to help him intercede with the occupation authorities on behalf of the starving population of Athens. Fahrner called it 'a passionate and dangerous undertaking'. Stauffenberg got Fahrner access to the staff of Fieldmarshal Wilhelm List, the Commander-in-Chief of German forces in the Balkans. Fahrner sought to have some of the olive oil produced in Crete released for the population of Athens, but got no support from List for this proposal.[29]

On 22 June 1941 German forces invaded the Soviet Union (Operation Barbarossa). On the following day the General Staff moved into its new headquarters, 'Camp Fritz' (later known as 'Mauerwald') near Angerburg in East Prussia.[30]

On the morning of 22 June Lieutenant-General Friedrich Olbricht, Chief of the General Army Office, said: 'Our army is a mere puff of wind on the vast Russian steppes.' He had professional knowledge of the armaments capacity of both Germany and her enemies. But other attitudes prevailed in the Army High Command: over-confidence and a failure to understand what advantages the enemy would draw from the vastness of his territory. The German strategy of rapid advance was defeated by distance, by bad roads, and by the Russian wide-gauge railway, which meant that German wagons had to be shifted on to Russian wide-gauge axles and vice-versa, or that all cargo and passengers had to be unloaded and reloaded. Stalin also derived a psychological advantage from the fact that his people were defending their Russian homeland.

But Hitler recklessly held to his blitzkrieg methods. Eleven days before the attack, he issued his Directive No. 32, which shifted armaments production to meet the needs of the Navy and Air Force and scheduled a reorganisation of the Army for the end of 1941. On 14 July Hitler announced a reduction of the Army and a concurrent increase of armoured divisions to 36 (although each was to have only two armoured battalions). In order to equip the new formations, he ordered 'the suspension of all supplies of motor-vehicles to the field army in the east' – just when that army was sustaining enormous losses.

In 1942 Hitler ordered his armed forces to attack the British in the Mediterranean and the Near East 'from Libya via Egypt, from Bulgaria through Turkey, and possibly also from Transcaucasia through Iran'. At the same time the Navy and Air Force were to prosecute the 'siege of England'.[31]

On 3 July the Chief of the General Staff, Lieutenant-General Halder, noted: 'I think I am not exaggerating when I say that the campaign against Russia was won in fourteen days. Naturally that does not mean it is over.'[32] On 13 July the Commander of 41st Panzer Corps, Lieutenant-General Georg-Hans Reinhardt, declared during a visit to the 6th Panzer Division: 'If the division reaches the Luga sector today, there will be a special news bulletin and the war will have been won.'[33]

In mid-July 1941 Stauffenberg visited General Guderian's 2nd Panzer

Group in Army Group Centre between Orsha and Smolensk. He also looked up Lieutenant-General Geyr von Schweppenburg, whom he knew from his visits to Ludwigsburg and London, in his forward command post as commander of the 24th Panzer Corps, and inquired whether his formations were well supplied. Stauffenberg lost his identification tag in the forward lines; it was recovered and sent back to him at Camp Fritz. Major-General von Loeper also commanded a formation in the 2nd Panzer Group, the 10th Infantry Division; Stauffenberg talked with him about the campaign and they both anticipated a successful conclusion, but they agreed that Hitler had made another big mistake by redirecting the drive on Moscow southward and had thus destroyed the chance of a blitzkrieg victory.[34]

On his return from the front Stauffenberg personally reported to Halder on the strain which the quick succession of breakthrough battles put on the mechanised formations; while their combat strength had declined, their confidence in their own superiority had dangerously increased.[35]

The campaign in fact turned into a debacle in its first four weeks. On 25 July Loeper's senior staff officer, Major (GS) Georg von Unold, wrote to Stauffenberg that the division had reached a high degree of exhaustion. Having had no rest, and lacking ammunition, the men were close to losing heart. The division was fighting as mere battalions instead of combat commands or brigades – 'without strength, without reserves, without tanks, rushing from one engagement to the next'. The leadership was inconsistent, but the responsibility for this state of affairs was at levels higher than army corps. The world's strongest air power could not even send up a few dive-bombers. The corps had orders for a 'deep thrust eastward', but instead of accomplishing this they had been defending themselves for a week against an enemy growing ever stronger. Unold concluded with an appeal to Stauffenberg: 'Help us before it is too late!' Loeper added a postscript: 'Dear Stauff, they are well on their way to hounding all our armoured corps – ours, in any case – to death, just as Murat hounded his splendid cavalry in 1812, while the Russians operate with shorter supply lines, reorganise, and go into battle refreshed. A child simply has to break his toy!'[36]

In October the Soviet T 34 tanks appeared before the 4th Panzer Army. The divisional artillery was powerless against them: only 10-centimetre guns could damage the tanks' front-plates. Weapons production was 50–60% below replacement level; the armoured regiments had to be reduced from three to two battalions, so that the armoured forces lost their punch. There were no plans to increase munitions production for a Russian campaign continuing into 1942; if the campaign did in fact continue, and production was resumed, it would not become adequate again before the end of 1942.[37]

Halder changed his sanguine view. On 11 August he noted: 'Our last resources have been expended. [. . .] Looking at the situation as a whole, it is becoming ever clearer that we underestimated the Russian colossus, which deliberately prepared for war with the entire absence of restraint proper to totalitarian states.' At the beginning of the campaign, Halder noted, German intelligence had estimated that there were 200 Russian divisions; now the estimate was 360, and when a dozen were annihilated, the Russians put another dozen in their place. The attacking German forces were stretched along an enormously long front without any depth, while the Russians were close to their supply bases.[38]

Halder also knew that winter equipment was available for only 58 divisions of occupying troops, not for the 150 divisions which were likely to be in Russia in December 1941. Almost at the same time, on 16 August, Fieldmarshal Keitel informed the heads of the authorities responsible for armaments and replacements that Hitler planned to disband 50 divisions, including 300,000 veterans of both wars.[39]

It was probably during his journey to the front in July 1941 that Stauffenberg visited Army Group Centre headquarters at Borissov and met the Commander's senior staff officer, Lieutenant-Colonel (GS) Henning von Tresckow, and his special missions officer, Second Lieutenant (Res.) Fabian von Schlabrendorff. The two officers were impressed by their visitor and understood 'that he was a non-Nazi, and indeed saw Hitler and National Socialism as a danger'.[40]

At the end of August Stauffenberg travelled to Army Group North. He gave Halder his findings from his visits to Lieutenant-General Reinhardt's 41st and Lieutenant-General von Manstein's 56th Army Corps. Both were well supplied; the 41st needed only personnel replacements. Upon the conclusion of the current operation – the encirclement of Leningrad – three to four days' rest would be sufficient before the two corps could attack again. General Hoepner, commanding 4th Panzer Group, and Fieldmarshal von Leeb, Commander-in-Chief of Army Group North, offered the same judgement on 31 August.[41]

On 20 September Stauffenberg again gave Halder his views after a visit to 2nd Panzer Group. This formation had suffered heavy losses in the battle for Kiev. Now it had orders to attack Moscow (Operation Typhoon), but it had only about sixty tanks left – not even half the full complement of an armoured division.[42] The 4th Panzer Group under General Hoepner was ordered to join in the attack on Moscow.

The change of fortune became apparent in October even to observers who did not know the details of what had been planned. At the beginning of October Berthold Stauffenberg wrote to his wife that 'things had progressed very well in the east', but that already there had been snowstorms. At the end of the month he wrote, after a telephone conversation with Claus, that advances in the east had become almost impossible because the roads had turned into bottomless quagmires; this was particularly unwelcome because the Russians had not many reserves left and in good weather it would have been possible to advance rapidly.[43] Claus Stauffenberg must have paid another visit to the front meanwhile; on 25 October he received the Royal Bulgarian Medal Fourth Class, First Grade for bravery.[44]

The General Staff hoped for frost to firm up the roads, but, as Berthold wrote to Mika, when the frost came it was so hard that engines would not start, and the vehicles froze into ruts and broke their axles. The mood at Naval High Command was bad, said Berthold, because there was no will to move against the Americans 'who are increasingly intervening in the naval war', thereby diminishing Germany's chances of defeating Britain. Japan's entry into the war would probably lead to war between Germany and the United States, however; and when the whole world was at war, the outcome would be even less foreseeable, but the lawyers' work would decrease.[45]

At the beginning of September Moltke met Claus Stauffenberg's cousin Hans Christoph, Baron von Stauffenberg, who worked in Admiral Canaris's Armed Forces Supreme Command Foreign Countries Group/Counter-intelligence Branch. Moltke was secretly seeking collaborators for a shadow administration that could spring into action after Germany had lost the war, as Moltke had no doubt she would. He asked the Baron: 'Don't you have a cousin in the Führer's Headquarters? Couldn't something be done with him?' The Baron relayed this to Berthold, and after a few weeks brought Moltke Berthold's answer: 'I spoke with Claus. He says we must win the war first. During the war one cannot do that sort of thing, particularly not during a war against the Bolsheviks. But afterwards, when we come home, we shall clean up that brown plague.' Claus Stauffenberg now hoped, as he indicated to Pezold, that the Armed Forces, sweeping from victory to victory, would be able to seize control.[46]

On 19 November Hitler said to Halder that neither of the opposing coalitions could now expect to defeat the other, and raised the subject of peace negotiations.[47] He virtually admitted defeat.

On 9 November Fieldmarshal von Brauchitsch suffered a serious heart attack. He returned to his desk within a few days, but never recovered. Hitler dismissed him on 19 December and himself assumed direct command of the Army. On 23 December he issued a statement in which he claimed to be justified by his successes and demanded obedience 'until the ultimate rescue of the Reich'. He had in fact led the Army into a catastrophic defeat, and he had good reason to fear that the Army commanders would refuse to obey him. Hitler's personal appeal to the German people to collect winter clothing for the soldiers at the eastern front only strengthened the impression that the leadership had lost control of the situation.[48]

Hitler had often overruled Brauchitsch; now Halder had 'heated altercations' and 'roaring scenes' with Hitler. Hitler wanted the front to hold where it was; his generals wanted to fall back to more tenable positions.[49] Endemic supply problems remained unsolved. If the General Staff Organisation Branch set aside equipment for ten new divisions, the SS or Air Force might appropriate it because their commander-in-chief had better contacts with Hitler. Stauffenberg ironically suggested making Himmler, the SS Leader, Commander-in-Chief of the Army – then he would have to look after it. But at Christmas time, in his annual letter to his old comrades in the 6th Panzer Division, Stauffenberg encouraged them to look to the future with hope, even though the situation seemed desperate; Japan's entry into the war compensated for the state of war between Germany and America.[50] There is strong evidence that Stauffenberg believed at this time that the war in Russia could still be won.

Major (GS) Ulrich Bürker, Blomberg's son-in-law, had served with Stauffenberg in the 6th Panzer Division and for some months in 1940/41 in the General Staff Training Branch; he was now senior staff officer in the 10th Panzer Division, which belonged to 4th Panzer Group. Bürker reported on the state of his division to 40th Corps Command on 9, 15 and 30 November. At the same time he sent the same information directly to Stauffenberg, because his reports to Corps Command since mid-October had had no effect. On 2 and 4 December Bürker, by order of his divisional commander, reported both to Corps Command and to Stauffenberg that the men had been in combat without interruption since 2 October – day and night since 19 November – and had become apathetic; when their own artillery fired they would advance a few yards and then sink down exhausted. It was bitter to have to give up so close to the goal (Msocow), but the division was unable to attack any more. The combat strength of No. 86 Mounted Infantry Regiment consisted of 7 officers, 44 non-commissioned officers and 186 men, 18 machine-guns, 3 anti-tank guns, 3 light infantry artillery pieces and 2 heavy mortars; No. 69 Mounted Infantry Regiment had 5 officers, 55 non-commissioned officers and 313 men with 41 machine-guns, 3 anti-tank guns, 7 light infantry artillery pieces, 1 heavy infantry artillery piece and 4 heavy mortars. On 2 October No. 7 Panzer Regiment had started out with 180 tanks. Now, the remnants of the regiment were led by the sole remaining captain; they had 7 Mark II tanks, 14 Mark IIIs and 7 Mark IVs. There was no effective defence against the heavy tanks of the Red Army. The corps commander passed the report up to 4th Panzer Group, whereupon the division's withdrawal was initiated.[51] Bürker added that fragments of the division had been assigned to as many other divisions and corps; the divisional staff was directing traffic at Gshatsk, and it would be better to dissolve the division altogether and use the battle-seasoned (but tankless) tank crews, the experienced (but gunless) armoured-artillery men, the maintenance technical sergeants and infantry commanders as cadres for new divisions. But Hitler opposed such ideas 'for political and propaganda reasons', refusing to admit openly that any German formations had been annihilated.[52]

Major (GS) Staedke, who since August 1941 had been senior staff officer in the 20th Panzer Division, wrote to Stauffenberg from Rusa on 5 January 1942 describing more or less the same conditions. He made more direct reproaches aimed at Stauffenberg's own branch as well as 'the leadership' at large. The supply requirements for the Russian campaign, he complained, had been sloppily calculated; available German forces and enemy forces had been misjudged; winter equipment could not be organised by collecting furs and woollens from the civilian population in January![53]

Another report from Bürker, this time to Major (GS) Golling in the General Staff Training Branch, gave an embittered account of mistakes and disregarded warnings as the frost had set in. The division had been too weak to continue the thrust toward Moscow, having come within 20 kilometres of the city, with its flanks exposed because adjacent divisions had not kept up. 'Then, on 28 October I wrote my first warning letter to you, and also to Tresckow, Stauffenberg and Bernuth. I followed this up with detailed reports on fighting power to corps command on 9, 15 and 30 November, copies of which went to *Stauffenberg* at the same time. All of them concluded that the rapid decline of our fighting power made it necessary to *limit the objectives*.' And again: 'I kept Stauffenberg constantly informed.' Unfortunately, all his warnings had been proven accurate. Since written reports were undoubtedly consigned to the waste-basket, Bürker added, an officer from the General Staff ought to visit the division – which after all had been the practice during the summer.[54]

Baroness von Lerchenfeld wrote to her son-in-law at General Staff headquarters, remarking that her husband did not understand some of the recent events. Stauffenberg replied on 11 January 1942. The year had not begun auspiciously, he conceded, and there was no hope of peace in 1942. But none of the rumours surrounding Brauchitsch's departure was true: it was not connected with the woollens collection, although it must look that way. The winter clothing for the troops in the east had been ready in time, it was only a question of transport. The current woollens collection was designed to replace losses and 'to supply replacement troops and convalescents, and to improve regulation equipment'. It would have been better to build up reserves earlier, Stauffenberg wrote, conceding that such reserves had been lacking; but the proposal from Army High Command had been disregarded.

Stauffenberg's frustration with the procedures in his area of responsibility has been noted.[55] But there is no direct evidence that he knew that twenty railway trains were used to send Jews from German cities and from Prague to Lodz between 15 October and 4 November 1941.[56]

The situation at the front, Stauffenberg continued in his letter, was undoubtedly 'difficult', and it had to be mastered by using every last resource. There had never been a war without setbacks. In this case no individual was to blame: the deeper reason for the difficulties lay in the incorrect estimate of the Soviet Union's material capacities. 'They were underestimated by all of us. That the Soviet Union was militarily close to collapse after the battles of Kiev, Bryansk and Vyazma I do not doubt even today.' The mud made it impossible to exploit the successes, and when the muddy weather ended the Soviets brought up newly organised formations. But it was right to continue the attempt to defeat the enemy. 'Full victory was so close that everything had to be staked on one card. The risk was of course that much greater.'[57]

In April 1942 Stauffenberg met Brigadier von Loeper in Wuppertal. Loeper told him that when his 10th Infantry Division had arrived outside Moscow in December, with only a tenth of its vehicles left, Halder had ordered him to continue the thrust eastward for another six hundred kilometres to Gorki. Stauffenberg still maintained that 'everything had to be staked on one card' to win such a critical prize as the enemy's capital. He evidently accepted that Hitler's demonic will was appropriate to the situation, in spite of his own professional knowledge of the German forces' physical limitations. Stauffenberg's forebear, Gneisenau, had likewise disregarded rational calculations when opposing Napoleon's crushingly superior forces; but he probably would not have agreed with Stauffenberg that Russia could be defeated on her own soil.[58] In April 1942 Stauffenberg still believed that the situation on the east front could be mastered, or at least stabilised. Longer than many of his fellow officers on the General Staff he went on wrestling with the question of how the Soviet Union might be defeated.[59] But he evidently no longer believed the war could be won. At the same time he remained critical of Hitler. He agreed with Loeper that Hitler had finally abolished the rule of law when he had declared himself (on 26 April) supreme judge and above all legal statutes.[60]

In his letter to his mother-in-law Stauffenberg repeated that Brauchitsch's dismissal was not as grave a matter as it appeared; for some time the Führer had reserved for himself most decisions on the conduct of the war – this was 'in the nature of such a superior and strongwilled personage'. The Commander-in-Chief of the Army had been wedged between the Führer and the General Staff and this had produced frictions, particularly when a campaign 'did not go according to plan'. Moreover, Brauchitsch had lately suffered several nasty heart attacks and had resigned of his own accord. Now the General Staff was working better than before, and thanks to 'the new solution' (Hitler acting as Commander-in-Chief of the Army) it had become possible to marshal all national resources for the Army's decisive battle.[61]

In the first few days after the change Stauffenberg maintained the same view in heated debate with his brother Alexander, his cousin Clemens Count Stauffenberg, Captain (GS) Wilhelm Bürklin of General Staff Foreign Armies West Branch and Peter Sauerbruch: the view that the Army could much better hold its own against Hitler if it was under his direct command. Stauffenberg went so far as to say that Hitler's personal command was a gift to the Army. He was evidently reflecting the feelings of the Chief of the General Staff himself, who at first seemed revitalised after Brauchitsch's departure and thought Hitler's being in direct command was 'beneficial'.[62] There is no reason to think that Stauffenberg did not mean what he said.

Stauffenberg's views were not exceptional, and not especially sanguine. His older cousin Cäsar von Hofacker, who strongly deprecated aspects of the regime's policies, likewise did not think Germany's military situation was hopeless. The sacrifices in blood made his heart ache, he wrote to his wife; not being at the front depressed him. But there was no reason to think that all was lost. The crisis was not over, but there could be 'no doubt that we shall *hold* the east front', and it did not matter if that front was a hundred kilometres farther east or west. 'It is a defeat. But *by no means* a decisive one.' If the leadership learned to practise moderation, then perhaps 'we shall regain the reins of world events and bring things to a good conclusion after all'.[63] Like Stauffenberg, Hofacker differentiated between their country's vital interests and its dubious leadership.

Major (GS) Bürker travelled to General Staff headquarters at 'Mauerwald' at the beginning of February and personally handed in the report on his division to the Operations Branch. He made a call on Stauffenberg, who had written to him at length and had convinced him that the assessments made by Bürker and the divisional commander, Brigadier Wolfgang Fischer, were understood and shared in Organisation Branch. Upon his return to the front Bürker wrote to Stauffenberg again, on 25 February, that the absurdities had now reached a culmination: 'an infantry battalion on foot' had been assigned to the division, with horse-drawn field kitchens and heavy weapons on sleds: assigned to an armoured division which had been one of the fastest formations with the greatest striking power in the German Army, while all its own cadres were idle or dispersed to other formations! In the second half of April the division was withdrawn and sent to France for reorganisation; Stauffenberg no doubt had a hand in this. In December 1942 the division was deployed in Tunisia.[64]

Bürker's experience was symptomatic. At the end of March 1942, only eight of 162 German divisions in the Soviet Union were ready for action; three more would be ready after a rest. The sixteen armoured divisions together had 140 tanks ready for action, less than the normal complement of one armoured division. By the end of April 1942 the casualties of the

German forces on the east front amounted to a third of their total strength as at 22 June 1941: 1,167,835 officers and men.[65]

It appears that in the spring of 1942 Stauffenberg still believed that matters could be improved by surrounding Hitler with more competent advisers. He suggested to Lieutenant Richard, Baron von Weizsäcker, then working in the Quartermaster-General's Section, who thought the war was lost, that the great pincer movement through southern Russia on the one hand and Iraq and Iran on the other to the Caspian Sea could succeed.[66] But Stauffenberg also uttered sentiments entirely at variance with these views.

His duties included a lecture on command structure, which he delivered to successive classes of the War Academy in Moabit, and later in Hirschberg in Silesia. During the first months of 1941 he developed the habit of introducing the subject by saying the German command structure was even more absurd than what the most qualified General Staff officers could have produced if they had been asked to invent the most absurd command structure possible. Down to 1944 he used to remark in his lectures that he was trying to explain something that he did not himself understand. He would cover a blackboard with names of command headquarters and criss-crossing lines, creating a hopeless maze, step back to survey his work, and ask the audience whether they thought one could possibly win a war with this 'command structure'.[67]

Early in 1942 Lieutenant Julius Speer, who worked under Lieutenant-Colonel (GS) Finckh in the Quartermaster-General Supply Section and had dealings with Stauffenberg on numerous occasions, expressed astonishment at the large photograph of Hitler hanging behind Stauffenberg's desk. Stauffenberg said it was there so that his visitors could see that the man was mad. Then he and Speer talked about how to contain Hitler's recklessness. Stauffenberg said finally: 'There is only once solution. It is to kill him.' But both agreed that this would have to be arranged by some prominent person who could immediately seize full powers over the state and the Armed Forces, completely excluding Party agencies.[68]

From time to time there was a good deal of talk among General Staff officers about 'changing the command structure', and about Hitler's numerous inappropriate interventions in military operations. But in Stauffenberg's case it was not just angry talk. He despised inconsequential criticism. Colsman put it thus: 'Stauffenberg considered Hitler an enemy worthy of his steel.'[69]

8

Stauffenberg turns against Hitler

On 2 June 1942 Stauffenberg reported to the Chief of the General Staff, General Halder on his visit to the Commander-in-Chief of the 6th Army, Lieutenant-General Friedrich Paulus, and to divisions in that army. Stauffenberg said he had been impressed by the German offensive successes, and believed the front could be stabilised. But he did not believe the war could be won militarily.[1]

After his visit Stauffenberg wrote to Paulus and described what he thought it meant to be a soldier. He thanked Paulus for his hospitality and continued: 'The days in and around Kharkov and the contacts with all the divisions I visited gave great joy and "much encouragement".' His visit had reminded him what one missed when one was not in the field, but in surroundings where the limits of every action were always immediately apparent and were 'by no means always based on factual considerations'. It was 'refreshing' to visit the front 'where the supreme commitment is made without hesitation, where life is sacrificed without grumbling, whereas the leaders and exemplars bicker over prestige or lack the courage to stand up for a view, or a conviction, that affects the lives of thousands.'[2] Stauffenberg was growing increasingly bitter about the inconstancy of senior commanders from the front who announced that they had come to General Staff headquarters to tell Hitler the plain truth, but never did.[3]

In mid-July Hitler moved his headquarters to camp 'Wehrwolf' in a patch of woodland near Vinnitsa in the Ukraine, and the General Staff headquarters to facilities nearby, where they remained until the end of October.[4]

Stauffenberg's Organisation Branch group was working on directives for armaments production, which had to be channelled through the office of the Chief of Army Equipment. They dealt with tank tracks, with penetration of shells, spare-parts production, re-equipment of formations, organisation of personnel replacements, creation of snow-removal units. In August 1942 – three years after Stauffenberg's post-action report of 1939 – the Army Staff, Quartermaster General and Organisation Branch jointly requested the creation of a central authority to co-ordinate everything to do with repairs

37. On a trip from 'Mauerwald' headquarters to Vinnitsa in the Ukraine, summer 1942. Stauffenberg, Lieutenant-Colonel (GS) Coelestin von Zitzewitz (centre) and Colonel (GS) Reinhard Gehlen (back to camera)

and spare parts. But the Supreme Command of the Armed Forces always created and expanded agencies that parallelled those of the General Staff, such as the Armed Forces Supreme Command Organisation Branch, making a mockery of any unity of command structure.[5] On 8 October Stauffenberg signed a draft order entitled 'Basic Order No. 1 (To Raise Combat Strength)' – apparently with ironic intent, since the first part of the title was identical with Hitler's directive that nobody was to know of any secret matters unless it was necessary, and even then he was to know no more, and no sooner, than he must.[6] Stauffenberg decreed a 10% reduction of personnel in the Army High Command and in army-group, army and army-corps commands, and a reduction of service and supply personnel and artillery crews 'as the Russians did long ago'; he also prohibited postings of troops from the field to higher command headquarters or administrative centres: 'Postings from the front to the rear are forbidden and will be replaced by postings from the rear to the front.'[7]

38. Stauffenberg and Mertz von Quirnheim at the Vinnitsa headquarters, 1942

Meanwhile Hitler prepared to attempt what the officers of the 1st Light Division had practised as a wargame in May 1939: to secure oil for the operations in the east from Baku on the Caspian Sea. But Hitler ruined his own plan by overextending available forces. Although plans showed that there were not enough resources for the summer offensives against the Soviet Union, men and material were drawn away from the eastern front to support operations in North Africa, aimed at tying up large forces belonging to Russia's western allies. Furthermore, in July 1942 Hitler took a fateful decision. Army High Command had planned an offensive towards Stalingrad on the lower Volga ('Operation Blue'). On 17 July Hitler split this offensive into two thrusts, one aimed at Stalingrad and the other at Rostov; on 23 July he ordered that, simultaneously with the attack on Stalingrad, the Caucasus must be brought under German control and Baku taken. Control of Stalingrad, on the lower Volga, was a strategic precondition for the Caucasus offensive, which might otherwise be cut off from its supply lines by a Soviet counter-offensive. But now the German forces had to prosecute both operations at the same time.[8] The Soviets retreated before the German offensive until the German thrust ran out of manpower, fuel and other supplies. The tanks could not force the Caucasus passes; during the winter the German forces had to retrace their two-thousand kilometre advance from the Terek to Kharkov – past the graves of thousands of their fallen comrades. Control of the city of Stalingrad was not a military necessity, but it became a matter of prestige for both dictators. However, once Hitler had made the error of splitting up 'Operation Blue' the position just west of the Volga had to be held until the retreat of the 1st Panzer Army from the Caucasus had been secured. When Hitler made his fateful decision, General Halder resolved to bring about his own dismissal (Hitler did not allow resignations). He received it, after several serious clashes with Hitler, on 24 September 1942. He was succeeded by Lieutenant-General Kurt Zeitzler, previously Chief of the General Staff in Army Group D.[9]

All this had been predictable, and predicted. German forces on the east front would be short of 800,000 men by 1 November 1942, and 1.2 million by the spring of 1943. The General Staff Organisation Branch war diary recorded as early as mid-September 1942 that 'a successful resumption of the offensive in North Africa can no longer be expected and the operations north of the Caucasus aimed at tying up strong Anglo-American forces in the Near East will not be effective this year.' In mid-October 1942 the army groups in the east 'were informed that from now on they could not count on replacements in any numbers worth mentioning.'[10] The great pincer strategy had collapsed in its initial stages.

At the end of 1942 the Führer's Headquarters and the heads of Armed Forces Operations Staff moved with Hitler to the Berchtesgaden area where Hitler had his 'Berghof' country house. The General Staff, however, moved back to 'Mauerwald' in East Prussia, so that the two vital military command centres were a thousand kilometres apart. The diary of the General Staff Organisation Branch, where Stauffenberg was in charge of such matters, noted: 'The separation (from the beginning of the crisis in Africa to the end of November) of the Führer's Headquarters from Army High Command headquarters reveals frictions and difficulties in the command structure. The intersecting lines of command are described in a report by Organisation Branch.' This led to a memorandum by Organisation Branch concerning the Army's command structure. Its contents were agreed at a meeting attended by Stauffenberg, Brigadier Schmundt, Lieutenant-General Buhle and Brigadier Friedrich Hofmann.[11]

The idea that the nations of the Soviet Union might support the German forces by turning against Stalin's rule found a good deal of favour in the German Army. It would have been the reverse of the process whereby the Third Supreme Army Command, with the aid of Lenin, had precipitated the Russian Revolution of 1917, leading to the Treaty of Brest-Litovsk which took Russia out of the First World War. The experts in the Foreign

Office, the General Staff and the Ministry for the Occupied Eastern Territories all agreed that the Soviet Union could be defeated only with the aid of its own population.[12]

In February 1942 Captain Hasso von Etzdorf, Foreign Office liaison officer to the General Staff, minuted proposals by the head of Quarter-master-General Group II (war administration), Major (GS) Hans-Georg Schmidt von Altenstadt, and his assistant, Captain (GS) Otto Hinrich Bleicken, 'for the subversion of Soviet resistance (eastern propaganda)': 1. Whoever could solve the land question would win over the Russian people, as the Bolsheviks did after 1917. 2. Use the national aspirations of the non-Russian peoples. 3. Since the Russian people were accustomed to following their governments in blind obedience, the establishment of separate puppet regimes in Ukraine and Caucasia was likely to fragment the Soviet state; the ultimate struggle against Bolshevism must be fought in the depths of the Asiatic territories by Russian forces. 4. Harness the religious needs of the population.[13]

In October 1941 two Turkish generals appeared in Army High Command headquarters to suggest organising a formation of Turkish-Muslim volunteers from (Soviet) Muslim prisoners-of-war to fight on the German side against the Red Army. As a result Armenian, Azerbaijan, Georgian, Turkestan and Volga-Tatar legions were formed in Poland in November 1941.[14] Hitler permitted these formations at first, in view of the desperate situation of December 1941 and January 1942; but in February 1942 he prohibited the organisation of any more.[15] In the twilight of uncertain policies, many formations were in fact raised for work behind the German front, and even to fight at the front.[16]

From spring 1942 Stauffenberg was convinced that the Soviet Union could not be defeated by Germany alone, nor by conventional military operations, but only with the support of the population. Others had observed this before him. Brauchitsch had understood it before his dismissal, and so had the senior staff officer in Army Group Centre command, Colonel (GS) von Tresckow, and the intelligence officer there, Major (GS) Baron von Gersdorff. Their view was shared by the chief of General Staff Foreign Armies East Branch, Lieutenant-Colonel (GS) Reinhard Gehlen, and his colleagues.[17] Large numbers among the nations under Soviet domination had welcomed German forces as liberators. This changed when hundreds of thousands of Soviet prisoners-of-war starved to death. Of the total 5.7 million in German custody during the war, 2 million were dead before 28 February 1942, 3.3 million by the end of the war. Executions, exploitation and brutal oppression were the order of the day in many parts of German-occupied Soviet territory. Guerilla ('partisan') bands grew to divisional and even army strength in vast unoccupied wooded pockets behind the German front. The Red Army fought better and better, the

Ukrainian and other volunteers on the German side fought poorly or not at all.[18]

Stauffenberg, aided by the Quartermaster General, Major-General Eduard Wagner, Schmidt von Altenstadt, Professor Gerhard von Mende and Captain (Res.) Otto Bräutigam of the Reich Ministry for the Occupied Eastern Territories, drew up an Organisation Branch order establishing equality for the volunteers in terms of uniform, care, pay, quarters and deployment.[19] Stauffenberg and the other General Staff officers involved succeeded in keeping the volunteers largely under Armed Forces control and out of the clutches of the anti-Slav SS. Stauffenberg also managed to organise more volunteer auxiliaries than Armed Forces Supreme Command would allow, and he succeeded in getting Lieutenant-General Ernst Köstring, the former Military Attaché in Moscow, appointed as General in Charge of Caucasus Affairs to keep the region under Army control and to keep out the black-shirted thugs and the 'brown plague' of Party bosses.[20]

In a conversation with Gehlen's assistant, Major (GS) Heinz Danko Herre, in April 1942 Stauffenberg expressed outrage at the brutal treatment of the civilian population in the German-occupied Soviet Union, the mass murder of 'racially inferior' persons, especially Jews, and the mass starvation of Soviet prisoners-of-war.[21]

In May 1942 Stauffenberg was informed of the mass murder of Jews by Lieutenant (Res.) Hans Herwarth von Bittenfeld, a former member of the German embassy in Moscow who had served in the campaigns in Poland and Russia and since March 1942 had been working in Foreign Office Section XIII (occupied and unoccupied USSR) under the former Ambassador Friedrich Werner, Count Schulenburg. Also in May 1942, Stauffenberg and Herwarth received an eye-witness report from an officer about how some SS men had rounded up the Jews in a Ukrainian town, led them to a field, made them dig their own mass grave, and then shot them. Upon hearing this report Stauffenberg said that Hitler must be removed. He believed that the senior commanders had the duty to put this into effect.[22]

At the end of June 1942 Major (GS) von Pezold, who was now working with the General Staff Foreign Armies East Branch, told Stauffenberg of a remark made to him by Fritz-Dietlof, Count Schulenburg, at the Berlin Bristol hotel on 22 June: 'we have won over Witzleben'. Pezold had answered that a coup d'état would be irresponsible because if there was internal fighting the fronts would collapse. But, Pezold continued, Schulenburg was such a radical that he might actually do something. Stauffenberg replied: 'Oh, never mind the little bomb-throwers.'[23] But from summer 1942 onwards, Stauffenberg uttered with growing frequency his verdict that 'the foolish and criminal' Führer must be overthrown.

A friend from Bamberg days, Major (Res.) Dietz, Baron von Thüngen, who served on the General Staff during 1942 and part of 1943, remarked on

Stauffenberg's many telephone conversations, and Stauffenberg responded by broaching the subject: 'You seem to believe that I am engaged in conspiracy here.' Then he said that things could not go on as they were, but the change that must come had to be 'new', not a 'restoration': history could not be turned back. Once in the casino of the Vinnitsa headquarters he said, referring to the regime: 'We must do away with that lot.'[24]

In August 1942 Major (GS) Oskar-Alfred Berger succeeded Lieutenant-Colonel (GS) Mertz von Quirnheim as head of Organisation Branch Group IV. Stauffenberg and Berger often went for two-hour rides together. During the second or third outing, in August 1942, Stauffenberg said suddenly: 'They are shooting Jews in masses. These crimes must not be allowed to continue.'[25]

Soon after this Stauffenberg told Berger about Halder's 1938 coup plan, which had been foiled by the Munich Agreement. After a while Stauffenberg was talking about tyrannicide during nearly every outing. He cited St Thomas Aquinas, who had declared that tyrannicide was permissible and meritorious in certain circumstances. He spoke of the Holy Reich, the remainder of which was in danger of being destroyed. Berger objected that tyrannicide was still murder, and that one could not bring about a better order by murder.[26]

During those weeks Stauffenberg also went riding with Lieutenant-Colonel (GS) Burkhart Mueller-Hillebrand, his Branch chief from April to October 1942. When the conversation turned to Hitler's frequent defamations of the officer corps, Stauffenberg said it was time that an officer went over there with a pistol and shot the dirty fink.[27]

Berger's and others' reactions to his attacks on Hitler showed Stauffenberg that no one on the General Staff wanted to take part in any drastic action against the Führer. There was some discussion among them about prevailing upon Hitler to relinquish his personal command of the Army, to effect 'a change in the command structure'. Berger, Heusinger, Stauffenberg and Colonel (GS) Helmuth Stieff, Mueller-Hillebrand's successor from October 1942, even considered writing a joint memorandum, but they never got round to it.[28]

Between 11 and 20 September 1942 Stauffenberg visited the 162nd Infantry Division in order to gain direct information on the raising of Turkic battalions. In the words of his uncle, Lieutenant-Colonel Count Üxküll, 'the whole organisation is Claus's child'.[29]

Count Üxküll had long wished for a field command. This was difficult to arrange because he was sixty-six years old, had received his basic and tactical training at the end of the previous century, had served in staff positions, and had not been in active service between the wars. Through Stauffenberg's efforts, Count Üxküll was posted with the 'eastern legions' on 10 September 1942, and was given command of the Azerbaijan Legion in the 162nd

Infantry Division in October. On his way to his new post, Count Üxküll visited his nephew at the Army High Command headquarters at Vinnitsa on 23 and 24 September. In the next few days they drove to divisional headquarters together; Stauffenberg returned to Vinnitsa on 28 September.[30]

Stauffenberg also visited Lieutenant-General von Sodenstern, Chief of the General Staff of Army Group B command (OC General von Weichs) in Starobielsk. He spoke with him for two hours. Sodenstern gathered that among the Army leaders who were not engaged directly at the front there was a new will to put a halt to Hitler's irrational and criminal conduct of the war, and to open negotiations with the western allies. Stauffenberg referred to 'the common fundamental ideals' and sought to win Sodenstern's support for, and participation in, such action. Sodenstern declined; his understanding of the military ethos did not permit mutiny in the face of the enemy. But he assured Stauffenberg that whatever the methods used to bring about a new regime, the Army Group would continue to discharge its duty at the front, and suggested that he would be able to take a more supportive position if he had a home command.[31]

In the same month, still before 23 September, Stauffenberg visited 40th Panzer Corps headquarters in a hut on the Terek, between the Black Sea and the Caspian. The corps, part of the 1st Panzer Army in Army Group A, was commanded by Lieutenant-General Geyr von Schweppenburg from June to 27 September. Their advance had stalled for lack of fuel. Stauffenberg and the 1st special missions staff officer, Captain Johann Dietrich von Hassell, a son of the former ambassador in Rome and later one of the leading conspirators against Hitler, agreed on the gravity of Hitler's mistake of splitting the Stalingrad and Baku operations. Then Geyr called Stauffenberg into his room. Stauffenberg got no further with him than he had with Sodenstern.[32] He flew on to General von Kleist's 1st Panzer Army headquarters at Shelesnovodsk.[33]

In the days after Halder's dismissal (24 September 1942), the chief of Organisation Branch, Lieutenant-Colonel (GS) Mueller-Hillebrand, held a meeting in his office with Stauffenberg and Captain (GS) Bleicken of Quartermaster-General War Administration Branch. Stauffenberg presented the subjects for the meeting, giving a shocking description of the field army personnel situation. The immediate occasion was Hitler's order to constitute ten Air Force mounted-infantry 'field divisions': because of an intervention by Göring, these divisions, contrary to original intentions, were not to be used for replacements on the eastern front. But the Army had to fully equip the new divisions with vehicles equivalent to the needs of four or five armoured divisions. Bleicken demanded to know who was responsible for withholding the urgently needed replacements from the field army and wanted Hitler to be told 'the truth'. At this point Stauffenberg jumped to his feet and shouted: 'Hitler is responsible. No fundamental change is possible unless he is removed. I am ready to do it.'[34]

It was mortally dangerous, even in the Army, to fail to report people who uttered such sentiments, and, of course, more so to utter them. More than 1000 German soldiers were put to death by order of courts martial in 1942 alone. About 300 Allied soldiers were killed by order of American, British and French courts martial during the entire Second World War.[35] Stauffenberg's superior officer, Mueller-Hillebrand, was a witness to Stauffenberg's threat. Bleicken immediately gave his special missions staff officer, Second Lieutenant (Res.) Walther Bussmann, an account of the meeting 'so I can refer to it later'. Bussmann did exactly the same by giving his university teacher an account.[36] It is unknown whether or not Mueller-Hillebrand reported the incident to Lieutenant-General Zeitzler, or whether Bleicken reported it to his superior officer. Bleicken's and Bussmann's depositions indicate, at any rate, that both took Stauffenberg's threat seriously.

While Stauffenberg deprecated the inconsequential talk of 'the little bomb-throwers', once he had decided to act he acted more firmly than other opponents of the Führer. Having failed to find anyone to lead or initiate a revolt, he declared himself ready to do it himself and looked for an opportunity.[37] Halder, Mueller-Hillebrand or Heusinger could have taken Stauffenberg along with them to a briefing with Hitler, but did not. If Stauffenberg did not ask them, it was because he knew he did not have their support; if he did ask them, they were silent about it after the war and had reason to be. Halder would say only that he had been aware of the direction his 'intimates', especially 'the passionate youth', were taking after his departure in September 1942 – namely, that they 'would be increasingly pushed onto the path of assassination'.[38] After the war Heusinger testified, in Halder's defence against the charge of having supported Hitler in his criminal courses, that the question of Hitler's 'removal' had 'naturally' occupied him and his colleagues on the General Staff 'a good deal and frequently'; but they had realised that they would have met only with lack of understanding from the population and the Armed Forces, and would have been accused of treason.[39]

In October 1942 Lieutenant-Colonel (GS) Schmidt von Altenstadt chaired a meeting of some forty General Staff officers. They heard reports on German agricultural policy in the east. Alexander Stauffenberg's brother-in-law Otto Schiller, formerly Agricultural Attaché in the German Embassy in Moscow and now Administration Counsellor in the Foreign Office Economic Staff East, spoke to the officers about the perniciousness of this policy. In the discussion that followed Stauffenberg said that Germany was sowing hatred and that German crimes would be revenged on the next generation. In view of the insufficiency of human and material resources on the German side, it was clear that the war in the east could only be won with the aid of the population there; it was scandalous that millions of soldiers should be risking their lives daily while no one had the courage to put on his helmet and tell the Führer these things, even though he might pay for this with his life.[40]

Early in December 1942 Colonel Wessel, Baron von Freytag-Loringhoven, the intelligence officer with the Army Group Don command, sent his specialist for indigenous volunteers, Lieutenant (Res.) Karl Michel, from staff headquarters in Kharkov to Stauffenberg at 'Mauerwald' to seek his support. Michel wanted assurances that the 5000 Kalmucks he had raised would not be exploited as mere cannon fodder. Stauffenberg took Michel to Lieutenant-Colonel (GS) Baron von Roenne in Foreign Armies East and declared that the volunteers represented a great hope that a liberated Germany would not fall victim to a Bolshevik dictatorship, since they would help to overthrow it. Stauffenberg thereby conspired against official government policy. Michel recalled Stauffenberg saying that Fate did not honour suffering but action: Germany must be saved from destruction by action.[41]

The Minister for the Occupied Eastern Territories, Rosenberg, called a meeting of eighteen of his own civil servants and fifteen military representatives to be held in the ministry in Berlin on 18 December 1942. On his way to this meeting Herwarth stopped off at 'Mauerwald' and looked up Stauffenberg, who was also going to attend. He found him thoroughly changed. Thus far Stauffenberg and Herwarth had not discussed organised resistance against the regime. Herwarth saw, again, that Stauffenberg no longer thought Hitler's advisers had to be removed, but that Hitler himself was the cause of the evil. But according to Herwarth, Stauffenberg still hoped that senior commanders would take the lead. Stauffenberg himself was about to receive a posting to the front.[42]

The meeting was convened in the ministry's Small Conference Room in the former Soviet embassy at No. 63 Unter den Linden on 18 December at 10.30 a.m. Stauffenberg was there as one of two General Staff representatives. Lieutenant-General Köstring was to speak for Army Group D but sent Lieutenant (Res.) von Herwarth in his stead. Rosenberg in his opening address told the meeting that the occupied territories were to be subordinated to German economic requirements; large non-autonomous regional organisations were being contemplated to discourage independence movements. He acknowledged that the mood among the population was 'strained by the treatment of prisoners-of-war and forced labour'; he intended to report to the Führer on these 'findings' and requested his audience to 'speak freely'.

Lieutenant-General Franz von Roques said, on behalf of Army Group North, that the exploitation of the population by mostly incompetent German rear-area authorities was intolerable: 27,000 farmers in Estonia were being prosecuted for failure to meet delivery quotas, but 24,000 of them owned only one cow; the Army Group required 6000 workers, 6 had volunteered, only 3000 could be forced; all this served only to swell the ranks of the partisans. Lieutenant-General Max von Schenckendorff of Army Group Centre told the same story. A golden opportunity to win over and enlist the population to help remove the Bolshevist yoke had been squandered by unchecked brutalities; instead of supporting the people's desire to be educated and learn German, instead of enlisting them to fight against marauding bands, they were being brutalised. High-ranking Red Army officers and trained parachute agents provided the partisans with superb leadership; labour for German needs was almost unavailable. Colonel (GS) Gustav Gillhausen said on behalf of Army Group B (Ukraine) that people who were asked to risk getting killed fighting for the Germans against the Soviets must be given a good reason – land, positions in government or commerce, home rule. Lieutenant (Res.) von Herwarth read a teletype message from Lieutenant-General Köstring saying that Russia could only be defeated with the help of the Russians. Schmidt von Altenstadt seconded these statements: the population would support the German cause if they were given 'an objective worth dying for'; the Führer was still being venerated in the east to an undreamt-of extent and could even today reverse the course of events by making an appropriate political announcement.

Stauffenberg kept silent. He had no illusions left about what could be done effectively, and what policy Hitler and his henchmen would follow.[43] After Stauffenberg had talked with police and SS authorities in Berlin early in December 1942, to discuss the status of Baltic auxiliary police units, the Organisation Branch war diary recorded: 'The regular police command is prepared to follow suggestions from Army High Command, but points out that this depends on the Reich SS Leader's decision. They hint that he is probably pursuing objectives which would make it difficult to achieve the arrangement the Army High Command is seeking.'[44]

In any case, Stauffenberg was now launched on another course. In this it appears that he was reflecting the view of the Chief of the General Staff, as he had done in January in his letter to his mother-in-law: because he could not accomplish what he believed to be necessary, he had been seeking to remove himself from the General Staff, just when Halder was doing the same thing.[45] Stauffenberg had for some time been hoping for a posting to an armoured division in the field. Evidently he had been making active efforts to obtain such a posting, for Frank wrote to Berthold on 18 July: 'It is bitter for Claus to be kept away from where he is really at home.'[46] On 23 July Stauffenberg wrote to Karl Josef Partsch that, as Partsch probably knew from Berthold, his wish for a field posting had not yet been fulfilled. 'The strain of working at the centre is not easy to bear in the long term – less because of the workload than for other reasons.'[47]

In November 1942 Count Üxküll wrote to his wife of Claus's wish for a posting as senior staff officer with a panzer division, adding that Stauffenberg's superiors were not likely to let him go. But by this time Stauffenberg had spoken out so often in favour of Hitler's removal that his presence on the General Staff was dangerous to his colleagues as much as to himself. He told his wife that 'he had got himself into some tight corners' and must retreat to the front for a time.[48] When he arrived at his new post, in mid-February 1943, he told his divisional commander that he had got into hot water at General Headquarters and was glad to be far away in Africa.[49]

General Zeitzler ordered Stauffenberg's field posting in the autumn of 1942.[50] In October or November Stauffenberg discussed with his brother Berthold the potential consequences for his family, for his friends and for Stefan George's legacy, but also his fruitless efforts to find allies against Hitler in the upper ranks of the Army.[51]

On 22 November 1942 Lieutenant-Colonel Henning von Blomberg, commander of No. 190 Panzer Battalion, fell in battle near Mateur in Tunisia. He had been Blomberg's only surviving son: his brother, Major Axel von Blomberg, had been shot down over Bagdad. Following established practice, Blomberg's son-in-law, Colonel (GS) Bürker, senior staff officer in the 10th Panzer Division in Tunisia, was withdrawn from the front on 15 December; he left his post on 5 January 1943.[52] His successor was Major (GS) Wilhelm Bürklin. Bürklin was badly wounded on 1 February 1943; on 3 or 4 February Stauffenberg received his orders to take over as senior staff officer in the 10th Panzer Division. It appears that Stauffenberg's posting had been deferred and Bürklin had been substituted, for on 27 December, at 'Mauerwald', Stauffenberg had told Herwarth that he was about to take up a posting as senior staff officer of an armoured division, and Berthold had told Frank (probably at the same time, and certainly well before 20 January) that Claus's wish to lead a panzer division was to be fulfilled.[53] It was also during this time, most likely in January, that Brigadier Oster and Lieutenant-General Olbricht told their fellow conspirator Hans Bernd Gisevius, a military counter-intelligence agent in the German consulate in Zürich, 'that Stauffenberg had now seen the light and was participating.'[54]

In the weeks after Halder's retirement, between the end of September and the end of 1942, Stauffenberg visited the former Chief of the General Staff at his house in Berlin. Halder later recalled being surprised at this, because he had settled with those who shared his views that they were not to keep in touch because he was being watched by the Gestapo: quite naturally, in a dictatorship the contacts of the erstwhile mighty who had fallen would come under suspicion. Halder also said he was 'concerned' for Stauffenberg.

Stauffenberg told Halder that he was in Berlin to talk with his brother Berthold because he faced some crucial personal decisions. He could not

39. Frank Mehnert at the front in Russia, February 1943

bear it in Army High Command any longer; since Halder had left, all efforts
to oppose Hitler had ceased, and one could no longer speak openly but could
only look on as Germany went to her destruction. He wanted to request a
field posting because he could no longer endure the psychological strain.[55] It
may also be assumed that Stauffenberg attempted to enlist Halder in a plot
against Hitler.[56]

Stauffenberg's activities in January 1943 had an almost palpable connec-
tion with the existing anti-Hitler conspiracy. Cryptic remarks in Count
Üxküll's letters to his wife point in that direction: whether or not Count
Üxküll would be given leave depended 'on Claus's view of things'; 'I shall
explain that to you some day'.[57] Older and younger conspirators held a
co-ordination meeting at Peter, Count Yorck's house in Lichterfelde on 8
January. Beck, Goerdeler, Hassell, Popitz, Jessen, Moltke, Yorck, Trott,
Schulenburg and Gerstenmaier were in attendance.[58] Goerdeler, Olbricht
and Tresckow met in Berlin on 25 January to co-ordinate plans for a
coup-d'état.[59] While these meetings took place, Lieutenant-Colonel (GS)
Reerink visited Stauffenberg at 'Mauerwald' on 14 January. Stauffenberg

told Reerink how the General Staff had striven to persuade Hitler to order a retreat by the 6th Army. They talked about the tragedy of the 6th Army, and how Göring had guaranteed that it would be supplied by air; Stauffenberg pronounced Göring a traitor. About the same time Stauffenberg told his friend Major (Res.) Baron von Thüngen that the Army leadership was also the leadership of the nation, 'and we shall take control of this leadership'.[60]

In November 1942 General Beck wrote to Fieldmarshal von Manstein, describing the wider strategic position as hopeless, and urging the consequences. Manstein replied that he agreed with Beck's assessment of the situation, but that a war was lost only if one gave it up as lost – and he thought that the war could still end in a draw.[61]

Tresckow visited Manstein at his 11th Army headquarters at Vitebsk on 16 November 1942 and spoke with him for two hours. Stauffenberg must have told Tresckow about the Air Force field divisions scandal, for Tresckow told Manstein that Göring had withheld 170,000 men from the front. Manstein asked Tresckow if he knew of a suitable special missions staff officer for him; Tresckow suggested Lieutenant (Res.) Alexander Stahlberg, who was related by marriage to Schlabrendorff and was a distant cousin of Tresckow's. Stahlberg remembers that on 17 November, just before he began work under Manstein, Tresckow told him to remember the names of Stauffenberg and Fellgiebel. This suggests that Tresckow had a hand in putting Stauffenberg in touch with Manstein.[62]

The ostensible context was the command structure and replacements. The impending doom of the 6th Army at Stalingrad made the topic acutely relevant. Lieutenant-General Hans Valentin Hube, OC 14th Panzer Corps, who saw Manstein frequently in those days, sought to suggest to Hitler and Zeitzler in December and January that losses of this magnitude threatened the prestige of a head of state, and in a telephone call to Zeitzler on 19 January Hube suggested that it would be better if the Führer put someone else in direct command of the Army.[63] Manstein, who since 20 November 1942 had been Commander-in-Chief of Army Group Don, wrote to Zeitzler on 22 January and urged that Hitler give up trying to be everything from political leader and war lord to field commander, show some confidence in his generals, and accept *one* advisor (the Chief of the General Staff) for the conduct of the war on all fronts.[64]

On 26 January 1943 Manstein received Brigadier Schmundt, the Führer's Chief Adjutant and Chief of Army Personnel; Lieutenant-General Erich Fellgiebel, Chief of Armed Forces and Army Communications; and Major (GS) Count Stauffenberg of the General Staff Organisation Branch at his headquarters in Taganrog. According to war diary entries, Schmundt was with Manstein for two hours and twenty minutes, Fellgiebel for ten minutes, and Stauffenberg for three-quarters of an hour. Contrary to the custom followed in the official diary, there is not even a hint of what was discussed.[65] But Manstein recorded in his private diary:

> 26.1. Schmundt came with Fellgiebel and Stauffenberg. Long talks in which I tried to convey the need to create a unified Armed Forces command, meaning that the Führer must choose a Chief of the General Staff whom he really trusts. I emphasised quite sharply that it was wholly inappropriate to think that the Führer might relinquish command of the Army: for one thing he would never do it, and for another, all confidence is focussed on his person. I said especially to Schmundt that immediately after I had heard of Hube's telephone call I had called Heusinger and told him that I distanced myself entirely from it, and that my own view was as here recorded – that is, an opposite one.

Manstein refers to Stauffenberg in familiar terms, equal to those he uses for Schmundt and Fellgiebel. On the following day Manstein spoke again with Schmundt, and apparently also with Fellgiebel, and wrote in his private diary:

> Conversation with Schmundt in the same vein as yesterday. I showed him how thus far decisions had always been taken too late, and I emphasised that the Führer must trust his advisors and eliminate any who were irresponsible.
>
> I attempted to make clear to him how, beginning with Blomberg, the Führer had been given a wrong concept of the attitude of the officer corps; that because of this, and because he chose Brauchitsch and Halder, and kept them on in spite of conflicts over the western offensive, the Führer had ceased to believe that his generals too had ability; and that this must be changed.
>
> Fellgiebel wants me to urge myself upon the Führer as Chief of the General Staff. That is out of the question. My being posted there would make sense only if I were invited – that is, if the necessary confidence were placed in me, without which my advice on operations would not be accepted. Any attempt to obtrude myself, if only by seeking an appointment for a briefing on these matters, would in my view only prevent him in advance from having any confidence in me. Without that one could serve neither the Führer nor the cause.

After the war Manstein nevertheless declared that he had attempted three times what, according to his diary, he rejected: once alone, immediately after the capitulation of the 6th Army at Stalingrad; once together with Fieldmarshal von Kluge in the summer of 1943, after the failed Kursk offensive ('Operation Citadel'); and once more alone in the winter of 1943/1944.[66] Manstein did indeed brief Hitler on 6 February 1943 and attempted to put forward his proposal to make a change in the 'leadership structure', but Hitler immediately assumed full responsibility for Stalingrad and cut Manstein off. On the other two occasions Hitler also rejected Manstein's suggestions, maintaining that he alone, the Führer, enjoyed the confidence of the people and the Army. Manstein, for his part, always refused to go any farther because he believed that a forcible removal of Hitler would very quickly destroy the fighting spirit of the troops.[67]

After the war Manstein declared that Stauffenberg had briefed him on behalf of Organisation Branch on replacements for the armies in Army Group Don. Afterward Stauffenberg had asked to speak to him 'privately', and had raised his concerns regarding Hitler's errors in generalship. Manstein could only agree: a change in military command was urgently desirable; he was thinking in terms of the appointment of a responsible Armed Forces Chief of the General Staff who would be in actual overall command. At the very least, Manstein believed, a Commander-in-Chief East should be appointed. Manstein clearly included his conversation with Stauffenberg in his diary entry for 26 January, and his post-war account only expands it. In the diary he goes on to say that he told Stauffenberg he would try to persuade Hitler to agree to a change. Manstein also recalled that Stauffenberg seemed in despair about all the things he was forced to witness in the Army High Command, and that he therefore advised him to have himself transferred to a General Staff post in the field in order to remove himself from the displeasing milieu of the Führer's Headquarters.[68]

But Stauffenberg was not interested in appeals to Hitler, by individuals or by fieldmarshals and senior commanders, either severally or all together. He sought only Hitler's removal by force. Manstein later once denied this, and on another occasion conceded it. But when Stauffenberg had spoken to him 'privately', he had threatened to have him arrested if he did not stop talking. (This account by Stauffenberg's divisional commander in Tunisia, Brigadier von Broich, of what Stauffenberg had told him is, of course, unimpeachable.)[69] Manstein later denied this, too, but admitted that he had 'warned' Stauffenberg. Stauffenberg had not come to be told to get himself posted to the front. On one occasion the fieldmarshal contemptuously explained that he could not have subordinated himself 'to a lowly major'. But Stauffenberg had not come to ask Manstein to subordinate himself to anyone, nor to join a conspiracy with persons unknown: Stauffenberg did not represent any such persons. Stauffenberg had come to urge Manstein to lead the Army and the Nation in an attempt to end the tyranny and the war.[70]

Stauffenberg was deeply disappointed with the results of his approaches to generals and fieldmarshals. Manstein's answer, he said, was not what one expected from a fieldmarshal. He put it more colourfully to Dietz von Thüngen: 'Those chaps have their pants full or straw in their skulls, they don't want to do anything.'[71]

9

In the front line

On 8 November 1942 American troops, commanded by General Dwight D. Eisenhower, landed at Casablanca, Oran and Algiers. They threatened to establish a staging base for the invasion of Europe and, more immediately, to attack the rear of the German-Italian Africa Corps and cut it off from its remaining supply line through Tunis while it was still facing the British 8th Army. Hitler reacted rapidly to prevent this, and to tie down two Allied armies in North Africa. On 11 November, German forces began to arrive in Tunisia, beginning with several parachute units, bombers and launches, parts of an armoured battalion, a light artillery battalion, and an anti-tank company. The 10th Panzer Division, one of three divisions transferred to Tunisia, reached Naples by rail, then crossed by boat. But 2,000 of its vehicles never left Italy, so it was severely weakened from the start.[1] By the beginning of December the German forces in Tunisia were organised – in intentional overstatement – as the 5th Panzer Army under General Hans-Jürgen von Arnim.[2]

After his visit to Manstein, Stauffenberg returned to 'Mauerwald' for a few days. He came to Berlin on 3 February 1943, the day when the 'Führer's Headquarters' announced that 'the battle of Stalingrad is over'. Stauffenberg expected to begin a short period of leave, during which he would receive orders for his next posting. But he learned on that day or the day after that he was to go to Tunis to replace the 10th Panzer Division's senior staff officer (Ia), Major (GS) Wilhelm Bürklin, who had been badly wounded when he and the divisional commander, Major-General Wolfgang Fischer, drove onto a mine on 1 February (Fischer was killed). Stauffenberg went and collected his Africa uniform.[3]

In the following weeks the anti-Hitler conspiracy feverishly sought to launch a coup. There was much discussion about the lack of a coup leader. Goerdeler did not think much of Manstein and considered Beck a procrastinator; he hoped to persuade the Commander-in-Chief of the Home Army, General Friedrich Fromm, to take the initiative. Lieutenant-General Olbricht was not generally expected to take any initiative. As a conspirator on Fromm's staff put it: Olbricht wanted to 'act' against Hitler when he received orders, Fromm wanted to give orders once 'action' had been taken. Whether Stauffenberg was proposed as a possible coup leader is unclear. The weight of the evidence is that he could not have agreed to a further deferral of his posting to the front; nor is there any evidence that he could have got the requisite key post in the Home Army at that time, nor that any attempt was made to put him there.

Because there was so evidently no alternative, Beck now gave his consent to the assassination of Hitler.[4] The conspirators' efforts produced two assassination attempts in March.[5]

During his brief sojourn in Berlin in the first days of February 1943 Stauffenberg visited his friend Peter Sauerbruch, who was in hospital with jaundice. Sauerbruch had contracted the disease while he was quartermaster of the 14th Panzer Division in the 6th Army, and he had left the field hospital in December 1942 to lead his division westwards over the last passable bridge across the river Don in order to keep it open for an operation to relieve the 6th Army. Stauffenberg talked about the oppressive atmosphere in the General Staff, and commented on his new posting, with despair in his voice: 'This is an escape to the front!'[6]

Before leaving Berlin on 4 February, Stauffenberg and his wife met with Colonel (GS) Bürker in the Kempinski Hotel: Bürker briefed his colleague on his new division. Bürker must have told Stauffenberg that he had himself advised Armed Forces Command Staff on 27 January to exploit the current weakness of the American and British forces in Tunisia by expanding the German bridgehead to the Bône-Tozeur line and by a thrust to Tebessa. Stauffenberg and his wife then left for a two-days' visit to Bamberg and three days at Lautlingen, instead of the three weeks' leave he had originally been given. On a visit with relatives in nearby Wilflingen, Stauffenberg said that if a first-year War Academy student on exercise had done anything analogous to letting the 6th Army become enveloped he would have been sent down; however, once the 6th Army was encircled and unable to break out, capitulation would not have prevented a catastrophe because the Soviets could not have fed and housed the large numbers of prisoners.[7]

On 10 February Stauffenberg travelled to Munich, flew from there to the 10th Panzer Division liaison command at Naples-Bagnoli, and went on to Tunis on 11 February. He visited his wounded predecessor, Major (GS) Bürklin, in the military hospital there and learned more about his division. On 14 February he arrived at the division's command post.[8]

Since 3 February the division had been commanded by Brigadier Friedrich Baron von Broich. Bürklin had been temporarily replaced by Major (GS) Josef Moll, the intelligence officer on the 5th Panzer Army command staff. Stauffenberg took over his duties as senior staff officer immediately upon his arrival, in the midst of an attack called 'Operation Spring Breeze' that had been launched on the previous day. Veterans say that he helped to fan the breeze quite considerably.[9] Moll stayed on until 18 February, after the battle of Sidi Bou Zid. Stauffenberg's aides were the 1st special missions officer Lieutenant Wilhelm Reile (succeeded on 20 March by Lieutenant Horst von Oppenfeld), Second Lieutenant Klaus Burk as 4th special missions officer, and Master Sergeant Bösenberg as divisional clerk.[10]

Stauffenberg's uniform had not yet been bleached by the African sun, and he looked very much the newcomer, but this impression faded more quickly than the colour of his uniform. He was his own person to a degree uncommon in the Army, not afraid to speak his mind (though with due respect) to superior officers; and he was usually right, which was not unproblematical. Besides military matters he liked to discuss history, geography, literature, politics. The division's 4th special missions officer, Second Lieutenant Burk, who became a banker after the war, recalled that Stauffenberg's religious views were part of his 'business principles'. Most of all Stauffenberg was happy to be in a combat division again, and he won his comrades' respect and affection with his competence, reliability, energy, personal courage, cordial and open manner. Burk wrote to his brother at the end of March: 'Commander and senior staff officer are terrific!'[11]

Stauffenberg drafted the orders for the troops – even those for rapid retreats – carefully and in good time, in clear language, so that the troops always felt that they were competently led. His habits of energetic and intensive work inspired others to greater efforts. He worked twelve or fourteen hours a day in the command car, a captured British bus, or in the jeep on visits to subordinate or superior command posts, making an effort to get to know all officers down to company commanders and to talk with as many men and non-commissioned officers as possible. He saw to it that visitors to his command post were offered coffee, cigarettes or wine. In the night before the battle of Médenine on 6 March it rained heavily and the command bus was crammed with officers, but when messengers arrived Stauffenberg gave orders to make room for them in the bus and to provide them with refreshments.[12]

Brigadier von Broich soon regarded Stauffenberg as a friend. He was pleased to have as senior staff officer 'an upright man, an anti-Nazi, and a very capable General Staff officer'. They often sat in the command bus late in the evening, after the orders had gone out, with Tunisian wine, talking about the removal of Hitler's rule, about philosophy or literature, and Stauffenberg liked to recite verses by Stefan George. Stauffenberg told his commander how pleased he was to be in Africa, as things had become rather uncomfortable for him in Germany. Here in North Africa he could practise everything he had learned at the War Academy – attack, defence, retreat, delaying action. (The senior staff officer, of course, assumed control of the division from the command post when the divisional commander was in the field.)[13]

Stauffenberg made no secret, to Broich and to other officers in the division, of his view that Hitler must be removed by force. Broich recounted this later; so did Lieutenant (Res.) Albrecht von Hagen, the 2nd special missions officer, when he was on trial before the 'People's Court' on 7 August 1944 for his part in the anti-Hitler conspiracy. The divisional adjutant Major Heinz von Schönfeldt once heard Stauffenberg say audibly, with obvious reference to Hitler, at the end of a situation briefing: 'Someone ought to kill that chap!'[14]

The German forces in Africa were under the tactical command of the Italian Armed Forces Supreme Command (*Comando Supremo*) and the German Commander-in-Chief South, Fieldmarshal Albert Kesselring. In case of immediate danger, however, Kesselring could act under direct orders from Hitler.[15] 'Operation Spring Breeze' was commanded by the permanent deputy Commander-in-Chief of the 5th Panzer Army, Major-General Heinz Ziegler. He convened a final briefing at his command post at La Fauconnerie on 13 February. In attendance were Ziegler; the Commander-in-Chief of the 5th Panzer Army, General von Arnim; the commander of the German-Italian Panzer Army 'Africa Corps', Fieldmarshal Erwin Rommel; the commander of Air Corps Tunis, Brigadier Hans Seidemann; and the commanders of the 10th and 21st Panzer Divisions which were part of the 5th Panzer Army, Brigadier von Broich and Colonel Hans-Georg Hildebrandt.

'Operation Spring Breeze' was a thrust against Sidi Bou Zid, Sbeitla, and generally in the direction of the Algerian ports on the Mediterranean. Formations of the 5th Panzer Army were to attack westward; Rommel was to advance with formations of the 'Africa Corps' northward through Gafsa and Feriana. The American commanders were expecting German-Italian attacks, but could not discover where the main thrust was planned because Arnim and Rommel kept changing their dispositions, and in addition used changes in structure and command terminology to confuse the enemy about both the size and the location of their formations. The German and Italian troops were battle-hardened veterans of desert warfare, whereas the Americans had not yet seen combat.[16]

At 4 a.m. on 14 February 110 tanks of the 10th Panzer Division drove forward in two parallel columns through Faid to Sidi Bou Zid. The division's forces for this attack consisted mainly of No. 7 Panzer Regiment, the 2nd (armoured) battalion of No. 69 Panzer Grenadier Regiment (II/69), the 2nd battalion of No. 86 Panzer Grenadier Regiment (II/86) which had half-tracks with a 37-mm gun and a machine-gun or two machine-guns, and a company of about a dozen Mark VI 'Tiger' tanks belonging to No. 501 Heavy Armoured Battalion. The 21st Panzer Division (at about a third of its full strength, with only two mechanised infantry battalions) drove forward on two roads from Maknassy to Sidi Bou Zid. The total strength of the

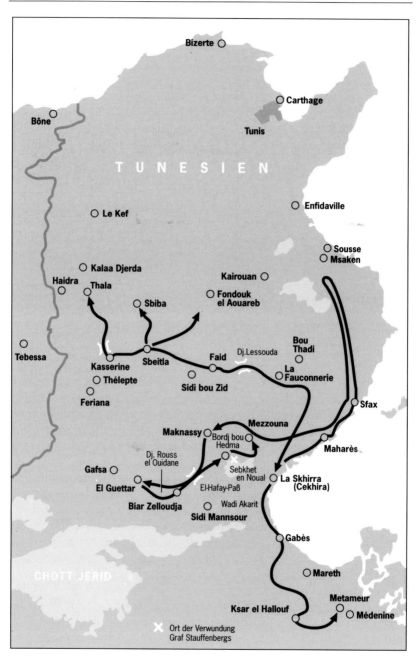

X Stauffenberg wounded here

40. Movements of the 10th Panzer Division in Tunisia while Stauffenberg was serving as its senior General Staff officer, 14 February to 7 April 1943

41. The Faid pass: looking towards Faid, 1943

attack force was equivalent to one division. Dive bombers and other bomber aircraft supported the attack.[17]

At 6 a.m. on 14 February the first tanks of the 10th Panzer Division reached a minefield eight kilometres west of Faid. A fierce sandstorm drowned out sight and sound during the advance, and also covered the clearing of mines, so that the Americans were taken by surprise. No. 7 Panzer Regiment outflanked an infantry position to its north on a mountain called Djebel Lessouda. Colonel Rudolf Gerhardt's combat command, with Mark III and Mark IV tanks, came upon fourteen American Sherman tanks standing uncamouflaged in a row; they disabled them one by one. Later that morning fifteen more American tanks were put out of action. The enemy withdrew towards Sbeitla. Shortly before 1 p.m. the first tanks of No. 7 Panzer Regiment entered Sidi Bou Zid. When an American tank formation, ranked five hundred metres deep, advanced on Sidi Bou Zid from the west, the Mark IV tanks and the armour of II/69 blocked the road and terrain on that side, while the main armoured force including the Tigers outflanked the American tanks in the south and then attacked them north-westward; the armour of the 21st Panzer Division attacked them from the rear. The 88-mm shells of the Tigers easily pierced the armour of the Shermans, and the Mark IVs were able to get in close enough to do decisive damage because the Americans were unpractised in the use of their long-range 75-mm guns. Soon the battlefield was strewn with burning tanks: the smoke and dust were so thick that the tank commanders fought standing in their open hatches.

By evening the tank battle of Sidi Bou Zid was over. The town was firmly in the hands of the 10th and 21st Panzer Divisions, while the remaining American forces retreated westward. Combat Command A of the American 1st Armoured Division lost 44 tanks, all their anti-tank guns and all their 155-mm howitzers. German losses were very much lighter.[18]

Rommel urged immediate pursuit to Tebessa and further north to cut off all enemy forces east of the Tebessa–Le Kef line, even hoping to force the rest to retreat towards the port of Bône – and this time there would be no Dunkirk. Eisenhower's anxious reports of those days seem to support Rommel's view. But Arnim kept German-Italian operations on a level more commensurate with available forces. In a short time the British 8th Army would be arriving at the Mareth position, which consisted of nothing but a few old French frontier fortifications, and Rommel would have to rush back to defend the Tunisian bridgehead there. If the advance to Tebessa took a week, and Tebessa as a major supply depot was adequately defended, so that the northward advance took a further week, it would be three weeks before Rommel could be back to defend the Mareth position 500 kilometres south-east. Montgomery could not be expected to wait for him. Moreover, the Americans were receiving a steady flow of reinforcements; the German-Italian forces were not, and were growing weaker.[19]

Eventually, however, the German-Italian command decided to advance northwards to Sbeitla – a decision which would have been less costly if it had not been so delayed, as Rommel pointed out later. German hesitation gave the Americans the opportunity to counter-attack on 15 February. Forty American Sherman tanks attacked shortly before noon. Without losing a moment the Germans counter-attacked: there were dramatic tank duels at a few metres' range, and the Germans disabled thirty-three American tanks, capturing six of them as well as artillery, machine-guns and a hundred vehicles. The division's own losses were thirteen Mark IV tanks, five 88-mm guns, and some other artillery.[20]

Rommel had asked for command over the 10th and 21st Panzer Divisions. The superior command authorities in Rome granted this during the night of 18/19 February, but only for an advance to Le Kef, not to Tebessa; and they withheld the Tigers Rommel had asked for (which were waiting for new tracks to be flown in to replace worn-out ones). Several assaults on the Kasserine Pass by Combat Command German Africa Corps, and on the Sbiba passage by the 21st Panzer Division, failed on 19 February. In the evening of that day Rommel and his Chief of the General Staff, Colonel (GS) Fritz Bayerlein, drove through Sbeitla and east to the 10th Panzer Division command post. They met with Broich and Stauffenberg. Broich was expecting the vanguard of his division by 8 p.m. that evening. Rommel

42. The Kasserine pass, 1943; below, looking towards Kasserine from the east

43. Fieldmarshal Rommel (centre) visiting the 10th Panzer Division command post on 19 February 1943. On Rommel's left (with maps) Colonel (GS) Bayerlein, Lieutenant Otto Metz (3rd special missions officer on the 10th Panzer Division staff), Lieutenant (Res.) Heino Bues (combat supply-train commander in the 10th Panzer Division); on Rommel's right, Brigadier Baron von Broich (back to camera), and Stauffenberg; behind Stauffenberg, on edge of picture, Second Lieutenant Burk

instructed Broich on deploying the 10th Panzer Division in support of the 21st; he arrived back at his command post at Feriana towards 7 p.m.[21]

On 20 February at 7.30 a.m. Rommel drove to Kasserine, where he found Broich. The 10th Motorcycle Infantry Battalion (K 10) of the 10th Panzer Division was en route to Kasserine. Rommel paid a visit to Italian troops south-west of Kasserine, who were to attack the Americans in the mountains; at 10.30 a.m. he met again with Broich at the Kasserine-Haïdra railway bridge that crossed the river Hatab. Broich had moved his command post into the railway station at Kasserine. Rommel ordered Broich to deploy his most forward battalion behind parts of Panzer Regiment 'Africa' and No. 7 Bersaglieri Regiment, both under the command of Colonel Menton. Rommel later dictated a diary entry: by 11.30 a.m. there was still no sign of the K 10; Broich had informed him that II/86 was intended for the attack but had not arrived yet (though it was about to), and he wanted to keep the K 10 for the support operation.[22] No. 7 Panzer Regiment was delayed because its tanks had been travelling all night on bad roads from Kairouan and needed maintenance. Rommel sharply repeated his orders to Broich, adding that all commanders must lead at the head of their troops. But Rommel's ruthless and insulting command style was a poor substitute for adequate resources. Towards noon Fieldmarshal Kesselring appeared at the 10th Panzer Division command post in Kasserine, met with Rommel, and had lunch with Broich and the Army Group Africa Chief of the General Staff, Brigadier Alfred Gause. Kesselring promised to restore the first battalions of No. 69 and No. 86 Panzer Grenadier Regiments to the 10th Panzer Division, but this was not done until late March.[23]

Towards 5 p.m. Rommel returned to the railway station at Kasserine, which briefly served as the combined command post of the German Africa Corps and the 10th Panzer Division, and ordered these two formations to take the Kasserine Pass. In the evening dusk Rommel observed, as he dictated for his diary, 'the exciting scene of the tank battle north of the pass'. He had special praise for the 7th Bersaglieri, who attacked fiercely and whose commander fell during the attack; they threw the American, British and French forces out of the pass in joint action with the II/86 and the K 10.[24]

During the night of 20/21 February, elements of the 10th Panzer Division launched their pursuit towards Thala and continued it during the day. Towards 12.30 p.m. Rommel drove up to the leading tanks of the combat command temporarily styled 'Group Rommel' in his armoured radio car. He took personal command, driving along on the left side of the lead tanks, while Broich in his jeep drove along on the right side. Stauffenberg also came forward to the II/86 during the attack.[25]

Urged on by Rommel, the lead tanks followed in hot pursuit in a cloud of dust behind the car of the commander of the British 26th Armoured Brigade, Brigadier A. L. Charles Dunphie, through the British defensive positions, whereupon the British opened fire on the rear of the German force. The lead tanks turned round and knocked out the British positions. East of the road the tanks disabled six enemy tanks, contributing to a total of thirty-two tanks disabled or captured during that day, besides many artillery pieces and nearly a battalion of prisoners. British soldiers who lay dead beside their anti-tank guns were robbed of their clothes by Arabs before the shooting ended. The 10th Panzer Division reached Thala by evening, but now the attack ran into the American reserves and stalled, losing ten tanks and several armoured personnel carriers. Broich wanted to attack again at 1 p.m. on 22 February, and requested air support. But even Rommel had doubts now. Broich agreed with him that a further advance without adequate infantry forces, in the absence of the division's I/69 and I/86, would only isolate the division.[26] During the night of 22/23 February the combat commands of the 10th Panzer Division and the German Africa

44. Brigadier Baron von Broich and Stauffenberg at the 10th Panzer Division command post in Kasserine station on 20 February 1943

Corps disengaged and withdrew to the Kasserine Pass. As always, Brigadier von Broich waited at the minefield until the last vehicle had passed through, before the pioneers installed the last mines; then he drove back to his command post. The enemy did not pursue. During the morning the pioneers destroyed railway bridges around the Kasserine Pass, and guns and tanks which had to be left behind. From 23 to 26 February the division retreated eastward through Faid and Bou Thadi to La Skhirra (Cekhira) north of Gabès, where they took up reserve positions.[27]

On 23 February the German-Italian forces were renamed Army Group Africa, and Rommel was their (nominal) Commander-in-Chief until he left Africa on 9 March.[28] On 28 February Rommel, Broich and Major-General Ziegler (who was deputy General Commanding the German Africa Corps from 23 February until Major-General Cramer took over on 5 March), along with other German and Italian officers discussed 'Operation Capri', an attack on Médenine. This was intended to disrupt the British assembly of troops for their attack on the Mareth position. On 2 March Rommel briefed Broich and Stauffenberg on the operation, which was set to begin on 4 March. Broich and Stauffenberg investigated the roads and found them poorly suited to tanks. Preparations forced a postponement of the attack until 6 March.[29]

The roads the 10th Panzer Division had to travel were narrow, full of curves and inclines; often they were sunken between high cliffs. The roads were so treacherous and progress so slow that the troops had to move in daylight, exposed to aerial observation; but the gorges and rocks also protected them against fighter-bomber attacks. Nevertheless, one well-placed bomb could have set fire to a munitions or fuel truck and blocked the road. Stauffenberg organised the division's march superbly, but it was strenuous and dangerous. Overtaking was forbidden on mountain roads, but some drivers tried it and there were accidents. On 5 March the division was in Ksar el Hallouf, where it formed the southern wing of the Mareth position.[30]

The British were well prepared. They had mounted 500 well-camouflaged anti-tank guns in a semi-circle around Médenine, and they had another 350 guns and 300 tanks. The German Africa Corps, under the command of Major-General Cramer, here consisted of the 10th, 15th and 21st Panzer Divisions, the 90th Light Africa Division, and the Italian Spezia Division; they had only 160 tanks and 200 guns.[31]

Broich and Stauffenberg knew that the situation of the German and Italian forces in Tunisia was hopeless. They were receiving no reinforcements or supplies, while the enemy grew stronger daily. But they regarded 'Capri' as a limited operation against the British positions at Médenine, which could succeed if the 160 tanks of the three divisions were concentrated against the left flank and the rear of the British 8th Army. They proposed this to Rommel but he rejected it, insisting that three separate armoured groups must attack the British positions in three places. Broich and Stauffenberg thought this was senseless. Nevertheless, Stauffenberg was obliged to formulate this order: 'On day X the German Africa Corps, together with forces from the entire Army, will attack the enemy forces between Médenine and the Mareth position, and annihilate them.'[32]

After a rainy night, the division attacked at 6 a.m. on 6 March. The 21st Panzer Division attacked on the left of the 10th, the 15th on the left of the 21st, an armoured reconnaissance battalion of the German Africa Corps on the right of the 10th. The mission of the 10th was to cut the British positions into a northern and a southern half, and so begin an envelopment. Since the German-Italian forces' approach had been observed, there was no suprise. It had proved impossible to lift the mines in the British minefields at the foot of the mountains around Ksar el Hallouf, so the tanks could not come storming out at full speed, but had to detonate the mines in front of them as they went along. The tanks of No. 7 Panzer Regiment succeeded in passing out of the narrow mountain road of the Hallouf valley under cover of darkness, but were unable to deploy rapidly. They had to move out of the Hallouf valley into the open plain in single file, which meant that several British batteries could concentrate their fire on one tank at a time. Nevertheless, the attack by three armoured regiments rolled on, with chains clanking, engines droning, tank guns bellowing, heavy artillery fire crashing, infantry running, in a thickening cloud of dust and smoke. It rolled up to the concentrated, lethal wall of British anti-tank fire, sustained heavy losses, and stalled even before daylight had broken through the early morning fog. Rommel noted that the German-Italian artillery had begun firing at the appointed time, at 6 a.m., but without much effect due to the lack of aerial reconnaissance; the panzer divisions' artillery had to shift its positions forward with the advance of the attack to stay in range; it had insufficient ammunition; the enemy controlled the air. The tanks and other vehicles turned round to seek cover in a wadi, but the British had calculated on that and immediately fired into the wadi.[33]

Brigadier Broich borrowed a personnel carrier and drove forward to look for his tanks. He found three of them on fire; several of his Mark IV tanks were standing in the bed of a stream, firing their 75-mm guns at the enemy, but were themselves pinned down, as was the infantry of II/69 and II/86. Broich regrouped them for a fresh assault.

Major-General Cramer had a view of the battlefield from his command post on Djebel Tebaga, but he could see only haze, dust and smoke, so he drove forward to the divisional command posts. At the 21st's command post a grim-faced Brigadier Hildebrandt stood beside his armoured reserve; at the 10th Stauffenberg was issuing orders 'with exemplary composure'. The 10th attacked again, but the supporting fire of No. 90 Armoured Artillery Regiment was too weak to shield the attacking forces against the rapid pounding from hundreds of British anti-tank guns. II/69 advanced only five-hundred metres before it got pinned down. Stauffenberg ordered the division's three batteries of *Nebelwerfer* (smoke-shell mortars) to fire on the enemy batteries, but the *Nebelwerfer* were knocked out by fighter-bombers after they had fired three rounds. Nor could the battle-seasoned K 10 force a breakthrough.[34]

At 4.15 p.m. sixteen dive bombers came to the support of the 10th Panzer Division assault force, which just managed to reach Mctameur and there held a line against enemy artillery and attacks from the air and on the ground. Rommel noted that the 10th Panzer Division was the only one which had renewed its attack successfully. Broich and Stauffenberg wanted to continue attacking during the night. But on Cramer's advice Rommel broke off the failed battle and ordered the troops to retreat into the mountains after nightfall.[35]

Stauffenberg's order for the retreat was one of his most impressive in terms of lucidity and style. His comrades later remembered that the dangerous retreat on narrow mountain roads succeeded through his superior organisational skill, but also because the British failed to pursue. Stauffenberg kept the command bus at the entrance to the Hallouf Valley and observed the terrain to see if any British troops were following the 10th

Panzer Division force as it disengaged. Broich was with the tanks of No. 7 Panzer Regiment, which was covering the retreat farther east in the open terrain. As was his custom, he waited until the retreat was completed, until the tanks had moved back into the mountains and the pioneers had mined their entrance.[36]

On 10 March the greater part of the 10th Panzer Division moved into reserve positions west of Sousse and south of Msaken. Stauffenberg prepared a comprehensive evaluation of the Chott-Akarit position in Wadi Akarit, exposing the insufficiency of the available heavy artillery. He concluded that an enemy attack on the position could be stopped only farther north, at the narrow passage of Enfidaville.[37]

On 20 March the division received orders to move into the area west of Maharès and to stand by for action at short notice. Stauffenberg sought to gather intelligence on roads. On the same day Fieldmarshal Montgomery launched his large-scale attack on the Mareth position, which was repulsed by the defenders with heavy losses to the attackers. Montgomery broke off the operation on 23 March.[38]

On 22 March the 10th Panzer Division was ordered to secure the western flank of the German-Italian forces in Tunisia. The division had to attack the American 1st Infantry Division along the Gabès-Gafsa road during the night of 22/23 March and attempt to arrive in the Americans' rear before daybreak. The division attacked at 3 a.m.: its tanks rolled through the American infantry positions and nearly reached the artillery behind them, but were then held up by a minefield which disabled eight German tanks, while the American artillery knocked out another thirty. The division was short of artillery ammunition and had hardly any tanks left; it attacked again in the afternoon, but could not drive the enemy out of his positions and did not reach El Guettar or Gafsa. An American infantry division, reinforced and with air support, had fought the battle-seasoned but weakened 10th Panzer Division to a standstill. The Americans, however, did not exploit their success by counter-attacking, so that the 10th Panzer Division had for the time being prevented an enemy breakthrough to Gabès, and had protected the retreat of the German-Italian formations from the Mareth position to the Akarit position.[39]

From now on the 10th Panzer Division had to defend and hold as much terrain as possible east of El Guettar. Combat Command Reimann drove northwards through the El-Hafay Pass, then west into the parallel valley to the north to secure the division's right flank. Colonel Hans Reimann had only the II/86, an artillery battalion, an 88-mm battery, and a company of 76.2-mm anti-tank guns mounted on Skoda tanks. Stauffenberg visited their positions in the days following 24 March. Farther north a combat command led by Colonel Rudolf Lang masterfully defended the Maknassy Pass from 23 March to 7 April against the breakthrough that Major-General George

Smith Patton had ordered. Lang's group consisted of mounted infantry of
I/69 and I/86, Italian infantry, the No. 9 Battery of No. 90 Armoured
Artillery Regiment, some 88-mm artillery, a 170-mm battery with a range of
27 kilometres, and a battalion of Tigers. They held the pass through to
Mezzouna against an American force consisting of three infantry batallions,
four artillery battalions, and two armoured companies which had several
75-mm tank-destroyers.[40]

From 30 March to 6 April the division had to repel daily American
infantry attacks which were supported by tanks. The division had to
abandon several hill positions. The American artillery fired 25,000 rounds
daily on the division's positions; the enemy also dominated the air.[41]

On 4 April the commander of the No. 90 Armoured Artillery Regiment
Combat Command, Major August Montada, was wounded; Second Lieutenant Edwin Schott took command. The group had to hold its position
against an attacking regiment. Schott related how on 5 April Stauffenberg
had sent him two 'assault guns' – guns which were bolted onto tank chassis,
so that the guns could be aimed roughly by manoeuvering the entire vehicle.
One of them had a defective chain and turned back, the other reached a
point beyond the group's position, and was damaged and immobilised.
When Schott reported this, Stauffenberg ordered him to destroy it with
explosives. When Schott said he had none, Stauffenberg handed the telephone to the artillery commander, who told Schott there was a sack of
hand-grenades in the driver's cabin; when Schott objected that he had no
fuses the officer told him to use a hand-grenade; now Schott objected that
the hand-grenade fuses lasted only four and a half seconds. At this point
Stauffenberg cut in, telling Schott that as a pioneer he ought to be able to
cope with the situation. Schott did use a hand-grenade to detonate the
sackful. He survived the explosion by lying flat on the ground only seven
metres from the vehicle, and only lost his hearing temporarily.[42]

Meanwhile the combat command was having a difficult time holding off
enemy infantry and mortar attacks. The terrain consisted of dozens of low
hills, all close together, so that the group's 22-mm and 88-mm guns were
useless. Schott placed machine-guns on the hills that had a sufficient view.
They fired until they ran out of ammunition or until they were knocked out
by mortar shells or hand-grenades. When the infantry attack suddenly
ceased it became clear that it had been a diversion from the main thrust
north of the Djebel Rouss el Ouidane mountains.

On 6 April the British 8th Army broke through the German–Italian
positions in Wadi Akarit. Patton ordered his II Corps to break through to
the coast on 7 April: the 10th Panzer Division was in danger of being cut off.
The American and British spearheads linked up north of the Wadi Akarit
position on 7 April between 4 and 5 p.m.[43]

On 5 April Broich and Stauffenberg were already calling urgently for a withdrawal of the division, but German Africa Corps command delayed the order until 6 April, too late for an orderly disengagement. On that day the divisional command post was under enemy artillery fire in an olive grove at the crossroads of Biar Zelloudja west of Sidi Mannsour.[44]

Lieutenant Friedrich Zipfel, posted to take command of a company in the division, reported to Stauffenberg on 6 April. He found the command post under bombardment. Stauffenberg, in an Africa uniform shirt and American trousers, shaking the glass of shattered windows from the maps, pointed through one of the windows: 'When that begins again, take the foxhole on the right, I shall take the one on the left.' Loud battle noise was audible from the west, and there was infantry fire nearby. While Zipfel was there, unit commanders kept ringing to ask for reinforcements or permission to withdraw; Stauffenberg had to insist that they hold out until 9 p.m.[45]

Second Lieutenant Schott recorded soon after the actual events that the senior staff officer of the division rang him toward 6 p.m. to say he must hold out until 7 p.m. and retreat toward Mezzouna at 7.05 p.m., taking the dead and wounded with him. When Schott and his combat command drove onto the bog road between Sebkhet Sidi Mannsour and the heights of Djebel Ben Kreir they were suddenly fired upon by six to eight tanks coming out of a depression between the many low hills. Schott's group got 'totally shot up at less than 100 metres range'. Behind Schott's small car there followed another one with a 20-mm gun hitched behind it, and behind that two 88-mm guns loaded on twelve-ton traction engines, some personnel carriers, and other vehicles. The first shots from the tanks were aimed at the largest guns and the traction engines, all of which were carrying as many passengers as they could hold. Most of these large vehicles received direct hits: within seconds there were great balls of fire, explosions, smoke, dust, dead soldiers everywhere, and very few survivors. Schott was sucked out of his open car by a grenade. His driver pulled him up and helped him back in; they escaped the inferno with the two passenger cars, the 20-mm gun and a munitions lorry which took a hit and went up in flames only moments later. Again and again Schott and his driver had to jump out of their car and scurry for cover among thorny cactuses. Out of the range of enemy fire at last, they came upon some German troops, and they stopped and slept until someone ordered Schott to report to the senior staff officer. Stauffenberg was still in his bus in the olive grove at Biar Zelloudja and remarked that the combat command had not fought well. Why had they not made mincemeat of the enemy with their large guns? Schott objected that the group had done its duty to the utmost, and that among the low hills there had been no field of fire for the artillery. Stauffenberg accepted this and dismissed Schott.[46]

That same evening Stauffenberg was still drafting orders for the retreat; but the units began moving back, under cover of darkness, before written

orders reached them; most orders were telephoned or otherwise orally
transmitted. By 8 a.m. on 7 April enemy artillery was shelling the positions
the division had just vacated, but it soon located the retreat route, which was
full of moving columns of vehicles. The intelligence section's action report
recorded:

> The movements [of the 10th Panzer Division] over the El-Hafay Pass were
> discovered and attacked by enemy aircraft in the morning hours of 7 April.
> The withdrawal of the division was disrupted during 7 April by heavy enemy
> artillery fire 5 kilometres north-west of Sebkhet en Noual, at Bordj bou
> Hedma, and by running fighter-bomber and bomber attacks south of Mez-
> zouna. The division was able to keep its material and personnel losses low only
> because a track was opened along the northern edge of the salt lake called
> Sebkhet en Noual, which permitted a successful retreat over difficult terrain.
> Enemy infantry were very slow to pursue.[47]

A dangerous jam of vehicles occurred at the south-west entrance to the
El-Hafay Pass. Hundreds of vehicles stood round the entrance without
cover or camouflage, four columns abreast, forced to merge into a single file.
After sunrise, first enemy reconnaissance fighters, and an hour later twin-
engined bombers, appeared and inflicted heavy losses upon the troops
waiting to pass through.[48]

The greater part of the division's vehicles moved eastward between the
heights of the El-Hafay Pass and the Sebkhet en Noual, onward round the
mountains south of Mezzouna, then northward; parts of No. 86 Panzer
Regiment took the more difficult route through the pass north of Sebkhet en
Noual between Djebel Chabita and Djebel Khetati. After the K 10 under
Major (Res.) Heinrich Drewes had travelled through the El-Hafay Pass, the
rearguard was able to retreat through the same pass towards 1 p.m. To
evade enemy air attacks, the K 10 travelled as far to the south as possible
along the boggy northern edge of Sebkhet en Noual. Nevertheless they, and
the rearguard which followed, had to traverse a plain without any natural
protection against air attacks, and a narrowing passage between the mountains south of Mezzouna and the salt lake. Here all vehicles came under
heavy artillery bombardment and fighter-bomber fire before they could
reach the relative safety of Mezzouna.[49]

The division, together with the 21st Panzer Division, took up defensive
positions near Mezzouna on 8 April. Since large numbers of enemy tanks
were assembling in the south, however, they retreated further to the
Faid-Sfax road on the same evening, moved farther north on 10 and 11
April, and took up their places in the Enfidaville position on 12 April.[50]

On 7 April at 5 a.m. Stauffenberg sent the 1st special missions officer,
Lieutenant von Oppenfeld, with the order of disengagement to the com-
mander of No. 90 Armoured Artillery Regiment, Colonel Heinz Schmid.
Later that morning Stauffenberg took his leave of Broich in order to direct

the division's retreat from his Horch jeep, after which he would drive on to the new command post near Mezzouna. Broich reminded Stauffenberg to look out for fighter-bombers; he himself would follow in about an hour, when the last battalion would have passed.[51]

With a few armoured radio cars Stauffenberg went through the El-Hafay Pass, drove along the northern edge of Sebkhet en Noual, and stopped near Bordj bou Hedma. When Lieutenant Reile arrived with the 5th company of K 10, he found Stauffenberg standing in his jeep, with his armoured radio cars stopped nearby, endeavouring to direct the improvised retreat. He said to Reile: 'We shall be lucky if we get out of this. As usual, we disengaged twenty-four hours too late.' The K 10 drove on and was attacked from the air several times, shot down one of the fighter-bombers, and suffered two casualties. Stauffenberg followed the K 10.[52] The next hour was one of the worst the division had ever gone through.

When Stauffenberg reached the narrow terrain between the Chabita-Khetati Pass and the Sebkhet en Noual, he got caught up in an inferno of fighter-bomber attacks. The planes attacked again and again, shooting into burning vehicles which presented easy targets; the wounded could not be retrieved, ammunition exploded. A battery of the 3rd Battalion of No. 90 Armoured Artillery Regiment arrived in the mêlée and the crews had to get out of their traction engines and lorries and run for cover. If they could not find cover in time, they could only wait until the fighter pilots were committed to an approach and could not change their aim, then fling themselves aside. Between sorties the survivors got hold of usable vehicles and tried to make their way out. In all this mayhem Stauffenberg was driving back and forth between the units to direct them, standing in his jeep, when his car came under fire. He threw himself out onto the ground, his face on his hands, and then he was hit.[53]

Schott arrived with the remnants of his group, the column stopped, someone shouted that the 'Ia' was wounded. Schott hurried forward and found two or three others already looking after Stauffenberg. The windscreen of Stauffenberg's jeep had a 20-mm bullet hole on the passenger side. An ambulance presently arrived. Schott recalls that Stauffenberg had no bandages when he was lifted into the ambulance.[54]

Reports on the details of the chaos naturally vary. Second Lieutenant Dr Hans Keysser, assistant medical officer of No. 361 Panzer Grenadier Regiment of the 90th Light Division, had joined the retreat to Enfidaville on 7 April, in a half-ton Bedford truck flying a Red Cross flag; but he had decided to drive inland in the direction of Gafsa. He came upon a jeep; a soldier was standing in it and waved him over. The jeep's driver was unhurt but his passenger, an officer, had head wounds, and his right hand had been hit. A dead lieutenant lay on the back seat. While the doctor was dressing the wounds, the officer asked him his name. Dr Keysser sub-

sequently indicated the direction of the nearest field hospital, presumably
No. 200 Field Hospital at Sfax, and drove on. He learned over a year later, as
a prisoner-of-war in America, that his patient had been Stauffenberg.[55]

When Broich and Burk finally followed the other units over the treeless
plain with their jeep, a radio car and two motorcycle messengers, they were
attacked twice by a dozen low-flying fighters, and each time managed to run
for cover without being hit. Driving on, they came upon Stauffenberg's
empty jeep, which was riddled with bullet holes. At the command post near
Mezzouna they learned that Stauffenberg had been gravely wounded, had
received first aid from a doctor belonging to a unit which did not belong to
the division and who had happened to be passing by with an ambulance, and
was now on his way to a clearing station.[56]

Stauffenberg was taken to No. 200 Field Hospital near Sfax. His right
hand was amputated above the wrist; the little finger and the ring finger on
his left hand and his left eye had to be removed as well. Three days later he
was driven in an ambulance to No. 950 Base Hospital at Tunis-Carthage.
He remembered the journey as an exceedingly uncomfortable and painful
one, disrupted again and again by enemy fighter-bombers.[57]

10

Conspiracy

Stauffenberg's family was without news of him between 3 and 12 April, when Berthold first learned that Claus had been seriously wounded and could not yet be transported back to Germany. A few days later Claus arrived by boat in Livorno and was put on a hospital train. Peter Sauerbruch arranged for him to be admitted to Ward II of the First General Military Hospital in the Lazarettstrasse in Munich because the chief surgeon there, Dr Max Lebsche, was reputed to be the best available. Stauffenberg was admitted on 21 April; he shared a room with Lieutenant Prince Löwenstein, son of the owner of Castle Haid where the 1st Light Division had been quartered during the occupation of the Sudetenland.[1]

Nina Stauffenberg saw her husband on Good Friday, 23 April, for the first time since he had left for Africa. On 26 April he had middle-ear surgery, which weakened him considerably. Shortly afterward he had a knee-joint operation during which the presence of virulent tetanus bacilli was discovered. Shrapnel under his scalp and in his arms caused inflammation. But Stauffenberg refused all painkillers and soporifics.[2]

Soon a steady stream of relatives, friends and comrades was passing through the hospital room. Cousin Clemens, Count Stauffenberg, came from Jettingen with his wife and his daughter Maria-Gabriele on 27 April. Stauffenberg's mother visited him daily in the weeks after 4 May; from 11 May Nina also came daily. Uncle Berthold paid a visit; Maria-Gabriele came again on 10 May with her fiancé, Captain (GS) Joachim Kuhn, who was with the General Staff Organisation Branch, and again with her mother on 26 May and 3 July.[3] Kuhn visited Stauffenberg again, alone, on 27 June. Stauffenberg told him that the generals would not act, that 'we' had to do it.[4] Maria-Gabriele's brother Markwart, who was a radio operator in the signal corps barracks next door, installed a radio for his cousin and occasionally accompanied him to the theatre. On those occasions Stauffenberg insisted on dressing himself and tying his own shoelaces. He asked about the 'White Rose' student group. Some of its members had staged a public protest in Munich University, and had been arrested, tried, and decapitated in February. Markwart suggested that most students were not in sympathy with the National Socialist regime, but did not support the White Rose and its revolt either. Stauffenberg commented that Germany evidently needed the 'Führer principle'.[5] Elizabeth, Baroness von und zu Guttenberg, a sister-in-law of cousin Clemens, visited Stauffenberg in mid-May. He told her that in Africa they had simply thrown away his hand with his ring on it, and radiated vitality. He dictated a letter to the widow of Lieutenant-Colonel Henning von Blomberg, saying that his own fate was not so pitiable compared to what he saw in hospital. When Partsch visited Stauffenberg he found him even keener on action than before he had been wounded. Herwarth also found him restless, and said in retrospect that Stauffenberg had the inner fire of a man who saw his life's mission awaiting him.[6]

Between March and June 1943 a number of high-ranking military officers stopped off to visit Stauffenberg on their way to Hitler's headquarters, which was then at Berchtesgaden. In May the Chief of the General Staff, General Zeitzler, brought him the Wound Badge in Gold, and some wine. Bürker came in the first days of June, and Stauffenberg, in Löwenstein's presence, said hard words about Hitler's generalship. Major (Res.) Drewes also came in June. He had led the K 10 at El Guetter, and gun in hand at the head of the K 10 he had fought off three American battalions, for which he had been awarded the Knight's Cross; he was still recovering from wounds received in Tunisia. Around the end of June Colonel (GS) Stieff, Mueller-Hillebrand's successor as Chief of Organisation Branch, came and expressed his condemnation of Hitler's leadership so freely that Löwenstein preferred not to hear it. The Quartermaster-General, Major-General Wagner, looked in, and sent two soldiers with a few cases of oranges. General Geyr von Schweppenburg came to see Stauffenberg and said he would like to have him as chief of staff for his panzer group, which was being organised in France. Stauffenberg said it was up to his superiors; in fact he did not want to work with Geyr.[7]

Claus's brother Berthold came to Munich as often as he could: for example, on 10 May on his way to Switzerland on official business concerning grain shipments to Greece, and again on his way back on 19/29 May. Berthold used the opportunity to see Robert Boehringer, the President of the Commission mixte de secours du Comité internationale de la croix-rouge, not only in order to do all he could to facilitate the passage of the grain ships through the maritime operational zones, but also to discuss the critical edition of the works of Hölderlin which had been launched in Stuttgart and Tübingen in 1941. Berthold and Robert both helped with the collection of Hölderlin manuscripts in Switzerland. As Frank had fallen at Staraja Russa on 26 February 1943, they discussed who should succeed him as one of Stefan George's heirs and trustees. Berthold had already chosen Claus and had told Robert of this in April, when Claus had just been wounded and could not yet be moved: Berthold said that there was no one he could trust 'so unreservedly'. Robert warned that whoever was appointed would have to be in a position to communicate with the other two and to act, but he accepted Berthold's decision.[8]

At the beginning of May, when Berthold found Claus already 'able to discuss anything', Uncle Nux came to visit. As commander of the Azerbaijan Legion in the 162nd Infantry Division at Priluki in 1942 and 1943, he had used his troops to intervene against mass shootings under German orders. He urged his nephew to take an active role in the existing coup-d'état conspiracy. Claus did not yet commit himself. But when his uncle visited him again, he said that since the generals had not achieved anything it was time for the colonels to get involved.[9]

On 8 June Stauffenberg wrote to Rudolf Fahrner, shakily with the three fingers of his left hand, that a visit after Whitsuntide would be welcome, but he wanted advance notice 'in order to avoid collisions'. Some time earlier Fahrner had written to Melitta, wife of Claus's brother Alexander, to say that Claus and Berthold approved of interventions to keep Alexander from getting posted to the front again. Claus had learned of this, and told Fahrner in his letter that neither he nor Alexander and Melitta themselves could support such 'protectionist manipulations'. Finally Stauffenberg asked Fahrner to send him some of the things he wanted to discuss with him, particularly Fahrner's translation of the 'Dialogue' by Dionysios Solomos, a nineteenth-century champion of Greek independence, and a modern German version of the *Chanson de Roland* which Fahrner had written in collaboration with Max Wetter and several other friends. Fahrner sent the *Chanson*, and Stauffenberg wrote on 25 June to say how much it had moved him. He expected to be well enough to see Fahrner on 28 June.[10] Fahrner brought his translation of the 'Dialogue': it concerned the relative merits of old Byzantine Church Greek and the living popular tongue. Fahrner's introduction said that neither could elevate a nation to a higher plane of existence: only poetry could do this. Stauffenberg thought that such questions were 'not our concern at the moment', but that the 'Dialogue' had 'occidental importance'. He suggested many changes in the translation and objected to Fahrner's pretentiously artificial style.[11]

On 3 July Stauffenberg travelled from Munich to Bamberg. His family was moving from Wuppertal into apartments in the house of his parents-in-law in Bamberg, but these were not yet habitable, so that Claus and Nina had to stay in a hotel. On 5 July he arrived at Lautlingen, where he stayed until 7 August. From here Stauffenberg sent Rudolf Fahrner his suggestions for shortening his version of the *Chanson de Roland*. Stauffenberg and his brothers also discussed the restoration of Frank's statue of a pioneer at Magdeburg. They edited passages of the translation of the seventh book of the *Odyssey*, which then went to press, and did some editorial work on Eberhard Zeller's adaptation of the history of Hannibal. By now Stauffen-

45. *Stauffenberg on leave in the summer of 1943 with (from left) his son Heimeran, his daughter Valerie, his niece Elisabeth, his nephew Alfred and his son Franz Ludwig*

berg was able to climb the lesser mountains around Lautlingen without using a stick. Early in August he spent a few days with Fahrner in Überlingen.[12]

The Chief of Staff in the General Army Office, Colonel (GS) Hellmuth Reinhardt, asked for a field posting in the spring of 1943. He suggested Stauffenberg as the best qualified candidate for his successor. The chief of General Army Office, Lieutenant-General Olbricht, of course knew Stauffenberg from the time when he had worked in the General Staff Organisation Branch. He asked Army Personnel to assign Stauffenberg to him, and this was done. It was a great distinction for Stauffenberg, a lieutenant-colonel, because the position was designated as a colonel's position with the possibility of accelerated promotion to brigadier. Olbricht evidently asked Stauffenberg in May, and Stauffenberg agreed immediately, saying he hoped to be available in three months. He expected that his new post would give him 'opportunities for decisive intervention'.[13] During the long weeks in hospital Stauffenberg had often said, as if in delirium: 'We must save Germany', or 'as General Staff officers we all are responsible.'[14]

But Stauffenberg also said repeatedly that he did not want to become a desk soldier, he wanted to go back to the front. General Zeitzler recalled that

Stauffenberg had requested a new field posting even before he had recovered from his wounds. But Zeitzler had wanted to give him time to recover fully, and put him at the disposal of the Commander-in-Chief of the Home Army. Stauffenberg eventually succeeded in getting the Home Army Command medical officer, Dr Carpentier, to pass him 'fit for active duty'.[15]

Stauffenberg's wish for a new field posting reflected the attitude common among Army officers.[16] It may also reflect his refusal to accept his injuries as permanently disabling.

Meanwhile, the conspirators' unsuccessful efforts to bring Hitler down showed only too clearly what was lacking: energetic central organisation and leadership.

Tresckow spoke to Manstein, without success, in February 1943. Tresckow also told Stieff in February 1943 that it was the historic duty of General Staff officers to remove Hitler, in the interest of the nation and to prevent the war from being lost. Stieff was a decided anti-Nazi, and as long as Tresckow himself could not gain access to the dictator, he was Tresckow's only hope. This was before the opportunity came up in March to place a bomb on Hitler's plane. When the bomb failed to detonate, a plan was made to attack him at a public appearance on 'Heroes' Day' a week later, which was frustrated by Hitler's unpredictability. When the conspirators were only just recovering from these blows the Secret State Police struck against their ranks in April and arrested several plotters in Admiral Canaris' Counter-espionage Branch. Tresckow once again pursued the assassination project with Stieff, and in August Stieff promised to carry out an attempt on Hitler's life.

In March Goerdeler hoped to win over General Heinz Guderian. But instead Guderian accepted from Hitler a country estate of about two thousand acres, worth over one and a quarter million marks. Attempts to win over Fieldmarshal Günther von Kluge, the Commander-in-Chief of Army Group Centre, seemed promising, but Kluge's commitment remained elusive or uncertain.[17]

Fritz-Dietlof, Count Schulenburg, was one of the most active plotters in 1943. What might have happened to Stauffenberg in autumn 1942 happened to him when he went looking for 'reliable' officers. He was arrested at the house of Rüdiger, Count von der Goltz, who had earlier acted as General von Fritsch's defence counsel, at 2.30 a.m. on 2 April 1943. Schulenburg put on a tremendous turn of outrage at such treatment of an old Party and SS member and he was released after a few hours. But it was a danger signal and a warning. The authorities were edgy, the 6th Army had been annihilated at Stalingrad, Hans and Sophie Scholl had tried to bring about a student revolt in Munich in February. Three days after Schulenburg's arrest the Secret State Police arrested Hans von Dohnanyi, Dietrich Bonhoeffer and Josef Müller, all long-time plotters in the Armed Forces

Supreme Command Foreign Affairs Bureau/Counter-espionage Branch, after they had discovered that the three officials were helping Jews to escape with false papers and money.[18]

The other conspirators continued their efforts. Tresckow spoke with the Chief of General Staff Operations Branch, Major-General Adolf Heusinger, in May. Tresckow hoped, with the help of his friend Brigadier Schmundt, Hitler's Chief Adjutant and Chief of the Army Personnel Office, to become Chief of Wehrmacht Operations Branch, or to replace Heusinger for two months and thus gain access to Hitler for an assassination attack; but Heusinger would not play.[19] In July Schulenburg was in Paris, urging his anti-Hitler friends there to take the initiative; but they told him that not even a single division could move without the knowledge of Armed Forces Supreme Command and of Hitler.[20] Efforts to persuade the Supreme Commander West, Fieldmarshal von Rundstedt, the most senior field-marshal, proved futile, although Rundstedt let the conspirators know that he would not object to a coup d'état. He too had accepted a great sum of money from Hitler.[21] At least Schulenburg was able to report to Olbricht on 2 August that the Military Governor in France, Major-General Karl-Heinrich von Stülpnagel, was willing to co-operate in a coup and even to take the initiative. Lieutenant-Colonel (Res.) Cäsar von Hofacker was put in place as Stülpnagel's special aide to act as liaison between the plotters in Berlin and in Paris.[22]

In the first days of July 'Operation Citadel', the last great offensive on the eastern front, stalled before Kursk and was broken off. On 10 July nine enemy divisions landed in Sicily. Turkey now gravitated towards the anti-German coalition. If Italy fell, Hitler would lose what control he still had in the Mediterranean and on Germany's southern flank. He gave up hope of defeating the Soviet Union and concentrated his resources on the growing menace in the west. On 25 July Mussolini was overthrown by generals who were willing to treat with the enemy; although he was eventually liberated by a German commando force, most of the Italian forces were no longer in alliance with Germany.[23]

At the end of July the coup d'état seemed imminent. Tresckow came to Berlin on the 29th and said that Kluge had decided to act against Hitler by ordering the Home Army to occupy all centres of government. On 31 July the Home Army issued, by special couriers, urgent new orders to all deputy corps headquarters and military district commands to prepare strong rapid-deployment units at once.[24] On 9 August Moltke told Hans Luka-schek that Hitler was about to be arrested at his headquarters by a panzer division.[25]

Goerdeler, called back to Berlin from Königsberg, arrived at Home Army Headquarters in Bendlerstrasse at 11 a.m. on 2 August to confer with Tresckow and Olbricht. Then Olbricht received news that German forces were occupying Italy, and that the armoured troops had been withdrawn from the Berlin area. There was now only one panzer battalion at Falling-bostel, seven hours' drive away; by afternoon it was revealed that this too had been moved. Moreover, there was no indication that Kluge or anyone else was actually about to take the lead.[26]

On 7 August Stauffenberg travelled to Jettingen to visit his relatives. On 9 August he went on to Munich for a series of operations to prepare him for a false wrist and hand. But a fragment of shrapnel caused a suppuration on his right arm and the operations had to be postponed for four weeks. Stauffenberg merely had himself fitted for a glass eye.[27] He did not commonly wear it, but if he was suddenly summoned to see very important superiors he would send his driver to 'fetch his eyesight'.[28]

It was at this juncture that Lieutenant-General Olbricht called Stauffen-berg to Berlin. There Stauffenberg immediately went to see the Chief of the General Staff of Military District III (Berlin), Brigadier Hans-Günther von Rost, who had been in the plot since the beginning of 1943. At Military District Command at No. 144 Hohenzollernstrasse Rost took the new emergency Home Army mobilisation orders code-named 'Valkyrie' from his safe and gave them to his special missions officer, Lieutenant (Res.) Heinz-Günther Albrecht, who immediately began revising them under Stauffen-berg's instructions to suit them for a coup d'état in the Berlin region. Stauffenberg gave Albrecht a draft of an order entitled 'State of Emer-gency'.[29]

Between mid-August and mid-October Stauffenberg went at least twice to see Tresckow in Babelsberg, to discuss details of Hitler's overthrow. Berthold Stauffenberg discussed them with Yorck, and generally assisted his brother's entry into the conspiracy.[30]

In the last days of August Stauffenberg travelled once again through Bamberg to Lautlingen. In Bamberg his wife found him changed and remarked to him that he seemed to be involved in a conspiracy. Stauffenberg confirmed it but did not mention any names. He merely said to Nina that the less she knew the better.[31]

The earliest date on which the coup might have been launched appears to be 13 August: the new 'Valkyrie' orders came into force on this date. Under the new system military district commanders could trigger 'Valkyrie' measures for their districts independently if the need arose.[32]

Tresckow gave up a cure which a physician had ordered him to take, as well as a vacation in Elmau with his family, and instead devoted himself to the military preparations for the uprising. During these weeks in August and September he and his wife lived in Berlin-Babelsberg at the house of his sister, Marie Agnes von Arnim. He worked out of Army Group Centre Rear Command on the Kaiserallee in Berlin to revise the coup plans, which Olbricht had kept. Little had been done in this regard, he told his wife, and he was glad and relieved to see that there was at last someone in the Home Army, Stauffenberg, who was getting a grip on the organisation of the coup.[33]

The conspirators were still looking for a fieldmarshal for supreme leadership. When Tresckow arrived in Berlin on 29 July, he believed that Kluge had been won for the role. Kluge sent his counter-intelligence officer, Colonel (GS) Baron von Gersdorff, to Manstein's Army Group South command headquarters at Saporoshe. Gersdorff spoke with Manstein on 8 August. In his personal diary Manstein recorded his response to 'Kluge's inquiries transmitted orally by Gersdorff' – inquiries, that is, about the foreign-policy question. Manstein said that peace was not currently a possibility because the enemy believed victory to be within his reach, but that if there was any chance of negotiation even with Russia it ought to be attempted; talks with Russia through Japanese mediation might induce the British to negotiate with the present German government and 'to give up their idiotic demand to negotiate only with a different government'. 'The main object is always to eliminate one enemy. Any talks initiated by others than the Führer would be bad because that would reveal to the enemy a disunity on our side. The Army can never be involved in anything like that.' Internally, a change of leadership could not be contemplated because the Führer was the only one who had the confidence of the people and the soldiers. 'Any suggestion that military leaders should interfere with the political leadership would mean that they thereby abandoned the principle of military subordination, and that will always work against themselves.' Manstein did express himself in favour of a change in command structure, so that Hitler would either have a chief of the general staff for all branches of the Armed Forces, or assume direct command of the Navy and Air Force in addition to the Army, and work directly with all three chiefs of staff. Manstein suggested that Kluge submit these proposals to Hitler. Gersdorff replied that any such approach to Hitler would be useless, even if Rundstedt, Kluge and Manstein made it jointly; it was necessary now to use 'any method' that could save Germany from catastrophe. Manstein said: 'Meaning that you want to kill him?' Gersdorff said that was the plan, whereupon Manstein reiterated that he as a soldier would not participate in an act which would tear the Army apart, but added that he would loyally serve a new regime after a coup d'état.[34] On the same day Manstein informed Zeitzler that every effort to decide the war must be concentrated in the east: after the defeat of Russia Germany would easily manage the western powers in Europe.[35]

The conspirators still expected Kluge to support the coup plan actively. Stieff visited Kluge on 13 August and reported afterward: 'In any case we can count on him.'[36] But Kluge had told Stieff that he was against 'forcing' Hitler.[37] Goerdeler nevertheless expected Hitler's overthrow in September, or at least well before 15 October.[38]

In October Tresckow was transferred to Army Group South officer reserve pool and posted as officer commanding No. 442 Grenadier-Regiment, which belonged to the 168th Infantry Division of the 8th Army in Army Group South. This temporary posting, for which he left on 10 October, completed his qualifications for promotion to brigadier and for his subsequent posting as Chief of the General Staff of the 2nd Army, which took effect on 1 December 1943. On his way to 2nd Army command headquarters Tresckow stopped at Manstein's Army Group South headquarters on 25 November. He wrote to his wife that there was 'some progress', that Manstein was 'despite continuing difference [of views] very cordial etc.' He and Manstein agreed that Hitler was 'leading us wrong', but Manstein's views were in all respects the same as those he had expressed to Beck, Stauffenberg and Gersdorff.[39]

Planning the coup: internal preparations

Stauffenberg was in Lautlingen again from 2 to 9 September 1943; his brother Berthold took a few days' leave to meet him there. Rudolf Fahrner came over from Überlingen for a day to see the brothers. They discussed the translation of the eighth book of the *Odyssey*, and also 'state and religion, labour issues, and agricultural matters'; and they again condemned the persecution of the Jews. Berthold was back in Berlin on 7 September and met with Moltke, Steltzer, Yorck and Trott.[1]

From 7 to 9 September Colonel (GS) Stieff was in Berlin for an armaments meeting. Tresckow visited him in his flat at Sybelstrasse on 9 September and told him of the two assassination attempts he had organised for 13 and 21 March of that year. A fresh attempt was expected on about 20 September. In fact, new anti-tank and infantry guns were scheduled to be shown to Hitler on 1 October. Stieff, as the head of General Staff Organisation Branch, could be expected to attend this, and he seems to have agreed to use the opportunity for an assassination attempt.[2] But nothing came of it.

Stauffenberg planned to start in his new position as Chief of Staff in the General Army Office on 1 November. On 9 September he travelled to Munich for the fitting of a false wrist and hand which he had postponed from the beginning of August. He moved into his old room in the reserve hospital. (Prince Löwenstein happened to be there, too, for treatment of his leg wound.) Shortly after Stauffenberg's arrival, Lieutenant-General Olbricht telephoned and told him that he must come to Berlin immediately. Stauffenberg protested that he was in Munich for necessary medical treatment, but Olbricht insisted.[3]

Stauffenberg took a train back to Berlin via Bamberg, where he saw his family and collected his pre-Africa uniform. On 14 September he wrote to Rudolf Fahrner from his brother's flat at no. 8 Tristanstrasse in Wannsee to say that his operation had been postponed once more, 'and since there is urgent work here I heeded my superiors' pleas and I am using the time to make myself familiar with my new duties and to help out'. Stauffenberg was

46. No. 8 Tristanstrasse in Berlin-Wannsee (photographed ca. 1988)

temporarily posted as General Army Office Chief of Staff effective from 15 September, and served full-time from 1 October; his permanent posting came into effect on 1 November. However, his predecessor, Colonel (GS) Reinhardt, remained in his post for several weeks after 1 October. Stauffenberg had in fact come earlier than would have been necessary if he was merely to be shown his new job.[4]

Soon Uncle Nux moved in with the Stauffenberg brothers to help Claus at home, and to help along the coup preparations. He knew it was too late to save Germany as an independent power, but he believed that it was still worth showing the world that there was opposition inside Germany to the evil regime. He also believed that if any hope remained of bringing about a coup, this was because Claus had joined the conspiracy. According to Uncle Nux, it was Claus who at last gave some solid form to the diffuse efforts of the conspirators.[5]

Annabel Siemens, who was a niece of Peter, Count Yorck, and thus related to the Stauffenbergs, started to come in daily to keep house for Claus, Berthold and Uncle Nux. When the Naval High Command building, where Berthold worked, was burned out in the great air raid on Berlin on 23 November, the Command's offices were moved first to Eberswalde and then in January 1944 to Bernau; Berthold took up his quarters in Bernau, but came to Berlin for briefings and at weekends. Claus Stauffenberg rarely saw Annabel; usually he left before she arrived and came home long after she had gone. After the great November air raids, Annabel took to living in so that she would not have to spend hours in a public shelter or underground station if there was an alert on her way home. On one of the rare occasions when she and Stauffenberg had a conversation that went beyond conventional civilities, in February 1944, he said: 'Now I must go back to my desk and send tens of thousands to their senseless deaths.' When Annabel asked what he meant by that, he explained that he had to provide replacements for the eastern front.[6]

On another occasion, the Catholic Stauffenberg wanted to know from Annabel, who was a Lutheran, whether she thought it would be right to sacrifice the salvation of one's own soul if one might thereby save thousands of lives. Without hesitation she said 'yes'. She did not know anything about the conspiracy, although there was a lot of coming and going, and every morning the used glasses told Annabel how many guests had been there the night before. In March or April 1944 Uncle Nux suddenly told Annabel that she was no longer needed. She felt hurt, but later understood that the intention had been to protect her from danger.[7]

Stauffenberg and his fellow-plotters prepared detailed plans for military and political action. They were based in part on old drafts and consisted of orders for military mobilisation and deployment, a new command structure, a list of political delegates to the military district commands, and policy statements.

About the time Stauffenberg assumed his new duties in September 1943, Colonel (GS) Bürker, Chief of Armed Forces Supreme Command Leadership Staff Branch II, learned from Major (GS) Klamroth (who had served in the 10th Panzer Division in Russia and now worked in the General Staff Organisation Branch), that a group of General Staff officers were preparing a coup d'état, and that Stauffenberg was one of them. Considering the importance of his position, Bürker's support could have been helpful. He asked Stauffenberg to come to see him at his office on the Tirpitzufer in Berlin, and after the usual preliminaries regarding 'the situation' he asked what people were backing those plans he had heard about. Stauffenberg named only Beck. Bürker said he thought Beck was indecisive; the plotters needed at least one fieldmarshal, with his command apparatus and resources. He also said that Himmler's police system was a dangerous threat. In 1923 Bürker, then an officer cadet in the Infantry School in Munich, had witnessed Hitler's attempted putsch. He concluded from Stauffenberg's answers that the proposed coup had no chance of success, and told him it looked as if he were preparing an ordinary military putsch. Stauffenberg remarked that he sometimes had the same impression himself. When Bürker said that now, after the failed Kursk offensive of July 1943, it was too late for a putsch, Stauffenberg retorted sharply: 'It is never too late!' A few days later Bürker summoned Stauffenberg again and told him his heart was with him and with his plans, but in his mind he could not justify supporting them. When Bürker visited Olbricht's office a few days later, he dropped in on Stauffenberg. Stauffenberg pointed to a photograph of his children on his desk and said, 'I am doing it for them.'[8]

Stauffenberg knew, of course, that the conspiracy needed broad support for a thoroughgoing renewal of the political fabric. In conversations with Peter Sauerbruch at the end of 1943 and at the beginning of 1944 he remarked that many who had been political leaders in the Weimar era had not understood the significance of the Republic; in particular, General von Seeckt, the Chief of Army Command, had isolated the Army politically and socially. Stauffenberg said that he had been much impressed by the stand the Social Democrats had taken in the Reichstag in March 1933 in their attempt to stop Hitler. An opportunity had evidently been missed in the Weimar Republic; therefore he intended to seek a dialogue with the union leaders and socialists. Peter, Count Yorck, did indeed arrange for Stauffenberg to meet the Social Democrat Julius Leber, who had been decorated for bravery as an officer in the First World War; in the Reichstag he had been his party's spokesman on military affairs. Leber and Stauffenberg shared a concern for the soldiers in the field, but they had more in common than that. Leber was a Catholic and felt so committed to his Church that in 1944 he had discussed with his Lutheran wife the question whether she should convert. Stauffenberg always spoke of Leber with great respect and affection.[9]

In the months after his arrival in Berlin Stauffenberg also met other conspirators: Ulrich, Count Schwerin von Schwanenfeld, Eduard Brückl-meier, Eugen Gerstenmaier, Carl Goerdeler, Jens Peter Jessen, Ulrich von Hassell, Johannes Popitz, Hermann Maass, Wilhelm Leuschner, Jakob Kaiser, Max Habermann. He discussed with them the composition of a transitional government; he opposed Goerdeler's candidacy and favoured a labour politician to head the cabinet. Leuschner and Leber wanted a large role for labour, but they did not want to attract once again the odium of liquidator after defeat that had haunted the Social Democrats since 1918;

they were willing to serve as vice-chancellor and interior minister respectively, but not to form a government.[10]

Stauffenberg's brother Berthold and their cousin Hans Christoph, Baron Stauffenberg, had been in contact with Moltke since before the war. Moltke had long hoped to win over Berthold for his own planning group. He thought that Germany would lose the war, be occupied by enemy forces and lose territory. He believed that 'the generals' would not overthrow Hitler, and that he himself and his friends could not do so: it was better for them to hold themselves in readiness until after the regime had collapsed, rather than risking their lives in hopeless coup plans.[11]

But while Moltke had no confidence in 'the generals', he evidently thought that Claus Stauffenberg's dynamism might after all produce results. Moltke had been opposed to a coup d'état mainly because it had so little promise of success. As early as September 1941 he had inquired whether 'something' could be done with Claus. Stauffenberg's reply – first the war must be won, but then 'we shall clean up that brown plague' – suggests that Moltke had not merely been talking about post-war plans.[12] Now, in the autumn of 1943, Moltke again sought to win over Stauffenberg, evidently this time for a coup. At the same time he was worried that Stauffenberg's charm and dynamism might induce some of his friends, particularly Yorck and Leber, to join the plotters and to lose their lives as a result; but he became less adamant once Stauffenberg had joined the conspiracy.[13]

Stauffenberg's energetic will led to friction in his relations with Moltke. Moltke was cool and haughty, and Stauffenberg did not find him personally attractive. He was impressed with Moltke's ideas on the voluntary redistribution of large landed estates. But he was put off by Moltke's disdain for Germany's status as a power and her territorial integrity, and by the seemingly abstract discussions of Moltke's group. He commented to Kuhn that the time for tea-parties and debates was over.[14] Stauffenberg naturally wanted to feel that his undertaking had support, rather than criticism from the sidelines.

One evening in November, Stauffenberg and Annabel Siemens drove to Yorck's house at 50 Hortensienstrasse for a meeting which included Moltke and Gerstenmaier. The women were making jam from dried plums; Gerstenmaier came into the kitchen to taste it. After an hour or two Stauffenberg came into the kitchen; his face was white. He said to Annabel only, 'we're going.' In the car he said: 'I can't stand that fellow Helmuth Moltke.' Moltke was oblivious to the irritation he might have caused. He valued Claus Stauffenberg more than his brother Berthold, who seemed to him effeminate. The collaboration between Moltke and Claus was not impaired by their differing personalities.[15]

Tresckow introduced Stauffenberg and Goerdeler to each other, apparently in mid-September. Goerdeler respected Stauffenberg; he found him high-minded, but presumptuous. In November 1944 in prison, two months after he had been sentenced to death, Goerdeler wrote that Stauffenberg had proved to be wrong-headed, had tried to play politics and pursued an 'unclear course' with leanings toward left-wing socialists and communists.[16] Goerdeler told Secret State Police interrogators that Stauffenberg had demanded to be kept 'fully informed of all political measures and of all personalities destined for high office', and that he had complied.[17]

Stauffenberg also raised doubts about Popitz, who had tried to conspire with Himmler against Hitler from May to August 1943. This was indeed a dangerous matter. Olbricht had taken Tresckow to Popitz's flat for a meeting at the beginning of August. Popitz's go-between Carl Langbehn, who was Himmler's solicitor, had been there; Langbehn was arrested in September and was interrogated about the background to his machinations over several weeks. After Stauffenberg had met Hassell and Popitz at Jessen's in November 1943, he told Hassell that Popitz was being watched closely by the police.[18]

But there were other differences. Stauffenberg's position on the issue of assassination was unequivocal. Goerdeler, on the other hand, was ambiguous: he opposed assassination on religious and moral grounds, but at the same time he urged it and desired its consequences.[19] On 26 May Stauffenberg and Goerdeler conferred in the Bendlerstrasse office of Captain (Res.) Hermann Kaiser, keeper of the Home Army Command's war diary. Immediately afterward Goerdeler told Kaiser that Stauffenberg needed no urging, but had agreed that he, Goerdeler, would be the only one to conduct negotiations with the Social Democrats and trade unions. Stauffenberg did not adhere to this division of labour between the civilian and military conspirators; but he kept Goerdeler informed of all dates planned for the coup d'état, and he did acknowledge Goerdeler as the civilian leader of the conspiracy. In May 1944 Goerdeler had written a letter for the 'enlightenment of the Chief of the General Staff, General Zeitzler, and had asked Stauffenberg to pass it on. In June or July Stauffenberg told Goerdeler that there was no need to do so, because when he, Stauffenberg, had reported to Zeitzler as General Fromm's Chief of the General Staff, he had told him that he considered the war as good as lost. Zeitzler had replied that many people thought so, but few would say so out loud.[20]

In June 1943 Carlo Mierendorff, formerly Secretary-General of the transport workers' union and a member of Moltke's Kreisau Circle, had advocated the inclusion of the Communists in a non-partisan 'people's coalition'. The socialists Adolf Reichwein and Leber as well as Moltke supported the idea of contacts with the Communists. Leuschner, Jakob Kaiser, and Stauffenberg, when first confronted with the suggestion, were opposed.

In January 1944 Reichwein and Leber embarked on preliminary talks with a former member of the Communist Students' League, Ferdinand Thomas, who acted as intermediary for the underground Central Committee of the Communist Party of Germany. By May 1944 the conspirators had accepted Reichwein's and Leber's view 'that Communism would have a decisive role in Germany after the war was lost: the conspirators must try and head off a radicalisation of their revolt. If the troops on the western front retreated, and if the eastern front could be stabilised, Germany might still be able to avoid occupation by the Red Army. Stauffenberg and his fellow-conspirators had of course no intention of exchanging a Nazi dictatorship for a Communist one; but Stauffenberg eventually agreed to talks with the Communists, and so did Fritz-Dietlof, Count Schulenburg, and Yorck.

A first meeting took place between Reichwein, Leber, and the Communist underground leaders Anton Saefkow and Franz Jacob in the flat of a Berlin physician, Dr Rudolf Schmid. A few days later Stauffenberg mentioned the meeting to Rudolf Fahrner and declared that contacts with 'the other opposition groups' were important.[21]

When Reichwein and Leber arrived at Dr Schmid's flat, they saw that Thomas had brought along not only Saefkow and Jacob, but also a third man unknown to them. Reichwein and Leber were trapped, but went through with the meeting, evidently trusting Thomas. The Communists declared they did not know whether or not their 'friends abroad' would disavow them, but they could assure their interlocutors that there were no plans to introduce the Bolshevik system into Germany: religious freedom would be guaranteed, the Christian trade unions would be tolerated, and private property would be respected. They talked as if they thought it quite inevitable that Germany would be occupied by the Red Army. The meeting ended with mutual assurances of co-operation. A further meeting was arranged for 4 July. Thomas was evidently unaware that the third man was a police informer, but Leber decided not to attend. Reichwein and the Communists were arrested when they turned up on the appointed date. Leber was arrested at home the next day.

In order to advance the organisation of the coup d'état, Tresckow arranged for Major (GS) Hans-Ulrich von Oertzen to be posted to III Deputy Corps Headquarters at 144 Hohenzollernstrasse, on the Fehrbelliner Platz in Berlin. Stauffenberg was also posted there so that he could become familiar with conditions in and around Berlin. Oertzen and Stauffenberg worked on the coup plans to occupy important points in Berlin, such as SS barracks, ministries, communications centres and broadcasting stations. They used the office of Lieutenant (Res.) Heinz-Günther Albrecht, Special Missions Officer to the Deputy Corps Chief of Staff,

Brigadier Hans-Günther von Rost. Albrecht unobtrusively provided them with information on troop strengths and deployments, and accompanied them to shield their work from unwelcome notice. The President of Berlin Police, Count Helldorf, looked in frequently, as did Admiral Canaris, Colonel (GS) Hansen, of Canaris's agency, who was in the plot, and Lieutenant-General Olbricht and Lieutenant (Res.) von Haeften. (Haeften was soon to become Stauffenberg's special missions officer; he was the brother of Hans-Bernd von Haeften, a diplomat who was in Moltke's 'Kreisau Circle'.)

Successive drafts of the plans were typed by Eta von Tresckow at her home in Potsdam; but she had her children to look after, and Stauffenberg could not be constantly going to Potsdam once Tresckow had gone back to the front. Now the typing chores were shared between Margarethe von Oven, a friend of the Tresckows whom he had installed in Army Group Centre's Berlin rear command, and Ehrengard, Countess von der Schulenburg, who was the secretary of III Deputy Corps Commander, Lieutenant-General Joachim von Kortzfleisch.[22]

Tresckow told Margarethe von Oven to wear gloves while typing, to use a borrowed typewriter, to type at home, to take both typewriter and drafts with her down to the air-raid shelter during alerts, and to burn obsolete drafts. Before leaving for the front on 10 October, he often came to Grunewald, where she lived with her mother, to hand over revised drafts and to meet with Stauffenberg. The two men took long walks together so that what they said would not be overheard. Once they were walking along Trabener Strasse with Margarethe von Oven, who was carrying all the current drafts under her arm, when a carload of SS men approached and stopped alongside them. Stauffenberg's and Tresckow's faces turned white. The SS men jumped out and entered a house across the street.[23]

Margarethe von Oven was upset when she read the first words of one of the drafts: 'The Führer Adolf Hitler is dead.' This must mean that the authors were implicated in plans to assassinate Hitler, and thus in high treason. But she recalled what Tresckow had told her during the summer: tens of thousands of Jews were being killed most cruelly, and it was this above all that had motivated him and his fellow-conspirators to enter into the conspiracy. Stauffenberg, a devout Catholic, so businesslike yet radiating an inner fire, gave her the same explanation. He read her a poem by Stefan George which seemed to fit the situation exactly:

> When once this generation has cleansed its shame
> Has thrown from its neck the villein's yoke
> In its entrails feels but hunger for honour:
> Then from the battlefield covered with endless graves
> Will flash the bloody gleam . . then through the clouds

Will rush roaring armies then through the fields
Will rage the horror of horrors the third storm:
The return of the dead!

If ever this nation from her cowardly slackness
Remembers her election, her mission:
She will receive the divine explanation
Of unspeakable dread . . then hands will be raised
And mouths will sound in praise of her worth
Then in the morning breeze a true emblem will flutter
The royal standard and bow itself in greeting
To the Noble· the Heroes!

Stauffenberg said one had to choose between two evils: action (against the regime), or inaction. He believed that God had assigned a mission to him, and he had devoted himself to it entirely. His inner calling gave him the certainty that was so convincing to others. Nevertheless he asked himself constantly whether his way was the only possible one.[24]

When Schulenburg and Rost initiated Ehrengard, Countess von der Schulenburg, she objected that the role of conspirator did not become a woman. But Rost told her that 'there is probably nothing else for it'. When reminded of the many whom Hitler was senselessly driving to their deaths, she agreed. After working hours, she and Albrecht typed the drafts. Since the building was centrally heated and had no open fires, she had to burn obsolete drafts in toilet bowls in the lavatory, and then scrub out the bowls. During the day she and Albrecht had to accommodate visitors in a small waiting room to keep them away from Oertzen and Stauffenberg; often they had to feign ignorance or give incorrect information. Rost came in on Sundays to work on coup preparations. It took Stauffenberg only three days to gather sufficient information about the military forces in the Berlin area; after this he went to work at the General Army Office in the Bendler-strasse.[25]

The orders for 'Operation Valkyrie', along with similar ones code-named 'Rhinegold', were first conceived during the winter 1941 catastrophe on the Russian front as a way of mobilising reserves. 'Valkyrie I' was designed to raise reserves for the front; Stauffenberg had worked on it in the General Staff Organisation Branch in the summer of 1942. 'Valkyrie II' organised combat-ready divisions, brigades, reinforced regiments and combat commands in three stages for 'deployment locally, at home or in frontier regions', to protect the coasts or to combat airborne enemy forces. The orders carried a high level of secrecy: 'Under no circumstances may agencies and individuals outside the Wehrmacht be informed of the intentions or of preparatory work.' This denied the police and the Secret State Police any knowledge of these measures (although they would inevitably be concerned in any internal emergency); nor is there any hint that the Waffen-SS was to be regarded as within the Wehrmacht. The 'Valkyrie' orders lay ready in sealed envelopes in the safes of the deputy corps commands and military district commands, and also in the safes of the military governors in the occupied territories.[26]

These orders became obsolete in October 1942, when five 'Valkyrie II' divisions were organised and deployed at the front. On 31 July 1943 Lieutenant-General Olbricht issued revised orders over the signature of the Commander-in-Chief Home Army, directing the deputy corps commands to combine replacement and training units into combat groups. This was described as a precaution against 'internal disturbances'.[27]

Six hours after the code word was issued, units had to be ready for deployment ('Valkyrie' stage 1); immediately afterward they were to be organised into combat commands ('Valkyrie' stage 2). This had to be done as rapidly as possible, but no time limit was set for the completion of stage 2 because of the variations in geographical conditions and equipment among the districts. Armoured units and armoured infantry units, with the armoured troop and infantry schools, were to form separate combat commands. Deputy corps commands had to be prepared to secure important objectives such as telephone exchanges, telegraph and radio transmitters, power plants, bridges. Secrecy was stressed, as it had been in the May 1942 version. Every Friday, deputy corps commands had to report the personnel and equipment on hand for 'Valkyrie' units to General Army Office. On 6 October 1943 Olbricht issued an amendment ordering that field army units temporarily stationed at home should be included in the 'Valkyrie' combat commands. Olbricht's and Tresckow's revisions also authorised deputy corps commands to activate 'Valkyrie' and to deploy troops independently in case of need.[28] The orders could be effective in emergencies – but also for the purpose of a coup d'état.

Rost furthered these preparations with energy and imagination. He ordered detailed plans for emergency deployment, and paid personal visits to SS and NSDAP installations to learn all he could about their personnel, equipment and weapons, and to gauge the 'reliability' of particular units. He thought No. 9 Replacement Training Battalion exceptionally 'reliable' under its commander Major Meyer and its adjutant Lieutenant von Gottberg; it was earmarked to occupy the ministries in Berlin. On the occasion of a heavy air raid on Berlin, Rost put on a dress rehearsal: the armoured vehicles of the Krampnitz Armoured Troops School rolled into Berlin's government quarter within just over an hour. Goebbels protested angrily.[29]

An important change in the 'Valkyrie' orders was signed by Stauffenberg on 11 February 1944. It provided for the organisation of reinforced regiments, and allowed deputy corps to draw on units from other deputy corps, in order to speed up the organisation of combat-ready formations. Unauthorised reorganisations of replacement and training units, and 'holding back personnel designated for field deployment', were forbidden. This made it possible to pull field replacements together quickly and without denuding a military district of all its troops – which might have serious consequences in an emergency. It would also enable the conspirators to draw on armoured troops from more than one deputy corps, or to deploy armoured units to isolate an SS garrison. (SS units were not under the control of deputy corps and military district commanders.)[30]

On 29 May 1944 the Minister for Armaments and Munitions, Albert Speer, wrote to the Chief of Armed Forces Leadership Staff, General Alfred Jodl, requesting him to make contingency plans in case air raids destroyed the Rhine bridges and cut off the German heartland from German forces west of the river, and in case of an Allied landing on the North Sea coast. There were hardly any troops on German territory which could oppose such an invasion. On 5 June Jodl commented in his diary that at any given time 300,000 men were at home on leave, the equivalent of ten or twelve divisions; he suggested the establishment of 'divisional shells' in which these men could be organised at short notice. Hitler approved Speer's and Jodl's suggestions in briefings on 3 and 5 June.

On 7 June Stauffenberg, accompanying General Fromm, attended his first briefing with Hitler, to discuss rapid-mobilisation measures. These discussions were continued during further visits to Hitler's headquarters on 6 and 8 July. On 6 July Stauffenberg reported on 'Valkyrie'. Hitler approved most of his proposals and decided that if enemy forces invaded German territory, the military commanders-in-chief were to have full 'executive powers', both military and civil, including authority over the Reich defence commissars – meaning the Gauleiters and other Party and government functionaries in the capital and in the provinces.[31]

In June and July 1944 the conspirators prepared special sets of orders for taking control of the capital. They were based on the authorisation of deputy corps commanders to take measures to protect vital installations, independently if need be. Since the conspirators were in the appropriate positions, they were able to adapt the measures to the requirements of a coup d'état.[32]

'Valkyrie' exercise orders were to be issued on the day before the uprising ('day X-1') to the armoured troops at Krampnitz, and to the infantry at Döberitz and Potsdam. On day X the military districts were to receive, on a staggered schedule, the 'basic order' beginning with the announcement that the Führer was dead. At hour X – shortly before or after Hitler's assassination – order no. 2 was to be issued to the Military Commander in Berlin, ordering a state of emergency, military government, and 'Valkyrie' for all units under his command. Speed of deployment might vary, of course, depending on the time of day, or the effects of the latest air raid. Government buildings were then to be occupied, as well as all SS headquarters, Party district offices, the homes of Reich ministers, communications installations, newspaper offices, the radio station at Tegel, the Berlin radio tower and the radio studios in the Masurenallee. The police would have orders to co-operate with the Army: the President of Berlin Police, Count Helldorf, and the Director of the Reich Criminal Police Office, Major-General of Police Arthur Nebe, promised to see to that. A shock troop, led by a general, was to inform the commandant of SS troops in Berlin that the Waffen-SS (military SS, as distinct from concentration camp guards) was now incorporated into the Army. Similar instructions were to be transmitted by the Berlin Military Commander to Regiment 'Göring'. SS units and Regiment 'Göring' were to be confined to barracks. At hour X the armoured-troops school would receive orders to move three of its own 'Valkyrie' battalions and two additional battalions from the officer cadet school and the school for non-commissioned officers in Potsdam to the Tiergarten-Bendlerstrasse area in Berlin. A company of armoured personnel carriers and a motorised infantry company were to occupy the radio transmitters at Königs-Wusterhausen and Zeesen, and to prohibit any political broadcasts. Vehicles of 170 metric tons would be obtained from Kanin, 24 kilometres south-west of Potsdam. The commander of the armoured-troop school had at once to report to General Fromm's headquarters to receive his orders; two of his battalions were to be placed under the Berlin Military Commander; the greater part of the forces from the armoured-troop school were to be at the disposal of the coup-d'état headquarters in the Bendlerstrasse, and some of them would conduct armed reconnaissance against the Waffen-SS barracks in Lichterfelde and Lankwitz. One company with armoured personnel carriers was to meet General Fromm and Colonel Stauffenberg at Tempelhof airfield to take them to the Bendlerstrasse.

The plotters relied on the Chief of Wehrmacht and Army Communications, Lieutenant-General Fellgiebel, and on some of his trusted subordinates, to ensure that certain exchanges and lines were blocked at the crucial time, and to keep others open for the use of the conspirators, giving them control of telecommunications. There was no question of destroying any facilities; they would be needed, and in any case the only effective way of interrupting the multitudinous lines and routings was through military orders.

General Fromm's attitude was a matter of some speculation, since it might decide the success or failure of the coup. Fromm had the reputation of a shrewd opportunist. When Olbricht suggested to him an 'intervention' against 'the leadership', Fromm merely thanked him. When in mid-June Stauffenberg became Fromm's Chief of the General Staff and reported to him, he told him that in his view the only way out of the war was through overthrowing the regime. Fromm thanked him for his frankness. Once Fromm said, without addressing anyone in particular: 'Supposing you go through with your putsch, be good enough not to forget Wilhelm Keitel.'

On 15 July, in anticipation of Hitler being assassinated, the Krampnitz Armoured-Troop School was mobilised, in vain as it turned out; Fromm reprimanded Olbricht and said that the mobilisation might have provoked Guderian, the Inspector-General of Armoured Troops, into transferring the armour to the front.[33] Stauffenberg made no secret of his poor opinion of Fromm; but it was reasonable for the plotters to expect that Fromm would join their side after Hitler's death.[34]

The coup-d'état planners prepared a list of 'political delegates' to be appointed and named by teletype message for each military district. The delegates were to have authority comparable to that of provincial governors and were to 'advise' the deputy corps commanders on the implementation of measures ordered by the Berlin coup leaders. Goerdeler prepared the list and submitted it to Beck and Stauffenberg.[35]

Each military district was also to receive a liaison officer. Stauffenberg himself prepared a list of sixteen names for fifteen of the seventeen military districts. He recruited the candidates through his powers of persuasion, and the authority derived from his experience on both the General Staff and the front line.[36]

In autumn 1943 Stauffenberg initiated Major Hans-Jürgen, Count Blumenthal, of General Army Office Replacement Group, into the conspiracy. His method on such occasions was to summon the candidate to his office, sketch the war situation, and draw the conclusion that the Armed Forces must take control. Major Ludwig, Baron von Leonrod, came to Berlin at Stauffenberg's request in mid-December. Stauffenberg told him that the Führer had become 'unsupportable' and must be done away with; liaison officers were required for the moment when the Armed Forces took over executive power; Leonrod had been designated for VII Deputy Corps and Military District (Munich). Leonrod objected that he had taken an oath of loyalty to the Führer. Stauffenberg said that an oath was sacred in principle, but no longer valid in the present emergency; Leonrod, as a practising Catholic, was in fact obliged (said Stauffenberg) and 'conscience-bound to act contrary to his oath'. On 20 December Stauffenberg summoned to Berlin Captain (Cavalry, Res.) Friedrich Scholz-Babisch from Silesia; in January 1944 Captain (Res.) Dietrich, Baron Truchsess von Wetzhausen, and Lieutenant-Colonel Hans Erdmann of I Deputy Corps (Königsberg).[37]

Stauffenberg's friend Peter Sauerbruch persuaded Major Roland von Hösslin, holder of the Knight's Cross, a frequent visitor to Sauerbruch in Wannsee, to participate in the rising. After the failure of the coup Hösslin was accused of high treason. He protected Sauerbruch, and testified only that Stauffenberg had told him on 1 April 1944 that the field army was losing the equivalent of one army corps every month; that replacements were not available; that Germany was drifting toward military collapse; and that Stauffenberg had persuaded him primarily by appealing to his honour as an officer: the honour of the officer corps demanded that they should do what they had failed to do in 1918, retain control. And: 'The Führer must go too!' The other nations would always regard the National Socialist state as a menace and would never make peace with it. One could not accept responsibility for continuing the struggle until Germany had been utterly destroyed. When Hitler was overthrown, the Army – the most conservative institution in the state and one rooted in the people – would have to maintain order.[38] Hösslin concealed from his interrogators his true assignment in I Military District, the province of East Prussia, by saying he had to 'implement the state of emergency in Königsberg'. In fact Hösslin was in command of the armoured reconnaissance and training battalion at Meiningen, and he was to lead three companies, one of them armoured, to 'protect' the Führer's Headquarters – that is to say, to isolate it.[39]

Lieutenant-Colonel (GS) Peter Sauerbruch, whom Stauffenberg had visited in hospital in January 1943, had gone on to serve as intelligence officer on No. 2 Panzer Army command staff, and subsequently as General Staff liaison officer with the General of Tactical Air Power at Berlin-Rangsdorf. In December 1943 Stauffenberg had Sauerbruch transferred to the General Army Office, and resumed the topic he had raised in January, trying to persuade him with military arguments. The war, he said, was lost. The new rockets had only tactical significance; there was no prospect of a separate peace in the west; the enemy alliance that was demanding Germany's unconditional surrender could not be divided. The only glimmer of hope was that the western powers would still have to land in France, and that Britain probably would not like to see Russia advance too deeply into central Europe. The generals were unpolitical and blinded by Hitler's successes, the fieldmarshals understood the peril but were indecisive; therefore the younger generation must assume responsibility. Anyone who realised the senselessness of the sacrifices that had been made and were being made in the pursuance of the war would be unable to face the relatives of the fallen unless he had done everything in his power to end this perversion of the soldier's commitment. The oath of loyalty could not be a question, for loyalty had to be mutual: Hitler had betrayed the military forces and the nation. Whether a military coup could be justified politically at the end of 1943 was to Stauffenberg a question of minor importance; the essential thing was to end the war. The government emerging after the coup could only be transitory, it would lack real authority; but it would have to concentrate on holding the eastern front against an irruption of Russian brutality. Stauffenberg also hinted at the 1938 attempts to remove Hitler, and at the reasons for their failure.

Sauerbruch considered what he had heard. Stauffenberg had not asked him to act as assassin, but Sauerbruch saw that the idea could not be far from Stauffenberg's mind.[40] He was soon relieved of the need to answer because he was transferred. Perhaps Stauffenberg would have been more successful had he appealed to Sauerbruch's moral convictions by citing the murders of Jews, Soviet prisoners-of-war and others; but Stauffenberg evidently had more confidence in strictly military arguments.

After the assassination, the temporary head of state (*Reichsverweser*) and supreme commander of military forces was to be General Beck. His draft decree on the 'provisional command structure' incorporated the views on unified command structure which Beck had advocated before his resignation, especially in memoranda of 1934 and 1938. They were based on the negative effects of divided command during the First World War, and also on Stauffenberg's long-standing criticism of the existing command structure.[41] The decree ordered the creation of a 'great general staff', a war ministry, an 'officer bureau' (personnel office), and a 'high command east'. Subordinated to the 'great general staff' was the Leadership Staff of the Armed Forces (*Oberkommando der Wehrmacht/Wehrmacht-Führungsstab*, or OKW/WFSt), excluding sections to be incorporated in the 'high command east'; the Air Staff (*Generalstab der Luftwaffe*); and the Foreign Countries Bureau/Counter-Intelligence Branch (*OKW/Amt Ausland/Abwehr*). The chief of the 'great general staff' would be the joint chief of staff; he would also be commander-in-chief of the Army, although this title is not mentioned in the decree. A new 'commander-in-chief east' was to command the field army in the areas of Army Group A, Army Group South, Army Group Centre and Army Group North, in the Ukraine, and in the 'East Land' (*Ostland*, comprising the Baltic States and White Ruthenia). The staff was to come from the present General Staff of the Army, but there is no mention of a 'chief of staff'. Everyone was to be subordinate to the supreme commander designate of military forces, Fieldmarshal von Witzleben. General Erich Hoepner, formerly the famous commander of the 4th Panzer Army and an opponent of Hitler since before the war, was to take command of the Home Army – that is, presumably, if Fromm refused to co-operate.[42]

Thus the military command was to be reorganised as Beck had demanded in 1934. In time of war, the commander-in-chief of the Army and chief of the 'great general staff' would be one and the same; the peace-time chief of the 'great general staff' would then become quartermaster-general. Theatres of war would be commanded by commanders-in-chief immediately subordinate to the supreme chief of the military forces. The chief of the 'great general staff' would be in charge of overall planning and the overall military direction of the war under the authority of the supreme commander of military forces, and of the whole of Army command.

Fieldmarshal von Witzleben, who had been in the officer reserve pool since March 1942, agreed in September or October 1943 to act as supreme commander of military forces in the coup, and thus his name appeared under the plotters' first general order to all military commanders. The order began by stating that Hitler was dead, and accused 'an unscrupulous clique of Party leaders' of attempting to stab the fighting armies in the back and to usurp power for selfish purposes; therefore the Reich government had declared a military state of emergency for the maintenance of law and order, and had named Fieldmarshal von Witzleben as supreme commander of military forces and head of executive authority. To the uninitiated, 'Reich government' would have meant the existing government headed by Hitler's officially designated successor, Reich Marshal Göring. But when the plotters talked about the 'maintenance of law and order', they really meant that law and order must be *restored*.[43]

Martial law decrees were prepared, forbidding outdoor or indoor gatherings and the carrying of weapons except by members of the military or police forces. They prohibited private long-distance travel for three days, restricted long-distance telephone calls and imposed a 9 p.m. curfew. Vital services, communications, social and public services were ordered to carry on under threat of penalties imposed by martial law. The functionaries of the NSDAP were forbidden to carry out Party orders; all the Party's property and files were to be confiscated; no such property or files could be removed, under penalities imposed by martial law.[44]

Disobedience, looting, violence, treason against the government or against the country, murder, unlawful detention, extortion and bribery all came under martial law. The summary courts martial were to follow the established criminal procedures, but in urgent cases they could take whatever decisions they considered appropriate. They were to hear the accused and the witnesses, then pass judgement immediately and have it carried out without delay. In particular, the graver crimes committed by the organs of the previous regime had evoked popular outrage and 'required stiff punishment'. The courts would therefore be required to sentence and execute the leading criminals of the Nazi government during the first hours of the new regime.[45]

In mid-September Stauffenberg began reviewing and revising draft proclamations of the coup government's fundamental views and intentions.[46] In October Berthold Stauffenberg telegraphed Rudolf Fahrner (who was in Überlingen) to come to Berlin.[47] Claus Stauffenberg had been to see Colonel (GS) Stieff at Army headquarters at 'Mauerwald', and had earnestly entreated his help. Stieff had pledged himself to help with the coup, and to join another conspirator in an assassination attempt.[48] Claus Stauffenberg told Fahrner, with his usual laugh, that 'action' was expected in ten to fourteen days' time, and asked him to help formulate the proclamations which were to be broadcast after Hitler's fall.[49]

Fahrner worked in a room in Berthold's flat at no. 8 Tristanstrasse. He noticed some comings and goings, but he himself met only members of the family. His presence was concealed from outsiders; common literary interests would have provided an explanation if necessary. Superseded drafts were burned, and when they became so numerous that burning them might have attracted notice, Fahrner or Nina Stauffenberg had to take them away. When Nina came to Berlin for Olga, Countess Üxküll's wedding with Fredy von Saucken on 28 October, she had to take a rucksack full of papers back to Bamberg with her. Cäsar von Hofacker and other conspirators, as well as one of the chief 'loyalists' on 20 July 1944, Lieutenant-General Joachim von Kortzfleisch, also attended the wedding. On the 29th, Claus Stauffenberg told Nina at no. 8 Tristanstrasse that on this day he would have the decisive discussion with his cousin.[50]

Count Üxküll (Uncle Nux) also participated in the editing of the drafts. Berthold's wife Mika became the guinea-pig for testing the effect on 'the people'. She remarked that 'the people' had no notion of what the drafts were saying – a reaction which the authors thought auspicious. Claus Stauffenberg and Fahrner wanted to avoid the faddish trivialities of current linguistic usage, which they considered outworn: they wanted to further new thinking with good style as they understood it.[51] Stauffenberg showed the drafts to Schulenburg, Beck, Goerdeler, and brought back critical comments and amendments which were then incorporated.

Fahrner left after a few days and gave Claus Stauffenberg a gold ring inscribed 'FINIS INITIUM'. Stauffenberg wore it on his left middle finger. It re-phrased Stefan George's 'I am an end and a beginning'.[52]

Claus Stauffenberg discussed the military and political draft documents mainly with his uncle Üxküll; Berthold worked with Fahrner on style, and on legal and administrative points. They intended to restore just laws and procedures, occupy the concentration camps, restore to the prisoners their rights and honour, punish their torturers. All ministers and Party leaders down to district and community leaders would be arrested. All SS and police barracks would be surrounded with heavy weapons; all SS and police officers and men were to be disarmed and arrested. Two energetic Army officers would demand to see the senior SS officer in every barracks and declare to him: 'The Führer is dead. A small clique of unscrupulous Party leaders, who are strangers to the front, have attempted a coup d'état. A military state of emergency has been declared and executive power has been placed in the hands of the military district commanders.' They would go on to explain that the Waffen-SS was to be subordinated to the military district commanders and incorporated into the Army; the Waffen-SS were to be confined to barracks until further notice; this order would be enforced, if necessary, with the heavy weapons surrounding the installation. The senior SS officer must issue the necessary orders at once, in the presence of the two Army officers. If he refused he was to be shot, and the guard and the entire force were to be disarmed.[53]

47. Wedding of Olga ('Dusi'), Countess Üxküll to Fredy von Saucken, Hotel 'Kaiserhof', Berlin, 28 October 1943. From left, seated: Alexandrine ('Lasli'), Countess Üxküll, Lieutenant-Colonel Nikolaus ('Nux'), Count Üxküll, Olga ('Dusi') von Saucken (née Countess Üxküll), Lieutenant Fredy von Saucken, Freda von Saucken (née Baroness von Hollen), Siegfried von Saucken-Loschen, Bertha ('Püzze') Siemens (née Countess Yorck, sister of Peter, Count Yorck), Brigadier Dietrich von Saucken (Armoured Troops). From left, standing: Lieutenant-General Joachim von Kortzfleisch, Edelgard von Kortzfleisch, Elisabeth Blume, Margarethe Blume, Siegrid von Bülow (née Saucken), Berthold Stauffenberg, Friedrich Carl ('Piggy') Siemens, Maria ('Mika') Stauffenberg, Peter, Count Yorck, Nina Stauffenberg, Edgar, Baron von Üxküll, Lieutenant-Colonel (GS) Claus Stauffenberg, Marion, Countess Yorck (née Winter), Lieutenant-Colonel (Res.) Cäsar von Hofacker, Elisabeth von Saucken (née von Saucken, wife of Brigadier Dietrich von Saucken), Corporal Alexander ('Julex'), Count Üxküll, Lieutenant Oskar von Saucken, Second Lieutenant Hans-Erich von Saucken (killed near Jassy, 30 May 1944), Friedrich Blume

The fiction of a Party or SS putsch was dubious insofar as the new authorities would claim to be defending the old regime. The fiction was dropped, moreover, in the next order: acts of revenge were forbidden on the grounds that the population must 'become conscious of the contrast with the arbitrary methods of the previous rulers'.[54]

After Hitler's death the radio transmitters, which were guarded by SS troops, were to be occupied at once, and the proclamations were to be broadcast to publicise the uprising. After the announcement that Hitler was dead, the intervention by the Army was to be justified by the actions of the Party leaders. After the return of the soldiers the nation would be called upon to decide freely on its future constitution. Law and justice were to be restored immediately; the crimes of the National Socialists would be punished by due process of law. Peace would be sought straight away, but 'in view of what had happened' (territorial) losses would have to be sustained. Germany would be cleansed internally and reconciled with the divine powers, giving hope for the future; all Germans were called upon to serve the fatherland to the best of their ability.

A separate proclamation to the military forces emphasised the crazy way that the war had been prosecuted, abjured any idea of menacing other nations, and vowed not to sacrifice one more human life for the war except for the immediate defence of the country, of women and children; prudent commanders would lead the armies home as soon as possible.[55]

Stauffenberg wanted no return to the politicians and conditions of the Weimar era: as he said to Jakob Kaiser early in 1944, 'Herr Kaiser, there must be no restoration'. Since Stauffenberg declared himself in favour of giving the trade unions a political role, Kaiser understood him to oppose people like Goerdeler or Popitz. At the same time Stauffenberg wanted the historical achievements of the nobility to be taken into consideration in the renewal of the state, but without being any more specific.[56]

At Lautlingen in September, Claus and Berthold had discussed with Fahrner how all classes of society could be drawn on to form a government, and how a national representative assembly could be created without old-style political parties. They thought the pre-1933 system of political parties which were geographically and socially rootless, with their leaders coming up through the ranks, had produced not true popular representation but only self-serving corruption. They favoured a more direct represen-tation through communities, professional and occupational associations and interest groups. They wished people to accept the inevitable differences among individuals in terms of positions and possessions; they wanted owners of large estates voluntarily to divide up their land; they hoped to preserve rural life rather than replace it by 'constructions calculated for advantages' (meaning industry). They wanted employers and employed to share responsibility; technology, industry and commerce must be sub-servient to the nation and must not be allowed artificially to stimulate demand and thus to dominate the people, nor must technology be permitted to control politics through so-called 'objective necessities'. The propertied classes must anticipate the solution of social problems and must not wait until confronted by the demands of the propertyless classes. International disputes in future must have no more importance than differences among ethnic groups within Germany.[57] Claus Stauffenberg himself laid emphasis on the concept of the identity of Army and Nation. In 1942 and January

1943 he responded to a friend who favoured intervention by senior military leaders: 'Yes, we are indeed the leadership of the Army and also of the Nation and we shall take control of this leadership.'[58]

Stauffenberg's own essential political programme, however, was the overthrow of Hitler. Although he took part increasingly in political considerations and planning, and although he showed considerable interest in pro-labour legislation and social insurance, he had neither the experience nor the leisure to develop political programmes beyond the most basic and general views.[59] He was undogmatic: he did not adopt ideas, but sought human beings, as he had said in 1923. He thought people who 'adopted a world view' were 'unfree'. But he also believed that a state needed a religious foundation.[60]

Mierendorff's programme of 14 June 1943 had contained the idea of a non-partisan national movement. Now, in 1944, Leuschner, Jakob Kaiser and Habermann, the union leaders, all opposed the restoration of the Weimar multi-party system, and favoured *one* party which would be an elite of politically conscious forces. Leber placed little importance on programmes, and more on action.[61] This was one of the points on which Stauffenberg heartily agreed with Leber. Nevertheless the draft policy statements present a tangible constitutional and government platform, and Stauffenberg accepted it.

The emergency decree issued on 28 February 1933 by the Hitler government had suspended the basic rights enshrined in the Reich Constitution of 1919: personal liberty, freedom of speech and of the press, freedom of assembly and association, freedom of communication (post, telegraph, telephone), protection against search and seizure at home, and freedom of property. The plotters' prepared policy statements declared that these fundamental rights were reinstated with immediate effect, except for restrictions required by military necessity.[62]

It appears that no more work was done on the draft statements between November 1943 and March 1944, at which time Berthold Stauffenberg dictated draft statements to his trusted secretary in Naval High Command, apparently in order to obtain additional copies.[63] At the end of June Stauffenberg asked Rudolf Fahrner to come from Athens to Berlin to help revise the drafts. Fahrner helped Berthold revise the 'Proclamation to the German Nation': the changes were mostly stylistic, to eliminate excess emotion. The address to women was replaced by a single sentence in the general proclamation. References to the fronts and to the prospects of peace needed to be updated; the whole text became shorter and more pointed; a warning against political adventures 'from the right, the left or the centre' was added.[64]

Beck received the new versions on the evening of 14 July, the eve of Stauffenberg's second or third attempt on Hitler's life. On 15 July

Goerdeler, the prospective head of government, and Gisevius, the ambitious conspirator, were waiting at the home of Beck – the prospective head of state – for the news of Hitler's death. Beck read the revised proclamations to his visitors, which took some time, 'since there were quite a lot of hand-written corrections in the well-thumbed papers'.[65]

According to Goerdeler's statement during his trial after the failure of the coup (which was confirmed by Hassell and Josef Wirmer), the draft 'Proclamation to the German Nation' was written by Stauffenberg. It contained accusations and announcements which Rudolf Fahrner recalled in 1945 (years before the document became accessible in the archives). It declared that the German nation had not chosen Hitler: he had usurped the government through the most reprehensible intrigues. He had brought upon Germany unconscionable extravagance, corruption, debt and want; he had set up a terror regime in order to keep himself in power; he had mocked the divine commandments, destroyed justice, trampled on the happiness of millions, set at naught the honour and dignity, liberty and life of others; he had besmirched the good name of the German people through cruel mass murder; he had thrown the nation into misery. His self-proclaimed genius for generalship had led brave soldiers into disaster; he had committed treason against the nation and its soul; he had broken, time and again, the oaths which he had sworn in 1933. 'We should be unworthy of our fathers, we should deserve the contempt of our children, if we had not the courage to do all we could to avert this fearful danger and regain our self-respect.' Thus the dictates of conscience and honour were squarely placed before all expediency.

The preliminary aims of the new government were to remain in force until the nation could decide upon them. The aim of the new government was 'the true national community based on respect, mutual assistance and social justice', justice and liberty, integrity of government and administration, restoration of German honour in the community of nations. The guilty ones, who had brought disgrace and distress upon the German nation and other nations, would be punished.[66] The 'Policy Statement' set forth the 'principles' and 'aims' of the new government under twelve headings: restoration of law and justice; restoration of morality; opposition to lying propaganda; restoration of the liberty of thought, conscience, faith and opinion; renewal of education on a Christian basis, but with complete tolerance of other beliefs; reorganisation of the administration and the civil service; a new constitution; acknowledgement of the principle of economic freedom; a policy of social justice; the reform of public budgets; continuation of the war only in defence of the fatherland; establishment of a just peace.[67] Judges who had broken or bent the law were to be punished; the fundamental liberties suspended by the Hitler government on 28 February 1933 were to be restored; the concentration camps would be disbanded.

There was to be a new constitution, drawn up with the consent of the nation and the soldiers in the field, whose participation would carry 'special weight'; until this could be achieved a temporary constitution, to be promulgated immediately, would fill the gap. There would be an immediate halt to the persecution of the Jews, 'which has been carried on in the most inhuman and unmerciful, deeply shameful and irreparable way'. The announcement of due punishment for all lawbreakers applied particularly to those responsible for the murder of the Jews.

The 'Policy Statement' emphasised the need for the German worker 'to participate creatively in responsibility': although he could not be 'exempted from the naturally dominant laws of the economy', social policy would emphasise social solidarity against the adversities of contemporary life. Private property was to be protected, but the state would intervene where the accumulation of capital was in conflict with the protection of the labourers' health and ability to work.

The following passage in the 'Policy Statement' was very probably drafted by Beck and Goerdeler: 'We warned against this war, which has brought so much misery upon all of mankind, and we may speak freely. We believed and still believe that there were other ways to safeguard our vital interests.' Germany must now 'courageously and patiently cleanse her much-dishonoured name' and regain the trust of other nations, in the belief that all statesmen were seeking a fruitful end to this struggle and would soon be ready to work with Germany to mitigate the hardships caused by this war. The new government, the 'Policy Statement' continued, took the view that the moral and material restoration of Germany was necessary for the peace of the world; that England and Germany together must protect Europe against Russia; that no white nation must collude in the expansion of Japan at the expense of white nations or of China; and that the entire world needed to co-operate economically. In order for Germany to recover morally, German criminals must be punished by Germany.

The same ideas occur in a draft 'Radio Address' which was among the papers deposited for Goerdeler in Berlin. It was evidently one of the drafts which Goerdeler attributed to Stauffenberg's authorship. The deeper motivations for the coup d'état are again apparent. The only hope of ending this Second World War with honour and safeguarding Germany's vital interests was to replace Hitler's terrorist and criminal regime by one based on 'law, liberty, honour and decency'. 'But this goal is not alone decisive. What we see as decisive is this: we must no longer tolerate impudent criminals and liars dishonouring our nation and soiling our good name. [. . .] We had to act under the dictates of conscience.'[68]

In an untitled draft, likewise attributed to Stauffenberg, there is a statement that the ideas of National Socialism had been largely correct, but had been turned into their exact opposites after Hitler became Chancellor.

Hitler's new leadership class represented the rule of the inferior and the corrupt. The Russian campaign had started with the order to kill the commissars, and continued with the starving of prisoners-of-war and the mass hunting down of civilian labourers. The leaders who had been incapable of avoiding a war on two fronts had no right to drag the entire German nation down with them. After the change of regime it would be necessary to use Germany's military might to preserve her as a power, and to exploit disagreements in the enemy camp as quickly as possible, before the Allied forces landed in France could become effective.[69]

A 'Proclamation to the Armed Forces' was drafted by Beck, Tresckow and Stauffenberg.[70] It declared that the previous government had unscrupulously taken advantage of the soldiers' faith in a just war for the redress of injustice done to Germany after the First World War and for the protection of freedom: it had abused them for the purposes of unlimited conquest and the exploitation of subjugated nations. The previous government could never have brought about peace, but had everywhere sown hatred.

Hitler believed he possessed the abilities of a strategist, but had never acquired the necessary ability 'in the various stages of hard military service'; 'through pigheadedness, incompetence and lack of moderation' he had exacted from the Armed Forces extreme, but avoidable sacrifices: the destruction of the 6th Army at Stalingrad, the collapse of the North African campaign, and the useless losses in Sicily. 'Hundreds of thousands of brave soldiers must pay with their lives, health and liberty for the temerity and the vanity of one man.' This must not be allowed to go on, lest the young condemn their elders for their lack of courage to save the fatherland. 'We must act because – this weighs most heavily – crimes have been committed behind your backs which besmirch the honour of the German nation and soil its good name in the world.'

Finally, the proclamation promised that no sacrifices would be demanded now that were not strictly necessary for defence.

12

Contacts abroad

Long before the outbreak of war, those who were trying to overthrow Hitler's government from within sought to enlist the political support of the governments of France, England and America, without any great success. After hostilities had begun, the war aims that the Allies developed precluded any serious collaboration with the German underground resistance. Contacts between the anti-Hitler plotters and the British government in the winter of 1939/40, through the intercession of Pius XII, only resulted in Allied demands for better 'guarantees' than they had got from the Versailles Treaty, meaning above all the more effective disarmament of Germany. Consequently, point 8 of the Atlantic Charter promulgated by the British Prime Minister and the American President at Placentia Bay on 14 August 1941 demanded the disarmament of 'nations which threaten, or may threaten, aggression'. This presupposed Germany's unconditional surrender. After America had officially entered the war, a coalition of twenty-six nations joined in the Washington Pact of 1 January 1942, which proclaimed the war aims of complete victory and unconditional surrender. The German-Russian Pact of 1939, the division of Poland between the two countries, the Russo-British alliance of July 1941, the Washington Pact, the extended Russo-British alliance of July 1942, and Western acceptance of extensive territorial acquisitions by Russia together implied that Germany must suffer territorial losses even greater than those of 1919, not to mention Allied agreement on the expulsion of German populations from the severed territories.[1]

Ulrich von Hassell fully understood the meaning and implications of these agreements, and even the sanguine Carl Goerdeler feared that the Allies would leave East Prussia and Silesia to Poland, and would control the German administration. On the other hand, Goerdeler found it possible to believe, even as late as September 1943, that England would grant Germany the territorial *status quo ante bellum* even including her eastern frontier of 1914, and he thought the French would be willing to negotiate a new status for Alsace and Lorraine. All this depended, of course, on the early overthrow of Hitler's regime from within.[2]

Julius Leber had hopes for an honourable peace, but acknowledged by autumn 1943 that the enemy coalition could not be separated, and that unconditional surrender and the military occupation of Germany could not be avoided. Moltke had been clear in 1940 that Germany would lose a great deal of her territory, with Silesia going to Czechoslovakia or Poland. He feared Russian dominance and Communism in Germany. In December 1943 he brought to Istanbul, for transmission to the American and British governments, an offer from the conspirators to facilitate the occupation of Germany by western Allied forces, if a minimum of agreement on political issues could be reached. Cäsar von Hofacker made clear to his cousin Stauffenberg that France would not make peace unless Alsace and Lorraine were returned – not just made autonomous as Goerdeler would have it.[3]

Adam von Trott zu Solz, a legation counsellor in the Foreign Office and one of Moltke's friends in the Kreisau group, reported at the last major meeting of this group over Whitsuntide 1943 (12–14 June) that there was no prospect of talks between the conspirators and the western Allied powers, but he thought the Soviets might be amenable. Many people believed that the Soviet government was in fact less terrible than Goebbels's propaganda portrayed it. Trott favoured an attempt to contact the Soviet envoy in Stockholm (the ambassador from 1944), Alexandra Michailovna Kollontay. But first he tried again clandestinely to contact the western powers, during an official trip to Istanbul in June and July 1943.[4]

On 13 July 1943 a 'National Committee Free Germany' was founded under Soviet auspices at Krasnogorsk. This seemed to support Trott's idea that Russia might be amenable to talks – although the conspirators had reason to be a little apprehensive in view of the fact that the League of Polish Patriots, which had also been founded under Soviet auspices, had in early 1943 demanded the annexation of Danzig, West Prussia and Upper Silesia. Moltke, however, wrote on 28 July 1943 that Stalin's pronouncements (on the occasion of the founding of the National Committee) had changed the situation fundamentally.[5]

There were signs that Stalin might be willing to discuss a separate peace with Hitler or with another German head of government, and there were rumours that the former ambassador in Moscow, Count Schulenburg, would be welcome as a negotiator. Since Hitler rejected the idea of any such peace overtures, Schulenburg discussed them with Goerdeler and Hassell, around the end of July.[6] Trott and Hassell still believed that England and America did not want Germany to pass under Soviet control. But Hassell, like Trott, would have sought an understanding with Russia if there was no alternative.[7]

Count Schulenburg, however, thought that it was still possible to reach an understanding with the western powers, and that there was no need to turn toward the Soviet Union. Beck did not favour it either, and emphasised the fact by confirming Hassell as his foreign-policy advisor.[8] But by mid-July 1944 Beck was willing to accept either Hassell or Schulenburg as foreign minister, depending on who could expect to obtain the better terms.[9]

Hard upon Trott's visit, Moltke was in Turkey on official business from 5 to 10 July 1943. Like Trott, he sought support for the German anti-Hitler movement. He made an extraordinary proposal: a German general-staff officer who was fully informed on the German positions in the west would be allowed to fall into British hands. He would help to plan the opening of the German front in the west and equally help plan an airborne invasion of western Europe by British-American forces; the German front in the east would continue to be defended. Moltke also intimated to his contacts that he opposed Hitler's assassination but not his overthrow by force.[10] There was in fact an Allied plan, codenamed 'Rankin', to occupy territories under German control before the launch of any full-scale invasion of the continent, if the German Armed Forces 'collapsed'. Moltke may have known of it. He hoped to complete the arrangements on a further visit to Istanbul in December. But the fact that the agent of the American intelligence organisation (Office of Strategic Services or OSS) in Istanbul, Alfred Schwartz, neglected to pass on Moltke's suggestion until 14 September did not augur well for a productive contact.[11]

In the meanwhile Fritz-Dietlof, Count Schulenburg, the former Vice-President of Berlin Police and former Governor of Silesia, who had served from 1940 in No. 9 Infantry Regiment in Potsdam and had fought on the Russian front, was sounding out people in Paris. On 2 August he reported to Olbricht and Tresckow that the military commanders there were ready to allow western Allied forces to march in as soon as they attacked – but until then they had no way of promoting the collapse of Hitler's regime.[12]

Stauffenberg also participated in discussions on foreign relations. He met Hassell at the beginning of November at the home of Captain (Res.) Jens Peter Jessen, who was advisor to Popitz, the Prussian Minister of Finance, and who headed the Quartermaster-General's travel pass office in Grossadmiral-Prinz-Heinrich Strasse in Berlin. Stauffenberg shared the hopes of Goerdeler, Ambassador Schulenburg, Trott and Moltke that negotiations would be possible after a coup. He wanted an honourable peace. With his brother Berthold, Fritz-Dietlof, Count Schulenburg and Captain (Res.) Count Schwerin von Schwanenfeld he discussed (with the 1919 precedent in mind) what to do if a weak or socialist government were to accept a dictated peace.[13]

Stauffenberg differentiated between negotiations with the Soviet Union on the one hand, and Soviet efforts to subvert the German military forces and the German state on the other. On one of his brief visits to Bamberg at the end of 1943 or beginning of 1944, he brought along a flyer issued by the National Committee Free Germany and commented: 'I am engaged in treason against the government. But those people are committing treason against the country.'[14]

Communist historians have attempted to show that Stauffenberg's aims had affinities with those of the Soviet-sponsored Free Germany movement. They maintain in particular that Stauffenberg's friend, Colonel (GS) Mertz von Quirnheim, had developed such sympathies, partly because of his experiences on the eastern front and partly because his brother-in-law, Brigadier Otto Korfes, had helped found the German Officers' League (on 11/12 September 1943, in the prisoner-of-war camp at Lunjovo) and was active on the National Committee. A further source for these contentions was the account given by Hans Bernd Gisevius, who was a counter-intelligence agent in Zurich from 1939 to 1944, but also acted as liaison between the conspirators and the American intelligence representative in Berne, Allen Dulles. Both the Communists' and Gisevius' claims were advanced in aid of their own respective political agendas.[15]

In autumn 1943 Stauffenberg was resolutely opposed to giving up either the eastern or the western front. Berthold said to his colleague in Naval High Command, Commander Alfred Kranzfelder, that as long as the fronts held it might be possible to use the prospect of negotiations with Russia to put pressure on the western powers; he amplified this with the comment that co-operation with the Soviet Union would mean total ruin, whereas England could not wish to turn over Europe to the Soviets and would probably negotiate with a German government that had removed Hitler.[16]

Trott and Moltke were already willing to 'open' the western front in autumn 1943; they must have had in mind the military governors of France and Belgium, Lieutenant-General von Stülpnagel and Lieutenant-General Baron von Falkenhausen. Towards the end of March 1944 Claus Stauffenberg told Peter Sauerbruch that all available forces ought to be moved to the eastern front, because an Allied landing in the west was inevitable. The war was lost; without a change of regime total ruin was assured, but after a change of regime there was a possibility at least of negotiations. Shortly before the Allied landing in Normandy, Stauffenberg discussed with Leber the idea of guiding western Allied forces through the German minefields in order to avert the collapse of the eastern front. Both thought it unlikely that the western Allies would co-operate, but the idea (nicknamed 'the western solution') was raised again and again. Stauffenberg indicated to Lieutenant (Res.) Michel in the summer of 1944 that he hoped the eastern front would hold, and that the western powers would advance as far as the German eastern front. This was tantamount to unconditional surrender.[17]

Moltke was misled by the Allied intelligence officers in Istanbul when he was there from 11 to 16 December 1943, and did not receive a response to the plotters' offer to open the western front after they had removed Hitler and his regime.[18]

Trott had accepted territorial and political changes to the *status quo ante bellum* as early as spring 1942. The plotters' draft policy statement of autumn 1943 also implied this. Moltke's message to the American and British governments was that the conspirators considered the defeat, unconditional surrender and occupation of Germany to be necessary for moral and political reasons, and that they would accept it before opening peace negotiations. They wished to co-operate with the western powers because they expected decent and dignified treatment from them; but only if the eastern front was defended, along a line approximately from Tilsit to Lvov, could the plotters hope to justify their actions to the German people and avert the accusation of having practised a 'stab in the back'. The group were willing to co-operate militarily with the Allies if such co-operation led to a western occupation of Germany in the shortest possible time; if this was agreed, the group undertook to form a provisional anti-National Socialist government simultaneously with the Allied landing. The group favoured liberty and democracy, and saw the rise of 'national communism' as the greatest danger for Germany and Europe; nonetheless, while they would conduct a non-communist internal policy, and intended to hold the front in the east, they wished to co-operate with Russia: their government would have strong links with the socialists and trade unions and would co-operate with 'independent Communists of personal integrity'.[19]

None of the ideas in Moltke's communication is unequivocally identifiable with Stauffenberg's views at the time. But the offer of military co-operation could not have been made without the support of the military plotters, meaning the group around Beck and Stauffenberg. Without Hitler's overthrow, which was evidently impossible without killing him, the offer of military co-operation could not have been honoured.

Brigadier Richard D. Tindall, the American Military Attaché in Ankara, saw Moltke mainly as an intelligence source, but did urge his superiors to impress upon President Roosevelt, General George Catlett Marshall (US Army Chief of Staff) and Colonel William Donovan (Director of the American intelligence agency, the Office of Strategic Services) that there was a possibility of ending the war in the west and saving perhaps hundreds of thousands of lives. Nothing came of it, and after Moltke's arrest on 19 January 1944 the contact was lost. After the failed July coup Donovan wrote to the President that in view of Russian suspicions it had been impossible to pursue Moltke's proposal. On 1 November 1943 the Allies had agreed to communicate 'immediately' to one another any peace feelers they received. But according to the published government documents the British and Soviet embassies were not notified of Moltke's 'peace feeler' until 14 May 1944.[20]

Stauffenberg spoke at length with his friend Mertz in Berlin between 11 and 13 December 1943. Mertz was on a short period of leave from his post as chief of staff in the 29th Army Corps. Stauffenberg said the war was lost and must be ended by removing the regime; any further military action must serve only to protect German territory. As long as the fronts held, even the defeated could still negotiate – if the enemy powers recognised the new German leaders and their commitment to reform. They might even see Germany as a useful potential ally against Bolshevism. Then honour could be restored, and reconstruction would be possible. The peace terms would undoubtedly be harsh, but this must be tolerated in view of the guilt on the German side. Mertz accepted this estimate and resigned himself to giving up his military profession.[21]

On 23 November 1943 a group of Swedish diplomats and experts, including the banker Jakob Wallenberg (a friend of Goerdeler's), arrived in Berlin to discuss the resumption of shipping between Göteborg and ports in Iceland, Spain, Portugal, Africa, Turkey and Greece. Senior Naval Judge Berthold, Count Stauffenberg and Commander Kranzfelder were to represent the German Navy. The night before the planned discussion, an air raid destroyed the buildings of the Swedish legation, so that the visitors were forced to return to Stockholm immediately. On the following night the hotel 'Kaiserhof', where they were to stay, was also destroyed. The same raids destroyed the Naval High Command building. Its offices were moved temporarily to a garrison at Eberswalde, sixty kilometres north of Berlin; on 22 January 1944 they were moved to camp 'Koralle', which was a collection of makeshift huts at Bernau, thirty kilometres north of Berlin.[22] The Swedes returned on 1 December for two days of negotiations. From 3 to 6 January 1944 Stauffenberg and Kranzfelder were in Stockholm with a German delegation that also included Minister Leitner and Trade Attaché Behrens of the Foreign Office, and Commander von Wahlert and Lieutenant-Commander Raehmel of Navy High Command.

Stauffenberg and Kranzfelder used the occasion to try through the Wallenberg brothers to set up a contact with the British government. The Naval Attaché in the Swedish legation in Berlin, Commander Moje Östberg, arranged for Kranzfelder to speak alone with Jakob Wallenberg during a lunch in the Stockholm naval officers' mess. No direct record of the result has been found. But there is evidence that Claus Stauffenberg believed he had a line of communication with Churchill.[23]

Berthold Stauffenberg was also concerned with food supplies to Greece. The Greek population under German occupation enjoyed the sympathy of the world, and the belligerents had been engaged in arrangements to allow food supplies to reach Greece under international controls since 1942. Shipping routes had to be charted through combat zones and minefields. Berthold Stauffenberg travelled to Switzerland on such business in May 1943, and there he met with Robert Boehringer, the President of the Commission mixte de secours du Comité international de la croix-rouge; he also represented Naval High Command in this matter in meetings with

OKW and the Foreign Office to consider the use of three more Swedish ships to supply Greece, and he was able to confirm that the Navy would give the necessary permissions. Boehringer credited Berthold Stauffenberg with personal merit in this matter. A further trip to Switzerland failed to materialise and no others were in prospect, as Berthold Stauffenberg wrote to Boehringer on 1 May 1944, adding significantly: 'Nevertheless I hope that we shall see each other again in the not-too-distant future.'[24]

Another line to the outside ran through Otto John, who had been working as a corporation lawyer for Lufthansa in Madrid since the beginning of 1942. He co-operated with the OKW intelligence bureau and had long been involved in anti-Hitler conspiracy. In autumn 1943 Captain Ludwig Gehre, who also worked in intelligence, told John that Olbricht's new chief of staff had got things moving towards Hitler's overthrow: he was a Swabian count who was a cut above that 'whole lot of Prussian counts' in the conspiracy.[25]

On 23 November 1943 Gehre instructed John to see if a line for rapid communication could be established through the American embassy in Madrid to General Eisenhower, the Supreme Commander of Allied Forces in North Africa and Europe, who had his headquarters in Algiers. At that time a coup was expected to take place in Germany within the next few days. John flew to Madrid and soon reported, through Klaus Bonhoeffer (Dietrich's brother) at the Berlin Lufthansa offices, that the line was available. When John tired of waiting for news of the coup he flew back to Berlin on 16 December, only to learn that Hitler had cancelled the occasion for which his assassination had been planned. John also reported that in Madrid he had been given reason to hope that negotiations would be possible after a coup. In January 1944 John met Stauffenberg at Werner von Haeften's house and suggested a contact between Roosevelt and Prince Louis Ferdinand of Prussia. But Stauffenberg took a dim view of the old monarchies and anything reactionary. He declared that the priority was to bring about 'a new situation'. After Hitler's fall soldiers on both sides of the conflict would best be able to determine what needed to be done. Stauffenberg gave John the same instructions Gehre had given him, and John flew back to Madrid at the beginning of February.[26]

John returned to Berlin on 10 March and wrote two reports. He wrote of intensive Allied preparations for the invasion of western Europe, somewhere between Bordeaux and Hamburg, in the second half of June. The British and Americans were resolved to force Germany to surrender unconditionally; Stalin wanted mainly to destroy the German Army and the National Committee Free Germany was a political deception; German agents were prone to believing rumours about east-west tensions.[27]

Stauffenberg relied particularly on the counsel of Adam von Trott. In the autumn of 1943 Moltke had told Trott, half-jokingly, that he would not allow him to become acquainted with Stauffenberg. In fact, Stauffenberg appears to have been acquainted with Trott since spring 1941, and had looked him up in his office early in 1943 before he left for Tunisia. From November 1943 Trott was a frequent visitor to Stauffenberg's office; early in November he reported to him the result of his October trip to Sweden, namely that England was not likely to consider a compromise peace after a coup.[28]

The relationship developed into a close friendship at the beginning of 1944. Trott told his wife at Easter (9 April) that he had met a highly capable, fiery young officer who had got things moving again.[29] Stauffenberg was Trott's senior, but younger than Tresckow, Hofacker, Olbricht, and appeared still younger than he was. Albrecht von Kessel, a friend of Trott's in the foreign service who met Stauffenberg at Schwerin's and Brücklmeier's residences in December 1943 described him thus: 'Although he had lost an eye and a hand in the Tunisian campaign he looked handsome and strong like a young war-god. With his wavy dark hair, the vigour of his harmonious features, his tall figure and the restrained passion of his personality he quite captivated us.'[30] Trott also referred to Stauffenberg, cryptically for the sake of caution, on 23 April: after Moltke's arrest he (Trott) had felt lonely at first, but was now enveloped and encouraged 'in a world of intense work and more than comradeship' for which he was grateful.[31]

Trott later told police interrogators that Stauffenberg had consulted him on the central issue: could a Germany that had rid itself of Hitler and National Socialism obtain a separate peace in the west or the east, in order to concentrate its forces on one side and force that side, too, to negotiate? Trott testified that Stauffenberg could never be quite persuaded that it was impossible to make an arrangement with the western Allied commanders to join forces with 'another Germany' against Russia. Stauffenberg had insisted on this possibility, claiming that Beck shared his conviction, until the last days, so that Trott had supposed that Stauffenberg must have had some commitments from the western side. Goerdeler also testified that Stauffenberg had said in June and July 1944 that he had a line of communication with Churchill, although he had not maintained that concessions might be secured from the Allies.[32]

At his trial before the 'People's Court' on 7 August 1944, Yorck stated that in June 1944, after the Allied landing in France, Stauffenberg 'did not vigorously object' to his, Yorck's, view that unconditional surrender would be demanded of Germany even after a successful coup d'état. At that time Hofacker considered that a compromise peace was no longer possible, and took the position that since the war had been lost militarily, the only thing that could be done was to end it politically and to render the inevitable defeat as bearable as possible. He advocated a well-timed capitulation so as to secure for Germany a 'tolerable position in central Europe'.[33]

On 18 June, the eve of his last trip to Stockholm, Trott wrote to his wife and hinted that he was expecting Stauffenberg. Later Trott told his interrogators that he had always disagreed with Stauffenberg about the willingness of the western powers to negotiate with an anti-Hitler government. Stauffenberg had insisted: 'I must know how England and the USA would act if Germany were forced to negotiate at short notice.' What Trott said was, of course, adapted to – or by – his interrogators. Stauffenberg had not been discouraged by Trott's scepticism, nor by that of Colonel Hansen (who had succeeded Canaris as head of Abwehr). He had insisted, even after Trott returned from Sweden empty-handed, that in view of the Soviets' rapid advance the West would negotiate with an anti-Hitler government.[34]

Trott's interlocutor in Stockholm, who (as Trott must have known) worked for British intelligence, asked him to put down his proposals in a memorandum. This memorandum reflects Stauffenberg's insistence on certain terms: the group for which Trott spoke could not consider co-operation with the Allies on the basis of unconditional surrender, for both psychological and political reasons; while they accepted military occupation, they must be granted territorial integrity and self-determination in order to allay fears of arbitrary annexations, a slave trade in German labourers and soldiers, and foreign justice against the criminals in the regime (all of which were provided for in the plan drawn up by Morgenthau, the American Secretary of the Treasury). If these things occurred, Hitler's enemies would be driven into resistance against the Allies. The anti-Hitler forces in Germany needed the support of senior military and police commanders, which they could obtain only if they could offer Germans a better prospect. If not, they did not wish to accept the odium of the defeat. The memorandum also raised the spectre of two opposing German states supported by the respective Great Powers: a 'national-bolshevik' one in the east and a western one with a nationalist opposition based on a Hitler legend. The West did not appear to be making any attempt to prevent this. The group capable of overthrowing the regime from within did not want a military dictatorship, but a democratic civilian government based on broad representation from which only Communist organisations advocating violent revolution were to be excluded. The memorandum then specified the plotters' own terms, which reflected their realisation that harsh conditions must be accepted, although their territorial expectations proved unrealistic. They demanded demobilisation under German administration; an interval of several weeks between surrender and military occupation; a return to the borders of 1936; no occupation of German territory by the Soviet Union; trial of war criminals in German courts.[35] This program would have preserved the existence of the Reich which was so close to Stauffenberg's heart. But there are indications that it was only meant to be a negotiating position.[36]

A few weeks after the successful Allied invasion of Normandy, prospects improved for a coup in concert with the commander of Army Group B in France, Fieldmarshal Rommel, who at first tolerated and finally supported the conspirators in the west. At the beginning of June Rommel had agreed to a plan worked out by the Military Governor of France, Lieutenant-General von Stülpnagel, and his Personal Aide, Lieutenant-Colonel (Res.) Cäsar von Hofacker, in consultation with Lieutenant-General Geyr von Schweppenburg, Brigadier Hans Speidel, Brigadier Count Schwerin and Vice-Admiral Ruge: to negotiate an armistice in the west and to arrest Hitler.[37] On Sunday, 9 July 1944, Rommel, with his Chief of the General Staff, Brigadier Hans Speidel, received Stauffenberg's cousin Lieutenant-Colonel (Res.) von Hofacker in his headquarters at La Roche-Guyon. Hofacker informed Rommel that Stauffenberg planned to kill Hitler and if possible Göring and Himmler at the same time, and to activate prepared plans to take over the government. Rommel said if Hitler were assassinated he would support the plot in every way he could.[38] On 16 July Rommel told Lieutenant-Colonel (GS) Elmar Warning, the senior staff officer of the 17th Luftwaffe Field Division near Le Havre, that he (Rommel) and the new Supreme Commander West, Fieldmarshal von Kluge, had given Hitler an ultimatum to end the war. If Hitler refused, Rommel would open the western front, 'for there is only one more important decision to make: we must see to it that the Anglo-Americans are in Berlin before the Russians'. On 17 July Rommel was seriously wounded in an air attack on his car on a road near Livarot. Kluge sent Rommel's ultimatum, with a supporting statement of his own, to OKW on 21 July.[39]

On 10 July Hofacker travelled to Berlin with instructions from his own superior, Stülpnagel, to report that in Stülpnagel's command everything was ready, and to urge immediate action. On the evening of 11 July Hofacker reported to Beck his 9 July conversation with Rommel, Rommel's readiness to act against Hitler, and Stülpnagel's instructions. Beck declared at the conclusion of the conversation that prominent negotiators would be sent to London and Moscow immediately following the coup d'état.[40]

By this time the situation was almost equally hopeless on all fronts. Army Group Centre in the east had collapsed: the defeat and losses were greater than those sustained at Stalingrad. Between the beginning of the Soviet offensive on 22 June and 8 July, twenty-eight German divisions with 350,000 men were annihilated. Army Group North was now in danger of being cut off by the Russian advance to Riga and being annihilated as well. The front in the west seemed only weeks away from collapse.[41]

Since all the efforts of Moltke, Trott, John and Gisevius had only gone to show that the enemies had no intention of negotiating with an anti-Hitler government, Stauffenberg's role in the conspirators' foreign relations consisted mainly in receiving bad news. Although his instructions to Trott of 18 June seem to indicate a different state of mind, he knew that nothing at all was in prospect other than unconditional surrender – as he told Peter, Count Yorck at the beginning of June. Stauffenberg also had no doubt that Germany would come under complete military occupation. On 1 July he told a friend, the sculptor and artillery lieutenant Urban Thiersch (who served as liaison between Stauffenberg and Colonel Hansen), that over-throwing the regime could not change the military position, which was hopeless; still it might prevent much bloodshed and cancel out the disgrace of the present government. But 'to sit idly by and abandon oneself to disgrace and paralysing duress' was worse than failure.[42]

In mid-July, and again on 18 July, Goerdeler asked Stauffenberg if East Prussia could be saved. Stauffenberg said no, it could not. As his remark to Yorck indicates, he had reached this conclusion not later than the beginning of June. After the start of the Soviet offensive in June, he had a fellow conspirator, Major Axel von dem Bussche, who had lost a leg, moved from the Insterburg military hospital in East Prussia to Hohenlychen near Berlin.[43]

Stauffenberg's close friend Colonel (GS) Mertz von Quirnheim, who on 17 June had succeeded him as Chief of Staff to Lieutenant-General Olbricht, said on 13 July: 'I realise that we shall bring about the end of the German military forces; whatever peace we shall have, it will remove the military class. Still, we must act, for the sake of Germany and the west.'[44]

On 16 July Stauffenberg and his brother Berthold met at Berthold's flat with Hofacker, Yorck, Trott, Schwerin, Fritz-Dietlof, Count Schulenburg, Mertz and Hansen. Trott said later, under interrogation, that Stauffenberg thought it might be possible to prevail upon the military commanders in the west to move the front back to the German frontier and 'to create the conditions for joint action by the western powers and Germany against the Soviet Union with the aim of putting an early end to the war' (the 'western solution'). Hansen said under interrogation that Trott had thought the enemy powers would be willing to negotiate if the regime in Germany were radically changed. In the subsequent discussion it was maintained – evidently by Stauffenberg – that such negotiations were to be conducted between soldiers, 'and *not only with the enemies in the west but also with the Soviets*, for which purpose old [former Ambassador] Schulenburg and the former Military Attaché in Moscow [Köstring], as experts, were to be involved in the negotiations'. A 'Berlin solution' was also considered: the plotters would seize control of the entire communications system and issue orders 'which would *start the fronts on a retreat* that *could not be reversed by Hitler's headquarters*'. After much discussion, the plotters reaffirmed their commitment to the 'central solution', which involved the assassination of Hitler.[45]

The evidence about those last discussions in June and July 1944 came mainly from arrested conspirators who were fighting for their lives, or who might even have been trying to suggest to their interrogators their own value as potential negotiators. After all, the interrogators had perhaps more reason to fear retribution after Allied occupation. But testimonies also came from many officers who were incapable of lying or unwilling to try. Moreover, the evidence given to Secret State Police officials is substantially confirmed by independent sources, so that the probability that it reflects the true views of the conspirators is high.

Stauffenberg understandably never quite abandoned hope of saving some of Germany's independence and greatness, as well as saving lives and ending the war. But on the whole the helplessness of the plotters, including Stauffenberg, emerges clearly enough from the evidence. No one wanted to negotiate with them. Attempts to seek a line of communication with the Soviet Union proved too dangerous, and indirectly led to the arrest of Reichwein and Leber on 4 and 5 July. Trott stated, under interrogation, that Stauffenberg might have had '*certain information from the opposite side*', from '*the English Supreme Command*'. But if that had been the case, Trott would have known and would not have had to guess at it. Otherwise, Trott stated, Stauffenberg 'with his deed "was acting in a void in terms of foreign policy"'. This is in fact what Stauffenberg and his fellow conspirators said in their prepared radio broadcast: 'We do not know what position foreign countries will take towards us. We had to act from the duty imposed by our conscience.'[46]

13

Assassination plans

When Lieutenant-General Olbricht telephoned Stauffenberg in hospital in Munich between 9 and 14 September 1943 and asked him to come to Berlin immediately, Hitler's assassination was planned for a date round 20 September. Colonel (GS) von Tresckow procured British plastic explosives from Army Group Centre and brought them to Berlin some time in September. Colonel (GS) Stieff, who as chief of the General Staff Organisation Branch had relatively frequent access to Hitler, had agreed to participate in the assassination if he did not have to do it alone. In the same month, Stauffenberg made an unsuccessful approach to Colonel (GS) Bürker when the latter was Chief of OKW/WFSt Branch II (Organisation). Also in September Stieff broached the matter to Colonel (GS) Joachim Meichssner, the Chief of OKW/Army Staff, who in November 1943 succeeded Bürker as Chief of OKW/WFSt Branch II (Organisation). Meichssner agreed, but after many postponements withdrew because he could not bear the stress of waiting.[1]

Goerdeler gave notice to Jakob Wallenberg in September that a coup d'état was imminent and asked him to dissuade the western powers from bombing Berlin, Stuttgart and Leipzig until 15 October. The coup was expected in September or before 15 October, but some time had to be allowed for the armistice negotiations which were to follow the coup.[2]

The plan was to bring the explosives, concealed in a briefcase, to a briefing with Hitler. One such briefing, at which Stieff was most likely in attendance, occurred on 1 October, but any attempt on Hitler at that time seems not to have gone beyond the discussion stage. Apparently Stieff had not even received – or definitively agreed to receive – the explosives. Stauffenberg took them to Stieff at 'Mauerwald' only at the end of October, and at that time appealed to him to carry out the attack, which Stieff agreed to do. Also at the end of October Stauffenberg expressed his hope to Rudolf Fahrner that the assassination attack would be carried out within ten to fourteen days.[3]

Evidently Meichssner had by now retreated and Stieff was not willing to act alone. Stauffenberg had repeatedly offered to carry out the assassination himself. The other conspirators argued against this, saying he was too important for the overall success of the coup.[4] They may have been apprehensive of Stauffenberg's radicalism. The events of July 1944 suggest that many high-ranking conspirators wanted to be quite certain of success. Apart from these considerations, Stauffenberg with his physical handicaps was of course not an ideal candidate for assassin. Stauffenberg said to Fahrner on 29 June 1944 that the assassination attack had failed to materialise in October 1943 because of 'the inaction of those who had agreed in October to carry it out'. Goerdeler was forced to notify Wallenberg that the action had been delayed.[5]

There followed an attempt to induce Hitler to visit Army Group Centre, as he had done in March 1943. On this new occasion Schlabrendorff, Colonel (GS) von Kleist, Captain Eggert, Lieutenant-Colonel (GS) von Voss, Major (GS) von Oertzen, Captain (Cav.) von Breitenbuch and Lieutenant von Boddien intended collectively to shoot Hitler with their pistols. The Army Group headquarters moved from Smolensk to Orscha and then to Minsk, but Hitler could not be prevailed upon to visit it. On 12 October Kluge suffered serious injuries in a road accident between Orscha and Minsk: this radically changed the environment at Army Group Centre, which had hitherto been favourable to the efforts of the plotters.[6]

Then in November Captain Axel, Baron von dem Bussche appeared on the scene. As an officer in the famous No. 9 Potsdam Infantry Regiment, he had been shot through the chest on three separate occasions (the first time while crossing the Marne in May 1940, the other times on the Russian front), and had been highly decorated. On 5 October 1942 he had witnessed the shooting of some three thousand Jews by SS and Ukrainian militia at Dubno in the Ukraine and concluded that Hitler must be killed. In November 1943 he obtained an indefinite leave, with the collusion of his regimental adjutant, Lieutenant Richard von Weizsäcker who knew what was on Bussche's mind, and who signed Bussche's service book for a leave without entering destination and dates. Bussche then went to see Count Lehndorff at his estate in East Prussia near Hitler's headquarters and suggested to Lehndorff that Hitler must be killed and that he, Bussche, could do it. Lehndorff made inquiries about Bussche and put him in touch with Fritz-Dietlof, Count Schulenburg who took him to see Stauffenberg at Camp Düppel on the western outskirts of Berlin.[7]

Bussche was enormously impressed by Stauffenberg's cool manner and appearance ('like one of Alexander the Great's generals'). He told Stauffenberg of the events at Dubno and found that Stauffenberg was aware of the mass-murder programme and in fact motivated by it to act against Hitler. Stauffenberg then began something of a lecture on tyrannicide, to the effect that the concept was easier to cope with for Catholics than for Protestants, but that Luther too had pronounced on the right to resist. Bussche set little store by these disquisitions and remarked that Lutheranism certainly permitted the shooting of mad tyrants, and in any case he had long transcended such considerations. When Stauffenberg raised the question of the soldier's oath, Bussche replied that it was founded on mutual loyalty, and that it had been broken by Hitler and was therefore null and void.

After these preliminaries, Stauffenberg said Bussche must go to 'Mauerwald' and see Stieff, who had regular access to Hitler's situation briefings and could get Bussche admitted to Hitler's presence as well. The unspoken but clearly understood presumption was that Bussche would assassinate Hitler. Bussche asked why Stieff had not done it. Stauffenberg said Stieff was as nervy as a racing jockey: he was not up to it. This was, among officers, an unequivocal verdict. Bussche was surprised that one who held the fate of Germany in his hand 'could not do that'. Stauffenberg, smoking a series of small Dutch cigars, told Bussche to go away and think about it.

Bussche went to lunch with Schulenburg and recounted the conversation to him. Then he went back to Stauffenberg and said yes. They discussed method. The use of a pistol seemed to them too uncertain because it would have to be concealed and might be discovered, perhaps through hidden x-ray equipment, and because alert guards might prevent a well-aimed shot. Stauffenberg then signed a travel order for Bussche to go to Army High Command headquarters and gave him the draft of the first coup announcement, which Fahrner had worked through, to take to Stieff. Bussche read the draft in a sleeping-car on his way to East Prussia. He was shocked by the plotters' lack of political confidence, since they evidently believed they must begin with the lie that an ambitious Party clique had murdered Hitler and aimed a 'stab in the back' against the armies in the field.[8]

At 'Mauerwald' Bussche stayed in the guest hut of Army High Command. He was to discuss the technical side of the assassination with Kuhn, Stieff's head of section III; and the 'general' questions – how and when he would be introduced into Hitler's presence – with Stieff. Stieff explained that the attack could be made during a presentation of new equipment, and that Göring and Himmler were expected to be present as well. Two or three soldiers had to wear and show the equipment: Bussche was to give the necessary explanations and act as their leader. Bussche asked Stieff about x-ray controls at the entrances to Hitler's headquarters. A long knife that he proposed to carry in one of his high boots was not likely to be detected, but he was concerned about the explosives. Bussche and Stieff agreed that the assassination would involve the death of the assassin. As no date for the equipment presentation had yet been set, Bussche returned to Berlin.[9] Stieff went on leave on 20 November. He asked Kuhn to take the explosives that Tresckow had procured and that Stauffenberg had brought to 'Mauerwald' back to Stauffenberg.[10]

On 22 November Bussche had dinner at the Crown Prince's palace on

Unter den Linden with his friend Karl Konrad, Count von der Groeben, and with Kurt, Baron von Plettenberg, the Crown Prince's financial administrator. Toward the end of the evening there began one of the great air raids on Berlin and everyone, including 'Empress Hermine', the second wife and now the widow of Emperor William II, retired to the air raid shelter. On 23 November Bussche travelled to Denmark to see his mother, who was Danish. (He never stayed more than three days for fear his presence might compromise her in the eyes of other Danes: as a German Army officer over six feet tall he was somewhat conspicuous.)[11]

Around 28 November he returned to Stieff at 'Mauerwald' to wait for the presentation date. Kuhn offered Bussche British explosives with acid time-fuses similar to those which Tresckow, Schlabrendorff and Gersdorff had employed in March 1943. The fuses contained acid in a glass vial. When the vial was broken and the acid released, it ate through a wire embedded in cotton which released a spring with the striker pin, and so triggered the explosive. The delay before the explosion depended on the temperature, and also on the concentration of the acid, the thickness and alloy of the wire, and the condition of the cotton that retained the released acid. These combined factors could produce relatively unpredictable variations between four-and-a-half and thirteen minutes. Bussche did not want to let the success of an assassination attack depend on something so uncertain. He requested German explosive and fuses he was familiar with, thinking also to avoid any implication that the enemy had supplied the materials. Kuhn and his special missions officer, Lieutenant (Res.) Hagen (who had served with Stauffenberg in the 10th Panzer Division in Tunisia, and whom Stauffenberg had won completely for the cause), were observed on 28 November as they buried the rejected materials at 'Mauerwald'. Luckily the men who conducted the subsequent inquiry were co-conspirators; Stieff was questioned by a colonel of the Abwehr, but was able to fend off all suspicion. There was considerable difficulty in obtaining substitute materials, because regulations were generally followed to the letter in the German Army, and it was essential not to arouse any suspicion. Kuhn asked a friend, Major Knaak, who commanded No. 630 Pioneer Battalion east of Orsha on the Dnieper and who had looked him up at 'Mauerwald', to procure the items Bussche needed; Knaak promised to do so. Then he asked Stieff to authorise a trip by Lieutenant (Res.) Hagen; Hagen flew to Minsk, where he was received by Major (GS) von Oertzen and obtained the explosives.

One evening, while Bussche was still waiting for the materials, he and Kuhn went to have dinner at the house of Marion, Countess Dönhoff, at Quittainen. After Hagen's return Kuhn brought Bussche a kilogram of explosives and an anti-tank mine, but no useful fuses. Bussche had wanted a hand-grenade fuse with a four-and-a-half seconds' delay, intending to cover the short hissing noise by clearing his throat vigorously; but it had proved impossible to procure a hand-grenade from the pioneers.[12]

Bussche went back to Berlin; Schulenburg and Schwerin went to see Lieutenant von Gottberg, adjutant of No. 9 Infantry Reserve Battalion at Potsdam, and explained to him that hand-grenade fuses were required. Gottberg provided two. Bussche went to see Gottberg at his flat in Potsdam, and together they cut off the wooden handle of a hand-grenade and attached the fuse, with a shortened lanyard, to Bussche's kilogram of explosives. The entire assembly fitted into Bussche's uniform-coat pocket. Gottberg and Second Lieutenant Ewald Heinrich von Kleist, who was serving in the same battalion, dropped the remnants of the hand-grenade off Glienicke Bridge into the River Havel.[13]

Bussche returned to 'Mauerwald' and again stayed in the guest hut. On the third day Stieff summoned him and expressed his regret, which was noticeably tempered by relief, that the equipment that was to be presented had been destroyed in air raids, so the assassination plan could not go forward. Bussche said that when a new date was set Stieff could inform the conspirators in advance, present the uniforms and equipment without him (Bussche) and carry out the assassination on that occasion. Stieff's reaction to this was nervous and unpleasant. Bussche returned to the east front and took over his battalion of the Potsdam regiment (I/G.R. 9) which he found in a 'totally frazzled' condition. On 31 January 1944 he had his left leg shot away. He was still in hospital on and after 20 July 1944; as he had kept the explosive and fuses with him, in a small suitcase on top of the wardrobe in his hospital room, he lived through some anxious moments when secret-police agents interrogated him about Stauffenberg's special missions officer and fellow conspirator, Captain Klausing of his own Potsdam regiment, who had visited him on 17 July. A few weeks later Count Groeben took the awkward items away with him and threw them into a lake.[14]

Stieff later testified that Stauffenberg had continued his search for an assassin, so that he needed a fresh supply of explosives. Kuhn, whose background was in the pioneer troops, was supposed to see to it.[15] According to what Goerdeler told the police and the 'People's Court', a new date for the assassination was expected to be set around Christmas. Stauffenberg had asked Goerdeler to alert the political delegates for the days from 25 to 27 December and to hold himself ready. Stauffenberg told Mertz between 11 and 13 December that the crucial event could occur any day now.[16]

When the occasion failed to materialise, Goerdeler reproached Stauffenberg for alerting the political delegates and endangering so many people. Stauffenberg agreed that they would not be alerted in advance again. Goerdeler also spoke against the assassination of Hitler, but Stauffenberg insisted on it and said he would do it himself rather than consider any other method of removing Hitler.[17]

In January 1944, in Schlabrendorff's Berlin flat, Tresckow, Stauffenberg, Freytag-Loringhoven (head of Abwehr Branch II), Gersdorff and Schlabrendorff discussed the procurement of additional explosives, which

Freytag-Loringhoven promised to arrange. They also talked about their experiences with the methods of assassination that they had tried to employ. Tresckow knew, from his visit with Kluge to Hitler's headquarters on 26 July 1943, that Hitler's midday situation briefing offered a good opportunity.[18]

Until mid-January 1944 Stauffenberg went on trying to bring Bussche back from the front. Stauffenberg sent a teletype order for Bussche to travel to General Army Office in Berlin. The adjutant of Bussche's regiment, the No. 9 Infantry Regiment, Lieutenant von Weizsäcker, thought the teletype message was incautiously phrased. Bussche's divisional commander decided on 21 January that Bussche could not be sent to Berlin unless a replacement were provided. Weizsäcker drove to the rear area in order to telephone Stauffenberg without being overheard, and explained what had happened. Before another request for Bussche could be prepared, he had his left leg shot away.[19]

On 28 January Second Lieutenant Ewald Heinrich von Kleist, son of Ewald Heinrich von Kleist-Schmenzin (a conservative politician and uncompromising enemy of Hitler), received a telegram. He belonged to the Potsdam No. 9 Regiment; after being wounded at the front he had been posted to the reserve battalion at Potsdam, and had just arrived at his father's house in Pomerania when the telegram ordered him to return to Potsdam at once. On the following morning, a Saturday, he was back in Potsdam. Schulenburg summoned him to the flat they shared in the officers' club and said, without any preliminaries, that he had a fairly unpleasant proposal for him: would he kill Hitler and sacrifice his own life to do it? Stieff was doing it too, with explosives. When Kleist asked why he was needed if Stieff was doing it, Schulenburg said it was to make quite sure, as Stieff was nervous. As Bussche had done, Kleist concluded that Stieff could not be relied on.[20]

On the same day Schulenburg took Kleist to Stauffenberg, who talked with him during the entire afternoon, for six hours. He explained that soon any attempt to save Germany by ending the war would be meaningless. But an opportunity to save Germany would exist shortly. He did not wish to press Kleist, only to ask him if he felt in duty bound to take a course that that might cost him his life. Bussche had been ready to kill Hitler, but was no longer available. A new opportunity had now offered itself: there was to be a presentation of equipment, new uniforms that had been tested at the front, before Hitler on 11 February. Kleist was to act as a front-line officer and lead the presentation. For this purpose he was to carry a briefcase containing an extensive written report – and plastic explosives.[21]

Kleist wanted twenty-four hours to think about it. He returned to Schmenzin and on Sunday explained Stauffenberg's proposal to his father. He rather hoped his father would dissuade him, on the grounds that it was too late for a compromise peace and that a new stab-in-the-back legend would arise. But his father said he must do it. If he failed to respond to such a challenge he would never be happy again. Kleist accordingly returned to Potsdam and informed Stauffenberg that he was ready to do it. He was to receive from Stauffenberg English plastic explosives and a hand-grenade fuse with a four-and-a-half seconds' delay. Schulenburg told Kleist to tie the explosive to his stomach.[22]

The day for the presentation passed without Kleist being called into action. He learned that this was because Stieff had been informed at the last moment that Himmler would not be present. The senior conspirators considered it necessary to eliminate Hitler's popular designated successor, Göring, simultaneously with the dictator himself; equally the conspirators believed Himmler must be eliminated at the same time because he commanded the enormous private army of the SS. In light of the events of 15 July 1944, however, it is difficult to dismiss the notion that there had been a lack of resolve.[23]

At about the same time, at the end of January 1944, Stauffenberg's special missions officer, Lieutenant (Res.) Werner von Haeften, decided he could shoot Hitler with a pistol. Haeften had been so badly wounded in Russia that he could no longer serve at the front. However, his brother, Hans-Bernd, asked him if he really wanted to break the Fifth Commandment, and Werner gave up his plan.[24]

Then Tresckow made another attempt to gain personal access to Hitler: he wrote a letter to Brigadier Heusinger, the Chief of General Staff Operations Branch, who daily reported the situation on the eastern front at Hitler's midday briefings, suggesting that Tresckow should replace him while he was away on leave. Tresckow also wrote to Stieff with instructions for detonating explosives intended for the assassination. Schlabrendorff took the letters to Heusinger and Stieff. Neither of them acted as Tresckow had hoped.[25]

But Tresckow did succeed in persuading Captain (Cav.) Eberhard von Breitenbuch to make an attempt on Hitler's life. Breitenbuch had been an opponent of the National Socialist regime ever since it had come to power. In 1940 he had served as Fieldmarshal von Witzleben's special missions officer, and through Tresckow's intervention he had been transferred to the same position with Fieldmarshal von Kluge in August 1943. Tresckow had explained to him that his real job was to influence the Fieldmarshal to support the conspiracy. Since then Breitenbuch had been kept up-to-date on assassination plans. After Kluge's road accident of 12 October 1943 he remained in his post with Kluge's successor, Fieldmarshal Busch.[26]

On 9 March 1944 Busch received orders to brief Hitler at his 'Berghof' headquarters near Berchtesgaden on 11 March. Hitler sent his Condor FW 200 for Busch and his aides. On the afternoon of 9 March Tresckow and Oertzen came to see Breitenbuch. Tresckow said he had learned that

Breitenbuch would be at Hitler's midday briefing on 11 March; therefore the fate of Germany, of the women and children threatened by enemy air raids and of the soldiers at the front, were all in Breitenbuch's hands and he was responsible for them. Oertzen produced a type of rifle grenade out of his briefcase, with a fuse in its base that allowed for delays from one second to three minutes. Breitenbuch was to carry it under his uniform, set it at an appropriate moment, and fling his arms round Hitler until the grenade exploded. Since Tresckow did not mention Göring or Himmler, he must have thought that the coup could not be delayed until all three could be killed together. Breitenbuch thought Tresckow's proposed method of assassination too uncertain, and said he preferred to use his pistol, which he would carry in his trouser-pocket. Tresckow pointed out that Breitenbuch would have to aim at Hitler's head or neck because he would be wearing protective clothing. Stauffenberg appears to have been informed of the plan: he arrived in Bamberg on 8 March and left during the night of 9/10 March.[27]

Busch and Breitenbuch arrived at Salzburg airport in the morning of 11 March; one of Hitler's 7.7-litre Mercedes took them to the 'Berghof'. As it happened, Busch, his operations officer Colonel (GS) Peter von der Groeben and Breitenbuch were the only officers who had come from the front. Among those waiting to be ushered into the great hall for the midday briefing were Göring, Keitel, Jodl and Goebbels. Presently an SS officer opened the door and they all entered in order of rank. Breitenbuch, the least senior, carrying maps and other items Busch needed for his report, was about to enter last when he felt his arm grabbed by the SS officer, who said that no special missions officers were to be admitted. The opportunity to kill Hitler had vanished.

Tresckow waited at Army Group Centre headquarters in Minsk when Busch, Groeben and Breitenbuch returned that evening. He said to Breitenbuch: 'Well, Breitenbuch, the plan has been betrayed.' He thought that someone must have overheard his telephone conversations with the conspirators in Berlin, in which he had notified them of the plan.[28]

Also at the beginning of 1944 Stauffenberg got Lieutenant-Colonel (GS) Peter Sauerbruch transferred to the General Army Office. During a conversation in the presence of one of Olbricht's section heads, Lieutenant-Colonel (GS) Bernardis, Stauffenberg recited Stefan George's poem 'The Anti-Christ' – without comment, but it was evident to Sauerbruch that Stauffenberg's intention was to win over Bernardis for the conspiracy. He also spoke of the crimes committed against the peoples in the German-occupied territories and against the Jews. In mid-March Stauffenberg informed Sauerbruch of the failed efforts involving Bussche and Kleist, and of Werner von Haeften's religious scruples. Finally he asked Sauerbruch whether he would be willing to do it. Sauerbruch expressed his view that there were still other ways of eliminating Hitler, and went on to say that he did not feel confident of an accurate pistol shot; that he did not wish to harm third parties by using explosives; and that there was the question of the oath of loyalty. Stauffenberg retorted that loyalty could only be reciprocal and that Hitler had long since broken his oath to the nation. Soon after this conversation Sauerbruch received a new posting, and when Sauerbruch came to say good-bye Stauffenberg remarked that it was a good thing that the issue had been decided in this way. On about 25 March Sauerbruch returned to the front as senior staff officer of the 4th Panzer Division.[29]

At about that time, during a trip by sleeping car from Berlin to Führer Headquarters at Berchtesgaden, Stauffenberg made an attempt to persuade Meichssner to act as assassin. Stauffenberg and Captain (Cav. Res.) Paulus van Husen of OKW/WFSt (at whose flat Stauffenberg commonly met with Yorck) shared a compartment; Meichssner was in another compartment on the same train. Meichssner had access to Hitler, he was a decided enemy of the Führer, and he was energetic. But lately he had shown himself not quite equal to the demands of his work and the stress of conspiracy: his nerves were in tatters. When the train had left Berlin, Stauffenberg extracted two bottles of burgundy from his suitcase and said, 'Now we shall have a talk with Meichssner.' He invited him into his compartment and began a wide-ranging disquisition on the military and political situation. The not-too-subtle subtext was the question of how Hitler could be removed. Finally, when the bottles were empty, Stauffenberg tried to get Meichssner to agree to a further meeting at Brücklmeier's; but Meichssner would not commit himself. When Meichssner had gone back to his own compartment, Stauffenberg said to Husen: 'It's easy to see that he does not want to go on.'[30]

Trescow and Stauffenberg had run out of resources to bring about Hitler's assassination. There was no lack of plotters willing to carry it out. Stauffenberg's cousin Hofacker, under Gestapo interrogation after the failed coup, insisted that he and Stauffenberg had been at odds because he, Hofacker had wanted a much more 'active' role; at his trial he told the presiding judge that he had only one regret, his inability to take Stauffenberg's place as assassin. Carl, Count Hardenberg, special missions officer to Fieldmarshal von Bock, recounted: 'And in any case, *all* those I knew in our immediate group had volunteered to do it.' This included Captain Klausing, who had been wounded at Stalingrad and had become special missions officer to Stauffenberg in April 1944. Klausing expressed surprise that conspirators such as Stieff, with the rank of general, had failed to act, while so many younger officers had volunteered but had not gained access to Hitler.[31]

New opportunities arose only at the end of June, when it was Stauffenberg himself who gained access to Hitler.

14

Launching the insurrection

Claus, Count Stauffenberg, had declared himself ready in 1942 to assassinate Hitler, and after his recovery from the severe wounds he had received in Tunisia, he continued to insist that he himself would kill the dictator. The other conspirators would not stand for it because he was physically handicapped, and because he was essential for the coup d'état in Berlin. In any case he had no access to Hitler until he was designated as General Fromm's Chief of the General Staff.[1]

At weekends Stauffenberg often went to stay with friends in the country. When he had to visit Army High Command Headquarters, which was moved, with Hitler's headquarters, to the Berchtesgaden area in March 1944, he would always, if possible, stop off at Bamberg, which was on his way. He spent the weekend of 1 and 2 April with Werner von Haeften on Hardenberg near Küstrin. Carl, Count Hardenberg, recognised in Stauffenberg 'the model of an intelligent and brave German officer', a man like a hero of antiquity, who was fully aware that he was sacrificing himself.[2]

When Ludwig Thormaehlen saw Stauffenberg in Berlin in April, Stauffenberg told him: 'Ludwig, I almost thought I would never recover. We still have a mission. And I despaired that I could not complete the mission that had fallen to me. [. . .] Ludwig, if what is now happening goes on happening, not one of us can go on living: family will be meaningless, family will no longer be possible, it will not exist any more.'[3] Later, in June, he remarked: 'Now it is not the Führer or the country or my wife and four children who are at stake: it is the entire German people.'[4]

Schulenburg took the same view. In July 1944 he told one of the young officers in his Potsdam regiment, who was in the plot, that it would be impossible to go on living if the coup failed; but it had to be attempted for the sake of history and justice.[5] On Maundy Thursday, 6 April, Schulenburg returned home to Trebbow after a four-week battalion commanders' training course at Antwerp and announced that Stauffenberg would join them for Easter. When he learned that his wife had already invited Captain Klausing, Stauffenberg's special missions officer, it occurred to him that the combination might be conspicuous; but he abandoned the thought, probably realising that the suspicion the conspirators feared was mostly in their own minds. Stauffenberg arrived on Easter Sunday afternoon, relaxed and cheerful, enjoyed the Schulenburgs' hospitality, and patiently endured the governess and the nanny, who were both National Socialists and who competed to cut his meat for him. After dinner the company told ghost stories and hunting stories, and discussed Shakespeare, Rilke and George. On Monday morning, which was still a holiday, Stauffenberg and Schulenburg took a long walk in the woods. Stauffenberg evidently gave Schulenburg some of his views on the future of Germany. On Tuesday morning at six Stauffenberg and Klausing returned to Berlin.[6]

On 7 April Berthold, Count Stauffenberg, wrote asking Rudolf Fahrner (who was still in Athens) to keep him up-to-date on various literary efforts, such as Alexander Stauffenberg's book-length poem on the death of Stefan George ('Der Tod des Meisters'), Karl Josef Partsch's 'Agis und Kleomenes' and Eberhard Zeller's 'Hannibal'. He reported that Willi Dette, who had been able to join the Air Force after 'aryanisation', was now a prisoner-of-war. Amongst all this he inserted the phrase: 'Regrettably nothing new to report on the move to Wannsee.' It meant that the uprising was not an immediate prospect.[7]

On 20 and 21 April Claus Stauffenberg met with Schwerin, Brücklmeier, and Botho von Wussow, one of Schwerin's friends who worked in the Foreign Office Information Branch and was currently serving in Lisbon. Wussow gave his assessment of the foreign-policy situation; Stauffenberg was so impressed that he suggested introducing Wussow to General Fromm. Wussow was doubtful, but Stauffenberg believed Fromm to be in sympathy with the plotters and said: 'Don't worry about Fromm. Just don't tell him we want to abolish the military; apart from that you can speak with him quite openly.'[8]

The decision to make Stauffenberg the Home Army Commander's Chief of the General Staff was taken before the middle of May. Albert Speer, then Minister of Munitions, later recounted that Hitler's Chief Adjutant, Major-General Schmundt, had designated Stauffenberg for the position in order to 'invigorate the work of Fromm, who had grown tired'. Schmundt had told Speer that Stauffenberg was considered one of the most efficient and able officers in the Army. Hitler himself had advised Speer to collaborate closely with Stauffenberg. Speer remembered Stauffenberg's youthful charm, and his unique way of being 'poetic and precise at the same time'.[9]

The Commander-in-Chief of the Home Army, General Fromm, had from time to time uttered sentiments which gave the conspirators reason to believe that he would not hinder their plans. When Stauffenberg reported to Fromm in mid-June as his new Chief of the General Staff, he told him he was working to overthrow the Führer. Fromm thanked him and did not comment further. On 3 July, as he admitted at his trial before the 'People's

Court', he even told Helldorf that it would be best if the Führer committed suicide.[10]

Stauffenberg's new posting must have been the reason for his promotion to colonel: the position was normally held by an officer with the rank of general. Two of Stauffenberg's predecessors in the position since March 1941 had been posted as colonels (GS) and promoted to brigadier while in post; Stauffenberg's successor was a brigadier.[11]

Stauffenberg's efforts to foster the uprising are reflected in Mertz's letters to his future wife in the spring of 1944. In January 1942, when Mertz was serving on the General Staff Organisation Branch, he had written that in a desk job his 'soldierly dreams were not being fulfilled'. After almost sixteen months' service at the southern end of the eastern front, as Chief of the General Staff of 29th Army Corps, Mertz wrote on 2 March 1944 that the struggle against the Russians was a battle against a force of nature, and one which was controlled by a keen intellect to boot:

> And therein lies the only inner resonance which making war evokes in me, from a purely soldierly point of view: there is enjoyment in fighting such a good opponent. It is rewarding and one learns more every day. You will understand these peculiar-sounding thoughts, which come back to me again and again, if you consider that, apart from all the further and deeper foundations of our struggle, my work here is the fulfilment and apogee of my professional life. The visible manifestations of war are slowly making clear to me the ultimate substance of my profession, which begins to fulfil itself only when and where other professions and objectives begin to recede. To lead men in those moments when we stand at the frontiers between this world and the next, and to wrestle with heart and mind over questions and decisions which always involve human lives.[12]

On 11 May Mertz wrote to his future wife that he was feeling 'mildly excited' because he had learned through a 'private official channel' that he had been posted to the officer reserve pool in anticipation of another posting, but he wanted to stay at the front: 'I do not know what those boys have in store for me. If they post me to OKH I shall declare my disinterest in the war.' Four days later he wrote:

> Most *awful* let-down! I am definitively posted as chief [of staff] to General Army Office (Stauffenberg's position). I am devastated. I had certainly hoped that, if I were reassigned, I should become an army chief [of the General Staff]; and now this home posting for which I am in no way suited. Just because I once sat in Organisation Branch for 2½ years! [. . .] Hilde, I am furious and very disappointed about this new posting. In this phase of the war I, of all people, at home.[13]

On 22 May Mertz was on his way home from the Rumanian front; from Vienna he announced that he would arrive in the Black Forest, where his fiancée Hilde Baier lived, on 24 May. On 23 May he came to see Stauffenberg and Olbricht in Berlin. They explained to him that any hopes of stabilising the fronts had to be abandoned. On 24 May Mertz telephoned Hilde Baier from Angerburg to say that he would not arrive until 25 May.[14]

The dates suggest that Stauffenberg sent Mertz to 'Mauerwald' to get hold of the explosives in Stieff's custody. All the most important offices and officers were in the Berchtesgaden area, where the Führer had his headquarters from February to mid-July. Brigadier Stieff, Chief of the General Staff Organisation Branch, was also at Berchtesgaden. From there he telephoned Stauffenberg's successor in Organisation Branch, Lieutenant-Colonel (GS) Klamroth, who was at 'Mauerwald'. (Klamroth had served as quartermaster in the 10th Panzer Division in Russia.) His colleague in Organisation Branch was Lieutenant (Res.) Hagen, who had served in the same division in Russia and in Tunisia. Klamroth and Hagen each packed half of the explosives into their briefcases and took the courier train to Berlin. On 25 May they handed the materials to Stauffenberg in his office.[15]

Mertz now felt 'liberated', because he could take an active part in preparations for the insurrection. On 13 July he explained his motives to a friend: 'It is quite clear to me that we shall bring about the end of the German military forces, for, whatever sort of peace we achieve, it will remove the military class once and for all; yet we must act for the sake of Germany and the West.' After a few days' leave in the Black Forest he set out for Berlin on 9 June, arrived on 10 June, and moved in with Stauffenberg at no. 8 Tristanstrasse on 14 June. On 17 June he wrote to Hilde Baier:

> Today at 14.00 p.m. I sat down on Stauff's chair, with an audible thud and all the self-confidence I could muster. My head is swimming after the 6 short days of 'introduction'. But it is high time for me to get down to business and to be permitted to take responsibility; in the last 2 days I got frustrated just sitting there and listening. Olbricht will have to be very patient with me in the first weeks, until I am 'up and running'. But I took over from St. a very well-trained staff with a number of really good General-Staff officers.[16]

This was, in theory, the breakthrough for the insurgency plan. Now there was a real prospect of access to Hitler for a man who was willing to kill him. Stauffenberg would have access to Hitler, and Mertz would conduct the coup d'état in Berlin.

As soon as Stauffenberg saw the merest prospect of being able to carry out Hitler's assassination himself, in the second half of April, he was ready to seize the opportunity. Wussow learned during his visit on 20 and 21 April 'that Stauffenberg would carry out the assassination'.[17]

In late May – certainly not later than 13 June – Stauffenberg asked his sister-in-law Melitta, Countess Stauffenberg, who was in charge of the test station for special flying equipment at the Air War Academy at Berlin-

Gatow, to fly him to the Führer's Headquarters and back again. After he had explained his plan, she agreed, but had to tell him that she could only use a Fieseler 'Stork', which was slow and would require fuelling stops.[18]

When Klamroth and Hagen brought the explosive on 25 May, Stauffenberg told Hagen that he intended to make an attempt on the lives of Hitler and his immediate associates (Göring and Himmler). On 26 May, after a discussion with Stauffenberg, Goerdeler told Hermann Kaiser, who kept the war diary in Home Army Command, that Stauffenberg had given him his word of honour to use force against the Führer.[19]

Nevertheless the arguments still continued, if only to re-affirm from time to time the commitments made. On 6 June 1944 American, British and Canadian forces landed in Normandy. Tresckow attended a meeting of army commanders convened in East Prussia by the Chief of the General Staff; Stauffenberg asked Count Lehndorff, who happened to be in Berlin and was about to return to Steinort, to ask Tresckow whether he thought the coup d'état was still meaningful, since no practical political objective was conceivable. Tresckow gave his answer through Lehndorff:

> The assassination of Hitler must take place *coûte que coûte*. Even if it does not succeed, the coup d'état must be attempted. The point now is not the practical purpose, but to prove to the world and before history that the German resistance have staked their all and put their lives on the line. Beside that, nothing has any weight.[20]

Stauffenberg also asked Rudolf Fahrner, on 4 July, whether he thought it was right that he, Stauffenberg, should assassinate Hitler. Fahrner believed that Stauffenberg only made up his mind to do it after receiving his affirmative answer.[21]

A few days before the actual assassination attack (it must have been on 10 July, the eve of an expected opportunity for an attack on Hitler), Stauffenberg and Yorck came to have dinner with Paulus van Husen. They talked about the urgency of overthrowing Hitler, which had been increased by the arrest of Reichwein and Leber on 4 and 5 July, and about whether it was 'ethically permissible to use force'. When Stauffenberg left to catch his overnight train to Berchtesgaden, he said: 'There is nothing for it, he must be killed.'[22]

On 29 May Stauffenberg, travelling in company with the Chief of the General Army Office Quartermaster Branch, Lieutenant-Colonel (GS) Herber, took the night train to Berchtesgaden, where he was to attend briefings of the General Staff Organisation Branch. These were undoubtedly in preparation for a briefing with Hitler himself, and besides that they gave Stauffenberg the opportunity for another attempt to persuade Stieff to take an active part in the assassination.[23]

On 1 June Stauffenberg arrived in Bamberg, apparently directly from

Berchtesgaden, for a few days' leave. During the night of 7 June, at 2.00 a.m., he took a train back to Berchtesgaden. In the afternoon, from 15.52 to 16.52 p.m., accompanying General Fromm, he took part in a 'special briefing' with Hitler, his first direct encounter with the dictator. Keitel and Speer were there, too. Hitler took Stauffenberg's left hand with both his own hands when he was presented to him. Then Hitler started shuffling situation maps with a shaking hand, repeatedly staring at Stauffenberg. Stauffenberg, sitting in conference at a round table with Hitler, Göring (who was obviously wearing make-up), Keitel, Himmler and Speer, reflected that Speer was the only sane person there; all the others were psychopaths. Hitler's eyes seemed to be veiled; the atmosphere was mouldering and rotten, making it hard to breathe. Hitler's personality made a poor, weak impression on Stauffenberg.[24]

The meeting discussed statistics for munitions production, anti-tank guns, aeroplane production, measures for rapid troop mobilisation, shelters for Hitler's special train, and induction fuses which responded to mine-sweepers.[25]

On 8 June Stauffenberg and Herber took part in the Corpus Christi Day procession in Berchtesgaden before they returned to Berlin.[26]

There is no indication that Stauffenberg intended an attempt on Hitler's life on 7 June. His remark to Stieff 'that in the presence of the Führer one could move quite freely' contained his own realisation of the fact and a reproach to Stieff. Mertz was still on leave and therefore not available to lead the insurrection in Berlin during Stauffenberg's absence. Stauffenberg's question to Tresckow, transmitted by Lehndorff, followed a few days later. Stauffenberg could not proceed on his own. After the Allied invasion of Normandy it was necessary to review the political decision to go ahead with the coup with the principals – Beck, Olbricht, Wagner, Fellgiebel, Hoepner and Witzleben. Moreover, Stauffenberg's remark to Stieff on the occasion of his second meeting with Hitler, on 6 July – that he had all the explosives with him – suggests that he did not carry them with him on 7 June.[27]

The urgency of the insurrection grew daily. Tresckow wanted Stauffenberg to travel to France, seek out Major-General Speidel (Rommel's Chief of Staff), and get him to create a large gap in the front so that the western Allied forces could invade Germany. Then, on 22 June, began the great Red Army offensive against Army Group Centre, which by 8 July had annihilated 28 German divisions. Also on 22 June Reichwein and Leber met with leaders of the German Communist Party, Anton Saefkow and Franz Jacob; on 4 July Reichwein and the Communists were arrested, and Leber was arrested the next day. Leber's arrest weighed heavily on Stauffenberg, since he perforce felt partly responsible for it.[28]

In the second half of June Lieutenant-General Olbricht gave a farewell party for Stauffenberg and a group head of General Army Office in the officers' mess of the Cavalry and Driving School at Krampnitz. The entire staff of General Army Office and some other officers were present. The Officer Commanding, Colonel Momm, a friend of Stauffenberg's, showed off riding-horses and trotters. Stauffenberg was persuaded to mount a horse, and performed a piaffer. At that time or soon afterward Momm promised Stauffenberg to send the school's armour to the Siegestor in Berlin after Hitler's assassination.[29]

Over the weekend from 24 to 26 June Stauffenberg was with his family in Bamberg. Toward the end of June Stauffenberg and a few generals and politicians met at the house of the famous surgeon Ferdinand Sauerbruch (father of Peter Sauerbruch) in Grunewald. When the company left, Stauffenberg stayed behind. He looked tired; Sauerbruch suggested a few weeks' rest. Stauffenberg said no, he had an important mission, and began to talk about the coup plans. Sauerbruch did not want to hear about them and quickly interrupted: Stauffenberg's injuries were too serious, his physical condition was poor, his nerves were not strong enough, he might make mistakes. Stauffenberg was hurt and got up to leave. Sauerbruch managed to placate him, but could not dissuade him.[30]

The Stauffenberg brothers hoped to save Germany from utter ruin, but they were prepared for the ultimate catastrophe. Under the sign of the Secret Germany, as it were, they drew together once more, to prepare their legacy.

Alexander Stauffenberg had been called up at the beginning of 1939 for service as a reserve non-commissioned officer in the 4th battery of No. 53 Motorised Heavy Artillery Reserve Battalion. At the beginning of September 1940 he was discharged and returned to 'freedom' in Würzburg University. He worked on Theoderic, the Ostrogoths and the Migrations, and thought the subject fascinating but intellectually sterile. In a letter to Theodor Pfizer he said he was looking forward to turning his attention to 'what is really important today, the Greeks', from Peisistratus to the fall of Athens. The writing of history was certainly 'not always very easy' these days, but he preferred it to being 'an acting servant of others while they make history', in which one 'might possibly want this or that to be different'.[31] But if he had to be a soldier he wanted to be at the front. When he was called up to serve in No. 389 Artillery Regiment in January 1942, he rejected the chance given to men of his advanced years to volunteer for a coastal battery in Norway: 'We shall go along to Russia, after all we must see where the old Ostrogoths did their wandering!' He was at the front with the 6th Army; in the autumn of 1942 he was wounded and thereby escaped the Stalingrad catastrophe, and after his recovery he was appointed Professor of Ancient History at the University of Strassburg. Promoted to Second Lieutenant, he was called to service again on 15 February 1943, and, 'artilleristically spruced up' by a training course in Berlin in April, he

48. Alexander Stauffenberg as an artillery second lieutenant, 1943

returned to the eastern front, and was sent to Normandy in June for more artillery training. Here he used his free time to translate the Seventh Book of the *Odyssey* and worked on his poem on 'Der Tod des Meisters' (which had been held up for years by criticisms from Blumenthal). Back in the east, he was a front-line artillery observer on the Dnieper from 5 October, and was wounded on 30 October near Novo Lipovo. Nearly insensitive to pain, he did not want to leave his unit and had to be moved from the clearing station back home by force. He worked on 'Der Tod des Meisters' again and finished it by New Year's Eve 1943, hoping to see it published semi-privately in 1944. After his recovery he wanted to return to his field unit at once, but he was posted to No. 69 Heavy Artillery Reserve and Training Battalion in St Avold in Lorraine in February 1944. Now he hoped to be posted to Strassburg in order to resume teaching at the university.[32]

Rudolf Fahrner had returned to Athens in the autumn of 1943, after completing his work on the draft proclamations. He succeeded in bringing Alexander to the German Institute in Athens in the spring of 1944 to give a lecture on 'Tragedy and State in Early Athens'. After the lecture, he persuaded Brigadier Kurt Schuster-Woldan, the Artillery Commander with 68th Army Corps, to appoint Alexander National Socialist Leadership Officer in Athens, effective from 1 June. When Alexander reported to his general and said that he was wholly unsuited for the position, the general replied that was why he had been appointed.[33]

At the beginning of June Alexander and Berthold discussed changes to 'Der Tod des Meisters'. Berthold opposed a reference to the death of Jesus and demanded a ranking of the friends according to their closeness to or distance from the Master. Claus Stauffenberg, too, even after a heavy day's work securing replacements for the front lines (and carrying on with the plot), found time to read Alexander's poetic memorial carefully and consult with his brothers about it.

On 28 June Fahrner flew from Athens via Prague to Berlin, arriving early on 29 June, and went directly to see Claus at the flat in Wannsee, before the latter left for work in the small Mercedes which Haeften usually chauffeured. Stauffenberg received Fahrner saying: 'Effendi, this may make you laugh, but I am engaged in high treason with all the means available to me.'[34]

At no. 8 Tristanstrasse Fahrner met Mertz, who was still living there, and participated in the discussions. Claus went to Alt-Friesland on Sunday, 2 July, with Haeften, Klausing and Georg von Oppen (who was in the plot). From Alt-Friesland he tried unsuccessfully to telephone Kluge, who took over as Supreme Commander West from von Rundstedt on 3 July. Fahrner spent 2 and 3 July in Berthold Stauffenberg's hut at Camp 'Koralle', in the room belonging to Commander Kranzfelder (who was away). He and Berthold took long walks together and swam in some of the many lakes. They revised the text of 'Agis und Kleomenes', passages of Fahrner's and Alexander's *Odyssey* translation, and the draft proclamations and policy statements. Moreover, at Claus's request they drafted an 'Oath' consisting of statements Claus had specified orally. Claus also worked through all of these pieces, using the three fingers of his left hand to write in changes, particularly to the 'Oath'. Then Fahrner dictated the final versions to Berthold's secretary, Maria Appel. Beck received the old drafts of policy statements with the handwritten revisions for his approval.[35]

There had been a change to the command structure. The Abwehr, headed by Canaris's successor Colonel (GS) Georg Hansen, was now incorporated in the Central Security Department (RHSA), which was a part of Himmler's SS empire. This meant that Hansen was dangerously surrounded by informers: Claus Stauffenberg needed a reliable officer who could be attached to him. He asked Rudolf Fahrner for advice. Fahrner named Lieutenant Urban Thiersch, a sculptor friend, who had been badly wounded in Russia and now commanded a replacement training battery at Regensburg. Stauffenberg sent a telegram summoning Thiersch to Berlin and received him on 1 July, with almost the same words he had said to Fahrner: 'Let us come straight to the point: I am engaged in high treason with all the means available to me.' The insurrection, he continued, would not change the military situation, which was hopeless; but it could still prevent much bloodshed and the final chaos, and it would remove the disgrace of the present government; information about crimes against the eastern nations and Jews never stopped coming in. He hoped no longer to save the Reich, but human lives. It was no longer a question of the fatherland, he said, but of the people. There was doubt that the coup would succeed, he told Thiersch, but worse than a failed insurrection was to passively observe the disgrace. They were not really good plotters, but they had a chance to act 'for honour'.[36]

Several utterances by conspirators in those weeks express their moral seriousness. Stauffenberg had said to Peter Sauerbruch that he could not look the widow of a fallen soldier in the eye if he did not assume responsibility by taking action against the criminals.[37] Only a few days before 20 July he said: 'It is now time that something was done. But the man who has the courage to do something must do it in the knowledge that he will go down in German history as a traitor. If he does not do it, however, he will be a traitor to his own conscience.'[38] Similarly, Berthold Stauffenberg said on 14 July: 'The most terrible thing is knowing that we cannot succeed and yet that we have to do it, for our country and our children.'[39]

Cäsar von Hofacker returned to Paris on 17 July, after meetings with his fellow conspirators, without having visited his wife and his children, knowing that he might never see them again. On the Berlin-Metz train he wrote to his wife that the nature and implications of his activities had reached an 'historic level', so that 'to allow even a few hours to pass unused for this purpose would have been a sin against the Holy Ghost, and not least a neglect of the duties of the husband of a German woman and the father of German children'.[40]

Urban Thiersch was impressed by Stauffenberg's appearance and energy. Stauffenberg appeared to command 'unassailable powers of genius' which imposed the conviction that he could banish the crude forces of the regime. Thiersch was less favourably impressed with the organisation of the coup. It seemed unsystematic because the military apparatus could not be openly used, and because Stauffenberg's official duties really took up all his time at the office and even at home. Stauffenberg hoped that, against all rational expectations, 'the right people' would in the right place at the right time.[41]

Stauffenberg had little hope of success or survival. Therefore he wanted a written statement of his and his immediate friends' fundamental views and aims. He wanted it to be taken to a safe place, and to serve as a testament when they were no longer able to speak for themselves. The 'Oath' was meant to strengthen the bond among the surviving friends after Germany's inevitable defeat and occupation. It was a manifesto for the *Vita Nuova* of the heirs of Stefan George's legacy, of the Secret Germany. It was 'naturally' not intended for publication; as Fahrner explained, it was meant also

Wir   glauben an die Zukunft der Deutschen.

Wir   wissen im Deutschen die Kräfte, die ihn berufen, die

      Gemeinschaft der abendländischen Völker zu schönerem Le-

      ben zu führen.

Wir   bekennen uns im Geist und in der Tat zu den grossen

      Überlieferungen unseres Volkes, das durch die Verschmel-

      zung hellenischer und christlicher Ursprünge in germa-

      nischem Wesen das abendländische Menschentum schuf.

Wir   wollen eine Neue Ordnung die alle Deutschen zu Trägern

      des Staates macht und ihnen Recht und Gerechtigkeit ver-
                                                      bewegen
      bürgt, verachten aber die Gleichheitslüge und fordern
      uns vor deren
      die Anerkennung der naturgegebenen Rängen

Wir   wollen ein Volk, das in der Erde der Heimat verwurzelt

      den natürlichen Mächten nahebleibt, das im Wirken in den

      gegebenen Lebenskreisen sein Glück und sein Genüge fin-

      det und in freiem Stolze die niederen Triebe des Neides

      und der Missgunst überwindet.

Wir   wollen Führende, die aus allen Schichten des Volkes wach-

      send, verbunden den göttlichen Mächten, durch grossen

      Sinnd, Zucht und Opfer den anderen vorangehen.

Wir   verbinden uns zu einer untrennbaren Gemeinschaft, die
                                Tun
      durch Haltung und Tat der Neuen Ordnung dient und den

                                                        —2—

49. *Carbon copy of the 'Oath', with changes in Claus Stauffenberg's hand*
(translation in Appendix VI)

−2−

künftigen Führern die Kämpfer bildet, derer sie

bedürfen.

    Wir geloben

        untadelig zu leben,

        im Gehorsam

        ~~gewissenhaft~~ zu dienen,

        unverbrüchlich zu schweigen,

        und füreinander einzustehen.

.−.−.−.−.−.−.−.−.−.−.−.−.−.−.−.−.−.−.−.

to establish Stauffenberg's own views, as distinct from the various prepared policy statements in which he had collaborated and which reflected many of his ideas, but at the same time represented 'many compromises' with the views of others such as Goerdeler, Beck, J. Kaiser, Gerstenmaier, Moltke. Stauffenberg spoke about this with his brother Berthold and Rudolf Fahrner; on about 1 July he asked them to formulate his ideas in an 'Oath'. Berthold Stauffenberg and Rudolf Fahrner wrote them down, in the form of short theses, in Berthold's quarters at Camp 'Koralle', and Maria Appel typed them at Fahrner's dictation.[42]

On 4 July, the last day of Fahrner's stay in Berlin, Stauffenberg wondered whether an insurrection would have any meaning now that Germany's defeat had been sealed; few people now expected the war to last longer than a few more weeks. Echoing Moltke's views, he asked whether it would not be better to preserve the constructive forces to stand ready for a new beginning. But so many lives could be saved by ending it all now, and the ethical imperative dictated that Germany should liberate herself from the criminals who governed her.[43]

During the night of 4/5 July, Stauffenberg spent most of the evening at home in bureaucratic battles to supply the fronts: Fahrner saw him, wrestling for hours on the telephone with their desperate needs, struggling with Army, Party and armaments agencies, while at the same time dealing with the effects of the latest enemy air raids upon armaments and replacements, and with thousands of refugees now fleeing the eastern provinces. Only after all this had been done, in the small hours, was he able to join Berthold and Fahrner (representing Alexander, who was in Athens) in reading the entire long poem 'Der Tod des Meisters'; they approved it and agreed to its publication. It was printed in a limited edition in 1945.[44] It was a manifesto of the Secret Germany. The Master's companions came 'from within the Reich's invisible frontiers', and they had sealed their union at the Master's burial. Claus and Berthold approved these words:

> And parting we knew: in our life
> Every breath and trembling pang
> With blood and spirit serves this grave.

Claus was mentioned in the last lines of the 'Conclusion':

> Yet you will remain with us, defining, leading,
> The war-god's lordly herald of the future world,
> Only enhanced by one eye's sacrifice.

Karl Wolfskehl (who received a copy of *Der Tod des Meisters* in his exile in Auckland) and other Jewish friends later objected to a passage in the 'Conclusion' which they considered offensive.[45] Alexander made a small change for the second printing of 1948. The original version ran:

> With the dispersed, whatever wicked
> Crime was done to them – guiltless yet ensnared
> In the thousand-year curse of their blood
> Which cut them off from the fruit and drink of the soil,
> Theirs Tantalus' fate – let there be no reckoning.

The altered lines ran:

> With the dispersed, whatever wicked
> Crime was done to them – where they became ensnared
> In the thousand-year curse of their blood. . .

The changed version does not seem to be a reaction to Wolfskehl's objections. The phrase 'the thousand-year curse of their blood' was intolerable to Jews after the mass murders of Auschwitz. It was certainly lacking in tact – although the Stauffenbergs were willing to sacrifice their lives to put an end to such crimes.

Fahrner had to be careful not to tell Alexander the few facts he knew about the conspiracy, because Alexander was incautious. But the two men shared and expressed the spirit of opposition to the regime. In the evenings, as they drank wine at the 'Phaleriotissa' tavern in Phaleron, they pounded the rhythm of the *skolia* of Harmodius and Aristogeiton on the table:

> ἐν μύρτου κλαδὶ τὸ ξίφος φορήσω
> ὥσπερ Ἁρμόδιος καὶ Ἀριστογείτων
> ὅτε τὸν τύραννον κτανέτην
> ἰσονόμουσ τ' Ἀθήνασ ἐποιησάτην.

> In a myrtle-branch I will carry my sword,
> As did Harmodius and Aristogeiton
> When they slew the tyrant
> And made Athens a city of equal rights.[46]

On 5 July Claus Stauffenberg learned that Reichwein and Leber had been arrested. He was upset and said to Trott: 'We need Leber, I'll get him out.' On 8 July Thiersch met Stauffenberg's special missions officer, Lieutenant von Haeften, at Bendlerstrasse. Haeften said it was absolutely necessary to act now; Stauffenberg wanted to do it himself. Thiersch also saw Stauffenberg on that day, briefly, and he appeared to be 'under a heavy dark burden'. It was the day after he had apparently given up hope on Stieff.[47]

The question of which troops could be used to seize power led to ever-renewed calculations. Home Army troops which could be mobilised under 'Valkyrie' plans were to occupy key points. But in the present crisis situation, all available 'Valkyrie' formations might be ordered to the front at a moment's notice, as had happened once before, in 1942.[48]

The garrisons in Military District III (Berlin and environs) were commanded by the Deputy General Commanding III Army Corps and Commander in Military District III, Lieutenant-General von Kortzfleisch. His Chief of the General Staff, Brigadier von Rost, was in the plot, and reliable.[49]

At the end of March 1944 Rost suddenly received a new posting as commander of the 3rd Panzer Grenadier Division. He had to leave his post in Berlin effective from 1 May, and he took with him Lieutenant Albrecht, his special missions officer, who was familiar with the coup preparations. Stauffenberg was as surprised as Rost and had no opportunity to intervene; there was no one in Army Personnel Office who could help. Rost's departure put the entire Berlin operation of the insurrection in jeopardy. Haeften took over from Albrecht all sensitive documents, but since the preparations were based largely on cues that only Rost and Albrecht understood, everything had to be re-done.[50]

Oertzen was attached to Rost's successor, Brigadier Otto Herfurth; the plotters believed they could reckon on Herfurth's support although he was at best superficially aware of their plans. But Herfurth was far from equal to Rost's strong personality, nor could he find his way about in the coup machinery. Herfurth's senior staff officer, Lieutenant-Colonel Mitzkus, did not have a strong position on the staff; he was initiated into the coup plans and took part in their revision, but he had to submit his work on them to Stauffenberg. The plan now was to carry the coup orders from General Army Office to III Deputy Corps Command at no. 144 Hohenzollerndamm by hand, and only on the day of the insurrection. Since the Commander, Kortzfleisch, was pro-Hitler, Olbricht planned to summon him to his offices on the day of the coup, arrest him, and replace him with a co-conspirator, Major-General Karl, Baron von Thüngen, the Inspector for Military Replacements in Berlin.[51] After Rost's departure, however, Deputy Corps Command could no longer be considered an active centre in the insurrection, able and willing to use 'Valkyrie' to seize an initiative.

Although the 'Valkyrie' orders had been drafted under Lieutenant-General Olbricht's supervision, he had not the authority to activate them. On one occasion General Army Office, through Olbricht and Mertz, tried to act as the superior command-level and give orders to the deputy corps commands. The result was questions, requests for confirmation by the Commander-in-Chief of the Home Army, failures to follow orders.[52]

Another unpredictable factor was the strength of forces in the military districts, particularly Berlin. The most powerful forces capable of rapid deployment were armoured units, which meant that the coup planners relied on these especially.

Armoured School II in Krampnitz near Potsdam was constantly engaged in organising fresh units, and its strength varied. At the beginning of July its motorised infantry battalion and other mechanised units were to be transferred to the eastern front. There were several mobilisation alerts and the troops were practised. This could aid the plotters, but only if the troops were not moved to the front before the coup.[53]

Although the plotters' control of the armoured troops was uncertain, these troops were assigned key missions in the coup plan. A good number of the Armour School troops were to protect the Bendlerstrasse buildings containing the Home Army command and the military communications centre of Berlin; others were to do reconnaissances against the Waffen-SS garrisons in Lichterfelde and Lankwitz. One company of armoured troops from the Armour School, with heavy weapons, had to stand by to tackle the Berlin SS commandant. Another company of armoured personnel carriers was to meet the Commander-in-Chief of the Home Army and his Chief of the General Staff at Tempelhof airfield. Fromm and Stauffenberg could be expected back from Berchtesgaden or Rastenburg approximately two-and-a-half hours after Hitler's death, by which time the armoured unit must be ready to meet them in Berlin. Therefore, if the coup was to succeed it seemed to the plotters that the armoured units must be alerted one or two hours in advance of the assassination. The dispositions showed that the armoured troops were expected to arrive in the centre of Berlin two hours after they had left their barracks.[54]

The Berlin Military Commander, Major-General von Hase, was in the plot and an important factor in it. He resided at no. 1 Unter den Linden next to the Brandenburg Gate. Besides the Greater Berlin Military Police Battalion at no. 12 Ziegelstrasse (which was headed by another co-conspirator, Lieutenant-Colonel Heinz), Hase commanded the Berlin Guard Battalion 'Grossdeutschland' at no. 15a Kruppstrasse in Moabit. The Guard Battalion was the only unit besides the Armour School troops that could be brought rapidly into the Berlin city centre. But the plotters did not firmly control this unit. On 1 May a former Hitler Youth leader and holder of the Knight's Cross, Major Remer, was appointed its commander. Apparently the conspirators did not give serious thought to the question of Remer's loyalty until July. Nothing is known of any attempt to win him over.[55]

At the end of June Hase rebuked Remer because the Guard Battalion had taken part in Propaganda Minister Goebbels's celebration of the solstice instead of helping to put out fires after an air raid. The President of Berlin Police, Count Helldorf, warned Hase that Remer was a faithful National Socialist. But Hase said Remer would follow orders like any other major. On the day of the uprising, martial law would be in force.[56]

On 18 July Hase held a briefing on 'internal disturbances' with the commanders under his authority at his headquarters. When Remer left, Heinz stayed behind to point out that Remer wore the Hitler Youth badge in gold on his uniform and would support the existing regime. He suggested sending Remer to Italy on some fictitious assignment. Hase waved it away;

Remer was highly decorated for bravery, he would follow orders.[57] This
view was tenable, of course, so long as Remer considered his orders
legitimate. Hase reckoned on Hitler's death and the new 'legitimacy' which
would follow it.

The plotters also counted on parts of the 'Brandenburg' Division at
Brandenburg near Berlin. Originally a special sabotage organisation at the
disposal of the OKW/Amt Ausland/Abwehr Branch, it had seen action at
the front in 1943, when it was nearly annihilated; the remnants returned
home for reorganisation. Troops of the division, which was under the
temporary command of Colonel Lahousen, would have been available to the
plotters. This remained the case when on 1 April 1943 Colonel Alexander,
Baron von Pfuhlstein was appointed commander; the conspirators atached
to him Captain (Res.) Count Schwerin von Schwanenfeld and Lieutenant-
Colonel Heinz.

But in the meanwhile Admiral Canaris, the Chief of the Abwehr, who
had tacitly supported the plot, was gradually losing control of both the
Abwehr and the 'Brandenburg' Division; by February 1944 he had been
eased out of office altogether. Towards the end of 1943 and into January
1944 there was a series of arrests and subsequent investigations by the senior
military judge, Manfred Roeder, which posed an acute threat to the conspiracy. Canaris told Pfuhlstein that Roeder had referred to the 'Branden-
burgers' as shirkers. On 18 January 1944 Pfuhlstein flew to seek out Roeder
at Morszyn near Lvov, confronted him and slapped him in the face. The
result was that Roeder was removed from his dangerous investigations, but
Pfuhlstein was also removed from command of the 'Brandenburg' Division
as from 1 April 1944; Schwerin was posted to the travel-pass office in
Branch II War Administration of the Quartermaster-General's Office at
Grossadmiral-Prinz-Heinrich-Strasse.[58]

Lieutenant-General Fellgiebel undertook to isolate Hitler's headquarters
on the day of the coup by shutting down all telephone, teletype and
telegraph communications. Major Hösslin, a veteran of the campaign in
North Africa, holder of the Knight's Cross, OC of Armoured Reconnaissance and Training Battalion Meiningen, was charged with 'implementing
the state of emergency in Königsberg', and with the 'protection' of the
Army High Command Headquarters a few kilometres away from Hitler's
headquarters: that is to say he was to help isolate the latter.[59]

Major (GS) von Oertzen, senior staff officer in Corps Detachment E in
the 2nd Army, where Tresckow was Chief of the General Staff, knew the
military installations in and around Berlin from his work with Stauffenberg
in September 1943. On 9 July he came to Olbricht on a fictitious mission to
request replacements of personnel, weapons and other equipment for the
2nd Army. In fact he was to assist Olbricht, Mertz and Stauffenberg in
filling gaps in the coup organisation.[60]

On 17 July Olbricht sent Oertzen to visit Motorised Infantry Replacement Training Brigade 'Grossdeutschland' at Cottbus. Oertzen was to discover how long it would take to raise its 'Valkyrie' units. The commander of the brigade's replacement and training regiment and deputy commander of the absent brigade commander, Lieutenant-Colonel Stirius, thought Oertzen was the senior staff officer of III Deputy Corps Command – perhaps because of indications from Oertzen that he was to be attached to III Deputy Corps Command. On the next day Stirius received a request from Stauffenberg to come to a briefing on 19 July at 10.00 a.m., without an indication of the subject matter. On the same day Oertzen and Lieutenant-Colonel von der Lancken went to see the adjutant of the brigade at Cottbus to inform themselves about its strength in personnel. It was only natural, of course, for Stauffenberg, himself a veteran of the armoured forces, to assure himself of the availability of the armoured troops, although he did not have direct authority over them, and mobilisation orders would have to be issued by III Deputy Corps Command. But he could hope that his own background in armoured combat, and the charm of his personality, would ensure compliance with the Bendlerstrasse orders on insurrection day. On 15 July, when the assassination was expected, the 'Valkyrie' units were called six hours before the probable time of the assassination. When the attack did not take place, Olbricht declared that the mobilisation had been a practice alert. The Cottbus 'Valkyrie' troops had been slow to cover the hundred kilometres to Berlin: they did not reach the Schulzendorf-Marienfelde-Lichtenrade area until the morning of 16 July.[61] On 19 July, Stauffenberg questioned Stirius about the strength and organisation of the brigade and the results of the 15 July 'exercise', and asked how much time the brigade would need to reach the area south of Hamburg. Stirius reported: distance 360 kilometres, time of march readiness $= x$; arrival of advance detachment $= x + 15$ hours, arrival of the main force $= x + 18$ hours, arrival of sections to be brought up $= x + 24$ hours. Stauffenberg declared himself satisfied. The calculation implied that the advance detachment could be in Berlin in four hours, the main force in five hours after march readiness. In fact, on 20 July the main radio transmitter for Germany was occupied by troops of the brigade one hour and forty-five minutes after they had received the order.[62]

All this illustrates the need to have a strong personality in authority in Berlin to control and command the diverse military forces on the day of the uprising. Lieutenant-General Olbricht was not such a personality; Colonel (GS) Mertz von Quirnheim's position did not give him sufficient authority; and Stauffenberg would be away during the crucial first three hours.

In view of the uncertainties, plans were laid to bring in a detachment from farther afield. This was organised by Brigadier von Tresckow, Chief of General Staff to the 2nd Army. The detachment consisted of several battalions of Cavalry Regiment Centre in Army Group Centre, now part of the 3rd Cavalry Brigade which was commanded by Lieutenant-Colonel Georg, Baron von Boeselager. Tresckow sent Boeselager from the eastern front to Paris on 7 July to persuade Fieldmarshal von Kluge to capitulate in the west. When Boeselager returned from this mission on 14 or 15 July, he spoke to his brother, Major Philipp von Boeselager, who commanded the I Battalion of No. 31 Cavalry Regiment. He said that Hitler would be assassinated shortly: Philipp must start assembling 1200 men (six squadrons) of the 3rd Cavalry Brigade and moving them to airfields in the Government General (German-occupied Poland).[63] From there they were to be flown to Tempelhof airfield immediately after the assassination, so that they could be in Berlin and at the disposal of the insurrectionists three hours after Hitler's death. Lieutenant-Colonel von Boeselager prepared to use the same method to move another two or three battalions to Berlin for the same purpose.[64] Major Philipp von Boeselager began to move the troops on 15 July; on 19 July all six squadrons in his regiment rode two hundred kilometres to Brest, arriving thirty-six hours later, in the afternoon of 20 July. Lorries stood ready to take them to an airfield. But they were not called upon on 20 July, and after the collapse of the uprising they returned to the front.[65]

15

Uprising

The briefings on rapid reserve mobilisations which had begun on 7 June were continued, again at Hitler's 'Berghof' headquarters, on 6 and 8 July. On 6 July Stauffenberg took part in two 'special briefings' with Hitler at the 'Berghof', one between 5 and 6 p.m. and one from shortly before midnight to 1 a.m. on 7 July. Stauffenberg presented the 'Valkyrie' plans. Hitler approved most of his points and decided that if enemy forces invaded German territory the military commanders were to have full military and civil executive powers, even over the Reich Defence Commissars (Gauleiters or other officials).[1]

There is evidence suggesting that at this stage Stauffenberg still hoped that Stieff would carry out the assassination, or at least help with it. When General Zeitzler pressed for the oft-postponed presentation of uniforms and equipment, it was probably at the prompting of Stauffenberg and Olbricht, and perhaps also of the Quartermaster-General. During briefings from 19 to 22 June with Speer, the Munitions Minister, Hitler agreed that the presentation should go foward. It took place at Klessheim near Salzburg on 7 July. On 6 July Stauffenberg said to Stieff that he had 'all that stuff with him', meaning the explosives. He had not brought 'all that stuff' along merely to show it to Stieff. Stieff testified, when on trial for his life, that he had prevented Stauffenberg from carrying out an assassination attempt on that occasion. On 8 July, Stauffenberg seemed 'under a heavy dark burden', and Haeften told Thiersch that Stauffenberg himself now wanted to carry out the assassination attack.[2]

On 11 July Stauffenberg flew to Berchtesgaden to attend Hitler's 'morning briefing' at the 'Berghof' from 1.07 to 3.30 p.m. He took Captain Karl Friedrich Klausing along as his special missions officer. A new obstacle appeared in the fact that Göring and Himmler were not present.

The assassination attempts between March 1943 and March 1944 had been undertaken regardless of whether Göring or Himmler were present or not. But the Fieldmarshals von Kluge and Rommel insisted to General Beck that Göring and Himmler must be eliminated at the same time as Hitler. The Quartermaster-General, Lieutenant-General Wagner, Lieutenant-General

Fellgiebel, Brigadier Stieff, Lieutenant-General Olbricht, General Hoepner and General Beck himself insisted that Himmler must be there to be assassinated along with Hitler. These demands were not wholly unreasonable, for Göring was Hitler's officially designated successor and Himmler controlled the SS, a potential civil war army. But Göring rarely attended briefings of the kind to which Stauffenberg was summoned. It was equally impossible to be sure that Himmler would be present, although it was more likely because the SS was to train the 'blocking divisions' which were to be organised for the wavering eastern front, and they were the subject of the briefing on 11 July.[3]

As it turned out, neither Göring nor Himmler was present. Stauffenberg had been informed of their absence in advance of the 'morning briefing' and had said to Stieff, 'Good God, oughtn't one to go ahead regardless?' On the next day Klausing expressed his displeasure that through Stieff's failure the attempt to kill Hitler had not been carried out. While Stieff's intended role and his actions are obscure in this reference and in Stieff's own later testimony, it is clear that Stauffenberg wanted to carry out the attack despite the absence of Göring and Himmler, and that Stieff prevented it.[4]

After Hitler's briefing Stauffenberg, Fellgiebel, Stieff and Klamroth met in the Frankenstrub barracks in Berchtesgaden and discussed preparations for the next occasion. By that evening Stauffenberg and Klausing were back in Berlin. Here Goerdeler and Witzleben had been alerted in anticipation of Hitler's assassination; a number of police officers and officers of No. 9 Grenadier Replacement and Training Battalion from Potsdam had been awaiting their cue in Berlin.[5]

Hans Bernd Gisevius, an Abwehr agent working out of the German consulate-general in Zurich, came back from Switzerland to Berlin on the morning of 12 July in order to take part in the uprising. He went to see Count Helldorf and heard from him little that was complimentary to Stauffenberg, as he later recounted. According to Helldorf as reported by Gisevius, Stauffenberg had seized control of the entire coup leadership and had prevented contacts between Helldorf and Beck, Olbricht and Schulenburg. No plan for the exact role of the police had thus far been submitted to Helldorf.[6]

In the afternoon Gisevius went to see Beck, who had no time for him because he was getting ready for a meeting of the scholarly 'Wednesday Society' to which he belonged. But Beck asked Gisevius to make contact with Stauffenberg as quickly as possible. Stauffenberg had been a great support of late and had carried the whole burden of preparing the insurrection, said Beck. Since Brigadier Oster had been removed from his Abwehr post, Stauffenberg was the only activist in the Armed Forces who was prepared to go all the way. Beck's praise apparently did not change Gisevius' reservations about Stauffenberg, in whom Gisevius understandably dis-

cerned an obstacle to his own ambitions. Stauffenberg was not likely to
agree to the position Gisevius expected for himself, namely that of a 'Reich
Commissar for Purges and Restoration of Public Order'; or to the suggestion that on the third day of the uprising he was to be put in charge of the
'entire civilian executive'. It was, after all, Julius Leber who was slated to
become Minister of the Interior.[7]

From Beck's house in Lichterfelde Gisevius went to see his old friends,
the Strüncks. Captain (Res.) Dr Theodor Strünck was an Abwehr officer
and had carried the conspirators' messages back and forth between Berlin
and Zurich, where Gisevius was their main contact with the American OSS
Resident, Alan Dulles, in Berne. The Strüncks had lost their flat in an air
raid and were now living in basement rooms in what had been Schacht's
villa in the west end. Goerdeler arrived there soon after Gisevius and
lamented, as had Helldorf before him, that Stauffenberg had isolated him.
Goerdeler complained that Stauffenberg wanted to lead not only 'tech-
nically' but also politically; he wanted to preserve the soldierly qualities of
the nation, make it socialist, and attain a tolerable peace through military
means. Gisevius commented that Goerdeler 'visibly' wanted democracy,
whereas Stauffenberg wanted 'the military dictatorship of the "true"
National Socialists': he was unwilling to give up either the totalitarian or the
military or the socialist principles, and was plotting with Leber to prevent
Goerdeler from becoming chancellor.[8]

A little later Stauffenberg and Hansen announced themselves. After a
meeting with Fromm they had decided to come over to Strünck's to see
Gisevius.[9]

The two colonels arrived after midnight. Stauffenberg's six feet of height
seemed even taller in the low-ceilinged basement rooms. Gisevius' impression of Stauffenberg during this first meeting was formed, of course, under
the influence of Helldorf's and Goerdeler's complaints, and Gisevius projected his own ambitions upon his rival. Gisevius' ignoble and mockingly
expressed sentiments do him no credit, but for that very reason they can be
accepted as sincere. It was easy, he said, to imagine how a cripple must think
and feel; 'this pitiable man' could hardly 'hope to create an atmosphere
among a wider audience, such as masses of people'. It was 'as if a merciless
fate had pushed him into the role of conspirator'. His manner had been
coarse: he had demanded coffee from Mrs Strünck. Apparently his
behaviour was an attempt 'to over-compensate for the inferiority complexes
which his mutilations had caused in him'. Gisevius did not get the impression that Stauffenberg was an opponent of the National Socialists; rather he
seemed to be 'the very type of the "new" General-Staff officer, such that
Hitler could not have wished for a better – or a born assassin'.[10]

Since Gisevius was one of the liaisons between the conspirators and the
enemy, the question of foreign policy arose. Stauffenberg naturally wanted

to hear from Gisevius what he knew of the Allies' attitude. Gisevius saw this as a soldier meddling in politics. His account describes Stauffenberg as an ignorant amateur politician who, in face of the collapse of Army Group Centre and the prospect that Stalin's troops would appear outside Berlin within a few weeks, intended to deal 'politically entirely with the East' but was at the same time irresolute. Gisevius 'gladly' informed Stauffenberg that the demand for Germany's unconditional surrender was immutable. If he did so in the same sarcastically superior tone in which he wrote his memoir, Stauffenberg must have been provoked.

When Gisevius, with unrivalled lack of tact, expressed his admiration of Stauffenberg's courageous willingness to carry out the assassination, Stauffenberg in some irritation asked Gisevius how he knew that he was going to 'throw the bomb'. Gisevius' memoir continues: 'This evening I really have the impression that someone here is going all out.' Yet he saw Stauffenberg as a disappointed praetorian who in the face of military defeat had suddenly lost his illusions and who, from exaggerated belief in his own mission, believed he must be 'soldier, politician, tyrannicide, saviour of the fatherland' all at once. After the coup there would inevitably be 'purges'. Gisevius says that Stauffenberg wanted to strictly limit the number of the 'guilty', especially in the Army, confining them to those who were 'undoubtedly' unprincipled 'Party generals of the Reinecke and Keitel type', and rejected the condemnation of Brauchitsch, Halder or the fieldmarshals on the grounds 'of their spineless toleration of Hitler's aggressions'. Finally, Stauffenberg annoyed Gisevius by warning him against contact with Oster: 'Oster was the officer who had fought most clear-sightedly, most resolutely and most unceasingly against the brown tyranny – and for the longest time. Between his outlook and that of Stauffenberg, who changed sides and joined the fronde only at the time of the Stalingrad catastrophe, there is an abyss: two officers, and two worlds.'[11]

Gisevius, evidently blinded by ill-will, refused to see the mortal danger to the conspiracy from contact with Oster, who was under constant Gestapo observation. Gisevius knew nothing of Stauffenberg's single-handed efforts to bring about Hitler's fall in 1942, and he forgot that Oster had never himself made an attempt to kill Hitler. Even after the failed uprising, after two of the Stauffenberg brothers had given their lives in the attempt to liberate the nation from the criminals, even after months of reflection, Gisevius showed no understanding of the position of a conspirator to whom name and honour had meant something and who had sacrificed both for the most thankless task in the conspiracy. Stauffenberg knew that there would be no room for the assassin in the new order.[12]

On 14 July Hitler moved his headquarters to 'Wolfschanze' in East Prussia.[13] On the same day, Fromm and Stauffenberg were told to be there on the morrow. Fromm, Stauffenberg and Klausing left Berlin by air

50. Stauffenberg and Hitler, 15 July 1944. From left: Stauffenberg, Rear-Admiral Karl-Jesko von Puttkamer, Air Force Lieutenant-General Karl Bodenschatz, Hitler, Fieldmarshal Wilhelm Keitel (with file)

shortly after 7 a.m. and arrived around 9.30 a.m. at Rastenburg airfield, south of 'Wolfschanze'. They were driven to the 'Kurhaus' casino inside security perimeter II and breakfasted with the headquarters commandant and three officers of his staff. From the casino Stauffenberg telephoned Stieff and Fellgiebel. Towards 11 a.m. Fromm, Stauffenberg and Klausing drove to Keitel's offices inside security perimeter I. After briefings preparatory to their presentations at Hitler's midday conference, Fromm and Stauffenberg went with Keitel to Hitler's briefing hut towards 1 p.m. The hut was a low wooden structure with brick facings covered by a thin coat of cement, with a concrete ceiling and windows with steel shutters, which were open. The bunker which Hitler was using as quarters at that time, and a hut for his bodyguard, were in a fenced and guarded enclosure within security perimeter I. A special pass was required to enter this 'Führer Perimeter'.[14]

Stauffenberg's method of assassination was determined not only by his physical handicaps. If there was to be any hope of a successful uprising, he had to survive and return to Berlin to lead the insurrection. Beck indeed ordered Stauffenberg not to attempt the assassination unless he thought he could survive it, because he was the only one who could lead the coup. The events of 15 and 20 July confirmed Beck's judgement. Olbricht lacked revolutionary energy, Mertz's position and authority were insufficient, Fromm could not be expected to do more than tolerate the coup. Stauffenberg understood these limitations: he had had ample experience with generals beset by scruples, hesitation and timidity. For these reasons, he had to use a time-fuse so that he could deposit the explosives near Hitler and withdraw before the explosion.[15]

The most suitable fuses available in German explosives ordnance were captured British acid fuses, which were silent. These fuses came with nominal time-delays of 10, 30, 90 minutes, 5 hours, 10 hours and 20 hours. But the delays varied with the air temperature and also as a function of the composition and thickness of the retaining wire, the acid, and the cotton. Ten-minute fuses, intended only for training purposes, could vary between 4.75 and 9.6 minutes even within a relatively narrow temperature range from 20 to 25°C; 30-minute fuses at the same temperatures had an actual range of between 14.5 and 28.75 minutes. Under the circumstances of the assassination attempt, 30-minute fuses were the most suitable. The assassin had to set his fuse before entering Hitler's briefing room, and he had to avoid observation while setting it. The role intended for Stieff – perhaps on 7 July, almost certainly on 11 and 15 July – must have been to set the fuse and then to bring Stauffenberg a briefcase with the explosives and the activated fuse. Since Stieff evidently failed in this, Stauffenberg had to contrive to set the fuse between his last preparatory meeting and Hitler's briefing, and he had to give himself enough time to walk from one to the other with the fuse running. On 15 July and again on 20 July he had to walk four hundred metres, which took about four minutes. The ten-minute fuse was clearly unsuitable.[16]

The meetings on 15 July dealt particularly with the 'blocking divisions' for the eastern front, to be organized by the Home Army and trained by the SS. The official stenographer in Führer's Headquarters listed for 15 July three meetings with Hitler in which Fromm and Stauffenberg participated: the situation briefing from 1.10 to 1.40 p.m.; a 'special briefing' on defensive positions from 1.40 to 2.20 p.m.; and another 'special briefing' from 2.20 to 2.25 p.m.[17]

Stauffenberg could either let Stieff activate the fuse or activate it himself, but only when he knew that Hitler was in the briefing room. The photograph of Stauffenberg waiting with other officers as Hitler arrived at the briefing hut on 15 July shows Stauffenberg without his briefcase. Stieff may have been holding it.[18]

Stauffenberg concluded from his experiences on 15 July that he must delay going to Hitler's briefing until he knew that Hitler was there; then he must set the fuse and take the briefcase with the explosives and activated fuse into the briefing room. This is probably why he camouflaged the explosives in his briefcase with a shirt, which he would say he wanted to change into just before going to the briefing with Hitler.[19]

Quite apart from these difficulties, something nearly incredible happened.

In Berlin, Mertz ordered the Army schools and reserve training units near Berlin to take up march readiness for 'Valkyrie' at about the same time as Stauffenberg's plane departed for East Prussia, five to six hours in advance of the expected time of the assassination: the purpose was to ensure the shortest possible delay between the assassination and the military occupation of key points in the capital. This advance order must mean that Stauffenberg had decided to carry out the assassination regardless of whether Göring or Himmler were present, since the advance alert that Mertz ordered could hardly be repeated. Although the Secret State Police commission investigating the events after 20 July found no evidence that anyone had understood what the 'practice alert' really was (who would have admitted it?), it found that the conspirators had been worried that it would be uncovered. In any case, Mertz's actions on 15 July had nothing tentative stemming from any reservations concerning Göring and Himmler.[20]

While Stauffenberg was getting ready to fly to 'Wolfschanze', and while he was en route, the generals in the plot neglected to tell him that they did not want him to act if Himmler was not there.

In a briefing with Major-General Thiele and Colonel Hahn, Fellgiebel's chiefs of staff for Army Communications in Berlin and for Wehrmacht Communications in 'Mauerwald', the Quartermaster-General, Lieutenant-General Eduard Wagner, insisted that the assassination must not be carried out unless Himmler was present. Thiele sent Hahn to 'Mauerwald' on the same evening with orders to inform and instruct Fellgiebel and Stieff accordingly. The message for Stieff was, of course, equally intended for Stauffenberg. In the hierarchy of the Army, Wagner was deputising for the Chief of the General Staff, Zeitzler, who had been ill since 30 June; Wagner, who was ambitious, evidently claimed analogous authority in the plot. The behaviour of Beck, Olbricht and Hoepner on the afternoon of 15 July showed, however, that they also did not want Stauffenberg to go ahead unless Himmler was there.[21]

Evidently, however, no one told Stauffenberg this until after his arrival at

'Wolfschanze'. Indeed, the plotting generals may even have left him in the dark until he met with Stieff at 'Wolfschanze'. Stieff's testimony in the 'People's Court', that on 15 July he had 'urgently admonished' Stauffenberg 'under no circumstances' to carry out the assassination, and Stauffenberg's report to Beck that Stieff had removed the briefcase with the explosives, illuminate this incredible development.[22]

Stauffenberg might well have ignored hierarchic constraints, but he could not ignore the fact that he did not have the support of the other principals in the plot. Because of the last-minute instruction not to go forward unless Himmler was present, Stauffenberg was expected to overturn everything that had been planned. One can well imagine the psychological stress and tension caused to him, already keyed up as he was to assassinate the head of state and supreme commander, by the sudden desertion of his fellow conspirators. Stauffenberg must have known that the armoured troops near Berlin had been alerted early that morning. He also knew that the Krampnitz Armoured School troops were to be moved out to East Prussia within the next five days.[23] The attempt of 15 July was not a casual experiment, but the deadly serious business of an uprising against powerful and dangerous rulers. Now Stieff, Fellgiebel and Wagner had prevented him from assassinating Hitler. He felt betrayed.

During the briefings with Hitler Stauffenberg twice left the briefing room to telephone his fellow plotters at Bendlerstrasse, trying to obtain their approval for the assassination without Himmler's presence. He did not receive it. When he finally spoke to Mertz and they agreed that he must go ahead, the meetings were over and Hitler had left.[24]

After the briefings Stauffenberg had some conversations in front of the briefing hut. Fromm and Keitel went to lunch in Keitel's special train, 'Braunschweig', which was standing at the Moysee halt. Then Stauffenberg walked over to building 8, where Klausing was waiting at the car with Stieff and Fellgiebel; he talked with them, telephoned Berlin once more, and then went off with Klausing to lunch in the 'Braunschweig's' dining car. Fromm, Buhle, Stauffenberg and Klausing then went to 'Mauerwald' (about twenty kilometres northeast, near Angerberg) by car. Fromm flew back to Berlin after meetings in 'Mauerwald'; Stauffenberg and Klausing took the courier train back to Berlin.[25]

Mertz had telephoned Stauffenberg's flat at 7 a.m. and had learned that Stauffenberg had left. Minutes later, quoting from a list of military installations he had before him, he instructed the duty officer at Bendlerstrasse to order maximum alert for the Army schools and other 'Valkyrie' organisations in and around Berlin. When Mertz left for his office that morning he took his pistol, which he had never done before. He was rested, calm and confident.[26]

In the afternoon, between 3 p.m. and 3.30 p.m. Mertz called home and said there was 'nothing in particular', but he might be late; he would bring his friend Siebeck for supper and to stay overnight. They arrived after 8 p.m., exhausted. They recovered, and spent a pleasant evening. Mertz's self-control was perfect: in Siebeck's presence he gave no indication of the stresses of that day, when he had been at the centre of what ought to have been a turning point in world history, and had been let down by his fellow conspirators.

When Siebeck had retired for the night, Mertz told his wife what had happened. Stauffenberg had telephoned after the start of the 'Führer briefing' to say that Himmler was again not there. He, Mertz, had told Olbricht and Beck. There had followed a long discussion, and other telephone conversations (with Hoepner, for example). Mertz got the impression of foot-dragging. He concluded that 'when it comes to unconditional courage and a willingness to accept the ultimate consequences, you will find yourself alone'. After about half an hour, he had been forced to tell Stauffenberg that the generals did not want him to do it, since Himmler was not there. Stauffenberg then said he and Mertz would decide: what did Mertz think? Mertz had said, 'do it'. After another interval Stauffenberg called again to say that the briefing had just ended when he had returned to the briefing room.[27]

Siebeck later recalled the moment when Stauffenberg's news arrived – that the assassination could not take place. The tension in Olbricht's offices at Bendlerstrasse had suddenly been replaced by a 'kind of euphoric mood', as if all felt that they had had a narrow escape. Helldorf also remarked that Olbricht acted as if he had been relieved of a tremendous burden. Olbricht gathered up his Ia/I/1 section head, Major (GS) Harnack, and Major (GS) von Oertzen, declared that the 'Valkyrie' alert had been an exercise, and went off to inspect the schools.[28] Olbricht was reprimanded by Fromm because his alert might have resulted in the armour being taken over by General Guderian, the Inspector-General of Armoured Troops.[29]

On the next day, a Sunday, Siebeck had to catch a train back to Hirschberg after breakfast. Mertz had to go to his office. Siebeck went with him. Stauffenberg was there and immediately pointed at Siebeck, saying: 'Who is this?' Mertz explained that Siebeck was 'reliable'. Stauffenberg then spoke of Saturday's failure caused by Himmler's absence. He and Mertz agreed that next time they would simply go ahead and pay no attention to the wishes of other conspirators who had not supported them. With that they acknowledged the likelihood of failure. They were willing to do it purely for the symbolic value of the attempt. Stauffenberg went to see Beck that evening to give him his report.[30]

Stauffenberg had supper with the Mertzes, who had an apartment at the Harnackhaus. Mrs von Mertz met Stauffenberg for the first time and found him quite extraordinary: 'Comprehensive knowledge, lively intellect, great intelligence, charm, dominant in everything, but nerves not in a good state. So his features did not show the composure, or radiate the purposefulness and sureness, that doubtless they usually owned. No political talk all evening – pleasant, although scarcely believable.' Mrs von Mertz also noticed the unconditional bond between soldiers which reminds the non-soldier so sharply that he does not belong.[31] Later, after the war, Mrs von Mertz expanded on her impressions:

> If you were informed you could see that Stauffenberg was feeling the effects of the previous day, when the failed assassination had made such enormous demands on him; and that he was also feeling the remorseless intellectual and psychological strain under which he was living. But the passionate dedication of the whole man, this vibration of every nerve under a calm surface, which I sensed so strongly, only enhanced my impression of him and gave me a more essential idea of the extraordinary quality of this strong, masculine personality.'[32]

Others, too, observed the strain under which Stauffenberg was living. Rudolf Fahrner, who never said anything negative about Stauffenberg, did once reveal that at the end of June he had noticed his friend's tiredness and hypertension: Stauffenberg had lost much of his dynamic energy of October 1943. At that time he had 'still' had great verve, he had been 'still so fresh and free of all those commitments, he had tremendous dash': if the assassination had succeeded at that time, he would 'certainly have had a smashing success'.[33] The disappointments of the last few days did not help. Klausing no doubt told the truth when he said during his trial, after freely owning up to his part in the uprising, that he would not have taken part had he known the sort of men (not including Stauffenberg, of course) who were to take command during the coup; he would have known that it could never succeed.[34]

On the same evening of 16 July there gathered at Stauffenberg's in Wannsee Berthold, Count Stauffenberg, Fritz-Dietlof, Count Schulenburg, Trott, Hofacker, Mertz, Schwerin and Hansen. They discussed how to solve the difficulties that had surfaced in the assassination attempts thus far, and whether the insurrection might be begun by opening the west front ('western solution'). This seemed inadvisable because Hitler would undoubtedly deploy SS and Army troops against the mutineers.[35]

Cäsar von Hofacker had been authorised by Rommel, Kluge, Stülpnagel and Speidel to arrange the co-ordination of coup activities in the west with those in the Führer's Headquarters, in Berlin and in Germany generally. There was discussion of a 'Berlin solution': to usurp the communications networks for twenty-four hours and issue retreat orders to all army groups. In the end it was agreed that the 'central solution' of murdering Hitler was the precondition of everything else. If subsequent testimony can be trusted,

Trott took the view that after the removal of Hitler and his entire government it would be possible to negotiate with both east and west. There was talk also of 'negotiations from soldier to soldier'. But in fact capitulation was the only option because of the demand for unconditional surrender, and because Allied military personnel were not authorised to conduct political negotiations.[36]

On 17 July Rommel was severely wounded in an air attack upon his car. On the same day the Reich Main Security Office issued orders for Goerdeler's arrest. On 18 July Goerdeler appeared in Berlin and learned of his impending arrest. He told Stauffenberg that he proposed to fly with Beck to Kluge to initiate the 'western solution'; Stauffenberg did not think it appropriate. In the course of 18 July it turned out that Stauffenberg would have to travel to 'Wolfschanze' again on 20 July to brief Hitler. On the same day Stauffenberg learned, through Kranzfelder, that rumour in Berlin had it that the Führer's Headquarters would be 'blown up' in the near future. He remarked: 'There is no choice. The Rubicon has been crossed.'[37]

On 19 July Stauffenberg and Mertz once more assured themselves of the armoured troops near Berlin. At 10 a.m. Lieutenant-Colonel Stirius reported to Stauffenberg on the organisation, strength and marching speed of his brigade. Mertz telephoned the Chief of Staff of the Inspector-General of Armoured Troops, Brigadier Thomale, and asked him to postpone the planned removal of the Armoured School's troops to East Prussia by a few days, saying they were needed for a 'Valkyrie' exercise. Thomale telephoned the Inspector-General, General Guderian, at Allenstein, Guderian gave his approval, and Thomale passed this on to Mertz.[38] It is likely that Thomale and Guderian understood the meaning of the 'exercise'.

In the afternoon of 19 July, while Stauffenberg held a meeting with some thirty officers of his staff, the conspirators (as they had done on 14 July) informed Fieldmarshal von Witzleben, General Hoepner, Major-General von Hase, the initiated officers of No. 9 Grenadier Replacement Training Battalion at Potsdam and Major von Leonrod at the Krampnitz Armoured School that the next day would be decisive. Hase and Olbricht once more discussed the prepared measures.[39]

Stauffenberg's driver Karl Schweizer had to fetch a briefcase from Lieutenant-Colonel von der Lancken in Potsdam and take it to no. 8 Tristanstrasse in Wannsee. It contained two packets tied with string. Lancken had charge of the explosives between assassination attempts.[40]

Towards 6 p.m. Stauffenberg looked up Lieutenant-General Wagner in Zossen, talked with him for an hour, and then for half an hour drove hares with him which Wagner's special missions officer killed with a shotgun.[41]

Later that evening Stauffenberg met Trott. On his way home he had Schweizer stop at a church in Steglitz and stepped inside for a while. At home his brother Berthold was waiting for him. Claus showed him the briefcase with the explosives covered by a shirt. Berthold stayed the night and next morning accompanied his brother to the airfield.[42]

Nina Stauffenberg and the children had gone to Lautlingen on 18 July for the summer holidays. On the 16th Stauffenberg had asked her to delay the journey, but he could not give her any reasons, and she had bought the tickets. He wanted to speak to her on the eve of the assassination attack: it was likely to be for the last time. When he tried to reach her by telephone on the evening of 19 July, he could not get through because some bombs had been dropped on Ebingen.[43]

On 20 July towards 7 a.m. Schweizer drove the two brothers to Rangsdorf airfield. Haeften was waiting there; Stieff came along on the same flight. Haeften told Schweizer to go to the uniform depot at Spandau and get himself a new uniform. Schweizer wanted to know why he needed one; Haeften said, 'you will get a lot more new things.' The courier plane was delayed by fog and left round 8 a.m., to land at Rastenburg at 10.15 a.m. Stauffenberg was met by a staff car and taken to the casino inside security perimeter II. Stieff had himself driven to 'Mauerwald', Haeften went with him. Stauffenberg breakfasted with members of the headquarters commandant's staff, including the adjutant, Captain (Cav.) von Möllendorf. Towards 11 a.m. he had himself driven to Compound I to meet the OKW Chief of Army Staff, Lieutenant-General Buhle, his former superior in the General Staff Organisation Branch. He discussed the 'blocking divisions' with Buhle and the Chief of the General Staff of I Deputy Army Corps (Königsberg), Major-General von Thadden. Up to this point a special missions officer of the headquarters staff had carried Stauffenberg's briefcase. Haeften had the one with the explosives. At about 11.30 a.m. Stauffenberg, Buhle, Thadden, Lieutenant-Colonel (GS) Lechler of Buhle's office and Haeften, who had rejoined Stauffenberg, went to Keitel's office hut for a further preparatory briefing.

Haeften had no part in this meeting and waited in the narrow hallway. He became conspicuous by an evident lack of calm. A special missions officer, Staff Sergeant Vogel, who worked with Keitel's adjutant, Major John von Freyend, noticed a parcel wrapped in a tarpaulin on the hall floor, which was otherwise completely empty. Vogel asked Haeften if that was his, and Haeften replied that Colonel Count Stauffenberg needed it for his presentation at the Führer's briefing. Shortly before noon, when Vogel looked down the hall again, the parcel was no longer there.[44]

Towards noon Hitler's personal servant, Linge, telephoned Keitel to remind him that the 'morning briefing' had been put back to 12.30 p.m. because Mussolini was due to arrive at 'Wolfschanze' on his special train that afternoon. At about 12.25 p.m. Keitel was informed that Major-General Heusinger, the General Staff Chief of Operations, had arrived on the local train connecting 'Mauerwald' and 'Wolfschanze'. Keitel became restless and hurried the meeting. At this point Stauffenberg had to try to delay things, to wait, to stay behind if possible until he knew that Hitler was in the briefing room. He asked Keitel's adjutant, Major John von Freyend, where he could freshen up and change his shirt – an operation that would justify both privacy and a call for Haeften's assistance. Stauffenberg and Haeften went into a sitting room that had been indicated. Vogel went by and noticed them handling an object. Keitel, Buhle and John, as well as Lechler and Thadden who were not going to the Führer's briefing, stood outside the hut waiting for Stauffenberg.[45]

Now Fellgiebel telephoned Keitel's office and asked to speak to Stauffenberg. John answered the telephone and sent Vogel to tell Stauffenberg that Fellgiebel had called and to urge him to hurry his departure for the briefing hut. Vogel went to the sitting room and opened the door (inwards), to find that the movement of the door was stopped by Stauffenberg's back. Vogel saw Stauffenberg and Haeften busy with some object while he was giving Stauffenberg the message. Stauffenberg answered, agitated and brusque, saying he was on his way. At the same moment Major John called from the front door: 'Stauffenberg, do come along!' Vogel remained for a few seconds standing at the sitting-room door, watching Stauffenberg and Haeften. As he stepped away towards his own office, Stauffenberg came rushing out of the sitting room and left the hut. Vogel had not realised what Stauffenberg and Haeften were doing. But Stauffenberg could not know that.

Outside Keitel's hut, John and Stauffenberg exchanged angry glances. John wanted to carry Stauffenberg's briefcase and already had his hand on it; Stauffenberg tore it away from him. Vogel admired the energy of the maimed officer.[46]

Stauffenberg and Haeften had brought with them two 975-gramme lumps of German plastic explosive with two British primer charges in each. In one of the lumps both the primer charges had British 30-minute fuses; in the other lump only one primer charge contained a 30-minute fuse.[47]

Stauffenberg had to aim at killing everyone in the briefing room because he could not be certain of Hitler's position in relation to the briefcase at the moment of the explosion. The sources establish this intention of Stauffenberg's, quite apart from the logic of the circumstances. In the judgement of the investigating experts the two lumps would have been sufficient to kill all those present.[48] But Stauffenberg went to the briefing with only one of the two lumps in his briefcase, having left the other with Haeften, evidently in the rush which had been heightened by Vogel's interruption. This was a flaw in the execution of the plan.

Setting the fuses was a ticklish job. Stauffenberg had with him a pair of pliers, one handle of which had been bent for easier use for a man with only three fingers. Evidently he felt he had to do it rather than Haeften, perhaps because he was the assassin; and evidently the intention was to activate all the fuses for maximum certainty of success (on 13 March 1943 only one had been used and it had failed). Stauffenberg had to remove the fuses from the primer charges and squeeze the copper casings to break the glass vials inside, so that the acid seeped into the cotton enveloping the retaining wires. A false angle of pressure, or too much pressure, might break the wire instead of it being slowly corroded to produce the calculated delay. Then he had to determine through an inspection hole that the spring with the striker pin was still compressed, remove a safety bolt, and then re-insert the fuses into the primer charges.[49] Vogel's interruption had interfered with these operations.

Haeften went to make certain of the car that was to take him and Stauffenberg back to the airfield. Stauffenberg talked animatedly with Buhle as they walked to the briefing hut, with John walking beside them. Just before they reached the front door of the briefing hut, Stauffenberg handed John his briefcase and asked him to give him a place near the Führer.

When Stauffenberg entered the briefing room, Major-General Heusinger was presenting the situation on the eastern front. Göring and Himmler were not there. Hitler and General Warlimont turned round and looked at Stauffenberg. Warlimont recalled the scene:

> The classic image of the warrior through all of history. I barely knew him, but as he stood there, one eye covered by a black patch, a maimed arm in an empty uniform sleeve, standing tall and straight, looking directly at Hitler who had now also turned round, he was, as I have said, a proud figure, the very image of the General Staff officer – the German General Staff officer – of that time.[50]

Keitel announced to the Führer Colonel Count Stauffenberg, who would report concerning the new organisations. Hitler let Stauffenberg shake him by the hand. John asked one of those standing near Hitler to relinquish his place at the map-table to Stauffenberg, and placed the briefcase on the floor in front of Stauffenberg. Now only Heusinger separated Stauffenberg from Hitler. Stauffenberg pushed the briefcase as close to Hitler as he could, but the massive table-support was between the briefcase and Hitler's legs. Stauffenberg murmured something, signalled to John and left the room with him, then asked him to get Lieutenant-General Fellgiebel on the telephone for him. John gave orders to the telephone operator in the briefing hut; Stauffenberg took the receiver, John returned to the briefing room, Stauffenberg put the receiver down and, leaving behind his belt and hat, he went off to the adjutants' building (no. 813), where he found Fellgiebel and Haeften. He stepped out of the building again at once, together with Fellgiebel, and while he was talking to him, they heard an enormous explosion from the direction of the briefing hut. It was between 12.40 and 12.50 p.m.

Fellgiebel testified later that he and Stauffenberg had seen a person covered with the Führer's cloak being carried from the briefing hut and had concluded that it was Hitler who had been killed. Stauffenberg was certainly convinced of it. Five-and-a-half hours later, as he entered his Bendlerstrasse office, he said Hitler was dead – he had seen him being carried out. In the first half-hour after his return Stauffenberg repeated this statement several times.[51]

After the explosion Stauffenberg and Haeften drove to the airfield. Under existing security regulations all gates had to be closed in case of an explosion. Stauffenberg got through the first guarded checkpoint by employing his considerable resources of sang-froid and military brusqueness. At the second gate, an outer-perimeter checkpoint on the road to the airfield, he was not allowed to pass until he had telephoned Captain (Cav.) von Möllendorf, who authorised the guard sergeant to let Stauffenberg and Haeften through. On the narrow road which took them the rest of the way to the airfield Haeften threw the second parcel of explosive out of the car into the wood. The Quartermaster-General had provided his own Heinkel He 111 for Stauffenberg's return flight so that at least he would not have to wait for the courier. They boarded and took off at 1.15 p.m.[52]

The flight to Berlin in a 'He 111' could take as little as an hour and a half, or as much as two hours with head winds. The investigating commission determined the time of landing in Berlin-Rangsdorf (not Tempelhof) as 'towards 3.45 p.m.'. Stauffenberg and Haeften found there neither the planned armoured personnel carrier nor Schweizer with his staff car. They had to ask the General of Tactical Air Power for a car; the general will certainly have recognised the name Stauffenberg because of Melitta's test flights with dive-bombers. Haeften telephoned the Bendlerstrasse towards 4 p.m. and reported the Führer's death. The 30-kilometre drive from Rangsdorf to Berlin took approximately half an hour. Stauffenberg and Haeften arrived round 4.30 p.m.[53]

Schweizer remembered later how he had waited in vain at Rangsdorf, and how he had finally been told that Stauffenberg was at Bendlerstrasse. The manager of the Bendlerstrasse motor-pool recounts that he received a telephone call in the afternoon requesting that Schweizer come and fetch Stauffenberg. Perhaps Schweizer drove out to Rangsdorf only then, too late; perhaps Schweizer had gone to the wrong airfield, expecting to meet a courier flight.[54]

One of Hitler's aides who had been in the briefing room during the explosion saw that Hitler had been only slightly bruised. He hurried over to the nearby telephone-exchange bunker and tried to take control of communications to prevent any information getting out without authorisation. The Headquarters Wehrmacht Communications Officer was summoned to the bunker. Fellgiebel walked towards it as well, and found that his own assignment coincided with the interests of the surviving Hitler regime. He only had to confirm the news blackout. This remained in place, more or less, for two to three hours. Although higher brass such as Fellgiebel, Wagner, Keitel or Himmler could use the telephone, all regular telephone and teletype connections were blocked. Then Fellgiebel, pacing up and down on the narrow road in front of the Führer's inner compound, observed Hitler taking a walk inside his compound. Fellgiebel went back to the communications bunker and telephoned Major-General Thiele that 'something terrible has happened, the Führer is alive'.[55]

There were evidently no provisions for the situation as it now existed, an overt but failed assassination attempt. The events of the rest of the day also showed that some of the Berlin conspirators hoped to distance themselves from the plot and escape the consequences.

Thiele received Fellgiebel's information shortly after 1 p.m. Only minutes later Fellgiebel's Chief of Staff at 'Mauerwald', Colonel Hahn, also told him the assassination attempt had been made and had failed. Thiele and Olbricht decided it would be best to do nothing for the time being and to go to lunch as usual. They contacted the Quartermaster-General, Lieutenant-General Wagner, who was at the Zossen Army High Command Headquarters, and agreed with him that it would be best to act as if they had no knowledge of what had happened. In the evening Olbricht told Gisevius that he had been informed by Fellgiebel, through Thiele, that the assassination attack had been carried out and had failed; he had decided to wait for what other news might come out of 'Wolfschanze'; then he asked Gisevius if perhaps they could still deny everything.[56]

Mertz must have received the news at the same time as Olbricht. He immediately sought to bring the 'Valkyrie' forces of the Armoured School at Krampnitz to Berlin. Towards 2 p.m. Major (GS) von Oertzen transmitted the alert under authority of the General Army Officer to the Armoured School's OC, who ordered march readiness and reconnaissance against the SS garrisons at Lichterfelde and Lankwitz. Major Rode, OC of the Armoured School's No. II Training Group, took two armoured reconnaissance vehicles camouflaged with driving-school signs to within sight of the SS barracks at Lichterfelde, reported that everything was calm, received new orders and proceeded to the Victory Column on Königsplatz near the Brandenburg Gate. The Infantry School at Döberitz also received 'Valkyrie' alert orders towards 2 p.m. Mertz ordered Major (GS) Harnack, who specialised in preparations for alerts in the deputy corps commands and military districts, to implement 'Valkyrie' immediately in all military districts.[57]

In the meantime Mertz summoned his General Staff officers of General Army Office and announced to them that Hitler had been assassinated and the military forces had taken over all executive powers to maintain order;

negotiations were under way to incorporate the Waffen-SS into the Army; Fieldmarshal von Witzleben was the new Wehrmacht Supreme Commander; General Beck had assumed the leadership of the State.

At 3 p.m. Thiele attempted to restore communications. From 4.05 p.m. normal communications with 'Wolfschanze' were restored. Shortly after 3 p.m. Thiele told Olbricht and Hoepner, who had arrived at Bendlerstrasse, that Führer's Headquarters was about to issue a radio communiqué. A radio was switched on and the generals waited but there was no communiqué. Mertz urged Olbricht to order the second level of 'Valkyrie'; Olbricht was doubtful and hesitant.[58]

Colonel (GS) Kratzer, from the Wehrmacht Propaganda Group, had been assigned on insurrection day to occupy the radio transmitter at Nauen and the national radio transmitter (*Deutschlandsender*). He had vehicles ready; at about 4.30 p.m. he asked Stauffenberg and Olbricht for his orders. Stauffenberg referred him to Olbricht. Olbricht said the situation was still unclear: some combat troops were on their way to the transmitters, but no one was to be drawn into insurrection activities at this juncture who was not already involved.[59] This shows that Olbricht considered the uprising a lost cause.

Mertz had finally given the orders for the next stage on his own initiative, shortly before 4 p.m., after hearing that Stauffenberg was back in Berlin. Olbricht said to Gisevius later that evening: 'Mertz outmanoeuvred me.' Olbricht wanted to play dead, as he called it. But round 4 p.m. he did agree, after all, that Mertz should issue further orders. He went with Mertz to Fromm, but Fromm refused his approval. He already knew from Keitel that Hitler had survived.[60]

The following orders now went out: 'Valkyrie Level 2'; the general order to all upper-level military commanders beginning with the words: 'The Führer Adolf Hitler is dead!'; and the proclamations of martial law. Since the orders were long, especially the second one, and they had to be typed on Enigma encoding machines, this took hours. In order to speed up the process Olbricht had one of his secretaries, Delia Ziegler, type more copies of the orders, and when his other secretary, Anni Lerche, returned at 5.30 p.m. from some errands she had to type more copies as well.[61]

When Stauffenberg and Haeften entered Stauffenberg's office at 4.30 p.m., they found there Berthold Stauffenberg in his Navy uniform, Fritz-Dietlof, Count Schulenburg, Colonel Jäger (OC of XXI Deputy Corps Armoured Troops, holder of the Knight's Cross), Lieutenant von Kleist and Captain Fritzsche. Stauffenberg announced: 'He's dead. I saw them carry him out.' Then he and Haeften went to Olbricht and gave him the same news. It had been like the detonation of a 150-millimetre grenade: hardly anyone could have survived it.[62]

When Olbricht said Fromm wanted to have Mertz arrested, Stauffenberg took Olbricht along to Fromm. Olbricht reported that Stauffenberg had just informed him of Hitler's death. Fromm said that was impossible because Keitel had just assured him of the opposite. Stauffenberg repeated that he had seen the dead Hitler being carried out: Keitel was lying as always. Olbricht added that therefore 'we' had activated 'Valkyrie'. Fromm pounded his desk with his fist and shouted that this was high treason and carried the death penalty, and demanded to know who had issued the orders. Olbricht said his Chief of Staff had issued them. Mertz was summoned to confirm it; he came accompanied by Kleist and Haeften. Fromm said they were all under arrest. But Stauffenberg retorted calmly that, on the contrary, Fromm was under arrest. He, Stauffenberg himself, had set off the bomb and he knew that Hitler was dead. Fromm said once more that the assassination attempt had failed. Stauffenberg must shoot himself. Stauffenberg, always imperturbable, declined, whereupon Fromm strode towards him with raised fists; Kleist and Haeften stepped in, Kleist pushed his pistol into Fromm's stomach, and Fromm became calm. Stauffenberg gave him five minutes to decide whether he would join the uprising or not and they all left Fromm's office. After five minutes Olbricht went back to Fromm; Fromm said he regarded himself as relieved of his command authority. He was placed under guard with his special missions officer in a side-room.[63]

The Chief of General Staff Organisation Branch, Brigadier Stieff, telephoned the Quartermaster-General, Lieutenant-General Wagner, between 4 and 5 p.m. to say he had heard from the Home Army Command offices that they had proclaimed a military government; but this, said Stieff, was madness. Wagner ordered Stieff to report all events concerning the insurrection to the Chief of Wehrmacht Supreme Command, Fieldmarshal Keitel.[64] He abandoned and betrayed his fellow conspirators.

Meanwhile, more plotters arrived at Bendlerstrasse: General Beck with Count Schwerin von Schwanenfeld, Oppen, Ludwig von Hammerstein. Gisevius came with Helldorf and the Potsdam Provincial Governor, Gottfried, Count von Bismarck, but Helldorf and Bismarck soon left again. When Gerstenmaier arrived after 6 p.m., the mood at Bendlerstrasse was already somewhat depressed. But Stauffenberg was constantly on the telephone to the command centres throughout Germany, answering inquiries about Hitler's death and requests for confirmation of orders received, doing all in his power to move the uprising forward.[65]

The conspirators had asked the III Deputy Corps Commander, Lieutenant-General von Kortzfleisch, to come and see Fromm, but he was received by Beck, Olbricht and Hoepner. He refused to believe in Hitler's death, tried to escape, and was arrested. Major-General von Thüngen was sent to III Deputy Corps Command at no. 144 Hohenzollerndamm to replace Kortzfleisch. Thüngen made no haste to get there, displayed no energy in his new role and made no effort to get hold of troops for the occupation of key government and Party buildings.[66]

Events in Cottbus illustrate how difficult it was for the plotters to move troops in support of the uprising. The Motorised Infantry Replacement Training Brigade 'Grossdeutschland' received the 'Valkyrie' order between 3 and 4 p.m., along with the long order beginning with the statement that the Führer was dead. Their specific assignment was to occupy the radio transmitter at Königs-Wusterhausen and the national transmitter at Herzberg; their main force was ordered to move into their 'Valkyrie' assembly area south of Berlin. The written orders that arrived over the teletype machine came from General Army Office, although the brigade was subordinated to III Deputy Corps. The OC of the 'Grossdeutschland' Brigade, Lieutenant-Colonel Stirius, who was standing in for the brigade commander, Colonel Schulte-Heuthaus, while the latter conducted exercises at the nearby training grounds, thought this curious. But he gave the requisite orders and the troops moved, occupied the transmitters and relieved the SS guards. After 6 p.m. the brigade commander's special missions officer came to Stirius and said that the adjutant of the Guard Battalion 'Grossdeutschland' (which belonged to the same division as the brigade) had told him over the telephone that there had been an assassination attempt on the Führer, who had been only slightly injured; it looked as if an insurrection were under way in Berlin. At 6.30 p.m. a radio broadcast announced that Hitler was alive and would speak later; but the brigade troops kept moving. Stirius informed Oertzen at III Deputy Corps Command of their progress. When Major Remer asked Stirius for a formation with heavy weapons as reinforcements, Stirius found that nothing needed to be done because the Cottbus 'Valkyrie' units were on their way. As Stirius himself was preparing to drive to III Deputy Corps Command after 8.30 p.m. he learned that 'Valkyrie' had been cancelled and the units of the brigade were on their way back to barracks. Colonel Schulte-Heuthaus, after his return to barracks, drove to III Deputy Corps Command as ordered and arrived there round 7 p.m. He found that all was confusion. He was told that the deputy commander had been summoned to Bendlerstrasse and had not been heard from since; apparently no one knew that Thüngen had been appointed Kortzfleisch's successor. But a second lieutenant of the Guard Battalion approached them and took them to see Major Remer at the Propaganda Ministry. Here they learned what had happened.

Meanwhile, Hitler had appointed Himmler Commander-in-Chief of the Home Army. Himmler designated SS-Lieutenant-General Jüttner as his deputy; Jüttner appeared at the Propaganda Ministry, which for an hour or two was the power centre of the loyalists in Berlin, and ordered Schulte-Heuthaus to reverse all 'Valkyrie' measures for his brigade, whereupon all units returned to barracks.[67]

The Infantry School at Döberitz also received its 'Valkyrie' orders between 4 and 5 p.m., with the specific assignment to occupy the broadcast studio building in Masurenallee. This was done: the commander of the Infantry School detachment requested that all broadcasts be suspended, he was taken to the 'main switching room' and shown that all the switches were turned off. What he did not know was that for security against air raids a new switching room had been built in a bunker next door, which he was not shown and which continued to function. Such matters were supposed to be taken care of by signals specialists to be provided by Major-General Thiele and his Berlin Chief of Staff, Colonel Hassel. But Thiele did not send any; Hassel sent his contingent to Major-General Hase's Berlin Military Command between 4 and 5 p.m., but when they arrived there they were not given any further orders. Other Infantry School detachments occupied the transmitter at Tegel and the overseas transmitter at Nauen, but for lack of specialists they could not determine whether or not transmissions had been suspended as ordered.[68]

The pattern was the same, more or less, at the rest of the military installations with potential 'Valkyrie' troops. A panzer battalion of Armour School II at Krampnitz arrived at the Victory Column towards 6 p.m. and was ordered on to the Fehrbelliner Platz. Two battalions of the Non-commissioned Officers' School at Potsdam were also ordered to the Victory Column. A company of armoured reconnaissance vehicles and an infantry company were sent to occupy the transmitters at Königs-Wusterhausen and Zeesen and to stop political broadcasts. But around 7 p.m. the battalion commanders began to receive information about the coup in progress and distanced themselves from it; they either learned that counter-orders existed or received them directly.[69]

Between about 6 p.m. and 10 p.m. Stauffenberg was almost constantly on the telephone to senior staff officers or chiefs of staff in the deputy corps commands throughout Germany. Few of the deputy corps commands took any action in conformity with the insurgents' orders; in most cases there were delays because orders arrived after duty hours, and officers with sufficient authority had to be contacted at home or were on their way home. Within a short time the news broke that Hitler had survived an assassination attempt. In many cases it arrived at the same time as the strange orders from Berlin.

In Prague, Vienna and Paris quite extensive measures were taken which cost those responsible their positions – and in the most extreme cases, in Paris, their lives. In Prague Lieutenant-General Schaal, an armoured troops man, telephoned Berlin asking Fromm to confirm the orders. Instead he got through to Stauffenberg. He then took steps to secure military installations and began to move against SS and Party leaders in Prague. That night he revoked everything he had done, but was imprisoned for his actions until

April 1945.[70] The commanding general in Vienna (XVII Deputy Corps Command) was another armoured-troop commander, Lieutenant-General von Esebeck, who had commanded a combat command of the 6th Panzer Division during the campaign in France in 1940. When the instructions arrived from Berlin he immediately ordered them to be carried out and arrested the heads of the Party organisation, the SS and the Secret State Police – but treated them to cognac and cigarettes. Some post offices and railway stations were occupied by the military, the President of Secret State Police was disarmed, the secret state police and SS subordinated to the Wehrmacht. But when Keitel called, Esebeck obeyed orders from the existing regime. Stauffenberg, aware of some stagnation in Vienna, called towards 10 p.m. to find out what was happening. When he was told that Esebeck was no longer following the coup orders he said to the Quartermaster, Captain Szokoll, 'Don't you people break down as well.' But Esebeck and his Chief of Staff, Colonel (GS) Kodré, were already making their apologies to the Party and SS leaders.[71]

There was a reliable group of fellow conspirators in Paris – Colonel (GS) Finckh, the Quartermaster West; Lieutenant-Colonel (Res.) von Hofacker; Lieutenant-General von Stülpnagel, the Military Governor – who had prepared everything well. They received news that Hitler was dead shortly after 2 p.m. and set the machinery in motion, ordering the occupation of key points and the arrest of all SS and Secret State Police officers. The sandbags in front of which they were to be shot were stacked up at the St Cyr military college. But the Supreme Commander West, Fieldmarshal von Kluge, summoned Stülpnagel and Hofacker to his headquarters at La Roche-Guyon, learned through a telephone call from Stieff that the assassination had failed, got through to the Bendlerstrasse, reached Stauffenberg and asked for Fromm. It was customary, of course, to speak with officers at the same rank or command level. Stauffenberg said Fromm was not available and turned Kluge over to Hoepner as Fromm's successor. Hoepner assured Kluge that Hitler was dead and the Berlin orders were to be followed, then the connection was interrupted and Kluge did not have it restored. Kluge did not believe Hitler was dead, and he wavered. Stülpnagel reminded him of the coup plan and of what the conspirators believed Kluge had agreed to. Kluge said he did not know what Stülpnagel was talking about, ordered all insurrection measures to be reversed and advised Stülpnagel to get into civilian clothes and go underground. The Paris SS establishment were arrested nevertheless, but released soon afterward. When Stauffenberg called the Military Governor's offices after 10 p.m., he got the Chief of Staff, Colonel (GS) von Linstow. Linstow told him it was all over: he could hear the regime's myrmidons tramping noisily up the hall.[72]

At 6 p.m. Stauffenberg had not yet given up. Colonel Hassel heard him say at that time: 'The fellow isn't dead after all, but the machine is running, one can't yet say how it will go.' But the national radio station was still broadcasting: something had to be done about that. Hassel reported that he had sent his contingent of signals specialists to the Berlin Military Command, where they would have to be given further instructions. Then he drove home.[73]

Between 5 and 6 p.m. Mertz informed the officers of his staff that Hitler was dead and that the Wehrmacht had assumed full executive powers. General Hoepner, as the new Commander-in-Chief of the Home Army, did the same with Stauffenberg's staff officers. At approximately 6 p.m. Stauffenberg informed the department heads on his staff that Fromm had failed to rise to the occasion and was in protective custody; full executive powers throughout the country had been turned over to the deputy corps commanders.[74]

Olbricht sent Kleist to see if the Guard Battalion had sealed off the government quarter. Kleist reported that tanks had taken up positions on the Charlottenburger Chaussee and that the SS had been disarmed by Guard Battalion troops in Hermann-Göring-Strasse. Then there appeared in Bendlerstrasse SS-Colonel Achamer-Pifrader of Reich Security Main Office (who was, incidentally, a veteran of the search for better methods of mass extermination), who had been sent to summon Stauffenberg to a 'meeting' with the Chief of the Secret State Police, SS-Major-General Heinrich Müller. Stauffenberg had the SS-Colonel arrested.[75]

Gisevius had irked Stauffenberg by pressing him concerning the occupation of the Secret State Police headquarters and urging that Goebbels be shot out of hand. Now Gisevius wanted to know why Stauffenberg had not shot the SS officer, who might 'later' give everything away. Stauffenberg was almost speechless in face of this defeatism. Gisevius immediately changed his tune (all this according to his own account) and urged that they should bring about some 'manifest facts' by at least shooting Heinrich Müller and Goebbels: it was essential to produce 'a few corpses' to make sure that the insurrection had burned its boats. Couldn't Stauffenberg see what duds he had around him? He, Gisevius, would lead a detail of officers to shoot Müller and Goebbels. No such officers seemed to be available, but Stauffenberg took Gisevius' point about the need to radicalise the uprising and sent Colonel Jäger to the Berlin Military Command to organise a raiding detail. Jäger had no success there. Gisevius went to Secret State Police headquarters to see Helldorf. When he returned to Bendlerstrasse toward 8 p.m., Olbricht told him that he no longer doubted that Hitler had survived; did Gisevius think one could still go back on it all?[76]

Gisevius' frivolous relation of the facts distorts the image. In the course of the evening Olbricht made a serious attempt to promote the success of the insurrection, although this could not make up for the crucial loss of time caused by his and Thiele's hesitation. Some time after 8 p.m. the bureau chiefs who had left the building and had then been recalled after Stauffenberg's return from 'Wolfschanze' arrived back at Bendlerstrasse. Olbricht told them that Hitler was dead and General Beck and Fieldmarshal von Witzleben had taken over the leadership; they objected that the radio had said that Hitler had survived an assassination attack, so they could not co-operate. Olbricht could not persuade them and did not attempt to prevent them from leaving.[77]

After this Gisevius related to Stauffenberg, Beck and Schulenburg how the President of Police had sat and waited for hours for directives from the Berlin Military Command so that he could order arrests. Stauffenberg said he had already instructed Hase to make contact with Helldorf; but Hase was no longer in a position to do so. Beck said they must have the proclamations and policy statements broadcast over the radio; the officer who was supposed to do this, Lieutenant-General Fritz Lindemann, General of Artillery to the Chief of Army Equipment and Home Army Command, was in Zossen at the Quartermaster-General's house, and later on he could not be found. Gisevius offered his services, but he did not have any of the proclamations – Lindemann had them. Gisevius began to draft a new one, using phrases variously offered by those present. Beck wanted to dispatch Gisevius, but then Gisevius said the broadcasting facilities had not yet been occupied. Stauffenberg said this would be accomplished by 8 p.m. when the tanks had arrived. They did not arrive; the insurrection centre did not control, or did not know whether they controlled, any transmitting facilities. Thus they lost their chance of bringing the population all over Germany into the streets and perhaps setting in motion a general revolt.[78]

At 7.55 p.m. Stauffenberg and Beck spoke by telephone with the Chief of the General Staff of Army Group North, Major-General Kinzel. Stauffenberg explained that according to his own information Hitler had not survived the assassination attack, contrary to what the radio had announced; General Beck was forming a new government; the new leadership considered an immediate withdrawal of the Army Group from Courland essential if East Prussia were to be saved. Then Beck spoke to Kinzel and said the Army Group must not allow itself to be encircled like the 6th Army at Stalingrad, but must break out westward: that was the Army Group Commander's responsibility before his conscience and before history.[79]

Fieldmarshal von Witzleben, the designated Supreme Commander of the Armed Forces, drove to General Staff Headquarters at Zossen, evidently on the assumption that he was to command from there. The Home Army Command Headquarters at Bendlerstrasse was, after all, subordinate. Witzleben learned from Lieutenant-General Wagner that the assassination attempt had failed. Now he arrived at Bendlerstrasse. When Stauffenberg reported to him he said only: 'A fine mess, this.' Then he went with Beck into Fromm's office. Beck gave Witzleben an account of the day's events.

They called in Stauffenberg to confirm Hitler's death; Witzleben did not believe it. Then Schwerin, who had been the conspirators' liaison with Witzleben, was called in. Witzleben hauled Stauffenberg and Schwerin over the coals, angrily banging his fist on the table. Whether Hitler was dead or alive, neither the capital nor the radio installations were in the conspirators' hands: Witzleben had reason to be angry. In a rage, he left and drove back to Wagner. When the Quartermaster-General had heard the Fieldmarshal's account he said: 'We're going home.'[80]

As the news of Hitler's survival spread through the various staffs in the Bendlerstrasse, some officers who were determined to make a display of loyalty to the old regime formed a counter-force. Fromm's special missions officer, Captain (Cav.) Bartram, did all he could to rouse his chief out of his lethargy. Colonel von Roell, head of Section II on Fromm's staff, telephoned Army Personnel at 'Wolfschanze' to find out if Hoepner had in fact been made Commander-in-Chief of the Home Army and was told that he had not. He was ordered to contact Brigadier Maisel at the Army Personnel office in Lübben; Maisel made certain that all deputy corps commands received orders countermanding those issued by the insurgents.[81] On Olbricht's staff a similarly determined and effective counter-offensive was organised. Three section heads and a sub-section head of Olbricht's staff demanded to see Olbricht, and gathered in his office round 9 p.m. Olbricht declared that responsible men had seized the initiative to save Germany; since the Guard Battalion detachment had been withdrawn, every General-Staff officer was obliged to help protect the building. The officers were dissatisfied but said nothing, apparently accepting Olbricht's orders, and departed to plan their next move. Sub-machineguns, pistols and hand-grenades were ordered and arrived; the officers armed themselves, and then returned to Olbricht and demanded to see Fromm. Olbricht offered to take them to Hoepner, the insurgents' replacement for Fromm. As they all moved down the hall, someone, apparently Klausing, fired a shot at the advancing group, aiming at Olbricht's quartermaster, Lieutenant-Colonel (GS) Herber. Then more shots were fired on both sides: Stauffenberg, wearing his white summer uniform jacket, fired his Belgian army pistol at Olbricht's section head, Lieutenant-Colonel (GS) Pridun, and himself took a bullet in his left shoulder.[82]

Stauffenberg retreated to Fromm's ante-room and asked one of Fromm's secretaries to get a line to Paris. He asked for Hofacker but was put through to Linstow, who said that the myrmidons were about to catch him. Olbricht and Herber came through into Fromm's office, where they found Hoepner and Beck. Stauffenberg, an indescribably sad expression on his face, said to Fromm's secretary: 'They've all left me in the lurch.'[83]

Then he followed Olbricht and Herber. Mertz and Haeften came along too. Herber accused Hoepner of interrupting supplies to the front by issuing

'Valkyrie' orders and demanded to know what was going on. Hoepner replied he was waiting for orders from Fieldmarshal von Witzleben. Haeften was burning papers on the floor.[84]

Fromm was now conducted back to his own office. His Chief of the General Staff glared at him darkly as Herber and the other loyalists confronted the leaders of the uprising with drawn pistols. Fromm said he was now going to do to the coup leaders what they had done to him that afternoon. He pronounced that they had been caught in the act of committing high treason, declared them under arrest and demanded their weapons. General Beck asked to keep his pistol in order to shoot himself, tried twice, and after the second shot collapsed, still alive.[85] Then Fromm asked the others if they had any last wishes. Hoepner said he was not involved and wanted to clear himself; Fromm allowed him to write down a statement. Olbricht also asked permission to write and did so. The writing lasted close on half an hour. Meanwhile Stauffenberg stood by in angry silence. Fromm became impatient and proceeded to declare that a court martial consisting of himself and the loyalists present had condemned to death Colonel Mertz von Quirnheim, Lieutenant-General Olbricht, the colonel whose name he would not mention, and Lieutenant von Haeften. Stauffenberg now spoke. In a few short sentences he assumed entire responsibility: all the others had acted as soldiers under his command. Fromm said nothing and stood aside at the door. Stauffenberg, Mertz, Olbricht and Haeften walked past him, hesitantly but calmly. They were led down into the courtyard, placed one after the other in front of a sandpile at the wall of the building, and shot by ten non-commissioned officers of the Guard Battalion under the command of Second-Lieutenant Werner Schady. When Stauffenberg was standing before the sandpile, he shouted before the soldiers fired: 'Long live holy Germany!'[86]

16

Epilogue

After the executions in the courtyard, Fromm ordered a staff officer to give Beck the *coup de grâce*; the officer ordered a member of the Guard Battalion to do it.[1] Soldiers loaded the bodies of the five dead officers onto a lorry and took them to the Matthäikirche cemetery in Schöneberg, where they were buried with their uniforms and decorations. On 21 July Himmler had them exhumed, cremated and their ashes scattered over open fields.[2]

One cannot imagine what Berthold Stauffenberg was thinking and feeling as his brother was led out and shot. It was the beginning for Berthold of a twenty-one-day martyrdom about which almost nothing is known except his verdict on National Socialism and some information he gave on the plans for the uprising; after that he was himself put to death with unbelievable cruelty.

Before they were even put on trial, Hitler had all the military men accused of having taken part in the uprising declared criminals unworthy to bear arms. His instrument was a 'Court of Honour' presided over by the most senior officer of the Army, Fieldmarshal von Rundstedt. The 'Court of Honour' expelled the accused from the Armed Forces so that they were not subject to military justice (although many of their cases were already before the Superior Court Martial), and were turned over to the 'People's Court'. This court had been formed in 1934 to deal with political crimes which had formerly come under the jurisdiction of the Supreme Court of the Reich. Nevertheless, the trials of military conspirators in the 'People's Court' violated the established procedures of the National Socialist state, for the Reich Court Martial had jurisdiction in cases involving former members of the Armed Forces if they were accused of acts committed while they were in the Armed Forces. Hitler arbitrarily altered the jurisdiction in favour of the 'People's Court'.[3]

The records of Berthold Stauffenberg's trial are lost. Berthold, Count Stauffenberg, Fritz-Dietlof, Count Schulenburg and Commander Alfred Kranzfelder were tried together in the 'People's Court' on 10 August 1944, sentenced to death and hanged in the most cruel manner on the same afternoon.[4]

Cäsar von Hofacker stood trial in the 'People's Court' on 30 August. When the presiding judge, the notorious Roland Freisler, who had represented the Ministry of Justice at the Wannsee Conference in January 1942, interrupted him, Hofacker said: 'Be silent, Herr Freisler, for today it is my head that is at stake. In a year it will be yours!' He concluded his speech: 'I uncommonly regret that I could not take the place of my cousin Stauffenberg, who was prevented by his disabilities sustained in combat from completing the deed.' Hofacker was sentenced to death, but for several months longer the Secret State Police continued to interrogate him, unsuccessfully, about the role of Rommel and Rommel's Chief of the General Staff, Major-General Speidel. Hofacker was hanged on 20 December 1944.[5]

Alexander, Count Stauffenberg, was brought back to Berlin from Athens by train on 26 July. The journey lasted four days and nights. Although it was soon clear that he was not involved in the plot, he remained in 'kith-and-kin' custody. In a speech to Party district leaders on 3 August Himmler declared, 'The Stauffenberg family will be exterminated down to its last member.' In fact, Himmler refused to issue uniform directives for the practice of 'kith-and-kin' detention and applied it arbitrarily.

Alexander managed to telephone his wife Melitta on the day before he left Athens. Only a few hours later she was arrested and remained in 'kith-and-kin' detention until 2 September; for a short time she was in the same prison as Claus, Count Stauffenberg's widow Nina at the Alexanderplatz in Berlin. After her release she resumed her research in aeronautics, which was of great importance to the war. Alexander Stauffenberg was held in various concentration camps and prisons, such as Stutthof in East Prussia, Buchenwald in Saxony, and Schönberg in Bavaria. Under police interrogation Alexander condemned the crimes of the National Socialists just as Berthold had done. A Secret State Police commissar, SS Major Paul Opitz, helped Alexander and Melitta with small favours – partly out of sympathy, partly in exchange for an assurance that they would attest to the humane treatment he had given them.[6]

Almost to the end of the war, Melitta Stauffenberg was able to look after her husband and some others who were held in 'kith-and-kin' detention. She exploited her 'war-essential' status to insist that she must see her relatives and bring them food. She visited Alexander at least once every month. Her work was 'naturally only a pretext for helping us', as Alexander wrote to Robert Boehringer on 8 May 1945. She performed test dives with the Junkers 88 and night flights with the Arado 96, the Focke-Wulf 190 and the turbo-jet fighter Messerschmitt 262, worked on night-landing instruments, and secured permission for flights at her own discretion. The bombers were not suitable for going to visit Alexander because there were generally no airfields near the camps and prisons where he was held. Only the slow Fieseler Stork could land in any small field, but it was constantly in danger of being shot down by the Americans who dominated the airspace over Germany.

Twice at least Melitta flew to Buchenwald. Although she possessed the necessary permissions, she always stood 'with one foot before a court martial'. She discovered the place where the children of the dead brothers and of Cäsar von Hofacker were held; the SS had taken them to Bad Sachsa in the Harz Mountains. At Christmas time she visited the children and brought them presents. In a long letter to Nina, who was still in prison, Melitta described her visit and the cheerful well-being of the children under the leadership of Claus Stauffenberg's eldest son Berthold.[7]

After Nina had given birth to Stauffenberg's daughter Konstanze at the end of January 1945, she and the child were transferred to St Joseph's Hospital in Potsdam. Melitta visited her there a few days later, arriving by bicycle and wearing the ribbon of the Iron Cross II and the Pilot Badge in Gold with Diamonds on her uniform jacket. The senior doctor, who had been with the Air Force, recognised her and thereafter saw to it that Nina Stauffenberg and her child had the best of care.[8]

On 8 April 1945 Melitta, on her way to see Alexander at Schönberg near Passau, flying a slow and unarmed Bücker 181 trainer, was shot down from behind near Strasskirchen by an American fighter. She landed her plane, but died two hours later of the bullet-wounds she had received.[9]

Alexander took the death of his courageous wife very hard. He was also distressed because his brothers had not taken him into the conspiracy. He would have preferred to die with them for their cause.[10]

Almost all the Stauffenbergs' close relatives were imprisoned for several months or longer. The head of the family, Uncle Berthold, who was eighty-five, died in solitary confinement in Würzburg in November 1944. Cousin Clemens developed heart disease and was given leave from Oranienburg concentration camp; through Melitta's intervention he was placed in St Joseph's Hospital in Potsdam. After his recovery Melitta flew him to Hof, whence he travelled to Guttenberg; his wife Elisabeth, who had been permitted to join him in hospital had to return to Buchenwald concentration camp, where she was imprisoned along with Alexander, Berthold's widow Mika, Elisabeth Stauffenberg and others. Twice they saw Melitta fly over the camp.[11]

The property of the conspirators and their relatives was confiscated, in Lautlingen, Jettingen, Wilflingen, Amerdingen, Greifenstein, although Hitler had requested that 'the bereaved be generously cared for'. After the war they had to struggle with the German bureaucracy for restitution, and to get widows' and orphans' pensions.[12]

Caroline, Countess Stauffenberg, the mother of the Stauffenberg brothers, was in Lautlingen on 20 July 1944, with her brother Count Üxküll (Uncle Nux), Berthold's wife Mika and Claus's wife Nina with their children. On 21 July she learned that Claus had been shot during the night as the leader of the uprising. Her brother told her: 'Never forget that he did this in supreme fulfilment of his duty.' Secret State Police officers came in the night of 22 to 23 July, arrested Count Üxküll and Nina Stauffenberg and imprisoned them in Rottweil. On the evening of 23 July they came again and took away Alexandrine Üxküll (Lasli), the erstwhile director of the Red Cross, and Caroline Stauffenberg, and put them in solitary confinement in the Balingen district-court prison. On 17 August the children were taken away. Alexandrine Üxküll was released after six weeks; Caroline Stauffenberg returned to Lautlingen on 2 November. Soon afterward eight Secret State Police officers moved in with their families. Only in December did Caroline Stauffenberg learn of the deaths of her son Berthold and her brother Nikolaus. Although she had had no knowledge of Claus's and Berthold's plotting, she declared to one of her few visitors in December 1944: 'I knew of my son's deed and I approve of it.'[13]

In April 1945 French troops occupied Lautlingen. As the Moroccans plundered and raped, six hundred villagers fled to the manor house and sought the protection of the old Countess. In June 1945 a former French prisoner-of-war who had been held in Lautlingen became commander of the troops here. He provided Alexandrine, Countess Üxküll and another relative with a military motorcar so that they could search for the children. They found them still in Bad Sachsa. Claus's sons made the journey back to Lautlingen in the car. Lasli procured a large bus in which the others travelled, only a few hours before the Red Army occupied the area. The Hofacker children were taken to Reichenbach; Berthold's children and Claus's daughter Valerie went to Lautlingen.

Mika and Alexander were detained by the Americans after Germany had capitulated. When Mika was set free, she inquired in Lautlingen to find out whether her children were still alive before she went there. Alexander was subjected to seemingly interminable interrogations in the same villa in Frankfurt am Main in which Fieldmarshal von Rundstedt was held. He encountered considerable difficulty convincing his American interrogators that he could not sit at the same table with von Rundstedt, who had presided over the expulsion of his brothers Claus and Berthold from the Armed Forces. Not until 15 September 1945 did he arrive in Überlingen to join Rudolf Fahrner, Gemma Wolters-Thiersch and Marlene Hoffmann. He spent three years there, writing poetry and history, before he felt able to face the world outside once more.[14]

In 1948 Alexander, Count Stauffenberg, was appointed to the Chair of Ancient History at the Ludwig-Maximilians-Universität in Munich. He translated Pindar and finished a major work on Sicily, *Trinakria*. In the 1950s he was one of the first to agitate against the threat to the entire world of atomic power. He died of cancer in 1963.[15]

The impulses which made the Stauffenberg brothers mortal enemies of the National Socialists arose from their views on service and justice. In 1933, like so many of their contemporaries, they saw a promise of German renewal, the restoration of internal order and external honour. They did not grieve over the destruction of what had been a disorderly and latterly ineffective democracy. But, unlike not a few of their relatives and friends – Nikolaus, Count Üxküll, Franz Schenk, Baron Stauffenberg, Albrecht von Blumenthal, Fritz-Dietlof, Count Schulenburg, Ulrich, Count Schwerin von Schwanenfeld – none of the Stauffenberg brothers joined the NSDAP. This was remarkable: their 'party' was the Secret Germany, their 'Führer' was Stefan George, their future was the 'vision' to which their small band was summoned.[16]

But even as they were repelled by the law-breaking, the outrages against Jews, the corruption and vulgarity of the new leaders, they approved of the policy of tearing up the hated and humiliating Treaty of Versailles, of the policy of 'racial purity', the strengthening of rural society. A friend commented that Claus Stauffenberg kept his distance from National Socialism, no more.[17] In fact Claus's 'distance' went deeper; it meant also the rejection of political meddling in the nation's sacred trust, the Army.[18] But the Stauffenberg brothers did not see, perhaps never saw, the inner link between Hitler's 'racial idea' and his policy of conquest. And although they learned the essential details of the abominable intrigues against Armed Forces Minister von Blomberg and against the Commander-in-Chief of the Army, General von Fritsch, and although their education and professions must have given them a clear understanding of the hierarchy of responsibility, they tended at the time to blame not the Reich Chancellor and Führer, but his henchmen.

They condemned the wilful causing of war. But when after the German attack on Poland Britain, France, Australia, New Zealand, South Africa and Canada declared war on Germany, they gave priority to defending their country: in Claus Stauffenberg's sober judgement of 1939, this was a struggle for survival. The Stauffenberg brothers put the nation first and its reprehensible regime second.[19]

Alexander put it clearly: 'Stauffenberg made his entry into the ranks of the Resistance very late, but once he had committed himself it was with his characteristic drive to action, and from the year 1942 onwards the warning, stirring voice of the officer from Army Headquarters Organisation Branch made itself heard among army staffs and army group staffs on the eastern front.' Alexander himself had reacted much sooner to the hollow ideology of the new rulers. His union with a woman of Jewish descent may have contributed to this. At the annual meeting of the German Historical

Association in 1937 he publicly expressed his uncompromising opposition to the official ideology.[20]

Claus Stauffenberg's radical change of position came in 1942, and it was provoked by the crimes of the regime – the mass murder of Jews, Poles, Russians, prisoners-of-war. The available evidence shows that other issues were secondary: the mistaken policy towards the peoples of the Soviet Union, which turned initial support for the German invaders into its opposite; and the repetition in 1942 of the strategy that had failed in 1941, that is, the attempt to achieve two geographically distant objectives at the same time, while the forces available were insufficient for either one. To Claus Stauffenberg all of this constituted treason against the Army and the Reich. Later, early in 1944, Stauffenberg said to another staff officer that the Führer always took decisions which brought his people nearer to ruin.[21] The readiness of the soldier to give his life for his country must be matched by rational objectives, and it must have meaning.

Only gradually did Stauffenberg come to understand that 'errors' in military leadership such as that at Dunkirk were not errors but the consequence of a perversion, namely the subordination of military action to ideological lunacy. Only gradually did it become clear to him that the shootings behind the combat lines, and the treatment of the populations in the Soviet Union, were not aberrations but conscious policy directed from the highest level. Nevertheless, some rather firm principles of military obedience had to be eroded and eventually thrust aside before Stauffenberg arrived at the conviction that military objectives, the unconditional protection of one's own nation and state, had to be subordinated to combatting those crimes.

When Stauffenberg finally concluded that Hitler had perverted military principles and intentionally involved the Armed Forces in crimes of unprecedented proportions, and that the leaders of the nation lacked all ethical integrity, he turned to senior Army leaders who were Hitler's direct subordinates once the Führer had assumed the status of Commander-in-Chief of the Army in December 1941. When all the senior leaders whom Stauffenberg approached in 1942 and early 1943 declined to act, he decided that the colonels had to do something if the generals would not.

The natural right to resist unjust rule is rooted in German history. Someone who sees iniquity in an ordered society will turn in the first instance to regular procedures, and will resort to self-help only if there is no hope of remedy from the proper authorities. Whether or not Claus Stauffenberg was familiar with the natural-law doctrine that the right to resist unjust rule devolves from the higher to the lower levels when the higher levels fail, he certainly came to apply it.[22]

Berthold Stauffenberg arrived at the same conclusion as Claus at the same time, based on information that came to him through his work. He told associates that those responsible in Germany must be punished for their crimes, 'such as concentration camps, persecution of the Jews', before Germany's total military defeat, and that no sacrifice was too great to achieve this.[23]

Both Berthold and Claus reached their decision that Hitler and his gang must be removed at a time when German forces controlled almost all of Europe. They were actively seeking to overthrow the regime from the summer of 1942, long before the Stalingrad disaster, but without joining the existing anti-Hitler conspiracy of which they were aware.

Claus Stauffenberg's letter to Lieutenant-General Paulus of 12 June 1942 is the first documentation of his appeals to senior commanders to recognise both their own responsibility and their right to act on it and resist. Several more such expressions followed, including the discussion with Fieldmarshal von Manstein in January 1943. By the end of 1942 Stauffenberg had endangered himself and his interlocutors so much that he had to discontinue his efforts and get himself transferred to the front. After his recovery from grave injuries received in Tunisia, Stauffenberg still hesitated to join the patchwork conspiracy. He believed that the leadership of the nation belonged to the Army and the officer corps, as Gneisenau had demanded. Stauffenberg had written to Sodenstern in March 1939 that 'the military forces and therefore their support, the officer corps, represent the most essential support of the state and the actual embodiment of the nation'. In the winter of 1942/43 he said to a comrade and friend, 'Yes, we are indeed the leadership of the Army and also of the Nation and we shall take control of this leadership.'[24] All of these utterances date from the time before the Stauffenbergs' entry into any conspiracy against the regime.

Claus Stauffenberg's 'Oath' seems to point in the same direction. Here, faced with the defeat of Germany, the Stauffenbergs expressed their true convictions: upright, self-confident, they trusted in the future of their nation even in face of the certainty of foreign occupation and moral humiliation. The Stauffenbergs rejected in advance the moral arrogance of the foreign conquerors. They wanted 'law and justice' and they understood that fate had made them co-responsible for Germany's disgrace; but they represented another Germany than the one the conquerors were defeating, and they gave their lives to restore its honour. Karl Wolfskehl said of the brothers that through them Spirit and Reich and Time were sanctified, and from the Rhine to the Mediterranean we now breathed freely: 'there grew a laurel forest of fame and woe for you, Harmodius and you, Aristogeiton'.[25]

In the end the 'colonels' were left alone, deserted by their senior leaders. The unbelievable events of 15 July 1944 must have been devastating, showing the lack of support from senior fellow conspirators. Any prospect of a successful uprising had vanished. It is one of the most painful insights into the events of 15 and 20 July 1944 that on the second occasion Stauffenberg was willing to make another attempt, without any hope.

Claus Stauffenberg always remained a faithful Catholic. Noble birth and family were deeply-felt obligations. Finally, he remained committed to the living Secret Germany to which the Stauffenbergs had become heirs through Stefan George's last will and testament. This neo-classicist and neo-romantic side-road of German intellectual history drove them to action with greater force than the intellectual milieu to which the other conspirators belonged. Claus and Berthold Stauffenberg gave their lives for the Secret Germany as well as for the Reich, and as sacrifice and atonement for the crimes of the Reich's leaders. They could not live without revolting against those crimes.[26] Claus sacrificed his life, his soul, his honour, his family.

The conspirators' self-sacrifice presents a continuing existential challenge to contemporaries and successors alike. That is the historical significance of the uprising.

Ultimately, the *manifest* act determines historical understanding and effect. All acts of resistance to the criminal regime participate in the legitimacy that Stauffenberg's act created. There is no indication that anyone else would have achieved it. And without Stauffenberg's manifest act there would never have been the host of individual martyrdoms which demonstrated the ethical foundations of the resistance, its existential response to inhumanity.

Alexander Stauffenberg wrote that a nation's secret destinies are revealed in its poetry, and that Poetry itself was the nation's destiny when through the Poet the man of action was moved to act, or to sacrifice himself if he failed.[27]

APPENDICES

I

School essay by Claus, Count Stauffenberg

The 24th January 1923

What do you want to do in life?

[essay no.] 8.
In-class essay.

For all those who have recognised the fatherland and the new Reich, there is only one exalted calling, of which the great Greeks and Romans gave us the visible example, and which knights displayed in its highest form: to become worthy of the fatherland and of fighting for the fatherland, and then to sacrifice oneself to the sublime fight for the nation; to live in full awareness of reality and battle. This calling must then be exercised in conjunction with one's actual profession; it must go before it as its guiding idea: everyone can produce in his profession something new, beneficial to the fatherland. However, if one is to do this one must dedicate all one's powers and interests to one's chosen profession, one must confine one's abilities within a given form. Eventually I want to build, to become an architect. I think it a fine thing and I am attracted by the co-ordination of spatial forms which are quite abstract in themselves into a beautiful, rationally arranged and meaningful, self-evident, circumscribed form, the harmony of plan and elevation, of internal and external appointments, the balancing of proportions, the perfection of line, all of it individual yet integrating itself into generally worthwhile values. To sum up at this detailed level: my delight in building, in setting stone upon stone. But on the whole, I want to put my thoughts into the building, but subordinated entirely to the experience of Germanness, of culture in general, so that every building will, so to speak, represent a temple dedicated to the German nation and fatherland. In order to become better acquainted with my nation, and with other nations and cultures that are models for us, which will show me the way more clearly – and also because it interests me and I enjoy it – I also want to study history especially. This is the direction of my will at present, I do not know whether it will turn out differently, but that is secondary, because the main thing is that we go on the chosen way with open eyes, with clarity and joy and manfully strive toward the goal.[1]

II

Letter from Claus, Count Stauffenberg to his father[2]

Bamberg Tuesday

[27 April 1926]

My Father!

Many · many thanks for your letter · to my dismay I hear that Duli[3] has broken her foot · I hope that it is nothing serious. The death of Otto Tessin[4] grieves me very much · especially when I think how your best friends are passing away: Stuttgart is changing more and more. – That the first years of my profession would not be very pleasant was always clear to me: it is after all not easy for one of us to act the commoner for a long time and to forgo all things intellectual almost completely · perhaps it is not easy either to keep focussing on the more ideal goals and motivations · the consciousness of which would make the unbearable bearable. I am now, as I was before, convinced that my decision was right, and if only the smallest hint of a benefit can accrue to the fatherland when more intellectual persons make themselves available (not merely the sporting and those who seek military service because they are keen on steel helmets and marching) I am richly rewarded for the sacrifice of a few years of my youth. Your confidence and acceptance of my choice · like that of my brothers and friends is infinitely valuable to me in this respect since I myself indeed easily tend towards pessimism with regard to the future we have to live through · not, however, that I lacked self-confidence! I thank you for your advice: I am in any case exceedingly cautious and reserved with people who do not possess my full confidence · my real self is in fact no one else's concern.

On 6 June we go to Grafenwöhr.[5] I do not yet know anything for certain about leave at Whitsuntide · if you can send me 50 marks for this month I can get by well for leave and purchases · if it is now inconvenient to you it will be all right. Please send me pictures: I was thinking of the two Dürer engravings in our room · also Berthold could select some of their pictures brought back from Italy · then also photographs of Duli · Berth. Alex and us together with you. I have one of you. Thanks for the laundry basket. Kiss Duli and tell her to get well. Regards to Mika.

I most cordially kiss your hand

your grateful son

Claus.

Money please in registered sealed letter

III

Letters from Claus, Count Stauffenberg to Brigadier Georg von Sodenstern[6]

Wuppertal-Barmen, 6.2.39
Lönsstr. 25.

Highly esteemed General!

As a reader of the *Militärwissenschaftliche Rundschau* may I be permitted to express, Sir, the gratitude of a younger man for the essay 'On the essence of being a soldier'. Not that the General's words had presented us with something new or unknown, for it would be a sad thing if we based ourselves – even if unconsciously – so little upon the permanent foundations of the soldier's ethos; nor is something aroused here which made us see for the first time a great question of our era, for every soldier who is worth a mention must today constantly strive, with open eyes or instinctively, after the guiding thoughts in the General's essay; your ideas are expressed so felicitously, with the honourable fire of our martial profession, and at the same time with such sharply measured intellectual clarity, that they help drown out the always audible clamour of our day. It is this which moves me, Sir, to write this letter of thanks.

I know well how unbecoming it is in me to address 'praise' or 'approval' to the General. All the more do I hope that the General will receive these lines as the thanks of a junior who was in harmony with the General's words and who wants 'to be led by men whose bearing commands his respect', and who remains ever
the General's
obedient
Count Stauffenberg.
Captain (Cav.).

Wuppertal, 13.3.39

Highly esteemed General!

An answer from the General to my letter is more than I had expected. I must be all the more grateful for the General's kind letter in that it again addresses *the* question which ought, more than any other, to arouse the whole officer corps and particularly those in my cohorts, whom one could call the 'link in the chain'; and which – I verily believe – consciously or unconsciously, clear-sightedly or rather more dimly, does stir them emotionally.

In the phrase about the danger 'of the universalisation of the soldier's life into something commonplace', the General has put his finger on the critical point – the position of the military and its responsible support, the officer corps, in the life of the nation – with such precision that, in view of the further deductions the General has made,[7] to address a personal assurance and a general request by the younger officer to the older, and in this I am assuredly not speaking only for myself.

The request: at the end of your letter, Sir, you express the fear that the admonitions of a generation which obviously provides the leadership of today's Armed Forces no longer find the right echo among the young. I know that coming from the General's mouth this does not signify resignation, as is already proved by the fact of publication in the *Rundschau*. But the General will perhaps understand that I see here an inchoate distancing from the younger generation which must ultimately end by hampering the active effectiveness of the very men who represent that great heritage – the men who have been purged of the dross of the merely conventional, the mere superficial everyday appearances, by the trial of the World War they fought through. I have encountered essentially the same attitude several times, and particularly among the officers of whom – the General will not take this to be an inappropriate value judgement! – we younger ones are accustomed to say, 'a splendid soldier, a true leader!' This attitude is more than comprehensible in face of the widely propagated and idolised losing of the self in the masses. But if there is any danger that the confidence in the absolute validity of the aristocratic foundation of the soldier's concept of the state and of life, the validity which spans the most diverse eras, may be lost to its best-qualified spokesmen and transmitters, then the crisis of which the General speaks and in which we already find ourselves becomes a grave danger.

No doubt we too, the officer corps, have already had to pay our tribute to the masses, and we ourselves have already partly become a 'mass', at least the younger generation: a mass with all its suffocating dangers, but also with its weaknesses. If some of us – even if we are imperceptibly few in number – succeed in awakening the incorruptible perception of what is genuine and essential, and confirm the immortal bearing of the officer and gentleman, then we shall have won half the battle.

In this connection another thing is close to my heart. Although I am rather suspicious of the catchword 'total', and although this catchword has been misused everywhere in our military environment, it is highly appropriate to the concept of the officer. We cannot afford to withdraw into the purely military, meaning a purely professional environment, although the best of us are particularly inclined to do so in view of the situation, and because of the tremendous effectiveness of forces outside our ranks which have expanded the Reich and put us in the saddle, seemingly by themselves, without any contribution from us. To be a soldier, especially a military leader, an officer, means to be a servant of the state, to be part of the state, and that includes overall responsibility. The sense of this must not be lost. To preserve and teach this comprehensive concept of the soldier's mission seems to me today our greatest task. What can be accomplished by an unshakable faith and a focussed determination that does not shy away from anything: that is before all our eyes. That we or our sons and grandsons should not have to begin anew here; that the link should not be broken here; that a generation should not deny itself which has not allowed itself to be distracted from the essence of being a soldier, either by the superficialities of the pre-war era or by four years of war or by the dislocations and confusions of the post-war era: that is my request. I believe my line of thinking is sufficiently consistent to allow a judgement of what this means. We must not only know how to fight for the Army itself: no, we must fight for our nation, for the state itself, in the knowledge that the military forces and their pillar, the officer corps, represent the most essential support of the state and the true embodiment of the nation.

I may hope not to be misunderstood by the General as I naturally often am by others: I am not concerned with this or that point of view, nor with opposition arising from personal background or education or profession, only with the Reich. For however one may twist and turn things, in the end, in the great battle, the national battle which will decide the existence or non-existence of the nation, responsibility will fall to the military forces; whether or not we are 'reserved' today, in the true fateful moments no political or other organisation could relieve us of one iota of responsibility. Again, if today's propaganda slogan, to the effect that we failed to 'toe the line' sufficiently before the Munich Agreement, seems to be justified, it must nonetheless be said that the caution displayed by a large part of the officer corps, while it was surely politically inexpedient, actually correspon-ded to a very true inner instinct. And if it revealed a disharmony between the political leadership and its resonance in the military forces, then perhaps it was due less to a lack of true soldierly attitudes among the officer corps than to the fact that the position of the officer corps within the state is purely professional and task-oriented, since the political leadership had not managed to concede to it the indispensable measure of confidence and co-responsibility which is, after all, indispensable for the leadership of the nation in arms, which will as ever fall to it in war.

The assurance of which I spoke at the beginning, Sir, is really contained in the preceding. It means the will, in spite of all dubious appearances and in spite of the nearly overwhelming force of a contrary line of development, to fight for the whole and not for a part. It means faith in a generation of leaders and teachers who represent for us more than merely the embodiment of a venerable tradition.

With German Greeting[8] I am
the General's ever
grateful and obedient
Count Stauffenberg.

IV

Letter from Claus, Count Stauffenberg to his mother-in-law[9]

H.Q. OKH, 11.1.42

Dearest Mami! Now in spite of all good intentions your birthday has arrived. Since a richly intensive work schedule, with all the attendant circumstances of night work and rush, have combined themselves with influenza, there was no space left for private letter-writing.

However: above all now, from all my heart, all good wishes upon your birthday! The year's beginning has not been so very confidence-inspiring, so that one can hardly harbour hopes and wishes for peace for this year, surely the best gift that could be offered to all of you. Actually I myself have no present for you, I do not even know what you will receive from Nina. – Many thanks for your letter. I should indeed like to explain this and that to you and Papi, but it is not entirely easy. Certainly I am informed about the rumours at home concerning Brauchitsch's departure and about combinations with the woollens collection. Not a true word in any of it. But it is quite natural that it should all look that way. *Woollens collection*: The winter clothing for the troops deployed in the east was made ready in good time. That it did not reach the troops is purely a question of transport and supplies. The current woollens collection serves to cover losses and wear, provide outfits for replacement troops destined for the east and convalescents, and improve regulation equipment. Certainly it would have been better to make the collection earlier: OKH suggested it as early as the beginning of September, though at the time it was aimed at creating sufficient reserves. – *Situation at the front*: It is no doubt very difficult just now. It is a situation which must be overcome by straining the last resources and means. No individual can be blamed here. The deeper reason lies in the incorrect assessment of the Soviet Union and her material capacity. They were underestimated by all of us. That the Soviet Union was on the point of military collapse after the battles of Kiev, Bryansk and Vyasma I do not doubt even today. When we were ready to exploit the success the bad weather returned, and as soon as the mud had been overcome, the Soviets just came up with their newly organised formations. A full victory lay so near that one had to stake everything upon one card. The risk was of course that much greater. That things are currently rather difficult I frankly admit. This is, however, essentially due to transport and supply difficulties in which respects the Russians are incomparably better off.

But after all there has never been a war without reverses and difficult situations. They have to be overcome in God's name. – *Brauchitsch*: The Führer had long since *de facto* reserved for himself decisions on almost all questions of warfare and operational leadership. This is in the nature of such

an outstanding and strong-willed personality. The existence of a commander-in-chief in between the Chief of the General Staff and the Führer
inevitably had an aggravating, hindering, delaying effect and inevitably
often led to misunderstandings and frictions. In short campaigns which ran
very much according to plan these difficulties could be tolerated – but not
really in difficult circumstances. In this sense Brauchitsch's departure was
only logical, the last step in a longer evolution. In addition there is the fact
that lately Brauchitsch had had several rather unpleasant heart attacks. In
any case the decision came absolutely from Brauchitsch.

It is obvious that our propaganda has not handled all this at all well.
There is also some feeling about the absence of any visible honours for
Brauchitsch. However, these can certainly still be provided at the next
opportunity. – Purely objectively, however, we can work better now than we
did before. With the new solution[10] it quickly became possible to capture
the entire resources of the nation and harness them for the Army's deciding
struggle. And that is decisive!

I myself am well again after a fashion. Again with all good wishes and
greetings to Papi

> Always your Claus.

V

Letter from Claus, Count Stauffenberg to Lieutenant-General Friedrich Paulus[11]

> H.Q. OKH. 12.6.42.

Highly esteemed General!

Army Group South informed me that I was not to report there any more,
since due to the Führer's visit on the day in question there was no time for
me. For this reason I decided to fly back in the OKW plane after all and so
gain an entire day.

These circumstances made it impossible for me to take my leave of the
General and to express to the General my most obedient thanks for my kind
reception at headquarters. I beg to make up for this in writing and especially
to be permitted to express my most obedient thanks for the hospitality
which I was allowed to enjoy as the General's personal guest.

The days in and around Kharkov and the contacts with all the visited
divisions gave great joy and 'much impetus'. Of course, it again brought
especially to mind what one misses far away from the troops in the field.
What can be more splendid than to be able to care for them and be effective
directly! Compared to that, all the satisfaction which, in a certain sense, one
can of course also find here is a pitiful surrogate. All the more so because an
insider – and I reckon myself to be one after 2 years' work here – must
always at once and everywhere recognise that his activity is circumscribed in

ways that are by no means always supported by objective fact. I am quite well aware that one must fight on regardless, and I try to make this clear to the other players again and again. But it is not always so easy to keep hold of one's own inner impetus in the process. The General will understand perfectly how refreshing it is, for one coming out of such an atmosphere, to visit where the supreme risk is ventured on without hesitation, where life is sacrificed without a murmur, while the leaders and exemplars bicker over prestige or lack the courage to stand up for a view, nay a conviction, which concerns the lives of thousands.

Seeing things in this way does not indeed make life here easier. But if one ceases to see this one ought to be hounded out of this institution as quickly as possible.

The General is again in the midst of an operation and with ardent hearts we follow every step of it. May this one and those that are to come be blessed by good fortune.

With esteem and gratitude
I am the General's
ever obedient
Stauffenberg.

VI

Stauffenberg's Oath[12]

We believe in the future of the Germans.

We know that the German has powers which designate him to lead the community of the occidental nations towards a more beautiful life.

We acknowledge in spirit and in deed the great traditions of our nation which, through the amalgamation of Hellenic and Christian origins in the Germanic character, created western man.

We want a New Order which makes all Germans supporters of the state and guarantees them law and justice, but we scorn the lie of equality and we bow before the hierarchies established by nature.

We want a nation which will remain rooted in the soil of the homeland close to the powers of nature, which will find its happiness and its satisfaction in its given surroundings and, free and proud, will overcome the low passions of envy and jealous resentment.

We want leaders who, coming from all classes of the nation, in harmony with the divine powers, high-minded, lead others high-mindedly, with discipline and sacrifice.

We unite in an inseparable community which through its bearing and actions serves the New Order and forms for the leaders of the future the fighters whom they will need.

We pledge to live blamelessly,
>   to serve in obedience,
>   to keep silent unswervingly,
>   and to stand for each other.

Alexander Stauffenberg may have received his first knowledge of the document from Marlene Hoffmann, who became his second wife. Marlene Hoffmann received the document from Rudolf Fahrner in 1944 in order to hide it. She had custody of it until Fahrner's return from captivity in the summer of 1945. In October 1947 Alexander Stauffenberg told Johann Dietrich von Hassell that 'he possessed Claus' "oath" which proved clearly how entirely Claus had been a part of western culture; that the "oath" had been drafted largely by Claus'; and that there was 'apparently nothing known for certain about the history of its genesis'.

Alexander reproduced the 'Oath' almost verbatim in a poem about his brothers, entitled 'On the Eve' (published in 1964), in which Berthold and Claus speak the lines alternately. There is no mention of Rudolf Fahrner in the poem.[13]

Of the few who helped in the writing of these theses, only Fahrner has testified to their origins. Fahrner stated essentially, and consistently, that Claus Stauffenberg was the author of all or almost all of them. Fahrner's gift for 'serving' supports his evidence.[14]

According to Fahrner's evidence, Claus Stauffenberg asked him and Berthold Stauffenberg to draft the 'Oath', which they did in the first days of July 1944. Berthold's secretary, Maria Appel, typed it at Fahrner's dictation. Claus made some changes in the carbon copy with his left hand and gave it to Fahrner on 4 July, asking him to hide it.

The idea of drafting the 'Oath' is to be attributed to Claus Stauffenberg, not only on the basis of Fahrner's evidence, but also based on a conversation between Fritz-Dietlof, Count Schulenburg, and Axel, Baron von dem Bussche.[15] It is consistent with Claus Stauffenberg's sense of ceremonial: he took an oath at his father's graveside.[16]

However, the idea of a manifesto for those who were to carry the torch after the probable demise of the principals is found in Rudolf Fahrner's books on Arndt and Gneisenau. In 1942 Stauffenberg wrote to a friend that he often referred to Fahrner's *Gneisenau* in the course of his official duties.[17] In both his works Fahrner stated that at the beginning of March 1812 Napoleon sent his troops to invade Prussia and imposed a treaty of submission: the whole of Prussia, except Silesia, was to be occupied; Prussia was to join the French in the war against Russia; the *Grande Armée* was to be provisioned and allowed free passage through Prussia. King Frederick William III signed the treaty:

The King surrenders. Gneisenau receives the discharge which he has repeatedly demanded; Scharnhorst goes on indefinite leave; Clausewitz, Groeben and others – 300 officers in all – demand and receive their discharge. Gneisenau and his friends feel that sacred honour has been desecrated, the very germ of future growth endangered. Fearing the spread of a slavish mentality and the consequent distortion of history, they set down their views in a common secret confession so that future times may learn, even if they themselves perish, that there have been men alive who have seen and felt the whole disgrace.[18]

Stauffenberg is likely to have known only this version – Fahrner's. Gneisenau's biographer Pertz, whose work Fahrner evidently used, dates the event to the spring of 1811 and describes it only as a project of Gneisenau's, which came to naught.[19]

The reasons for Fahrner's involvement in the formulation of the 'Oath' are transparent. Fahrner, as a philologist, literary critic, poet, adherent of Stefan George and friend, was the Stauffenberg brothers' indispensable assistant in the writing of proclamations and the casting of their ideas in an elevated style removed from everyday clichés. They called on him in the autumn of 1943, and again in June 1944. Stauffenberg did not have a secretary to whom he could dictate things such as the 'Oath'; his duties did not leave him time to sit down and formulate his thoughts himself. Fahrner said that Stauffenberg was not a drafter of programmes and was not systematic.[20] Berthold, however, had a reliable secretary and less hectic working conditions.

But the impulses lie deeper. Although Fahrner may never have said it *expressis verbis*, he must have been conscious of the parallel between Arndt-Gneisenau and Fahrner-Stauffenberg. This may seem an unimportant consideration in view of the fact that the uprising failed. But the control of the state was at stake, and it could have been a turning point in world history.

A comparison of the 'Oath' with Claus Stauffenberg's independently documented views reveals a thoroughgoing correspondence.

In his poem 'Abendland I' ('Occident I'), of 1923, Stauffenberg wrote of Germany's mission to the west and the universal Christian empire of the Middle Ages. He wrote the same ideas into a letter of 1936: for a German, the sublime heights of culture were always linked to 'universal effectiveness: the Holy Empire, humanism, [German] classicism'.[21] The reference to the 'lie of equality' coincided with Stauffenberg's own view.[22]

VII

Gisevius and the alleged 'eastern orientation' of Stauffenberg

Gisevius went underground on 20 July 1944 after the failure of the uprising. He stayed in hiding until 23 January 1945, when he succeeded in escaping to Switzerland using a passport which had belonged to Carl Deichmann, a brother of Moltke's wife Freya. Allen Dulles had had it modified; through the help of Georg Federer, of the German Legation in Berne, it had received the required visa.[23]

On 25 January Dulles cabled to Washington that Gisevius had told how Stauffenberg, the motive force of the attempted uprising in July 1944, had planned to proclaim a 'workers' and peasants' regime in Germany' and to conclude a separate peace with the Soviet Union. The situation on Germany's eastern front and the general situation in Germany, Dulles continued, suggested the conclusion that an 'eastern solution' must be attractive to Germany. If the resistance of German forces in the west was not broken soon, the Russians might meanwhile penetrate deeply into Germany. The French Foreign Minister, Georges Bidault, had intimated that the French were horrified at the thought of a Soviet-dominated government on their eastern border.

Then Dulles revealed the heart of the manoeuvre: he was seeking a secret contact with Rundstedt. He already had one with Kesselring in Italy.[24] This, of course, led to a separate surrender of the German forces there. Dulles proposed a discreet announcement that the (western) Allies would accept a partial surrender, so that western Germany, at least, would be occupied by American and British troops before the Russian advance caused complete chaos in Germany. Many Germans believed Germany could get along with Russia if she accepted a Bolshevik government.[25] This is precisely what Gisevius had written in a memorandum he had left for Dulles in Zurich on 11 July 1944 – hours *before* he travelled to Berlin, and *before* he learned of Stauffenberg's alleged views on 12 July.

Dulles repeated his remonstrations more urgently on 28 January 1945, still basing himself on Gisevius' information: Stauffenberg and his close associates in the conspiracy had resolved to bring about an 'eastern solution' and had intended to open the eastern front at once, without even an attempt at negotiating with the Russians. According to Dulles based on Gisevius, Stauffenberg had claimed that he had received, via Ambassador Kollontay and the National Committee Free Germany, assurances that Russia would grant a 'fair peace' and insist on only partial disarmament of German forces. Some months earlier Trott had attempted unsuccessfully to contact the British in Stockholm, after which he had himself embraced the 'eastern solution' and supported Stauffenberg.[26] In further reports, and in his memoirs, Gisevius repeated his claim that the inner Stauffenberg circle had sought an 'alliance with the extreme left, the Communists', had wanted the Russians to occupy Germany and recreate it according to the Soviet model.[27]

Gisevius also harboured hopes for his personal career which might be salvaged to some extent, even after the failure of the uprising, if he succeeded in supplying the decisive impulse for Dulles's policy and if this policy succeeded. Before he left Zurich for Berlin in July 1944, he told Dulles's intermediary, Mary Bancroft, that he claimed the position of foreign minister.[28]

The Secret State Police investigated this aspect with particular vigour, hoping to confirm Martin Bormann's premature verdict that the conspirators had committed treason in concert with the National Committee Free Germany. The police findings showed the opposite: there had been no contacts with the National Committee Free Germany or with any foreign power.[29]

In his February 1945 report to Dulles, which he corrected in his own hand, Gisevius claimed that after the coup d'état a directory of five was to hold power; it was to consist of Beck, Goerdeler, Leithäuser (?), Leuschner and Gisevius. Three days later a cabinet would have been formed under the authority of Beck as head of state, consisting of these personages: Reich Chancellor Goerdeler; Vice-Chancellor Leuschner; Interior Minister Leber, with Fritz-Dietlof, Count Schulenburg, as his secretary of state; Economics Minister Lejeune-Jung; Justice Minister Wirmer; Cultural-Affairs Minister Bolz; Finance Minister Löser; Foreign Minister Friedrich Werner, Count Schulenburg, with Hassell as his secretary of state; War Minister Oster or Olbricht, secretary of state Stauffenberg; Armed Forces Supreme Commander Witzleben; and Reich Minister to the Chief of State: Gisevius, who would be concurrently 'Reich Commissar for Purges and Restoration of Public Order'. Following Beck's explicit wish martial law was to be suspended on the third day and the entire civil executive turned over to Gisevius.[30]

VIII

The military career of Claus, Count Stauffenberg

1 April 1926	joins No. 17 Cavalry Regiment in Bamberg
18 Aug. 1927	promoted corporal, appointed officer cadet
15 Oct. 1927	promoted sergeant
17 Oct. 1927–9 Aug. 1928	Infantry School in Dresden
1 Aug. 1928	officer cadet with rank of staff sergeant
1928	wins bronze medal for sport
Oct. 1928–Aug. 1929	Cavalry School in Hanover

17 Aug. 1929	sword of honour for superior performance
1 Jan. 1930	promoted second lieutenant
30 July–12 Aug. 1930	pioneer course
18 Nov. 1930–14 Feb. 1931	mortar course
1 May 1933	promoted lieutenant
1 Oct. 1934–1 Oct. 1936	adjutant, Cavalry School Hanover
1935	interpreter examination in English
1936	*Wehrkreisprüfung* (qualifying examination for admission to the War Academy)
2 Oct. 1936	distinguished service badge, IVth class
6 Oct. 1936–31 July 1938	War Academy Berlin
1 Jan. 1937	promoted captain (cavalry)
1 April 1938	distinguished service badge, IIIrd class
1 Aug. 1938	detailed as quartermaster officer (Ib) to 1st Light Division at Wuppertal (from 18 Oct. 1939 renamed 6th Panzer Division)
1 Nov. 1939	permanently transferred to General Staff as captain (GS) (*Hauptmann im Generalstab*) and posted as quartermaster to 6th Panzer Division
31 May 1940	posted to Army High Command/General Staff of the Army/Organisation Branch as Section Head II
	Iron Cross Ist Class
1 Jan. 1941	promoted major (GS)
25 Oct. 1941	Royal Bulgarian Order for Bravery IVth Class, 1st Level
11 Dec. 1942	Finnish Liberty Cross IIIrd Class
1 Jan. 1943	promoted lieutenant-colonel (GS)
15 Feb. 1943	posted as senior staff officer (Ia) to 10th Panzer Division
7 April 1943	seriously wounded in Tunisia
10 April 1943	transferred to officer reserve pool of Army High Command; duties under direction of V Deputy Corps Command (Stuttgart)
14 April 1943	Wound Badge in Gold
20 April 1943	Italian-German Remembrance Medal Command (Stuttgart)
15 Sept. 1943	detailed to Chief of Army Equipment and Commander-in-Chief of the Home Army/General Army Office
1 Nov. 1943	posted as Chief of Staff to Chief of Army Equipment and Commander-in-Chief of the Home Army/General Army Office

1 April 1944	promoted colonel (GS)
20 June 1944	posted as Chief of the General Staff to Chief of Army Equipment and Commander-in-Chief of the Home Army
20 July 1944	shot by order of court martial
4 Aug. 1944	expelled from *Wehrmacht* by the Führer at the recommendation of the Army Court of Honour

IX

Hitler's East Prussian Headquarters 'Wolfschanze'

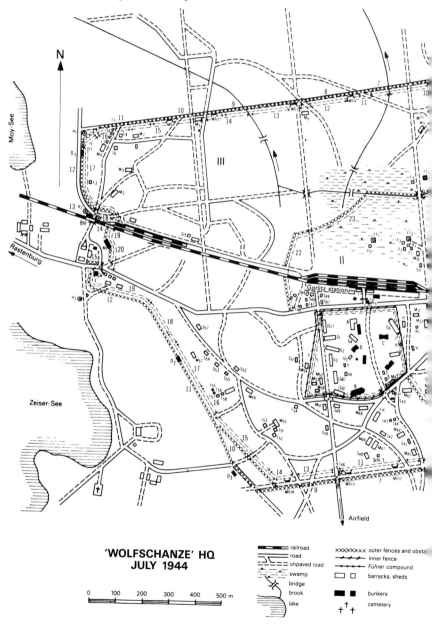

51. *Plan of Hitler's East Prussian Headquarters 'Wolfschanze'*

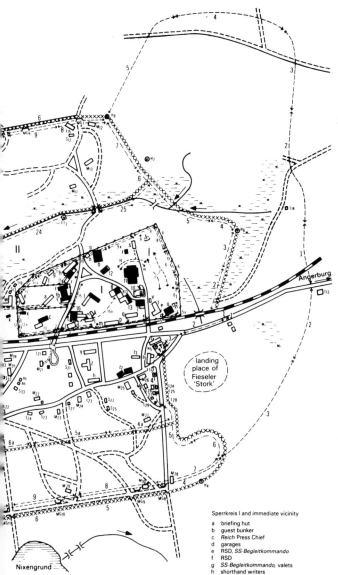

z_1 quarters
z_2 general shelters
z_3 liaison staff, Naval High Command
z_4 liaison staff, Air Force High Command
z_5 liaison staff, Naval High Command

7   Chief OKW
8   *Führer's* Personal Adjutants
10   Casino I and Teahouse
11   *Führer*
12   M. Bormann
13   *Führer's Wehrmacht* Adjutants
813   Army Personnel Office
16   communications bunker
     (teleprinter exchange)

Compound II and other parts of installation

G_1 WFSt
G_2 WFSt
G_3 WFSt
G_4 Commandant *Führer* HQ
G_5 Staff FBB
G_6 – $[G_6]$ WFSt

A   casino WFSt, casino *Führer* HQ
B   communications bunker
     (telephone exchange)
C   Staff FBB
D   heating plant, teleprinter exchange

I   Commandant
II   Commandant's quarters
III   General Warlimont's quarters
IV   sick bay
V   sick bay
VI   wash rooms
VII   Sauna II

M_1 – M_{10} FBB quarters
M_{11} III Platoon 2nd Comp. FBB
M_{12} guard platoon 7 FFA
M_{13} search light section
M_{14} II Platoon 1st Comp. FBB
     (2nd Lt. Jansson)
M_{15} II Platoon 1st Comp. FBB
     (2nd Lt. Christiansen)
M_{16}, M_{17} quarters
M_{21} 1st Comp. FBB
M_{22} signal platoon
M_{23} 1 Platoon 1st Comp. FBB
M_{24} 1 Platoon 1st Comp. FBB
     (2nd Lt. Stumpf)
M_{25} III Platoon 1st Comp. FBB (Lt. Seldte)
M_{26} – M_{30} quarters (M_{28}, formerly
     South Guard House)
M_{31} communications barracks
M_{32} Sergeant-Major Hildebrand
M_{33} troop quarters
M_{34} supplies and provisions
M_{35} officers' quarters
M_{41} supply section, 1st Comp. FBB
M_{42} Special Commando 'W'
m_{43} sergeant, Staff Commandant
M_{44} quarters
M_{45} Special Commando 'W'
M_{46} Fire-fighting comp.
M_{47} quarters
M_{48} enlisted men, Staff Commandant
M_{51} II Platoon 3rd Comp. (2nd Lt. Krieger)
M_{52}, M_{53} non-commissioned officers and
     enlisted men, WFSt
M_{54} III Platoon 3rd Comp. (Lt. Grotesmann)
M_{55} FBB (Lt. Pieper)
M_{56} office, 3rd Comp.
M_{57} I Platoon 3rd Comp. (Lt. Wegmann)
M_{58}, M_{59}, M_{61} quarters

L_1 – L_6 quarters
L_7 Guard House West
L_{13} Guard House East
L_{14} guard quarters
L_{15} guard quarters
L_{16} guard quarters
L_{21} Guard House I
L_{22} Lt. Kessel
L_{23} office, 1st Comp.
L_{24} – L_{29} quarters
L_{31} Guard House II
L_{41} Special Commando 'W' Accountant
L_{42} quarters
L_{43} Special Commando 'W' office
L_{44} quarters Major Gnass
L_{46} Guard House South
     (formerly Southwest Guard)
L_{47}, L_{48}, L_{51}, L_{52} quarters
L_{53} officers' casino 3rd Comp. FBB
L_{55} – L_{58} quarters

Ab   latrines
D   gun emplacements (bunkers)
F   anti-aircraft gun emplacements
FT   anti-aircraft gun towers
H   machine-gun towers
Hy   hydrant
MG   machine-gun emplacements

a – z, A – D   non-official designations

Sperrkreis I and immediate vicinity

a   briefing hut
b   guest bunker
c   *Reich* Press Chief
d   garages
e   RSD, *SS-Begleitkommando*
f   RSD
g   *SS-Begleitkommando*, valets
h   shorthand writers
i   RSD (Rattenhuber, Högl), mail room
j   liaison persons of high *Reich* authorities
     (Bodenschatz, Hewel, Voss, *SS-Obergruppen-*
     führer Wolff, later Fegelein), Dr. Morell, barber
     Wollenhaupt (from Hotel 'Kaiserhof' in Berlin)
k   cinema
l   drivers
m   heating plant
n   sauna
o   general shelter
p   Casino II
q   Chief WFSt
r   anti-aircraft bunker
s   water basin
t   *Reich* Marshal's house
u   Göring's bunker
v   Old Teahouse
w   *SS-Begleitkommando*
x   bunker
y   liaison staff of Foreign Minister
z   Speer, guests

LEGEND

– – – –   patrol paths of FBB guards, daytime
•   sentries, daytime
– – –   patrol paths of FBB guards, nighttime
⬭   sentries, nighttime

In the western part of Compound I, patrol routes were
slightly modified when *Führer* Compound was in use. Within
and outside of fences throughout the HQ area there were
also telephones, water taps, foxholes and short trenches,
dugouts, munitions depots, minefields (details for these not
available). Automobile sheds and revetments partly not
shown to preserve clarity.

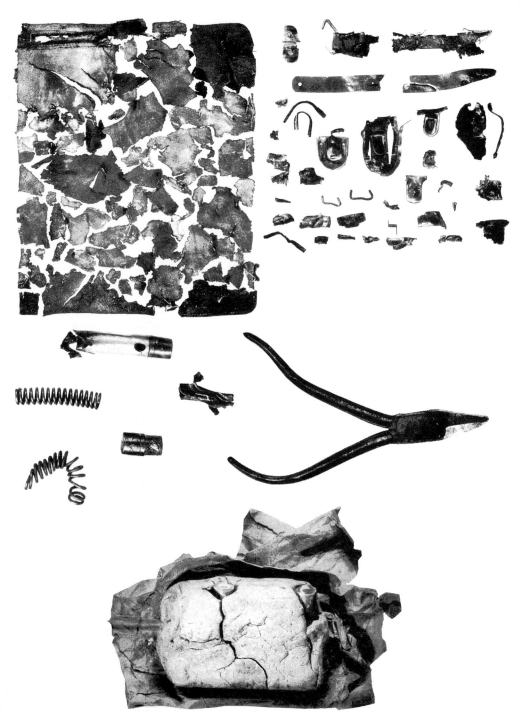

52. *Above: Remains of Stauffenberg's briefcase. Centre: Remains of fuses used in Stauffenberg's 'bomb', and the pliers he used to break the glass phial of the fuse. Bottom: Discarded parcel of explosive with primer charges*

NOTES

Prologue

1 Bismarck to Alvensleben 5 May 1859 in Bismarck, *Werke in Auswahl* 2 276.
2 NS in Kramarz 132.
3 Yorck 6 Aug. 1944; M. Yorck 10 Aug. 1972.
4 *Spiegelbild* 110; *Trial* XXXIII 424.
5 Bussche, interview 19 July 1984.
6 *Spiegelbild*, p. 471.
7 Pezold 25 April 1965.
8 See below p. 246 and appendix VI.
9 Halder to Kramarz 26 Jan. 1962.

1. Childhood, a World War, and a new beginning

All abridged citations of archival sources, personal information to the author, letters, depositions and published works are listed in full in the Bibliography. See also List of Abbreviations.

1 Wunder 1–17, 154, 196, 220, 253, 321, 335–348, 381–390, 465, 472–479.
2 Olga von Saucken (née Countess von Üxküll-Gyllenband), 27 July 1972; CSA; NS, Lautlingen; TP, 'Brüder' 491.
3 *Gothaisches Genealogisches Taschenbuch der Gräflichen Häuser A 1936* 590–591; *Genealogisches Handbuch der gräflichen Häuser A III, 1958* 445–446.
4 Dipper 14 June 1919; Daur; TP, 'Brüder' 491–492.
5 CSA July 1905.
6 CSA 15 Oct. 1907.
7 CSA Oct. 1907; Lautlingen guest book.
8 NS 19 Dec. 1991.
9 CSA July, Oct. 1912, Nov. 1913, Jan. 1914, Jan., May 1916.
10 CSA 17 Dec. 1907, May 1909, Oct. 1912, Feb., Nov. 1913, July 1914.
11 CSA July 1917, Feb., Aug. 1911; Daur 16 Sept. 1983.
12 CSA Feb. 1913.
13 CSA Sept. 1916, Dec. 1917.
14 CSK Jan. 1917, July 1918; TP 25 April 1981; Dr Koch.
15 For this paragraph CSA Oct. 1913, March, Dec. 1915, Feb., July 1917; ClS, 'Betreff: Gesuch'; ELG final examinations 1923 and 1926; Federer; HCSt.

16 CSK July, Aug. 1914.
17 CSK March 1915; CS Album.
18 Poetry album; CSK July–Sept. 1915, March 1916; BS to Uncle Berthold 27 July 1915, Nl MS.
19 CSK Sept.–Dec. 1915, May 1916.
20 CSK 1916, 1917; Lautlingen guest book; excerpt from Hofacker's military personnel record, Nl Hofacker.
21 CSK Nov. 1917–Jan. 1918.
22 CSA July 1918; *Hof- und Staatshandbuch 1914*, 7–8; BS to CS 11 and [13] July 1918, StGA.
23 ClS to CS 12 July 1918, StGA.
24 CSA July 1918; BS to AS 29 July, 2 Aug. 1918, StGA.
25 BS to AS 3, 12 Aug. 1918, StGA; CSK July–Aug. 1918; CSA Sept. 1918; Dipper 3 July 1919; Lautlingen guest book; Üxküll, *Schwesternleben* 11–74.
26 Riezler 222–229; Ludendorff 473–490, 457, 552–553.
27 CSK and CSA Oct. 1918.
28 CSK Nov. 1918; Weller, *Staatsumwälzung* 99, 104–112; Strecker; Köhler 27, 137–147, 154–155; Hegelmaier 232; Pistorius 21–27, 30–39, 46–47; *Schwäbischer Merkur* 9 Nov. 1918; Gönner 360; Blos 24.
29 CSK Nov. 1918; CSA April 1919; CM 32, 89.
30 Hegelmaier 239; Weimar Constitution art. 153–155 in *RGBl.* 1919, 1412–1413.
31 *Schwäbischer Merkur* 10 Jan. 1919, 5; TP, *Schatten* 46; CSK Feb. 1919.
32 CSK March–June 1919; Lautlingen guest book; NS Sept. 1982.
33 For this and the following three paragraphs: Lautlingen guest book; CSA June–Sept. 1919; Dipper 14 June, 3, 6 July 1919; Daur 16 Sept. 1983.
34 *Adress-Buch . . . Stuttgart* 1918–1929.
35 Elsbet Zeller; Dipper 3 Sept. 1919; CSA Sept. 1919–Jan. 1921; TP 31 July, 5 Aug. 1972; AS to TP 22 Dec. 1919, PP; Zeller 518 note 2b.
36 TP, 'Brüder' 496–497; TP, *Schatten* 59; AS to TP 5 Jan. 1920, PP; Held.
37 For this and the next three paragraphs: Wunder 484, 492; Rilke-Salomé 347, 586; Rilke-Nostiz 75–76; Schack 479; CS to Rilke 24 Feb., 8 March, 12 May 1918, 28 Jan., 11 Feb. 1919, Rilke-Archiv, c. in StGA; Rilke to CS 28 Feb., 7 March 1918, 23 Jan., 5 Feb. 1919, c. in StGA; Rilke, *Briefe . . . 1914 bis 1921* 178–189, 226–231; the 'certain work' which Dr v. St. had indicated was Rilke's 'Elegies': Schack 592; cf. Rilke's 'Requiem auf den Tod eines Knaben' in Rilke, *Werke* 2 104–107; the note in Rilke, *Briefe . . . 1914 bis 1921* 413 is inaccurate in referring only to one book beside Dr v. St.'s bed (De Coster's *Ulenspiegel*; cf. Charles de Coster, *Tyll Ulenspiegel und Lamm Goedzak: Legende von ihren heroischen, lustigen und ruhmreichen Abenteuern im Lande Flandern und andern Orts*, Eugen Diederichs, Jena 1912); there were also Arnold Bennett, *The Old Wives' Tale*, Chapman & Hall, London 1908, 1912 etc.; Mary Hamilton, *Dead Yester-day*, Duckworth & Co., London 1916; the photograph is reproduced in RB, *Bild*, Plate 139.
38 B. Graf Uxkull-Gyllenband 8, 37; Seekamp 286; Morwitz to StG 23 Aug. 1918, StGA.
39 'Hermes' 1 no. 1 [1919].
40 Artaud; Stevenson.

41 AS to TP 3 Jan. 1921, PP; TP; AS to Aunt Osch 10 May 1921, Nl AS; Held.
42 TP 25 April 1981.
43 N.d., Nl Ida, Countess Üxküll; Lautlingen guest book.
44 TP, 'Brüder' 496, 500; TP, *Schatten* 48–49; ClS, 'Gesuch'; CSA 1920; Mühlberger; Schneiderhan; NS; AS to CS Jan./Feb. 1926; BS to MS 23 Dec. 1923, Nl MS; Neerforth; Denk; Hamma; Bopp; Buck; Lutz.
45 TP, 'Brüder' 497–498; TP, *Schatten* 48–49; Hock; Schefold; Schefold, *Erinnerung* 3.
46 RO; RO, Ideenlehre 1923; Pfleiderer (a friend of O. at Tübingen University); BS's dedications to RO are here given in translation; Hölderlin, *Werke* 2 (ed. Seebass) 164–165; StG, *GA* IX 17; CS to Osch n.d. with postscript by BS; BS, Empedokles, PP; AS to CS 22 May 1923, Nl AS.
47 Kommerell, 'Zwiesprache' and BS, 'An Frank', StGA; K. Mehnert 62.
48 AS to TP 8 April, 27 June 1923, PP; AS to CS [16 or 17 June 1923], Nl AS; BS to CS [20 June 1923], Nl MS; Bürklin; NS, Lautlingen; NS; for ClS see below pp. 25, 46–49, Appendix II.
49 The exact amount calculated was 37,583 metres of beams, planks and boards, and 98,867 metres of telegraph poles: *Reparation Commission* 117–146. Federer; Pfleiderer; TP; *RGBl.* 1919 no. 140; Salewski 212–218, 222–223, 227–228, 231, 240–242, 365–374; Meier-Welcker 349, 357, 364–367; Rabenau 324–327; Buchrucker *passim.*
50 AS to TP 8 April, 27 June 1923, PP; AS to CS [6, 10 June 1923], Nl AS; AS, 1923 poems in StGA.
51 BS to CS [20 June 1923], Nl MS.
52 BS to CS [May/June 1923], Nl MS; AS to CS 3 May 1923, [6 June 1923], Nl AS; Heidelberg University Archive, AS and BS files; Seekamp 185, 294, 297, 309, 311, 320.
53 BS to CS [20 June 1923], Nl MS; AS to CS [14 Aug. 1923], Nl AS; Kraemer (classmate, roommate in Gmünd); TP; *Rangliste* 1923 40, 66; *Staatshandbuch* 1922 458–459; AS to StG 1 July 1923, StGA; AS to TP 29 Aug. 1923, PP.
54 Jena University Archive; BS to CS [Nov. 1923], Nl MS.
55 AS to TP 11 June 1923, PP; Tübingen University Archive 258/18258; AS to CS [4 Feb. 1927], Nl AS; AS to StG 4 Dec. 1923, StGA.
56 Two weeks after taking up the post in 1921, Dr Fehling began taking books from the Cotta archive and selling them to antique book sellers; there is evidence to suggest that she was trying to please her friend. She later made a suicide attempt, after which Blumenthal abandoned her and denounced her to George; in 1929 she actually killed herself. See Fehling-Kröner correspondence and related files in Cotta-Archiv, DAL; AB to StG [July 1925], StGA; M. Mommsen 1, 27. The Stauffenberg brothers were informed of the suicide attempt and the suicide; NS 15 June 1982. Also on the Stauffenberg-StG connection: AB to StG 23 Sept. 1922; NS in Kramarz 24 and Stettler 28; Federer; Lautlingen guest book; M. Mommsen 23a, 44–46; AB, 'principi iuventutis' (poems to Berthold, 1924), StGA; AS to StG 1 July 1923, 28 Feb., 29 March 1924, StGA; AS to CS [4 June 1923], Nl AS; AS to TP 14 May 1923, PP; AS to RF 23 Jan. 1943, Nl RF; cf. notes 204–210 in Hoffmann, *Stauffenberg* 484–485 for more details.
57 LT, 'Grafen' 686, 690, 692–695; LT, *Erinnerungen* 223; *Erzählungen* 26–27; StG,

'B.v.St.', *GA* IX 108–109; Seekamp 251, 334; EL 153; Wolters and Petersen 192–196, 322; RF in AS, *Denkmal* 58; AS to StG 20 March and 20 May 1924, StGA.

58 StG, *GA* VIII 85; EL 162.

59 Hoffmann, 'Stauffenberg und George' 522–524 and StGA.

60 BS, poems, StGA; AS to TP 27 June 1923, PP; TP, 'Brüder' 500; TP; AS, 'Einleitung'; Kramarz 24.

61 Hoffmann, 'Stauffenberg und George' 523–524.

62 AS, poems May–June 1923, StGA.

63 *Jahrbuch* III, pages VI–VII; Wolters, *George* 383; Seekamp 228; Keilson-Lauritz 37; *Malleus maleficarum* 1489.

64 AS to CS [16 or 17 June 1923], Nl AS; Seekamp 327; EK to LT 10 March 1956, StGA; MaS; NS; TP; AS, 1923 poems, StGA; NS, Lautlingen.

65 ClS, essays, Nl ClS; Kramarz 20.

66 Bopp, 'Leistung'; Bopp; Mühlberger; Neerforth; Vollmer; Wirth; Partsch to RB 24 Sept. 1969, StGA; NS; Kramarz 18.

67 ClS, essays, Nl ClS; Hoffmann, 'Stauffenberg und George' 523; Dipper 20 June 1919; Bopp; Lowinsky; Wirth; Kramarz 18–19; RF 21 Aug. 1982.

68 K. Hoffmann; Wirth; Lowinsky; Eckardt; Schneiderhan; Vollmer.

69 ELG, Reifeprüfung 1923; Lowinsky; Wirth; TP; Schneiderhan; H.Hofacker; Cantz; Dolderer; Haug; Hosemann; Müller-Gmelin; Ströhle.

70 Bopp; Mühlberger; Orthuber; cf. Landmann, *George* 368–369.

71 ELG, Reifeprüfung 1923, 1926; Bopp; Buck; Hosemann; Bach.

72 Buck; Bopp; Woellwarth; Hosemann.

73 Lowinsky.

74 Lowinsky; Müller-Gmelin; Buck.

75 Pfizer; Hosemann; Bach.

76 AS to CS [10 and 16 or 17 June 1923], Nl AS; BS to CS [20 June 1923], Nl MS; NS.

77 Lautlingen guest book; Schefold; Schefold, 'Erinnerung' 3.

78 RF, Frank 5; K. Mehnert 62–63; Stettler 27–30; F to BS 28 Jan., 31 Jan., 7 Feb. 1924, StGA; F, 'Chronologie', StGA.

2. Secret Germany

1 StG, *GA* IX 32, 108–109; AB, 'principi iuventutis', StA; MK, 'Konradin', Nl JA; MK, 'Lieder an C., StGA. The references to the 'Staufen mountain' and to 'Kyffhäuser' evoke the belief that Frederick II (or later his grandfather, Frederick Barbarossa) was sleeping under a mountain, and would one day return to rule.

2 ClS, poems, StGA and Hoffmann, 'Stauffenberg und George' 522–524; Appendix VI.

3 AS to StG 9 Feb., 5 April 1924, StGA; Vogt.

4 Vogt; AB, 'Reise'.

5 AB to StG 4, [20/21] April, 20 May 1924, StGA; AS to TP 15 April 1924, PP; AS to Countess Üxküll, n.d., Nl AS; AB, 'Reise'; Vogt.

6 AB, 'Reise'; BS to StG [20 April 1924], StGA.

7 E. Wolters to StG 17 April 1924, StGA; EK to StG 30 April 1924, StGA; Wolters-Thiersch.

8 Wolters-Thiersch; Zierold 19; Helbing 256–265.

9 EK to StG 30 April 1924, StGA.

10 Vogt.

11 EK, *Friedrich II* [7], 631–632.

12 Salin, *Kantorowicz*; EK to StG 26 Dec. 1926, StGA; Seekamp 347; Grünewald 59–74; Stockert; proof-reading notes in collaboration with BS, Jan. 1927, Nl JA.

13 Hölderlin, ed. Hellingrath, IV 1916 129–131, 181–185; cf. Hölderlin, *Werke* 2 (Grosse Stuttgarter Ausgabe), 3–5, 9–11, 149–152, 388. I do not wholly accept Michael Hamburger's translation of the quoted verses, cf. Hölderlin, *Poems* 400–407, 610–615.

14 Schiller, *Nationalausgabe* 2 I 431–436, 1 320–321.

15 Grünewald 79–80, citing Hebbel 6 378.

16 Heine 8/1 496–497, referring to the 'Witches' Kitchen' scene in Goethe's *Faust*.

17 Lagarde, *Deutsche Schriften* (1878) 68, 101–102, 248–249; Lagarde, *Deutsche Schriften* (1892) 98, 125, 241–242; Lagarde, 'Das verborgene Deutschland' [1–2].

18 Langbehn 262–267, 309; Podach 198.

19 Seekamp 3; M. Mommsen; EL 50; *Blätter* VII 1904 3–4.

20 *Jahrbuch* 1910 14–15; K. and H. Wolfskehl 95; StG, F. Gundolf 254; Plato, *Politeia*, end of book 9, adapted from the translation by E. Salin, *Von Mensch und Staat*, Schwabe, Basel, 1942; EK, 'Deutschland' 2; Hellingrath, *Hölderlin* 16–17, 40–41; Wolters, *George* 418–419, 426.

21 MK, *Dichter* 461, 474–477; Wolters, *George* 418–432.

22 MK, *Dichter* 483; Lübbe 196–202; MK to JA 7 Dec. [1930], StGA, printed in RB 1 186–188.

23 Cf. Walter Benjamin's review in *Literarische Welt* VI (1930) no. 33/34, 9 11; Benjamin, *Schriften* III 252–259; MK to JA 25 Sept. 1930 considered the review 'very Jewish' and declared it desirable to be described as a representative of the Secret Germany in which, amidst a thunder of words, 'the magic hat hangs next to the steel helmet'. Further evidences of MK's political inclinations in RB, 1 182; ES 253; MK to JA 24 June, 9 Sept., 25 Sept. 1930, StGA; MK to F Oct. 1930 in MK, *Briefe* 188–190; StG to MK 4 Jan. [1928], Hellmut Strebel to RB 29 July 1954, StGA; MK to StG 25 June 1931, StGA; MK, *Briefe* 202–204, 219–223; LT, *Erinnerungen* 245, 263–264; Pawlowsky 26–37; Grünewald 149–157.

24 Stefan George 399; Landmann, *George* 368; Seekamp 356; Pawlowsky 18.

25 Wolters, *George* 426, 527; RB, 1 136–137; Seekamp 347, 355, 364; Schulz; MK, *Briefe* 276; Hildebrandt to Brodersen 7 Jan. 1935, CP.

26 EK, 'Deutschland' 3; Salin, *Um* 263–264; RB, 2 165; Seekamp 359; StG, *GA* IX 59–65; EM to StG 11 July 1918, StGA; cf. Grimm 14.

27 EM to StG 11 July 1918, StGA.

28 Wolters, *George* 545; Seekamp 364–367.

29 Curtius (1950) 153.

30 Vallentin 47–48, 54; Breysig 26–27; Salin, *Um* 143–144, 158; EM to StG 10 July 1924, StGA.

31 Vallentin 101–103 (19 Feb. 1928).

32 LT, *Erinnerungen* 248–249; Seekamp 364, 367; EL 207; EK to EM [c. Sept. 1926], StGA; Wolters, *Reden*; RB, 1 134–136; Salin, *Um* 143; MK, *Briefe* 190.

33 ClS to MK 19 July [1928], DLA and Nl MK.

34 Justizministerium, list of candidates; TP, 'Brüder' 500; *Minerva* 1926.

35 Seekamp 336; B. v. Bothmer 11 March 1983; Markees 23 June 1984; RB, *Bild* 1 T. 138; LT, *Erinnerungen* 223.

36 For this and the following paragraph: Justizministerium, list of candidates; CS to TP [10 April 1925], PP; Lautlingen guest book; AS to StG 19 June 1925, StGA; Frank's chronology, StGA; BS to CS [14 July 1925], Nl MS; Seekamp 340, 347; Stettler 28; Mehnert 63; TP, 'Brüder'500; *Kürschners* 1926 col. 97; BS to TP's mother 17 Jan. [1927], PP; LT, *Erinnerungen* 227–228; memoranda on readings of EK's *Friedrich II*. Nl JA; EK to StG [26 Dec. 1926], StGA; BS to MS 2 March 1927, [4 and 29 June, 12 Nov. 1927], 26 Dec. 1927, 17 Feb. and 27 March 1928, 3 Jan. 1929; BS, 'curriculum vitae'.

37 BS to MS [22 and 27 June, 2, 4, 6, 9, 12, 15, 22 and 26 July, 3 and 7 Sept. 1927]; BS's appointments diary 29 June–3 Aug. 1927; Federer 23 Sept. 1983. I am indebted to my colleague V. Boss for his translation of the Russian letters.

38 BS to StG 18 Aug. 1927, StGA; Lautlingen guest book; BS to MS [24 and 28 Aug., 12 and 22 Sept., 30 Oct., 15 and 25 Nov. 1927, 26 Jan. 1928].

39 JA to StG [1 Feb. 1928], 11 July [1928], StGA; Stockert 5 Mai 1982; BS to CS 28 Feb. 1928, Nl MS; BS to MS [17 Feb., 6 and 26 March 1928].

40 For this and the following paragraph: BS to MS [22 and 24 March 1927, 26 March, 17 and 19 June 1928], 26 July and 25 Oct. 1928, [2, 9, 17 and 20 Jan., 24 Feb., 26 Dec. 1929]; BS, 'curriculum vitae' and business schedule, Nl BS; UAT 189/Prom. 1929; promotion certificate, Nl BS; BS to CS 16 March [1936], AS to CS [June/July 1928], Nl CS; 'Vorausschuss'; 'Geschäftsverzeichnis', Nl BS; Makarov, 'Vorkämpfer' 362; BS to Alexandrine, Countess Üxküll 17 Jan. [1929].

41 Pick 386.

42 BS to MS [27 Nov., 10 and 17 Dec. 1931], 2 Jan. 1932, 8, 15, 24 and 27 April, 12 Nov., 25, 27 and 29 Dec. 1932, 2 Jan. 1933, [15 Dec. 1935], 13 Jan., [5 March, 10 April 1936], Nl MS; BS to RB, 13 June 1936, RB to BS 17 June 1936, StGA; Schlayer 6 Jan. 1984; CS to TP 16 April 1936, PP.

43 BS to MS [26 Dec. 1929, 1 July, 4 and 13 Aug., 18 Sept., 6 and 13 Nov. 1931, 16 Jan. 1933]; BS to CS [Jan. 1932], Nl MS; AA/PA Pers. II E Bd. I and Völkerbund, Gerichtshof vol. 9; Makarov, 'Vorkämpfer' 362; Strebel, 'Stauffenberg' 14–15; LT, *Erinnerungen* 263; Elbe 127; Just IV 1, 3 Abschnitt 172.

44 University of Halle, Archive 16 July 1982; AS to StG 28 Jan., 14 May, 20 July 1927, 10 and 22 July 1930; AS to TP [May 1927, 20 July 1931]; AS to CS [4 Feb. 1927], 4 June 1928; Vogt 20 Apr. 1984; Der Reichs- und Preussische Minister für Wissenschaft, Erziehung und Volksbildungs Vorschlag zur Ernennung (proposal to appoint AS to a chair); Lauffer, 'Stauffenberg' 846.

45 Seekamp 335–336, 359, 368–377, 388; contract between StG and Georg Bondi 6 Oct. 1927, StGA; LT, *Erinnerungen* 242–244, 254; MK to StG, passim, StG; StG to F [15 Aug. 1927], StGA; RB 1 176, 182, 186–189, 195; WK 7 Jan. 1984; EM 465; MK to JA 18 June, 25 Sept., 24 Dec. 1930, JA to StG 11 July [1928], StGA; JA, *Dichtungen* 75–79; Salin 253 and 347 note 7; MK, *Dichter* 474–477; Partsch 14 July 1972; ClS to StG [June 1930], StGA; MK to ClS 26 Sept. 1930,

DLA; MK, *Briefe* 19–20, 177, 182–202; MK to ClS 23 Aug. 1931, StGA; MK to AS 17 Nov. 1931, DLA; AS to StG [21 Nov. 1931], StGA; BS to StG [10 Oct. 1933], StGA; NS 16 May 1989; MK to Lilly Anton 3 March 1931, papers of Dr F. v. Stockert.

46 StG, last will and testament 15 June 1930 and 31 March 1932, StGA; BS, last will and testament 31 Dec. 1933 and 16 April 1943, StGA; RF to StG 10 July 1933, StGA.

47 RF to StG 10 July 1933, StGA.

3. Reichswehr

1 ClS, 'Gesuch'; CSA 1920; TP, 'Brüder' 500; Mühlberger; Schneiderhan; NS; AS to CS [Jan./Feb. 1926]; BS to MS 23 Dec. 1932, Nl MS.

2 Eberhard-Ludwigs-Gymnasium, list of school leavers; *Regierungsblatt* 1911 no. 13; *Amtsblatt* 4 (1911) no. 9; ClS, 'Gesuch'; ClS to StG [Oct. 1924], StGA; LT, *Erinnerungen* 223–224.

3 AB to StG 5 Nov. 1924, StGA; Seekamp 336; RB 1 192–193 and T. 138; LT, *Erinnerungen* 218, 223–224 (incorrectly dating Claus's final examination to 1925).

4 ClS to StG [April 1925], StGA; Lautlingen guest book; AB to StG 6 Jan. 1925, [July 1925], StGA; ClS, 'Gesuch'; NS 12 Aug. 1982; *Amtsblatt* 17 (1924) 181; Jettingen guest book; Seekamp 340–341.

5 TP, 'Brüder' 499; Lautlingen guest book; AS, 'To C.', Aug. 1924, StGA; AB to StG [July and ca. 5 Oct. 1925], StGA; MK to StG [18 March 1926], StGA; Seekamp 343–344.

6 ClS, 'Gesuch'; Eberhard-Ludwigs-Gymnasium, final examinations 1926.

7 ClS to StG 11 July 1931, StGA; ClS to MK 19 July [1928], DLA; TP, 'Brüder' 500; NS 2 Oct. 1964, 12 Aug. 1982, 9 Jan. 1992; Kramarz 39.

8 Loeper 24 March 1971, 29 Aug. 1972; Wunder 474; ClS, essay 24 Jan. 1923, Nl ClS, see Appendix I.

9 AS, 'Der Krieger', May 1926, PP.

10 *Rangliste* 1917, 1926–1932; ClS to Uncle Berthold 18 Aug. 1939, papers of NS; NS in CM 66–67 and to Venohr Feb. 1987; NS 22 Oct. 1961; RF 21 Aug. 1982; Wehrstammbuch; *Aus der Geschichte* [2, 5].

11 ClS to his father [27 April 1926], Nl MS, printed in Appendix II; ClS to R. Lerchenfeld 6 March 1934, Nl Lerchenfeld; Pezold 1 July 1972; see the 'Oath' in Appendix VI.

12 ClS to his father [27 April 1926], Nl MS; Leuze 59, 63; Wehrstammbuch; Wilcke 23 April 1985; Theilacker 16 March 1971; Pezold 22 Aug. 1972; Canstein 25 Sept. 1988; *Rangliste* 1927–1928. Of ClS's room-mates, Wilcke survived, Hempel and Huffmann fell in the war (Morgenstern was not a room-mate.

13 Wilcke 23 April 1985; Walzer in Kramarz 38–39; Pezold 1 Sept. 1972; Finker 39; Luz 22 Aug. 1972; ClS's written work among his papers; Teske, *Spiegel* 41; Loeper, Thüngen in Kramarz 18.

14 Wilcke 23 April 1985; AS to CS [July 1928]; Pezold 1 Sept. 1972; ClS to J.Schmidt [Jan. 1928].

15 ClS to J.Schmidt [Jan. 1928]; Wolters, *Reden* 5–29; cf. Lübbe 196–207.

16 Wilcke 23 April 1985; Pezold 22 Aug. 1972; Sachenbacher 12 July 1972.

17 Wilcke 23 April 1985; Sachsen-Meiningen 10 Jan. 1973; Brauchitsch, interviewed on DDR 1 television in 1989.
18 ClS to MK [between Nov. 1929 and Feb. 1931], DLA.
19 Kramarz 36–39; Loeper 29 Aug. 1972; NS 13 Aug. 1968; Pezold 1 Sept. 1972.
20 LT, *Erinnerungen* 232; Seekamp 359, 362; ClS to MK March [1929], Nl MK; StG to F 10 Feb. 1929, StGA; MK, *Gespräche* 33–35.
21 Hildebrandt 228; Seekamp 262–268; cf. Vallentin, *Napoleon* (1923), *Napoleon und die Deutschen* (1926).
22 ClS to MK 19 July [1928], DLA; Truppenkrankenbuch; *Aus der Geschichte* [5]; AB to StG 8 July 1928, StGA; Seekamp 357.
23 Wehrstammbuch; Pezold 1 Sept. 1972; Leuze 64, 66; *Aus der Geschichte* [5]; *Rangliste* 1928–1929.
24 Pezold 1 Sept. 1972; ClS's papers; Wilcke 21 Sept. 1988; NS 7 Feb. 1979, 12 Oct. 1988; ClS to J. Schmidt Jan. [and between 16 and 23 Aug. 1929]; *Rangliste* 1930; Lautlingen guest book; Loeper 24 March 1971, 29 Aug. 1972; CM 73; Wehrstammbuch.
25 NS 23 April 1993.
26 Wehrstammbuch; Leuze 68; Luz 22 Aug. 1972; NS 12 Oct. 1988; Wilcke 21 Sept. 1988, 17 Jan. 1989; ClS to J. Schmidt [between 16 and 23 Aug. 1929].
27 Luz 2 March 1971; ClS to J. Schmidt Jan. [1929]; Sachenbacher 12 July 1972.
28 Schlieffen, *Cannae* 3–4 and *Schriften* I 8–9, II 442; Elze, *Schlieffen* 8–19; Freytag-Loringhoven 78; Elze, *Tannenberg* 26–27, 30–35, 39–40, 86. Neither Schlieffen nor Elze noted that Hannibal actually lost the Second Punic War.
29 ClS to F 28 March 1934, Nl F. 'Strategy of '66' refers to the Austro-Prussian War of 1866; 'Potato War' to the Bavarian War of Succession, 1778–9.
30 ClS, 'Schlacht'; Clausewitz, *Vom Kriege* 257, 259, 261–265. ClS did not comment on the sequel: after Darius had fled and the Persian left wing had given way, the Persians attempted a flanking attack with their right wing; Alexander, having gained more operational freedom in the course of the battle, successfully countered this attack by an encircling manoeuvre without which he might have lost the battle.
31 *Bamberger Tagblatt* 23 Sept. 1930; Leuze 71.
32 NS, 'Halsband' 89–91, 186–187; NS 7 Feb. 1979, 16 May 1989; Venohr 60.
33 NS 17 March 1962.
34 Schußtafel 1930, Nl ClS; Wehrstammbuch; *Rangliste* 1931, 1932; ClS, 'Vorschlag', Nl ClS; Pezold 1 Sept. 1972; NS 7 Feb. 1979; Einwohnermeldeamt Bamberg 17 Jan. 1989; Mannschatz 7 July 1972.
35 F's 'Chronologie', StGA; NS 13 Aug., 11 Sept. 1968, 12 Aug. 1988; Seekamp 379–382; ClS to StG 11 July 1931, StGA; Auszug aus dem Krankenmeldebuch; Just IV, 1, III (Schwarz) 172.
36 Just IV, 1, III (Schwarz) 176–177; Schulze, *Weimar* 363–364; Brüning 17–40, 148–150, 161–162, 273–274, 387; Bennett 169, 191–196, 236; Castellan 77–85; Hillgruber, *Großmacht* 63–76; VB 12 July 1932; Der Reichswehrminister, No. 600.32. W I a, 29 Jan. 1932, and No. 3650. 32. W III, 14 Aug. 1932, and Wehrkreiskommandant VII [illeg.] 2.a/m Ic, 1 Oct. 1932, BA-MA RH 26–17/116; *New York Times*, Late City Edition 8 Aug. 1932 1, 8; Vogelsang, *Reichswehr* 135–142, 147–151, 154, 295–304. Bennett 195–196 cites *Documents*

diplomatiques français 1932–1939 1, I, no. 100, according to which an unnamed French visitor told the French Military Attaché in Berlin that the Reichswehr Press Officer, Major Erich Marcks, had told him (the visitor) that the Reichswehr was in the habit of dismissing soldiers before they had served their full term, in defiance of the Treaty of Versailles; neither the *Documents* nor Bennett supply any confirmation of this hearsay.

37 Schorr 259. A loaf of brown bread, the most frequently consumed variety, cost about RM 0.38 in Berlin in 1931, RM 0.36 in 1932 (though the price dropped to RM 0.33 in December 1932), and RM 0.33 in the first six months of 1933, when the prices were evidently more strictly controlled. *Statistisches Jahrbuch* 1932 253, 1933 251.

38 Huber 3 606–607; cf. Hamilton, *passim*; Falter, *passim*.

39 Just IV, I, III (Schwarz) 192–193; Spuler II, 4, 148–152, 478.

40 Kramarz 40–41; Metz 30 May 1971; Loeper 29 Aug. 1972; Leuze 60, 63; *Aus der Geschichte* [3]; CM 82; Sauerbruch 9 Feb. 1977; NS 24 April 1981.

41 Theilacker 16 March 1971; Manteuffel 28 Feb. 1971; Metz 30 May 1971; H.Süsskind-Schwendi 4 July 1972; CM 79–82; Hofacker, 'Lebenslauf'; Hofacker to Herbert von Samson-Himmelstjerna 1 Sept. 1930, and notes for election speech, Nl Hofacker.

42 *Aus der Geschichte* [7]; *VB*, Munich edn 6 Feb. 1933 1.

4. Sea change

1 *Trial* XXXV 42–4l8.

2 *Regierung Hitler* 1 3; *VB* Munich edn 6 Feb. 1933 1; Vogelsang, *Dokumente* 434–435; Bracher, Sauer, Schulz 710–711, 719.

3 *RGBl.* I 1933 35–41; *Ministerial-Blatt* 1933 c. 169–170.

4 *RGBl.* I 1933 83; Michaelis, Schraepler 9 38–40.

5 *RGBl.* I 1933 83, 135–136, 141, 479; Grundmann 346–347; Repgen 67–98; Just IV 2 IV (Hofer) 20, 25.

6 *RGBl.* I 1933 1016, I 1934 529, 747; Just IV 2 IV (Hofer) 25–36; Mau 119–137; KJM, *Heer* 88–141; Höhne, *Mordsache*; *VB* 15, 16 July 1934 1–2.

7 *Regierung Hitler* I 683; Rautenberg, *Dokumente* 105; Bennett 471–490.

8 Cf. Moeller; Bormann 13 June 1939.

9 F to MK 8 Oct. 1930, MK, *Briefe* 190; Brodersen 19 July 1988; Stockert, 'George' 69.

10 See chapter 2 above; StG to F 4, 16 March 1932, F to StG 15, 20 Oct. 1933, StGA.

11 Wolfskehl, *Werke* I 280. For those who joined the NDSAP see: Elze (joined 1 May 1933): BDC; Hildebrandt: BDC; Hildebrandt to Brodersen 7 Jan. 1935, CP; Thormaehlen: BDC; Brodersen 19 July 1988; Fahrner: BDC. Blumenthal did not succeed in joining the Party until 1939, two years after admissions, closed in 1933, had been re-opened, and after he had lodged a formal protest against his non-admission: BDC; M. Mommsen, 'Anlage', StGA; RB 1 194; Volz 54, 73; *Stefan George 1868 · 1968* 335; Hildebrandt, *Erinnerungen* 227–230; Hildebrandt, *Individualitaet* 18–19, 26–30; Seekamp 385.

12 F's bust of Hitler was completed by April 1933; Hanfstaengl sold at least 30

copies; F's correspondence 1933–1937, Nl F; F to StG 25 Sept., 1 Oct. 1933, StGA; F to his mother 14 and 15 June 1936, 23 Oct. 1937, StGA; Pilz, 'Bildnis'; Pagels; RF 9 May 1977; StG said to F early in 1933 that he must do 'him' on horseback; WK 6/7 Jan. 1984. Stettler 38 is misleading.

13　W. Uxkull 8; he was quoting from StG, *GA* IX 39: 'dass einst / Des erdteils herz die welt erretten soll..'

14　W. Uxkull 22–23; BS to F 10 Jan. 1935, EK to StG 26 Nov. 1933, StGA.

15　RF to StG 10 July 1933, StGA; RF, 'Frank' [13]. In Nov. 1916 Kurt Breysig said to StG that in the course of the fifty years after the war people would have to be changed completely. StG replied: 'Yes, that is our business': Breysig 27.

16　Wolfskehl to Verwey 15 Sept., 26 Oct. 1932, Nijland-Verwey 266–267, 270–273.

17　Walzer 22 Dec. 1965; BS to MS [14, 20, 23 April 1933], Nl MS; EK to StG [5 June] 1933, StGA; Seekamp 385 (G. P. Landmann mistakenly has EK and StG meet in Berlin at Easter 1933); EK, 'Gesuch', copy, Frankfurt University 17 May 1978; ES, *Kantorowicz* 6. EK, as a 1914 volunteer, frontline soldier and veteran of the Freikorps, was exempt from the 'Law for the Restitution of the Professional Civil Service' of 7 April 1933 (*RGBl.* I 1933 175–177), which excluded Jews from university posts, and he declared his support for 'a nationally governed Reich'.

18　EK to StG [5 June], 10 July 1933, StGA; Grünewald 121–122, with erroneous date 4 June.

19　EK to StG 26 Nov. 1933, StGA; ES, *Kantorowicz* 6–7; EK, 'Deutschland', Nl EK and Nl ES. EK wanted his lecture published by Bondi, but StG died on 4 Dec. 1933, and ES advised EK against publication: EK to StG 26 Nov. 1933, StGA; ES to EK 21 Dec. 1933, Nl ES.

20　S. Vallentin to Wolfskehl 8 Dec. 1934, ES to WK 9 Nov. 1934, Hildebrandt to WK 28 Nov. 1934, WK to Hildebrandt 4 Dec. 1934, StGA; StG, *GA* VIII 41.

21　EL 209; ES 244; F, notes 1933–1938, StGA.

22　For instance, StG wrote to Melchior Lechter saying that Munich, where there were 'only people and youth' was 'a thousand times better than this Berlin mishmash of low-ranking civil servants Jews and whores!' (StG to Lechter [27] April 1905, StGA). Boehringer and G. P. Landmann (see George-Gundolf 163) reduced this to 'a thousand times better than this Berlin mishmash'. Quoted out of context in *Stefan George 1868 · 1968* 164. Ernst Robert Curtius, recording a visit to StG on 16 April 1911, noted StG's comments on Jews in his circle: 'Jews are the best conduits. They are skilled in the transmission and transposition of values. To be sure, they do not experience things as deeply as we do. They are in any case different people. I never allow them to become a majority in my society or in the Yearbook.' Curtius 153. When writing his essay 'George in Gespräch' ('George in Conversation'), Curtius evidently drew on his own diary, which the author has seen: Curtius had torn out all the pages from 154 onwards, i.e. the entries for 1910 from August and for 1911 entirely, noting at the end 'St.G. S. 171–179'. Seekamp suppressed the passage because of its content, but its authenticity was not in doubt: Keilson 28 Oct. 1985.

　　Hildebrandt to Brodersen 7 Jan. 1935, CP: 'Even as far back as the war St.G. taught that the Jews were agents of decomposition in the political and the intellectual state. [. . .] He was increasingly dissatisfied with their attitude. In 1932 he told me the Jews ought not to be surprised if he joined the N.S.' StG also told Hildebrandt that he wished at least to avoid any antagonism between himself and the National Socialists – 'except that he would hold to the best of his Jewish followers'. On 19 Sept. 1933 StG spoke to EL in Basel concerning the persecutions of Jews: 'I will tell you something: when I think of what Germany will have to face in the next fifty years, then the Jewish matter in particular is not very important to me.' EL 209.

In 1920 F. Gundolf said that he did not feel Jewish, only German; but if he accepted a teaching post at Berlin University, he would be afraid of 'the pogrom-rumpus that now, at the slightest inducement, fills all rooms where Jews are lecturing'; EL 96; George-Gundolf 339; Seekamp 307.

On 28 Nov. 1923 W. Üxküll wrote to StG (StGA) that he and some other friends – Thormaehlen, Morwitz, Blumenthal and Percy Gothein – believed that EK ought to be left off a list for a series of lectures because 'for a gesture by [StG's] state the Jewish element was not appropriate today· indeed the effect might be diminished or disrupted'; on 3 May 1924 Üxküll wrote to StG (StGA) from Oxford, saying that it was entirely free from 'the abominable (with the Master's intonation, please) type of intellectual Jew· or the hyperblond Aryan under his spell'.

On 11 July [1928] Johann Anton wrote to StG (StGA) that the periodical *Litterarische Welt* was collecting comments on StG on the occasion of his birthday and 'all Jews were being asked for their sinapis'.

On 16 July 1931 Thormaehlen wrote to StG (StGA) that 'the Jews' were busying themselves, with the assistance of the Socialists, to frustrate government measures for order and recovery.

23 Jens, *Dichter* 9, 45, 66, 181–218.
24 EM to StG 10, 12, 25 May 1933, StG to EM 10, 15 May 1933, EM to Zierold 10 Sept. 1933, EM to Wolfskehl 25 Dec. 1933, StGA; *VB Südd.A.* (supplement *Kulturpolitik*) 5 Dec. 1933. There survive one draft by StG's hand, two by F's hand, and copies by EM from Sept. and Dec. 1933. EM's copy of May 1933 appears not to have survived. The excerpt in *VB* may have come from his May 1933 or his Sept. 1933 copy. The essential texts are consistent, apart from small spelling variations; what StG wanted transmitted was transmitted. StG told WK concerning the offer of large amounts of money that if one accepted so much as five pennies 'from such people' one would be lost: WK 6 Jan. 1984.
25 Hildebrandt to Brodersen 7 Jan. 1935, CP; Hildebrandt, *Erinnerungen* 227–230; EL 209; StG, *GA* IX 38–39. Hans Naumann, 'Stefan George und das Neue Reich', *Zeitschrift für Deutschkunde* 48 (1934) 276, claims, without giving a source, that StG had often enjoyed the society of young SA troopers; Glöckner, *Begegnung* 200, in a letter of 6 Dec. 1933, appears to repeat Naumann's story – which cannot be verified.
26 WK and Schlayer 6–7 Jan. 1984; RB 10 June 1968; G. P. Landmann 31 Aug. 1968; Partsch to Greischel March 1963, LT to F 30 Sept. 1937, StGA; BDC files on F; EL 209; RB 2 182–183. StG often discouraged political conversations in his presence in the years 1931–1933: Partsch in *Wie* 75; Seekamp 381; RB 10 June 1968.

27 Seekamp 386; RB 2 188; LT, *Erinnerungen* 281–283; LT to F 30 Sept. 1937, StGA.

28 StG to F [ca. 19 and 20] July 1933, BS to StG 27/28 June 1933, ClS to StG 21 June 1933, StGA; BS to MS [beginning of Aug., 17 Aug., between 25 and 31 Aug., and 31 Aug. 1933], Nl MS; Partsch to Greischel March 1963; Partsch 14 July 1912; LT, *Erinnerungen* 283; RB 2 188, 300; WK 6 Jan. 1984; Seekamp 386–387; Hildebrandt, *Erinnerungen* 233.

29 *Spiegelbild* 447–457. Reinhardt 1–9 ascribes the creation of the notion of 'Volks-gemeinschaft' to Hitler; it is true that he 'created' a perversion of it, but the original concept came from the *Romantik*: J. and W. Grimm 12 col. 481.

30 AS to TP 17 April 1933, PP; BS to MS [3 March, 2, 12 May 1933], Nl MS.

31 BS to MS [17, 18, 24, 27, 30 Oct., 14 Nov. 1933], Nl MS; BS to StG [27 Oct., 1, 10, 18 Nov. 1933], StGA; Zech to AA 23 Oct. 1933, AA/PA Völkerbund, Gerichtshof vol. 10; Partsch 3 March 1977.

32 BDC.

33 *Spiegelbild* 1984 664; Gabriele, Countess Stauffenberg, 29 Aug. 1978; Linden 19 Aug. 1985; R. Lerchenfeld 20 July 1972; Guttenberg, *Beim* 112–115; Donohoe 111–112; CM 32, 89; NS 6 May 1981.

34 M. L. Lerchenfeld 18 May 1989.

35 ClS to StG 21 June 1933, StGA; Bauch 17 Dec. 1956; Beelitz 21 April 1964, 6 June 1973, 9 Sept. 1985; Benzmann 15 Nov. 1977; Buhle as reported by Pezold 1 Sept. 1972; RF in Zeller 239–241; Elze 18 July 1972; Greiner 15 May 1964, 9 March 1971; Th. Guttenberg in CM 92; Hammerstein, *Spähtrupp* 267; Harteneck 15 March 1971; Herwarth, *Zwischen* 246–247; Heusinger 29 March, 14 April 1977; Heyde 3 Jan., 8 June 1972; E. Koch-Erpach 28 March 1964, 1 July 1972; Kratzer 19 July 1972; Kuhn 7 Aug. 1972; Lamey 12 July 1971; R. Lerchenfeld 23 March 1971, 20 July 1972; Loeper 24 March 1971, 29 Aug. 1972; Luz 2 March 1971, 17 July, 22 Aug. 1972; Mannschatz 7, 11 July 1972; Manteuffel 18 July 1972; Merk 25 May 1972; Metz 30 May 1971; Moltke as reported by HCSt 5 July 1972; Niemack 24 March 1971; Partsch to Greischel March 1963, StGA; Partsch 14 July 1972; Pezold 1 Sept. 1972; Pfizer 31 July, 5 Aug. 1972; Sachenbacher 18 Feb. 1971, 12 July 1972; Saucken 27 July 1972; Sauerbruch to a son of ClS ca. 1964; Sauerbruch 9 Feb. 1977; Schack 10 March 1971; Schiller 14 May 1989; Seefried 13 April 1971; HCSt 28 July 1971, 5 July 1972; Markwart Stauffenberg 4 June 1973; Marlene Stauffenberg 23 Aug. 1972, 30 Aug. 1978; H. Süsskind-Schwendi 4 July 1972; Teske 31; Teske 8 May 1973; Theilacker 16 March 1971. Perfall 11 Feb. 1966 denied that any of his regiment's officers were enthusiastic about the Nazi regime. M. Süsskind-Schwendi 22 Jan. 1972 said that ClS was 'sceptical to negative' about National Socialism; NS 7 Aug. 1972, Viebig 24 Aug. 1971, and A. Üxküll 17 May 1973 gave a similar description of him.

36 For this and the following paragraph: the following, although not themselves eyewitnesses (none could be found), had the account from ClS himself: Sauer-bruch in Zeller 519 note 19, to a son of ClS ca. 1964, to Kramarz 24 July 1964, in Kramarz 42, and 9 Feb. 1977, 15 Nov. 1980; Mannschatz reporting Leonrod 11 July 1972; Teske 8 May 1973. For a critical review of the sources see Hoffmann, *Stauffenberg* (German edn) 507–509 note 115. Another incident in which ClS

was an involuntary participant has been confused with the torchlight procession: ClS, returning from a ride, met and joined his regiment's training squadron, which was accompanied by the regimental band. They passed the town hall, where the swastika flag was just being hoisted in the presence of a large crowd; Lieutenant von Manteuffel, the squadron commander, ordered his men to salute as they rode past. As the swastika was still, in law, only a party flag, Manteuffel was reprimanded. This incident most likely occurred on 13 March 1933: Manteuffel and Walzer in Kramarz 42–46; Manteuffel 20 June 1964, 18, 22 July 1972; Pezold 1 Sept. 1972; M. Th. Süsskind-Schwendi 22 Jan. 1966; *Bamberger Tageblatt* 14 March 1933 3; *RGBl.* I 1933 no. 21, I 1935 no. 100. See also Hoffmann, *Stauffenberg* (German edn)509 note 116.

37 M. Lerchenfeld 18 May 1989.
38 Loeper 24 March 1971.
39 Dienstlaufbahn; *Rangliste* 1927–1932.
40 ClS to StG 21 June 1933, StGA; ClS to R. Lerchenfeld 6 March 1934, Nl Lerchenfeld; Harteneck 15 March 1971.
41 Rautenberg, 'Dokumente' 105–110, 113, 120 and note 142; NS 12 Oct. 1988.
42 ClS to StG 21 June 1933, StGA.
43 NS 18 May, 12 Oct. 1988; CM 107–108; Venohr 74; BS to MS [27 Sept. 1933], Nl MS.
44 StG to F [23 Sept. 1933], BS to F 29 Sept. 1933 and RB, 'Bericht', StGA; BS to MS [27 Sept. 1933], Nl MS; AS, *Tod*; RB 2 189–192; Seekamp 389–390.
45 RB, 'Bericht'; RB 2 191; ClS's lists for the vigil, StGA; AS, *Tod* says that eleven people took part in the wake; TP, 'Brüder' 490 reports twelve, presumably based on conversations with AS or BS; Venohr 75 merely adds to the confusion.
46 RB, 'Bericht'; Seekamp 389–390; *Weizsäcker-Papiere* 77 with incorrect date; RB to BS and F 15 Nov. 1934, StGA.
47 RB, 'Bericht'; Schlayer 6 Jan. 1984; WK 6 Jan. 1984; F, notes 26 Sept. 1937, StGA; ES, *Kantorowicz* 7. Wolfskehl arrived at 7 a.m. on 6 Dec.; allegations that F prevented Wolfskehl from arriving on time are as unfounded as the contention that F had prevented Wolfskehl from visiting StG during his illness; M. Landmann in *Neue Zürcher Zeitung* 14 Nov. 1971; G. P. Landmann, notes [Dec. 1971], Stettler to M. Landmann 8 June 1972, RB to Stettler 6 July 1972, StGA.

5. In the Third Reich

1 LT, 'Aufzeichnungen'; Staatsarchiv Magdeburg 7 Oct. 1988; Piper 39–100; F's papers relating to the monument in Nl F; *Kurhessische Landeszeitung* 13 April 1934; WA to StG [March/April 1933], F to StG 23 Oct. 1933, F to BS 14 Jan. 1934, StGA; WK 6 Jan. 1984; BS to MS [9 July 1934].
2 F's papers relating to the monument in Nl F; LT, 'Aufzeichnungen'; ClS to BS 14 March 1934, Nl BS; NS 7 Aug. 1972 said that F also worked in the Stauffenbergs' flat; F was in Bamberg from about 2 to 25 March 1934: F to BS 4, 23 March 1934, StGA; LT to F 27 Nov. 1933, 14 Feb. 1934, Nl F; Giesau 121–122; Gerling 19 Aug. 1988; Staatsarchiv Magdeburg 7 Oct. 1988.
3 ClS to BS 27 Dec. 1936, LT to BS [8 Aug. 1937] (postcard of model with 'common private's' features, Nl MS.

4 BS to MS [3, 8, 15, 18 April 1935], Nl MS; F's papers relating to the 'pioneer', Nl BS; F to his mother 8 Oct. 1937, F to C. Farenholtz 5/8 Aug. 1941, F to BS 29 May 1942, BS to RF [Aug. 1943], BS to ClS 6 Aug. 1943 (carbon copy), StGA; F to RB 29 Dec. 1939, Nl RB; *Magdeburger General-Anzeiger* 3 Dec. 1939; Wunder 479; F to RF 16 May 1942, Stettler 114; LT, 'Aufzeichnungen'.

5 ClS to BS 14 March 1934, StGA; *Der Stürmer* 12 (1934) no. 10 4; BA-MA RH 1/v.53.

6 Pezold in Kramarz 46; Pezold's comments on Kramarz's Ms 1965; Pezold 1 July 1972; Walzer in Kramarz 49–50.

7 NS in CM 136, 141–142.

8 *Aus der Geschichte* [8].

9 NS 22 April 1964, 7 Feb. 1979, 12 Oct. 1988, 3 Dec. 1990; Pezold 1 Sept. 1972; Fremerey (succ. Perfall) 20 June 1962; Venohr 84; Kramarz 34–35, 51, 53; CM 116; ClS to Erffa 22 Nov. 1936, papers NS; NS to Venohr Feb. 1987.

10 NS 23 April 1993.

11 NS 16 May 1989; CM 116; Kramarz 35; Krankenblatt; Teske, *Spiegel* 36–37; BS to MS 2 June [1936], Nl MS; Cramer 20 Feb. 1963; NS to Venohr Feb. 1987.

12 BS to MS 20 May [1936], Nl MS; ClS, 'Bemerkungen zur taktischen Übungs-reise 1936', Nl ClS; CM 117; ClS to Erffa 22 Nov. 1936, P NS; ClS to Partsch 22 April 1940, PPa.

13 Loeper 29 Aug. 1972; CM 117–118 confuses the two trips without giving precise dates; NS to Venohr Feb. 1987 with incorrect date 1935; ClS to [Pfau] (his English teacher) 4 Sept. 136; Lautlingen guest book; Geyr 12; NS 3 Dec. 1990. ClS letters from England were confiscated by the Gestapo from his Bamberg home in July 1944 and have not re-surfaced.

14 Handliste; Wehrstammbuch; *Handbuch* 137; Saucken 25 Feb. 1989; *Berliner Adressbuch* 1926–1938.

15 NS 7 Feb. 1979; BS to RB 6 Oct. 1936, StGA; BS to MS [30 Sept., 3 Oct., 12 Dec. 1937], Nl MS; *Berliner Adressbuch* 1935–1939; C. v. d. Schulenburg 12 Aug. 1968 and in CM 136–137; Krebs 96, 157–158; Ehrensberger in Roon, *Neuordnung* 83–84; Kessel 22–27; Yorck 57; T. Schulenburg 98.

16 Erfurth 171–172; Teske, *Spiegel* 39, 50; 30–40% of the 100 admitted annually were posted to the General Staff between 1936 and 1938.

17 Mappe Taktik, Aufgaben und Lösungen, II Lehrgang: plan for autumn manoeuvres of the 17th Inf. Div. [January] 1938, Nl ClS.

18 Teske, *Spiegel* 39, 43, 46–47; Erfurth 223–224; Beck, 'Lehre', *Studien* 227–228; Wedemeyer 47, 50–52, 61; Wedemeyer, G-2 Report; Lamey 26 July 1972.

19 Wedemeyer 22 July 1962.

20 Wedemeyer 56; Wedemeyer 9 May 1962.

21 Beelitz (classmate) 21 April 1964, 6 June 1973; Huhs (classmate) 20 Sept. 1972, 10 May 1973 relates that ClS acknowledged Hitler's political talent and energy, but regarded the Nazi leaders with contempt and Hitler as an upstart without profound education or character.

22 Roosevelt, 1937 Volume 406–411.

23 Wedemeyer 22 June 1962; NS 23 May 1962.

24 Bachert 11 June 1973; Teske, *Spiegel* 31; Beelitz 21 April 1964, 6 June 1973;

Loeper 29 Aug. 1972; Pezold 1 Sept. 1972; HCSt 28 July 1971, 5 July 1972; *Spiegelbild* 447–450.

25 Bachert 11 June 1973; *Rangliste* 1928, 1932; BAZ, Mertz's career details 14 July 1966; Beelitz 21 April 1964; Teske, *Spiegel* 31–32 and 8 May 1973, somewhat at variance with other sources; KJM, *Heer* 39; Mertz to AM 7, 8 May 1935.

26 Mertz to AM 8, 12, 23 May 1935; *VB Norddeutsche Ausgabe* 22 May 1935.

27 Teske, *Spiegel* 46; Wedemeyer in Name Index; Wedemeyer 52; ClS to F [25, 26 June 1937], StGA.

28 ClS to F 15 July, 15 Aug. 1937, StGA; Lautlingen guest book.

29 ClS to F 15, 25, 29 Aug., 2, 9 Sept. 1937, StGA; Teske, *Spiegel* 39, 46, 48.

30 AA/PA Pol. Abt. Ref. Russland Pol. Verschluss Nr. 73; excerpts in *ADAP* D I 729–730; Herwarth drafted the lecture; Herwarth 24 Aug. 1972.

31 Noakes and Pridham 408–409; *DGFP* C 5 853–862.

32 Finckh in *Spiegelbild* 305; Huhs 1 Nov. 1972; Lamey 26 July 1972; Loeper 29 Aug. 1972; Pamberg 26 Jan. 1971; Pezold 1 Sept. 1972; Reinhardt 1 July 1972; Teske, *Spiegel* 41–42; Topf; Varnbüler 19 Jan. 1971; Zeller 228.

33 ClS to F 15 Aug. 1937, StGA; CM 121.

34 Zeller 227; Kramarz 52.

35 ClS, 'Kavallerie als operative Waffe', Nl ClS; RF 15 July 1963; Witzleben to ClS 27 May and 1 Nov. 1938, Nl ClS; 'Schule des Sieges' 5; Kramarz 52 and CM 124 offer unsupported contentions.

36 Roon, *Neuordnung* 80; ClS to Franz, Baron von Stauffenberg 16 Aug. 1937, Nl F. v. Stauffenberg.

37 ClS to Teske 29 Aug. 1937. Pius XI's Encyclical 'With burning anxiety' is dated 14 March 1937; ClS's use of the title in his letter to Teske suggests that he knew the encyclical, had thought about it, and identified with it.

38 ClS's speech in Lautlingen guest book.

39 NS in CM 144.

40 Friedrich, Baron von Stauffenberg, 10 Aug. 1972; Loeper 29 Aug. 1971; Lamey 26 July 1972; Pezold 1 Sept. 1972; R. Lerchenfeld 23 March 1971; NS to Venohr Feb. 1987 giving Schulenburg as ClS's source of information.

41 Huhs 20 Sept. 1972, 10 May 1973; Loeper 29 Aug. 1972; Partsch 14 July 1972; Pezold 1 Sept. 1972; cf. Heilfron 4 2648.

42 June 1938 exercise papers in Nl ClS; April–June 1938 General Staff exercises in BA-MA WI/IF 51502 pp. 1–109; Beck, memorandum 15 July 1938 in KJM, *Beck* 537–542.

43 Zeller 227 gives no source, but Loeper 29 Aug. 1972 and I. Reinhardt 1 July 1972 confirm ClS's delight in giving guided tours of medieval cathedrals in general; ClS to F 15 Aug. 1937, 23 and 27 June 1938, StGA; ClS to BS 14 March 1934, StGA.

44 'Die Schule des Sieges', Nl Teske; Goethe, *Tasso* 304.

45 ClS to F 23 and 27 June 1938, StGA; Teske, 'Zwiespalt'; Teske, *Spiegel* 41.

46 Handliste. During the war Stauffenberg's fellow officers remarked on his talent in all matters of organisation: Herwarth, *Zwischen* 247; Loeper 29 Aug. 1972.

47 Dienstlaufbahn.

48 R[olf] K[ratzer] in Kramarz 70; Keilig 42 II 1–2.

49 BS to MS [2 Jan., 3, 16, 28 April 1935], Nl MS.

50 BS to RB 17 Sept. [1934], 4 and 9 Nov. 1935, BS to F 10 Sept., 25 Nov. [1934],
    F to RB 31 Oct., 8, 11, 14 Nov. 1935, StGA; BS to MS 20 Nov., [16 Dec. 1934,
    6 Oct. 1935], Nl MS.

51 BS to MS 16 and 31 Dec. 1934, [26 Feb. 1935], 21 Aug. 1935, [17 Sept., 1 Dec.
    1935, 18 May, 5 June 1936], Nl MS; Lautlingen guest book; BS to RB 14 Sept.
    1935, 27 April [1936], 18 May 1936, StGA; BS to ClS 21 Sept. [1935], Nl ClS; F
    to RB 13 May 1936, StGA; MS, pocket diary 27 April, 8 and 10 May 1936.

52 Partsch 3 March 1977, 7 April and 15 May 1989; BS to MS [2, 14, 26 Jan., 9, 20
    Feb., 20 March, 21 July,16 Dec. 1934, 28 April, 22 June 1935], Nl MS; BS to F
    6 Feb. [1934], StGA; ClS to BS 14 March 1934, StGA; Makarov, 'Vorkämpfer'
    365.

53 *RGBl.* I 1933 480, 538–539; BS, 'Entziehung'.

54 A few years later, Stauffenberg could have added that no state had changed its
    legislation to admit Jews who were trying to leave Germany: *Palestine*; Stimson
    31 March 1944; Wyman 5–15, 260–268; Nicosia 157, 159, 162–163; Wasserstein
    17–39, 81–96, 143–155, 169–182, 205, 269, 278, 330–331, 339, 342–343, 352.

55 *Spiegelbild* 447–457.

56 Rönnefarth, Euler 125–127, 130–132; Kennan, *Fateful*.

57 *VB Norddeutsche Ausgabe* 8 March 1936 1–5; BS to Uncle Berthold [draft, after 7
    March 1936], Nl MS; BS, 'Vorgeschichte'; *RGBl.* II 1925 no. 52; 'Traité
    d'assistance mutuelle entre la France et l'Union des Républiques Soviétiques
    Socialistes', 2 May 1935, in Société des Nations, *Recueil des Traités* CLXVII
    1936 no. 3881; *Zeitschrift für ausländisches öffentliches Recht und Völkerrecht* V
    (1935) 599–611; *ADAP* C V 1–5, 14–22.

58 Handakten Gladisch.

59 BS to TP 2 Nov. [1936], PP; Makarov 363; minutes of 'Studienausschuss KR',
    NA T-1022 R. 1903; Ernennungsurkunde 24 Oct. 1936, Nl BS; Moltke, *Briefe*
    67; Bürkner to Gladisch 14 Aug. 1940, Handakten Gladisch, BA-MA III M
    501/1; Moltke, Balfour, Frisby 95, 122; Wengler 297–305; Moltke to his wife 22,
    25, 26 April 1940, *Briefe* 132–133 and Nl Moltke (more complete).

60 Mosler 25 July 1972; [Werner Traber] to Prof. Dr. W. Baum 28 May 1957, Nl
    MS; Makarov 363.

61 Moltke, *Briefe* 548–549; Wengler 303; Moltke, *Völkerrecht* 20.

62 F to BS 18 Dec. 1933, F to RB 19 Aug. 1935, StGA; correspondence BS-F-RB
    with attorney Plum, StGA; BS to MS *passim*, Nl MS; RB, 2 188; RB to BS and
    F [29 March] 1934 and *passim*, StGA.

63 BS to MS [8, 15, 24, 27 April 1932, 15 Dec. 1935], Nl MS; BS to RB 13 June
    1936, RB to BS 17 June 1936, StGA; Schlayer 6 Jan. 1984.

64 Wunder 390–391, 479; BS to MS 13 Jan., [5 March, 10 April 1936], Nl MS; CS
    to TP 16 April 1936, PP; NS 18 May 1989.

65 MS's pocket diary 14, 25 Feb., 29 March 1936; BS to ClS 16 March [1936], Nl
    ClS; O. v. Saucken 14/15 Aug. 1994.

66 BS to RB 6 Oct. 1936, StGA; MS's pocket diary 7 Sept. 1936.

67 BS to RB 3 March [1934], 13 June 1936, RB to BS 17 June 1936, EM to E.
    Gundolf 5 Oct. 1936, StGA.

68 BS to MS [23 Nov. 1935], Nl MS; AS to BS 25 Oct. 1940, StGA; Giessen

University Archive 5 Aug. 1981; [AS] 'Vorschlag'; *Kürschners* 1950 col. 1774; CS to TP 9 July 1938, PP; F to StG 11 Oct. 1933, StGA; TP 31 July, 5 Aug. 1972.

69 AS, 'Germanen' 406–419; *Deutsche Allgemeine Zeitung* 8 July 1937; *Frankfurter Zeitung* 6, 8, 9 July 1937.

70 ClS to F 15 July 1937, StGA; *VB* 7 July 1937, 8.

71 Bracke esp. 116, 118, 131; Schiller 24 June 1993.

72 CS Album 1927; Schiller 15 May, 28 Sept. 1989, 24 June, 9 Aug. 1993; *Schlesische Flieger Nachrichten*; Handel; Wunder 480.

73 Dette to F 2 Feb. 1938, StGA; Partsch 14 July 1972.

74 F to Farenholtz 28 July 1939, to M. Farenholtz 1 Aug. 1939, Farenholtz to F 4 Aug. 1939, ClS to BS 16 Feb. [1937], StGA; G. P. Landmann, *George* 129; M. Mommsen ca. 1963; BDC files; Volz 54; AB to F [April and May 1937], Nl F StGA; Giessen University Archive 18 Aug. 1989.

75 RF, 'Leben' 1.

76 LT to BS 17 Dec. 1940, StGA; RF 20 Dec. 1961, 9 May 1977; Seekamp 326, 368; RF to StG 29 Nov. 1930, StGA; RF file, BDC.

77 RF, F [6]; RF, 'Zum 20. Juli' 291; RF, 'Leben' 1–2; RF 4 Sept. 1977, 6 Aug. 1981, 21 Aug. 1982; Seekamp 386; AS to BS 25 Oct. 1940, StGA.

78 MS to RF 23 June 1946, RF to MS 28 March 1946, 3 Aug. 1948, Nl MS.

79 RF 10 March 1977; StG to Hindenburg July 1928, draft in *Stefan George* 301–302; Vallentin 104; StG, *GA* IX 31; F to RB 20 Dec. 1939, Nl RB; photograph of statue in StGA; F's papers and correspondence on Hindenburg in Nl F; OC Magdeburg garrison to Farenholtz 5 June 1936, Brigadier [Oskar] von Hindenburg to Farenholtz 17 Oct. 1936, StGA; F to BS [28 Aug. 1939], Nl MS; Stettler 38, 154–155; BS to RF [Aug. 1943], StGA.

80 RF to F 25 April 1937, StGA; StG's ambivalence in 'Der Krieg', *GA* IX 27–34; F's file on Sophocles, and F to AB 10 June 1936, StGA; G.P.Landmann, *George* 371.

81 RF, *Arndt* 9, 12–13, 75, 171–182; RF, 'Frank' [8].

82 RF, 'Frank' [8]; F to RF 19 Jan. 1936, StGA.

83 ClS, Bemerkungen; Partsch to F [early summer 1937], StGA; RF, 'Frank' [8].

84 RF, 'Frank' [9]; F to BS 29 May 1942, StGA; cf. *Blätter*, Zehnte Folge 1914 156: 'As in the previous sequences so in this latest one all names of authors were omitted as not indispensably relevant.'

85 RF, *Gneisenau*, Vorrede.

86 RF, *Gneisenau* 25–26; RF, *Arndt* 18–19; Delbrück 1 130.

87 RF, *Gneisenau*, Vorrede and 48–51; Thimme 97–100; Zeller 246.

88 Stern, 'Gneisenaus Reise' 15–16, 32–33; Thimme, 'Zu den Erhebungsplänen' 78–110; Pertz, *Gneisenau* 1 395–396; Delbrück 1 129–130; RF, *Arndt* 18–19; Loeper 29 Aug. 1972; Reerink 27 Feb. 1987.

89 Envelope postmarked München-Solln 17 Oct. 1944 in StGA.

90 Hölderlin, *Werke* 3 269, 4 320–326; Beck, Raabe 53; Hölderlin, *Werke* (Insel edn 1961) 1 307; F to E[dith?] L[andmann?] 2 Nov. 1937, StGA; F to Partsch 22 April 1936, Stettler 102; F, *Agis*; Partsch to F [April 1937], StGA; RF, 'Frank' [16]; F to Partsch 19 July 1942, StGA; Partsch 3 March 1977.

6. Crisis and war

1 ClS to F 6 July 1938, StGA.
2 Handliste; Keilig 105 I 1–6; Reerink June 1963, 4 Nov. 1971; Kriegsrangliste 1. LD 1938; 'Darstellung'; Schöne 5 March 1971; Kielmansegg 24 Aug. 1991; Lamey 26 July 1972.
3 Reerink 1963; Topf; Teske, *Spiegel* 41; Teske 8 May 1973; Teske, 'Zwiespalt'.
4 ClS to F 29 Aug. 1938, StGA.
5 ClS to F 29 Aug. 1938, F to BS 8 Sept. 1938, StGA; 'Darstellung'.
6 'Darstellung'; Reerink 1963, 24 March 1965; Tessin 2 31; Keilig 105 I 1–3.
7 F to RB 20 Sept. 1938, StGA.
8 Reerink 1963.
9 Haid guest book.
10 'Darstellung'.
11 Zeller 232.
12 NS 31 Aug. 1972, 12 Aug. 1982; Heimeran, Count Stauffenberg 17 Jan. 1987.
13 Reerink 1963; Heyde 8 June 1972; Kratzer 19 July 1972; Pezold 1 Sept. 1972.
14 NS Oct. 1962, 31 Aug. 1972, 12 Aug. 1982; TP 31 July, 5 Aug. 1972, 10 March 1977.
15 ClS to Sodenstern 13 March 1939.
16 Deutsch, *Hitler* 220–230; Hoffmann, review of Deutsch, *Hitler* in *Militärgeschichtliche Mitteilungen* 2/76, 197–199.
17 Gisevius II 71; Halder, 'Protokoll' 69, 71; Krausnick, 'Vorgeschichte' 346; Bücheler, *Hoepner* 75–77; Mueller-Hillebrand I 161; Leibstandarte orders 14, 16, 19, 22, 26 Sept. 1938, NA T-354 roll 214/3878609–43 and roll 612/000250–304; Weingartner 31; Guderian 57; Reerink 1963; Schöne 17 Dec. 1962, 5 March 1971; RF 10 March 1977 could not substantiate his suggestion that ClS had wanted to 'win over' Hoepner. Cf. suggestive statements in Zeller 242; Kramarz 71; CM 145.
18 *Wuppertaler Zeitung* 11 Nov. 1938.
19 NS Oct. 1962; Reerink 1963; R. Lerchenfeld 23 March 1971, 20 July 1972; Loeper 29 Aug. 1972.
20 AA/PA Völkerbund, Abrüstungskonferenz 1932 vol. 2 and Vbd. Gerichtshof Prof. Schücking.
21 BS to RB 25 April, 1 May 1938, BS to F 25 June 1938, F to RB 7 May 1938, RB to BS 28 April, 11 May, 19 June 1938, StGA; ClS to RB, draft for BS ca. 26 June 1938, ClS to F 26 June 1938, StGA; Jappe-Schubring 42.
22 RB to F 4 Jan. 1939, StGA; RB to BS and F 1939 *passim*, StGA and Nl RB. F to RB 27, 23 May, 7 Nov., 12 Dec. 1938, Nl RB; Schlösser 38–39, 365; Wolfskehl to Mann 10 July 1937, Mann 529–531; Wolfskehl, *Werke* I 216–219.
23 Thiersch 21 Jan. 1978; Partsch in G. P. Landmann, *Wie* 77; RF, 'Bericht' 3; RF 10 March 1977; Willi [Dette] to F 2 Feb. 1938, 6 Jan., 7 June 1939 (Dette had applied for 'Aryanisation'), F to Dette 27 Jan. 1939, F to BS 18 July 1942, Partsch to BS 26 Dec. 1942, StGA. M. Landmann's statement that in 1933 F had prevented Wolfskehl from seeing StG has no basis, and RB declared it 'invented': Landmann, 'Literatur'; Stettler to M. Landmann 8 June 1972, RB to Stettler 6 July 1972, StGA.

24 NS 7 Feb. 1979; Blomberg 24 July 1962, 4 Dec. 1990; at Christmas 1940 ClS gave precedence to Mertz: Mertz to AM 7 Dec. [1940].

25 Schöne 5 March 1971; Reerink 1963.

26 For this and the following: RF, 'Gneisenau', typescript, Nl ClS; Reering 1963, 27 Feb. 1987; RF 10 March 1977; NS 12 Aug. 1991; ClS's son Berthold (27 Jan 1987)remembers the event; Zeller 232–233; Delbrück II 81–83.

27 RF in Zeller 233; RF in CM 150; Reerink 1963.

28 RF in Zeller 242; RF 10 March, 9 May 1977.

29 For this and the following Sodenstern, 'Wesen'; Sodenstern, 'Vorgeschichte'; Giessler 552–554.

30 Nettesheim 17, 22 August 1968.

31 RF, *Gneisenau* 17–19; HCSt, 'Rede' 125–126.

32 KJM, *Beck* 552.

33 *Militärwissenschaftliche Rundschau, Sonderheft*, March 1937 8; Beck, *Studien* 62; Clausewitz II 1 618.

34 Thüngen 25 Jan. 1946.

35 *VB Norddeutsche Ausgabe* 28 Sept. 1938 3–5.

36 *Debates* vol. 345 col. 2415.

37 *VB Norddeutsche Ausgabe* 1 April 1939 1–2 and March–April *passim*; Hofer, 'Diktatur' 154–156.

38 Loeper 29 Aug. 1972; Pezold 1 Sept. 1972; RF 15 July 1963, 9 May 1977; F to BS 16 July [1939], Nl BS.

39 RF in Zeller 242–243; RF 10 March 1977; ClS to F 3 April, 2 July 1939, StGA; MS to BS [25 May 1939], Nl MS.

40 ClS to F 2, 5 July 1939, StGA; Partsch, 'Bild' 3199; Partsch 14 July 1972.

41 Lautlingen guest book; ClS to F 2, 5 July 1939, StGA.

42 ClS to F 16 July 1939, StGA; KTB 1.LD.

43 ClS to Uncle Berthold 18 Aug. 1939, Nl ClS.

44 Nettesheim 22 Aug. 1968; F. Frh. v. Stauffenberg 10 Aug. 1972.

45 KTB 1.LD.

46 MS to BS [ca. 24 Aug., Sept., Oct. 1939], Nl MS; Luise Mehnert to F 22 Aug. 1939, BS to MS [23 Sept. 1939], StGA; I. Üxküll to TP 18 Oct. 1939, PP; Dr Hans-Heinrich Ambrosius to MS 17 April 1946, StGA.

47 KTB 1.LD; Halder I 31; Paul, *Brennpunkte* 23–24; Cmd. 6144, *Accounts and Papers: eight volumes. (7.) State papers. Session 28 November 1939–20 November 1940*, vol. XII, *1939–40*, London 1939; *The Times* (Royal edn), 26 Aug. 1939, p. 9; with secret protocol as Cmd. 6616, *Accounts and Papers: five volumes. (4.) Law, miscellaneous, state papers. Session 29 November 1944–15 June 1945*, vol. X, *1944–5*, London 1945.

48 Halder I 41; Paul, *Brennpunkte* 25.

49 Paul, *Brennpunkte* 30, 32; Reerink 1963.

50 Reerink 1963; Kramarz 67.

51 [ClS to NS] 10 Sept. [1939], StGA; KTB 1.LD; 6. Pz. Div. Abt. Ib, Erfahrungsbericht 15 Nov. 1939; Paul, *Brennpunkte* 36–37.

52 KTB 1.LD; [ClS to NS] 10, 17, 23 Sept. [1939], 13, 14 Sept. 1939, StGA; Reerink 1963; Paul, *Brennpunkte* 33–37.

53 Reerink 1963; [ClS to NS] 10 Sept. [1939], 13, 14 Sept 1939, StGA; Domarus 1377–1393; *Soviet Documents* III 389.

54 [ClS to NS] 17, 23 Sept. [1939], StGA; KTB 1.LD; Paul, *Brennpunkte* 38; *West Point Atlas* II 2 7.

55 [ClS to NS] 17, 27 Sept. [1939], StGA.

56 Loeper 29 Aug. 1972.

57 KTB 1.LD; Loeper, 'Bericht'; Paul, *Brennpunkte* 45–46; Vormann 112–113; [ClS to NS] 25 Sept. 1939, StGA.

58 [ClS to NS] 30 Sept. [1939], StGA; *West Point Atlas* II, 2 7; Umbreit, 'Kampf' 271–272.

59 KTB 1.LD; NS to the family 2 Oct. 1939, StGA; divisional chaplain Prof. Bross, sermon 17 Oct. 1939, Nl ClS; Tessin 3, 6.

60 Loeper 29 Aug. 1972; 6. Pz. Div. Abt. Ib KTB 1–6 Feb. 1940; Heerespersonalamt, filmed cardfile; Paul, *Brennpunkte* 56; Schöne 17 Dec. 1962; Keilig 211/160, 202.

61 C. v. d. Schulenburg 5 Nov. 1984; Sauerbruch 12 Feb. 1963.

62 Handliste; BS to F 20 Nov. [1939], StGA; MS to BS [end of Nov. 1939], Nl MS; 6. Pz. Div. Abt. Ib KTB 5 Nov. 1939, 12–15 Jan. 1940; Mertz to AM 29 Oct. [1939].

63 TP 31 July, 5 Aug. 1972.

64 CM 169–171; Zeller 243; Kramarz 73; RF 19 Nov. 1985; NS 15 Sept. 1964, 31 Aug. 1972; O.K.H. Gen. St. d.H.-Zentr. Abt., Kriegs-Stellenbesetzung Stand: 15.11.39. On timing see also Hoffmann, *Stauffenberg*, German edn 523 note 129.

65 As regards the war in the air, for example, it was in fact Britain which first intentionally bombed civilian targets, in August 1940. Warsaw was a fortress when the German air force bombed it, so was Rotterdam; the bombing of Coventry was not even an act of retaliation, for the targets were munitions factories. Britain refrained from bombing German civilian targets in the first months of the war mainly because of French fears of German retaliation, and because British bombers were not capable of extensive long-range attacks. See Boog. The British position, somewhat veiled in *The Times* of 19 April 1941, was stated clearly in a press release issued from the Prime Minister's residence on 18 April 1941: 'The following statement is issued from No. 10, Downing Street. [. . .] It is a mistake to describe the bombing of Berlin last night by the R.A.F. as a reprisal for the raid on London the night before. It is not a reprisal but part of the regular policy adopted by the R.A.F. under instructions of His Majesty's Government of bombing all objectives in the two guilty countries [Germany and Italy] which are most likely to weaken their military or industrial capacity. This policy will be continued to the end of the war, it is hoped on an ever-increasing scale, irrespective of whether any further attacks are made on the British Islands or not.' P.R.O. CAB 120/300/1207.

66 ClS to TP 30 Dec. 1939, PP; RF on ClS's view of 'revolutions' in Zeller 246. See also below, pp. 152–161.

67 Partsch to F 27 Jan. 1940, StGA; RB to BS and F 10 March 1940, Nl RB.

68 6. Pz. Div. KTB No. 2. A General-Staff quartermaster branch responsible for roads, 9. Abt. Ib/Stra, distributed a memorandum dated 5 May 1939 which said that the condition of Polish roads made invasion or transit by a mechanised army

'completely impossible'. ClS on Schlieffen to C. Farenholtz 5 Feb. 1940, C. Farenholtz's papers.

69 Staedke 13 Jan. 1963.

70 Handliste; Pezold in Kramarz 58 and 6 Feb. 1966; Kielmansegg 24 Aug. 1991; Colsman; Schöne 17 Dec. 1962; Staedke 13 Jan. 1963; Kempf 7 Jan. 1963.

71 6. Pz. Div. Abt. Ib KTB 1/6 Feb. 1940; Paul, *Brennpunkte* 56; Kramarz 65; Staedke 13 Jan. 1963.

72 Manstein, notes; Manstein, *Siege* 93, 109. Colonel (GS) Rudolf Schmundt was Hitler's Personal Adjutant for Wehrmacht affairs.

73 Halder I 206; Jacobsen, *Fall Gelb* 119–130; Umbreit 254.

74 6. Pz. Div. Abt.Ib KTB 27 Feb.–3 March 1940; ClS to Partsch 22 April 1940, Partsch papers; 6. Pz. Div. KTB No. 2.

75 F to BS 9 March, 15 April 1940, StGA; ClS to Partsch 22 April 1940, Partsch papers.

76 Anlagen-Band C KTB 6. Pz. Div. Feldzug Frankreich 6.4.40–19.5.40.

77 Halder I 213 and map 'Situation West 10 May 1940 0 hours'; 6. Pz. Div. KTB No. 2 10 May 1940.

78 6. Pz. Div. Ia Anlagen-Band A, 10 May–1 July 1940.

79 Anlagen-Band C KTB 6. Pz. Div. Feldzug Frankreich 6 April–19 May 1940; 6. Pz. Div. KTB No.2 11–12 May 1940.

80 6. Pz. Div. KTB No. 2, 13 May 1940; Paul, *Brennpunkte* 59–61.

81 6. Pz. Div. KTB No. 2 14 May 1940; Paul, *Brennpunkte* 64.

82 6. Pz. Div. KTB No. 2 summary in T-315 roll 320/193 *et seq.*

83 Hitler, *Weisungen* 50–51.

84 6. Pz. Div. KTB No. 2 15 May 1940; Kempf's order in Anlagenband C; Paul, *Brennpunkte* 66–72.

85 6. Pz. Div. KTB No. 2 16–18 May 1940; Paul, *Brennpunkte* 71.

86 6. Pz. Div. KTB No. 2 18 May 1940; Paul, *Brennpunkte* 73.

87 ClS to NS 18, 27 May 1940, NS to relatives 22 May 1940, StGA.

88 Topf.

89 6. Pz. Div. Ia Originalbefehle und Meldungen zum KTB No. 2 19 May 1940, T-315 roll 321/169–170; Umbreit 290.

90 Ia-Befehl 20 May 1940, 6. Pz. Div. Ia Originalbefehle und Meldungen zum KTB No. 2 16–21 May 1940; 6. Pz. Div. KTB No. 2 20 May 1940.

91 Radio command, XXXXIst Army Corps to 6th Pz. Div. 13.45, received 14.35, Originalbefehle und Meldungen zum KTB No. 2 16–21 May 1940.

92 Ellis 110; Jacobsen, *Dünkirchen* 68; 6. Pz. Div. KTB No. 2 21 May 1940; Ia to combat command Ravenstein 21 May 1940 in Anlagen-Band C KTB 6. Pz. Div.

93 6. Pz. Div. KTB No. 2 22 May 1940.

94 Halder I 314, 316; Jacobsen, *Dünkirchen* 83; Ellis 158–159, 386.

95 Jacobsen, *Dünkirchen* 54–59, 70–85, 88–102; Halder I 318–319; *Meyers Lexikon* 7th edn vol. 4 (1926), 'Flamen'; *Meyers Lexikon* 8th edn vol. 4 (1938), 'Flamen'.

96 6. Pz. Div. KTB No. 2 23–24 May 1940 and Ia Anlagenband C.

97 6. Pz. Div. KTB No. 2 24 May 1940; ClS to NS 27 May 1940, StGA; R. v. Ribbentrop 19 March 1991; Weizsäcker 205; Schmidt, *Statist* 482–483; Kordt 385–391.

98 6. Pz. Div. KTB No. 2 25–30 May 1940; Ellis 187–188, 215–216.

99 Kempf to Generalkommando XXXXI.A.K. 30 May 1940 in 6. Pz. Div. Abt. Ia KTB No. 2 Originalbefehle und Meldungen and KTB No.2 28–30 May 1940; Ellis 215–216.
100 [ClS to NS] 27 May, 17 June 1940, StGA; Anlagen-Band D zum KTB 6. Pz. Div. Feldzug Frankreich; Halder I 299.
101 6. Pz. Div. KTB Ib 12 July, 14 Sept. 1940.
102 Staatsarchiv Sigmaringen, Nl Stauffenberg.
103 ClS to NS 27 May 1940, NS to family 2 June 1940, StGA; 6. Pz. Div. KTB No. 2 31 May 1940.

7. On the General Staff

1 [ClS to NS] 17 June 1940, StGA; Zeller 234; Pezold 1 Sept. 1972.
2 Pezold in Kramarz 79; Pezold's ms. corrections in Kramarz's typescript 1965, Slg Kramarz; Kriegs-Stellenbesetzung des GenStdH.
3 [ClS to NS] 17 June 1940, StGA.
4 [ClS to NS] 17 June 1940, StGA; Reinhardt 1 July 1972; Halder I 363.
5 [ClS to NS] 17 June 1940, StGA; Reinhardt 1 July 1972; OKH Gen. St. d.H. Zentr. Abt., Kriegs-Stellenbesetzung.
6 NS 15 July 1965; Mertz to AM 28 Aug. [1940].
7 NS in Kramarz 79–80; [NS to BS] 2 June 1940, StGA; Halder I 329–330, II 5, 155; Mertz to AM 24, 28 Aug., 1, 4, 28 Sept., 17, 30 Oct. [1940].
8 [ClS to NS] 19, 21 June 1940, StGA; ClS's mood may have been influenced by StG's poem 'Der Krieg', StG, *GA* IX 28–34.
9 Lerchenfeld 20 July 1972; Lautlingen guest book; F. Frh. v. Stauffenberg 10 Aug. 1972; Mannschatz 7 July 1972; Beelitz 6 June 1973; Zeller 243; Reinhardt 1 July 1972; Loeper 29 Aug. 1972; Halder II 5; RF 15 July 1963, 10 March 1977.
10 NS 11 Sept. 1968; Nettesheim 14 June, 17, 22 Aug. 1968.
11 Halder I 67, 79, 98; Keilig 91; *Trial* XXXV 91–93; Groscurth 241, 245, 357–359; Jodl in Hubatsch 70; Krausnick, *Einsatzgruppen* 80–106; Jacobsen, *1939/1945* 606. Halder told Groscurth on 9 Sept. 1939 'that it was the intention of the Führer and of Göring to destroy and exterminate the Polish nation'; Groscurth diary 9 Sept. 1939, Groscurth 202.
12 Major (GS) Heinz Hoppe in McCloy II 67; Mannschatz 7 July 1972; Hübner 17 July 1972; Metz 30 May, 1 Aug. 1971; Reinicke; Roidl 28 April 1984; Zeller 234, 243–244.
13 Hofacker to F.-D.Schulenburg 27 Oct. 1941, Hofacker to his wife 14 Dec. 1941, Nl Hofacker.
14 *KTB OKW* I 371; Halder II 335–337; Irving, *Hitler* 295–296, 331–332; Bussmann, Politik 8, and 27 Aug. 1974; Richthofen 28 Nov. 1978 (he received the same request from ClS).
15 CvdS 5 Nov. 1989.
16 Deichmann, pocket diary 16, 20 March 1942; Deichmann 23 July 1989; Moltke, *Briefe* 355–356 (20 March 1942, abridged in *Letters* 208).
17 F. v. Moltke 24 July 1989.
18 Moltke, *Briefe* 420 (10 Oct. 1942); *Letters* 252.
19 Balfour, Frisby 214, 218–219.

20 Hoffmann, *History* 255–258.
21 Kramarz 82; Hoppe in McCloy II 67; Hübner 13 July 1972; Ferber 29 May 1973; Berger 7 May 1984; Herwarth, *Zwischen* 246; Maizière 3 Sept. 1985. For an extensive consideration of Halder's evidence see Hoffmann, *Stauffenberg* 529–531 note 35.
22 Halder I 324, 357, 360–363; Mueller-Hillebrand I 136–137, 153, II 62–63; Mueller-Hillebrand and Maizière in Kramarz 78–79; Maizière 20 Jan. 1963, 3 Sept. 1985.
23 Halder I 372, II 49, 58, 79; *KTB OKW* I 38.
24 Lautlingen guest book; Heyde 3 Jan. 1972; Halder II 218–219; Hitler, *Weisungen* 79–81; Ferber 29 May 1973.
25 BS to MS [ca. 24 Sept. 1940], MS to BS [between 26 and 30 Sept. 1940], Nl MS; BS to F [ca. 10 Oct., received by F 12 Oct. 1940], StGA.
26 BS to F [ca. 10 Oct. 1940], F to BS 4 Dec. 1940, 2 Jan. 1941, StGA; Mertz to AM 7 Dec. [1940]; H. Mertz (Mertz's father), pocket diaries Dec. 1940, Jan. 1941.
27 Hillgruber, Hümmelchen 59, 66, 75.
28 A., Count Stauffenberg (Amerdingen) 15 Aug. 1985.
29 RF in Zeller 235–236, 244; Zeller 31 Dec. 1994; A., Count Stauffenberg (Amerdingen) 15 Aug. 1985; F to BS 5 July 1941, StGA; NS 3 Dec. 1990; Hitler, *Weisungen* 122–129; H. Mertz, diary April–May 1941; RF March 1984; Halder III 143; Olshausen 246; *ADAP D* XII 703–705; Fleischer 120; Hoffmann, 'Roncalli' 77–82. Apparently during the time he spent with RF in Greece, ClS commented on the question of Hitler's overthrow by saying: 'He is still winning too many battles.' Zeller 244; RF 10 March 1977. Whether or not ClS shared Halder's setback theory (that Hitler could be deposed only after he had suffered serious setbacks in the war), he had changed his mind by the time the campaign against Russia was in progress.
30 Halder III 8.
31 Hermann G. Lüben in *Süddeutsche Zeitung* No. 179, 7 Aug. 1986 9 (a slightly variant version based on Lüben's ms. in Kroener 857); Kroener 857–870; Hitler, *Weisungen* 129–133, 136–139; Paulus 49; Organisations-Abteilung (III) 11 Aug. 1941, Notizen für KTB, Beiträge zum KTB 1941–43, T-78 roll 414/6382358–6382361; Halder III 169–171, 345.
32 Halder III 38.
33 6. Pz. Div. Ia KTB 13 July 1941.
34 Halder III 88; Klink 459; Rotberg 8 May 1975, 28 July 1990; Tessin 2 2–3; Unold to ClS 25 July 1941, Nl ClS; Loeper 29 Aug. 1972; Keilig 211/202; Tessin 3 166–167.
35 Halder III 88.
36 Unold to ClS 25 July 1941, Nl ClS.
37 Notizen für K.T.B. [end Oct. 1941], and Lt. Col.(GS) Christ (head of Org. Branch Group III), [minutes] 5 Nov., 13 Dec. 1941, 15 June 1942, T-78 roll 414/6382362–6382365, 6382377–6382379, 6382407–6382410.
38 Halder III 170.
39 Reinhardt, *Wende* 127; Kroener 867–868; *KTB OKW* I 1047–1054.
40 Schlabrendorff 86.
41 Halder III 210; Klink 462, 546.

42 Halder III 242.

43 BS to MS [9 Oct. 1941], 28 Oct. [1941], Nl MS.

44 Wehrstammbuch.

45 Halder III 280; BS to MS [ca. 22 Nov. and between 7 and 11 Dec. 1941], Nl MS.

46 Moltke, *Briefe* 279; HCSt 1963, 28 July 1971, 5 July 1972; Wunder 460–487; HCSt, 'Rede' 125–126; on timing see Hoffmann, *Stauffenberg* 533 note 98; Pezold 1 Sept. 1972.

47 Halder III 295; *KTB OKW* IV 55–56, 1712, 1721; Irving, *Hitler* 794 note 13 based on Schmundt in T-77 roll 17/8168–75 and Dr. ing. Walter Rohland, sworn statements 24 Nov. 1948 and 16 May 1964.

48 Domarus 1815; *VB Norddeutsche Ausgabe* 21 Dec. 1941 1–2.

49 Halder III 320–322, 366, 371–373, 375–377.

50 Reerink 1963; J. Speer 22 Feb. 1966; Stahl 6 May 1987.

51 Bürker 18 Oct. 1972; Bürker to Paulus 4 Aug., 17 Nov. 1941 in Paulus 142, 146; OKH Gen. St .d.H. Zentr. Abt., Kriegs-Stellenbesetzung Stand: 15.2.41; OKH/PA-Kartei; KTB Nr. 3 XXXX.A.K.2 Dec. 1941; [Bürker] to XXXX.Pz. A.K. 8, 9, 15, 30 Nov. 1941, KTB XXXX.A.K. Ia VI. Abschnitt T-314 roll 988/495–496, 506–507, 542–543, 569–570; Bürker to ClS 4 Dec. 1941 and 2 Jan. 1942; Tessin 3 62.

52 Bürker 2 Feb. 1942 in KTB No. 6 10. Pz. Div. Anlagen VII T-315 roll 569/662; KTB Org. Abt. 19–25 March, 8–15 April, 1–10 Aug., 1–10 Sept. 1942; *KTB OKW* II 317.

53 OKH/PA file; Staedke to ClS 5 Jan. 1942, Nl ClS; Staedke visited ClS frequently in Gen. St. hqs and occasionally stayed with him overnight, discussing all his concerns: Staedke 13 Jan. 1963.

54 Bürker 2, 9 Jan. 1942, T-315 roll 569/313–315; Kriegs-Stellenbesetzung 1.11.41, 1.3.42. Bernuth: Lt.Col. (GS), Head, Training Branch in Gen. Staff.

55 [ClS to NS] 17 June 1940, StGA; Reinhardt 1 July 1972.

56 W. Meyer 7.

57 NS 3 Dec. 1990; ClS to Baroness von Lerchenfeld 11 Jan. 1942, copy in Nl ClS; *KTB OKW* I 1072–1074; Halder III 279–283; Kroener 867–868; Klink 587; KTB Org. Abt. 26 Feb. 1942, T-78 roll 414/6382393–6382397.

58 Cf. RF, *Gneisenau* 57–59.

59 Loeper in Kramarz 94; Loeper 29 Aug. 1972; Bürklin in Kramarz 92; Bürklin 15 July 1962; Bussmann 27 Aug. 1974; Pezold 1 Sept. 1972.

60 Loeper in Kramarz 94; *RGBl.* I 1942 247; Domarus 1874.

61 ClS to Baroness Lerchenfeld 11 Jan. 1942.

62 *Weizsäcker-Papiere* 286 cited by Wegner 995; NS 7 Aug. 1972, 3 Dec. 1990; Saucken 27 July 1972, 3 March 1991; Marlene, Countess Stauffenberg 23 Aug. 1972; Bürklin in Kramarz 92; Bürklin 15 July 1962; Sauerbruch in *Spiegelbild* 395; M., Count Stauffenberg 4 June 1973.

63 Hofacker to his wife 29 Dec. 1941, Nl Hofacker.

64 Schick 5 March 1991; Bürker to ClS 25 Feb. 1942; Tessin 3 171; Captain (GS) Butler (quartermaster of 10th Pz. Div. and deputy senior staff officer) to Bürker 15 April 1942, KTB No. 6 10. Pz. Div. Anlagen VIII T-315 roll 569/1177–1178.

65 *KTB OKW* II 46.

66 Herwarth 3 Feb. 1963, 24 Aug. 1972, 20 July 1984, 3 Jan. 1985; Herwarth, *Zwischen* 250–251, 287; Kielmansegg 1 June 1973; Weizsäcker 26 April 1975, 2 Dec. 1990, 28 Jan. 1992.

67 Reerink 1963; Keilig 52 IX 5; Rotberg 8 May 1975, 28 July 1990; Weckmann 18 Feb. 1971; command-structure diagrams in files of Org. Abt. T-78 roll 414/6382879–6382890; Herwarth, *Zwischen* 190, 223, 239–241, 248; Herwarth 24 Aug. 1972; Hükelheim 15 March 1977.

68 J. Speer 18 Oct. 1945, 7 Sept. 1965, 22 Feb. 1966; Zeller 244; CM 217, 542; Bussmann 24 April 1985 remembers Speer's account of ClS saying 'töten, töten, töten' ('kill, kill, kill').

69 Maizière 3 Sept. 1985; Bräutigam, *So* 482–484; Bräutigam 7 Sept. 1985; Woellwarth 5 June 1973; Weizsäcker 26 April 1975; variations in Herwarth, *Zwischen* 287 and Seiffert 18 May 1973; Colsman in Zeller 520 note 29; similarly Michel 23 Aug. 1979.

8. Stauffenberg turns against Hitler

1 KTB Org. Abt. 1–5 June 1942; Halder III 453; ClS to Paulus 12 June 1942 in Appendix V; Pezold 1 Sept. 1972; Herre 7 Dec. 1986; J. Speer 22 Feb. 1966.

2 ClS to Paulus 12 June 1942.

3 Herwarth, 'Meine'; Herwarth 25 Aug. 1972; Berger 7 May, 12 July 1984; Kielmansegg 1 June 1973.

4 KTB Org.Abt. 11–20 July, 31 Oct. 1942; *KTB OKW* II 570; Hoffmann, *Security* 226–229.

5 KTB Org.Abt. 6–12 May, 1–20 Aug. 1942.

6 Hitler in conference with the heads of the Armed Forces and their Chiefs of Staff in the New Chancellery on 23 May 1939, *Trial* XXXVII 556; explicit order 11 Jan. 1940 in *Trial* VIII 263; see also *Trial* X 602, XXI 591; Jacobsen, *1939–1945* 643; an obscure reference in Halder I 234 note.

7 OKH GenStdH Org.Abt.g.Kdos. 1942–1944.

8 Heeres-Quartiermeisterreise 1939, Nl ClS; Zeller 232; Ed. Wagner 87; Hitler, *Weisungen* 196–200; Wegner 761–778, 868–898, 951–961.

9 Keilig 211/374; Halder III 489, 493, 513, 518, 520, 524.

10 KTB Org. Abt. 11–20 Sept., 11–20 Oct., 1 Nov. 1942.

11 KTB Org. Abt. 18 Nov., 12 Dec. 1942; Hoffmann, *Security* 188–189, 226; HPA Kartei NA RG 242. Schmundt was Hitler's Chief Adjutant; Buhle was Chief of Army Staff in Armed Forces Supreme Command; Hofmann was Head of E (H) in Army High Command.

12 Herwarth, 'Deutschland' 5–6, 10, 14, 18; Bräutigam, *So* 482–486; Bräutigam 7 Sept. 1985; Thorwald 54–57, 87; Dallin 146–167; R.-D. Müller 995.

13 Förster 1078; Etzdorf, Aufzeichnungen V.A.A., AA/PA and T-120 roll 748/337851; OKH Gen.St.d.H.Zentralabteilung, Kriegs-Stellenbesetzung Stand 1.3.42.

14 Mende 25.

15 KTB Org. Abt. 1–5 Jan., 6–10 Feb. 1942, and Anlagen T-78 roll 414/6382669–6382675; Michel, *Ost* 44, 48; Mende 24–29; Kramarz 97–111; *Hitlers Lagebesprechungen* 252–268; Förster 1077–1078.

16 Herre in Thorwald 53–58; Thorwald 71 (not wholly compatible with other evidence) 87; Dallin 535–536; KTB Org. Abt. 19–25 March, 1–12 May 1942; Kramarz 104.

17 Strik-Strikfeldt 35–37, 40–45, 59–61, 84; Strik-Strikfeldt 11 Aug. 1963; Gersdorff, *Soldat* 115 (omitting reference to the issue for 1941); Thorwald 54–69; 82–84; OKH/Gen.St.d.H./Zentralabteilung, Kriegs-Stellenbesetzung Stand 1.3.42; *Trial* XXV 156–161.

18 Mende 19 Sept. 1963; Strik-Strikfeldt 11 Aug. 1963; Herwarth, 'Deutschland' 5–6, 10, 14, 18; Streit 9–10.

19 KTB Org. Abt. 21–25 June 1942; Mende in Kramarz 104–105.

20 Herwarth, 'Andenken' 766–768; Herwarth 24 Aug. 1972; Herwarth, 'Meine'; Herwarth, *Zwischen* 253–258, 261; Thorwald 67, 72–73, 106–109; Bräutigam [ca. 1963]; Keilig 211/173; Dallin 239; KTB Org. Abt. 21–31 Aug. 1942.

21 Herre 7 Dec. 1986; Thorwald 54–65, 70–73; Major (GS) Heinz Hoppe in McCloy II 67; Herwarth, 'Meine'; Herwarth, *Zwischen* 250; Herwarth 3 Jan. 1985, 8 May 1986; Loos 39.

22 Herwarth, *Zwischen* 250; Herwarth 3 Jan. 1985; Michel 23 Aug. 1979.

23 Pezold 1 Sept. 1972.

24 Thüngen 25 Jan. 1946; Maizière 3 Sept. 1985; Herre 9 Sept. 1972.

25 Berger 7 May 1984.

26 Berger 7 May, 12 July 1984.

27 Mueller-Hillebrand 27 Oct. 1945–April 1947 422–423 ('Schmutzfink') and 30 April 1962 ('Schwein'); ClS may well have employed a term stronger still; Keilig 211/228; Seiffert, a colleague in the Org. Branch, 18 May 1973 dates ClS's thorough disenchantment to 'July 1942 or mid-1942'; J. Speer 22 Feb. 1966 'would think it was autumn 1942'.

28 Berger 7 May, 12 July 1984.

29 KTB Org. Abt. 11–20 Sept. 1942; Truppenveränderungsmeldungen, Deutsche Dienststelle; Personalkartei, BA-Z; N. Üxküll to I. Üxküll 12 Sept., 19, 20 Oct. 1942, Nl I. Üxküll; Späth 190; Saucken 4 Feb. 1989.

30 Sodenstern, 'Vorgeschichte'; Keilig 211/359.

31 J. D. Hassell 9, 14 Aug., 5 Sept. 1990; J. D. Hassell, 'Kaukasusfeldzug'; Herwarth 3 Feb. 1963; Broich 14, 20 June 1962.

32 Prinz Wilhelm-Karl of Prussia, Second Lieutenant, 2nd special missions staff officer in 1st Panzer Army operations staff, letter 23 June 1993.

33 KTB Org. Abt. 11–30 Sept., 11–20, 25 Oct. 1942; Bleicken, 'Jahre' 80; Bleicken 15 Sept. 1990; Bussmann 27 Aug. 1974, 24 April 1985, 17 Aug. 1990; Bussmann, 'Entwicklung' 29; Bussmann, 'Politik' 10.

34 Wagner, *Volksgerichtshof* 945; Messerschmidt, Wüllner 49–50, 70, 73.

35 Bleicken did not answer the author's question about the situation in which he expected to be able to 'refer to it'; Bleicken 25 Dec. 1990; Bussmann 27 Aug. 1974, 24 April 1985, 17 Aug. 1990.

36 Kramarz 114 misinterprets ClS' account to Broich (Broich 14, 20 June 1962) to read that ClS had approached 'primarily the fieldmarshals', or 'most of the commanders-in-chief on the eastern front' and that this could not be confirmed. But Broich only mentioned 'all commanders-in-chief' and only one fieldmarshal; 'all' is colloquially imprecise. ClS's efforts, to which he added an appeal to

Manstein in January 1943 (see below pp. 159–161) show a quite wide-ranging
effort.

37 Halder, 'Protokoll' 60, 78c.
38 Halder, 'Protokoll' 108.
39 N. Üxküll to I. Üxküll 23, 24, 26, 27 Sept. 1942, Nl I. Üxküll.
40 Otto Schiller in Zeller 246; Herwarth, Zwischen 265, 286; K. Schiller 18 March
   1992.
41 Michel, *Ost* 40–52, 57–58; Michel 23 Aug. 1979. Rothfels, *German Opposition* 72
   note 49, 129 note 170 and *Deutsche Opposition* 1977, 227 note 86, declares, despite
   critical reservations, that Michel's account contains 'genuine and valuable information' on ClS's activities regarding volunteers; Kramarz does not mention
   Michel's account; CM 545 note 62 declares it 'scientifically completely useless'.
   Although Michel's account is highly subjective, it is confirmed by others such as
   Strik-Strikfeldt 170, 178, 182–183; Herre 26 April 1985; Herwarth, *Zwischen*
   332–334, N. Üxküll, letters to I. Üxküll, 1942, Nl I. Üxküll.
42 Herwarth, *Zwischen* 286–287; Berger 12 July 1984. Bussmann 27 Aug. 1974
   relates that Tresckow had said to him, to Gersdorff and to Bleicken (who was
   now posted as senior staff officer with 46th Panzer Corps): 'We must rest our
   hopes on Stauffenberg. He will be the soul of the revolution.' Bleicken, 'Jahre'
   84–85, and 15 Sept. 1990 in response to a question, did not confirm this
   account.
43 KTB Org. Abt. 19 Dec. 1942; Gillhausen, 'Niederschrift', KTB Befh. H. Geb.
   B, BA-MA RH 22/77; 'Grundsätzliche Gedanken aus der Aussprache des
   Reichsministers für die besetzten Ostgebiete mit den Befehlshabern der Heeres-
   gebiete im Osten 22 Dec. 1942', Der Chef der Sicherheitspolizei und des SD,
   Kommandostab, *Mitteilungsblatt* No. 15 20 [?] Jan. 1943, Akten des Reichs-
   sicherheitshauptamts, BA R 58/225; Dallin 152–153 with abstruse speculations
   based on the names of those present; Herwarth, *Zwischen* 287–288; J. Speer 22
   Feb. 1966.
44 KTB Org. Abt. 4 Dec. 1942; MS to BS [Nov.], 2, 3 Dec. [1942], Nl MS.
45 Maizière 3 Sept. 1985; Georg Reinicke 16 March 1971; Berger 7 May, 12 July
   1984; Kielmansegg 1 June 1973.
46 F to BS 18 July 1942, StGA.
47 ClS to Partsch 23 July 1942, Partsch Papers.
48 N. Üxküll to I.Üxküll 26 Nov., 6 Dec. 1942, Nl I. Üxküll; NS 3 Dec. 1990;
   Zeller 248 without source ref.; for Jan. 1943 Thüngen 25 Jan. 1946.
49 Broich 20 June 1962.
50 Kramarz 121; Zeitzler 3, 26 July 1962.
51 Halder 26 Jan. 1962; NS 12 Aug. 1991.
52 *Genealogisches Handbuch, Adelige B* XVI 99; Personalkartei, RG 242; Reile,
   'Einsatz'.
53 Herwarth, *Zwischen* 289; [Partsch] to BS 26 Dec. 1942 (ClS was expected in
   Berlin for the end of Dec.); F to BS 20 Jan. 1943, StGA.
54 Gisevius 8 Sept. 1972; Gisevius II 254–257.
55 26 Jan. 1962; Halder in Kramarz 119; Halder 5 July 1969 in Schall-Riaucour
   304–305. Halder's report that ClS broke down in tears is questionable in the
   absence of any other such report for any point in ClS's adult life, and in light of

Halder's own tendency to lachrymose outbursts: Groscurth 223, 246; Hartmann 75.

56 Halder, 'Protokoll' 60, 78c.

57 N. Üxküll to I. Üxküll 6 Jan. 1943, Nl I. Üxküll.

58 Hoffmann, *Widerstand* 443–446; Hassell 345–347; cf. Kaiser, diary 18, 21, 25, 29 Jan. 1943; Tresckow to his wife 14 Jan. 1943, Nl Tresckow; K. L. Guttenberg, appointments diary 21 Dec. 1942. Dr Carl Goerdeler was the former Lord Mayor of Leipzig and Reich Prices Commissioner; Ulrich von Hassell was Ambassador in Rome until Feb. 1938; Professor Johannes Popitz was Prussian Minister of Finance; Dr Jens Peter Jessen was a Professor of Political Science in the University of Berlin; Dr Gerstenmaier was a Counsellor of the Consistory in the Evangelical Church Foreign Countries Bureau and a member of Moltke's 'Kreisau Circle'.

59 Kaiser, diary 25 Jan. 1943; Schlabrendorff 61–63, 67–70.

60 Reerink 1963; NS in CM 266; Thüngen 25 Jan. 1946.

61 Manstein's evidence at the Nuremberg Trials on 10 Aug. 1946, *Prozess* XX 680; Manstein to R. v. Manstein 30 Dec. 1967; Manstein 5 Feb. 1968; Gisevius at Nuremberg 25 April 1946, *Prozess* XII 264; Schlabrendorff 126. R. v. Manstein 21 June 1991 informed the author that he had not yet found his father's correspondence with Beck.

62 Manstein, private diary 16 Nov. 1942; R. v. Manstein 21 June 1991, 26 Feb. 1992; Manstein, *Soldat* 192; Tresckow to E. v. Tresckow 17 Nov. 1942; Stahlberg 18 July 1984; Stahlberg, *Pflicht* 224–230; Wegner 1031.

63 *KTB OKW* II 1200; Manstein, *Siege* 382–383; Kehrig 453, 630–631.

64 Manstein to Zeitzler 22 Jan. 1943 in Kehrig 631–632; Wegner 1031; Goerdeler, 'Idee' 23; Schlabrendorff 72; Gersdorff, *Soldat* 78, 118.

65 Anlage KTB HGr Don; Manstein, private diary 26–27 Jan. 1943; Manstein in Kramarz 115–116; Manstein to R. v. Manstein 30 Nov. 1967; Manstein 30 Oct. 1972; Busse (Manstein's senior staff officer, from March 1942 Chief of Staff) in Kramarz 116–117; Stahlberg, information to Scheurig 15/16 Sept. 1965; Stahlberg 18 July 1984; Stahlberg, *Pflicht* 262–271 with the incorrect claim that Manstein's subsequent recommendation was the reason for ClS's transfer to the front, and with questionable accounts of conversations between Manstein and Zeitzler on ClS's new posting which Zeitzler had long since ordered (Zeitzler in Kramarz 121; Herwarth, *Zwischen* 289; F to BS 20 Jan. 1943, StGA); Stahlberg's reliability is also impaired by his incorrect dating of the encounter for 18 Jan. 1943 in all his accounts before 1987 (when the author informed him of the correct date as given in KTB HGr Don) and by his omission in all his accounts before 1987 of Schmundt and Fellgiebel, and of Manstein's discussions with Schmundt and Fellgiebel on the next day (Manstein, private diary 27 Jan. 1943).

66 Manstein, 'Notizen'; Manstein, 'Richtigstellung'; Manstein in Kramarz 116; Manstein to R. v. Manstein 30 Dec. 1967; Gersdorff, *Soldat* 134–136.

67 Kehrig 530 note 223a; Manstein, private diary 26–27 Jan. 1943; Manstein, 'Richtigstellung'; Manstein in Kramarz 116.

68 Manstein in Kramarz 115–118; Manstein 15 Nov. 1962; Manstein to Williams 30 Oct. 1972.

69 Broich 20, 25 June 1962.

70 Manstein 15 Nov. 1962; Broich 14, 20, 25 June 1962.
71 Herwarth 3 Feb. 1963; Broich 14, 20, 25 June 1962; NS in Kramarz 116; Thüngen 25 Jan. 1946.

9. In the front line

1 Arnim 570. On the movements and engagements of the 10th Pz. Div. see Schick, *Die 10. Panzer-Division*, 521–656.
2 *KTB OKW* II 151, 921–922, 946, 951; Tessin 1 281–282; Tessin 3 170–171; Keilig 211/7; Howard, *Grand Strategy* IV 171–190, 337–355; Burk 14 Aug. 1985.
3 Kaiser, diary 2–3 Feb. 1943; Gisevius 8 Sept. 1972; NS 30 July 1968; *VB* Berlin edn 4 Feb. 1943 1.
4 Kaiser, diary 1, 3, 19–23 Feb. 1943; Gisevius II 259; Schwerin 321.
5 Kaiser, diary 19 Feb., 3, 12 March 1943; Hoffmann, *Widerstand* 350–360; Schlabrendorff 69–70.
6 Sauerbruch 9 Feb. 1977, 5 Sept. 1990; Sauerbruch, 'Bericht' 139–142; ClS then said the same to Major Roland von Hösslin, a comrade from No. 17 Cavalry Regiment; *Spiegelbild* 373 with incorrect date; Colsman in Zeller 248.
7 Bremme in Kramarz 121 note 3; NS in CM 282–283; Bürker's promotion is apparently pre-dated to 1 Jan. 1943 in HPA files, since during his visit to Armed Forces Command Staff on 27 Jan. 1943 he was still identified as a lieutenant-colonel; *KTB OKW* III 77; NS 30 July 1968; Lautlingen guest book; CS to TP 15 March 1943, PP; ClS to Pezold's wife 9 Feb. 1943, Pezold Papers; Friedrich, Baron Stauffenberg 10 Aug. 1972.
8 Lautlingen guest book; CS to TP 15 March 1943, PP; ClS to Pezold's wife 9 Feb. 1943, Pezold Papers; Lüke 20 Feb. 1991; Kramarz 121 based on Bürklin 15 July 1962 has the hospital in Tunis; Burk 6 Dec. 1990 says the hospital was in Kairouan; Reile, 'Einsatz', corrected by Schick 30 May 1991.
9 Schick 25 Jan. 1994.
10 Howe 407; Keilig 211/85; Kramarz 122; Schick 30 May, 10 Dec. 1991; Burk 6 Dec. 1990; Reile, 'Einsatz'; Oppenfeld 27 May 1984.
11 Burk 14 Aug. 1985; Oppenfeld 14 Aug. 1985; Colonel Heinz Schmid (OC No. 90 Pz. Art. Rgt. in 10th Pz. Div.) in Kramarz 123; H. Schmid 23 Sept. 1962; Broich 14 June 1962; Bürklin 15 July 1962; Kleikamp 18 Dec. 1962; Reimann in Kramarz 124; Adalbert Eibl of ASR 961 in 999th Div. in Burkhardt, *Schein* 371; Burk to Otto Burk 27 March [1943]; Lüke 6 March 1991.
12 Reile 17 [March] 1991; Reimann 17 July 1962 and in Kramarz 124; Broich 14 June 1962; Oppenfeld 27 May, 20 July 1984, 14 Aug. 1985; Zipfel in Kramarz 126.
13 Broich 14, 20 June 1962 and in Kramarz 122; Reile 17 [March] 1991.
14 Reile 5 April 1991; Hagen was posted to General Staff Organisation Branch under Stieff, Klamroth and Major (GS) Joachim Kuhn; *Trial* XXXIII 328–329; KTB 10. Pz. Div. Ic Tätigkeitsbericht 22 March–19 April 1943; Broich 14 June 1962 and in Kramarz 126; Schönfeldt 22 March, 22 April 1991; Burk 6 Dec. 1990.
15 Stumpf 572–573.
16 Howe 406–416; Lüke 437–438; Rommel, 'Tagesberichte' 13, 23 Feb. 1943; KTB

10. Pz. Div. Ic Tätigkeitsbericht 14 Feb. 1943; Reile, 'Einsatz'; Keilig 211/375; Stumpf 719; 21. Pz. Div. Ia Divisionsbefehl für den Angriff auf Sidi bou-Zid 12 Feb. 1943, NA T-315 roll 570/371; Rommel, *Krieg* 349–355; *Eisenhower Papers* II 952–982; Hinsley II 757–763.

17 KTB 10. Pz. Div. Ic Tätigkeitsbericht, *passim*; Lüke 346; Lüke 28 Jan., 20 Feb. 1991; Reile, 'Einsatz'; Arnim 570.

18 Schick 30 May 1991 based on Burk, Moll, Reile, and correcting Burk 27 Oct. 1990 as well as Reile, 'Einsatz'; Oehlert 18 April 1991; Leyendecker 18 April 1991; KTB 10. Pz. Div. Ic Tätigkeitsbericht 14 Feb. 1943; Lüke 437–439; Howe 410–422. Arnim 572 recorded an American counterattack at 5 p.m. on 14 Feb., which was repulsed with great losses to the enemy, but perhaps confuses it with the action of 15 Feb.

19 Cf. *KTB OKW* III 52–53, 77; Schick 5 Feb. 1992; Burk 27 Oct. 1990; Rommel, *Krieg* 349–353; *Eisenhower Papers* II 952–982; Hinsley II 577–597, 757–763; *Rommel Papers* 394.

20 Rommel, *Krieg* 349–350; Howe 416–422; Reile, 'Einsatz'; KTB 10. Pz. Div. Ic Tätigkeitsbericht 15 Feb. 1943.

21 Rommel, 'Tagesberichte' 18–19 Feb. 1943; Howe 438–440, 453; Rommel, *Krieg* 353–354; Reile, 'Einsatz'; Schick 30 May 1991 based on Moll; Arnim 572–573.

22 Rommel, 'Tagesberichte' 20 Feb. 1943; KTB 10. Pz. Div. Ic Tätigkeitsbericht 20 Feb. 1943; Howe 455, 472; Kramarz, illustration facing p. 64; Burk 14 Aug. 1985; Reile 17 [March] 1991; Schick 30 May 1991 based on Moll. K 10 (Krad-Schützen-Bataillon 10) consisted of 1 armoured reconnaissance company, 1 company with armoured personnel carriers, 2 infantry companies with side-car motorcycles, 1 company with 2 infantry-artillery troops with 4 75-mm guns, 1 anti-tank-gun troop, 1 anti-tank rifle troop.

23 Howe 441–442, 452–453; KTB 10. Pz. Div. Ic Tätigkeitsbericht 19 Feb. 1943; Reile, 17 [March] 1991 and 'Einsatz'; Rommel, 'Tagesberichte' 20 Feb. 1943; Keilig 211/95.

24 Rommel, 'Tagesberichte' 20–21 Feb. 1943; Leyendecker 18 April 1991; Lüke 449–450.

25 Rommel, 'Tagesberichte' 21 Feb. 1943; Leyendecker 18 April 1991; Reile 17 [March] 1991.

26 KTB 10. Pz. Div. Ic Tätigkeitsbericht 21 Feb. 1943; Rommel, 'Tagesberichte' 21–22, 24 Feb. 1943 and Reile, 'Einsatz' both give higher numbers of prisoners; Lüke 450–451; Rommel, *Krieg* 358–360, 364–367; Howe 456, 459–466, 469; Heiner, 'Unterlagen'; Reile, 17 [March] 1991. Contrary to what he had said at the time, Rommel in *Krieg* 359–360 blamed Arnim's retention of nineteen Tigers for the failure to attain the larger objectives of the operation.

27 Reile, 'Einsatz'; Rommel, 'Tagesberichte' 23 Feb. 1943; KTB 10. Pz. Div. Ic Tätigkeitsbericht' 22 Feb. 1943.

28 Rommel, 'Tagesberichte' 23–24, 27 Feb. 1943; Stumpf 737. General von Arnim and Lieutenant-General Gustav von Vaerst were summoned to Rome for briefings without Rommel's knowledge, although they were nominally his subordinates, whereupon Rommel had a furious telephone conversation with Fieldmarshal Kesselring.

29 Rommel, 'Tagesberichte' 28 Feb. 1943; Reile, 'Einsatz'; KTB 10. Pz. Div. Ic

Tätigkeitsbericht 23 Feb.-1 March 1943; Rommel, *Krieg* 364–367; Howe 514–519; Cramer 7. Brigadier Karl Bülowius, General of Pioneers in the German Africa Corps, warned that all British mines around the defensive perimeter at Médenine were secured against being lifted so that they must be detonated, which would make surprise impossible.

30 Reile, 'Einsatz'; Heiner, 'Unterlagen'; Weist 19 Feb. 1991; Rommel, 'Tages-berichte' 28 Feb. 1943; Lüke 458.

31 Howe 515–516; Hertel 18 April 1991.

32 Rommel, 'Tagesberichte' 5 March 1943; Cramer 7; Colonel Heinz Schmid in Kramarz 123; H. Schmid 23 Sept. 1962; Burk 14 Aug. 1985, 27 Oct., 6 Dec. 1990; Lüke 459; KTB 10. Pz. Div. Ic Tätigkeitsbericht 6 March 1943; Howe 516–517.

33 Reile, 'Einsatz' and 10 Feb. 1991; Heiner, 'Unterlagen'; Balser 4 March 1991; Cramer 7; Weist 19 Feb. 1991; Rommel, 'Tagesberichte' 6 March 1943; Breiten-berger in Lüke 474.

34 Reile 17 [March] 1991; KTB 10. Pz. Div. Ic Tätigkeitsbericht 6 March 1943; Cramer 7–8; Lüke 462–463.

35 Rommel, 'Tagesberichte' 6 March 1943; Cramer 8; Reile, 'Einsatz'.

36 Oppenfeld 14 Aug. 1985; Reile 10 Feb., 17 [March] 1991 and Einsatz; Lüke 466; Hertel 18 April 1991: 'The order to retreat arrived toward 3 a.m., the lines of command worked well, when the sun came up we had gone! We are still proud of this triumph of organisation.'

37 KTB 10. Pz. Div. Ic Tätigkeitsbericht 10 March 1943; Reile, 'Einsatz'; 10. Pz. Div. Ia No. 70/43 14 March 1943 in KTB 10. Pz. Div. Ia Anlage No. 6; Schott 20 April 1991.

38 Teleprinter message HGr Afrika Ia 1386 20 March 1943 in 10. Pz. Div. Ia Anl. KTB No.6; Howe 531–537; Rommel, *Krieg* 374–375.

39 Hertel 18 April 1991; Howe 559–563; KTB 10. Pz. Div. Ic Tätigkeitsbericht 22–27 March 1943 and II Anl. with CIS's reports on the interrogation of prisoners on 24 and 31 March and 1, 2, 3, 6 April; Lüke 474.

40 Hertel 18 April 1991; Schick 10 Dec. 1991, 5 Feb. 1992; Lüke 483–497; Howe 554–557; Lang.

41 KTB 10. Pz. Div. Ic Tätigkeitsbericht 30 March-6 April 1943.

42 Schott 20 April, 27 May 1991.

43 Howe 539, 576.

44 Burk 6 Dec. 1990; CIS in Reile 10 Feb. 1991.

45 Zipfel 18 Jan. 1964 and in Kramarz 124–125; Burk 12 Feb. 1991; Schott 13 March, 20 April 1991; Schick 5 Sept., 10 Dec. 1991.

46 Schott 20, 26 April, 27 May 1991; Balser 23 Jan. 1991.

47 KTB 10. Pz. Div. Ic Tätigkeitsbericht 7–12 April 1943.

48 Balser 23 Jan., 4, 25 March, 12 Dec. 1991.

49 Burk 12 Feb. 1991; Balser 23 Jan. 1991; Reile 10 Feb. 1991.

50 KTB 10. Pz. Div. Ic Tätigkeitsbericht 7–12 April 1943.

51 Oppenfeld 27 May 1984; KTB 10. Pz. Div. Ic Tätigkeitsbericht 7–12 April 1943; Broich 14 Feb. 1962 and in Kramarz 127–128; Burk 27 Oct., 6 Dec. 1990, 12 Feb. 1991; Balser 23 Jan., 4, 25 March, 12 Dec. 1991.

52 Reile 10 Feb. 1991.

53 Balser 23 Jan., 4 March 1991; Schönfeldt 22 March 1991; Schott 13 March, 20, 26 April 1991; NS 9 Aug. 1991; Lüke 28 Jan., 12 Feb. 1991 (based on no longer identifiable sources) places the wounding of ClS by the Maknassy-Mezzouna railway, evidently in error.

54 Schott 20 April 1991.

55 Keysser 6, 12, 23 Feb., 1, 21 April 1991. Balser 23 Jan., 21 Feb. 1991 relates that the medical officer of IIIrd Btl. of No. 90 Armoured Artillery Rgt, Dr. Biskamp, gave ClS first aid. Balser's reports are vivid but contain confusions and contradictions. From where Balser was while Dr Biskamp was allegedly treating ClS, Balser could not have observed this. Dr Biskamp died in 1981 and could not be interviewed; his widow and one of his sons, who is also a doctor, assert that Dr Biskamp occasionally mentioned ClS but never said he had treated him. Mrs Biskamp 21 Feb. 1991; Dr Klaus Biskamp 7 March 1991. Dr Keysser's version is confirmed by Burk 28 Feb. and 27 April 1991: when Burk arrived at the new command post near Mezzouna he heard that ClS had been given first aid by a medical officer from a 'strange unit', meaning one not in 10th Panzer Division, who had happened to be passing.

56 Burk 28 Feb. 1991.

57 NS 30 July 1968; Deutsche Dienststelle 30 Oct. 1991; BA-MA 15 Nov. 1991.

10. Conspiracy

1 CS to TP 11 April 1943, PP; BS to RF 13 April [1943], Nl RF; BS to RB [12 April 1943], Nl RB; Krankenmeldung to Wehrmacht-Auskunftstelle Berlin, Deutsche Dienststelle 30 Oct. 1991; NS 30 July 1968, 19 Jan. 1969; Bragadin 243; Rohwer, Hümmelchen 343, 361; Walter Anton to BS n.p.n.d., StGA: 'There may be *chirourgoi* who are superior to L. in knowledge and skill but I doubt that anyone would employ his great art so appropriately and in such a balanced manner as one always saw L. doing.' Löwenstein 15 Jan. 1992.

2 NS 30 July 1968, 19 Jan. 1969, 3 Dec. 1990; BS to MS [10] May 1943, Nl MS; Marie-Gabriele, Countess Stauffenberg 16 Aug. 1985; BS to RB 27 May 1943, Nl RB; BS to RF 24 May [1943], Nl RF; *Spiegelbild* 305.

3 M.-G., Countess Stauffenberg 16 Aug. 1985; G. Frh. v. Fritsch in Kramarz 130; M., Count Stauffenberg 15 Aug. 1985; NS 10 Nov. 1991.

4 M.-G., Countess Stauffenberg 16 Aug. 1985; Herwarth 24 Aug. 1972.

5 M., Count Stauffenberg 4 June 1973, 21 July 1984; HCSt 1963 129; M., Count Stauffenberg 15 Aug. 1985 thought he had told ClS that most of the students in Munich could be mobilised against the regime. By 'the Führer principle' Stauffenberg meant authoritarian leadership.

6 Guttenberg, *Beim Namen* 176–177; Blomberg 24 July 1962; Partsch 3 March 1977; Herwarth, *Zwischen* 290–291.

7 Zeitzler 3, 26 July 1962 in Kramarz 130; Sachenbacher 12 July 1972; M., Count Stauffenberg 16 Aug. 1985; Bormann, 'Daten'; Junge/Linge; Bürker 18 Oct. 1972; ClS to Bürklin 9 June 1943, facsimile in Kramarz between 128 and 129; BA-Z Verleihungskartei; Phillips 15; the timing of Stieff's visit to before 8 June 1943 in Stieff 247 note 1 for letter no. 100 is not supported by the evidence cited

in I. Stieff, Hellmuth Stieff Bl. 75; Löwenstein 15 Jan. 1992; NS in Kramarz 130; Joest 7 June 1978; NS 10 Nov. 1991.

8 BS to MS from Munich [10] May 1943, Nl MS; M.-G., Countess Stauffenberg 16 Aug. 1985 whose mother's pocket diary dates the visit; RF, 'Bericht'; on Greece see also below pp. 218–219); on Hölderlin see W. Hoffmann, 'Neue' 43–48; W. Hoffmann, 'Stuttgarter' 12; Lohrer 289–300; BS to RB [before 21] April 1943, RB to BS 2 May 1943, StGA; Stettler 55.

9 NS Oct. 1962 in Kramarz 130; NS 15 Sept. 1964, 3 Dec. 1990; BA-Z 24 Feb. 1977; Bürklin in Kramarz 131; BS to MS [10] May 1943, Nl MS; Saucken 29 March 1965, 25 Nov. 1990.

10 BS to RF 24 May [1943], Nl RF; BS to RB 29 April 1943, Nl RB; ClS to RF 8, 25 June 1943, Nl RF; RF, Bericht has 'in May', which is incorrect.

11 RF 10 March 1977, 9 May 1977; ClS to RF 4 July 1943, Nl RF (the letter is dated from Munich but was sent from Lautlingen); Solomos, 'Gespräch', draft with ClS's ms. entries, StGA; Solomos, *Neugriechisches Gespräch*.

12 BS to RB 29 June [1943], Nl RB; M.-G., Countess Stauffenberg 16 Aug. 1985; NS 13 Aug. 1968; Lautlingen guest book; CS to TP 21 July 1943, PP; ClS to RF 20 July 1943, StGA; BS to ClS 6 Aug. 1943, carbon copy to RF in StGA.

13 Reinhardt 13 Sept. 1969, 1 July 1972; Kramarz 130; personnel file in NA RG 242; KTB Org. Abt. 6–10 June, 1–10 and 21–31 Aug. 1942; Zeller 238 based on RF as CM 291 established. Timing: RF recalls that ClS was asked and consented in May; CM 291; equally NS Oct. 1962 in Kramarz 130; NS 3 Dec. 1990; CM 336 based on Keilig 203 1942.

14 NS in HCSt 1963 129; NS 3 Dec. 1991 dates the first such utterance to end of April or beginning of May 1943; NS in Kramarz 132.

15 Zeitzler 3 July 1962; Kramarz 131 gives an inaccurate paraphrase of Zeitzler; Kleikamp 21 Jan. 1963 confirms ClS's desire to return to the front and dates ClS's request after his discharge from hospital; Anni Lerche, Olbricht's secretary, in Zeller 521 note 36; Kaiser, diary *passim*.

16 Kleikamp 21 Jan. 1963; Tresckow to his wife 9 July [1943], Nl Tresckow; Hofacker to his wife 17 Jan. 1943, Nl MS; Schwerin 303; H. Mertz, diary 22, 26 May 1944.

17 Manstein, 'Richtigstellung' denies that Tresckow sought to win him for a coup but allows for the timing Feb. 1943; according to R. v. Manstein 21 June 1991 there is no reference to Tresckow's visit in Manstein's private diary; Stahlberg in Scheurig, *Tresckow* 136–137; Stahlberg, *Pflicht* 281–282; Kaiser, diary 6 April 1943 based on information from Tresckow on that day; Kaiser, diary March–June 1943, particularly 29 March, 6, 7, 8 April, 9, 12, 15 May, 9 June, 29 July 1943; BA R 43 II/1092, R 43 II/985b; Rothfels, 'Briefe' 305 note 18; Stieff in *Spiegelbild* 87–88 and *Trial* XXXIII 307–308; I. Stieff to Ricarda Huch 17 July 1947; Stieff 170; Hassell 350; Gersdorff in Graml, 'Militäropposition' 473–474.

18 Kaiser, diary 6 April 1943; Hoffmann, *Widerstand* 363–366; W. Meyer 383–385.

19 Kaiser, diary 28 May 1943; Stieff in *Spiegelbild* 88; Schlabrendorff in *Spiegelbild* 401; Bussche 18 Sept. 1967.

20 Krebs 252–258; FDS to CvdS 10 June, 15 July 1943, Nl CvdS; Falkenhausen, 'Erinnerungen' 12–13; Teuchert 7–8; Kaiser, diary 14 May, 2 June, 1 July 1943;

Hassell 372; Gisevius II 259; Ritter, *Goerdeler* 337, 389–390, 404; Nebgen 164, 184, 198.

21　Teuchert 9; BA R 43 II/985a; Bürker, 'Im Wehrmachtführungsstab'; BDC personnel file on Rundstedt's aide, Major (Res.) and SS-Major Hans-Viktor von Salviati, with excerpts from his diary.

22　Kaiser, diary 7 June, 2–3 Aug. 1943; Hassell 382; Heinemann, *Rebell* 150–152; Hofacker to the Reich Finance Ministry 13 Oct. 1943, Nl Hofacker; Bargatzky 1–3; Falkenhausen, 'Erinnerungen' 5, 12; cf. Moltke, *Briefe* 541.

23　Hillgruber, Hümmelchen 175–176; *Hitlers Lagebesprechungen* 377; Hitler, *Weisungen* 233–241; Hillgruber, *Weltkrieg* 122–123, 128.

24　Kaiser, diary 29, 31 July 1943; Moltke, *Briefe* 512–519 expecting 'stormy days'; on operation 'Valkyrie', 31 July 1943, see below pp. 196–205.

25　Schwerin 317–319, 537 note 38; cf. Moltke, *Briefe* 523–524; Albrecht, 'Vorbereitungen'.

26　Kaiser, diary 29 July, 2 Aug. 1943.

27　Jettingen guest book; M.-G., Countess Stauffenberg 29 Aug. 1978, 16 Aug. 1985; Lautlingen guest book; BS to RB 29 June [1943], Nl RB; NS 13 Aug. 1968.

28　Schweizer 18 June 1965.

29　RF 10 March 1977; NS 3 Dec. 1990; CS to TP [25 Aug. 1943], PP: 'Bertholds back in Berlin – Claus too – operation postponed.' Albrecht, 'Vorbereitungen' and 27 Aug. 1967.

30　E. v. Tresckow 26 July 1971; M. Yorck 5 Sept. 1963; Husen 2 July 1963.

31　NS in Kramarz 135; NS 3 Dec. 1990; CM 295, 312–313 misdates several episodes.

32　Kaiser, diary 29 July 1943; Schwerin 319; 'Walküre' 31 Aug. 1943, BA-MA WK XVII/91.

33　Tresckow to E. v. Tresckow [4 July], 9 July [1943], Nl Tresckow; Ritter, *Goerdeler* 365, 539–540 notes 41, 43 based on information from E. v. Tresckow; E. v. Tresckow 26 July 1971; the offices of GFM v. Bock and Count Hardenberg (his personal aide) were in the building which served as the Federal Building (Bundeshaus) in Berlin after the war. L. v. Hammerstein 10 Dec. 1990; Schulenburg in *Spiegelbild* 88; E. v. Tresckow 1 May 1969.

34　Gersdorff, 'Beitrag'; Gersdorff in *Prozess* XX 680; Gersdorff, *Soldat* 134–136; Manstein, private diary 8 Aug. [1943]; Manstein, 'Richtigstellung'; cf. Manstein, *Soldat* 185.

35　Manstein, private diary 8 Aug. [1943]; excerpt with editorial changes affecting meaning in Manstein, *Soldat* 184–185; Kaiser, diary 6 Apr. 1943.

36　Stieff 173; Rothfels, 'Briefe' 305; Stieff's evidently false testimony in *Spiegelbild* 87–88, which CM 330–331 accepted.

37　Kaiser, diary 2 Aug. 1943; Stieff in *Spiegelbild* 87–88.

38　Goerdeler, 'Idee' 25; Ritter, *Goerdeler* 337.

39　Tresckow to E. v. Tresckow 13 Oct., 27 Nov. 1943; E. v. Tresckow 26 July 1971; HPA personnel files, NA RG 242; HPA/P3 list in NA T-78 roll 39/6000561; Tessin 7, 156–157; Manstein to his wife 25 Nov. 1943; R. v. Manstein 30 Nov., 30 Dec. 1963.

11. Planning the coup: internal preparations

1 Lautlingen guest book; BS to RB 10 Sept. 1943, StGA; BS to RF, telegram from Lautlingen 2 Sept. 1943, Nl RF, StGA; Thiersch 21 April 1943, 21 Jan. 1978; Moltke, *Briefe* 537. Lt.Col. Steltzer, with the military government in Norway, belonged to Moltke's 'Kreisau Circle' (named after Moltke's estate).

2 Tresckow had told Stieff in Feb. 1943 that it was his patriotic duty to use his access to Hitler to kill him. From a letter Stieff wrote to his wife on 6 Aug. 1943 she concluded that he had agreed to do this. I. Stieff 13 July 1947; I. Stieff, 'Hellmuth Stieff' 75; the indictment against Goerdeler has 'beginning September 1943'; the judgement on Goerdeler and *Spiegelbild* 532 date it to 'late autumn 1943'; in Goerdeler, 'Idee' 25 the time-frame is mid-Sept. to mid-Oct. 1943; Ritter 337 says 'in September' without source reference; [RF] in Zeller (1st edn) 185; AS, 'Der zwanzigste Juli 1944'; *Spiegelbild* 410–411; NA Hoffmann Collection Prints Box IV, Photo with Hitler entitled 'viewing new weapons 1 Oct. 43'; KTB Org. Abt. 3 Oct. 1943, NA T-78 roll 414/6382527–28 notes: 'Demonstration at the Führer's on 1 Oct. 43'; this concerned mainly anti-tank guns and circular field-of-fire guns; Boelcke 296–306; Stieff 170.

3 Löwenstein 15 Jan. 1992; BS to RB 10 Sept. 1943, StGA: 'Claus is much better. He is in Munich once more for an operation on his arm to prepare it for an artificial hand. He will be back on duty by about 1 November.'

4 ClS to RF 14 Sept. 1943, BS to RF 20 Sept. [1943], StGA; NS 12 Aug., 4 Nov. 1991; Handliste; Zeller (1st edn) 150, 154; Zeller 255–256; Reinhardt 1 July 1972; Keilig 211/266. Evidently in September Reinhardt had not yet shown ClS his job; BS to RB 1 May [1944], Nl RB: 'Claus has been back on duty since Oct and has got over his serious injuries amazingly well.'

5 Olga von Saucken 29 March 1965, 27 July 1972; Johnston 10 Aug. 1982.

6 Johnston 21 July 1972, 10 Aug. 1982, 16 Aug. 1991; Saucken 27 July 1972; BS to RF 16 Jan. [1944], StGA; BS to RB 1 May [1944], Nl RB; Jessen 26 Aug. 1946; Graf 28 Aug. 1978.

7 Johnston 21 July 1972, 10 Aug. 1982.

8 Bürker, 'Im Wehrmachtführungsstab'; Bürker to Reile from Wien-Miedling on 8 Nov. 1943: 'I saw Drewes here, quite his old self. Also my second successor has been patched back together and despite the loss of an eye and a hand he is busily active again.' Reile 17 [March] 1991; Liste I; BA-Z Personalkartei; Schick 5 Sept. 1991.

9 Sauerbruch 9 Feb. 1977; Leber, *Mann* 169; A. Leber in Kramarz 174 note 17; RF 15 July 1963. Leber apparently objected to the proposed new government's having a Christian colouring (*Spiegelbild* 234–235).

10 Yorck in Kramarz 137; Schwerin 326–327; indictment against Goerdeler; Leber, *Den toten* 11; Leber, *Mann* 290–291. ClS celebrated his birthday in Brücklmeier's flat; Schwerin 327. Captain (Res.) Count Schwerin was a farmer and landowner; he had been on Witzleben's staff from Nov. 1939, and from March 1943 on the 'Brandenburg' Division's staff in Berlin; on 1 May 1944 he moved to the General Staff/Quartermaster-General pass office in Grossadmiral-Prinz-Heinrichstrasse (now Hitzigallee) in Berlin (Schwerin 374, 460–461). Dr Brückl-

meier was a Legation Counsellor in the Foreign Office; D. Dr Gerstenmaier was a Counsellor of the Consistory in the Evangelical (Lutheran) Church's Foreign Bureau and a member of Moltke's 'Kreisau Circle'; Dr Goerdeler was the former Lord Mayor of Leipzig and Reich Prices Commissioner; Dr Jessen was a Professor of Political Science at the University of Berlin; Hassell was Ambassador in Rome until Feb. 1938; Professor Popitz was Prussian Minister of Finance; Maass was a Social Democrat and former Secretary of the Reich Committee of Youth Organisations. Dr Leber had been decorated for bravery in the First World War and was subsequently Member of the Reichstag for the SPD; Leuschner was a Social Democrat, 1929–1933 Minister of the Interior in Hesse, Trade Union Secretary; J. Kaiser was Secretary of the Christian trade unions in the Rhineland and Westphalia 1924–1933; Habermann was Chairman of the German National Shop Clerks' Association 1918–1933.

11 HCSt 2 Aug 1963, 28 July 1971, 5 July 1972; Moltke, *Briefe* 279, 454–458, 490 and *passim*; Moltke, Balfour, Frisby 156, 232–251; Steltzer 154–169; Roon 561–571; Kennan 121 (in 1940 Moltke already expected Germany to lose the war); in a memorandum dated 24 April 1941 (Roon 507–517) Moltke left no doubt that Germany would lose. Balfour, Frisby 184–185, 215–224, 271–273; F. v. Moltke 19 May 1991, 18. Feb. 1992; Moltke, *Völkerrecht* passim; W. Hoffmann 27 and 31 May 1977.

12 See p. 140 above.

13 Moltke, *Briefe* 450, 454, 519–520, 522, 537–541, 562–567, 573, 575, 580, 583, 588–589; F. v. Moltke 2–3 Dec. 1978, 19 May 1991; M., Countess Yorck 5 Sept. 1963, 25 Sept. 1983; Yorck, *Stärke* 61, 69; Furtwängler, *Männer* 215–216; John, 'Männer' (II, IV); A. Leber in Kramarz 136 (Schulenburg introduced ClS and Leber) contradicts *Spiegelbild* 210 (Goerdeler introduced ClS and Leber); Albrecht, *Sozialdemokrat* 213; NS 1 July 1964, 3 Dec. 1990; Moltke to G. Jaenicke in Moltke, *Völkerrecht* 289. Kramarz 138 cites W. v. Götz 5 Sept. 1962 for November, but the letter cited does not say this; K. Jessen 1962; Falkenhausen in Roon 336; Roon 317–322; Balfour, Frisby 270; Wengler; Hoffmann, *Widerstand* 279, 736 note 68a; Gerstenmaier 14 Jan. 1971.

14 Yorck, *Stärke* 58; RF 9 May 1977; Gerstenmaier 14 Jan. 1971; Moltke, Balfour, Frisby 186; Herwarth 24 Aug. 1972.

15 Moltke, *Briefe* 557 does not mention ClS; Johnston née Siemens 21 July 1972, 19 Aug. 1982, 16 Aug. 1991; M., Countess Yorck 3 May 1977, 25 Sept. 1983; Moltke, Balfour, Frisby 360 note 4; Sauerbruch 8 May 1986; F. v. Moltke 18–19 Aug. 1977; Moltke, *Briefe* 580.

16 Goerdeler, 'Idee' 25; Tresckow to E. v. Tresckow 13 Oct. 1943; E. v. Tresckow 26 July 1971; Tessin 7, 156–157; indictment against Goerdeler; Tresckow introduced ClS and Goerdeler before 10 Oct. 1943, the date he left for the front.

17 *Spiegelbild* 523.

18 K. Jessen 1962; Hassell 394, 399, 418, 608 note 9; Hoffmann, *Widerstand* 367–368.

19 Hassell 400; *Spiegelbild* 101, 409; Nebgen 198; on 11 July 1944 Goerdeler told ClS through H. Kaiser 'to break through forwards'; judgement against Kaiser in *Spiegelbild* 1984 729.

20 Goerdeler, 'Idee' 28; judgement against Kaiser in *Spiegelbild* 1984 728–729; Goerdeler in *Spiegelbild* 523; also *Spiegelbild* 118, 179, 212–213.

21 For this and the following paragraph: Roon 271, 274–275, 589–590; Nebgen 175–176; indictment against Thomas *et al.*; Hoffmann, *Widerstand* 447–448, 790–791 note 218; RF 19 Nov. 1985; Sänger, 'Stauffenberg' and 15 Dec. 1980; judgement against Saefkow *et al.*; judgement against Schmid; judgement against Thomas. On 15 July 1944 Mertz, and on the following day Stauffenberg and Mertz, stated that they had not established contacts with the Communists or the SS; Siebeck, 'Erinnerung'; Siebeck 17 April 1973, 5 Nov. 1980, 6 March 1981; they can only have meant that there were no working contacts. Gerstenmaier, 'Sie wollten' and 2 July 1979 says that Sänger's version is unsubstantiated, but bases his own objections on impressions and suppositions.

22 M., Countess Hardenberg 20 Aug. 1985; Rantzau; for Tresckow's transfer to the front see above p. 189.

23 M., Countess Hardenberg 26 Nov. 1961, Interview 1984, 20 Aug. 1985.

24 M., Countess Hardenberg 2 Dec. 1961, 20 Aug. 1985; StG, *GA* IX 114.

25 Albrecht, 'Vorbereitung'; Rantzau, 'Selbstmord'.

26 'Walküre II' 26 May 1942; Verwendungsbereitschaft des Ersatzheeres 13 Oct. 1942; Rüdt von Collenberg 3 Feb. 1964; H. Reinhardt 12 Nov. 1967, 1 and 2 July 1972; KTB Org. Abt. 6–10 June, 1–10 Aug., 21–31 Aug. 1942; Tagebuch BdE/Chef des Stabes Aufnahme 557. On 2 March 1942 Colonel (GS) Friedrich von Unger, Chief of the General Staff III Deputy Corps (Berlin), told Colonel (GS) Karl-Erik Koehler, Chief of Staff in General Army Office, that disturbances might be caused by the SS or by a change of mood in the population, so III Military District wanted approval for preparatory troop deployments; Koehler warned Unger against any 'independent' measures, adding that the SS alone should deal with disturbances, and 'the Walküre II formations were intended for unforeseen incidents'.

27 'Walküre' 31 July 1943; Zeller 303; Hoffmann, *Widerstand* 374–380.

28 Hoffmann, *Widerstand* 376–378; *Spiegelbild* 163; 'Walküre' 31 July, 6 Oct. 1943.

29 'Selbstmord'; Rantzau; Albrecht, 'Vorbereitung'; Pfuhlstein, 'Meine Tätigkeit'; *Wehrmacht-Fernsprechverzeichnis Gross-Berlin Teil II*; Hoffmann, *Widerstand* 383–384.

30 'Walküre' 11 Feb. 1944 in *Spiegelbild* 165–166; Koch-Erpach 28 March 1964; Hoffmann, *Widerstand* 768 note 169.

31 Boelcke 372; Speer, *Erinnerungen* 387–388; Hitler, *Weisungen* 255–264; for details of CIS's visits see below, pp. 238–240, 253, 256–260.

32 For this and the following: *Spiegelbild* 35–41, 68; 'Walküre' 31 July 1943; *Volksgerichtshof-Prozesse* 49–51; Hoffmann, *Widerstand* 415–428.

33 Hoepner quoting Olbricht in *Trial* XXXIII 397.

34 Olbricht in *Spiegelbild* 44; Ziegler 23 Aug. 1965; Hassell 338, 348, 350, 362; Kaiser, diary 20 Feb., 7 June, 19 July 1943; Dulles, *Germany's Underground* 149; Winterfeldt 30 Aug. 1966; Ritter 358–359; Blumentritt, 'Stellungnahme'; Colonel (ret.) J.R. in Kramarz 184–185; Kiessel 14; Gisevius II 331; CM 337 cites Ziegler in IfZ Slg Zeller.

35 *Spiegelbild* 145; indictment against Goerdeler *et al.*; judgement against Goerdeler

et al. in *Spiegelbild* 533; Hoffmann, *Widerstand* 439–441; J. Kaiser, 'Deutschlands Trennung'; Nebgen 140, 165, 177; Gisevius II 302–303 records some of Goerdeler's complaints against ClS; Ritter 366–369, 543 note 61, 618.

36 *Spiegelbild* 145, 305–307, 312–313; Herwarth, *Zwischen* 246; Hoffmann, *Widerstand* 381–383, 430–432; no one was nominated for military districts V and VI; for VII there was a liaison officer and a substitute.

37 *Spiegelbild* 258–259, 307, 312–313, 333–334, 435.

38 Mrs P. Sauerbruch 8 May 1986; *Spiegelbild* 373.

39 Liste I; *Spiegelbild* 372.

40 Sauerbruch, 'Bericht' 139–149.

41 See p. 145 above.

42 *Spiegelbild* 70–82; *Trial* XXXIII 403.

43 *Spiegelbild* 24–25; Witzleben's statement in *Spiegelbild* 42–43 that he had offered himself as c-in-c Army probably reflects a communication error; Hoffmann, *Widerstand* 897; on Göring's succession: BA Nl Hitler/23, R 43 II/1660 containing the law on the succession of the Führer and Reich Chancellor, 13 Dec. 1934; decree on the Führer's deputy, 23 April 1938; minute 11 March 1944.

44 *Spiegelbild* 75.

45 *Spiegelbild* 70–75; Schramm, *Aufstand* 139.

46 M., Countess Hardenberg 26 Nov. 1961.

47 Timing varies between beginning and end of October: RF, 'Bericht'; RF 15 July 1963, 10 March, 9 May 1977; RF, 'Zum 20. Juli'; RF 1962/63 in Zeller 327; AS, 'Der zwanzigste Juli 1944' III, 3; Zeller, 1st edn 182, 185.

48 See chapter 13 (Kleist's evidence, and Stieff's for July 1944).

49 Zeller 328.

50 RF, 'Bericht'; NS Oct. 1962, 1 July 1964, 3 Dec. 1990; Saucken 27 July 1972; RF 10 March, 9 May 1977.

51 RF 10 March, 9 May 1977.

52 Zeller 365, 528 note 29; StG, *GA* VIII 27.

53 *Spiegelbild* 41; RF, 'Bericht'.

54 *Spiegelbild* 24–26.

55 RF, 'Bericht' and in Zeller 328–329; RF 15 July 1963; Saucken 29 March 1965; Hoffmann, *Widerstand* 896–906 based on originals; Secret State Police copies printed in *Spiegelbild* 24–33; also *Spiegelbild* 139, 147–156, 199, 213, 235–239, 249, 265–270; on the authorship of the drafts see below, pp. 208–212.

56 Nebgen 173–174; Thüngen 25 Jan. 1946; RF in CM 307; Maass in *Spiegelbild* 205, 212, 465.

57 RF in Zeller 253–255 (not in the 1st edn); RF 9 May 1977, 6 Sept. 1979; BS in *Spiegelbild* 447–448, 453; see the 'Oath' in Appendix VI below, pp. 293–294; *Spiegelbild* 19; Gisevius II 302–303 identified the weak point – how the rulers were to be found – but his critique is overstated and hostile.

58 See ClS's correspondence with Sodenstern in appendix III; Thüngen 25 Jan. 1946; 'Oath' in Appendix VI, pp. 293–294.

59 *Spiegelbild* 205–206, 465; Goerdeler, 'Idee' 25; Nebgen 103.

60 'Oath' in appendix VI, pp. 293–294; *Spiegelbild* 212, 500; Schefold, 'Erinnerung' 3, 15 Oct. 1973, 9 Sept. 1981; Pezold 25 April 1965; RF 15 July 1963; cf. Leber, *Mann* 280–281.

61 *Spiegelbild* 205; Roon 589; Leber, *Mann* 280–281.
62 *Die deutsche Reichsverfassung* Art. 114, 115, 117, 118, 123, 124, 153; *RGBl.* I 1933 no. 17.
63 Pfohl 14 March 1957.
64 RF, 'Bericht'; RF in Zeller 362–363; RF, 'Zum 20. Juli'; RF 9 May 1977; *Spiegelbild* 131, 138–142, 147–156, 535–536; Thierack to Bormann 8 Sept. 1944 in Osas 98; Ritter 544 note 66; papers collected by H. R. Trevor-Roper while investigating Hitler's death, on film DJ38 prepared by David Irving, contain the 23rd copy (of 90) of 'Schriftstücke' – 'Papers found in "Hospiz am Askanischen Platz" in an envelope addressed to Dr Goerdeler' and registered as such by the Secret State Police under 3 August 1944, which are the drafts that Beck, Tresckow, ClS and RF had worked on; on Goerdeler's drafts see Ritter 373–374, 543–545 notes 64, 66; O. v. Saucken 29 March 1965.
65 RF in Zeller 362–363; RF, 'Zum 20. Juli'; RF 5 July 1962, 10 March 1977, 9 May 1977; *Spiegelbild* 131, 139–140, 200; Gisevius II 333–334; Thierack to Bormann 8 Sept. 1944 in Osas 97–99.
66 Judgement against Goerdeler in *Spiegelbild* 535–536; Thierack to Bormann 8 Sept. 1944 in Osas 98; *Spiegelbild* 199–203; Pechel 304–305; Nebgen 8.
67 'Presse. Regierungserklärung Nr. 2 (3. Fassung)' in 'Schriftstücke' 19–34; *Spiegelbild* 145–156, 249–255; Ritter 586–592; Thierack to Bormann 8 Sept. 1944 in Osas 94–97; Goerdeler, Rundfunkrede; Goerdeler, Regierungsprogramm.
68 'Schriftstücke' 12–18; *Spiegelbild* 213–217.
69 Report of the Secret State Police commission on '20.7.1944' (RSHA/Amt IV), dated 24 July 1944, *Spiegelbild* 33–34, also 448 (BS's testimony).
70 *Spiegelbild* 199–202; Thierack to Bormann 8 Sept. 1944 in Osas 98.

12. Contacts abroad

1 Christie's report of 1937 in Christie Papers CHRS 1/21 A; Conwell-Evans 91–92; Reynolds, *Treason* 11–115, 297 note 81; Hoffmann, 'Question'; *The Times* (Late London edn) 15 Aug. 1941 4 and 3 Jan. 1942 4; *FRUS* 1941 I 1–38; *The Conference at Washington, 1941–1942, and Casablanca, 1943* 362–376; *Parliamentary Debates* Fifth Ser., *House of Commons*, Vol. 377 col. 242–243 (20 Jan. 1942); *VB Norddeutsche Ausgabe* 5 Jan. 1942 1.
2 Hassell 267; Goerdeler, 'Aufzeichnung'; Goerdeler, 'Ausarbeitung', *Spiegelbild* 250, 411; judgement on Kaiser; Goerdeler, 'Idee' 33–40. Goerdeler cherished nearly identical hopes in May 1943, and May and Nov. 1944.
3 Leber, *Mann* 285; Kennan 121; Balfour, Frisby 184–186, 215–224, 271–273; Hofacker in *Spiegelbild* 136.
4 F. v. Moltke 24 July 1989; CvT 253; Roon 317–322.
5 Roon 254; Hillgruber, Hümmelchen 170, 174, 176; Moltke, *Briefe* 512–513.
6 Fleischhauer, *Chance* 110–112; Schwerin 299: through Brücklmeier they met in Kessel's flat at 4 Marienstrasse, where Brücklmeier lived.
7 Moltke, *Briefe* 568, 575; Hassell 382; Anderson 30 Oct. 1943.
8 F. W. Schulenburg in *Spiegelbild* 308–309.
9 Goerdeler in *Spiegelbild* 309, 360; Gisevius II 332–344.

10 Roon 317–322 (reporting only Moltke's opposition to assassination); Balfour, Frisby 270; Wengler; Hoffmann, *Widerstand* 279 and 736 note 68a.

11 Pogue 102–106, 339–343; Ehrman 8–10, 110, 389; Howard 629; Wedemeyer 245; Hinsley 3 44–45; CvT 231–232; Moltke, *Briefe* 575; DOGWOOD [= Alfred Schwartz] 14 Sept. 1943, F. v. Moltke's papers.

12 Krebs 177–178, 191, 209–234; Teuchert 8; Kaiser, diary 14 May, 2 June, 2 Aug. 1943; Hassell 372, 382.

13 Johnson (the American Chargé d'Affaires in Stockholm) to Secretary of State Hull 12 Sept. 1944, *FRUS* 1944 I 550–551; Anderson 17 Sept., 6 and 30 Oct. 1943; CvT 251; Hassell 418, 608 note 9; *Spiegelbild* 189. On British attempts to exploit Trott's feelers see Hoffmann, *Widerstand* 284–285, 290–291. ClS is said to have thought Papen might be a useful go-between for talks with the Allies: Friedrich, Count Pfeil (aide to Fromm) in *Prozess* XI 579; cf. Gottfried, Count Bismarck-Schönhausen in *Prozess* XII 581.

14 NS 23 Aug. 1969, 19 Jan. 1973; Dieckmann 30 Jan. 1979 reports the same rejection by ClS and Mertz for June 1944.

15 Hillgruber, Hümmelchen 185; Finker 167–170; Wegner-Korfes 539–542; Hoffmann, *Widerstand* 743–746 notes 132–139; Melnikow; see Appendix VII. Wegner-Korfes interpreted Mertz's references to 'Otto' (in letters to Hilde Baier, widow of Lieutenant-Colonel (Res.) Dr Otto Baier who had fallen on the eastern front on 9 May 1942, and whom Mertz married on 31 May 1944) as expressions of support for Otto Korfes's activities; but Mertz was referring to Lt-Col. Dr Otto Baier: Mertz to Hilde Baier 8 and 10 May 1944, BA-Abt. Potsdam Me6 Nl Mertz v. Quirnheim; Mertz to Hilde von Mertz 15 June 1944, and H. v. Mertz's diary 22 May 1945, H. v. Mertz's papers.

16 Kranzfelder in *Spiegelbild* 115–116.

17 Sauerbruch 12 Feb. 1963, 24 July 1964, 9 Feb. 1977, 15 April 1991; Sauerbruch, 'Bericht' 147–148; *Spiegelbild* 402–403; John, 'Bericht'; Michel 23 Aug. 1979; cf. Michel, *Ost* 40–52; Leber, *Mann* 286.

18 DOGWOOD 30 Dec. 1943, F. v. Moltke's papers; Brigadier Richard G. Tindall (American Military Attaché in Ankara) to Schwartz 29 Dec. and report 31 Dec. 1943, F. v. Moltke's papers; Colonel William Donovan (Director of OSS) to Roosevelt 29 July 1944, F.D.R. Library PSF OSS File.

19 Rothfels, 'Zwei' 394; Rothfels, 'Trott' 308, 318–322; Hoffmann, *Widerstand* 265–267, 285; 'Schriftstücke' 14; *Spiegelbild* 214. Moltke to Freya v. Moltke 7 Jan. 1944 in Moltke, *Briefe* 587 repeated what he had said to his contacts in Istanbul in July 1943 and also in a letter to Alexander Kirk, the American Minister in Cairo (whom he had known in Berlin) in December 1943, that Germany must undergo a rapid western occupation; Balfour, Frisby 271–273. The memorandum for transmission to the American authorities that resulted from Moltke's visit was drafted in German by Moltke's friends Professors Hans Wilbrandt (OSS codename HYAZINTH) and Alexander Rüstow, then translated into English. The present author has followed the German original draft from the papers of F. v. Moltke. Roon 582–586 reproduces the original version; the English translation appears in Balfour, Frisby 273–277; Moltke, Balfour, Frisby 264–268 contains a re-translation from English into German.

20 Donovan to Roosevelt 29 July 1944, F.D.R. Library PSF OSS File; *FRUS* 1943

I 680, 687, 737, 752–754; *FRUS* 1944 I 510–513; Tindall, report 29 Dec. 1943, DOGWOOD 30 Dec. 1943, Tindall to Schwartz 31 Dec. 1943, papers of F. v. Moltke.

21 Kranzfelder in *Spiegelbild* 116; Dr v. Mertz, pocket diary 1943; H. Mertz, 'Albrecht Ritter Mertz von Quirnheim'.

22 Ambassador Ritter to Minister Richert 23 Nov. 1943, Richert to Ritter 25 Nov. 1943. The Swedish legation moved temporarily to Alt Döbern: Kungliga Utrikesdepartement Stockhom H 60 G/Allm. Göteborgstrafiken 1 March–15 May 1944; Jessen to Graf 26 Aug. 1946, Graf 28 Aug. 1978; BS to RF 16 Jan. [1944], StGA; BS to RB 1 May [1944], Nl RB.

23 Goerdeler, 'Idee' 29; *Spiegelbild* 126–127, 247–248; H. Kaiser in *Spiegelbild* 126: ClS had 'two contacts with the English side'. P[ro] M[emoria]; 'Verhandlungen'; Graf 28 Oct. 1950; Graf 7 April 1978; J. Wallenberg 16 Sept. 1977; Mårtensson, with a photograph of Östberg displaying the guest book which has Kranzfelder's signature but not BS's; Ståhle to Post 5 Jan. 1944, Kungliga Utrikesdepartement Stockholm H 60 G/Allm. Göteborgstrafiken 1 Jan.–29 Feb. 1944.

24 Minister Leitner, minute 17 Feb. 1944, AA/PA Rechtsabteilung/Völkerrecht, Rotes Kreuz Nr. 9, Hilfstätigkeit ausländischer Wohltätigkeitsorganisationen in Griechenland aus Anlass des Krieges, vol. 16; Hoffmann, 'Roncalli' 77–82; Hoffmann, 'Stauffenberg und George' 542; BS to RB 1 May [1944], Nl RB.

25 John, *Zweimal* 85–93, 107, 139–140; Beaulac 200.

26 John, *Zweimal* 139–141, 147–148; Dulles, telegrams 1888–9 and 1890–3 from Berne dated 27 Jan. 1944, CIA/OSS Archive; Beaulac 201–202.

27 John, *Zweimal* 148; John, 'Bericht'; John, 'Zum Jahrestag' 5; John, 'Some Facts' 41–47; John, *Zweimal* 156–158. Klemperer 352 says ClS was without illusions due to John's reports; but John reproached himself for having failed to convince ClS that he could not, as ClS demanded, provide for direct talks with Eisenhower, soldier to soldier, after the coup: John, 'Some Facts' 41–47; John, *Zweimal* 155–160; Lamb 288.

28 Malone 215; Moltke, Balfour, Frisby 282 and note 5 confuse the provenance of Moltke's remark; Balfour had it from C. Bielenberg in 1970: Balfour, Frisby 291 and note 4. Kramarz 138 says H.-B. v. Haeften had introduced ClS to Trott, but the source he cites (Waltraut von Götz, a cousin of Trott's, to Kramarz 5 Sept. and 24 Nov. 1962) does not say this; Yorck in *Spiegelbild* 110 says that Trott became familiar with ClS through W. v. Haeften; see also *Spiegelbild* 440, 505; Ziegler 1963. Trott was in Stockholm from 27 Oct.–3 Nov. 1943; CvT 251; Lindgren 278–279.

29 CvT 261–262.

30 Kessel 253–254.

31 CvT 260–262; Trott to CvT 23 April 1944, papers of CvT; Götz 5 Sept. 1962.

32 Götz 5 Sept. 1962; *Spiegelbild* 110, 126–127, 247–248; 367, 507; Goerdeler, 'Idee' 29 mentioned a 'representative of Churchill' in Madrid and a 'representative of Roosevelt' in Berne, while the ground for contacts with Russia was prepared through Wallenberg in Stockholm. The last reference may refer to Dulles; the Madrid reference may reflect a misunderstanding of John's efforts which had remained entirely unsuccessful on the British side. John, *Zweimal* 147.

33 *Trial* XXXIII 422–423; *Spiegelbild* 136.

34 Papers of CvT; Lindgren 281; *Spiegelbild* 175.
35 Lindgren 281, 289–291 (text of memorandum); Morgenthau, *passim*. One can only marvel at the accuracy of the memorandum's predictions, although the movement based on the Hitler legend remained quite weak during most of the post-war years.
36 See below p. 223. There are sources referring to attempts by intermediaries, particularly Willy Brandt, to put Trott in contact with the Soviet Embassy in Stockholm; none alleges that Trott sought the contact or that contact was made; some say Trott cancelled whatever arrangement had been made, others say the Soviets refused to have any contact with Trott: Cole 72–82 (calling the report of the American Chargé d'Affaires in Stockholm, Herschel V. Johnson, in *FRUS* 1944 I 523–525 an 'overly abbreviated form' of his own 'long and urgent telegram' of 26 June 1944, which has not been found in NA); Scott, 'Mail Story' 17 Sept. 1944; CvT 252–253; Gerstenmaier 2 July 1979. Klemperer 340 believes that 'no doubt' Trott sought out Ambassador Kollontay and even states that 'the visit to Mme Kollontay had been arranged upon Trott's initiative', without offering evidence.
37 Speidel, *Invasion* 91–93; Eberbach 11 April 1967; *Spiegelbild* 175.
38 Ruge 11 June, 2 and 13 July 1944; Ose 197; Irving, interview with Colonel Hans Lattmann, OC II Btl. no. 67 Art. Rgt, in Irving, Selected Documents Film 97049/3; G. Falkenhausen, 'Erinnerungen' 18; *Spiegelbild* 136; Speidel, *Invasion* 133.
39 Ruge 13 July 1944 with later addition, and 17 July 1944; A. Falkenhausen, 'Bericht' 38; G. Falkenhausen, 'Erinnerungen' 19; Irving, interview with Warning 11 Dec. 1976, in Irving, Selected Documents Film 97049/3; Irving, *Trail* 413; Ose 190–191, 334–340; Speidel, *Invasion* 136–141.
40 G. Falkenhausen, 'Erinnerungen' 18; *Spiegelbild* 136.
41 Hillgruber, Hümmelchen 217, 221; Niepold 9 and *passim*; *KTB OKW* IV 858–859; Ruge 13 July 1944; Ose 190–191, 199, 334–340.
42 Papers of CvT; RF 15 July 1963; U. Thiersch 1949 in Zeller 361.
43 Goerdeler, 'Idee' 29; Hammerstein, *Spähtrupp* 291; Krebs 291–292.
44 Plassmann 10 March 1947; H. Mertz 31 Jan. 1980.
45 *Spiegelbild* 56–57, 91–92, 101, 111, 174–176.
46 *Spiegelbild* 111, 198; 'Schriftstücke' 16.

13. Assassination plans

1 *Spiegelbild* 89–90, 128, 178, 194; I. Stieff 13 July 1947; RF 10 March, 9 May 1977; RF to W. Baum 25 July 1962, IfZ ZS 1790; Gehlen 3 Sept. 1972; Weniger, 'Vorgeschichte' 490; Zeller (1st edn) 189; Hammerstein, *Spähtrupp* 235; Kleist 4 Dec. 1990; Bussche, 'Eid' 4; Husen 2 July 1963, 16 Jan. 1968.
2 I. Stieff 13 July 1947; I. Stieff, 'Hellmuth Stieff' 75; indictment against Goerdeler *et al.*; judgement on Goerdeler *et al.*; Goerdeler, 'Idee' 25; Zeller 525 note 1.
3 *Spiegelbild* 89–90; Gichtel; *Trial* XXXIII 308–310, 314; Org. Abt. (IIIb), Beitrag zum KTB 3 Oct. 1943, NA T-78 roll 414/6382528; Boelcke 296–301; Schlabrendorff 121; RF in Zeller 327; cf. Hillgruber, Hümmelchen 189–190.

4 Kleist 14 Feb. 1946.

5 RF 9 May 1977; RF in Zeller 362; Ritter 337.

6 Schlabrendorff 124–125 with confused chronology; Keilig 211/51.

7 For this and the following: Bussche 1 March 1966, 18 Sept. 1967, 25 Aug. 1978, 29 Aug. 1980, 19 July 1984, 26 Oct. 1985, 27 Nov. and 2 Dec. 1990, 29 March 1991; BA-Z, Militärische Dienstlaufbahn Frhr. von dem Bussche-Streithorst (Axel) 26 May 1970 and 24 Jan. 1991; Bussche's Soldbuch; Weizsäcker 8 May 1995; Hoffmann, *Widerstand* 399–400 and note 49; *Trial* XXXI 446–448; Groeben 29 March 1991; Krebs 259; Herzer 21 Aug. 1991.

8 Bussche, 'Eid'; Bussche 2 July 1948 in Records 1147–1149; Bussche in 'Freiheitskämpfer'; Bussche 9 Feb. 1966, 29 Aug. 1980, 2 Dec. 1990.

9 *Spiegelbild* 129; Bussche 27 Aug. 1978, 29 March and 16 Aug. 1991; Bussche, 'Eid'; Bussche in 'Freiheitskämpfer'.

10 I. Stieff, 'Hellmuth Stieff' gives 20 Nov. 1943 as the date when Stieff arrived at Thalgau near Salzburg for his 'short period of leave', and notes that he visited his parents-in-law at Mittelsteine Kreis Glatz in Silesia from 23 to 27 Dec. 1943; presumably Stieff had returned to 'Mauerwald' at the end of November.

11 Groeben 29 March, 16 Aug. 1991; Bussche 16 Aug. 1991; *VB* Berlin edn 25 Nov. 1943 4.

12 Hagen 15 Jan. 1972; Bussche 9 Feb. 1966, 18 Sept. 1967, 27 Aug. 1978, 27 Nov. 1990, 29 March and 16 Aug. 1991; Bussche in Records 1148; Hoffmann, 'Warum' 458; *Spiegelbild* 55, 89, 128–129, 194, 318–319; Hagen in the People's Court on 7 Aug. 1944, *Trial* XXXIII 330–333; I. Stieff, 'Hellmuth Stieff'; Stieff in *Trial* XXXIII 311; Kleist 14 Sept. 1967; Dönhoff 25 April 1991. Stieff and Hagen sought to obfuscate the chronological link between the procurement of explosives and Bussche's presence at 'Mauerwald' and claimed the explosives had not been usable in any case; and Bussche was never mentioned.

13 Gottberg 22 April 1966; Bussche 9 Feb. 1966, 18 Sept. 1967, 16 Aug. 1991.

14 BA-Z Personalkartei; Bussche in 'Freiheitskämpfer'; Bussche 18 Sept. 1967, 27 Aug. 1978, 27 Nov. 1990; 16 Aug. 1991; John, *Zweimal* 141. Schwerin 334 (without source ref.; on 31 Dec. 1991 to the author he named Bussche as the source) said Stieff had sent Bussche back to his battalion and had *put him off* until January.

15 Hagen in *Trial* XXXIII 333. Hoffmann, *Widerstand* 403 did not distinguish between the two procurements of Nov. and Dec.

16 Indictment against Goerdeler; judgement on Goerdeler in *Spiegelbild* 533. Confirmations: Gisevius, 'Bericht' 28 for 26 Dec.; see also Gisevius II 321; Leonrod (for 19–25 Dec.) in *Spiegelbild* 54, 262, 321; Kessel 1944/45 253–257, in Schwerin 334, and Schwerin to the author 1 Sept. 1991 based on Kessel's pocket diary (between 12 Dec. and Christmas on the occasion of an expected visit by Hitler to Zossen); H. Mertz, 'Albrecht'; Dr v. Mertz, pocket diary 1943; Herzer 21 Aug. 1991. Some circumstances suggest that by Christmas the opportunity was no longer expected to materialise at that juncture: ClS was at Bamberg with his family 24–26 Dec.; BS was in Lautlingen 24–27 Dec.; Stieff was in Mittelsteine Kreis Glatz in Silesia with his parents-in-law and his wife; F.-D. Schulenburg was with his family in Trebbow for Christmas; Schwerin was with his family in Göhren. NS 31 Aug. 1972; Heimeran Stauffenberg 18 June 1986; BS to RF 16

Jan. [1944]; CS to TP 5 Jan. 1944, PP; I. Stieff, 'Hellmuth Stieff'; Schwerin 540 note 28; Schwerin 31 Dec. 1991.

17 Indictment against Goerdeler. Gisevius II 321 erroneously stated that the assassination had by then been indefinitely postponed because ClS's group wanted to 'give Hitler a last chance to beat back the invasion'; this is absurd in view of the events described below.

18 Gersdorff 9 June 1962; Tresckow in *Spiegelbild* 88; Hitler, *Lagebesprechungen* 380; Rommel, 'Tagesberichte' 1943; Hoffmann, *Widerstand* 413–414.

19 Weizsäcker [May 1970]; BA-Z Personalkartei; Bussche in 'Freiheitskämpfer'.

20 Kleist 27 Nov. and 4 Dec. 1990, 10 July 1991; Kleist to AS 14 Feb. 1946 (28 Jan.); Kleist to Kunrat v. Hammerstein 14 May 1944 (end of Jan.), Hammerstein, pocket diary; Hammerstein, *Spähtrupp* 235; Bussche 25 Aug. 1978, 16 Aug. 1991.

21 Kleist in Zeller 1st edn 190; Kleist 14 Sept. 1967, 10 July 1991. On the matter of chronological confusion see Hoffmann, *Stauffenberg* 583 note 58. On the production of German plastic explosive see Hoffmann, *Widerstand* 413–414; perhaps Kleist was offered the other half of the explosive that was found and confiscated at 'Mauerwald' on 28 Nov. 1943.

22 Kleist in Hammerstein, *Spähtrupp* 235; Kleist in Zeller 1st edn 190; Kleist 19 July 1964, 14 Sept. 1967, 10 July 1991. ClS said at one point that the delay could be varied, which would imply acid fuses or the rifle grenade which Tresckow offered to Breitenbuch in March; see below, pp. 231–232.

23 Kleist in Zeller 1st edn 190; Kleist 10 July 1991; Stieff in *Spiegelbild* 90; decrees on Hitler's successor 1934–1944 in BA NS 20/129, Nl Hitler/23 and R 43 II/1660; *Trial* xxxi 222; Domarus 1316; see below, pp. 258–262.

24 *Spiegelbild* 90; Schlabrendorff 1946 121; Sauerbruch 9 Feb. 1977, 21 Sept. 1983; R. Müller 4 April 1947; Roon 157–158; Gollwitzer, Kuhn, Schneider 175; Barbara von Haeften (Hans-Bernd's widow) 26 Aug. 1991.

25 Schlabrendorff 123–124.

26 Breitenbuch 8 Sept. 1966; Ritter 365.

27 Diary of NS's mother.

28 Breitenbuch 8 Sept. 1966; Hoffmann, *Widerstand* 407–410. Degner 24, 25 Aug. 1965, 14 Oct. 1966, 1 Oct. 1968 and Burchardt 13 July 1965 (section heads in Fellgiebel's command) report a plan to shoot down Hitler's plane around 20 March; it failed because Hitler decided to go by train instead.

29 Sauerbruch, 'Bericht' 145–148; Sauerbruch 12 Feb. 1963, 25 July 1964, 9 Feb. 1977, 15 April 1991; *Spiegelbild* 404.

30 Husen 2 July 1963, 16 Jan. 1968.

31 *Spiegelbild* 522; Schramm, *Aufstand* 192–203; Lotte von Hofacker (Cäsar's widow) to MS 4 Sept. 1945, Nl MS; W. Wagner 688–691; Hardenberg 1945; Hausmann 23 Dec. 1945; M. Klausing 1 Sept. 1980; R. Hardenberg 20 Oct. 1946; *Trial* xxxiii 431.

14. Launching the insurrection

1 Kleist 14 Feb. 1946; see above, p. 153.

2 Lerchenfeld, Kalender 29 April–1 May 1944; NS 12 Aug. 1991; Schwerin 379; *Spiegelbild* 417; Hardenberg.

3 LT, 'Aufzeichnungen' reproduces this in quotation marks, i.e. as a near-verbatim statement.
4 Ziegler, 'Bericht'; similarly Topf.
5 Oppen 11 Aug. 1984.
6 Hausmann 23 Dec. 1945; Oppen 11 Aug. 1984; Krebs 291–292; Zeller 523 note 31 based on information from Bussche (see below pp. 243–246, 294–295); CvdS 12 Aug. 1963, 15 Aug. 1990; Tisa Schulenburg 124.
7 BS to RF 7 April [1944], StGA; RF 4 Sept. 1977; Dette to F 2 Feb. 1938, StGA.
8 Wussow; Schwerin 362–363, 462. 'Abolish the military' was ironic hyperbole: what Stauffenberg meant was that there was no need to tell Fromm everything.
9 Speer 13 July 1972; Speer, *Erinnerungen* 388.
10 Hammerstein, *Spähtrupp* 209; Schlabrendorff 137–137; Kramarz 184–185; Kiessel; Hopf to Bormann 10 March [1945], *Spiegelbild* 1984 756–759; C. Hardenberg 1945; Hoffmann, *Widerstand* 463–464.
11 Keilig 55 II 2. Nikolaus, Count Üxküll, wrote to Theodor Pfizer on 20 June 1944 (TP's papers) that ClS had become a colonel and Chief of Staff to Fromm, 'a position appropriate to a general'.
12 Mertz to A. Zacharias 14 Jan. [1942]; Mertz to H. Baier 2 March 1944; HPA Personalkartei; cf. above, pp. 108–110.
13 Mertz to H. Baier 11 May 1944, H. Mertz's papers; Mertz to H. Baier 13/15 May 1944; H. Mertz, diary 22 May 1944; HPA Karteiblatt in NA RG 242 201 Files of General Staff Officers records 20 May 1944 as the day of Mertz's new posting and departure; Mertz to H. Baier, telegram from Vienna [21 May 1944]: 'Posted to Berlin. Fly east from Vienna tomorrow. Hope for leave soon.' Mertz to A. Zacharias 21 June 1944: '4 weeks ago I was posted to OKH in Berlin.'
14 H. Mertz, diary 24 and 25 May 1944.
15 G. Wagner 17 Nov. 1964; Liste I; Schick 5 Sept. 1991; judgement against Klamroth; Klamroth, Hagen, Stieff in *Trial* XXXIII 311, 328–329, 334–334, 339; KTB 10. Pz. Div. Ic, Tätigkeitsbericht 22 March–19 April 1943; *Spiegelbild* 55, 94. There must have been a further consignment, since on 20 July 1944 ClS used hexonite, not the regular German Army issue material; *Spiegelbild* 55.
16 H. Mertz, diary 20, 23, 26, 30 May, 9–11 June 1944; H. Mertz, 'Albrecht Ritter Mertz von Quirnheim'; Plassmann 10 March 1947; H. Mertz 31 Jan. 1980; Mertz to H. Mertz 13 June 1944; Mertz to H. Mertz 17 June 1944.
17 Wussow.
18 Bracke 173, 178–181, 183.
19 Hagen in *Trial* XXXIII 339; judgement on Kaiser in *Spiegelbild* 1984 728; Hoffmann, *Stauffenberg* (German edn) 586 note 35 discusses some further evidence.
20 Schlabrendorff 128–129; Boeselager 19 Nov. 1964, 21 Sept. 1983, 25 June 1984; Hobe 98–101.
21 RF in Zeller 364–365; RF 19 Nov. 1985; Thiersch 21 April 1953; there may be confirmation in the fact that W. v. Haeften wrote to Sauerbruch, two or three weeks before 20 July, that ClS was thinking of doing it himself; Sauerbruch in Kramarz 189.
22 Husen 2 July 1963, 16 Jan. 1968.
23 Herber 25 Jan. 1966.
24 Lerchenfeld, Kalender 1–6 June 1944; NS 1 July 1964, 11 Sept. 1968, 12 Aug.

1991; Herber 25 Jan. 1966; Peschel in *Spiegelbild* 1984 666; *Spiegelbild* 91; Speer, *Erinnerungen* 388.

25 Boelcke 377–379.

26 Herber 25 Jan. 1966 gave the (apparently incorrect) date of 11 June, evidently thinking it was a Sunday; but Corpus Christi Day is the Thursday after Trinity, and ClS can hardly have stayed at Berchtesgaden for several days.

27 Stieff in *Spiegelbild* 90–91, 130.

28 Schlabrendorff 129; Hillgruber, Hümmelchen 217, 221; Niepold 9 and *passim*; Leber, *Den toten* 11–12; Leber, *Mann* 292; RF, 'Zum 20. Juli'; Thiersch, 'Bericht'; Thiersch 21 April 1943, Nl RF; see above p. 196.

29 Hendrichs; NS 12 Aug. 1991; NS to Kramarz [10] Oct. 1962 dating the occasion July 1944; Momm 206.

30 Lerchenfeld, Kalender 24–26 June 1944; Sauerbruch, *Leben* 552–554. These memoirs are inaccurate in many details; 550–551 they mention a bullet that had remained stuck in ClS's head, which NS 11 Sept. 1968 declared had never happened; but ClS's driver Schweizer confirmed the visit to Sauerbruch's some time in June 1944; P. Sauerbruch 9 Feb. 1977 confirmed his father's assessment of ClS's physical condition.

31 AS to Partsch 3 Nov. 1941, Partsch's papers; AS to TP 10/23 Nov. 1941, PP; [AS], 'Deutsche'.

32 Bracke 100–101; AS to RF 23 Jan. 1943, Nl RF; AS to TP 13 April 1943, PP; AS to BS 24 June 1943, StGA; AS to CS 11 Oct. 1943, Nl AS; [AS], 'Deutsche'; CS to TP 5 Jan. 1944, PP; Siegfried Lauffer in AS, *Macht* 433; BS to RB 1 May [1944], Nl RB dates AS's wounding 'on the Dnieper' erroneously to Nov. 1943; Melitta, Countess Stauffenberg, in Bracke 129; AS to TP 8 Feb. 1944, PP; BS to RF 7 April 1944, Nl RF; Marlene, Countess Stauffenberg 15 Feb. 1992.

33 BS to RB 1 May [1944], Nl RB; RF 4 Sept. 1977, 6 Sept. 1979, 19 Nov. 1985; AS, *Dichtung*; *Rangliste 1944/45* 37, 322; BS to RF 10 June [1944], StGA; [AS] 'Deutsche'.

34 BS to RF 7 April, 10 June [1944], StGA; BS to AS [10 April 1944], StGA; RF 4 Sept. 1977, 19 Nov. 1985; RF, 'Zum 20. Juli'; Cords 24 Oct. 1967.

35 RF, 'Zum 20. Juli'; Appel 15 April 1946, 12 Aug. 1948, 14 March 1957; see above pp. 202, 209–210; Schwerin 379. M. Appel destroyed remaining copies of drafts for the coup on 21 July 1944. When she was subsequently interrogated by Admiral Judge Dr Curt Eckhardt and by the Gestapo she was able to explain RF's visit by the *Odyssey* translation in her desk-drawer.

36 Thiersch, 'Bericht'; Richthofen 28 Nov. 1978; Ziegler, 'Bericht'; RF, 'Zum 20. Juli'; Thiersch, 21 April 1953, Nl RF; Thiersch 21 Jan. 1978.

37 Sauerbruch 9 Feb. 1977.

38 ClS to the wife of B. v. Pezold, who had been taken prisoner at Stalingrad, in Kramarz 201.

39 Leber, *Das Gewissen steht auf* 126; MS was the source: HCSt 7 May 1981.

40 Hofacker to his wife [17 July 1944], Nl Hofacker.

41 Thiersch, 'Bericht'; Thiersch 21 Jan. 1978; RF in Zeller 365; Winterfeldt 30 Aug. 1966; Ziegler, 'Bericht'; John 1971.

42 RF, 'Zum 20. Juli'; RF 9 May 1977, 19 Nov. 1985; Appel 15 April 1946, 14 March 1957; see pp. 244–245 for facsimile text and Appendix VI for translation of Stauffenberg's 'Oath'.

43 RF in Zeller 364.
44 AS to RB 8 May 1945, StGA; RF in Zeller 364, 366; *Der Tod des Meisters*, Delfinverlag, Munich 1945.
45 See Wolfskehl, *Gesammelte Werke* I 280–281.
46 Athenaeus VII 223–225.
47 Hoffmann, *Widerstand* 448; Leber, *Den toten* 11–12; Leber, *Mann* 292; RF, 'Zum 20. Juli'; Thiersch, 'Bericht'; Thiersch 21 April 1953, Nl RF, and 21 Jan. 1978.
48 See above pp. 198–200; Directive No. 51 of 3 Nov. 1943 in Hitler, *Weisungen* 233–238; Bürklin 15 July 1962.
49 See above pp. 198–200.
50 Keilig 211/278; Albrecht, 'Vorbereitungen'; Mitzkus, 'Um den 20. Juli'.
51 Mitzkus, 'Um den 20. Juli'; cf. *Spiegelbild* 196.
52 Mitzkus, 'Bericht'; Mitzkus, 'Um den 20. Juli'; Stirius; *Spiegelbild* 196; Ritgen, 'Schulen' 104–195; Rothkirch 14 Jan. 1989; Hoffmann, *Widerstand* 477, 893.
53 Ritgen, 'Schulen' 104–195; Rothkirch 14 Jan. 1989.
54 *Spiegelbild* 40; see above pp. 200–209.
55 *Wehrmacht-Fernsprechverzeichnis Gross-Berlin* Part II 1943 37, 41, 43; Keilig 211/267; Zeller 351 without source reference.
56 Heinz, 'Offener Brief'; M. Hase 3 March 1964; Gisevius II 317.
57 Heinz, 'Offener Brief'.
58 Pfuhlstein, 'Tätigkeit'; Pfuhlstein, '12 Abhandlungen'; Lahousen, 'Sidelights'; Lahousen, 'Zur Vorgeschichte'; Heinz, 'Von Wilhelm Canaris'; Heinz 8 March 1966; Leverkuehn; Erasmus 29 Aug. 1965; *Spiegelbild* 370–371, 405–406; M. Schwerin, 'Ulrich-Wilhelm Graf Schwerin von Schwanenfeld'; Handliste der Generalstabsoffiziere 1943; cf. Hoffmann, *Widerstand* 343–344; Schwerin 374, 461.
59 *Spiegelbild* 372; HPA-Liste.
60 'Selbstmord'.
61 Stirius 2 Feb. 1967; *Spiegelbild* 158; 'Selbstmord'; Mitzkus, 'Um den 20. Juli'.
62 Stirius 2 Feb. 1967.
63 Therefore this force would not have been available for Stauffenberg's previous attempts in July to overthrow Hitler.
64 Boeselager, *Widerstand* 21.
65 Boeselager 28 Aug. 1969; Boeselager, *Widerstand* 21–23.

15. Uprising

1 Peschel; *Spiegelbild* 130; Speer, *Erinnerungen* 387–388; Boelcke 372; Hitler, *Weisungen* 255–264.
2 Boelcke 385, 397; *Spiegelbild* 90, 130. Kopkow-Cordes (head of the investigating commission at the scene of the 20 July attack) recalled in 1946 that Stieff was to carry out the attack on 10 July; *Trial* XXXIII 313, 319–320; H. Mertz, diary 3–4 July 1944, 15 July 1945 (noting that on 15 July CIS had gone down that horrible road in vain for the *third* time); Thiersch, 'Bericht'.
3 *Spiegelbild* 17, 21, 44, 49, 91, 130, 329–330; Haeften to NS 11 July 1944, Nl CIS; Gisevius II 295, 321, 339–340; Hausmann 13 Sept. 1980; H. Mertz, diary 15 July 1944; cf. above pp. 221–223 on Kluge and Rommel; Verfügung 7 Dec. 1934, BA NS 20/129; *Trial* XXXI 222; Gesetz über den Nachfolger des Führers und

Reichskanzlers 13 Dec. 1935; Erlass über die Stellvertretung des Führers 23 April 1938; Aufzeichnung 11 March 1944; all in BA Nl Hitler/23 and R 43 II/1660; Domarus 1316; Linge, 'Record'; Himmler, appointments diary and notebook; Heusinger 9 Sept. 1967; Puttkamer 10 Sept. 1967.

4 Peschel; *Trial* XXXIII 319–320, 358–359, 384–394, 427, 432–433, 437; *Spiegelbild* 44, 49, 91, 125, 130, 146; Klausing to Hausmann 12 July 1944, Hausmann 23 Dec. 1945, 13 Sept. 1980. Stieff also claimed that on 11 July he had prevented the attack by 'not letting Stauffenberg out of his sight'.

5 *KTB OKW* IV 1754 note 1; Kramarz 191; *Spiegelbild* 125 has the meeting at the 'Berchtesgadener Hof'; Hoffmann, *Widerstand* 470.

6 Gisevius II 290–292, 295–296.

7 Gisevius II 299–300, 304–305; Gisevius, 'Bericht' does not mention the events of 12 July; see Appendix VII, pp. 296–297; Hoffmann, *Widerstand* 453.

8 Gisevius II 298, 300–305.

9 Ibid. 306.

10 Truppenkrankenbuch; Gisevius II 306–307.

11 Gisevius II 310–313.

12 Kramarz 201.

13 Hoffmann, 'Zu dem Attentat' 257; Hoffmann, *Widerstand* 471.

14 Geisberg; Streve; *Spiegelbild* 1984 179; Hoffmann, 'Zu dem Attentat' 258–264.

15 *Spiegelbild* 130; Klausing in *Trial* XXXIII 432; Hammerstein, *Spähtrupp* 269; Thiersch 21 Jan. 1978; RF, 'Zum 20. Juli'; Sauerbruch, *Leben* 431.

16 *Field Engineering* 7; *British Booby Traps* 21–23; Hoffmann, 'Warum' 457–459; *Spiegelbild* 94.

17 Himmler, notebook 15 July 1944; Peschel; *Spiegelbild* 49–50.

18 Geisberg.

19 *Spiegelbild* 21, 130.

20 H. Mertz, diary 15 July 1944, 15 July 1945; *Spiegelbild* 158–159.

21 *Spiegelbild* 329–330; Stieff in *Spiegelbild* 91; Heusinger 330; Warlimont 469. Fromm's presence may have been another hindrance: it may have been more than a coincidence that Zeitzler was ill and that Fromm stayed in Berlin on 20 July; Heusinger's irritation because he had not been warned (Heusinger 6 Aug. 1964) points in that direction.

22 Geisberg; *Trial* XXXIII 319–320; Gisevius disclosed immediately after his escape from Germany to Switzerland in Jan. 1945, as Dulles cabled to Washington on 28 Jan. 1945 with minor inaccuracies (Dulles to Donovan 28 Jan. 1945, OSS archive): '2 prior coups had been planned, 1 failed on July 6 in Munich due to Hitler's sudden departure and further attempt on July 16 in East Prussia, failed when Stauffenberg's collaborator, General Stieff lost his nerve.' Only later in his book does Gisevius give his story a hostile twist against ClS, building up Stieff's reputation at ClS's expense (however, Gisevius, *End* 531 does not include, as the original Gisevius II 350 does, the first sentence below):

> It was as Beck had feared beforehand, the horse [Stauffenberg] had actually refused the jump. Stauffenberg blamed his friend and contemporary, General Stieff. This talented officer was one of Hitler's youngest generals, who had behind him a brilliant career on the General Staff. For the past six months he had been one of the main activists in Stauffenberg's group. For

months the bomb had been locked in his safe, awaiting its great hour. According to Stauffenberg's description, Stieff had suddenly lost his nerve on Saturday. While Stauffenberg was telephoning the Bendlerstrasse, Stieff had taken the briefcase with its deadly contents and carried it out of the room. That was all very well. But this account did not answer our pressing question of why it had been necessary for Stauffenberg to make that telephone call.'

23 Hoepner quoting Olbricht in *Trial* XXXIII 397; Thomale 11 Aug. 1971.

24 Hoepner in *Spiegelbild* 45; Hoepner in *Trial* XXXIII 394; Yorck in *Trial* XXXIII 427; Gisevius II 339–340 based on information from Helldorf; Gisevius 8 Sept. 1972 (not insisting that ClS had talked only with Haeften); H. Mertz, diary 15 July 1945; cf. Hoffmann, *Widerstand* 475.

25 Geisberg; Reinecke 31 May 1964, 30 April 1965, 7 Nov. 1967; H. Mertz, diary 15 and 16 July 1944 and 1945; cf. Gisevius II 345.

26 H. Mertz, diary 15 July 1945.

27 H. Mertz, diary 15 July 1944 and 1945; Siebeck 17 April 1973; *Spiegelbild* 45; *Trial* XXXIII 394; Gisevius II 339–340.

28 Siebeck 17 April 1973; Gisevius II 340; 'Selbstmord'; Harnack 29 Aug. 1966; Hoffmann, *Widerstand* 805–806 note 349.

29 Hoepner quoting Olbricht in *Trial* XXXIII 397.

30 Siebeck 1 Oct. 1971 (with timing errors), 17 April 1973; H. Mertz, diary 16 July 1944, 16/17 July 1945; H. Mertz 21 Aug. 1991; Herzer 13 Sept. 1991; Gisevius II 345.

31 H. Mertz, diary 16 July 1944.

32 H. Mertz, 'Albrecht Ritter Mertz von Quirnheim'.

33 RF 9 May 1977; both H. Mertz and RF thus support F. Sauerbruch, *Leben* 532–533.

34 *Trial* XXXIII 433–434; *Spiegelbild* 182.

35 F.-D. Schulenburg and Hansen in *Spiegelbild* 91–92, 101, 136 (Hansen: towards 7 p.m.); Gisevius II 345–352; Hammerstein, *Spähtrupp* 264; G. Falkenhausen 24 March 1947.

36 *Spiegelbild* 91–92, 101, 136, 175–176; see above pp. 222–223; judgement on Klamroth; cf. Hoffmann, 'Colonel' 638–639.

37 Hoffmann, *Widerstand* 480–483; *Spiegelbild* 116–117.

38 See above pp. 251, 260; Thomale 11 Aug. 1971.

39 *Trial* XXXIII 359, 395–396, 485–486.

40 Schweizer 18 June 1965.

41 Kanitz 23 March 1964, 28 Aug. 1972.

42 Götz in Kramarz 200; Zeller 376 apparently based on information from Schweizer's sister (with the variant that the church was in Dahlem); *Spiegelbild* 21; Schweizer 18 June 1965 (church in Steglitz); Schweizer 1971 (church in Wannsee).

43 NS 31 Aug. 1972 based on Lerchenfeld, Kalender 18 July 1944; CM 451, 456.

44 Schweizer 18 June 1965; *Spiegelbild* 84, 112; Busse 13 March 1984; Dosch 10 April 1984; Ferber 8 March 1984; Salm-Salm 26 March 1984; Vogel, 'Betr.'; Vogel 1 July 1971, 5 Sept. 1985; John von Freyend; Hoffmann, *Widerstand* 486–487; Hoffmann, 'Zu dem Attentat' 268; Hoffmann, 'Warum' 450–451.

45 John von Freyend; Lechler; Vogel, 'Betr.'; Wehner, 'Spiel' 31; *Spiegelbild* 21.
46 John von Freyend; Vogel, *Betr.*; Vogel 1 July 1971, 5 Sept. 1985.
47 Hoffmann, 'Warum' 451–455.
48 *Trial* XXXIII 320, 402; C. Hardenberg 1945; *Spiegelbild* 92; Widmann 30 July 1968; Wehner, 'Spiel' 31; Wehner, *Täter* 254; Gisevius 8 Sept. 1972; Krausnick, Wilhelm 543, 548–550.
49 Hoffmann, *Widerstand* 895; *Spiegelbild* 84; Hoffmann, 'Warum' 451–460.
50 Warlimont, Interview.
51 Reinecke 31 May 1964; Fritzsche 14 July 1972; *Trial* XXXIII 402; Major-General von Thüngen and an anonymous witness in *Volksgerichtshof-Prozesse* 77 and 80–81; Schlabrendorff 148 based on Fromm's account given in prison; Bartram; cf. below p. 268.
52 Hoffmann, *Widerstand* 488–493 with a discussion of some discrepancies in the accounts of the investigating commission (1944) and the driver (1965 and 1966). Recently another driver, Karl Fischer, claimed to have chauffered CIS; his story concerning this trip at least is an obvious invention.
53 On flight times see Hoffmann, *Widerstand* 823–825 note 93; *Spiegelbild* 22; Hoepner in *Trial* XXXIII 400–404; Bartram; Schlabrendorff 147 based on Fromm's account; Hopf.
54 Thon 13 Aug. 1971; Bäke 9 Aug. 1972; Schweizer 18 June 1965. Thon times the events an hour earlier.
55 Hoffmann, *Widerstand* 499–503, 507–511.
56 Wagner, 'Verlauf'; Gisevius II 389; Gisevius 4 Aug. 1971, 8 Sept. 1972; Hoffmann, *Widerstand* 503, 506–507.
57 Ritgen, 'Schulen' 106; Glaesemer 10 June 1986; Hoffmann, *Widerstand* 511 and 826–282 note 99; Schobess; Harnack 20 July 1948. Remer timed the receipt of his first orders variously between 2.30 and 4.10 p.m.: Remer, 'Ablauf' (1944); Remer 15 Aug. 1945, 28 Oct. 1949; Grenzendörfer; see also Hoffmann, *Widerstand* 827 note 99; Rode 24 July, 14 Aug. 1971, 27 Dec. 1989 claims he received his orders before noon and refused to carry them out, but neither Glaesemer nor Schauss confirms this.
58 Hoffmann, *Widerstand* 510; F.-D. Schulenburg in *Spiegelbild* 97; Gisevius 4 Aug. 1971 based on information from F.-D. Schulenburg, and 8 Sept. 1972.
59 Kratzer 25 July 1963.
60 Gisevius (who was friendly with Olbricht) 4 Aug. 1971, 8 Sept. 1972; Schulenburg in *Spiegelbild* 97; Hoepner in *Trial* XXXIII 402.
61 Hoffmann, *Widerstand* 512–516; Ritgen, Schulen 106; Stirius 2 Feb. 1967; Lerche 30 June 1946; see the orders in Hoffmann, *History* 754–759.
62 *Trial* XXXIII 402; Major-General von Thüngen and an anonymous witness in *Volksgerichtshof-Prozesse* 77 and 80–81; Schlabrendorff 148 based on Fromm's account.
63 Hopf, report on Fromm's trial; Kleist 2 Oct. 1968; Schlabrendorff 148 with some apparently apocryphal variations.
64 Wagner, 'Verlauf'; Burchardt 13 July 1965; Schramm, 'Vorgänge'; Schramm, 'Mitteilungen'.
65 Hoffmann, *Widerstand* 521–523; Gerstenmaier, 'Zur Geschichte'.
66 Mitzkus, 'Bericht'; Hoffmann, *Widerstand* 525–526.
67 Delius 28 July 1965; Stirius 2 Feb. 1967; Remer, 'Ablauf'; Grenzendörfer.

68 Hoffmann, *Widerstand* 531–533.
69 Glaesemer 10 June 1986; Ritgen, 'Schulen' 106; Rothkirch 14 Jan. 1989; Hoffmann, *Widerstand* 534–536, 540; BBC Monitoring Service 21 July 1944.
70 Hoffmann, *Widerstand* 543–557, 560–573.
71 HPA Kartei; Hoffmann, *Widerstand* 573–581.
72 Hoffmann, *Widerstand* 581–588.
73 Hassel 11 Dec. 1964.
74 Harnack, 'Bericht'; Herber, 'Was ich'; Heyde, 'Verschwörung'; Pridun; Roell; Hoepner in *Trial* XXXIII 407–408.
75 Kleist 15 Sept. 1964, 2 Oct. 1968; V. Hoffmann; Gisevius II 384–386, 389; Gisevius 8 Sept. 1972; Huppenkothen, '20. Juli'; John, 'Zum Jahrestag'; Krausnick, Wilhelm 179, 548, 568 (on Achamer-Pifrader).
76 Gisevius II 385–386, 389; Gisevius 8 Sept. 1972.
77 Hoffmann, *Widerstand* 616.
78 Gisevius 1954 628, 630; Gisevius II 393; Hoffmann, *Widerstand* 533, 614.
79 KTB HGr Nord 20 July 1944, Zimmermann and Jacobsen 139; Gisevius II 396–397.
80 Gisevius II 397–398; John, 'Some Facts' 67; Roell; Bernt 598; Witzleben in *Trial* XXXIII 360–370; Wagner, 'Verlauf'.
81 Hoffmann, *Widerstand*, 617–622.
82 Ziegler, 'Wer schoss'; Winterfeldt 30 Aug. 1966; L. v. Hammerstein in Hammerstein, *Spähtrupp* 281.
83 Winterfeldt 30 Aug. 1966; Schramm, *Aufstand* 98–99.
84 Harnack, 'Bericht'; Herber, 'Was ich'.
85 Hoepner in *Trial* XXXIII 416; Herber, 'Was ich'; Bernt 599–600; Bartram.
86 Bartram; Harnack, 'Bericht'; Oppen 11 Aug. 1984; Pridun, 'Vermerk'; Schlee; Hoepner in *Trial* XXXIII 417–418. The eye witness Winterfeldt 30 Aug. 1966 relates that Haeften jumped in front of Stauffenberg and was shot first, so that only the next salvo killed Stauffenberg; Lerche 9 July 1946 reports second hand that Mertz jumped in front of Stauffenberg and was shot first; Schlee merely lists those shot in this order: Olbricht, Stauffenberg, Mertz, Haeften; eye witness Thon (head of Bendlerstrasse motor-pool) 13 Aug. 1971 says no one jumped in front of Stauffenberg. Stauffenberg's exclamation is recalled by several witnesses, with variations. Röhrig 29/30 June 1965 ('es lebe das geheiligte Deutschland' or 'es lebe das heilige Deutschland'); Winterfeldt 30 Aug. 1966 ('es lebe das geheiligte Deutschland'); Schweizer 18 June 1965 ('es lebe das heilige Deutschland'); Ziegler, 'Bericht' ('heiliges Deutschland'); Lerche 9 July 1946 second hand ('heiliges Deutschland'); Thon 13 Aug. 1971 ('es lebe Deutschland, ohne den Führer'). Salin 324 note 123 surmises an exclamation containing the words 'das geheime Deutschland'; one may speculate that this would have been so uncommon that the witnesses simply perceived the word as 'heilige' or 'geheiligte' instead of 'geheime'.

Epilogue

1 Bartram.
2 Bernt 601; Himmler, 'Rede' 382; Goetzke 14 July 1965.
3 W. Wagner 13–49, 662–665; *RGBl.* 1935 I 839.

4 Hoffmann, *Widerstand* 649–650; W. Wagner 679–681; C. Bussche 21 Sept. 1983.

5 Lotte von Hofacker (Cäsar's widow) to MS 4 Sept. 1945, Nl MS; W. Wagner 688–691. Hofacker told police interrogators that 'he had had a run-in with Claus Stauffenberg because he, Hofacker, had not wanted to be a fellow-traveller but an active player': *Spiegelbild* 522.

6 Himmler, 'Rede' 385; Kaltenbrunner to M. Bormann 25 Oct. 1944, BA EAP 105/34; NS, 'Litta'; CS, 'Lautlingen'; Bracke 188–193, 210, 221–244; AS to RB 8 May 1945, StGA; RF, 'Leben' 10–12; Bethge 1032–1034; F. Hassell 173–214; *Spiegelbild* 168, 436, 450.

7 AS to RB 8 May 1945, StGA; NS, 'Litta'; CS, 'Lautlingen'; Bracke 194–198, 202–205, 210, 215, 218, 221.

8 NS, 'Litta'; Bracke 193–194.

9 AS to RB 8 May 1945, StGA; Bracke 223–244 cites 'USAAF European Theater World War 2 Victory Credits: 040845' according to which the American Second-Lieutenant Norboune A. Thomas shot down Countess Stauffenberg.

10 AS to RB 8 May 1945, StGA; NS, 'Litta'; O.P. Stauffenberg 20 Feb. 1973; Marlene, Countess Stauffenberg 23 Aug. 1972.

11 CS, 'Lautlingen'; NS, 'Litta'; Clemens, Count Stauffenberg 27 Oct. 1946; Bracke 194.

12 AS to RB 8 May 1945, StGA; CS, 'Lautlingen'; Thierack 24 Oct. 1944; Schwerin von Krosigk and Thierack to the heads of the Higher Revenue Service and the Chief Prosecutor at the 'People's Court' 13 Nov. 1944.

13 CS, 'Lautlingen'; NS, 'Lautlingen'; W. Hoffmann 10 March, 12 Sept. 1977, 6 Sept. 1979.

14 CS, 'Lautlingen'; RF, 'Leben' 12, 15–16; AS to RB 8 May 1945, StGA.

15 RF, 'Leben' 39–42.

16 ClS in Hoffmann, 'Claus' 522.

17 Saucken 27 July 1972; Thiersch 21 Jan. 1978.

18 See below, Appendix III.

19 Nettesheim 22 Aug. 1968.

20 AS, 'Der zwanzigste Juli 1944' III, 2; Saucken 27 July 1972.

21 Harnack 2 Oct. 1984.

22 Wolzendorff 95–104, 206–209; Bèze 18–63.

23 [Werner Traber] to Baum 28 May 1957.

24 RF, *Gneisenau* 17–19; ClS to Sodenstern 13 March 1939, BA-MA N 594 (see Appendix III); Thüngen 25 Jan. 1946.

25 Wolfskehl, *Werke* I 280–281.

26 AS, 'Erinnerung'; NS in Kramarz 132; Yorck 6 Aug. 1944; M. Yorck 10 Aug. 1972; *Spiegelbild* 110; *Trial* xxxiii 424.

27 AS, 'Erinnerung'.

Appendices

1 Nl ClS.

2 Ms., ink pencil. The punctuation adapted to StG's style is preserved here. Many of the peculiarities of ClS's style, and the orthography adapted to StG's manner,

are lost in the English translation; see the German in Hoffmann, *Stauffenberg* (German edn) 456. ClS also used StG's script which, of course, only the original shows.

3 The brothers' nickname for their mother.

4 Colonel (Ret.) Otto Freiherr von Tessin, Royal Chamberlain in Württemberg.

5 Training area near Hof.

6 Ms., ink, notepaper with family crest; BA-MA N 594; printed with some variant readings in Giessler, 'Briefwechsel' 560, 562–564; printed with the original spelling in Hoffmann, *Stauffenberg* (German edn) 457–460. Cf. pp. 107–110 above.

7 The words missing from ClS's sentence would perhaps have been 'to beg' or 'it only remains'.

8 An approved substitute for the otherwise prescriptive 'Heil Hitler'.

9 Ms. copy by ClS's mother-in-law Anna, Baroness Lerchenfeld, papers of Nina, Countess Stauffenberg; the original is lost. German in Hoffmann, *Stauffenberg* (German edn) 460–462. Cf. pp. 142–144 above.

10 Hitler himself took over the function of Commander-in-Chief of the Army.

11 Copies of the ms. in Slg Hilfswerk 20. Juli 1944, IfZ ZS/A 29/3 and in E. A. Paulus to the author 15 Sept. 1990; printed in Kramarz 226 with errors; partially printed in Görlitz, *Paulus* 168 with distorting errors; printed according to the original in Hoffmann, *Stauffenberg* (German edn) 462–463. Cf. p. 146 above.

12 Carbon copy with ms. changes by ClS, deposited in StGA by RF 1977; further information on the 'Oath' from J. D. von Hassell, 'Aufzeichnung'; RF 6 Sept. 1979, 19 Nov. 1985; RF, 'Leben' 9–10; Marlene, Countess Stauffenberg, 21 March 1977, 12 March 1992; BS to RF 10 June [1944], StGA; AS, Deutsche. The top copy may be presumed to have remained in Claus's or Berthold's possession; it has not turned up since and may have been destroyed or confiscated on or after 20 July 1944. RF had the carbon copy and for safekeeping gave it to a friend, Marlene Hoffmann, who lived in Ramsau below the Dachstein, a remote region of the Alps. Most likely the carbon copy passed into Alexander's possession in 1945. Of the 191 words in the 'Oath', 95 were published verbatim in Zeller 1952 295, 1965 489. The entire 'Oath' is reproduced, mostly verbatim, with only a few variations, in AS's poem 'Vorabend', published in 1964; AS, *Denkmal* 21–25. The 'Oath' was published verbatim and in full in Hoffmann, *Stauffenberg* (German edn) 396–397 (facsimile).

13 AS, *Denkmal* 21–25.

14 LT to BS 25 Nov., 17 Dec. 1940, Nl BS; LT to F 11 Jan. 1941, StGA; Vallentin 136; Seekamp 378.

15 Krebs 291–291; Zeller 523 note 31 based on Bussche.

16 Cf. above p. 17; ClS to Teske 29 Aug. 1937. According to RF 15 July 1963 the 'Oath' was to be sworn after the uprising, but before Germany's occupation, in order to bind together those who espoused its ideas.

17 RF, *Arndt* 15; RF, *Gneisenau* 56–57; ClS to Partsch 23 July 1942.

18 RF, *Gneisenau* 56–57; RF, *Arndt* 15 has a slightly different version; both are offered without source reference.

19 Pertz, *Gneisenau* II 89–91; Gneisenau used 'Knoth' as a cover name; Griewank 159.

20 RF 9 May 1977.

21 Hoffmann, 'Claus' 522–523; ClS to Erffa 22 Nov. 1936, Nl ClS; cf. AS, 'Germanen' in *Die Welt als Geschichte* I 72–100, II 117–168, III 345–361; AS, 'Theoderich' in *Macht* 406–419; *Deutsche Allgemeine Zeitung* Nr. 310–311, 8 July 1937; *Frankfurter Zeitung* 6, 8, 9 July 1937; *VB* 7 July 1937 8; Hölderlin, *Sämtliche Werke* IV ed. by Norbert v. Hellingrath 181–185; Fichte 7 456–457; Lbbe 196–202; Ferry 21–53; Seeley 13–19, 340–359; Gilbert 60–66, 71–73, 76–77; Crewe; EK, 'Deutschland'; StG, *GA* IX 39.

22 See ClS, letters to his father and to Sodenstern, above pp. 287–290; StG, *GA* IX 39; RF, *Arndt* 31, 181; Lehmann 2 559–561; Hofacker to Herbert von Samson-Himmelstjerna (Puka, Estland) 1 Sept. 1930, Nl Hofacker; RF 19 Nov. 1985; AS, *Denkmal* 24.

23 Gisevius, *Wo, passim*; Gisevius's dedication in Federer's copy of Gisevius I; Federer 29 March 1977; Dulles to Donovan 28 Jan. 1945.

24 *FRUS, Malta and Yalta* 957; Dulles to Donovan 25 Jan. 1945.

25 Dulles to Donovan No. 4077 25 Jan. 1945; Dulles, *Underground* 172–173; Dulles, *Surrender, passim*; Smith, Agarossi, *passim*; Harriman to Stettinius 10 Jan. 1945 in *FRUS, Malta and Yalta* 453–454; Cheston 27 Jan. 1945.

26 Dulles 28 Jan. 1945; Cheston 1 Feb. 1945; similarly Gisevius to Bancroft 4 Feb. 1945; Dulles, *Underground* 170 toned down these statements considerably; see also above p. 216.

27 Gisevius, 'Bericht' 28; Gisevius II 279.

28 Bancroft to Dulles [11 May, 11 July 1944].

29 *Spiegelbild* 507; *Spiegelbild* 1985 592.

30 Gisevius, 'Bericht' 31; Gisevius II 304–305, 325 without the words 'the entire civil executive'.

BIBLIOGRAPHY

I. Unpublished primary sources

a. Papers in public and private hands

Papers without an archive reference are in the author's possession. Collections described as 'papers' are papers of deceased persons in private or public archives, or papers of surviving persons. 'Nl' is a designation for papers of deceased persons in the possession of heirs or archives. Individual letters within a discrete group of papers are identified in the notes.

Akten der Reichskanzlei [re: gifts to civil servants, military officers and others, 1933–1945], BA R 43 II/984, R 43 II/985, R 43 II/985a, R 43 II/985b, R 43 II/985c, R 43 II/986, R 43 II/1087, R 43 II/1092, R 43 II/1092a, R 43 II/1092b

Akten des Studienausschusses KR, NA T-1022 roll 1903

Akten betreffend Vbd., Verwaltungs- und technische Fragen. Personal. Deutsches Personal im Internationalen Gerichtshof, Dec. 1926–Sept. 1935, Pers. II E Bd. 1

Albrecht, Heinz-Günther, 'Die militärischen Vorbereitungen der damaligen Führungsstelle der Widerstandsbewegung im Generalkommando Berlin im Hinblick auf den geplanten Umsturz. Niedergeschrieben im Sommer 1946/47', typed (copy)

Amerdingen guest book 1918–1945

Anderson, Ivar, diary, Kungliga Biblioteket, Stockholm, Ivar Anderson Papper L 91:3

Anklageschrift gegen Dr Karl Goerdeler, Wilhelm Leuschner, Josef Wirmer, Ulrich von Hassell, Dr Paul Lejeune-Jung, Der Oberreichsanwalt beim Volksgerichtshof o J 17/44 gRs, Berlin 3 Sept. 1944, IfMLbZKdSED, ZPA NJ 17584

Anklageschrift gegen Ferdinand Thomas, Dr. med. Rudolf Schmid, Dr. phil. Adolf Reichwein, Dr. rer. pol. Julius Leber, Der Oberreichsanwalt beim Volksgerichtshof 8 J 170/44g 1 H 244/44, Berlin 9 Aug. 1944, IfMLbZKdSED, ZPA NJ 1583

Anlage [I] zum Kriegstagebuch der Heeresgruppe Don bezw. Heeresgruppe Süd vom 22.11.42–23.3.43 (O.B.-Gespräche), BA-MA RH 19 VI/42

Anton, Johann, Nl in possession of Dr Franz von Stockert and StGA

Appel, Maria, 'Eidesstattliche Erklärung', typed copy, Hamburg-Gross-Flottbek 12 Aug. 1948, Nl RF (see also Pfohl)

[Army High Command, Chief of Army Munitions and Commander of Home Army,
    = Chef der Heeresrüstung und Befehlshaber des Ersatzheeres], Geschäfts-
    einteilung der Abt. Ia des AHA/Stab [4 Feb. 1944], BA-MA RH 15/120
[Army High Command, Chief of Army Munitions and Commander of Home
    Army], (telephone directory) Stand 1.1.1943, BA-MA RHD 46/3
Fernsprechverzeichnis des Oberkommandos des Heeres/Generalstab des Heeres,
    Stand vom 15.10.1942, BA-MA RHD 46/2
Fernsprechverzeichnis der Vermittlung OKW/OKH mit Übersicht über die
    Ausweichunterkünfte, Stand 1.11.44, BA-MA RHD 46/1
2. Abteilung, Generalstab des Heeres, Geschäftseinteilung der 2. Abteilung
    (Organisationsabteilung) des Generalstabes des Heeres, 27 Dec. 1938, BA-MA
    RH 15/130
[Army High Command, General Staff of the Army/Organisation Branch], g.Kdos.
    Bei-Akte zur Akte 1a, 'Grundlegende Befehle' Nr. 1–28, 1942–1944, NA T-78
    roll 414
Auswärtiges Amt, VM, Akten betreffend: Völkerbund. Errichtung eines inter-
    nationalen Gerichtshofs, Sept. 1929–Nov. 1931, Völkerbund, Gerichtshof Bd.
    9, 10, AA/PA
Auszug aus dem Krankenmeldebuch, Hannover 28 Nov. 1936, Krankenbuchlager
    Berlin
Auszug aus dem Offz.-Krankenmeldebuch des Standortes Bamberg, Bamberg 30
    May 1931, Krankenbuchlager Berlin
Auszug aus dem Truppenkrankenbuch, Fähnrich Graf Stauffenberg, 1./R.R.17,
    Hannover 15 Aug. 1929, Krankenbuchlager Berlin
Auszug aus dem Truppenkrankenmeldebuch der Inf.Schule Dresden, Bamberg 30
    May 1931, Krankenbuchlager Berlin
[Bancroft, Mary,] Letters to Allen Welsh Dulles, typed, 1943–1945
    Report (for Allen Welsh Dulles, Feb. 1945), typed, Princeton University Library,
    A. W. Dulles Papers, Box 203
    'The Background and Story of the 20th of July', typed, [Feb. 1945]
Bargatzky, Walter, 'Persönliche Erinnerungen an die Aufstandsbewegung des 20.
    Juli 1944 in Frankreich', mimeographed, Baden-Baden 20 Oct. 1945
Bartram, Heinz-Ludwig, '20. Juli 1944', typed, n.p. [1954], BA H90–3/4
Bauch, [Prof. Dr Kurt], Letter to Prof. Dr Walter Baum 17 Dec. 1956, IfZ ZS-
    1789
BBC Monitoring Service, Daily Digest of World Broadcasts, Part I, No. 1830 [for
    20 July 1944], mimeographed, [London] 21 July 1944
Beumelburg, Werner, 'Der bittere Weg', typed, n.p. n.d., IfZ ED 100 Slg Irving
[Blumenthal, Albrecht von], 'Reise nach Italien und Sizilien 7. März bis 10. Mai
    1924', StGA
    Letters to Stefan George, StGA
    'Principi iuventutis' [poems to Berthold, Count Stauffenberg, 1924], StGA
Blumentritt, [Günther], 'Stellungnahme zu dem Buch "Offiziere gegen Hitler".
    Nach einem Erlebnisbericht von Fabian v. Schlabrendorff bearbeitet und
    herausgegeben von Gero v. S. Gaevernitz 1946 Europa Verlag Zürich', typed,
    [England] Nov. 1946, Slg John
Boehringer, Robert, Correspondence re Stefan George and his circle, StGA

'Bericht über das Verhalten beim Tode und bei der Bestattung von Stefan George, Locarno, 9 Dec. 1933', StGA

Bormann, M[artin], Rundschreiben Nr. 127/39 (Nicht zur Veröffentlichung.), Munich 13 June 1939, Landeszentrale für politische Bildungsarbeit Berlin

'Daten aus alten Notizbüchern', Hoover Institution, NSDAP Hauptarchiv roll 1

'Brunhilde-Ost', [order], Der Chef der Heeresrüstung und Befehlshaber des Ersatzheeres AHA Ia(I) Nr. 4940/42 g. Kdos., 28 Oct. 1942, BA-MA RH 15/v. 173

Bürker, Ulrich, 9, 15, 30 Nov. 1941, 4 Dec. 1941, 25 Feb. 1942 to Claus, Count Stauffenberg, KTB 10. Pz.Div. Anlagen, NA T-314 roll 988/495–496, 506–507, 542–543, 569–570 and BA-MA RH 27–10/42

2 Jan. 1942 to Lt.-Col. (GS) Mueller-Hillebrand, BA-MA RH 27/10–44

9 Jan. 1942 to Maj. (GS) Golling, OKH /GenStdH/Ausbildungsabteilung/Gr. II

'Bericht über 10. Pz.Div. und Division Fischer (Stab 10. Pz.Div.)', typed, 2 Feb. 1942, Anlagenband Nr. VII der 10. Panzer Division Nr. 6, Meldungen vom 1.1.42–28.2.1942, NA T-315 roll 569/662–665

Buhle, [Walther], 'Geschäftseinteilung der 2. Abteilung (Organisationsabteilung) des Generalstabes des Heeres', typed, Berlin 27 Dec. 1938, BA-MA RH 15/130

Burchardt, Heinz, 'Zugehörigkeit zur Widerstandsbewegung vom 20. Juli 1944', typed copy, Munich 1946, Nl Degner

[Burk], Klaus, Letters from the front to Otto [Burk], 1943, in possession of Klaus Burk

Bussche, Axel [Freiherr] von dem, [Testimony in] Records of the United States Nuernberg War Crimes Trials. United States of America v. Ernst Von Weizsaecker et al. (Case XI). December 20, 1947–April 14, 1949, NA Microfilm M897

'Er wollte Hitler töten', Sender Freies Berlin, Berlin 19 July 1984

Soldbuch, Nl Bussche

Butler, Peter von, 15 April 1942 to Claus, Count Stauffenberg, KTB Nr. 6 der 10. Pz.Div., Anlagen VIII, NA T-315 roll 569/1177–1178

Cheston, Charles S., Memorandum for the President, 27 Jan. 1945, F.D.R. Library PSF Box 170 OSS Jan. 1945

Memorandum for the President, 1 Feb. 1945, F.D.R. Library PSF Box 171 OSS Feb. 1945

Christie, M. G., Christie Papers, Churchill College, Cambridge

[Colsman, Erwin,] 'Erhaltung der Manneszucht im Kriege (Zersetzung). Notizen zum Vortrag vor den Offizieren der rückwärtigen Dienste am 6. Januar 1940', typed, n.p. [Jan. 1940], Nl ClS

Cotta-Archiv, Deutsches Literatur-Archiv, Marbach a.N.

Curtius, Ernst Robert, diary, ms., Nl Curtius

'Darstellung der Ereignisse, 1. Leichte Division. Begonnen am 5.9.1938. Geschlossen am 19.10.1938', typed, Reerink Papers

Deichmann, Hans, pocket diary 1942, Hans Deichmann Papers, typed excerpt of 14 Nov. 1988

'Dienstanweisung für den Chef des Generalstabes des Heeres im Frieden', 31 May 1935, BA-MA RH 2/V. 195

'Die militärische Dienstlaufbahn des Oberst i.G. Claus Schenk Graf von Stauffen-berg, geb. am 15.11.1907 in Jettingen/Schwaben + 20.7.1944 in Berlin', BA-Z 24. Feb. 1977

Dipper, Elisabeth (married name Daur), letters to her parents from Lautlingen 14 June, 3 July, 4 Sept. 1919, in Elisabeth Daur Papers

Dulles, Allen Welsh, Reports from Bern to the Director of the Office of Strategic Services in Washington, D.C., in OSS-Archive, Central Intelligence Agency, Washington, D.C.

  Papers, Princeton University Library

Eberbach, Heinrich (General of Armoured Troops) to Militärgeschichtliches For-schungsamt, Freiburg i.Br. 11 April 1967, typed copy in Irving, Selected Documents Film 97049/3

Eberhard-Ludwigs-Gymnasium Stuttgart, Abgangs-Zeugnis. Der Schüler Klaus v. Stauffenberg [. . .], Stuttgart 18 Sept. 1924, Staatsarchiv Ludwigsburg E 202 Büschel 1630

  Reifeprüfung 1923, Anmeldungs- und Zeugnisliste, beurkundet 3 März 1923 Reifeprüfung 1926

Etzdorf, Dr Hasso von, 'Aufzeichnungen V.A.A.' [1939–1943], AA/PA 1247 and NA T-120 roll 748

Fahrner, Rudolf, Nl in possession of von Gemma Wolters-Thiersch and StGA

  'Das Gespräch des Dionysios Solomos', typed, n.p. [1943] with ms. entries by Stauffenberg, Nl RF, StGA

  'Bericht, Biessenhofen 26 July 1945', typed, Nl RF

  'An das Kultusministerium Baden/Württemberg', Karlsruhe 20 Dec. 1961, typed carbon copy, Nl RF

  'Zum 20. Juli', typed, n.p. n.d., Nl RF

Falkenhausen, [Alexander] von, ['Bericht über meine Stellung zur N.S.D.A.P. und ihrem Regime'], typed, [Frankfurt a.M.] 15 Nov. 1946, NA RG 338 MS No. B 289

Falkenhausen, Gotthard Freiherr von, 'Erinnerungen an die deutsche Widerstands-bewegung', typed, n.p. 1945

Fernsprechverzeichnis, *see* [Army High Command]

Frank, *see* Mehnert

Geisberg, [Wilhelm], 'Meldung', typed, [Wolfschanze] 23 July 1944, BA EAP 105/34 and *Spiegelbild* 1984 668–669

G[isevius], H[ans] B[ernd], 'Memorandum for A[llen] W[elsh] D[ulles]', typed, n.p. July 1944

  'Bericht [an Mary Bancroft für Allen Welsh Dulles]', typed [Zürich] Feb. 1945, Princeton University Library, Allen W. Dulles Papers, Box 20

[Goerdeler, Carl], [notes for Jacob Wallenberg], typed, [Stockholm 19–21 May 1943], BA Nl Goerdeler 23

  'Praktische Massnahmen zur Umgestaltung Europas', typed, n.p. n.d., BA Nl Goerdeler 23

  'Vorgesehene Rundfunkrede bei Übernahme der Reichsregierung', typed copy, n.d., Hoover Institution Germany G 597 (the same publ. from Nl Goerdeler; *see* II. Printed sources)

  'Unsere Idee', typed, Nov. 1944, BA Nl Goerdeler 26

  see also Anklageschrift

Graf née Klaeger, Ruth, ['Bericht'], typed, Landau 28 Oct. 1950
  see also Klaeger; Jessen
Greifenstein guest book 1939–1944
Greischel, Dr Walther, to Dr Robert Boehringer 12 April 1966, StGA
[Grenzendörfer, Wilhelm], 'Notizen von der Schilderung des Generalmajors Remer von den Vorgängen am 20. Juli 1944 in Berlin, gehalten am 24. Juli 1946 in dem englischen Internierungslager 2221/Q in Belgien', typed, n.p. n.d., Nl Paul Collmer
Guderian, Heinz Günther, 'Kommentar', typed, n.p. April 1966, Slg David Irving, Rommel Papers 97049/2, also IfZ Slg Irving
Guest book, *see* Amerdingen, Greifenstein, Jettingen, Lautlingen
Guttenberg, Karl Ludwig Freiherr von und zu, Termin-Kalender für das Jahr 1942, Nl Guttenberg
[Halder, Franz], 'Protokoll aus der Verhandlung Halder. Spruchkammer X München [15.–21. Sept. 1948]', mimeographed [Munich 1948], BA-MA H 92–1/3
Halder, Franz, 'Zu den Aussagen des Dr. Gisevius in Nürnberg 24. bis 26.4.1946', typed carbon copy, Neustadt, 4 Feb. 1948, BA-MA N 124/10
Hammerstein, Ludwig Freiherr von, 'Tages-Notizkalender' 1943, 1944, Hammerstein Papers
Handakten des Ministerialdirigenten Dr. Bräutigam als Bevollmächtigter des RMbO beim Oberkommando der Heeresgruppe A über die Besetzung des Kaukasus und die Behandlung der kaukasischen Völker, 1941–1945, BA R6/66
Handakten des Vorsitzenden des Vorausschusses KR, Admiral Gladisch, BA/MA III M 501/1
Handliste der Generalstabsoffiziere, OKH/HPA Amtsgr. 3, Stand 1. Juli 1943, NA T-78 roll R57 and BA-Zentralnachweisstelle
Hardenberg, Margarethe, Countess, 'Bericht' [1982, audio-tape copy] and typed transcript, n.p. Sylvester 1945, Nl Hardenberg
[Hardenberg-Neuhardenberg, Carl-Hans, memoir], ms. and typed transcription, n.p., 31 Dec. 1945, Nl Hardenberg
Harnack, Fritz, 'Bericht über die Vorgänge des 20.7.44 in der Bendlerstrasse', typed, Brunswick 20 July 1948
[Heerespersonalamt], Von P 3 freigegebene Offiziere, 1943–1944, NA T-78 roll 39
Heerespersonalamt, filmed cardfile, NA RG 242
Heinz, Friedrich Wilhelm, 'Von Wilhelm Canaris zur NKWD', typed, n.p. n.d. [ca. 1949], NA microfilm R 60.67
Herber, Franz, 'Was ich am 20.7.44 in der Bendlerstrasse erlebte', typed, n.p. n.d. [ca. 1948], BA H 90 3/4
'Hermes' [ms. mimeographed 'periodical', vol. 1, no. 1, with contributions by Berthold, Alexander and Claus, Count Stauffenberg], Nl Berthold Graf Stauffenberg
[Herwarth von Bittenfeld, Hans], 'Deutschland und die ukrainische Frage 1941–1945', typed, n.p. n.d., Herwarth Papers
Himmler, Heinrich, [appointments diary], ms., 2 Jan.–16 Dec. 1943, 3 Jan.–31 May 1944, BA EAP 21–b/1–5
  [notes on briefings with Hitler and others], ms., May 1934–Dec. 1944, BA NS 19/275 and NS 19/331

[Hofacker, Cäsar von], 'Lebenslauf', ms. [incomplete, n.p. ca. 1937], Nl Hofacker Kriegsranglisten-Auszug, Heeresarchiv Stuttgart 30 Dec. 1937, Nl Hofacker

Hopf, [Werner], 'Vorlage an Herrn Reichsleiter Bormann. Betrifft: Prozess um den Verrat am 20.7.1944 [trial of Fromm 7 March 1945]', typed, [Berlin] 10 March [1945], BA EAP 105/30 and *Spiegelbild* 1984 756–758

Huppenkothen, [Walter], 'Der 20. Juli 1944', typed copy, n.p. [1953], IfZ ZS 249/II

Indictment *see* Anklageschrift

Irving, David, Selected Documents on the Life and Campaigns of Field-Marshal Erwin Rommel, E. P. Microform Ltd., East Ardsley, Wakefield, Yorkshire, England, films 1–11 (*also* IfZ Slg Irving)

Jessen, Sydney, 'Alfred Kranzfelder geb. 10.2.08 gest. 10.8.1944, ein Bild nach den Aufzeichnungen von Frau Ruth Graf, geb. Kläger', typed, n.p. 1945/58, IfZ ZS 1803

[Notes for Prof. Walter Baum], typed, n.p. 24 Jan. [1957], IfZ ZS 1484

Jettingen guest book 1919–1949

Jodl, Alfred, [pocket appointments diary 1944], NA T-84 roll R149

John, Otto, 'Bericht. Betrifft: Spanien/Portugal', typed copy, n.p. Feb./March 1944, Nl Dr Walter Bauer

'Bericht' [from Madrid, for Colonel Hansen], typed copy, n.p. March 1944, Nl Dr Walter Bauer

'Some Facts and Aspects of the Plot against Hitler', typed, London 1948, IfZ Slg John

Interview with Joachim Fest, Bavaria Atelier GmbH, Munich 1971

[Judgement of People's Court, Senate I], 15 Aug. 1944, against Bernhard Klamroth, Hans-Georg Klamroth, Egbert Hayessen, Wolf Heinrich Graf Helldorf, Dr Adam von Trott zu Solz, Hans Bernd von Haeften, typed copy, AZ I L 292/44 OJ 3/44 gRs., AA/PA Inl. II, NA T-120 roll 1038

[Judgement of People's Court, Senate I, 8 Sept. 1944 against Dr Karl Goerdeler, Wilhelm Leuschner, Josef Wirmer, Ulrich von Hassell, Dr Paul Lejeune-Jung], typed copy, [ref.] 1 L 316/44 O J 17/44g Rs., IfMLbZKdSED, ZPA NJ 17584 (Abdruck: Osas 80–95; *Spiegelbild* 530–542)

[Judgement of People's Court, Senate I, 17 Jan. 1945 against H. Kaiser and B. Thoma], typed copy, Az. I L 454/44 O J 7/44 g Rs, [Berlin 17 Jan. 1945], BA EAP 105/30; also in *Spiegelbild* 1984 726–731

[Judgement of People's Court, Senate I, 5 Sept. 1944] against Anton Emil Hermann Saefkow, Franz Edmund Jacob, Bernhard Karl Bästlein, typed copy, Az. 1 H 208/44 8 J 157/44 [Berlin 5 Sept. 1944], IfMLbZKdSED, ZPA NJ 1500

[Judgement of People's Court, Senate I, 12 Oct. 1944] against Dr med. Rudolf Schmid, typed copy, Az. 1 H 281/44 8 J 170/44g [Berlin 12 Oct. 1944], IfMLbZKdSED, ZPA NJ 1583

[Judgement of People's Court, Senate I, 4 Oct. 1944] against Ferdinand Thomas, typed copy, Az. 1 H 244/44 8 J 179/44g [Berlin 4 Oct. 1944], IfMLbZKdSED, ZPA NJ 1583

Judgement *see also* Anklageschrift; Prozessbericht

[Junge, Hans and Heinz Linge, 'Record of Hitler's Activities 23 March–20 June 1943]', ms., Hoover Institution, Stanford, California Ts Germany R 352 Kh

Justizministerium, 'Kandidatenliste für die erste höhere Justizdienstprüfung im Frühjahr [May] 1927', Universitätsarchiv Tübingen, 258/18258; 129/Paket 73 Frühjahr 1927 L2

[Kaiser, Hermann, diary 1 Jan.–3 Aug. 1943], ms., BA Kl.Erwerb. 657
    Tagebuch [diary Jan.-Aug. 1943], transcript by Ludwig Kaiser [Frankfurt/M. 1950], NA RG 338 MS B-285

Kaiser, Ludwig, 'Ein Beitrag zur Geschichte der Staatsumwälzung vom 20. Juli 1944 (Goerdeler-Bewegung), Teilbericht', typed, Kassel-Wilhelmshöhe n.d., NA RG 338 MS no. B-285

Kaltenbrunner, Ernst (Chief of Security Police and SD) to Head of Party Chancery (Leiter der Parteikanzlei) Reichsleiter Martin Bormann 25 Oct. 1944, typed, BA EAP 105/34

Kanitz, Rainer Graf von, letters to Mrs Elisabeth Wagner 23 March, 14 April 1964, 14 July 1972, copies in Kanitz Papers

Kantorowicz, Ernst, letters to Stefan George, StGA
    'Abschrift. Gesuch um Beurlaubung des o.ö.Prof.Dr.Ernst Kantorowicz für das Sommer-Semester 1933. Frankfurt a.M., den 20. April 1933. An den Herrn Minister für Wis., Kunst u. Volksb. Berlin (d.d.Herrn Dekan der Phil. Fak. d. Univ. Frankfurt a.M.)', Johann Wolfgang Goethe-Universität [Frankfurt a.M.], Archiv
    'Das geheime Deutschland. Vorlesung gehalten bei Wiederaufnahme der Lehrtätigkeit am 14. November 1933', [Frankfurt/M., 1933], Nl Salin C 34, Universitätsbibliothek Basel
    ['Das Geheime Deutschland'], n.p. n.d., AR 7216, Ernst H. Kantorowicz Collection, Leo Baeck Institute, New York

[Kessel, Albrecht von], 'Verborgene Saat. Das 'Andere' Deutschland', typed, Vatican City September 1944 to April 1945

Kiessel, Georg, 'Das Attentat des 20. Juli 1944 und seine Hintergründe', typed, Sandbostel 6 Aug. 1946, Slg H.R.Trevor-Roper on David Irving film DJ38

Klamroth, *see* Judgement

[Kommerell, Max], 'Zwiesprache, Für Berthold inmitten des vollen Lebens ein Schatte früheren Lebens, Frühjahr 1923, Winter 1924', ms., Nl Johann Anton in possession of Dr Franz von Stockert
    'Konradin: Für B. und A. von St.', Marburg 1924, Nl Johann Anton in possession of Dr Franz von Stockert
    'Lieder an C.', Cannstatt, [Jan.–March] 1925, StGA
    Letters to Stefan George, StGA
    Letters to Johann Anton, StGA
    Nl in possession of Mrs Erika Kommerell

Kopkow-Cordes, Horst, 'Account of the Plot of 20 Jul 44', typed, n.p. 9 April 1946

Kramarz, Joachim, Slg Kramarz, Gedenkstätte Deutscher Widerstand, Berlin

Krankenblatt Berichtsjahr 1936, Standortlazarett Hannover, Krankenabteilung II, Krankenbuchlager Berlin

Krankenmeldebuch, *see* Auszug

Kriegsrangliste der 1. leichten Division 1938, Reerink Papers

Kriegstagebuch, Generalstab des Heeres, Organisations-Abtlg. vom 1.1.–31.12.42, NA T-78 roll 417

Kriegstagebuch der Heeresgruppe Don (Süd), *see* Anlage
Kriegstagebuch Nr. 3 der Führungsabteilung (Ia) des Gen.Kdo. (mot.) XXXX vom
    31.5.1941–26.12.1941, BA-MA KTB XXXX. A.K. Bd. 31093,1
Kriegstagebuch Nr. 2 der 6. Panzer-Division. Begonnen: 10.5.1940. Abgeschlossen:
    3.7.1940, NA T-315 roll 337
Kriegstagebuch *see also* Tagebuch, War Diary
[Lahousen, Erwin], 'Sidelights on the Development of the "20 July" in the Foreign
    Countries/Intelligence Service (Amt Ausland/Abwehr) for the Period of Time
    from the End of 1939 to the Middle of 1943', typed, n.p. n.d. [ca. 1945], NA
    RG 238
    'Zur Vorgeschichte des Anschlages vom 20. Juli 1944', typed carbon copy,
    Munich 1953, IfZ ZS 652
Lang, Rudolf, 'Report on the Fighting of Kampfgruppe Lang (10th Pz Div) in
    Tunisia (Dec 42–15 Apr 45)', Department of the Army, Office of the Chief of
    Military History, Washington, D.C. MS D-166
Lautlingen guest book 1906–1947
Leibstandarte SS 'Adolf Hitler', Befehle, NA T-354 rolls 214, 612
Lerche, Anni to Dr Hans Bernd Gisevius 30 June 1946, intercepted and translated
    by British Censor IRS 3 D.C.S., typed, n.p. 17 July 1946, Slg Trevor-Roper
    and David Irving film DJ 38
Lerchenfeld, Anna Alexandrowna Freifrau von, née Freiin von Stackelberg, pocket
    diary 1944, papers of Nina, Countess Stauffenberg
Leumunds-Zeugnis. Dem Klaus, Philipp, Maria Schenk Graf von Stauffenberg in
    Lautlingen, Schultheissenamt Lautlingen, 8 Oct. 1924, Staatsarchiv Ludwigs-
    burg E 202 Büschel 1630
Linge, Heinz, 'Record of Hitler's Activities 11 August 1943–30 December 1943',
    typed transcript, n.p. 1952, NA RG 242 Misc. Box 13
[List], Aus der Haft bei dem SD sind folgende bisher in den Listen II-IV
    enthaltenen Offiziere entlassen worden, typed [Heerespersonalamt Sept. 1944],
    BA EAP 105/2
[List], Durch den Führer wurden auf Vorschlag des Ehrenhofes des Heeres aus der
    Wehrmacht ausgestossen: Am 4. August 1944. [dto] Am 14. August 1944. [dto]
    Am 24. August 1944. [dto] Am 14. September 1944, typed [Heerespersonalamt
    Sept. 1944], BA EAP 105/2
[List], Durch den Führer wurden auf Vorschlag des Ehrenhofes des Heeres aus der
    Wehrmacht entlassen: Am 14. August 1944. [dto] Am 24. August 1944. [dto]
    Am 14. September 1944, typed [Heerespersonalamt Sept. 1944], BA EAP
    105/2
List I [of officers arrested, released or sentenced, to 29 Aug. 1944, Heerespersonal-
    amt, typed, Aug. 1944], BA EAP 105/2
Liste I. Generalstabsoffiziere [officers of the General Staff who were expelled or
    dismissed from the Armed Forces, sentenced, executed, arrested or released
    from detention to 1 Sept. 1944], typed [Heerespersonalamt Sept. 1944], BA
    EAP 105/2
Liste II. Offiziere von Ref. II [expelled or dismissed from the Armed Forces, or
    released from detention], typed [Heerespersonalamt Sept. 1944], BA EAP
    105/2
Loeper, Friedrich-Wilhelm Freiherr von, 'Bericht über das Gefecht der [1. Leich-

ten] Division zwischen Warschau und Modlin vom 17.–21.9.39', typed copy, Rykaly 24 Sept. 1939, Reerink Papers

Manstein, Erich von, personal diary, Nl Manstein

Letters to his wife, typed, 25 and 26 Nov. 1943, Nl Manstein

Manstein, [Erich] v[on], 'Persönliche Notizen', typed carbon copy, Bridgend, 20 May 1947, Slg John

'Richtigstellung zur Darstellung der Haltung des Feldmarschalls v. Manstein im Buch "Offiziere gegen Hitler"', typed, n.p., n.d., Slg John

Letter to the editor of *Alte Kameraden*, typed copy, Irschenhausen/Isartal 5 Feb. 1968, Nl Manstein

Manstein, Rüdiger von, [notes on communications from Erich von Manstein], ms., n.p. 30 Nov. and 30 Dec. 1967

Mehnert, Frank, Nl, StGA

Mertz von Quirnheim, Albrecht Ritter, letters to Anneliese Edle Mertz von Quirnheim née Kraudzun, Nl Alice Bachert

Letters to Hilde Baier, subsequently Hilde Edle Mertz von Quirnheim, Hilde von Mertz Papers and BA Abt. Potsdam, 90 Me6 Nl Mertz v. Quirnheim

Letters to Anna Luise Zacharias née Kessler, Gedenkstätte Deutscher Widerstand, Berlin

Mertz von Quirnheim, Hermann Ritter von, pocket diaries and other papers 1940–1944, BA Abt. Potsdam, 90 Me6 Nl Mertz v. Quirnheim

Mertz von Quirnheim, Hilde Edle, diaries 1944–1945, ms., Hilde von Mertz Papers

'Albrecht Ritter Mertz von Quirnheim, Oberst i.G.. Gefallen am 20. Juli 1944', typed carbon copy, n.p. n.d.

Mitzkus, [Bruno], 'Bericht über die Ereignisse im stellv. Generalkommando III. A.K. am 20. Juli 1944', typed, n.p. 9 Aug. 1945, Stiftung 'Hilfswerk 20. Juli 1944'

'Um den 20. Juli und das Ende im Wehrkreiskommando III', Berlin, typed, Bad Homburg v.d.H. April 1947, Stiftung 'Hilfswerk 20. Juli 1944'

Moll, Josef, 'Kriegsschauplatz Nordafrika 1942–43' n.p. [1944 or 1945], Nl Moll

Moltke, Freya von, Papers

Mommsen, M[omme], [enclosure for letter to RB ca. 1963], StGA

Morwitz, Ernst, letters to Stefan George, StGA

Name Index to Correspondence of the Military Intelligence Division of the War Department General Staff, Watf-Wee, NA M1194 roll 249

Oberkommando des Heeres, Chef H Rüst und BdE, 'Dienstplan für den Stab A.H.A.' 28 March 1940, BA-MA RW 4/v. 148

Oberkommando des Heeres, *see also* Army High Command, Kriegstagebuch, War Diary

Obermüller, Rudolf, papers in Nl BS, StGA Inv. P4

[Obermüller, Rudolf], 'Sokratische Ideenlehre im Phaidros', typed, n.p. April 1923

'Platon: Huldigung des liebenden Sokrates im Phaidros', ms. with dedication 'Zur Ehre Berthold Stauffenbergs', n.p. [April 1923], Nl BS, StGA Inv. P4

Oertzen *see* Selbstmord

Office of Strategic Services, Archive, Central Intelligence Agency, Washington, D.C. and Langley, Virginia

Office of Strategic Services *see also* Cheston; Dulles; Bancroft

Offz.-Krankenmeldebuch *see* Auszug

O.K.H.   Gen.St.d.H.-Zentr.Abt.,   Kriegs-Stellenbesetzung.   Stand: 15.11.39,
    15.2.40, 10.5.1940, 1.7.40, 1.12.40, 15.2.41, 1.11.41, 1.3.42, BA-MA
Partsch, Karl Josef, Papers
    'Erinnerungen an Robert Boehringer', typed, n.p. [1976], StGA
Personnel files of HPA and Military District commands [etc.], BA-Z, NA
Peschel, [Kurt], [minute], typed, [Wolfschanze] 22 July 1944, BA EAP 105/34, NA
    T-84 roll 21
Pfohl, Maria [née Appel], 'Meine Erinnerungen an den 20. Juli 1944', typed, Villa
    Angela [Argentina] 14 March 1957, Nl RF
Pfuhlstein, Alexander von, 'Meine Tätigkeit als Mitglied der Berliner Verschwörer-
    zentrale der deutschen Widerstandsbewegung vom 1. Oktober 1936–20. Juli
    1944', typed and mimeographed, Kreuzwertheim am Main May 1946, IfZ ZS
    592
    '12 Abhandlungen über persönliche Erlebnisse', typed, Kreuzwertheim am Main
    24 June 1946, IfZ ZS 592
Plassmann, Clemens, to Annemarie Koch 10 March 1947, typed copy in Hilde von
    Mertz's papers
Poetry album of Caroline Schenk, Countess Stauffenberg, StGA
Political Memorandum [based on information from Trott through Inga Almstrom
    née Carlgren (later married Kempe)], typed, [Stockholm] 23 March 1944,
    P.R.O. FO371/39059/139936
Pridun, Karl, 'Vermerk. Betrifft: 20. Juli 1944, Stellungnahme', typed, Bregenz 30
    Oct. 1953, IfZ ZS 1769
P[ro] M[emoria] angående svensk-tyska förhandlinger rörande Göteborgs trafiken i
    Berlin den 1–2 december 1943, Stockholm 4 Dec. 1943, Kungliga Utrikesde-
    partement, Stockholm, H 60 G/Allm. Göteborgstrafiken 1.–30.11.43
Prozessbericht, *see* Bormann; Lautz; Thierack
Records of the United States Nuernberg War Crimes Trials. United States of
    America v. Ernst Von Weizsaecker et al. (Case XI). December 20, 1947–April
    14, 1949, NA M897
Reichssicherheitshauptamt, files, BA R58/225
Remer, [Otto Ernst], 'Der Ablauf der Ereignisse am 20.7.1944 wie ich sie als
    Kommandeur des Wachbtl. Grossdeutschland erlebte', typed copy, Berlin 22
    July 1944, BA EAP 105/32 and *Spiegelbild* 1984 637–642
    'The 20 Jul 44 Plot', Interview, typed, PW Camp No. 26, 15 Aug. 1945, NA RG
    338 ETHINT 63
    [Interrogation], Oberstaatsanwalt bei dem Landgericht, Oldenburg 28 Oct. 1949,
    Az. -9 Js 164/49
Richert, [Arvid Gustav] (Swedish Minister in Berlin) to Ambassador in AA [Karl]
    Ritter 25 Nov. 1943, Kungliga Utrikesdepartement, Stockholm, H 60 G/Allm.
    Göteborgstrafiken 1.11.43–30.11.43
Ritgen, Helmut, 'Die Schulen der Panzertruppen des Heeres, 1918–1956', typed,
    Celle-Boye 1990
Ritter, [Karl], to [Arvid Gustav] Richert 23 Nov. 1943, Kungliga Utrikesdeparte-
    ment, Stockholm, H 60 G/Allm. Göteborgstrafiken 1.–30.11.43
Roell, [Ernst Günter] von, 'Bericht über die Ereignisse des Nachm. und Abends des
    20.7.1944', typed carbon copy, Berlin 21 July 1944, BA H 90 3/2
Rohowsky, Johannes, Nl in BA-MA N 124

[Rommel, Erwin], 'Tagesberichte' 3 Oct. 1942, 24 Oct.–23 Dec. 1942, 25 Dec. 1942–26 March 1943, NA T-84 roll 259, typed transcript of stenographic notes in IfZ Slg David Irving

'Tagesberichte' 9.5.43–6.9.43. Original. Privattagebuch O.B. (geheim) in [David Irving], Selected Documents on the Life and Campaigns of Field Marshall Erwin Rommel, E. P. Microform Limited, East Ardsley, Wakefield, Yorkshire, England 1978 roll 97049/11

Ruge, Friedrich, 'Tagebuch geführt beim Stabe der Heeresgruppe B (Fm. Rommel) 20.12.1943–1.8.1944', typed transcript of stenographic notes in Irving, Selected Documents Film 97049/2 and IfZ Slg Irving

Sauerbruch, Peter to Dr Gerd R. Ueberschär, Militärgeschichtliches Forschungsamt, 2 Feb. 1990

Schlee, [Rudolf], 'Bericht', typed copy, Berlin 23 July 1944, BA EAP 105/30

Schmidt, Jürgen, Nl in possession of Ursula Mannschatz née von Berg, Schmidt's widow

'Schriftstücke, die in dem "Hospiz am Askanischen Platz" in einem für Dr. Goerdeler bestimmten Umschlag vorgefunden wurden', [typed copy, RSHA] Amt IV/Sonderkommission 20.7.44, Berlin 3 Aug. 1944, 90 Ausfertigungen/ 23. Ausfertigung, Slg H.R. Trevor-Roper on David Irving film DJ38

'Die Schule des Sieges. Schlussbericht des Hörsaals IIb der Kriegsakademie', typed and mimeographed, Bingen/Rhein 23 June 1938, Nl Teske

Schulenburg, Fritz-Dietlof, Count, letters to Charlotte, Countess Schulenburg, in Nl Charlotte, Countess Schulenburg

Schulenburg, [Friedrich Werner, Count], 'Politische Beziehungen Deutschlands zur Sowjetunion', typed, n.p. end 1937, Herwarth Papers and AA/PA Pol. Abt.Ref.Russland Pol. Verschluss Nr. 73 and Botschaft Moskau/Politische Beziehungen zwischen Deutschland und der UdSSR Bd. 2

Schweizer, Karl, interview with Joachim Fest, television film 'Operation "Walküre"', Bavaria Atelier GmbH, Munich 1971

Schwerin von Krosigk, [Lutz Graf], Reichsminister der Finanzen, and Reichsminister der Justiz Georg Thierack to Oberfinanzpräsidenten und Oberreichsanwalt bei dem Volksgerichtshof 13 Nov. 1944, copy, BA Slg Schumacher 242

Scott, John, 'Mail Story. Confidential for the information of the Editors [*Time*], not for publication. Stockholm 17 Sept. 1944', NA 811.91258/9–2144

'Selbstmord des Majors Ulrich von Oertzen, Ia der Korps-Abteilung E der 2. Armee, im Dienstgebäude des Wehrkreiskommandos III', typed carbon copy, Amt V [des RSHA], Berlin 22 July 1944, BA R 58/1051

Siebeck, Eberhard, 'Erinnerung an Oberst i.G. Ritter Mertz von Quirnheim', typed carbon copy, Munsterlager 18 Dec. 1946, Siebeck Papers

Sodenstern, [Georg] von, 'Zur Vorgeschichte des 20. Juli 1944', typed, Frankfurt/ M. 1947, NA RG 338 MS B-499

Speer, [Julius], 'Betrifft: Bericht über meine Kenntnis der Vorgänge des 20. Juli 1944 im Führer-Hauptquartier', typed, Freiburg i.Br. 18 Oct. 1945, IfZ ED 88

Speidel, Hans, 'Zur Vorgeschichte des 20. Juli 1944', typed, Freudenstadt 16 June 1947, NA RG 338 Ms. B-721

Ståhle, Amtschef, to Chargé d'Affaires Eric von Post [Berlin] 5 Jan. 1944, Kungliga Utrikesdepartementet, Stockholm, H 60 G/Allm. 1.1.–29.2.44

Stahlberg, Alexander, 'Gespräch Manstein/Stauffenberg am 18.1.1943 in Taganrog, Niederschrift Dr. Bodo Scheurig, 16. Sept. 1965 nach persönlicher Befragung (am 15./16. Sept. 1965)', IfZ ZS A 31 Bd. 3

'Tresckow, Niederschrift Dr. Bodo Scheurig 16. Sept. 1965 nach Befragung Stahlbergs am 15. Sept. 1965', IfZ ZS A 31 Bd. 3

[written statement], typed, Hannover 31 Jan. 1957, IfZ 2651/57

Standesamt Ludwigsburg, Familienregister

Stauffenberg, Alexander Schenk, Count, Nachlass

'Der Reichs- und Preussische Minister für Wissenschaft, Erziehung und Volksbildung, Vorschlag zur Ernennung von einem Dozenten zum planmässigen ausserordentlichen Professor', Berlin 24 Dec. 1936, BA-Dokumentationszentrale (Berlin) ZA V 117

'Der Tod des Meisters. Zum zehnten Jahrestag', ms., n.p. [1944], StGA

'Der zwanzigste Juli 1944', typed, n.p. n.d. [ca. 1948], Slg H.R.Trevor-Roper on David Irving film DJ38

Deutsche Dienststelle (WASt), Bescheinigung, Berlin 30 Oct. 1991

'Einleitung zur St.G.-Rede im Ebelu', typed carbon copy, n.p. [1959], StGA

'Erinnerung an Stefan George. Gedenkfeier am 4. XII.1958 in Berlin', typed carbon copy, StGA

[Stauffenberg, Berthold Schenk, Count] 'Vortrag gehalten von Berthold Stauffenberg am 12.5.20', typed carbon copy with ms. amendments

'Des Empedokles Gestalt in Geschichte und Drama', typed carbon copy, n.p. n.d., Nl Pfizer

[Poems], StGA Umschlag II Berthold Stauffenberg Gedichte 1923

[Stauffenberg, Berthold, Alexander und Claus Schenk Graf von], 'Weihnachten 1915. Programm', ms., [Stuttgart 1915], Nl BS

[Stauffenberg, Caroline, Countess Schenk von], notes on her children, ms., 1905–1922/1945.

Letters to Rilke, Rilke-Archiv and copies in StGA

['War diary', 1914–1919, ms., ca. 1919, Papers NS]

'Lautlingen 1944/45 für Hupa', ms., [Lautlingen 1945], Nl AS

Letter to Mrs Britta Hammarskjöld 9 Jan. [1934], Kunglika Biblioteket, Stockholm, Nl Hammarskjöld

Stauffenberg, Claus Schenk, Count, 'Bemerkungen zu Gneisenau', Nl ClS

'Betreff: Gesuch von Claus Schenk Graf von Stauffenberg um Zulassung zur Reifeprüfung im Februar 1926 als ausserordentlicher Teilnehmer', Stuttgart, 12 Oct. 1925', Staatsarchiv Ludwigsburg E 202 Büschel 1630

Letters to Brigadier Georg von Sodenstern, BA-MA Nl 594

Stauffenberg, Claus Schenk Graf von, Nachlass

'Die Schlacht bei Issos', typed, Bamberg, 15 Oct. 1930, Nl ClS

'Vorschlag für die Winterausbildung des Minen-Werfer-Zuges', Bamberg, 14 Oct. 1931, typed, Nl ClS

Stauffenberg, Claus Schenk, Count, *see also* Leumunds-Zeugnis

Stauffenberg, Clemens Schenk, Count, 'Zu Anfrage zwecks Ergänzung der Karthotek über Zusammenhänge mit dem 20. Juli 1944', typed, Jettingen 27 Oct. 1946, Slg Stiftung 'Hilfswerk 20. Juli 1944'

[Stauffenberg, Hans Christoph Schenk Freiherr von], 'Rede von Hans Christoph

Freiherr von Stauffenberg am 2. August 1963' [in Bad Boll], typed and mimeographed, n.p. n.d.

Stauffenberg née Classen, Maria Schenk, Countess, Nachlass (partly in StGA)

[Stauffenberg, Nina Schenk, Countess], 'Lautlingen', typed, Bamberg 1966

[Stieff, Ili], 'Hellmuth Stieff, Generalmajor (seit 30. Januar 1944). Aufstellung das Attentat des 20. Juli 1944 betreffend', typed, n.p. n.d., BA-MA N 114/4

Stimson, Secretary of State for War Henry L., letter to John W. Pehle, Executive Director, War Refugee Board, Department of the Treasury, 31 March 1944, National Archives, Washington, RG 59, Department of State decimal file 840.48, Refugees/5499

Streve, [Gustav], Betr.: 'Besuch Oberst Graf Stauffenberg im FHQu. am 15.7.44', typed, [Wolfschanze] 23 July 1944, BA EAP 105/34 and *Spiegelbild* 1984 667

'Tagebuch Chef d. Stabes [with Chief of Army Munitions and Commander of Home Army] ab 19. XII. 41–[2.3.42]', NA T-78 roll 659

Tätigkeitsbericht *see* [War Diary, 10th Panzer-Division]

Teletype message ['Der Führer Adolf Hitler ist tot'], Aufnahmekopie des Chef des Stabes der Seekriegsleitung, [Berlin] 20 July [1944] 19.28 [hours], BA-MA III M 1005/11

Teletype message ['Innere Unruhen. Eine gewissenlose Clique frontfremder Partei-führer . . .'], typed copy of message received in Military District X (Hamburg), [Hamburg] 20 July 1944, files of Gauleitung Schleswig-Holstein and Der Höhere SS- und Polizeiführer bei den Reichsstatthaltern und Oberpräsidenten in Hamburg, in Oldenburg und in Bremen, in Hannover und in Schleswig-Holstein im Wehrkreis X vom 21. July 1944, Slg Trevor-Roper on David Irving film DJ 38

Teuchert, Friedrich Freiherr von, [notes on 20 July 1944], typed, Munich [1946]

Thierack, [Georg], Reichsminister der Justiz, to Heinrich Himmler 24 Oct. 1944, BA Slg Schumacher

Thierack *see also* Schwerin von Krosigk

[Thiersch, Urban], 'Bericht von Urban Thiersch, ehm. Oberleutnant der Art., über seine Begegnungen mit Oberst Graf Stauffenberg im Juli 1944', typed, Munich-Nymphenburg 1949, IfZ ED 88 Bd. 2

 'Eidesstattliche Erklärung', typed, Munich 21 April 1953, Nl RF

Thormaehlen, Ludwig, [Aufzeichnungen], typed, [Bad Kreuznach 1946], Nl Dr Walther Greischel

Thüngen, Dietz, Baron, Major (Res.), ['Aufzeichnung über Claus Graf Stauffenberg'], typed, Thüngen, 25 Jan. 1946, IfZ ED 88

Tresckow, E[ta] v[on], Befragung durch Bodo Scheurig 1 May 1969, IfZ Slg Scheurig

[Trott zu Solz, Clarita von], 'Adam von Trott zu Solz. Eine erste Material-sammlung, Sichtung und Zusammenstellung', typed and mimeographed, [Berlin 1958]

Trott *see also* Political Memorandum

Truppenkrankenbuch *see* Auszug

Truppenkrankenmeldebuch *see* Auszug

Truppenveränderungsmeldungen, Deutsche Dienststelle (WASt) Berlin

Unold, Georg von, Major i.G., 25 July 1941 to Claus, Count Stauffenberg, Nl ClS

Üxküll-Gyllenband, Ida, Countess, Nl

Üxküll-Gyllenband, Woldemar, Count, letters to Stefan George, StGA

Verhandlungen über technische Fragen des Göteborgverkehrs am 3. Januar 1944, Kungliga Utrikesdepartement, Stockholm, H 60 G/Allm. Göteborgstrafiken 1.1.–29.2.44

Verwendungsbereitschaft des Ersatzheeres, [order], Chef der Heeresrüstung und Befehlshaber des Ersatzheeres AHA Ia(I) Nr. 4810/42 g.kdos., 13 Oct. 1942, BA-MA RH 15/v. 174

[Waetjen, Eduard], Waetjen memorandum, typed, [Bern 1944], Princeton University, Allen W. Dulles Papers, Box 20

    Waetjen notes, typed, n.p. [1945/46], Princeton University, Allen W. Dulles Papers, Box 20

Wagner, [Eduard], 'Der Verlauf des 20. Juli (aus dem Gedächtnis)', typed, [Zossen] 21 July 1944, IfZ ED 95

'Walküre II', [order], Der Chef der Heeresrüstung und Befehlshaber des Ersatzheeres AHA Ia VII Nr. 1720/42 g Kdos. 26 May 1942, signed Olbricht, BA-MA RH 15/v. 175

'Walküre', [order], Der Chef der Heeresrüstung und Befehlshaber des Ersatzheeres AHA/Ia (I) Nr. 3830/43 g. Kdos., 31 July 1943, MFA WK XVII/91

Walküre, [order], Oberkommando des Heeres Chef H Rüst und BdE AHA Ia(I) Nr. 5413/43 g. Kdos., 6 Oct. 1943, MFA WK XVII/91

Walküre *see also* Brunhilde; Verwendungsbereitschaft

War Diary, [Kriegstagebuch, Generalstab des Heeres/Organisationsabteilung, Bd. III] 1.1.–31.7.1942, BA-MA RH 2/821 and NA T-78 roll 417

[Kriegstagebuch, Generalstab des Heeres/Organisationsabteilung, Bd. IV] 1.8.–31.12.1942, BA-MA RH 2/824 and NA T-78 roll 417

[Commander in Army Group Area B, Dec. 1942], BA-MA RH22/77

[Generalkommando XXXX. Panzer-Korps, Ia, Anlagen], VI. Abschnitt vom 2.10. bis 17.11.41, NA T-314 roll 977

OKM/1. Skl. Teil C VIII 1.1.44–29.4.45, BA-MA RM 7/219

[6th Panzer-Division, Abt. Ib]. 6. Panzerdivision, Abt. Ib, K.T.B. 5.11.39–9.5.40, 22.5.40–3.7.40, NA T-315 roll 322

[6th Panzer-Division.] Anlagen-Band A zum Kriegstagebuch der 6. Pz.-Div. Ia. Feldzug Frankreich 10.5.40–1.7.40, NA T-315 roll 337

[War Diary no. 2 of 6th Panzer-Division]. Anlagen-Band C zum Kriegstagebuch der 6. Pz.-Div. Feldzug Frankreich 19.5.40–6.6.40, NA T-315 roll 337

[War Diary no. 2 of 6th Panzer-Division]. 6. Panzer-Division, Ia. Anlagenband C z. KTB. Nr. 2. Operationsbefehle, Meldungen, Ferngespräche. C40–C113. Teil II. 19.5.1940–6.6.1940, NA T-315 roll 320

[War Diary no. 2 of 6th Panzer-Division]. 6. Pz.Div.-Ia Anl.Bd. D z. K.T.B. Nr. 2, Gefechtsberichte, Erfahrungs-Berichte über besondere Vorkommnisse 21.5.–17.7.1940, NA T-315 roll 320

[War Diary no. 2 of 6th Panzer-Division]. 6. Panz.Div.-Ia. k: Anl.Bd. F, G, H z. K.T.B. Nr. 2, Kriegsrangliste d.Stab., Verlustliste d.Stb. u.d.gesamt.Div. Gef.u.Verpfl.Stärken dsgl. l: Anl.Bd. J z. K.T.B. Nr. 2, Wichtige Vernehmungen, Tagesbefehle, Vorschläge z. Ritterkreuz 30.5.–19.6.1940, NA T-315 roll 320

[War Diary no. 2 of 6th Panzer-Division]. 6. Pz.Div.-Ia Funksprüche 22.5.1940, NA T-315 roll 321

[War Diary no. 2 of 6th Panzer-Division]. 6. Panzer-Division, Ia. Original-Befehle und Meldungen zum KTB. Nr. 2. 16.5.1940–21.5.1940, NA T-315 roll 321

[War Diary no. 2 of 6th Panzer-Division]. 6. Pz.Div. Abt. Ia. Kriegstagebuch No. 2. Orig.Befehle u. Meldungen 25.5.–3.6.1940, T-315 roll 321

[War Diary no. 2 of 6th Panzer-Division.] Anlagen-Band C zum Kriegstagebuch der 6. Pz.-Div. Feldzug Frankreich. 6.4.40–19.5.40. Heimat, Frankreich, Operationsakten, NA T-315 roll 337

[War Diary of 6th Panzer-Division.] 6. Panzer Division Ia K.T.B. 17.6.1941–15.9.1941, NA T-315 roll 323

[War Diary of 6th Panzer-Division.] Abt. Ia Nr. 1323/40 geh., Erfahrungsbericht der 6. Panzer-Division: Feldzug Frankreich vom 10.5.–1.7.1940, typed and mimeographed, Wuppertal 18 July 1940, Nl ClS

[War Diary of 6th Panzer-Division.] Abt. Ib, Zu Fragebogen D: Heeresversorgung, typed and mimeographed, n.p. 12 July 1940, Nl ClS

[War Diary of 6th Panzer-Division.] Abt. Ib Nr. 1833/40 geh., Erfahrungsbericht über die Versorgung der 6. Pz.Div. während des Feldzuges in Frankreich. (10.5. bis 3.7.1940), typed and mimeographed, Wuppertal 14 Sept. 1940, Nl ClS

[War Diary, 10th Panzer-Division.] Anlagenband Nr. V zum Kriegstagebuch der 10. Panzer Division Nr. 6, BA-MA RH 27–10/42 and NA T-315 roll 568

[War Diary, 10th Panzer-Division.] Anlagenband Nr. VII zum Kriegstagebuch der 10. Panzer Division Nr. 6. Meldungen vom 1.1.42–28.2.1942, NA T-315 roll 569

[War Diary, 10th Panzer-Division.] 10. Panzer-Div. – Abt. Ia – Anlagenb. z. K.T.B. Nr. 6. 29.10.1942–19.4.1943, NA T-315 roll 570

[War Diary, 10th Panzer-Division.] 10. Panzer Division Abtl. Ic, Tätigkeitsbericht, angef.: 29.11.42, abgeschl. 15.3.43, NA T-315 roll 570

[War Diary, 10th Panzer-Division, Abt. Ic, Tätigkeitsbericht 22. März 1943–24. April 1943], NA T-315 roll 570

[War Diary, 10th Panzer-Division.] 10. Panzer-Division Abt. Ic Tätigkeitsbericht 22.3.–24.4.1943. II. Anlagen 2.4.1943–22.4.1943, NA T-315 roll 570

War Diary *see also* Kriegstagebuch

Warlimont, Walter, Interview with Joachim Fest, Bavaria Atelier GmbH, Munich [1971]

Wedemeyer, Albert C., G-2 Report. Germany (Combat). Subject: German General Staff School, typed, 11 July 1938, NA RG 407

Wedemeyer *see also* Name Index to Correspondence

Wehrmacht-Fernsprechverzeichnis Gross-Berlin Teil II, Druck: Heeresfachschule für Technik Berlin [1943], NA T-78 roll 659

Wehrstammbuch des Schenk, Graf von Stauffenberg, Claus Philipp Maria, Oberst, BA-Z

Wussow, Botho v[on], 'Einige Sätze zu dem SS-Bericht über den 20. Juli 1944, der in den *Nordwestdeutschen Heften* veröffentlicht wurde u.z. 1947 Heft 1/2', typed, n.p. 1947, Nl Schwerin von Schwanenfeld

Yorck von Wartenburg, Peter Graf, letters to Marion Gräfin Yorck von Wartenburg, Nl Yorck and (part) BA NS 6/50

Zeller née Miller, Elsbet, letter to Ricarda Huch 10 Dec. 1946, IfZ ZS/A 26/3
Ziegler, Delia, 'Bericht über den 20.7.1944', typed, n.p. [ca. 1947], IfZ ED 88 Bd.2

b. Letters to the author, unless other recipients are indicated

Stauffenberg family and relatives
Johnston, Annabel von née Siemens, 10 Aug. 1982
Lerchenfeld, Rudolf Baron, Colonel (Ret.), 23 March 1971
Saucken, Olga von, née Countess Üxküll, 29 March 1965 to Kramarz
    Nov. 1988, 4 Feb. 1989, 25 Nov. 1990, 3 March 1991
Schiller, Klara, 28 Sept. 1989, 24 June, 9 Aug. 1993
Stauffenberg, Heimeran [Count] von, 18 June 1986 to Jeff Myrow
Stauffenberg, Nina, Countess, 12 Feb. 1964, 13 Aug. 1968, 11 Sept. 1968, 8 Feb.
    1977, 26 Sept. 1988, 12 Oct. 1988, 10 Nov. 1991
    22 Oct. 1961, 17 March 1962, 23 May 1962, 16 Nov. 1962, 1 July 1964, 15 Sept.
    1964, 16 Sept. 1964, 2 Oct. 1964, 25 June 1965, 2 July 1965, 15 July 1965 to
    Kramarz
    to Wolfgang Venohr Feb. 1987
Stauffenberg, [Otto Philipp], Count, 20 Feb. 1973

Classmates of Berthold and Alexander
(a, b = form; Berthold and Alexander were in form b)
Gross, Paul (a), 19 April 1981
Held, Robert (b), 17 April 1981
Hock, Otto (b), 21 April 1981
Kraemer, Walter (a), 27 Nov. 1981
Marchtaler, Elisabeth von (widow of Hans Ulrich von Marchtaler, classmate of the
    twins, b), 7 Sept. 1981
Schefold, Karl (a), 15 Oct. 1973, 9 Sept. 1981, 18 May 1982, 22 Aug. 1988

Classmates of Claus
(a, b = form; Claus was in form b)
Bach, Margot (widow of ClS's classmate Alfred Bach, b), 11 July, 22 Dec. 1985, 29
    Sept. 1986, 5 Feb. 1988
Bopp, Alfons (b), 6 Aug., 30 Dec. 1983, 10 Nov. 1984
Buck, Eberhard (b), 13 Dec. 1969
Cantz, Rudolf (a), 5 Nov. 1969, 1 Dec. 1969, 9 Feb. 1983
Eckardt, Heinrich von (a), 17 Feb. 1983
Hamma, Franz (b), 19 Nov. 1971
Haug, Friedrich (a), 8 Nov. 1969, 5 March 1983
Hofacker, Helmut (form below ClS), 4 Feb. 1983
Lowinsky, Eduard (b), 2 Nov. 1983, 10 Jan., 24 May 1984, 1 June 1985
Lutz, Walther (b), 12 Nov. 1969
Mühlberger, Siegfried (b), 9 March 1971
Müller-Gmelin, Carl (b), 28 Nov. 1969, 2 and 20 March 1983, 30 Nov. 1984
Orthuber, Richard (b), 13 Dec. 1983
Schneiderhan, Kurt (b), 14 Feb. 1983

Vollmer, Walter (b), 22 Dec. 1969, 12 and 25 Feb. 1983
Wirth, Eugen (b), 12 Feb. 1983

Military comrades of Claus, Count Stauffenberg
Albrecht, Heinz-Günther, 11 May 1966, 1 Aug. 1966, 27 Aug. 1967
Anz, Otto, Lt. Col.(Res.), summer and autumn 1943 IIa in 168th Inf. Div., 13 June 1971
Bäke, Dr Franz, 9 Aug. 1972
Balser, Udo, Major (ret.), in April 1943 Lt. and commander of staff battery III./Pz. Artl. Rgt. 90 in 10th Pz. Div., 4 March 1991, 25 March 1991
   23 Jan. 1991 to Albert Schick
   12 Dec. 1991 to H. v. Schönfeldt
Beelitz, Dietrich, Brigadier (ret.), 28 April 1964, 25 Aug. 1964
Benzmann, Heinrich, Major (ret.), 19 April 1978
Berger, Oskar-Alfred, Brigadier (ret.), Aug. 1942–summer 1943 Org. Branch./ Section Head I, 10 March, 30 April, 7 May, 30 June, 27 July 1984
Biskamp, Dr Klaus, son of Dr E. Biskamp, 7 March 1991
Bleicken, Otto Hinrich, Colonel (GS, ret.), 1942 Section Head Qu.4 in Army Gen. Staff/Gen. Qu. M./Branch II (War Administration), 15 Sept., 25 Dec. 1990
Boeselager, Philipp Freiherr von, Major (Res., ret.), CO I. Btl. No. 31 Cav. Rgt., 15 Jan. 1965, 28 Aug. 1969, 16 Aug. 1984
Breitenbuch, Eberhard von, 8 Nov. 1966
Broich, Friedrich Freiherr von, Major General (ret.), 14, 20, 25 June 1962 to Kramarz
Bürker, Ulrich, Colonel (GS, ret.), 18 Oct. 1972, 20 Jan. 1977
Bürklin, Wilhelm, Colonel (GS, ret.), 15 June, 15 July 1962, 6 April 1965 to Kramarz
Burk, Klaus, Lt. (ret.), special missions officer (O IV) to CO 10th Pz. Div., 27 Oct., 6 Dec. 1990, 12 Feb. 1991, 28 Feb. 1991, 7 April 1991, 27 April 1991
Bussche, Axel Freiherr von dem, Major (ret.), 9 Feb., 1 March 1966, 18 Sept. 1967
Busse, Markus von, 13 March 1984
Busse, Theodor, Lt. Gen. (ret.), 1943 Chief of Gen. Staff to Manstein, 29 Nov. 1962 to Kramarz
Canstein, Raban Freiherr von, Brigadier (ret.), 25 June 1988, 25 Sept. 1988
Cords, Dr Helmuth, Captain (ret.), 24 Oct. 1967 to Kramarz
   23 Aug. 1981 to E. Zeller, IfZ ED 88 Bd. 2
Cramer, Hans, Lt.Gen. (ret.), 1934–1936 instructor at Cav. School in Hanover, 1943 Rommel's successor as General Commanding German Africa Corps, 20 Feb. 1963 to Kramarz
Degner, Friedrich, 1 Oct. 1968
Dosch, Rolf, Captain (ret.), 10, 29 April 1984
Erasmus, Dr Johannes, 1944 Ia in Div. 'Brandenburg', 29 Aug. 1965
Ferber, Ernst, 8 March 1984
Fremerey, Max, Major General (ret.), Oct. 1934 Perfall's successor as CO No. 17 Cav. Rgt., 20 June 1962 to Kramarz
Fritsch, Dr Georg Freiherr von, Colonel (ret.), 1943 in OKW/WFSt, 26 Nov., 7 Dec. 1963 to Kramarz

Fritzsche, Dr Hans, Captain (ret.), 1943 Deputy CO No. 9 Res. Btl., 6, 9 Aug. 1971, 23 Aug. 1984

Gersdorff, Rudolf-Christoph Freiherr von, Brigadier (ret.), 9 June 1962 to Kramarz

Glaesemer, Wolfgang, Brigadier (ret.), 10 June 1986 to Major (ret.) Werner Rode, 13 Feb. 1989 to Ritgen

Goetzke, Claus-Peter, Lt. (Res.), Chief Techn. Officer in Bendlerstrasse Communications Centre, 14 July 1965

Gottberg, Helmut von, Lt. and Adj. in No. 9 Inf. Res. Btl. in Potsdam, 22 April, 16 June 1966

Greiner, Heinz, Brigadier (ret.), 9 March 1971
6, 5 May 1964 to Kramarz

Hagen, Erica von, widow of Lt. (Res.) Albrecht von Hagen, 15 Jan. 1972

Halder, Franz, General (ret.), 26 Jan., 23 March, 18 May 1962 to Kramarz

Harnack, Fritz, Major (GS, ret.), 1944 Section Head in AHA, 2 Oct. 1984

Harteneck, Gustav, Lt. Gen. (ret.), 15 March 1971

Hassell, Johann Dietrich von, Major (GS, ret.), 15 July 1942–30 Sept. 1942 1st special missions officer to Lt. Gen. Leo Freiherr Geyr von Schweppenburg, General-Commanding XXXXth Pz. Corps, 9, 14 Aug., 5 Sept. 1990

Hausmann, Ulrich, Second Lt. in No. 9 Inf. Rgt., 23 Dec. 1945 to Mrs Maria Sybille Klausing

Heinz, Friedrich Wilhelm, 8 March 1966

Herber, Franz, Lt. Col. (GS) in AHA, 25 Jan. 1966

Hendrichs, Dr Victor, Lt. Col.(ret.), 16 Feb. 1971

Hertel, Hans-Joachim, Colonel (ret.), Feb.-April 1943 Captain and Adj. in Pz. Gren. Rgt.86, and Ia of an armoured combat command, 11 March 1991, 18 April 1991

Herwarth von Bittenfeld, Hans Heinrich, Legation Secretary, Captain (Cav., Res.), 3 Jan. 1985

Heusinger, Adolf, Lt. Gen. (ret.), 29 March, 14 April 1977

Heyde, Bolko von der, Colonel (GS, ret.), 3 Jan., 8 and 30 June 1972

Hübner, Werner, Lt. Col. (ret.), June 1940–May 1941 Captain in OKH/Org. Branch/Section I, 13 June, 13 July 1972

Huhs, Wilhelm, Colonel (ret.), 1 Nov. 1971, 20 Sept. 1972, 10 May 1973

Husen, Paulus van, Captain (Cav., Res.) in OKW/WFSt/Garrison Section in Berlin, 16 Jan. 1968
2 July 1963, 5 April 1965 to Kramarz

Kanitz, Rainer Graf von, 23 March 1964 to Mrs E. Wagner

Kempe, Ludwig, Major (ret.), 2 May 1965, 2 Jan. 1970

Kempf, Werner, Lt. Gen. (ret.), 7 Jan. 1963 to Kramarz

Keysser, Dr C. Hans, 6, 12, 23 Feb., 1, 21 April 1991

Kielmansegg, Johann Adolf, Count, Lt. Gen. (ret.), 23 Aug. 1971, 13 March 1984, 15 Aug. 1990

Kleikamp, Helmut, Brigadier (ret.), Chief, P3 Branch in OKH/Army Personnel Office, 18 Dec. 1962, 15, 21 Jan. 1963 to Kramarz

Kleist, Ewald Heinrich, Second Lt. in No. 9 Gren. Rgt., 15 Sept. 1964, 14 Sept. 1967, 2 Oct. 1968
14 Feb. 1946 [to Alexander, Count Stauffenberg], IfZ ED 88 Bd. 2

Kratzer, Rolf, Colonel (GS, ret.), 19 July 1972

Lamey, Hubert, Brigadier (ret.), War Academy instructor, 12 July 1971

Leyendecker, Wilhelm, Major (ret.), Feb.-23 March 1943 CO II./No. 86 Pz. Gren. Rgt. in 10th Pz. Div., 12 Feb. 1991, 18 April 1991

Loeper, Friedrich-Wilhelm Freiherr von, Major-General (ret.), 24 March 1971

Lüke, Hans, 1943 Lt.Col. in I./No. 69 Pz. Gren. Rgt. in 10th Pz. Div., 28 Jan., 20 Feb., 6 March 1991

Luz, Helwig, Major General (ret.), 2 March 1971, 17, 31 July 1972

Maass, Karl-Heinz, Major (GS, ret.), 1943 Captain and Company Commander 4./No. 7 Pz. Rgt. in 10th Pz. Div., 20 March, 20 May 1991

Maizière, Ulrich de, Lt. Gen. (ret.), 13 March 1984
 31 Oct. 1963 to Kramarz

Mannschatz, Diethelm, Lt. Col. (ret.), 21 Aug. 1972

Manstein, Erich von, Fieldmarshal, 15 Nov. 1962 to Kramarz, 30 Oct. 1972 to Williams (carbon copy in Nl Manstein)

Manteuffel, Hasso von, Lt. Gen. (ret.), 28 Feb. 1971, 18, 22 July 1972
 20 June 1964 to Kramarz

Merk, Ernst, Brigadier (ret.), 25 May 1972

Metz, Lothar, Brigadier (ret.), with Claus, Count Stauffenberg in Inf. School, War Academy and OKH, 30 May, 1 Aug. 1971

Mueller-Hillebrand, Burkhart, Major-General, 15 July 1962 to Kramarz

Niemack, Horst, Brigadier (ret.), 24 March 1971

Oehlert, Wilhelm, Feb.-April 1943 Lt., Adj. to C.O. II./No. 86 Pz. Gren. Rgt., 18 April 1991

Pamberg, Bernhard, Brigadier (ret.), 26 Jan. 1971

Perfall, Gustav Freiherr von, Major General (ret.), 11 Feb. 1966

Pezold, Bernd von, Colonel (GS, ret.), 12 Feb. 1963, 6 Feb. 1966 to Kramarz

Reerink, Werner, Lt. Col. (GS, ret.), 1938–1940 1st special missions officer and war diary keeper in 1st Light Div. and 6th Pz. Div., respectively, 24 March 1965 to Kramarz
 4 Nov. 1971, 27 Feb. 1987

Reile, Wilhelm, 10 Feb. 1991, 17 [March] 1991, 5 April 1991

Reimann, Hans, Colonel (ret.), 17 July 1962 to Kramarz

Reinecke, Hermann, Lt. Gen. (ret.), 31 May 1964, 7 Nov. 1967

Reinhardt, Hellmuth, Brigadier (ret.), 12 Nov. 1967, 2 July 1972

Reinicke, Georg, Major General (ret.), 16 March 1971

Ribbentrop, Rudolf von, 19 March 1991

Richthofen, Prof. Dr Bolko Freiherr von, 28 Nov. 1978

Ritgen, Helmut, Colonel (ret.), 18 Feb. 1991

Rode, Werner, Major (ret.), 14 Aug. 1971, 27 Dec. 1989
 to Dr H. Pigge 24 July 1971

Roidl, Wolfgang, Major (ret.), 1940–beginning 1941 in OKH/Org. Branch, 28 April 1984

Rotberg, Arnold Freiherr von, Brigadier (ret.), 1941 1st special missions officer to General Commanding XXIVth Pz. Corps, Lt. Gen. Geyr von Schweppenburg, 28 July 1990

Rothkirch[-Trach], Karl-Christoph, Count, 1944 Lt. and special missions officer to OC Pz. Troops School II Krampnitz, to Ritgen 14 Jan. 1989

Rüdt von Collenberg, Ludwig Freiherr, Brigadier (ret.) 3 Feb. 1964
Sachenbacher von Schrottenberg, Alfred, Colonel (ret.), 18 Feb. 1971
Salm-Salm, Nikolaus Leopold Prince, 26 March 1984
Sauerbruch, Peter, Colonel (GS, ret.), 15 Nov. 1980, 5 Sept. 1990, 14 Nov. 1990, 14
    April 1991
    [ca. 1964] to a son of CIS, in Slg Kramarz
    24 July 1964 to Kramarz
Schack, Hans von, Major (ret.), 10 March 1971
Schick, Albert, 1940–1941 Sergeant in 10th Pz. Div., 1944 in Pz. Instruction Div.,
    author of history of 10th Pz. Div., 30 May 1991, 10 Dec. 1991, 5 Feb. 1992,
    25 Jan. 1994
Schmid, Heinz, Colonel (ret.), 23 Sept. 1962 to Kramarz
Schobess, Herbert, Lt. Col. (ret.), 9 Dec. 1971
Schöne, Volkmar, Colonel (ret.), 5 March 1971
    17 Dec. 1962 to Kramarz
Schönfeldt, Heinz von, Major (ret.), to mid-March 1943 O.C. II. Btl. No. 90 Pz.
    Art. Rgt. in 10th Pz. Div., from mid-March 1943 Adjutant and IIa in 10th Pz.
    Div., 22 March 1991, 22 April 1991
Schott, Edwin, Second Lt. (Res.), 20 April 1991, 26 April 1991, 27 May 1991
Schulte-Heuthaus, Hermann, 20 Sept. 1965
Schweizer, Karl, Corporal, 2 Nov. 1967
Seefried, Adolf Freiherr von, Colonel (Ret.), 13 April 1971
Seraphim, Dr Hans-Günther, 1942 Captain and Quartermaster in the Armenian
    Legion, 23 March 1980, 17 Aug. 1990
Siebeck, Dr Eberhard, Major (ret.), 1 Oct. 1971, 17 April 1973, 5 Nov. 1980, 6
    March 1981
Spannenkrebs, Walter, Brigadier (ret.), 30 Nov. 1971
Speer, Dr Julius, 22 Feb. 1966
Staedke, Helmut, Major General (ret.), 13 Jan. 1963, 5 April 1965 to Kramarz
Stahl, Paul, Colonel (ret.), 6th Pz. Div., 6 May 1987
Stirius, Hans-Werner, Lt. Col. (ret.), 2 Feb. 1967
Strik-Strikfeldt, Wilfried, Captain (Res., ret.), 1, 11 Aug. 1963 to Kramarz
Süsskind-Schwendi, Hugo Freiherr von, Colonel (GS, ret.), 7 March 1971
Süsskind-Schwendi, Max Theodor Freiherr von, Lt.Col. (ret.), 22 Jan. 1966
Tempelhoff, Hans-Georg von, Brigadier (ret.), 7 July 1977
Theilacker, Eugen, Brigadier (ret.), 16 March 1971
Thomale, Wolfgang, Major General (ret.), 11 Aug. 1971
Thon, Albert, motor pool dispatcher in OKH in Berlin, Bendlerstrasse, 21 July
    1971 to Westdeutscher Rundfunk Cologne
    13 Aug., 15 Sept. 1971
Varnbüler, Ulrich Freiherr von, Colonel (ret.), 19 Jan. 1971
Viebig, Wilhelm, Brigadier (ret.), 24 Aug. 1971
Voll, Paul Theo, 28 Aug. 1964, 28 July 1972
Wagner, Gerhard, Rear Admiral (ret.), 17 Nov. 1964
Walzer, Hans, 22 Dec. 1965 to Kramarz
Weckmann, Kurt, Major-General (ret.), 1942–1944 OC General Staff Course and
    War Academy, 18 Feb. 1971

Wedemeyer, A. C., General (ret.), 5 June 1972
   9 May, 22 June 1962 to Kramarz
Weist, Heinz-Dietrich, 1943 Lt., OC 2nd platoon/6th comp./No. 69 Pz. Gren.
   Rgt./10th Pz. Div., 19 Feb. 1991
Weizsäcker, Richard Freiherr von, [May 1970], 28 Jan. 1992
Wilcke, Henning, Brigadier (ret.), 3 July, 21 Sept. 1988
Zeitzler, Kurt, General (ret.), 3, 26 July 1962 to Kramarz
Zipfel, Friedrich, 1943 Lt. in 10th Pz. Div., 3 May 1961 to Dr Walter Hammer, IfZ
   ED 106/91

Stefan George circle
Boehringer, Robert, 23 Aug. 1968
Brodersen, Arvid, 19 July 1988
Curtius, Ilse, 6 Dec. 1985
Elze, Walter, 28 Aug. 1968
Fahrner, Rudolf, 6 Aug. 1981, 10 July 1982, March 1984
   5 July 1962 to Prof. Walter Baum, IfZ ZS 1790
   15 July 1963 to Kramarz
Landmann, Georg Peter, 31 Aug. 1968
Partsch, Karl Josef, 7 April, 15 May 1989
   March 1963 to Walter Greischel, StGA
Strebel, Hellmut, 21 Aug. 1988
Wolters-Thiersch, Gemma, 11 May 1982

Friends and others
Appel, Maria, Secretary to Berthold Graf Stauffenberg, 15 April 1946 to Fahrner
Auswärtiges Amt, 15 Jan. 1992
Bach, Rudolph D., 28 July 1983
Bauch, Kurt to Maria, Countess Stauffenberg, 25 June 1946, Nl MS
Blomberg, Ruth von, 24 July 1962 to Kramarz
Bremme, Beate, wife of fellow officer of ClS in 6th Pz. Div., 3 Oct. 1962 to Kramarz
Bundesarchiv-Zentralnachweisstelle, 24 Feb. 1977
Daur, Elisabeth née Dipper, 16 Sept. 1983, 1 Feb. 1984, 23 April 1985
Deutsche Dienststelle für die Benachrichtigung der nächsten Angehörigen von
   Gefallenen der ehemaligen deutschen Wehrmacht (Wehrmacht-Auskunft-
   Stelle) Berlin, 30 Oct. 1991
Dieckmann, Erika, sister of Albrecht Ritter Mertz von Quirnheim, 30 Jan. 1979
Dönhoff, Marion, Countess, 25 April 1991
Eibl, Adalbert, Corporal, 5 March 1987
Falkenhausen, Dr Gotthard Freiherr von, 24 March 1947 to Dr Clemens Plassmann
Gerling, Heinz, Bureau of Monuments, Magdeburg, to Dr Ruth Mövius, 19 Aug.
   1988
Gerstenmaier, Eugen, 2 July 1979
Götz, Waltraud von, cousin of Trott, 5 Sept., 24 Nov. 1962 to Kramarz
Graf née Klaeger, Ruth, 7 April 1978
Hardenberg-Neuhardenberg, Renate, Countess, 20 Oct. 1946 to Mrs Marie-Sybille
   Klausing

Hase, Margarethe von, to Brigadier (ret.) Friedrich von Unger, March 1964
Herzer, Maria, step-daughter of Hans-Jürgen Graf von Blumenthal, 13 Sept. 1991
Hoffmann, Konrad, 15 Sept. 1984
Jessen, Sydney, 28 Aug. 1946 to Ruth Klaeger, Graf Papers
Keilson-Lauritz, Marita, 28 Oct. 1984
Koch, Oberarzt Dr med., Karl-Olga-Krankenhaus Stuttgart, 15 May 1981
Kröner, Margot, 14 Aug. 1981
Malone, Henry O., 10 Dec. 1978
Mannschatz, Ursula, 11 July 1972
Mannschatz, Diethelm, Lt. Col. (ret.), 21 Aug. 1972
Manstein, Rüdiger von, 21 June 1991, 26 Feb. 1992
Mende, Gerhard von, 26 July, 19 Sept. 1963 to Kramarz
Mertz von Quirnheim, Hilde Edle, 31 Jan. 1980
Mommsen, Momme, 14 April 1982
Müller, Ruth, 4 April 1947 to Ricarda Huch, IfZ Slg Ricarda Huch
Nettesheim, Kurt, 22 Aug. 1968
Obermüller, Rudolf, 2[8] Oct. 1978, 14, 15 Aug, 30 Oct. 1981, 6 May 1986
Reinhardt, Irmengard, 2 July 1972
Rohwer, Dr Jürgen, 7 Jan. 1969
Sachsen-Meiningen, Clara, Duchess of, 10 Jan. 1973
Sänger, Fritz, 15 Dec. 1980
Schmölders, Professor Dr G[ünter], 1 and 5 July 1963 to Kramarz
Schulenburg, Charlotte, Countess, widow of Fritz-Dietlof, Count Schulenburg,
     [8 May 1990], 15 Aug. 1990
   12 Aug. 1963 to Kramarz
Schwerin von Schwanenfeld, Detlef, Count, 1 Sept. 1991, 31 Dec. 1991
Staatsarchiv Magdeburg, 7 Oct. 1988
Stadt Heidelberg, Stadtarchiv, 29 April 1988
Stieff, Ili, widow of Brigadier H.Stieff to [Ricarda Huch] 13 July 1947, IfZ Slg
     Ricarda Huch ZS/A 26/3
Stockert, Franz K. von, 7 March 1982, 5 May 1982, 9 June 1988
[Traber, Werner] to Prof. Dr W. Baum (University of Freiburg i.Br.), 28 May 1956,
     Nl MS
Tresckow, Eta von, widow of Tresckow, 26 July 1971
Ueberschär, Gerd R., 17 Dec. 1990
Universität Halle-Wittenberg/Archiv, 16 July 1982
Voll, Paul Theo, 28 July 1972
Waetjen, Eduard, 3 July 1987
Wallenberg, Jacob, 16 March 1977
Wallenberg, Marcus, 5 April 1978, 3 Jan. 1979
Weddigen, Fritz, 19 Oct. 1962 to Kramarz
Wehner, Dr Bernd, member of 'Sonderkommission 20. Juli', 27 Oct. 1965
Yorck zu Wartenburg, Marion, Countess, 10 Aug. 1972
   5 Sept. 1963 to Kramarz
Zeller, Eberhard, 31 Dec. 1994
Zeller née Miller, Elsbet, 23 Sept. 1983, 25 Jan. 1984

c. Unpublished memoirs

Stauffenberg family and relations

Handel, Paul von, 'Erinnerungen an Litta', typed, n.p. [1974]

Kaehne, Brigittte von née von Hofacker, 'Meine Brüder', typed, Tübingen, 1987

Stauffenberg, Nina Schenk, Countess, 22 April 1964, Slg Kramarz
  'Das Halsband der Anna Iwanowna. Geschichte und Geschichten meiner Eltern',
    typed, Bamberg, 1966
  'Litta', typed, [Bamberg, 1966]

Military comrades of Claus, Count Stauffenberg

Benzmann, Heinrich, Major (ret.), 15 Nov. 1977

Bleicken, Otto Hinrich, Colonel (GS, ret.), 'Bewegte Jahre – Erinnerungen eines
    Generalstabsoffiziers', typed, Hamburg, 1990

[Bürker, Wilhelm], 'Im Wehrmachtführungsstab 1943. Mein Gespräch mit
    Stauffenberg (etwa Sept. 43)', typed, n.p., [ca. 1975]

Burchardt, Heinz, Major, in Office of Chief of Army Signals/Central Section
    (Personnel), 13 July 1965

Bussche, Axel Freiherr von dem, 27 Nov. 1990

Delius, Kurt, Lt. Col. (ret.), 'Der 20. Juli 1944', typed, Hoberge-Uerentrup, 28 July
    1965

[Hassell, Johann-Dietrich von], 'Aus dem Kaukasusfeldzug 1942/43', typed, n.p.,
    [1943]
  'Aufzeichnung – Besuch in Lautlingen am 11./12.10.1947', typed carbon copy,
    Tübingen, 17 Oct. 1947

Heiner, Ernst, 'Unterlagen über die ehemalige 6. Kompanie (Feldpostnummer
    18503) des Panzer-Grenadierregiments 69 (10.Panzerdivision) für die Zeit vom
    Mai 1942 bis März 1943', typed, Aalen, 1979

Mueller-Hillebrand, Burkhart, 'Briefe an meinen Sohn Burkhart', ms., 4 quarto
    notebooks, [Prisoner-of-War Camp] Grizedale near Windermere,
    Gefangenenlager Camp 1 [and other camps, from Feb. 1946], Allendorf Krs
    Marburg/Lahn, 27 Oct. 1945–[April 1947], Nl Mueller-Hillebrand

Oppenfeld, Horst von, 'Erinnerungen an Stauffenberg in Nordafrika, nach 41
    Jahren', typed, n.p., 27 May 1984

Reerink, Werner, ['Aufzeichnung über Claus Graf Stauffenberg'], typed, n.p., June
    1963

Reile, [Wilhelm], 'Einsatz der 10. Pz. Div. in Frankreich 1942 und in Tunesien',
    typed, [Ehringshausen, ca. 1986]

Sauerbruch, Peter, 12 Feb. 1963, 24 July 1964 for Kramarz

Vogel, Werner, Betr.: '20.7.1944 – eigene Erlebnisse', typed, n.p., 26 June 1970

Zipfel, Friedrich, 'Bericht über meine Begegnung mit Claus Graf Schenk von
    Stauffenberg', typed, Berlin, 18 Jan. 1964

Stefan George circle

Fahrner, Rudolf, 'Frank', ms., n.p., n.d., StGA
  'Mein Leben mit Offa', ms., n.p., 1985

Mommsen, Momme, 'Maria Fehling und die Stauffenbergs: Auf Grund persönlicher Erinnerungen an Maria Fehling und Albrecht von Blumenthal', typed,
[Palo Alto, 1982]

Friends and others
Gichtel, Hermann, 'Bericht über die Verhandlung gegen Oberst Jochen Meichssner
vor dem Volksgerichtshof', typed copy, n.p., 16 Oct. 1946
Nettesheim, Kurt, 'Bericht', typed, Wuppertal, 14 June 1968
Rantzau, Ehrengard, Countess [von, née Countess Schulenburg], 'Erinnerungen an
die Vorbereitungen zum 20. Juli 1944', typed, n.p., n.d., Stiftung 'Hilfswerk
20. Juli 1944'
Schwerin von Schwanenfeld, Marianne, Countess, 'Ulrich-Wilhelm Graf Schwerin
von Schwanenfeld', typed, [Heidelberg, 1964]
[Waetjen, Eduard, 'Kommentar zu Allen W. Dulles' Manuskript für Germany's
Underground', typed, n.p., ca. 1946/1947], Princeton University Library,
Allen W. Dulles Papers Box 20

d. Interviews

Stauffenberg family and relations
Johnston, Annabel von, née Siemens, 21 July 1972, 16 Aug. 1991
Lerchenfeld, Maximilian Ludwig Freiherr von (nephew of NS), 18 May 1989
Lerchenfeld, Rudolf Freiherr von, Colonel (ret.), (cousin of NS), 20 July 1972
Linden, Ines née Schenk, Countess Stauffenberg, 19 Aug. 1985
Saucken née Countess Üxküll, Olga von, 27 July 1972
Schiller, Klara, 15 May 1989, 18 March 1992
Stauffenberg, Friedrich Schenk, Baron, 10 Aug. 1972
Stauffenberg, Hans Christoph Schenk, Baron, 28 July 1971, 5 July 1972, 7 May
1981
Stauffenberg, Gabriele Schenk, Countess, 29 Aug. 1978, 16 Aug. 1985, 11 Jan. 1992
Stauffenberg, Alfred Schenk, Count (Amerdingen), 15 Aug. 1985
Stauffenberg, Markwart Schenk, Count, 4 June 1973, 21 July 1984, 15, 16 Aug.
1985
Stauffenberg, Marlene Schenk, Countess, 23 Aug. 1972, 28 Feb., 21 March 1977,
16 Jan., 30 Aug. 1978, 14 Aug. 1982, 15 Feb. 1992, 12 March 1992
Stauffenberg, Nina Schenk, Countess, 11 Sept. 1968, 7, 31 Aug. 1972, 31 May 1977,
15 June, 12 Aug. 1982, 16, 17, 18 May 1989, 27 Jan., 3 Dec. 1990, 9, 12 Aug.,
4 Nov. 1991
    Oct. 1962 to Kramarz
Üxküll-Gyllenband, Alexander, Count, 17, 18 May 1973
Yorck von Wartenburg, Dr Marion, Countess, 3 May 1977, 25 Sept. 1983, 9 Dec.
1990

Classmates of Berthold and Alexander
(a, b = form; Berthold and Alexander in form b)
Federer, Georg (b), 8 Dec. 1976, 29 March 1977, 5 Aug. 1982, 23 Sept. 1983
Held, Robert (b), 28 April 1981

Hock, Otto (b), 10 May 1981
Pfizer, Theodor (b), 31 July, 5 Aug. 1972, 4 Jan., 16 Feb., 10 March 1977, 3 Jan.
    1978, 25 April 1981, 14 March, 22 Sept., 24 Sept. 1983
Strecker, Max (b), 26 July 1971

Classmates of Claus
(a, b = form; Claus in form b)
Bopp, Alfons (b), 5 June 1971
Buck, Eberhard (b), 10 June 1971
Denk, Hans (b), 26 July 1971
Dolderer, Erich (b), 5 June 1971
Hosemann, Hubert (b), 3 June, 2 July 1971, 4 Nov. 1984
Neerforth, Karl-Heinz (a), 22 Aug. 1971
Schneiderhan, Kurt (b), 22 May 1971
Wirth, Eugen (b), 1, 5 June 1971

Military comrades of Claus, Count Stauffenberg
Balser, Udo, 21 Feb. 1991
Beelitz, Dietrich, 21 April 1964, 6 June 1973, 9 Sept. 1985
Berger, Oskar-Alfred, 12 July 1984
Boeselager, Philipp Freiherr von, Major (Res., ret.), 19 Nov. 1964, 21 Sept. 1983,
    25 June 1984
Breitenbuch, Eberhard von, 8 Sept. 1966
Burchardt, Heinz, 13 July 1965
Burk, Klaus, 14 Aug. 1985
Bussche, Axel Freiherr von dem, 11 Sept. 1977, 25, 27 Aug. 1978, 26 Oct. 1985,
    2 Dec. 1990, 29 March 1991
Bussmann, Walter, 27 Aug. 1974, 24 April 1985
Degner, Friedrich, 24, 25 Aug. 1965, 14 Oct. 1966
Etzdorf, Hasso von, 24 Aug. 1972, 6 Sept. 1985
Ferber, Ernst, Lt. Gen. (ret.), 1942–1944 OKH/Org. Branch, 29 May 1973
Fritzsche, Dr Hans, 14 July 1972
Gehlen, Reinhard, Brigadier (ret.), 3 Sept. 1972
Groeben, Karl Konrad, Count, 29 March 1991
Hammerstein, Ludwig Freiherr von, 6 July 1984, 10 Dec. 1990
Harnack, Fritz, 29 Aug. 1966
Hassel, Kurt, Colonel (ret.), 11 Dec. 1964
Hausmann, Ulrich, Professor of Archeology, Lt. in No. 9 Inf. Rgt., 13 Sept. 1980
Herre, Heinz Danko, Lt. Gen. (ret.), 9 Sept. 1972, 26 April 1985, 7 Dec. 1986
Herwarth von Bittenfeld, Hans Heinrich, 24 Aug. 1972, 20 July 1984, 8 May 1986
    3 Feb. 1963, Slg Kramarz
Hükelheim, Heinz, Brigadier (ret.), 1943–1944 Major (GS), Head, OKH/Gen. Qu.
    M./Qu. 2 Section, 15 March 1977
John von Freyend, Ernst, 14 May 1964
Kanitz, Rainer, Count, 28 Aug. 1972
Keysser, Dr C. Hans, 12, 21 Feb. 1991
Kielmansegg, Johann Adolf, Count, 1 June 1973, 12 Aug. 1984, 24 Aug. 1991

Kleist, Ewald Heinrich, 19 July 1964, 27 Nov. 1990, 4, 10 Dec. 1990
Koch-Erpach, Rudolf, Lt.Gen. (ret.), 28 March 1964
Kratzer, Rudolf, Colonel (GS, ret.), 25 July 1963 to Kramarz
Kretz, Erich, 29 Aug. 1965, 31 Aug. 1966
Lamey, Hubert, Brigadier (ret.), 26 July 1972
Lechler, Otto, 5 June 1964
Loeper, Friedrich-Wilhelm, Baron, 29 Aug. 1972
    [1962] to Kramarz
Löwenstein, Dr Johannes, Prince, 15 Jan. 1992
Luz, Helwig, Major-General (ret.), 22 Aug. 1972
Maizière, Ulrich de, 3 Sept. 1985
    20 Jan. 1963 to Kramarz
Michel, Karl, 23 and 28 Aug. 1979
Oppen, Georg von, 11 Aug. 1984
Oppenfeld, Horst von, 20 July 1984, 14 Aug. 1985, 14 Dec. 1990, 8 May 1995
Pezold, Bernd von, 1 Sept. 1972
Reinecke, Hermann, 30 April 1965
Reinhardt, Hellmuth, Brigadier (ret.), 1 July 1972
Röhrig, Wolfram, Captain, O.C. Communications Services in OKH, Berlin,
    Bendlerstrasse, 29/30 July 1965
Rotberg, Arnold, Baron, 8 May 1975
Sachenbacher von Schrottenberg, Alfred, Colonel (ret.), 12 July 1972
Sauerbruch, Peter, 9 Feb. 1977, 8 May 1986
    Feb. 1963 to Kramarz
Sauerbruch, Mrs Peter, 8 May 1986
Schott, Edwin, 13 March 1991, 23 April 1991
Schweizer, Karl, 18 June 1965
Seefried, Adolf, Baron, Colonel (ret.), 12 July 1972
Seiffert, Wolf, Captain, 1 April 1941–1 Oct. 1942 posted to Army General Staff in
    OKH/Org. Branch/Section I, 18 May 1973
Speer, Julius, 7 Sept. 1965
Speidel, Hans, Lt. Gen. (ret.), 26 May 1977
Speth, Hans, Lt. Gen. (ret.), 7 June 1973
Stahlberg, Alexander, Captain (ret.), 18 July 1984
Süsskind-Schwendi, Hugo, Baron, 4 July 1972
Teske, Hermann, Colonel (GS, ret.), 8. May 1973
Vogel, Werner, 1 July 1971, 5 Sept. 1985
Weizsäcker, Richard, Baron, 26 April 1975, 2 Dec. 1990, 8 May 1995
Wilcke, Henning, Brigadier (ret.), 23 April 1985, 1 July 1995
Winterfeldt, Alix von, Secretary to Gen. Fromm, 30 Aug. 1966
Woellwarth, Konrad, Baron, Lt. Col. (GS, ret.), 5 June 1973
Ziegler, Delia, Secretary to Olbricht, July 1963 to Irma von Buch-zu Dohna
Ziegler, Delia, 23 Aug. 1965

Stefan George circle
Boehringer, Robert, 10 June 1968
Bothmer, Bernhard von, 11 March 1983

Elze, Walter, 18 July 1972
Fahrner, Rudolf, 20 July 1964, 10 March, 9 May, 4 Sept. 1977, 6 Sept. 1979, 21 Aug. 1982, 19 Nov. 1985
Kempner, Walter, 6/7 Jan. 1984
Markees, Silvio, 23 June 1984
Partsch, Karl Josef, 14 July 1972, 27 May 1973, 3 March 1977
Schlayer, Clothilde, 6/7 Jan. 1984
Stettler, Michael, 24 March 1977
Thiersch, Urban, 21 Jan. 1978
Wolters-Thiersch, Gemma, 21 Aug. 1982

Friends and others
Bachert, Alice (divorced Anneliese Edle Mertz von Quirnheim), 11 June 1973
Biskamp, Mrs, widow of Dr Erich Biskamp, 21 Dec. 1991
Blomberg, Ruth von, 4 Dec. 1990
Bräutigam, Otto, 7 Sept. 1985
Bundesarchiv-Militärarchiv (Archivamtsrat Meyer), 15 Nov. 1991
Bussche, Camilla, Baroness née Acheson (divorced Schenk, Baroness Stauffenberg), 21 Sept. 1983
Deichmann, Hans, 23 July 1989
Farenholtz, Christian, 27 Jan. 1990
Gerstenmaier, Eugen, 17 Aug. 1965, 27 May 1977
Gerstenmaier, Maria, 28, 29, 30 May, 2 June 1977
Gisevius, Hans-Bernd, 4 Aug. 1971, 8 Sept. 1972
Graf née Klaeger, Ruth, 28 Aug. 1978
Haeften, Barbara von, 26 Aug. 1991
Hardenberg, Margarethe, Countess née von Oven, 20 Aug. 1985
Hardenberg, Margarethe Countess née von Oven, 16, 26 Nov., 2 Dec. 1961 to Kramarz
Hilberg, Raul, 10 Aug. 1990
Hoffmann, Konrad, 19 Dec. 1983
Hoffmann, Wilhelm, 10 March, 27 May, 31 May, 12 Sept. 1977, 6 Sept. 1979
Jessen, Käthe, June 1962 to Kramarz
Joest, Elsa Renata von, 7 June 1978
Klausing, Dr Mathilde (sister of Friedrich-Karl Klausing), 1 Sept. 1980
Knoll, Martha, 28 May 1977
Koch-Erpach, Emmy, 1 July 1972
Krauss, Barbara von née Oster, daughter of Brigadier Oster, 1 Nov. 1985
Kuhn, Friedrich, attorney in Bamberg, NSDAP Old Fighter, 7 Aug. 1972
Malone, Henry O., 2 June 1977
Mannschatz, Ursula, 7 July 1972
Mertz von Quirnheim, Hilde Edle, 21 Aug. 1991
Moltke, Freya von, 18–19 Aug. 1977, 2–3 Dec. 1978, 24 June 1984, 24 July 1989, 19 May 1991, 18 Feb. 1992
Mosler, Hermann, 25 July 1972
Nettesheim, Kurt, 17 Aug. 1968
Pfleiderer, Otto, 5 Aug. 1982, 23 Oct. 1985, 14 June 1986

Reinhardt née Koch-Erpach, Irmengard (daughter of O.C. No. 17 Cavalry Regiment), 1 July 1972
Schulenburg, Charlotte, Countess, 5 Nov. 1989
Speer, Albert, 13 July 1972
Vogt, Joseph, 3 Jan. 1978, 20 April 1984
Waetjen, Eduard, 5 Dec. 1986
Widmann, Albert, explosives expert in RSHA Amt V, 30 July 1968

II. Published primary sources

(Note: superscript number indicates number of edition or printing, e.g. [4]1966 = 4th edition 1966)
A., G., 'Letzte Begegnung mit Graf Stauffenberg', *Stuttgarter Zeitung*, 20 July 1950, p. 3
Adress-Buch der Landeshauptstadt Stuttgart mit dem Stadtbezirk Cannstatt, der Vorstadt Berg, den Vororten Degerloch, Gablenberg und Gaisburg, der Karlsvorstadt Heslach, dem Stadtteil Ostheim, der Vorstadt Untertürkheim und dem Vorort Wangen für das Jahr 1918 [dto 1919, 1920, 1922], Union Deutsche Verlagsgesellschaft, Stuttgart, [1917, 1918, 1919, 1921]
Adress-Buch der Landeshauptstadt Stuttgart für das Jahr 1923 [dto 1925, 1926, 1927], Union Deutsche Verlagsgesellschaft, Stuttgart, [1922, 1924, 1925, 1926]
Adressbuch see also Amtliches; Berliner
Akten der Reichskanzlei see Regierung Hitler
Akten zur deutschen auswärtigen Politik 1918–1945. Serie C: 1933–1936. vol. V, Vandenhoeck & Ruprecht, Göttingen, 1977; vol. XII, Vandenhoeck & Ruprecht, Göttingen, 1969
Akten zur deutschen auswärtigen Politik 1918–1945. Serie D (1937–1945), vol. I, Imprimerie Nationale, Baden-Baden, 1950; vol. XII, Vandenhoeck & Ruprecht, Göttingen, 1969
Amtliche Urkunden zur Vorgeschichte des Waffenstillstandes 1918. Auf Grund der Akten der Reichskanzlei, des Auswärtigen Amtes und des Reichsarchivs herausgegeben vom Reichsministerium des Innern. Second, enlarged edition, Deutsche Verlagsgesellschaft für Politik und Geschichte m.b.H., Berlin, 1924
Amtliches Stuttgarter Adressbuch 1928, Union Deutsche Verlagsgesellschaft, Stuttgart, [1927]
Amtliches Stuttgarter Adressbuch 1929, Union Deutsche Verlagsgesellschaft, Stuttgart, [1928]
Amtsblatt des Königlich Württembergischen Ministeriums des Kirchen- und Schulwesens, 4. Jahrgang, 1911
Amtsblatt des Württembergischen Ministeriums des Kirchen- und Schulwesens (Kultministerium), 17. Jahrgang, 1924
Anton, Johann, *Dichtungen, Blätter für die Kunst*, Berlin, 1935
Arndt, Ernst Moritz, *Ein Lebensbild in Briefen*, ed. Heinrich Meisner and Robert Geerds, Verlag von Georg Reimer, Berlin, 1898
Erinnerungen 1769–1815, ed. Rolf Weber, Verlag der Nation, Berlin, 1985
Arnim, [Hans-Jürgen] v[on], 'Gedanken über die Kriegführung in Tunesien im Februar 1943', *Wehrwissenschaftliche Rundschau* 2 (1952), pp. 567–576

Athenaeus, *The Deipnosophists*. With an English Translation by Charles Burton Gulick, Ph.D. 7 vols. Harvard University Press, Cambridge, Massachussetts, William Heinemann Ltd., London, 1941

Beaulac, Willard L., *Franco. Silent Ally in World War II*, Southern Illinois University Press, Carbondale and Edwardsville, 1986

Beck, Ludwig, *Studien*, K. F. Koehler Verlag, Stuttgart, 1955

Below, Nicolaus v., *Als Hitlers Adjutant 1937–45*, v. Hase & Koehler Verlag, Mainz, 1980

Berliner Adressbuch 1926 [and 1927–1936], 3 vols., August Scherl Deutsche Adressbuch-Gesellschaft m.b.H., Berlin, [1926–1936]

Berliner Adressbuch für das Jahr 1937, 3 vols., August Scherl Deutsche Adressbuch-Gesellschaft m.b.H., Berlin, [1937]

Berliner Adressbuch für das Jahr 1938, 3 vols., Verlag August Scherl Nachfolger, Berlin, [1938]

Berndt, Alfred-Ingemar, *Der Marsch ins Grossdeutsche Reich*, Eher Verlag, Munich, ⁴1940

Bernt, Adolf, 'Der 20. Juli in der Bendlerstrasse (Bericht eines Augenzeugen)', *Die Gegenwart* II (1956), pp. 597–601

Bismarck, Otto von, *Werke in Auswahl. Zweiter Band. Das Werden des Staatsmannes 1815–1862. Zweiter Teil: 1854–1862*, ed. Gustav Adolf Rein, W. Kohlhammer, Stuttgart, 1963

Blätter für die Kunst. Siebente Folge. Begründet von Stefan George. Ed. Carl August Klein, Verlag des Herausgebers, [Berlin], 1904

Blätter für die Kunst. Elfte und zwölfte Folge. Begründet von Stefan George. Ed. Carl August Klein, Verlag des Herausgebers, [Berlin], 1919

Blos, Wilhelm, *Von der Monarchie zum Volksstaat. Zur Geschichte der Revolution in Deutschland insbesondere in Württemberg*, Bergers Literarisches Büro und Verlagsanstalt, Stuttgart, [1922]

Boehringer, Robert, *Mein Bild von Stefan George*, Helmut Küpper vormals Georg Bondi, Munich and Düsseldorf, [1951], ²1968

Boelcke, Willi A., ed., *Deutschlands Rüstung im Zweiten Weltkrieg. Hitlers Konferenzen mit Albert Speer 1942–1945*, Akademische Verlagsgesellschaft Athenaion, Frankfurt am Main, 1969

Boeselager, Philipp Freiherr von, *Der Widerstand in der Heeresgruppe Mitte* (Beiträge zum Widerstand 1933–1945, [Nr.] 40), Gedenkstätte Deutscher Widerstand, Berlin, 1990

Bopp, A[lfons], 'Die Leistung!' *Kirchen-Anzeiger* [Kathol. Dekanat Tettnang] Nr. 30, 19 May 1964

Bräutigam, Otto, *So hat es sich zugetragen ... Ein Leben als Soldat und Diplomat*, Holzner Verlag, Würzburg, 1968

Breysig, Kurt, 'Stefan George. Gespräche, Dokumente', *Castrum Peregrini* XLII (1960), pp. 9–45

British Booby Traps. Field Engineering Pamphlet No. 9. 1943, The War Office, [London], 1943, reprinted in Canada 1944

Brüning, Heinrich, *Memoiren 1918–1934*, Deutsche Verlags-Anstalt, Stuttgart, 1970

Buchrucker, Ernst, *Im Schatten Seeckts. Die Geschichte der Schwarzen Reichswehr*, Kampf-Verlag, Berlin, 1928

Bussche, Axel [Freiherr] von dem, 'Eid und Schuld', *Göttinger Universitätszeitung* 2 (1947) No. 7, 7 March 1947, pp. 1–4

Bussche *see also* Freiheitskämpfer

Bussmann, Walter, 'Politik und Kriegführung. Erlebte Geschichte und der Beruf des Historikers', *Fridericiana. Zeitschrift der Universität Karlsruhe*, Heft 32, 1983, pp. 3–16

Clausewitz, Carl von, *Schriften – Aufsätze – Studien – Briefe. Dokumente aus dem Clausewitz-, Scharnhorst und Gneisenau-Nachlass sowie aus öffentlichen und privaten Sammlungen*, ed. Werner Hahlweg, 2 vols. (in 3), (Deutsche Geschichtsquellen des 19. und 20. Jahrhunderts, vols. 45, 49), Vandenhoeck & Ruprecht, Göttingen, 1966, 1990

Vom Kriege, Ferd. Dümmlers Verlag, Bonn, 1972

'Zwei Briefe des Generals von Clausewitz. Gedanken zur Abwehr', *Militärwissenschaftliche Rundschau* 2 (1937) Sonderheft, pp. 1–11

Cole, R. Taylor, *The Recollections of R. Taylor Cole. Educator, Emissary, Development Planner*, Duke University Press, Durham, North Carolina, 1983

Conwell-Evans, T. P., *None So Blind. A Study of the Crisis Years, 1930–1939*, Harrison & Sons, London, 1947

Cramer, [Hans], 'Die letzte Panzerschlacht des deutschen Afrikakorps', *Kampftruppen* (1962) No. 1/2, pp. 7–8

Crewe, Eyre, 'Memorandum on the Present State of British Relations with France and Germany', 1 Jan. 1907, in *British Documents on the Origins of the War. 1898–1914*, vol. III, His Majesty's Stationery Office, London, 1928, pp. 397–420

Curtius, Ernst Robert, *Kritische Essays zur europäischen Literatur*, A. Francke, Bern, 1950

Degras, Jane, ed., *Soviet Documents on Foreign Policy*. Vol. III: 1933–1941, Geoffrey Cumberlege, Oxford University Press, London, New York, Toronto, 1953

Die deutsche Reichsverfassung vom 11. August 1919. Textausgabe und Register mit einem Vorwort von Reichsminister a.D. Prof. Dr. Hugo Preuss, Reichszentrale für Heimatdienst, Berlin, 1919

Deutsches Hof-Handbuch. Adressbuch der Mitglieder, Hofstaaten und Hofbehörden der regierenden deutschen Häuser. Jahrgang 1914, Verlag des Deutschen Hofhandbuches, Berlin, [1914]

Documents diplomatiques français 1932–1939. 1ʳᵉ série (1932–1935), vol. 1, Imprimerie nationale, Paris, 1964

Domarus, Max, *Hitler. Reden und Proklamationen 1932–1945*, Schmidt, Neustadt a. d. Aisch, 1963

Dülffer, Jost [ed.], 'Überlegungen von Kriegsmarine und Heer zur Wehrmachtspitzengliederung und zur Führung der Wehrmacht im Krieg im Februar-März 1938', *Militärgeschichtliche Mitteilungen* 1971 No. 1, pp. 145–171

Dulles, Allen [Welsh], *The Secret Surrender*, Weidenfeld & Nicolson, London, 1967

Germany's Underground, The Macmillan Company, New York, 1947

Ebert, Friedrich, *Schriften, Aufzeichnungen, Reden*. 2 vols. Carl Reissner-Verlag, Dresden, 1926

[Eisenhower, Dwight David], *The Papers of Dwight David Eisenhower. The War*

Years, I-V, ed. Alfred D. Chandler, The Johns Hopkins Press, Baltimore and London, 1971

Elbe, Joachim von, *Unter Preussenadler und Sternenbanner. Ein Leben für Deutschland und Amerika*, C. Bertelsmann Verlag, Munich, 1983

Elze, Walter, *Clausewitz* (Schriften der kriegsgeschichtlichen Abteilung im Historischen Seminar der Friedrich-Wilhelms-Universität Berlin, Seminar-Reihe: Heft 6), Junker und Dünnhaupt Verlag, Berlin, 1934

Deutsche Geschichte und deutsche Freiheit. Briefe eines Hochschullehrers an seine Schüler im Feld, Rütten & Loening, Potsdam, [1940]

Graf Schlieffen (Veröffentlichungen der Schleswig-Holsteinischen Universitätsgesellschaft No. 20), Ferdinand Hirt, Breslau, 1928

Marburg. Bemerkungen zu dem einstigen Kreis dort, [printed in ms., privately published], Freiburg im Breisgau, 1961

Stefan George, Friedrich Wolters, Johann Anton, [printed in ms., privately published], Freiburg im Breisgau, 1959

Der Streit um Tauroggen, Ferdinand Hirt, Breslau, 1926

Tannenberg. Das deutsche Heer von 1914. Seine Grundzüge und deren Auswirkung im Sieg an der Ostfront. Im Einvernehmen mit dem Reichsarchiv, Ferdinand Hirt, Breslau, 1928

Von der Bedeutung der Westfront im Weltkriegsgeschehen. Rede bei der Feier der Erinnerung an den Stifter der Berliner Universität, König Friedrich Wilhelm III., in der Alten Aula am 27. Juli 1934 gehalten von Walter Elze, Preussische Druckerei- und Verlags-Aktiengesellschaft, Berlin, [1934]

Die Erzählungen aus den tausendundein Nächten, 8th vol. [2nd edn], Insel-Verlag, Leipzig, 1914

[Engel, Gerhard], *Heeresadjutant bei Hitler 1938–1943. Aufzeichnungen des Majors Engel*, ed. Hildegard von Kotze (Schriftenreihe der *Vierteljahrshefte für Zeitgeschichte* No. 29), Deutsche Verlags-Anstalt, Stuttgart, 1974

Escher, Max, 'melitta schiller-stauffenberg. eine begegnung', *Kulturwarte*, February 1972

Fahrner, Rudolf, *Arndt. Geistiges und politisches Verhalten*, W. Kohlhammer, Stuttgart, 1937

Gneisenau, Delfinverlag, Munich, 1942

Gneisenau, Delfinverlag, Munich, ²1942

Fahrner *see also* Solomos

Fehling, Maria, *Bismarcks Geschichtskenntnis*, J. G. Cotta'sche Buchhandlung Nachfolger, Stuttgart and Berlin, 1922

ed., *Briefe an Cotta. Das Zeitalter Goethes und Napoleons 1794–1815*, J. G. Cotta'sche Buchhandlung Nachfolger, Stuttgart and Berlin, 1925

Ferry, Jules, *Le Tonkin et la Mère-Patrie*, Victor-Havard, Paris, 1890

[Fichte, Johann Gottlieb], *Johann Gottlieb Fichte's sämmtliche Werke*, ed. J. H. Fichte. 8 vols. Verlag von Veit und Comp., Berlin, 1845–1846

Field Engineering (All Arms). Military Training Pamphlet No. 30. Part IV: Booby Traps. 1941, The Chief of the Imperial General Staff, [London, 1941], reprinted in Canada, September 1941

Foertsch, Hermann, *Schuld und Verhängnis. Die Fritsch-Krise im Frühjahr 1938 als*

Wendepunkt in der Geschichte der nationalsozialistischen Zeit, Deutsche Verlags-Anstalt, Stuttgart, 1951

Foreign Relations of the United States. Diplomatic Papers. 1941, vol. 1, United States Government Printing Office, Washington, 1958

Foreign Relations of the United States. Diplomatic Papers. 1942, vol. 1, United States Government Printing Office, Washington, 1960

Foreign Relations of the United States. The Conference at Washington, 1941–1942, and Casablanca, 1943, United States Government Printing Office, Washington, 1968

Foreign Relations of the United States. Diplomatic Papers. 1943, vol. 1, United States Government Printing Office, Washington, 1963

Foreign Relations of the United States. Diplomatic Papers. The Conferences at Malta and Yalta 1945, United States Government Printing Office, Washington, 1955

Foreign Relations of the United States. Diplomatic Papers. 1944, vol. 1, United States Government Printing Office, Washington, 1966

[Frank, Hans], *Das Diensttagebuch des deutschen Generalgouverneurs in Polen 1939–1945*, ed. Werner Präg and Wolfgang Jacobmeyer (Quellen und Darstellungen zur Zeitgeschichte, vol. 20), Deutsche Verlags-Anstalt, Stuttgart, 1975

Frank, Victor, *Agis und Kleomenes. Nach dem Plutarch*, Delfinverlag, Munich, 1944

[Frantz, Gunther], *Die Vernichtungsschlacht in kriegsgeschichtlichen Beispielen*, ed. Gunther Frantz, E. S. Mittler & Sohn, Berlin, 1928

'Freiheitskämpfer gegen Hitler', *Die Zeit* 22 July 1948, p. 2

Frenssen, Gustav, *Jörn Uhl*, G. Grote'sche Verlagsbuchhandlung, Berlin, 1902
  Gesammelte Werke, vols. 1–6, G. Grote'sche Verlagsbuchhandlung, Berlin, 1943

Die Friedensbedingungen der Alliierten und Assoziierten Regierungen, Verlag von Reimar Hobbing, Berlin, 1919

Fritzsche, Hans Karl, *Ein Leben im Schatten des Verrates. Erinnerungen eines Überlebenden an den 20. Juli 1944*, Verlag Herder, Freiburg im Breisgau, Basel, Vienna, 1984

Furtwängler, Franz Josef, *Männer, die ich sah und kannte*, Auerdruck, Hamburg, 1951

Genealogisches Handbuch der adeligen Häuser. Adelige Häuser A, vol. IV, C. A. Starke Verlag, Limburg an der Lahn, 1960

Genealogisches Handbuch der adeligen Häuser. Adelige Häuser B, vols. XIV, XVI, C. A. Starke Verlag, Limburg an der Lahn, 1981, 1985

Genealogisches Handbuch der freiherrlichen Häuser. Freiherrliche Häuser B, vol. II, C. A. Starke Verlag, Glücksburg/Ostsee, 1957

Genealogisches Handbuch der gräflichen Häuser. Gräfliche Häuser A, vols. II, III, C. A. Starke Verlag, Glücksburg/Ostsee, 1955, [1958]

George, Stefan, *Gesamt-Ausgabe der Werke. Endgültige Fassung*, 18 vols. in 15, Georg Bondi, Berlin, 1927–1934

George, Stefan, Friedrich Gundolf, *Briefwechsel*, ed. Robert Boehringer with Georg Peter Landmann, Helmut Küpper vormals Georg Bondi, Munich and Düsseldorf, 1962

Gersdorff, Rudolf-Christoph Frhr. v., *Soldat im Untergang*, Ullstein, Frankfurt am Main, Berlin, Vienna, 1977

Gerstenmaier, Eugen, 'Zur Geschichte des Umsturzversuchs vom 20. Juli 1944', *Neue Zürcher Zeitung* Nos. 979 and 983, 23 and 24 June 1945
'Der Kreisauer Kreis: Zu dem Buch Gerrit van Roons »Neuordnung im Widerstand«', *Vierteljahrshefte für Zeitgeschichte* 15 (1967), pp. 221–246
'Sie wollten Hitler nicht mit Stalin tauschen', *Die Zeit* No. 37, 8 Sept. 1978, p. 26
Geyr von Schweppenburg, [Leo] Freiherr, *Erinnerungen eines Militärattachés. London 1933–1937*, Deutsche Verlags-Anstalt, Stuttgart, 1949
Giessler, Klaus-Volker, 'Briefwechsel zwischen Claus Graf Stauffenberg und Georg von Sodenstern von Februar/März 1939. Gedanken zum Wesen des Soldatentums', in Friedrich P. Kahlenberg, ed., *Aus der Arbeit der Archive. Beiträge zum Archivwesen, zur Quellenkunde und zur Geschichte. Festschrift für Hans Booms*, Harald Boldt Verlag, Boppard am Rhein, 1989, pp. 552–564
Gisevius, Hans Bernd, *Bis zum bittern Ende*, 2 vols., Fretz & Wasmuth Verlag, Zürich, 1946
Bis zum bittern Ende, Fretz & Wasmuth Verlag, Zürich, [revised edn, 1954]
To the Bitter End, Houghton Mifflin Company, Boston, 1947
Wo ist Nebe? Erinnerungen an Hitlers Reichskriminaldirektor, Droemer, Zürich, 1966
Glöckner, Ernst, *Begegnung mit Stefan George. Auszüge aus Briefen und Tagebüchern 1913–1934*, Lothar Stiehm Verlag, Heidelberg, 1972
Gneisenau *see* Fahrner; Griewank; Stern; Thimme
Goebbels, [Joseph], *Tagebücher aus den Jahren 1942–43*, ed. Louis P. Lochner, Atlantis Verlag, Zürich, 1948
Die Tagebücher von Joseph Goebbels. Sämtliche Fragmente, ed. Elke Fröhlich, Part I, vols. 1–4, K. G. Saur, Munich, New York, London, Paris, 1987
[Goerdeler, Carl], 'Das Regierungsprogramm vom 20. Juli 1944. Karl Goerdelers geplante Rundfunkrede nach Übernahme der öffentlichen Gewalt. Aus dem Nachlass herausgegeben von Professor Dr. Gerhard Ritter, Freiburg', *Die Gegenwart* 1 (1946) No. 12/13, 24 June 1946, pp. 11–14
'Wiedergewinnung der sittlichen Grundlage. Carl Goerdelers Regierungsprogramm – Eine vorgesehene Rundfunkrede bei Uebernahme der Reichsregierung', *Stuttgarter Zeitung* No. 164, 20 July 1967, p. 11
Gollwitzer, Helmut, Käthe Kuhn, Reinhold Schneider, eds., *Du hast mich heimgesucht bei Nacht. Abschiedsbriefe und Aufzeichnungen des Widerstandes 1933–1945*, Chr. Kaiser Verlag, Munich, ³1962
Gothaisches Genealogisches Taschenbuch der Freiherrlichen Häuser, Teil B, 91. Jahrgang 1941, Justus Perthes, Gotha, [1940]
Gothaisches Genealogisches Taschenbuch der Gräflichen Häuser 1919, 92. Jahrgang, Justus Perthes, Gotha, [1918]
Gothaisches Genealogisches Taschenbuch der Gräflichen Häuser, Teil A, 109. Jahrgang 1936, Justus Perthes, Gotha, [1935]
Grant Duff, Shiela, *The Parting of Ways. A Personal Account of the Thirties*, P. Owen, London, 1982
[Grant Duff, Shiela and Adam von Trott zu Solz], *A Noble Combat. The Letters of Shiela Grant Duff and Adam von Trott zu Solz 1932–1939*, ed. Klemens von Klemperer, Clarendon Press, Oxford, 1988
Griewank, Karl, ed., *Gneisenau. Ein Leben in Briefen*, Koehler & Amelang, Leipzig, 1939

Groener, Wilhelm, *Das Testament des Grafen Schlieffen. Operative Studien über den Weltkrieg*, E.S.Mittler & Sohn, Berlin, 1927

Groener, Wilhelm, *Der Feldherr wider Willen. Operative Studien über den Weltkrieg*, E.S.Mittler & Sohn, Berlin, [2]1930

Groscurth, Helmuth, *Tagebücher eines Abwehroffiziers 1938–1940*, ed. Helmut Krausnick and Harold C. Deutsch, Deutsche Verlags-Anstalt, Stuttgart, 1970

Guderian, Heinz, *Erinnerungen eines Soldaten*, Motorbuch Verlag, Stuttgart, [11]1979

Guttenberg, Elisabeth von [und zu], *Holding The Stirrup. As Told to Sheridan Spearman*, Duell, Sloan and Pearce, New York, Little, Brown and Company, Boston, 1952

Beim Namen gerufen. Erinnerungen, Verlag Ullstein, Berlin-Frankfurt am Main, 1990

Halder, [Franz], *Kriegstagebuch*, vols. I–III, W. Kohlhammer Verlag, Stuttgart, 1962, 1963, 1964

Hammerstein, Kunrat Freiherr von, *Spähtrupp*, Henry Goverts Verlag, Stuttgart, 1963

Handbuch für das Deutsche Reich 1936, ed. Reichs- und Preussisches Ministerium des Innern. Sechsundvierzigster Jahrgang, Carl Heymanns Verlag, Berlin, 1936

Hassell, Fey von, *Hostage of the Third Reich. The Story of My Imprisonment and Rescue from the SS*, Charles Scribner's Sons, New York, 1989

Hassell, Ulrich von, *Vom andern Deutschland. Aus den nachgelassenen Tagebüchern 1938–1944*, Atlantis Verlag, Zürich, [2]1946

Die Hassell-Tagebücher 1938–1944. Aufzeichnungen vom Andern Deutschland, Siedler Verlag, Berlin, 1988 (expanded edn: source references based on this edn unless otherwise indicated)

Hebbel, Friedrich, *Sämtliche Werke. Historisch-kritische Ausgabe*, ed. Richard Maria Werner, 6th vol., B.Behr's Verlag, Berlin, 1902

[Hegelmaier, Leopold], *Beamter und Soldat. Lebenserinnerungen von Dr Leopold Hegelmaier, Wirklichem Staatsrat und Major der Landwehr a.D.*, Verlag von A. Bonz' Erben, Stuttgart, 1937

Heilfron, Ed[uard], ed., *Die Deutsche Nationalversammlung im Jahre 1919 in ihrer Arbeit für den Aufbau des neuen deutschen Volksstaates*, 9 vols., Norddeutsche Buchdruckerei und Verlagsanstalt, Berlin, [1920]

Heine, Heinrich, *Buch der Lieder*, Hoffmann und Campe, Hamburg, [48]1882

Historisch-kritische Gesamtausgabe der Werke, ed. Manfred Windfuhr, vol. 8/1, Hoffmann und Campe, Hamburg, 1979

Heintz [really: Heinz], F[riedrich] W[ilhelm], 'Offener Brief an Herrn Remer', *Deutsche Wirklichkeit* No. 18, 1 Sept. 1949, pp. 8–9

Hellingrath, Norbert von, *Hölderlin. Zwei Vorträge*, Hugo Bruckmann Verlag, Munich, 1921

Herwarth [von Bittenfeld], Hans von, 'Dem Andenken des Generals der Kavallerie Ernst Köstring', *Zeitschrift für Geopolitik, Weltwirtschaft, Weltpolitik und Auslandswissen* XXV (1954), pp. 766–768

'Meine Verbindung mit Graf Stauffenberg', *Stuttgarter Zeitung* No. 162, 18 July 1969, p. 7

Zwischen Hitler und Stalin. Erlebte Zeitgeschichte 1931 bis 1945, Propyläen Verlag, Frankfurt am Main, Berlin, Vienna, 1982

Heusinger, Adolf, *Befehl im Widerstreit. Schicksalsstunden der deutschen Armee 1923–1945*, Rainer Wunderlich Verlag Hermann Leins, Tübingen and Stuttgart, 1950

Heyde, B[olko] von der, 'Die Verschwörung des 20. Juli. Beteiligte sagen aus', *Die Welt*, 31 July 1947, p. 2

Hildebrandt, Kurt, *Individualitaet und Gemeinschaft. Festrede auf dem Herbstfeste des sudetendeutschen Kameradschaftsbundes in Schloss Heinrichsruh bei Teplitz*, Verlag Die Runde, Berlin, 1933

Erinnerungen an Stefan George und seinen Kreis, H. Bouvier & Co. Verlag, Bonn, 1965

[Himmler, Heinrich], 'Die Rede Himmlers vor den Gauleitern am 3. August 1944', *Vierteljahrshefte für Zeitgeschichte* 1 (1953) pp. 357–394

[Hinks, Roger], *The Gymnasium of the Mind. The Journals of Roger Hinks. 1933–1963*, ed. John Goldsmith, Michael Russell, The Chantry, Wilton, Salisbury, Wiltshire, 1984

Hitler, Adolf, [speech in the Reichstag on 13 July 1934], *Völkischer Beobachter*, North German ed., Berlin, 15/16 July 1934, pp. 1–2 and supplement

Hitlers Lagebesprechungen. Die Protokollfragmente seiner militärischen Konferenzen 1942–1945, ed. Helmut Heiber (Quellen und Darstellungen zur Zeitgeschichte, vol. 10), Deutsche Verlags-Anstalt, Stuttgart, 1962

Hitlers Weisungen für die Kriegführung 1939–1945. Dokumente des Oberkommandos der Wehrmacht, ed. Walther Hubatsch, Bernard & Graefe Verlag für Wehrwesen, Frankfurt am Main, 1962

Monologe im Führerhauptquartier 1941–1944. Die Aufzeichnungen Heinrich Heims, ed. Werner Jochmann, Albrecht Knaus Verlag, Hamburg, 1980

Hitler *see also* Domarus; Treue

Hölderlin, [Friedrich], *Sämtliche Werke. Historisch-kritische Ausgabe begonnen durch Norbert v. Hellingrath, fortgeführt durch Friedrich Seebass und Ludwig v. Pigenot*, vols. 1–6, Propyläen-Verlag, Berlin, 1923 (vols. 1, 4, 5 = 2nd edn)

Sämtliche Werke. Historisch-kritische Ausgabe unter Mitarbeit von Friedrich Seebass besorgt durch Norbert v. Hellingrath. Vierter Band. Besorgt durch Norbert v. Hellingrath. Gedichte 1800–1806, Georg Müller, Munich and Leipzig, 1916

Sämtliche Werke (Stuttgarter Hölderlin-Ausgabe im Auftrag des württembergischen Kultministeriums herausgegeben von Friedrich Beissner), vols. 1–8, W. Kohlhammer Verlag, J. G. Cottasche Buchhandlung Nachfolger, Stuttgart, 1946–1985

Sämtliche Werke, ed. Friedrich Beissner, Insel-Verlag, Frankfurt am Main, 1961

Poems and Fragments, translated by Michael Hamburger, Cambridge University Press, 1980

Hof- und Staatshandbuch des Königreichs Württemberg, ed. by the Königliches Statistisches Landesamt 1913, printed by W. Kohlhammer, Stuttgart, 1913; dto 1914

Hoffmann, [Konrad], [Richard] Lempp, [Paul] Stadelmann, *Worte an der Bahre und am Grabe des verewigten Herzogs Wilhelm zu Württemberg, bis 30. November 1918 König von Württemberg, Gedächtnisrede in der Liederhalle und Gedächtnispredigt in der Schlosskirche gesprochen zu Stuttgart, Bebenhausen und Ludwigsburg,* Chr. Scheufele, Stuttgart, [1921]

Hoffmann, Volkmar, '"Nie wieder bin ich solch einem Menschen begegnet": 20. Juli – 20 Jahre danach/Interview mit Stauffenbergs Sekretärin und anderen Beteiligten/"Ich würde es wieder tun"', *Frankfurter Rundschau* 18 July 1964, p. 3

Hubatsch, Walther, 'Quellen zur neuesten Geschichte III. Das dienstliche Tagebuch des Chefs des Wehrmachtführungsamtes im Oberkommando der Wehrmacht, Generalmajor Jodl, für die Zeit vom 13. Okt. 1939 bis zum 30. Jan. 1940', *Die Welt als Geschichte* 12 (1952), pp. 274–287 and 13 (1953), pp. 58–71

Hubatsch *see also* Hitler

Huber, Ernst Rudolf, ed., *Dokumente zur deutschen Verfassungsgeschichte,* 3 vols., W. Kohlhammer Verlag, Stuttgart, Berlin, Cologne, Mainz, 1961, 1964, 1966

Insel Almanach auf das Jahr 1919, Insel-Verlag, Leipzig, [1918, after 9 Nov. 1918], copy with ms. dedication by Rilke for Countess Stauffenberg in Theodor Pfizer's library

Jahrbuch für die geistige Bewegung, ed. Friedrich Gundolf and Friedrich Wolters, [Erster und] Dritter Jahrgang, 1910, 1912, Verlag der *Blätter für die Kunst,* Otto von Holten, Berlin, [1910, 1911]

Jappe-Schubring, Gioia, 'Aus meiner Kindheit und Jugend' in Georg Peter Landmann, ed., *Wie jeder ihn erlebte,* privately printed, Basel, [1977], pp. 34–47

Jodl *see* Hubatsch

John, Otto, 'Zum Jahrestag der Verschwörung gegen Hitler – 20. Juli 1944', *Wochenpost* 18 July 1947, pp. 4–6

'Männer im Kampf gegen Hitler (II)', *Blick in die Welt* 2 (1947), No. 7

'Männer im Kampf gegen Hitler (IV): Wilhelm Leuschner', *Blick in die Welt* 2 (1947), No. 9

Zweimal kam ich heim. Vom Verschwörer zum Schützer der Verfassung, Econ Verlag, Düsseldorf, Vienna, 1969

Kaiser, Jakob, 'Deutschlands Trennung war vermeidbar', *Das Parlament,* 20 July 1954

Kantorowicz, Ernst, *Kaiser Friedrich der Zweite,* Georg Bondi, Berlin, 1927

Keilig, Wolf, *Das deutsche Heer 1939–1945. Gliederung – Einsatz – Stellenbesetzung,* Verlag Hans-Henning Podzun, Bad Nauheim, 1956–[1970]

Kennan, George F., *Memoirs 1925–1950,* Little, Brown and Company, Boston, Toronto, 1967

Köhler, [Ludwig] v[on], *Zur Geschichte der Revolution in Württemberg. Ein Bericht,* Verlag W. Kohlhammer, Stuttgart, 1930

Kommerell, Max, *Der Dichter als Führer in der deutschen Klassik. Klopstock, Herder, Goethe, Schiller, Jean Paul, Hölderlin,* Georg Bondi, Berlin, 1928

Gespräche aus der Zeit der deutschen Wiedergeburt, Verlag der *Blätter für die Kunst,* Otto von Holten, Berlin 1929

Briefe und Aufzeichnungen 1919–1944, Walter-Verlag, Olten und Freiburg im Breisgau, 1967

Kordt, Erich, *Nicht aus den Akten . . .,* Union Deutsche Verlagsgesellschaft, Stuttgart, 1950

Kriegstagebuch des Oberkommandos der Wehrmacht (Wehrmachtführungsstab), vols.

I–IV, Bernard & Graefe Verlag für Wehrwesen, Frankfurt am Main, 1965, 1963, 1963, 1961

Kürschners Deutscher Gelehrten-Kalender 1931 [dto 1935, 1950], Walter de Gruyter & Co., Berlin, Leipzig, [1931, 1935, 1950]

[Lagarde, Paul de], *Ueber die gegenwärtige lage des deutschen reichs, ein bericht, erstattet von Paul de Lagarde*, Dieterichsche verlagsbuchhandlung, Göttingen, 1876

Deutsche Schriften, Dieterichsche verlagsbuchhandlung [*sic*], Göttingen, 1878

Deutsche Schriften. Gesammtausgabe letzter Band, Vierter Abdruck, Dieterichsche Verlagsbuchhandlung [*sic*], Göttingen, 1892

'Das verborgene Deutschland', [privately printed] Gebr. Klingspor, Offenbach am Main, 1920

Landmann, Edith, *Gespräche mit Stefan George*, Helmut Küpper vormals Georg Bondi, Düsseldorf and Munich, 1963

Landmann, Georg Peter, ed., *Wie jeder ihn erlebte. Zum Gedenken an Robert Boehringer*, privately printed, Basel, [1977]

Landmann, Michael, *Figuren um Stefan George*, 2nd vol., Castrum Peregrini Presse, Amsterdam, 1988

[Langbehn, Julius], *Rembrandt als Erzieher. Von einem Deutschen*, Verlag von C. L. Hirschfeld, Leipzig, 1890

Leber, Annedore, *Den toten, immer lebendigen Freunden. Eine Erinnerung zum 20. Juli 1944*, Telegraf Verlag, Berlin, 1946

[Leber, Julius], *Ein Mann geht seinen Weg. Schriften, Reden und Briefe von Julius Leber*, Mosaik-Verlag, Berlin-Schöneberg, Frankfurt am Main, 1952

Lenin, W. I., *Staat und Revolution. Die Lehre des Marxismus vom Staat und die Aufgaben des Proletariats in der Revolution* (Bücherei des Marxismus-Leninismus, vol. 17), Dietz Verlag, Berlin, 1957

Leverkuehn, Paul, *Der geheime Nachrichtendienst der deutschen Wehrmacht im Kriege*, Athenäum Verlag, Frankfurt am Main, [2]1957

Lindgren, Henrik, 'Adam von Trotts Reisen nach Schweden 1942–1944', *Vierteljahrshefte für Zeitgeschichte* 18 (1970), pp. 274–291

Linge, Heinz, *Bis zum Untergang. Als Chef des Persönlichen Dienstes bei Hitler*, ed. Werner Maser, F. A. Herbig Verlagsbuchhandlung, Munich, Berlin, [2]1980

Lohrer, Liselotte, 'Hölderlin-Ausgabe und Hölderlin-Archiv. Entstehung und Geschichte', in *In libro humanitas. Festschrift für Wilhelm Hoffmann zum sechzigsten Geburtstag 21. April 1961*, Ernst Klett-Verlag, Stuttgart, 1962, pp. 289–314

Ludendorff, Erich, *Meine Kriegserinnerungen 1914–1918*, Ernst Siegfried Mittler und Sohn Verlagsbuchhandlung, Berlin, 1919

Mann, Thomas, *Briefwechsel mit Autoren. Rudolf Georg Binding, Bertolt Brecht, Hermann Broch [et al.]*, ed. Hans Wysling, S. Fischer, Frankfurt am Main, 1988

Manstein, Erich v[on], *Verlorene Siege*, Bernard & Graefe Verlag für Wehrwesen, Frankfurt am Main; 1969 ([1]1955 Athenäum Verlag, Frankfurt am Main)

Soldat im 20. Jahrhundert. Militärisch-politische Nachlese, ed. Rüdiger von Manstein and Theodor Fuchs, Bernard & Graefe Verlag, Coblenz, [2]1983

[Mehnert, Frank] *see* Frank, Victor

Mehnert, Klaus, *Ein Deutscher in der Welt: Erinnerungen 1906–1981*, Deutsche Verlags-Anstalt, Stuttgart, 1981

Mende, Gerhard von, 'Erfahrungen mit Ostfreiwilligen in der deutschen Wehrmacht während des Zweiten Weltkrieges', in *Vielvölkerheere und Koalitions-kriege* (Auslandsforschung. Schriftenreihe der Auslandswissenschaftlichen Gesellschaft e.V., No. 1), C. W. Leske Verlag, Darmstadt, 1952, pp. 24–33

Michaelis, Herbert und Ernst Schraepler, ed., *Ursachen und Folgen. Vom deutschen Zusammenbruch 1918 und 1945 bis zur staatlichen Neuordnung Deutschlands in der Gegenwart. Eine Urkunden- und Dokumentensammlung zur Zeitgeschichte*, 26 [and 2 index-] vols., Dokumenten-Verlag Dr Herbert Wendler & Co., Berlin, [1959–1979]

Michalka, Wolfgang, ed., *'Volksgemeinschaft' und Grossmachtpolitik 1933–1939* (Das Dritte Reich. Dokumente zur Innen- und Aussenpolitik. Vol. 1), Deutscher Taschenbuch Verlag, Munich, 1985

Michel, Karl, 'Stauffenberg – der neue Dynamismus. Ein Beitrag zur Geschichte des Offiziersputsches gegen Hitler', *Die Tat* [Zürich], 25 Nov. 1946

Michel, Karl, *Ost und West: Der Ruf Stauffenbergs*, Thomas-Verlag, Zürich, 1947

Ministerial-Blatt für die Preussische innere Verwaltung. Teil I, ed. in the Prussian Ministry of the Interior, 94th year 1933, Carl Heymanns Verlag, Berlin, 1933

Moeller van den Bruck, *Das dritte Reich*, Hanseatische Verlagsanstalt, Hamburg, ^{3}1931

Moltke, [Helmuth] Graf von, *Ausgewählte Werke*, 4 vols., Reimar Hobbing, Berlin, 1925

   Gesammelte Schriften und Denkwürdigkeiten, 8 vols., Ernst Siegfried Mittler und Sohn Königliche Hofbuchhandlung, Berlin, 1891–1893

Moltke, Helmuth James von, *Briefe an Freya 1939–1945*, ed. Beate Ruhm von Oppen, Verlag C.H.Beck, Munich, 1988

   Völkerrecht im Dienste der Menschen. Dokumente, ed. Ger van Roon, Siedler Verlag, Berlin, 1986

Momm, Harald, *Pferde, Reiter und Trophäen*, Copress-Verlag, Munich, 1957

Morgenthau, Henry, *Germany Is Our Problem*, Harper, New York, 1945

Morwitz, Ernst, *Kommentar zu dem Werk Stefan Georges*, Helmut Küpper vormals Georg Bondi, Düsseldorf and Munich, 1960, ^{2}1969

Nebgen, Elfriede, *Jakob Kaiser. Der Widerstandskämpfer*, Verlag W. Kohlhammer, Stuttgart, Berlin, Cologne, Mainz, ^{2}1970

Nijland-Verwey, Mea, ed., *Wolfskehl und Verwey. Die Dokumente ihrer Freundschaft 1897–1946*, Verlag Lambert Schneider, Heidelberg, 1968

Offiziere im Bild von Dokumenten aus drei Jahrhunderten (Beiträge zur Militär- und Kriegsgeschichte, vol. 6, ed. Militärgeschichtliches Forschungsamt), Deutsche Verlags-Anstalt, Stuttgart, 1964

Osas, Veit, *Walküre. Die Wahrheit über den 20. Juli 1944 mit Dokumenten*, Deutschland-Verlag Adolf Ernst Schulze & Co., Hamburg, 1953

Pagels, Hermann Joachim, 'Victor Frank: Führerbüste 1933 in der Industrie- und Handelskammer Magdeburg', *N.S.B.Z. Nationalsozialistische Beamten-Zeitung* 5 (1936), No. 9, 20 April 1936, pp. 348

'Palestine. Statement of Policy. Presented by the Secretary of State for the Colonies to Parliament by Command of His Majesty, May, 1939', in *Accounts and Papers* XII, vol. XXVII, His Majesty's Stationery Office, London, 1939

Parliamentary Debates. Fifth Series. House of Commons. Official Report, vols 345, 377, His Majesty's Stationery Office, London, 1939, 1942

Partsch, Karl Josef, 'Stauffenberg. Das Bild des Täters', *Europa-Archiv* 1950, pp. 3196–3200

['Erinnerungen an Robert Boehringer'], in Georg Peter Landmann, ed., *Wie jeder ihn erlebte*, privately printed, Basel, [1977], pp. 74–87

[Paulus, Friedrich], *Paulus und Stalingrad. Lebensweg des Generalfeldmarschalls Friedrich Paulus. Mit den Aufzeichnungen aus dem Nachlass, Briefen und Dokumenten*, ed. Walter Görlitz, Athenäum Verlag, Frankfurt am Main, Bonn, 1964 [1]1960

Pechel, Rudolf, *Deutscher Widerstand*, Eugen Rentsch Verlag, Erlenbach-Zürich, 1947

Pfizer, Theodor, 'Die Brüder Stauffenberg' in *Robert Boehringer. Eine Freundesgabe*, ed. Erich Boehringer and Wilhelm Hoffmann, J. C. B. Mohr (Paul Siebeck), Tübingen, 1957, pp. 487–509

'Die Hölderlin-Gesellschaft: Anfänge und Gegenwart', *Hölderlin-Jahrbuch* 21 (1978–1979), pp. 14–35

Im Schatten der Zeit 1904–1948, W.Kohlhammer Verlag, Stuttgart, 1979

Pick, Albert, ed., *Aus der Zeit der Noth 1806 bis 1815. Schilderungen zur Preussischen Geschichte aus dem brieflichen Nachlasse des Feldmarschalls Neidhardt von Gneisenau*, Ernst Siegfried Mittler und Sohn, Berlin, 1900

Pilz, Kurt, 'Das Bildnis des Führers', *N.S.B.Z. Nationalsozialistische Beamten-Zeitung* 5 (1936), No. 9, 20 April 1936, pp. 351–354

Piper, Ernst, *Ernst Barlach und die nationalsozialistische Kunstpolitik. Eine dokumentarische Darstellung zur 'entarteten Kunst'*, R. Piper & Co. Verlag, Munich, Zürich, 1983

Pistorius, Theodor v[on], *Die letzten Tage des Königreichs Württemberg. Mit Lebenserinnerungen und Lebensbekenntnissen von seinem letzten Finanzminister, dem nachherigen Hochschullehrer, Prof. Dr. und Dr. e.h. Theodor v. Pistorius*, W. Kohlhammer, Stuttgart, [2]1936

Der Prozess gegen die Hauptkriegsverbrecher vor dem Internationalen Militärgerichtshof Nürnberg 14. November 1945–1. Oktober 1946, 42 vols., Sekretariat des Gerichtshofs, Nuremberg, 1947–1949.

Rangliste der Offiziere der Königlich Bayerischen Armee. Stand vom 21. April 1917, Drucksachen-Verlag des Kriegsministeriums, Munich, n.d.

Rangliste des deutschen Heeres 1944/45, ed. Wolf Keilig, Verlag Hans-Henning Podzun, Bad Nauheim, 1955

Rangliste des Deutschen Reichsheeres. Nach dem Stande vom 1. April 1923, ed. Reichswehrministerium (Heeres-Personalamt) [dto 1 May 1927–1932], E. S. Mittler & Sohn, Berlin, [1923, 1927–1932]

Rautenberg, Hans-Jürgen, 'Drei Dokumente zur Planung eines 300 000 Mann-Friedensheeres aus dem Dezember 1933', *Militärgeschichtliche Mitteilungen* 22 (1977), pp. 103–138

Die Regierung Hitler. Teil I: 1933/34, vol. 1, ed. Karl-Heinz Minuth (Akten der Reichskanzlei. Regierung Hitler 1933–1938 ed. for Historische Kommission bei der Bayerischen Akademie der Wissenschaften by Konrad Repgen, for the Bundesarchiv by Hans Booms), Harald Boldt Verlag, Boppard am Rhein, 1983

Regierungsblatt für das Königreich Württemberg vom Jahr 1911, Buchdruckerei Chr. Scheufele, Stuttgart, [1911]

Reichs-Gesetzblatt 1919, ed. Reichsministerium des Innern, Berlin, [1919]

Reichsgesetzblatt. Teil II. 1925, Verlag des Gesetzsammlungsamts, Berlin, 1925
Reichsgesetzblatt. Teil I. 1933 [dto 1934, 1935], Reichsverlagsamt, Berlin, 1933–1935
Reichsverfassung see Deutsche
Reinhardt, Fritz, 'Vom Wesen der Volksgemeinschaft' in *Grundlagen, Aufbau und Wirtschaftsordnung des nationalsozialistischen Staates*, ed. H.-H. Lammers and Hans Pfundtner, 3 vols., Industrieverlag Spaeth & Linde, Berlin, 1936–1939, no. 8
Reparation Commission, V. Report on the Work of the Reparation Commission from 1920 to 1922, His Majesty's Stationery Office, London, 1923
Riezler, Kurt, *Tagebücher, Aufsätze, Dokumente*, Vandenhoeck & Ruprecht, Göttingen, [1972]
Rilke, Rainer Maria, *Sämtliche Werke, Zweiter Band, Gedichte, Zweiter Teil*, Insel-Verlag, Frankfurt am Main, 1982
  Briefe aus den Jahren 1914 bis 1921, ed. Ruth Sieber-Rilke und Carl Sieber, Insel-Verlag, Leipzig, 1937
  [and] Lou Andreas Salomé, *Briefwechsel*, ed. Ernst Pfeiffer, Insel, Frankfurt am Main, 1975
  [and] Helene von Nostiz, *Briefwechsel*, ed. Oswalt von Nostiz, Insel, Frankfurt and Main, 1976
Röhm, Ernst, *Die Geschichte eines Hochverräters*, Verlag Franz Eher Nachfolger, Munich, 1928
Rommel, Erwin, *Krieg ohne Hass*, Heidenheimer Verlagsanstalt, Heidenheim (Brenz), [1950], 5th edn n.d.
  The Rommel Papers, ed. B. H. Liddell Hart, Collins, London, 1953
Roosevelt, Franklin D., *The Public Papers and Addresses. 1937 Volume*, Macmillan, New York, 1941
R[othfels], H[ans], ed., 'Ausgewählte Briefe von Generalmajor Helmuth Stieff (hingerichtet am 8. August 1944)', *Vierteljahrshefte für Zeitgeschichte* 2 (1954), pp. 291–305
  'Trott und die Aussenpolitik des Widerstandes', *Vierteljahrshefte für Zeitgeschichte* 12 (1964), pp. 300–323
  ed., 'Zwei aussenpolitische Memoranden der deutschen Opposition (Frühjahr 1942)', *Vierteljahrshefte für Zeitgeschichte* 5 (1957), pp. 388–397
Sänger, Fritz, 'Stauffenberg: Auch mit der KP. Streit um den 20. Juli 1944 – Falsche Argumente gegen Wehner', *Die Zeit* No. 34, 18 Aug. 1978, supplement *Politik*, p. 8
Salin, Edgar, *Um Stefan George. Erinnerung und Zeugnis*, Helmut Küpper vormals Georg Bondi, Munich and Düsseldorf, 2nd edn, 1954
  Ernst Kantorowicz 1895–1963, privately printed, [Basel, 1963]
Sauerbruch, Ferdinand, *Das war mein Leben*, Kindler und Schiermeyer Verlag, Bad Wörishofen, 1951
Sauerbruch, Peter, 'Bericht eines ehemaligen Generalstabsoffiziers über seine Motive zur Beteiligung am militärischen Widerstand', in *Vorträge zur Militärgeschichte 5. Der militärische Widerstand gegen Hitler und das NS-Regime 1933–1945*, Verlag E. S. Mittler & Sohn, Herford, Bonn, 1984, pp. 135–152
Schaal, Ferdinand, 'Der 20. Juli 1944 in Prag: Der Attentatstag im Spiegel militärischer Befehle', *Schwäbische Zeitung*, 26 July 1952

Schefold, Karl, 'Erinnerung an Alexander Schenk Grafen von Stauffenberg', *Mitteilungen des Vereins der ehemaligen Schüler des Eberhard-Ludwigs-Gymnasiums* 27 (1981) No. 37, June 1981, pp. 1–6

['Erinnerungen an Robert Boehringer'] in Georg Peter Landmann, ed., *Wie jeder ihn erlebte*, privately printed, Basel, [1977], pp. 99–104

Schematismus für das k. u. k. Heer und für die k. u. k. Kriegsmarine für 1914. Separatausgabe, Druck und Verlag der k.k. [*sic*] Hof- und Staatsdruckerei, Vienna, 1914

Schiller, [Friedrich], *Schillers Werke. Nationalausgabe. Erster Band. Gedichte in der Reihenfolge ihres Erscheinens 1776–1799*, ed. Julius Petersen and Friedrich Beissner, Hermann Böhlaus Nachfolger, Weimar, 1943

Schillers Werke. Nationalausgabe. Zweiter Band. Teil I. Gedichte, ed. Norbert Oellers, Hermann Böhlaus Nachfolger, Weimar, 1983

Schiller, K[lara], 'Melitta Gräfin Schenk von Stauffenberg, geb. Schiller (1903–1945)', *Schlesische Flieger Nachrichten* 6 (1988) No. 5, pp. 2–6

Schlabrendorff, Fabian v[on], *Offiziere gegen Hitler*, Europa Verlag, Zürich, 1946

Schlieffen, Graf Alfred v[on], *Gesammelte Schriften*, 2 vols., Ernst Siegfried Mittler und Sohn, Königliche Hofbuchhandlung, Berlin, 1913

Cannae. Mit einer Auswahl von Aufsätzen und Reden des Feldmarschalls sowie einer Einführung und Lebensbeschreibung von General der Infanterie Freiherrn von Freytag-Loringhoven, E. S. Mittler & Sohn, Berlin, 1925 [re-ed. of *Gesammelte Schriften* of 1913, with omissions]

Schmidt, Paul, *Statist auf diplomatischer Bühne 1923–45. Erlebnisse des Chefdolmetschers im Auswärtigen Amt mit den Staatsmännern Europas*, Athenäum-Verlag, Bonn, 1949

[Schmundt, Rudolf], *Tätigkeitsbericht des Chefs des Heerespersonalamtes General der Infanterie Rudolf Schmundt fortgeführt von General der Infanterie Wilhelm Burgdorf 1.10.1942–29.10.1944*, ed. Dermot Bradley and Richard Schulze-Kossens, facsimile edn, Biblio Verlag, Osnabrück, 1984

[Schramm, Percy Ernst], 'Vorgänge im FHQu am 20.7.44 (Attentat auf den Führer)', in H[erbert] Kraus, *Die im Braunschweiger Remerprozess erstatteten moraltheologischen und historischen Gutachten nebst Urteil*, Girardet Verlag, Hamburg, 1953, pp. 139–141

'Mitteilungen des Stellv. Chefs WFSt 21.7.44, 20 Uhr', in H[erbert] Kraus, *Die im Braunschweiger Remerprozess erstatteten moraltheologischen und historischen Gutachten nebst Urteil*, Girardet Verlag, Hamburg, 1953, pp. 142–145

Schroeder, Christa, *Er war mein Chef. Aus dem Nachlass der Sekretärin von Adolf Hitler*, ed. Anton Joachimsthaler, Albert Langen, Georg Müller Verlag GmbH, Munich, Vienna, 1985

Schulenburg, Tisa [Gräfin von der], *Zeichnungen, Aufzeichnungen*, Praesentverlag Heinz Peter, Gütersloh, [2]1979.

Schulz, Günter, 'Stefan George und Max Kommerell', *Das Literarische Deutschland* 2, 5 Feb. 1951, p. 3

Schwäbischer Merkur, October–November 1918

Seeley, J.R., *The Expansion of England. Two Courses of Lectures*, Macmillan and Co., London, 1931

Shakespeare, William, *The Sonnets and A Lover's Complaint*, ed. John Kerrigan, Penguin Books, Harmondsworth, Middlesex, 1986

Shirer, William L., *Berlin Diary. The Journal of a Foreign Correspondent, 1934–1941*, Alfred A. Knopf, New York, 1941

Société des Nations, Recueil des Traités. *Traités et Engagements internationaux enregistrés par le Secrétariat de la Société des Nations*, Secrétariat de la Société des Nations, Geneva, 1936

Sodenstern, [Georg] von, 'Vom Wesen des Soldatentums', *Militärwissenschaftliche Rundschau* 4 (1939), No. 1, issued mid-January 1939, pp. 42–60

[Solomos, Dionysios], *Neugriechisches Gespräch. Der Dialog des Dionysios Solomos*, transl. Rudolf Fahrner, Verleger Irmgard Böhm, Munich, 1943

Soviet Documents see Degras

Speer, Albert, *Erinnerungen*, Propyläen Verlag, Berlin, 1969

Speidel, Hans, *Invasion. Ein Beitrag zu Rommels und des Reiches Schicksal*, Rainer Wunderlich Verlag Hermann Leins, Tübingen, 1949

Spengler, Oswald, *Der Untergang des Abendlandes. Umrisse einer Morphologie der Weltgeschichte. Erster Band. Gestalt und Wirklichkeit*, Wilhelm Braumüller K. K. Universitäts-Verlagsbuchhandlung Gesellschaft m.b.H., Vienna and Leipzig, ^{2}1919

Spiegelbild einer Verschwörung. Die Kaltenbrunner-Berichte an Bormann und Hitler über das Attentat vom 20. Juli 1944. Geheime Dokumente aus dem ehemaligen Reichssicherheitshauptamt, Seewald Verlag, Stuttgart, 1961

'Spiegelbild einer Verschwörung'. Die Opposition gegen Hitler und der Staatsstreich vom 20. Juli 1944 in der SD-Berichterstattung. Geheime Dokumente aus dem ehemaligen Reichssicherheitshauptamt, ed. Hans-Adolf Jacobsen, 2 vols., Seewald Verlag, Stuttgart, 1984

Staatshandbuch für Württemberg 1922, ed. Württembergisches Statistisches Landesamt, Druck von W. Kohlhammer, Stuttgart, 1922

Stahlberg, Alexander, *Die verdammte Pflicht. Erinnerungen 1932 bis 1945*, Ullstein, Berlin, Frankfurt am Main, 1987

Stauffenberg, Alexander Schenk Graf von, *Die römische Kaisergeschichte bei Malalas. Griechischer Text der Bücher IX–XII und Untersuchungen*, W. Kohlhammer, Stuttgart, 1931

    König Hieron der Zweite von Syrakus, W. Kohlhammer, Stuttgart, 1933

    'Die Germanen im römischen Reich', *Die Welt als Geschichte* I 1935, pp. 72–100, II 1936, pp. 117–168, III 1937, pp. 345–361

    Der Tod des Meisters. Zum zehnten Jahrestag, Delfinverlag, Munich, 1945

    Der Tod des Meisters. Zum zehnten Jahrestag, Delfinverlag, n.p., 1948

    Dichtung und Staat in der antiken Welt, Verlag Hermann Rinn, Munich, [1948]

    Denkmal, Helmut Küpper vormals Georg Bondi, Düsseldorf and Munich, 1964

    Macht und Geist. Vorträge und Abhandlungen zur Alten Geschichte, Verlag Georg D. W. Callwey, Munich, 1972

    Trinakria. Sizilien und Grossgriechenland in archaischer und frühklassischer Zeit, R. Oldenbourg Verlag, Munich, Vienna, 1963

Stauffenberg, Berthold Schenk Graf von, *Die Rechtsstellung der russischen Handelsvertretungen* (Beiträge zum ausländischen öffentlichen Recht und Völkerrecht, No. 14), Walter de Gruyter & Co., Berlin und Leipzig, 1930

    Statut et règlement de la Cour permanente de Justice internationale. Éléments d'interprétation, Carl Heymanns Verlag, Berlin, 1934

'Die Zuständigkeit des Ständigen Internationalen Gerichtshofs für die sogen-annten politischen Streitigkeiten', *Deutsche Juristenzeitung* 39 (1934), cols. 1325–1330

'Die Abberufung des Präsidenten des Memeldirektoriums und das Urteil des Ständigen Internationalen Gerichtshofs vom 11.8.32', *Völkerbund und Völker-recht* 1 (1934), pp. 291–295

'Die Entziehung der Staatsangehörigkeit und das Völkerrecht, Eine Entgegnung', *Zeitschrift für ausländisches öffentliches Recht und Völkerrecht* IV (1934), pp. 261–276

'1. Das Urteil des Ständigen Internationalen Gerichtshofs vom 15. Dezember 1933 (Série A/B Nr. 61): Berufung gegen eine Entscheidung des ungarisch-tschechoslowakischen Gemischten Schiedsgerichts (Die Universität Peter Pázmány % tschechoslowakischen Staat)', *Zeitschrift für ausländisches öffent-liches Recht und Völkerrecht* IV (1934), pp. 395–403

'Die Vorgeschichte des Locarno-Vertrages und das russisch-französische Bündnis', *Zeitschrift für ausländisches öffentliches Recht und Völkerrecht* VI (1936), pp. 215–234

Stauffenberg, [Claus] Graf Schenk von, 'Gedanken zur Abwehr feindlicher Fall-schirmeinheiten im Heimatgebiet', *Wissen und Wehr. Monatsschrift der Deutschen Gesellschaft für Wehrpolitik und Wehrwissenschaften* 19 (1938), pp. 459–476
see also Giessler

Stauffenberg, Nina Gräfin, 'Sie wollten Hitler nicht mit Stalin tauschen', *Die Zeit* No. 37, 8 Sept. 1978, p. 26

Steltzer, Theodor, *Von deutscher Politik. Dokumente, Aufsätze und Vorträge*, ed. Friedrich Minssen, Verlag Josef Knecht, Carolusdruckerei, Frankfurt am Main, 1949

Stern, Alfred, 'Gneisenau's Reise nach London im Jahre 1809 und ihre Vor-geschichte', *Historische Zeitschrift* 85 (1900), pp. 1–44

Stettler, Michael, ed., *Erinnerung an Frank. Ein Lebenszeugnis*, Düsseldorf and Munich, 1968

Stieff, Hellmuth, *Briefe*, ed. Horst Mühleisen, Siedler Verlag, Berlin, 1991
see also Rothfels

Strik-Strikfeldt, Wilfried, *Gegen Stalin und Hitler. General Wlassow und die russische Freiheitsbewegung*, v. Hase & Koehler Verlag, Mainz, 1970

Ströhle, Albert, *Der Vertrag von Versailles und seine Wirkungen für unser deutsches Vaterland*, Zentral-Verlag G.m.b.H., Berlin, [1923]

Strölin, Karl, *Verräter oder Patrioten? Der 20. Juli 1944 und das Recht auf Widerstand*, Friedrich Vorwerk Verlag, Stuttgart, 1952

Teske, Hermann, *Die silbernen Spiegel. Generalstabsdienst unter der Lupe*, Kurt Vowinckel, Heidelberg, 1952

Teske, Hermann, 'Der Zwiespalt', *Schwäbische Donauzeitung* 19, 20, 21, 26 Aug. 1952 [resp.] p. 7

Teske, Hermann, ed., *General Ernst Köstring. Der militärische Mittler zwischen dem Deutschen Reich und der Sowjetunion 1921–1941* (Profile bedeutender Soldaten. Herausgegeben vom Bundesarchiv/Militärarchiv, vol. 1), Verlag E. S. Mittler & Sohn, Frankfurt am Main, n.d. [1965]

Thimme, Friedrich, 'Zu den Erhebungsplänen der preussischen Patrioten im Sommer 1808. Ungedruckte Denkschriften Gneisenau's and Scharnhorst's', *Historische Zeitschrift* 86 (1901), pp. 78–110

Thormaehlen, Ludwig, 'Die Grafen Stauffenberg, Freunde von Stefan George', in *Robert Boehringer. Eine Freundesgabe*, ed. Erich Boehringer und Wilhelm Hoffmann, J. C. B. Mohr (Paul Siebeck), Tübingen, 1957

Thormaehlen, Ludwig, *Erinnerungen an Stefan George*, Dr Ernst Hauswedell & Co., Hamburg, 1962

Topf, Erwin, 'Klaus Graf Stauffenberg', *Die Zeit* 18 July 1946

Treue, Wilhelm, Hrsg., 'Rede Hitlers vor der deutschen Presse (10. November 1938)', *Vierteljahrshefte für Zeitgeschichte* 6 (1958), pp. 175–191

Trial of the Major War Criminals before the International Military Tribunal. Nuremberg 14 November 1945–1 October 1946, 42 vols., Secretariat of the Tribunal, Nuremberg, 1947–1949

Trott zu Solz, A[dam] v[on], 'Der Kampf um die Herrschaftsgestaltung im Fernen Osten', *Zeitschrift für ausländisches öffentliches Recht und Völkerrecht* IX (1939), pp. 264–283

   see also Grant Duff; Lindgren; Rothfels

Üxküll[-Gyllenband, Alexandrine] Gräfin von, *Aus einem Schwesternleben*, W. Kohlhammer Verlag, Stuttgart, ²[1957]

Uxkull-Gyllenband [*sic*], Bernhard Victor Graf, *Gedichte*, ed. Ernst Morwitz, Helmut Küpper vormals Georg Bondi, Düsseldorf and Munich, 1964

Uxkull-Gyllenband [*sic*], Woldemar, Count, *Das revolutionäre Ethos bei Stefan George* (Philosophie und Geschichte. Eine Sammlung von Vorträgen und Schriften aus dem Gebiet der Philosophie und Geschichte, 45), Verlag von J. C. B. Mohr (Paul Siebeck), Tübingen, 1933

Vallentin, Berthold, *Napoleon*, Bondi, Berlin, [1922]

Vallentin, Berthold, *Napoleon und die Deutschen*, Bondi, Berlin, 1926

Vallentin, Berthold, *Gespräche mit Stefan George. 1902–1931*, Castrum Peregrini Presse, Amsterdam, 1961

Völkischer Beobachter 1933–1945

Vogelsang, Thilo, 'Neue Dokumente zur Geschichte der Reichswehr', *Vierteljahrshefte für Zeitgeschichte* 2 (1954), pp. 397–436

Volksgerichtshof-Prozesse zum 20. Juli 1944. Transkripte von Tonbandfunden, Lautarchiv des deutschen Rundfunks, [Frankfurt am Main], 1961

Vormann, Nikolaus von, *Der Feldzug 1939 in Polen. Die Operationen des deutschen Heeres*, Prinz-Eugen-Verlag, Weissenburg, 1958

Wagener, Carl, 'Der Vorstoss des XXXX. Panzerkorps von Charkow zum Kaukasus Juli-August 1942. Ein Beispiel für weitreichende Operationen mit schnellen Truppen', *Wehrwissenschaftliche Rundschau* 5 (1955), pp. 397–407, 447–458

Wagner, Gerhard, ed., *Lagevorträge des Oberbefehlshabers der Kriegsmarine vor Hitler 1939–1945*, J. F. Lehmann, Munich, 1972

Warlimont, Walter, *Im Hauptquartier der deutschen Wehrmacht 1939–1945. Grundlagen, Formen, Gestalten*, Bernard & Graefe Verlag für Wehrwesen, Frankfurt am Main, 1962.

Wedemeyer, Albert C., *Wedemeyer Reports!* Henry Holt & Company, New York, 1958

[Wehner, Bernd], 'Das Spiel ist aus – Arthur Nebe: Glanz und Elend der deutschen Kriminalpolizei', *Der Spiegel* No. 12, 23 March 1950, pp. 23–32

Dem Täter auf der Spur. Die Geschichte der deutschen Kriminalpolizei, Lübbe, Bergisch Gladbach, 1983

[Weizsäcker, Ernst Freiherr von], *Die Weizsäcker-Papiere 1933–1950*, ed. Leonidas Hill, Propyläen Verlag, Frankfurt am Main, Berlin, Vienna, 1974

Wengler, Wilhelm, 'Vorkämpfer der Völkerverständigung und Völkerrechtsgelehrte als Opfer des Nationalsozialismus: 9. H. J. Graf von Moltke (1906–1945)', *Die Friedens-Warte* 48 (1948), pp. 297–305

Wolfe, Robert, ed., *The Wannsee Protocol and a 1944 Report on Auschwitz by the Office of Strategic Services* (*The Holocaust*, vol. 11), Garland Publishing, New York, London, 1982

Wolfskehl, Karl, *Gesammelte Werke. Erster Band. Dichtungen. Dramatische Dichtungen. Zweiter Band. Übertragungen. Prosa*, ed. Margot Ruben and Claus Victor Bock, Claassen Verlag, Hamburg, 1960

Die Stimme spricht, Bücherei des Schocken Verlags 17, Schocken-Verlag, Berlin, n.d. [1934]

und Hanna, *Briefwechsel mit Friedrich Gundolf 1899–1931*, ed. Karlhans Kluncker. II. (Publications of the Institute of Germanic Studies, University of London, vol. 24.) Castrum Peregrini Presse, Amsterdam, 1977

see also Nijland-Verwey

Wolters, Friedrich, *Vier Reden über das Vaterland*, Ferdinand Hirt, Breslau, 1927

Stefan George und die Blätter für die Kunst. Deutsche Geistesgeschichte seit 1890, Georg Bondi, Berlin, 1930 [actually November 1929]

und Carl Petersen [ed.], *Die Heldensagen der germanischen Frühzeit*, Ferdinand Hirt, Breslau, 1921

Wuppertaler Zeitung, 1938

Yorck von Wartenburg, Marion, *Die Stärke der Stille. Erzählung eines Lebens aus dem deutschen Widerstand*, Eugen Diederichs Verlag, Cologne, 1984

Ziegler, Delia, 'Wer schoss auf Stauffenberg?' *Die Welt* 21. Aug. 1947, p. 2

Zierold, Kurt, *Begegnungen. Einige Abschnitte aus meinen Lebenserinnerungen* [printed in ms, n.p., 1966]

Zimmermann, Erich and Hans-Adolf Jacobsen, ed., *20 July 1944*, Berto Verlag, Bonn, [4]1961

III. Secondary literature

Adam, Uwe Dietrich, *Judenpolitik im Dritten Reich*, Droste Verlag, Düsseldorf, 1972

Albrecht, Richard, *Der militante Sozialdemokrat Carlo Mierendorff 1897 bis 1943. Eine Biografie*, Verlag J. H. W.Dietz Nachf., Berlin, Bonn, 1987

Artaud, Denise: 'Die Hintergründe der Ruhrbesetzung 1923. Das Problem der interalliierten Schulden', *Vierteljahrshefte für Zeitgeschichte* 27 (1979), pp. 241–259

Aus der Geschichte des Kavallerie-Regiments 17, Wilhelm Limpert, Berlin, n.d., BA-MA O III b 19

Bach, Hans I., 'Zur Geschichte einer schwäbisch-jüdischen Familie', 5731, in *Pessach-Festschrift der israelitischen Religionsgemeinschaft Württembergs*, April 1971, pp. 26–28

'Zur Geschichte einer schwäbisch-jüdischen Familie', 5732. *Rosch Haschana*, Stuttgart, September 1971, pp. 37–49

Baedeker, Karl, *Mittelitalien und Rom*, Karl Baedeker, Leipzig, [15]1927

Sachsen, Karl Baedeker, Leipzig, [2]1928

Balfour, Michael and Julian Frisby, *Helmuth von Moltke. A Leader against Hitler*, Macmillan, London and Basingstoke, [1972]

Barkai, Avraham, '"Schicksalsjahr 1938". Kontinuität und Verschärfung der wirtschaftlichen Ausplünderung der deutschen Juden', in Walter H. Pehle, ed., *Der Judenpogrom 1938. Von der 'Reichskristallnacht' zum Völkermord*, Fischer Taschenbuch Verlag, Frankfurt am Main, 1988, pp. 95–117

Baum, Walter, 'Marine, Nationalsozialismus und Widerstand', *Vierteljahrshefte für Zeitgeschichte* 11 (1963), pp. 16–48

Baumgart, Winfried, 'Die Mission des Grafen Mirbach in Moskau April–Juni 1918', *Vierteljahrshefte für Zeitgeschichte* 16 (1968), pp. 66–96

Beck, Adolf und Paul Raabe, ed., *Hölderlin. Eine Chronik in Text und Bild*, Insel-Verlag, Frankfurt am Main, 1970

Benjamin, Walter, 'Wider ein Meisterwerk. Zu Max Kommerell: Der Dichter als Führer in der deutschen Klassik', *Die literarische Welt* VI (1930) No. 33/34, pp. 9–11

Benjamin, Walter, *Gesammelte Schriften*, vol. III, Suhrkamp Verlag, Frankfurt am Main, 1972

Bennett, Edward W., *German Rearmament and the West, 1932–1933*, Princeton University Press, New Jersey, [1979]

Bethge, Eberhard, *Dietrich Bonhoeffer. Theologe, Christ, Zeitgenosse*, Chr. Kaiser Verlag, Munich, [3]1970

Bethge, Eberhard, 'Dietrich Bonhoeffer und die Juden', in Ernst Feil und Ilse Tödt, *Konsequenzen. Dietrich Bonhoeffers Kirchenverständnis heute* (Internationales Bonhoeffer-Forum, No. 3), Chr. Kaiser Verlag, Munich, 1980

Bèze, Théodore de, *Du droit des magistrats*, Librairie Droz, Genève, 1970

Bock, Claus Victor, *Wort-Konkordanz zur Dichtung Stefan Georges*, Castrum Peregrini Presse, Amsterdam, 1964

Boog, Horst, 'The Luftwaffe and Indiscriminate Bombing up to 1942', in Horst Boog, ed., *The Conduct of the Air War in the Second World War. An International Comparison. Proceedings of the International Conference of Historians in Freiburg im Breisgau, Federal Republic of Germany, from 29 August to 2 September 1988*, Berg, New York, Oxford, 1992

Bracher, Karl Dietrich, Wolfgang Sauer, Gerhard Schulz, *Die nationalsozialistische Machtergreifung. Studien zur Errichtung des totalitären Herrschaftssystems in Deutschland 1933/34*, Westdeutscher Verlag, Cologne and Opladen, [2]1962

Bracke, Gerhard, *Melitta Gräfin Stauffenberg. Das Leben einer Fliegerin*, Langen Müller, Munich, 1990

Bragadin, Marc' Antonio, *The Italian Navy in World War II*, United States Naval Institute, Annapolis, Maryland, 1957

Brandt, Otto, Meyer, Arnold Oskar, Just, Leo, *Handbuch der Deutschen Geschichte*, *see* Just

Bucher, Peter, *Der Reichswehrprozess. Der Hochverrat der Ulmer Reichswehroffiziere 1929/30*, Harald Boldt Verlag, Boppard am Rhein, 1967

Bücheler, Heinrich, *Hoepner. Ein deutsches Soldatenschicksal des zwanzigsten Jahrhunderts*, Mittler, Herford, 1980

Burkhardt, Hans, Günter Erxleben, Kurt Nettball, *Die mit dem blauen Schein. Über den antifaschistischen Widerstand in den 999er Formationen der faschistischen deutschen Wehrmacht (1942 bis 1945)*, Militärverlag der Deutschen Demokratischen Republik, Berlin, ²1986

Bussmann, Walter, *Die innere Entwicklung des deutschen Widerstandes gegen Hitler*, Morus-Verlag, Berlin, 1964

Castellan, Georges, *Le Réarmement clandestin du Reich, 1930–1935. Vu par le 2ᵉ Bureau de l'État-Major Français*, Plon, Paris, 1954

Dallin, Alexander, *German Rule in Russia 1941–1945. A Study of Occupation Policies*, Octagon Books, New York, 1980 (reprinted from edn publ. by Macmillan, London, and St. Martin's Press, New York, 1957)

Dehlinger, Alfred, *Württembergs Staatswesen in seiner geschichtlichen Entwicklung bis heute*, 2 vols, W. Kohlhammer, Stuttgart, 1951, 1953

Deist, Wilhelm, *The Wehrmacht and German Rearmament*, University of Toronto Press, Toronto, Buffalo, 1981

Delbrück, Hans, *Das Leben des Feldmarschalls Grafen Neidhardt von Gneisenau*, 2 vols, Verlag von Georg Stilke, Berlin, ³1908

Deutsch, Harold C., *Hitler and His Generals. The Hidden Crisis, January–June 1938*, University of Minnesota Press, Minneapolis, 1974

Doepgen, Heinz W., *Georg v. Boeselager. Kavallerie-Offizier in der Militäropposition gegen Hitler*, Verlag E. S. Mittler & Sohn, Herford and Bonn, 1986

Donohoe, James, *Hitler's Conservative Opponents in Bavaria 1930–1945, a study of Catholic, monarchist, and separatist anti-Nazi activities*, E. J. Brill, Leiden, 1961

Ehrman, John, *Grand Strategy, Volume V. August 1943–September 1944*, Her Majesty's Stationery Office, London, 1956

Ellis, L. F., *The War in France and Flanders 1939–1940*, Her Majesty's Stationery Office, London, 1953

Erfurth, Waldemar, *Die Geschichte des deutschen Generalstabes von 1918 bis 1945*, Musterschmidt-Verlag, Göttingen, Berlin, Frankfurt, 1957

Esposito, Vincent J., *West Point Atlas of American Wars. Vol. II: 1900–1953*, Fredrick A. Praeger, New York, 1959

Finker, Kurt, *Stauffenberg und der 20. Juli 1944*, Union Verlag, Berlin, ⁴1973

Fischer, Josef Ludwig, 'Wilhelm II.' in *Wilhelm II. Württembergs geliebter Herr*, Greiner und Pfeiffer, Stuttgart, [1928], pp. 1–104

Fleischer, Hagen, *Im Kreuzschatten der Mächte: Griechenland 1941–1944 (Okkupation – Resistance – Kollaboration)*, Verlag Peter Lang, Frankfurt am Main, Berne, New York, 1986

Fleischhauer, Ingeborg, *Die Chance des Sonderfriedens. Deutsch-sowjetische Geheimgespräche 1941–1945*, Siedler Verlag, Berlin, 1986

Förster, Jürgen, 'Die Sicherung des "Lebensraumes"' in *Das Deutsche Reich und der Zweite Weltkrieg*, vol. 4, ed. Militärgeschichtliches Forschungsamt, Deutsche Verlags-Anstalt, Stuttgart, 1983, pp. 1030–1078

Freytag-Loringhoven, Freiherr von, *Generalfeldmarschall Graf von Schlieffen. Sein Leben und die Verwertung seines geistigen Erbes im Weltkriege*, Historia-Verlag Paul Schraepler, Leipzig, 1920

Geyer, Michael, 'Das Zweite Rüstungsprogramm (1930–1934)', *Militärgeschichtliche Mitteilungen* 17 (1975), pp. 125–172

Giesau, Hermann, *Der Dom zu Magdeburg*, August Hopfer, Burg bei Magdeburg, ²1936

Gilbert, Bentley B., *The Evolution of National Insurance in Great Britain*, Joseph, London, 1966

Gönner, Eberhard, 'König Wilhelm II. (1891–1921)' in Robert Uhland, ed., *900 Jahre Haus Württemberg. Leben und Leistung für Land und Volk*, Verlag W. Kohlhammer, Stuttgart, Berlin, Cologne, Mainz, 1984, pp. 341–362

Görlitz, Walter, *Kleine Geschichte des deutschen Generalstabes*, Haude & Spenersche Verlagsbuchhandlung, Berlin, ²1977
see also Paulus

Graml, Hermann, 'Die deutsche Militäropposition vom Sommer 1940 bis zum Frühjahr 1943', in *Vollmacht des Gewissens II*, ed. Europäische Publikation e.V., Alfred Metzner Verlag, Frankfurt am Main, Berlin, 1965, pp. 411–474.

Graml, Hermann, *Reichskristallnacht. Antisemitismus und Judenverfolgung im Dritten Reich*, Deutscher Taschenbuch Verlag, Munich, 1988

Grimm, Jacob und Wilhelm Grimm, *Deutsches Wörterbuch*, 16 vols., Hirzel, Leipzig, 1854–1960

Grünewald, Eckhart, *Ernst Kantorowicz und Stefan George. Beiträge zur Biographie des Historikers bis zum Jahre 1938 und zu seinem Jugendwerk 'Kaiser Friedrich der Zweite'* (Frankfurter Historische Abhandlungen vol. 25), Franz Steiner Verlag, Wiesbaden, 1982

Grundmann, Herbert, *Die Zeit der Weltkriege* (Bruno Gebhardt, *Handbuch der deutschen Geschichte*, vol. 4), Union Verlag, Stuttgart, ⁸1959, second rev. reprint, 1961

Hartmann, Christian, *Halder. Generalstabschef Hitlers 1938–1942*, Ferdinand Schöningh, Paderborn, Munich, Vienna, Zürich, 1991

Heinemann, Ulrich, *Ein konservativer Rebell. Fritz-Dietlof Graf von der Schulenburg und der 20. Juli*, Siedler Verlag, Berlin, 1990

Helbing, Lothar, Claus Victor Bock, Karlhans Kluncker, ed., *Stefan George: Dokumente seiner Wirkung. Aus dem Friedrich Gundolf Archiv der Universität London*, Castrum Peregrini Presse, Amsterdam, ²1974

Hilberg, Raul, *The Destruction of the European Jews. Revised and Definitive Edition*, 3 vols., Holmes & Meier, New York, London, 1985
'German Railroads/Jewish Souls', *Society* 14 No. 1, November/December 1976, pp. 60–74
Sonderzüge nach Auschwitz, Horst-Werner Dumjahn Verlag, Mainz, 1981

Hillgruber, Andreas, *Die gescheiterte Grossmacht. Eine Skizze des deutschen Reiches 1871–1945*, Droste Verlag, Düsseldorf, ³1982

Hillgruber, Andreas, *Der Zweite Weltkrieg 1939–1945. Kriegsziele und Strategie der grossen Mächte*, Verlag W. Kohlhammer, Stuttgart, Berlin, Cologne, Mainz, ²1983

Hillgruber, Andreas [und] Gerhard Hümmelchen, *Chronik des Zweiten Weltkrieges*, Athenäum/Droste, Königstein/Taunus, Düsseldorf, 1978

Hinsley, F. H. [*et al.*], *British Intelligence in the Second World War. Its Influence on Strategy and Operations*, 5 vols. in 6, Her Majesty's Stationery Office, London, 1979, 1981, 1984, 1988, 1990

Hobe, Cord v., Walter Görlitz, *Georg von Boeselager. Ein Reiterleben*, Verlag Sankt Georg, Düsseldorf, 1957

Höhne, Heinz, *Mordsache Röhm. Hitlers Durchbruch zur Alleinherrschaft 1933–1934*, Rowohlt Taschenbuch, Reinbeck bei Hamburg, 1984

Hofer, Walther, 'Die Diktatur Hitlers bis zum Beginn des Zweiten Weltkrieges', in Leo Just, ed., *Handbuch der Deutschen Geschichte*, vol. IV, 2nd Part, Akademische Verlagsgesellschaft Athenaion Dr. Albert Hachfeld, Konstanz, 1965, pp. 1–257

Hoffmann, Peter, *Claus Schenk Graf Stauffenberg und seine Brüder*, Deutsche Verlags-Anstalt, Stuttgart, 1992, ²1992 (cited: Hoffmann, *Stauffenberg*, German edn)

'Claus Graf Stauffenberg und Stefan George: Der Weg zur Tat', *Jahrbuch der Deutschen Schillergesellschaft* XII (1968), pp. 520–542 (cited: Hoffmann, 'Stauffenberg und George')

'Colonel Claus von Stauffenberg in the German Resistance to Hitler: Between East and West', *The Historical Journal* 31 (1988), pp. 629–650

'Generaloberst Ludwig Becks militärpolitisches Denken', *Historische Zeitschrift* 234 (1982), pp. 101–121

'Harold C. Deutsch: Das Komplott oder Die Entmachtung der Generale. Blomberg- und Fritsch-Krise. Hitlers Weg zum Krieg. Aus dem Amerikanischen von Burkhardt Kiegeland. Zürich: Neue Diana-Press 1974. 461 Seiten' [review], *Militärgeschichtliche Mitteilungen* 1976 No. 2, pp. 196–201

The History of the German Resistance 1933–1945, Macdonald and Jane's, London, MIT Press, Cambridge, Massachusetts, 1977

Hitler's Personal Security, Macmillan, London and Basingstoke, 1979

'Peace through Coup d'État: The Foreign Contacts of the German Resistance 1933–1944', *Central European History* XIX (1986), pp. 3–44

'Roncalli in the Second World War: Peace Initiatives, the Greek Famine and the Persecution of the Jews', *Journal of Ecclesiastical History* 40 (1989), pp. 74–99

'The Question of Western Allied Co-operation with the German Anti-Nazi Conspiracy, 1938–1944', *The Historical Journal* 34 (1991), pp. 1–28

'Warum misslang das Attentat vom 20. Juli 1944?' *Vierteljahrshefte für Zeitgeschichte* 32 (1984), pp. 441–462

Widerstand, Staatsstreich, Attentat: Der Kampf der Opposition gegen Hitler, R. Piper-Verlag, Munich, Zürich, ⁴1985

'Zu dem Attentat im Führerhauptquartier »Wolfsschanze« am 20. Juli 1944', *Vierteljahrshefte für Zeitgeschichte* 12 (1964), pp. 254–284

Hoffmann, Wilhelm, 'Neue Arbeiten am Werk Friedrich Hölderlins', *Schwaben. Monatshefte für Volkstum und Kultur*, No. 1, 1942, pp. 42–48

'Die Stuttgarter Hölderlin-Ausgabe. Vorgeschichte und Aufbau', in [Theophil Frey, ed.,] *Die Stuttgarter Hölderlin-Ausgabe. Ein Arbeitsbericht*, J. G. Cotta'sche Buchhandlung Nachfolger, Stuttgart, 1942

Howard, Michael, *Grand Strategy. Volume IV. August 1942–September 1943*, Her Majesty's Stationery Office, London, 1970

Howe, George F., *Northwest Africa: Seizing the Initiative in the West* (*United States Army in World War II: The Mediterranean Theater of Operations*), Office of the Chief of Military History, Department of the Army, Washington, D.C., 1957

Hubatsch, Walther, 'Der Weltkrieg 1914/1918' in Leo Just, ed., *Handbuch der*

Deutschen Geschichte, vol. IV, 1st Part, Akademische Verlagsgesellschaft Athen-aion, Frankfurt am Main, 1973

Huber, Wolfgang und Tödt, Ilse, *Ethik im Ernstfall. Dietrich Bonhoeffers Stellung zu den Juden und ihre Aktualität* (Internationales Bonhoeffer-Forum, No. 4), Chr. Kaiser Verlag, Munich, 1982

Irving, David, *Hitler's War*, Hodder and Stoughton, London, Sydney, Auckland, Toronto, 1977
  The Trail of the Fox, E. P. Dutton, New York, 1977

Jacobsen, Hans-Adolf, *Dünkirchen. Ein Beitrag zur Geschichte des Westfeldzuges 1940*, Kurt Vowinckel Verlag, Neckargemünd, 1958
  Fall Gelb. Der Kampf um den deutschen Operationsplan zur Westoffensive 1940, Franz Steiner Verlag, Wiesbaden, 1957
  1939–1945. Der Zweite Weltkrieg in Chronik und Dokumenten, Wehr und Wissen Verlagsgesellschaft, Darmstadt, ⁵1961

Jens, Inge, *Dichter zwischen rechts und links. Die Geschichte der Sektion für Dichtkunst der Preussischen Akademie der Künste dargestellt nach den Dokumenten*, R.Piper & Co. Verlag, Munich, 1971

Just, Leo, *Handbuch der Deutschen Geschichte*, vol. IV, 1st Part, Akademische Verlagsgsellschaft Athenaion, Frankfurt am Main, 1973

Kehrig, Manfred, *Stalingrad. Analyse und Dokumentation einer Schlacht* (Beiträge zur Militär- und Kriegsgeschichte, vol. 15), Deutsche Verlags-Anstalt, Stuttgart, 1974

Keilson-Lauritz, Marita, *Von der Liebe die Freundschaft heisst. Zur Homoerotik im Werk Stefan Georges*, Verlag rosa Winkel, Berlin, 1987

Kennan, George F., *The Fateful Alliance: France, Russia and the Coming of the First World War*, Pantheon Books, New York, 1984

Kernig, C. D., *Marxism, Communism and Western Society. A Comparative Encyclo-pedia*, 8 vols., Herder and Herder, New York, 1972–1973

Keynes, John Maynard, *The Economic Consequences of the Peace*, Macmillan and Co., London, 1920

Klemperer, Klemens von, *German Resistance against Hitler. The Search for Allies Abroad, 1938–1945*, Clarendon Press, Oxford, 1992

Klink, Ernst, *Das Gesetz des Handelns. Die Operation 'Zitadelle' 1943*, Deutsche Verlags-Anstalt, Stuttgart, 1966
  'Der Krieg gegen die Sowjetunion bis zur Jahreswende 1941/42. I. Die Operationsführung. 1. Heer und Kriegsmarine' in *Das Deutsche Reich und der Zweite Weltkrieg*, vol. 4, ed. Militärgeschichtliches Forschungsamt, Deutsche Verlags-Anstalt, Stuttgart, 1983, pp. 451–652

Kramarz, Joachim, *Claus Graf Stauffenberg 15. November 1907–20. Juli 1944. Das Leben eines Offiziers*, Bernard & Graefe Verlag für Wehrwesen, Frankfurt am Main, 1965 (this edn cited)
  Stauffenberg. The Architect of the Famous July 20th Conspiracy to Assassinate Hitler, transl. R. H. Barry, Macmillan, New York, 1967

Krausnick, Helmut, 'Judenverfolgung' in Hans Buchheim, Martin Broszat, Hans-Adolf Jacobsen, Helmut Krausnick, *Anatomie des SS-Staates*, 2 vols., Deutscher Taschenbuch Verlag, Munich, 1965, 1967

Krausnick, Helmut, 'Vorgeschichte und Beginn des militärischen Widerstandes gegen Hitler', in *Vollmacht des Gewissens I*, ed. Europäische Publikation e.V., Alfred Metzner Verlag, Frankfurt am Main, Berlin, 1960

Krausnick, Helmut, Hans-Heinrich Wilhelm, *Die Truppe des Weltanschauungskrieges. Die Einsatzgruppen der Sicherheitspolizei und des SD 1938–1942* (Quellen und Darstellungen zur Zeitgeschichte, vol. 22), Deutsche Verlags-Anstalt, Stuttgart, 1981

Krebs, Albert, *Fritz-Dietlof Graf von der Schulenburg. Zwischen Staatsraison und Hochverrat* (Hamburger Beiträge zur Zeitgeschichte, vol. 11), Leibniz-Verlag, Hamburg, 1964

Kroener, Bernhard R., 'Die personellen Ressourcen des Dritten Reiches im Spannungsfeld zwischen Wehrmacht, Bürokratie und Kriegswirtschaft 1939–1942' in *Das Deutsche Reich und der Zweite Weltkrieg*, vol. 5, First Half, ed. Militärgeschichtliches Forschungsamt, Deutsche Verlags-Anstalt, Stuttgart, 1988, pp. 691–1001

Lamb, Richard, *The Ghosts of Peace 1935–1945*, Michael Russell, Wilton, Salisbury, Wiltshire, 1987

Landmann, Georg Peter, *Stefan George und sein Kreis. Eine Bibliographie*, Dr. Ernst Hauswedell & Co., Hamburg, ²1976

Landmann, Michael, 'Literatur um Stefan George', *Neue Zürcher Zeitung*, Fernausgabe No. 312, 14 Nov. 1971, pp. 49–50

Lauffer, Siegfried, 'Alexander Schenk Count Stauffenberg+', *Gnomon* 1964, pp. 845–847

Leber, Annedore, *Das Gewissen steht auf. 64 Lebensbilder aus dem deutschen Widerstand 1933–1945*, Mosaik Verlag, Berlin-Frankfurt am Main, ⁹1960

Lehmann, Max, *Scharnhorst*, 2 vols., Verlag von S. Hirzel, Leipzig, 1886, 1887

Leithäuser, Joachim G., *Wilhelm Leuschner. Ein Leben für die Republik*, Bund-Verlag, Cologne, 1962

Leuze, [Walter], *Das 17. (Bayerische) Reiter Regiment*, Attenkofersche Buchdruckerei, Straubing, [1932]

Loos, Werner, *Oberkommando des Heeres/Generalstab des Heeres. Bestand RH 2*, Part 2 (Findbücher zu Beständen des Bundesarchivs vol. 33), Bundesarchiv, Coblenz, 1988

Lübbe, Hermann, *Politische Philosophie in Deutschland. Studien zu ihrer Geschichte*, Benno Schwabe & Co. Verlag, Basel, Stuttgart, 1963

Lüke, Hans, *Die Geschichte des Regiments 69*, Traditionsgemeinschaft ehem. 69er/394er, Hamburg, 1986

Makarov, A.N., 'Vorkämpfer der Völkerverständigung und Völkerrechtsgelehrte als Opfer des Nationalsozialismus: 8. Berthold Schenk Graf von Stauffenberg (1905–1944)', *Die Friedens-Warte* 47 (1947), pp. 360–364

Malone, Henry O., *Adam von Trott zu Solz. Werdegang eines Verschwörers 1909–1938*, Siedler Verlag, Berlin, 1986

Mårtensson, Ola, 'Vi tänker öppna västfronten', *Sydsvenska Dagbladet Snällposten*, 20 July 1984

Martin, Bernd, 'Verhandlungen über separate Friedensschlüsse 1942–1945. Ein Beitrag zur Entstehung des Kalten Krieges', *Militärgeschichtliche Mitteilungen* 1976 No. 2, pp. 95–113

Mau, Hermann, 'Die "Zweite Revolution" – der 30. Juni 1934', *Vierteljahrshefte für Zeitgeschichte* 1 (1953), pp. 119–137

McCloy II, John J., *Die Verschwörung gegen Hitler. Ein Geschenk an die deutsche Zukunft*, Friedrich Vorwerk Verlag, Stuttgart, 1963

Meier-Welcker, Hans, *Seeckt*, Frankfurt am Main, 1967

Melnikow, Daniil, *20. Juli 1944. Legende und Wirklichkeit*, VEB Deutscher Verlag der Wissenschaften, Berlin, 1966

Messerschmidt, Manfred [und] Wüllner, Fritz, *Die Wehrmachtjustiz im Dienste des Nationalsozialismus. Zerstörung einer Legende*, Nomos Verlagsgesellschaft, Baden-Baden, 1987

Meyer, Winfried, *Unternehmen Sieben. Eine Rettungsaktion für vom Holocaust Bedrohte aus dem Amt Ausland/Abwehr im Oberkommando der Wehrmacht*, Verlag Anton Hain, Frankfurt am Main, 1993

Minerva. Jahrbuch der gelehrten Welt 28 (1926), Walter de Gruyter & Co., Berlin und Leipzig, 1926

Moltke, Freya von, Michael Balfour, Julian Frisby, *Helmuth James von Moltke 1907–1945. Anwalt der Zukunft*, Deutsche Verlags-Anstalt, Stuttgart, [1975]

Mommsen, Hans, 'Gesellschaftsbild und Verfassungspläne des deutschen Widerstandes', in Schmitthenner, Walter and Hans Buchheim, ed., *Der deutsche Widerstand gegen Hitler. Vier historisch-kritische Studien*, Kiepenheuer & Witsch, Cologne, Berlin, 1966, pp. 73–167

Moser, Jonny, 'Die Entrechtung der Juden im Dritten Reich. Diskriminierung und Terror durch Gesetze, Verordnungen, Erlasse', in Walter H. Pehle, ed., *Der Judenpogrom 1938. Von der 'Reichskristallnacht' zum Völkermord*, Fischer Taschenbuch Verlag, Frankfurt am Main, 1988, pp. 118–131

Müller, Christian, *Oberst i.G. Stauffenberg. Eine Biographie*, Droste Verlag, Düsseldorf, [1970]

Müller, Klaus-Jürgen, *Das Heer und Hitler. Armee und nationalsozialistisches Regime 1933–1940*, Deutsche Verlags-Anstalt, Stuttgart, 1969

    General Ludwig Beck. Studien und Dokumente zur politisch-militärischen Vorstellungswelt und Tätigkeit des Generalstabschefs des deutschen Heeres 1933–1938 (Schriften des Bundesarchivs 30), Harald Boldt Verlag, Boppard am Rhein, 1980

Müller, Rolf-Dieter, 'Das Scheitern der wirtschaftlichen "Blitzkriegstrategie"' in *Das Deutsche Reich und der Zweite Weltkrieg*, vol. 4, ed. Militärgeschichtliches Forschungsamt, Deutsche Verlags-Anstalt, Stuttgart, 1983, pp. 936–1029

Mueller-Hillebrand, Burkhart, *Das Heer 1933–1945*, vol. I: E. S. Mittler & Sohn, Darmstadt, 1954; vols. II–III: E. S. Mittler & Sohn, Frankfurt am Main, 1956, 1959

Nicosia, Francis R., *The Third Reich and the Palestine Question*, University of Texas Press, Austin, 1985

Niepold, Gerd, *Mittlere Ostfront Juni '44. Darstellung, Beurteilung, Lehren*, Verlag E. S. Mittler & Sohn, Herford und Bonn, 1985

Olshausen, Klaus, *Zwischenspiel auf dem Balkan: Die deutsche Politik gegenüber Jugoslawien und Griechenland von März bis Juli 1941*, Deutsche Verlags-Anstalt, Stuttgart, 1973

O'Neill, Robert J., *The German Army and the Nazi Party, 1933–1939*, Cassell, London, 1966

Ose, Dieter, *Entscheidung im Westen 1944. Der Oberbefehlshaber West und die Abwehr der alliierten Invasion* (Beiträge zur Militär- und Kriegsgeschichte, vol. 22), Deutsche Verlags-Anstalt, Stuttgart, 1982

Paul, Wolfgang, *Brennpunkte. Die Geschichte der 6. Panzerdivision (1. leichte) 1937–1945*, Höntges-Verlag, Krefeld, 1977, Biblio Verlag, Osnabrück, ²1984

Das Potsdamer Infanterie-Regiment 9. 1918–1945. Preussische Tradition in Krieg und Frieden, Biblio Verlag, Osnabrück, 1983

Pawlowsky, Peter, *Helmut Küpper vormals Georg Bondi 1895–1970*, Helmut Küpper vormals Georg Bondi, Düsseldorf and Munich, 1970

Pertz, G. H., *Das Leben des Ministers Freiherrn vom Stein*, 6 vols., G. Reimer, Berlin, 1849–1855

(continued by Hans Delbrück), *Das Leben des Feldmarschalls Grafen Neithardt von Gneisenau*, 5 vols., Georg Reimer, Berlin, 1864–1881

Phillips, Henry Gerard, *El Guettar. Crucible of Leadership. 9th U.S. Infantry Division Against The Wehrmacht in Africa, April 1943*, Henry Gerard Phillips, Penn Valley, California, 1991

Podach, Erich F., *Gestalten um Nietzsche, mit unveröffentlichten Dokumenten zur Geschichte seines Lebens und seines Werks*, Erich Lichtenstein Verlag, Weimar, 1932

Pogue, Forrest C., *United States Army in World War II. The European Theater of Operations. The Supreme Command*, U.S. Government Printing Office, Washington, D.C., 1954

Rabenau, Friedrich von, *Seeckt. Aus seinem Leben 1918–1936*, Leipzig, [1940]

Reinhardt, Klaus, *Die Wende vor Moskau. Das Scheitern der Strategie Hitlers im Winter 1941/42* (Beiträge zur Militär- und Kriegs-Geschichte, vol. 13), Deutsche Verlags-Anstalt, Stuttgart, 1972

Repgen, Konrad, 'Ein KPD-Verbot im Jahre 1933?' *Historische Zeitschrift* 240 (1985), pp. 67–98

Reynolds, Nicholas, *Treason Was No Crime. Ludwig Beck, Chief of the German General Staff*, William Kimber, London, 1976

Ritter, Gerhard, *Carl Goerdeler und die deutsche Widerstandsbewegung*, Deutsche Verlags-Anstalt, Stuttgart, ³1956

Rock, Christa-Maria, 'Stefan George', *Der Stürmer. Deutsches Wochenblatt zum Kampfe um die Wahrheit*, ed. Julius Streicher, 12 (1934) No. 10, March 1934, p. 4

'Stefan Georges Tod', *Der Stürmer. Deutsches Wochenblatt zum Kampfe um die Wahrheit*, ed. Julius Streicher, 13 (1935) No. 11, March 1935, p. [6]

Rössner, Hans, *Georgekreis und Literaturwissenschaft. Zur Würdigung und Kritik der geistigen Bewegung Stefan Georges*, Verlag Moritz Diesterweg, Frankfurt am Main, 1938

Rohwer, J[ürgen], Hümmelchen, G[erhard], *Chronik des Seekrieges 1939–1945*, Gerhard Stallin Verlag, Oldenburg und Hamburg, 1968

Roon, Ger van, *Neuordnung im Widerstand. Der Kreisauer Kreis innerhalb der deutschen Widerstandsbewegung*, R. Oldenbourg Verlag, Munich, 1967

Rothfels, Hans, *Die deutsche Opposition gegen Hitler. Eine Würdigung*, Fischer Taschenbuch Verlag, Frankfurt am Main, 1958, expanded edn 1977

The German Opposition to Hitler, Henry Regnery, Hinsdale, Illinois, 1948

Salewski, Michael, *Entwaffnung und Militärkontrolle in Deutschland 1919–1927*, R. Oldenbourg Verlag, Munich, 1966

Schack, Ingeborg, *Rainer Maria Rilke. Chronik seines Lebens und seines Werkes*, 2 vols, Insel Verlag, n.p., 1975

Schall-Riaucour, Heidemarie Gräfin, *Aufstand und Gehorsam. Offizierstum und Generalstab im Umbruch. Leben und Wirken von Generaloberst Franz Halder, Generalstabschef 1938–1942*, Limes Verlag, Wiesbaden, 1972

Scheel, Heinrich, 'Die "Rote Kapelle" und der 20. Juli 1944', *Zeitschrift für Geschichtswissenschaft* 33 (1985), pp. 325–337

Scheffler, Wolfgang, *Judenverfolgung im Dritten Reich*, Colloquium Verlag, Berlin, ²1964

Scheurig, Bodo, *Claus Graf Schenk von Stauffenberg*, Colloquium Verlag, Berlin, 1964

    Henning von Tresckow. Eine Biographie, Gerhard Stalling Verlag, Oldenburg und Hamburg, 1973, ³n.d.

Schick, Albert, *Die 10. Panzer-Division 1939–1943*, Traditionsgemeinschaft der ehemaligen 10. Panzer-Division, J. Pohle, Cologne, 1993

Schlösser, Manfred, *Karl Wolfskehl 1869–1969. Leben und Werk in Dokumenten*, Agora Verlag, Darmstadt, [1969]

    Karl Wolfskehl. Eine Bibliographie, Erato-Presse, Darmstadt, [1971]

Schorr, Helmut J., *Adam Stegerwald: Gewerkschaftler und Politiker der ersten deutschen Republik. Ein Beitrag zur Geschichte der christlich-sozialen Bewegung in Deutschland*, Kommunal-Verlag, Recklinghausen, 1966

Schramm, Wilhelm von, *Aufstand der Generale. Der 20. Juli in Paris*, Kindler Verlag (paperback edn), Munich, 1964

Schulze, Hagen, *Weimar. Deutschland 1917–1933*, Siedler Verlag, Berlin, 1982

Schwerin, Detlef Graf von, *'Dann sind's die besten Köpfe, die man henkt'. Die junge Generation im deutschen Widerstand*, Piper, Munich, Zürich, [1991]

Seekamp, H.-J., R. C. Ockenden, M. Keilson, *Stefan George. Leben und Werk. Eine Zeittafel*, Castrum Peregrini Presse, Amsterdam, 1972

Smith, Bradley F. and Elena Agarossi, *Operation Sunrise. The Secret Surrender*, Basic Books, New York, 1979

Späth, Alfred, 'Zum Andenken von Nikolaus Graf von Üxküll', *Vierteljahrshefte für Zeitgeschichte* 8 (1960), pp. 188–192

Stefan George 1868 · 1968. Der Dichter und sein Kreis. Eine Ausstellung des Deutschen Literaturarchivs im Schiller-Nationalmuseum Marbach a.N., ed. Bernhard Zeller, Kösel Verlag A.G., Munich, 1968

Steinert, Marlis G., *Hitlers Krieg und die Deutschen. Stimmung und Haltung der deutschen Bevölkerung im Zweiten Weltkrieg*, Econ Verlag, Düsseldorf, Vienna, 1970

Stevenson, D[avid], *French War Aims against Germany 1914–1919*, Clarendon Press, Oxford, 1982

Stockert, Franz K. v., 'Stefan George und sein Kreis. Wirkungsgeschichte vor und nach dem 30. Januar 1933', in Beda Allemann, ed., *Literatur und Germanistik nach der 'Machtübernahme'. Colloquium zur 50. Wiederkehr des 30. Januar 1933*, Bouvier Verlag Herbert Grundmann, Bonn 1983, pp. 52–89

Strebel, [Hellmut], 'Berthold Schenk Graf von Stauffenberg (1905–1944)', *Zeitschrift für ausländisches öffentliches Recht und Völkerrecht* 13 (1950/51), pp. 14–16

Streit, Christian, *Keine Kameraden. Die Wehrmacht und die sowjetischen Kriegs-gefangenen 1941–1945*, Deutsche Verlags-Anstalt, 1978

Stumpf, Reinhard, 'Der Krieg im Mittelmeerraum 1942/43: Die Operationen in Nordafrika und im mittleren Mittelmeer', in *Das Deutsche Reich und der Zweite Weltkrieg*, vol. 6, ed. Militärgeschichtliches Forschungsamt, Deutsche Verlags-Anstalt, Stuttgart, 1990, pp. 569–757

Tessin, Georg, *Verbände und Truppen der deutschen Wehrmacht und Waffen SS im Zweiten Weltkrieg 1939–1945. Zweiter Band: Die Landstreitkräfte 1–7*, Biblio Verlag, Osnabrück, [2]1973

Thorwald, Jürgen, *Wen sie verderben wollen. Bericht des grossen Verrats*, Steingrüben-Verlag, Stuttgart, 1952

Turner, Jr., Henry Ashby, *German Big Business and the Rise of Hitler*, Oxford University Press, New York, Oxford, 1985

Umbreit, Hans, 'Der Kampf um die Vormachtstellung in Westeuropa' in *Das Deutsche Reich und der Zweite Weltkrieg*, vol. 2, ed. Militärgeschichtliches Forschungsamt, Deutsche Verlags-Anstalt, Stuttgart, 1979, pp. 233–327

Venohr, Wolfgang, *Stauffenberg. Symbol der deutschen Einheit. Eine politische Biographie*, Ullstein, Frankfurt am Main, Berlin, 1986

Vogelsang, Thilo, *Reichswehr, Staat und NSDAP. Beiträge zur deutschen Geschichte 1930–1932*, Deutsche Verlags-Anstalt, Stuttgart, 1962

Volz, Hans, *Daten der Geschichte der NSDAP*, Verlag A. G. Ploetz, Berlin, Leipzig, [11]1943

Wagner, Walter, *Der Volksgerichtshof im nationalsozialistischen Staat* (Quellen und Darstellungen zur Zeitgeschichte, vol. 16/III, 'Die deutsche Justiz und der Nationalsozialismus', Part III), Deutsche Verlags-Anstalt, Stuttgart, 1974

Wasserstein, Bernard, *Britain and the Jews of Europe 1939–1945*, Institute of Jewish Affairs, London, Clarendon Press, Oxford, 1979

Wegner, Bernd, 'Der Krieg gegen die Sowjetunion 1942/43', in *Das Deutsche Reich und der Zweite Weltkrieg*, vol. 6, Deutsche Verlags-Anstalt, Stuttgart, 1990, pp. 761–1102

Wegner-Korfes, Sigrid, 'Der 20. Juli 1944 und das Nationalkomitee "Freies Deutschland"', *Zeitschrift für Geschichtswissenschaft* 27 (1979), pp. 535–544

Weingartner, James J., *Hitler's Guard. The Story of the Leibstandarte SS Adolf Hitler 1933–1945*, Southern Illinois University Press, Feffer & Simons, Carbondale and Edwardsville, London and Amsterdam, [1974]

Weisenborn, Günther, ed., *Der lautlose Aufstand. Bericht über die Widerstandsbewegung des deutschen Volkes 1933–1945*, Rowohlt Verlag, Hamburg, 1953

Weller, Karl, *Die Staatsumwälzung in Württemberg 1918–1920*, W. Kohlhammer, Stuttgart, 1930

'Beiträge zur Geschichte der Novembertage 1918 in Württemberg', *Württembergische Vierteljahrshefte für Landesgeschichte* 37 (1931), pp. 177–192

Der Weltkrieg 1914 bis 1918, ed. Reichsarchiv, vols 1–14, E. S. Mittler, Berlin, 1925–1944

Weniger, Erich, 'Zur Vorgeschichte des 20. VII. 1944: Heinrich von Stülpnagel', *Die Sammlung* 4 (1949), pp. 475–492

Westpoint Atlas see Esposito

Wolzendorff, Kurt, *Staatsrecht und Naturrecht in der Lehre vom Widerstandsrecht des Volkes gegen rechtswidrige Ausübung der Staatsgewalt. Zugleich ein Beitrag zur*

Entwicklungsgeschichte des modernen Staatsgedankens (Untersuchungen zur deutschen Staats-und Rechtsgeschichte 206, Alte Folge, No. 126), 2nd reprint of Breslau edn of 1916, Scientia Verlag, Aalen, 1968

Wunder, Gerd, *Die Schenken von Stauffenberg. Eine Familiengeschichte*, Müller & Gräff, Stuttgart, 1972

Wyman, David S., *The Abandonment of the Jews. America and the Holocaust 1941–1945*, Pantheon Books, New York, [1984]

Zeller, Eberhard, *Geist der Freiheit. Der zwanzigste Juli*, Verlag Hermann Rinn, Munich, [1952], [3]1956, Gotthold Müller Verlag, Munich, [4]1963, [5]1965 (cited from 5th edn unless otherwise indicated)

Oberst Claus Graf Stauffenberg. Ein Lebensbild, Ferdinand Schöning, Paderborn, Munich, Vienna, Zürich, 1994

INDEX